Strategic Management in the Asia Pacific

Harnessing Regional and Organizational Change for Competitive Advantage

To my parents,
Dr C. and Nandini Venkatesan,
and my grandparents,
Vasudev and Indira Bellare

Strategic Management in the Asia Pacific

Harnessing Regional and Organizational Change for Competitive Advantage

Edited by

Usha C. V. Haley

OXFORD AUCKLAND BOSTON JOHANNESBURG MELBOURNE NEW DELHI

Butterworth-Heinemann
Linacre House, Jordan Hill, Oxford OX2 8DP
225 Wildwood Avenue, Woburn, MA 01801-2041
A division of Reed Educational and Professional Publishing Ltd

A member of the Reed Elsevier plc group

First published 2000

British Library Cataloguing in Publication Data
A catalogue record for this book is available from the British Library

Library of Congress Cataloguing in Publication Data
Strategic management in the Asia Pacific: harnessing regional and organizational
    change for competitive advantage/edited by Usha C. V. Haley
    p. cm.
    Includes index.
    ISBN 0-7506-4129-0
    1. Strategic planning–Asia.   2.   Strategic planning–Pacific Area.
    3. Industrial management–Asia.   4.   Industrial management–Pacific Area.
    5. Finance–Asia.   6.   Finance–Pacific Area.   7. Investments, Foreign–Asia.
    8. Investments, Foreign–Pacific Area.   9.   Asia–Foreign economic relations.
    10. Pacific Area–Foreign economic relations.   11.   Asia–Economic conditions
    –1945   12.   Pacific Area–Economic conditions.   I. Haley, Usha C. V.
    HD70.A72S77   99–34094
    658.4'012'095–DC21   CIP

ISBN 0 7506 4129 0

Typeset by Avocet Typeset, Brill, Aylesbury, Bucks
Printed and bound in Great Britain by Biddles Ltd, Guildford and King's Lynn

FOR EVERY TITLE THAT WE PUBLISH, BUTTERWORTH-HEINEMANN
WILL PAY FOR BTCV TO PLANT AND CARE FOR A TREE.

Contents

Contributors

◼ About the editor

Usha C. V. Haley, editor of this book and author of Chapters 1, 4.1, 9, 9.1, 12, 12.1, 13, 13.1, 14, 14.1, 15, 16.1, 17 and 27, is Associate Professor in the School of Management, New Jersey Institute of Technology, Newark, New Jersey, USA and the Graduate Faculty of Management, Rutgers University, Newark, USA, and Research Associate in the Managing Business in Asia Program at the Australian National University, Canberra, Australia. She received her PhD in Business Administration, specializing in International Business and Management, from the Stern School of Business, New York University. She also completed Masters degrees in Business at Stern, in Political Science at the University of Illinois at Urbana-Champaign, and in Journalism at the University of Wisconsin-Madison. She has published her research in major international academic journals and presented her findings at professional conferences and to audiences of managers, government officials and academics. She has just published *The New Asian Emperors: The Overseas Chinese, their Strategies and Competitive Advantages* (with George T. Haley and Chin-Tiong Tan) for Butterworth-Heinemann, Oxford, and has two forthcoming books besides: *From Catalysts to Chameleons: Multinational Firms as Participants in Political Environments* and *The Chameleon in the Cactus Patch: Managing Multinational Firms in Mexico*. Her current research interests include managing organizational change; exploring and improving strategic decision-making in large organizations; understanding and influencing organizations' complex interactions with their global environments; managing business–government relations; and doing business successfully in the Asia Pacific and Mexico.

Prior to entering academia, she worked at the United Nations Organization and as a journalist. She has taught Strategic Management and International Business at New York University (New York), American University (Washington, DC), the Instituto Tecnologico y de Estudios Superiores de Monterrey (Monterrey, Mexico), the National University of Singapore (Singapore), the Queensland University of Technology (Brisbane, Australia) and Harvard University (Cambridge, MA). Additionally, she has taught in major corporate and universities' executive development programmes, for top and middle managers, in the USA, Australia, Mexico, Italy, India, Vietnam and Singapore. She also serves as a consultant on issues concerning strategic management and foreign direct investment for several multinational corporations in North America, Australia, Europe and Asia.

Currently, she is the Regional Editor, Asia Pacific, for *Management Decision* (UK) for which she has guest edited the special double issue on Strategic Management in the

Asia Pacific, and the Regional Editor, Asia Pacific, for the *Journal of Organizational Change Management* (USA) for which she has guest edited a special double issue on Strategic Dimensions of Organizational Change and Restructuring in the Asia Pacific. She also serves on the Editorial Advisory Board of the *Journal of Leadership and Leaders* (USA). She can be contacted through e-mail at uhaley@asia-pacific.com

■ About the contributors

Mette Bak, author of Chapters 18 and 18.1, is a graduate of the University of Copenhagen, and of the EAP European School of Management from which she holds the degrees of Diplom-Kauffrau (Germany) and Diplome Grande Ecole de Gestion (France). She is an Associate Member of the Centre for Cross-Cultural Management Research. Following two years in the human resources function of BASF in Shanghai, China, she is now Communications Manager in BASF covering Japan, China and Hong Kong.

Chris Christodoulou, author of Chapters 22 and 22.1, is an Associate Professor and researcher in the field of Strategic Management with extensive publications. He currently serves as the Deputy Director of the Swinburne Graduate School of Management, Australia and as Director of the Center for Organizational and Strategic Studies. In the past twenty years he has been a major contributor to the development of postgraduate management education, especially at the Swinburne University of Technology. He was also responsible for the establishment of the Swinburne Experiential Learning Center and the Caravan Management Game industry simulation. At present he is particularly interested in collaborative research of an international nature.

Dang Thi Kim Chi, author of Chapter 19, is an MBA graduate from the School of Management, Asian Institute of Technology, Bangkok, Thailand. She is working at present as a Project Analyst for the Mekong Project Development Facility (MPDF), a programme of the International Finance Corporation (IFC)/World Bank in Ho Chi Minh City, which provides financial sourcing for SMEs (small and medium enterprises) in Vietnam.

Ranjan Das (PhD), author of Chapters 24 and 24.1, is a Professor of Strategic and International Management at the Indian Institute of Management, Calcutta, India (a business school set up in collaboration with the Alfred P. Sloan School of Management, Massachusetts Institute of Technology (MIT), USA). He had twenty years of industry experience before joining academia. He is also a corporate adviser to a number of leading Indian and multinational corporations. His research and professional interests are in the areas of strategy, corporate restructuring, international business, change management and human resource development. He has written two books and published a number of articles in India and abroad. He has close interaction with Indian industry and is currently the Chairman of the Marketing Sub-Committee of Confederation of Indian Industry (Eastern region), India's largest and apex industry association.

Peter J. Dowling (PhD, Flinders University of South Australia), author of Chapters 25 and 25.1, is Foundation Professor of Management and Dean of the Faculty of Commerce and Law at the University of Tasmania, Australia. Previous teaching appointments include Monash University, the University of Melbourne and Cornell University. His current research interests are concerned with the cross-national transferability of human resource management practices and strategic management.

André M. Everett, author of Chapters 11 and 11.1, is a Senior Lecturer in the Department of Management at the University of Otago, New Zealand. He received an MBA and PhD in Management and Information Systems from the University of Nebraska-Lincoln, with prior studies at schools in Germany, France, Iceland, and Pennsylvania. He instructs commerce students in international management, operations strategy, and survey methodology. His research interests include internationalization of quality management, cross-functional integration of management philosophies, and cultural influences on international business. His writings on quality and international management topics have been published or presented in over fifteen countries. He is a member of the Decision Sciences Institute, the Pan-Pacific Business Association, the Academy of Management, the Academy of International Business, the Institute for Operations Research and the Management Sciences, the Association for Computing Machinery and numerous New Zealand societies.

Gary Fontaine, author of Chapter 16, completed his education in social psychology at the University of Washington, Duke University, and the University of Western Australia, receiving his PhD from the latter in 1972. He is currently an Associate Professor in the Department of Communication at the University of Hawaii, Honolulu, Hawaii, USA, and on the faculties of the Intercultural Management Program of the Japan America Institute of Management Science (JAIMS) in Honolulu and the Organizational Design and Effectiveness Program of the Fielding Institute in Santa Barbara, California. He is principal consultant of his own Strange Lands International Assignment Specialists with over twenty-five years' experience providing training for personnel from over 100 organizations in the Americas/Asia/Pacific region. His primary professional interests centre on helping assignees and organizations deal with the new people, places and technologies encountered on international assignments in contexts such as international business, diplomacy, foreign study, knowledge creation and transfer, immigration, justice, tourism, service delivery and intercultural marriage.

George T. Haley, author of Chapters 8, 8.1, 14, 17, 17.1, 20 and 20.1, is currently Associate Professor and Director of the Marketing and International Business Programs at the University of New Haven, West Haven, Connecticut, USA. He received his PhD in Marketing from the University of Texas at Austin. His research interests include new product development, cross-cultural marketing, strategic marketing management, industrial marketing management, ecological marketing, overseas business networks and channel management. He has particular research interests in marketing and strategic decision-making in the Asia Pacific and Mexico. Besides currently researching strategic and industrial marketing in South and Southeast Asian economies, he is also examining the effects of using financial models in new product decision-making. He has presented his research at major professional conferences and to audiences of managers and academics. He has just published *The New Asian Emperors: The Overseas Chinese, their Strategies and Competitive Advantages* (with Chin-Tiong Tan and Usha C.V. Haley for Butterworth-Heinemann, Oxford) and has two more forthcoming books. Additionally, his research has been published in *Industrial*

Marketing Management, the *International Journal of Physical Distribution and Materials Management*, the *Journal of Advertising*, *Management Decision*, the *Journal of Organizational Change Management*, the *Journal of Business and Industrial Marketing*, and *Advances in Consumer Research*, among others. He has taught Marketing and International Business at Harvard University (Cambridge, MA), DePaul University (Chicago), Baruch College (New York), Fordham University (New York), the Instituto Tecnologico y de Estudios Superiores de Monterrey (Monterrey, Mexico), the National University of Singapore (Singapore), Queensland University of Technology (Brisbane, Australia) and, Thammasat University (Bangkok, Thailand). He has also taught in executive-development programmes for major universities in the USA, Australia, Mexico, Singapore and India; and consulted on strategic and industrial marketing with companies in the Americas, Australia and Asia. He currently serves as Regional Editor, Asia, for the *Journal of Business and Industrial Marketing* (USA), and has guest edited a special issue on Business-to-Business Marketing in Asia for the journal. He also serves on the Editorial Advisory and Review Board of the *International Marketing Review* (UK), *Industrial Marketing Management* (USA) and *Marketing Intelligence and Planning* (UK). He is currently guest editing a special issue for *Marketing Intelligence and Planning* on Strategic Marketing in the Emerging Economies.

Mike Hobday, author of Chapters 5 and 5.1 and of *Innovation in East Asia: The Challenge to Japan* (Edward Elgar, 1995), is a Professorial Fellow specializing in corporate strategies for high technology in the Pacific Asia region at the Science Policy Research Unit (SPRU), the University of Sussex, UK. Prior to his training as an industrial economist, he worked for the US semiconductor corporation, Texas Instruments, for ten years. His PhD thesis on science and technology (later a book) analysed how Brazil had responded to changes in the world telecommunications industry. Since joining SPRU in 1984, he has published extensively on the global semiconductor and telecommunications industries, as well as public policies for information technology. He has acted as a consultant to the Malaysian, Brazilian and Venezuelan Governments, the House of Commons, the European Union, the Department of Trade and Industry (DTI), the Organization for Economic Co-operation and Development (OECD), the United Nations Industrial Development Organization (UNIDO), the United Nations Conference on Trade and Development (UNCTAD) and several private corporations. His recent work funded by the Economic and Social Research Council (ESRC) has shown how latecomer firms from South Korea, Taiwan, Singapore and Hong Kong (the four 'dragons') caught up technologically to become formidable international competitors in electronics.

Llewellyn D. Howell, author of Chapters 2 and 2.1, is currently a Professor of International Studies at Thunderbird, The American Graduate School of International Management, Glendale, Arizona, USA. At Thunderbird, he teaches in the areas of Political Risk Analysis and the Southeast Asian Regional Business Environment. He is also the Director of the Washington (DC) Winterim Program which focuses on US foreign economic policy. He has previously taught at the University of Hawaii, The American University (Washington, DC), the Naval Postgraduate School, and the Monterey Institute of International Studies. He began his work in the field of international affairs as a US Peace Corps Volunteer in Malaya. He has subsequently conducted research in each of the ASEAN countries, was a Fulbright lecturer at the Malaysian National Institute of Public Administration (INTAN), worked in Program Analysis and Evaluation in the Office of the US Secretary of Defense, and was a Senior

Research Associate at Third Point Systems in California, a defence research firm. He is editor/author of *The Handbook of Country and Political Risk Analysis*, second edition and is co-editor of *Malaysian Foreign Policy: Issues and Perspectives* and *International Education: The Unfinished Agenda*. He has authored more than seventy scholarly articles and chapters in the areas of political risk, foreign policy, and Southeast Asian studies. He is Senior Adviser for The PRS Group and consults widely on political risk for investors, foreign policy issues, and investment in Southeast Asia. He received his PhD in Political Science from Syracuse University in 1973, with related fields at Cornell University and the University of Michigan.

Terence Jackson, author of Chapters 18 and 18.1, is the Director of the Centre for Cross Cultural Management Research at EAP European School of Management, a pan-European graduate business school with campuses in Paris, Oxford, Berlin and Madrid. He has a Bachelors degree in Social Anthropology, a Masters degree in management education, and a PhD in organizational psychology.

P. S. Kirkbride, author of Chapters 21 and 21.1, is the Managing Director of the Change House, UK, a consulting business that specializes in organizational change and development, strategic human resources management, corporate culture and aspects of international management. He is also a Retained Associate at Ashridge Management College, UK, where he used to be on the full-time staff as a Team Leader on the college's core change programmes. In addition he is Visiting Professor and former British Aerospace Professor of Organizational Change at the University of Hertfordshire. His Asian connections stem from a five-year stint as Reader in Management at the City University of Hong Kong and from continuing consulting to leading clients such as the Hong Kong Bank, Cathay Pacific and the Mass Transit Railway Corporation. Other clients in Europe have included Zeneca, Digital Equipment, the Glaxo Group and the Department of Health. His academic background includes degrees in Management Studies and Industrial Relations and a PhD from the University of Bath. He has more than fifty articles, ten book chapters and two books to his credit.

Kam-hon Lee, author of Chapters 7 and 7.1, is Professor of Marketing and Dean of Business Administration at the Chinese University of Hong Kong, Hong Kong SAR. He obtained his B.Comm. and M.Comm. from the Chinese University of Hong Kong, and his PhD in Marketing at Northwestern University in Evanston, Illinois, USA. His research areas include cross-cultural marketing, strategic marketing and marketing ethics. He has published in the *Journal of Marketing, Journal of Management, Journal of Business Ethics, The World Economy, International Marketing Review, European Journal of Marketing, Marketing Education Review* and other international refereed journals. He has taught in executive programmes, or rendered consulting services to different institutions including the World Bank, Hang Seng Bank, Coca-Cola (China), Proctor and Gamble (Guangzhou), Digital Equipment Corporation, Du Pont Asia Pacific Ltd., Dentsu Advertising Agency, and Chinese Arts and Crafts (Hong Kong).

Peter Ping Li, author of Chapters 23 and 23.1, is an Associate Professor of Management at California State University at Stanislaus, USA. He received his PhD in International Business from George Washington University. His primary research interest lies in the development of holistic, dynamic and paradoxical theories with regard to strategic management of multinational corporations.

Linda Low, author of Chapters 9 and 12, is currently an Associate Professor in the Department of Business Policy, National University of Singapore, Singapore. She obtained her PhD in Economics from the National University of Singapore in 1984. Her research interests include public-sector economics and public policy, public enterprises and privatization, social security, human resource development, health and education, development and trade in the service sector (communications, business and finance, tourism, professional services), science and technology, information technology and telecommunication. She has been consultant to many international and local agencies. In Singapore, she has been consultant to the Ministry of Trade and Industry, the Population Planning Unit, the Ministry of Health, the National Productivity Board, the Singapore Tourist Promotion Board, the Port of Singapore Authority, the Trade Development Board and the Institute of Southeast Asian Studies. She was a resource person to the Services Subcommittee in the Economic Planning Committee that prepared the Strategic Economic Plan for Singapore, under the Ministry of Trade and Industry. At international level, she was consultant to the Asian Development Bank, United Nations Economic and Social Commission for Asia Pacific (UNESCAP) and Asia Pacific Development Corporation.

Ian Marsh, author of Chapters 6 and 6.1, is an Associate Professor at the Australian Graduate School of Management, Australia. His most recent publication is a study of Australia's political and economic future, *Beyond the Two Party System: Political Representation, Economic Competitiveness and Australian Politics* (Cambridge University Press, 1995). He has also edited a study of *Australian Business in the Asia Pacific: The Case for Strategic Industry Policy* (Longman Cheshire, Melbourne, 1994). He was educated at the University of Newcastle (New South Wales) and Harvard and has held visiting positions at Keio University (Tokyo) and the European University Institute (Florence). He is currently engaged on a collaborative research project on political developments in a number of Asian regional states, including the implications for business and business-government relations.

Lindsay Nelson (BA Honours Tasmania, MSc Hull University), author of Chapters 25 and 25.1, is a Lecturer in management in the School of Management at the University of Tasmania, Australia. Previous appointments include management level positions in industrial relations and human resource management. His research interests are in workplace change including decentralized bargaining new patterns of work and organizational change.

Boon Siong Neo, author of Chapters 26 and 26.1, is an Associate Professor and the Dean of the Nanyang Business School at the Nanyang Technological University, Singapore. He has varied experience in accounting, finance and Information Technology (IT) over the past fifteen years. He has contributed actively to major research and consulting projects including those undertaken by the Singapore National Computer Board, the Economic Development Board, the Trade Development Board and other major corporations. He obtained his Bachelor of Accountancy from the National University of Singapore, and Master of Business Administration and PhD from the University of Pittsburgh, USA. His research in the strategic exploitation and management of IT has been published in many journals. He is the co-author of a paper on IT infrastructure that won the Best Paper Award at the 17th International Conference on Information Systems in December 1996. He edited a book, *Exploiting IT* *for Business Competitiveness* (Addison-Wesley, 1996) which won a Singapore National Book Award in 1996.

Anthony Saunders, author of Chapter 4, is John M. Schiff Professor of Finance at the Stern School of Business, New York University (NYU), USA. He holds a PhD from the London School of Economics. He has taught at NYU since 1978, specializing in courses related to financial institutions. He was research adviser at the Federal Reserve Bank of Philadelphia from 1984 to 1989 and is an academic consultant to the Federal Reserve Board of Governors. He has also held visiting positions at the Comptroller of the Currency and the International Monetary Fund. He is the Editor of the *Journal of Financial Markets, Institutions and Instruments*, and the *Journal of Banking and Finance*, as well as an Associate Editor of six other journals. His research has been published in all the major finance journals, and he has recently published a book on *Modern Financial Institutions* for Irwin publishers.

Siew Kien Sia, author of Chapters 26 and 26.1, is a Lecturer in Strategy and Information Systems at Nanyang Technological University, Singapore. He is a certified public accountant and a certified information systems auditor. He obtained his Master of Information Systems from the University of Queensland (Australia) and his PhD (Business) from the Nanyang Technological University. His research interests are in the fields of information systems auditing and business process re-engineering. His work has been published in both local and international journals.

Sam K. Steffensen, author of Chapters 10 and 10.1, holds an MA in Socio-Technological Planning and a PhD from University of Copenhagen in Denmark and from Kyushu University in Japan. He is Assistant Professor at the Asian Research Center of the Copenhagen Business School, Denmark, but is presently based as an invited fellowship researcher at the Institute of Socio-Information and Communication Studies (ISICS), University of Tokyo, Japan. His current research focuses on information network businesses, the cyber economy, and new entrepreneurial cultures in Japan. His professional experiences include several years as a consulting director with Ernst and Young and numerous international consulting assignments undertaken as a private business consultant and service provider. He is adviser to a number of Japanese new business organizations, mentor to the Japan Market Entry Competition programme, and board member of the Asia-Pacific Business Club of Denmark.

Fredric William Swierczek (PhD), author of Chapters 19 and 19.1, is currently an Associate Professor at the School of Management, Asian Institute of Technology in Bangkok, Thailand. For several years, he has been a Visiting Professor at the Paris Graduate School of Management (ESCP) and the European School of Management (EAP) in Paris, France. He is the author of numerous publications on cross-cultural management, leadership styles, joint ventures, and technology parks in Asia.

Chin-Tiong Tan, author of Chapter 8, recently joined the new Singapore Management University, Singapore, as Distinguished Professor and Deputy Provost. Previously he was a Professor of Marketing and Director of Continuing Education at the National University of Singapore. He received his PhD from Pennsylvania State University. He taught at Pennsylvania State and the University of the Pacific, and has been a Visiting Professor at the Helsinki School of Economics and the University of Witwatersrand (Johannesburg, South Africa) and a Visiting Scholar at Stanford University. Active in management development and consulting, he designs and teaches in programmes around the world. He has lectured throughout Asia, the USA, Europe, Australia and South Africa. He is currently Academic Adviser to Singapore Airlines' Management Development Centre, acts as strategic adviser to several other firms and sits on the board of directors of two companies. He is immediate Past President of the Marketing Institute of Singapore and is Director of the Board of the Asia-Pacific Federation of Marketing and the World Marketing Federation. He is co-author of *Marketing Management: An Asian Perspective* and *Cases in Marketing Management and Strategy: An Asia-Pacific Perspective* (both Prentice-Hall), and *New Asian Emperors: The Overseas Chinese, their Strategies and Competitive Advantages* (Butterworth-Heinemann). He has published in the *Journal of Consumer Research, European Journal of Marketing, International Marketing Review, International Journal of Bank Marketing, Journal of International Business Studies, International Journal of Marketing, Marketing and Psychology, Research in Marketing* and *Marketing Intelligence and Planning,* among others.

Kong-Yam Tan (BA Hons [1979] Princeton University, MA [1983] and PhD [1984] Stanford University), author of Chapters 3 and 3.1, is currently Associate Professor and Head of the Department of Business Policy at the National University of Singapore (NUS), Singapore. Prior to joining NUS, he worked at the Hoover Institution, World Bank, the Monetary Authority of Singapore, and was the Director of Research at the Ministry of Trade and Industry in Singapore. His research interests are in international trade and finance, growth and development in the Asia Pacific region and economic reforms in China. He has published in major international journals including *American Economic Review, Long Range Planning* and *Australian Journal of Management* on economic and business issues in the Asia Pacific region. He has consulted for many organizations including Citibank, IBM, ATT, BP, Samsung, Bank of China, Ikea and Mobil. He was a board member of the Central Provident Fund Board from 1984 to 1996. He is currently Chief Editor of the *Asia Pacific Journal of Management.*

Mun-Heng Toh, author of Chapter 9, is an Associate Professor in the Department of Business Policy at the National University of Singapore, Singapore. He obtained his doctoral degree in Economics and Econometrics from the University of London, London School of Economics. His research interests and publications are in the areas of econometric modelling, input-output analysis, international trade and investment, human resource development, and household economics and development strategies of emerging economies in the Asia Pacific. He has co-authored and edited several books such as *The Economics of Education and Manpower Development: Issues and Policies in Singapore, Economic Impact of the Withdrawal of the GSP on Singapore, Challenge and Response: Thirty years of the Economic Development Board, Public Policies in Singapore: A Decade of Changes* and *ASEAN Growth Triangles.* He has been engaged as consultant in various economic projects sponsored by agencies in the private and public sectors. These include UNESCAP, the United Nations Organization, the Asian Development Bank, the Association of South East Asian Nations (ASEAN) Secretariat, Singapore Contractor's Association, Port of Singapore Authority, Singapore Telecom, the Singapore Tourist Promotion Board, the Ministry of Health (Singapore) and the Ministry of Trade and Industry (Singapore).

Truong Quang (PhD), author of Chapters 19 and 19.1, is a Visiting Faculty of international business, human resource management, and organizational behaviour and change at the School of Management, Asian Institute of Technology in Bangkok,

Thailand. He is also a Visiting Professor at Thammasat International Institute of Technology and the National Institute of Development Administration (NIDA) in Thailand, ENAG in Laos, and Europa Institut in Zaarbrucken, Germany.

Ingo Walter, author of Chapter 4, is the Charles Simon Professor of Applied Financial Economics at the Stern School of Business, NYU, USA; he also serves as Director of the New York University Salomon Center, an independent academic research institute founded in 1972 to focus on financial institutions, instruments and markets. He also holds a joint appointment as Swiss Bank Corporation Professor of International Management, European Institute of Administrative Affairs (INSEAD), Fontainebleau, France. Professor Walter received his AB and MS degrees from Lehigh University and his PhD in 1966 from NYU. He taught at the University of Missouri-St Louis from 1965 to 1970, and has been on the faculty at NYU since 1970. From 1971 to 1979 he was Associate Dean for Academic Affairs, and subsequently served a number of terms as Chairman of International Business and Chairman of Finance. His joint appointment with INSEAD dates from 1985. Professor Walter's principal areas of academic and consulting activity include international trade policy, international banking, environmental economics and economics of multinational corporate operations. He has published papers in various professional journals in these fields and is the author or editor of twenty-three books, the most recent of which include *Global Banking* (with Professor Roy C. Smith) published by Oxford University Press in 1996, and *Financial System Design: Universal Banking Considered* (co-edited with Professor Anthony Saunders) published in 1996 by Irwin Professional. His books on the Asia Pacific include *High Performance Financial Systems* published by the ASEAN Economic Research Unit of the Institute of Southeast Asian Studies, Singapore, in 1993 and *Restructuring Japan's Financial Markets* (with Professor Takato Hiraki) published by Irwin in 1993. At present, his interests focus on competitive structure, conduct and performance in the international banking and financial services industry, as well as international trade and investment issues. He has served as a consultant to various government agencies, international institutions, banks and corporations, and has held a number of board memberships.

Ho-Ching Wei (PhD), author of Chapters 22 and 22.1, is currently a Lecturer at the University of Western Sydney, Macarthur, Australia, where he is also the Coordinator of the Bachelor of Commerce (Management). Before commencing his career in academe, he served as a senior executive for over ten years in large companies in Taiwan. He was also an owner-manager of an SME (small or medium sized enterprise) and has had foreign direct investment experiences with his own company. His current research interests are the decision-making processes of top management and/or owner-managers, and the part that the networks around the owner-managers play in the decision-making processes.

R. I. Westwood, author of Chapters 21 and 21.1, is Senior Lecturer and Director of PhD Programs at the Graduate School of Business, University of Sydney, Australia. Educated in the UK, he has spent the past fifteen years working at universities in the Asia Pacific region, for most of that time at the Chinese University of Hong Kong. He has research interests in cross-cultural management issues, gender and organization, the meaning and experience of work, power-language issues in organization theory, and postmodernist approaches to conceptualizing organization and management. He has published numerous articles and book chapters in these areas and is the editor of and chief contributor to *Organizational Behavior: Southeast Asian Perspectives*. He is currently co-editing a book, *Language and Organization*, to be published by Sage in 1998–99.

Donald Xie, author of Chapter 2, is Director of Finance at Gates Rubber Company in Denver, Colorado, USA. He was born in Shanghai, China, and received his early education there. He worked as an accountant in Shanghai from 1982 to 1986 with the China National Native Produce and Animal By-Products Import and Export Corporation. He received a BA in Economics at Goshen College in the USA in 1990 and subsequently worked as an international project manager with CTB, Inc. He completed a Master of International Management degree at Thunderbird in 1996. He joined Gates Rubber Company after working as a business consultant in Shanghai.

Acknowledgements

This book about strategic management in the Asia Pacific required co-ordinating authors and topics across Asia, Australia, New Zealand, Europe and the USA – and over three years spanning some of the most momentous changes in the region's history. I hope the book demonstrates that global joint ventures can achieve desired goals and meet stakeholders' expectations. I wholeheartedly thank all the authors for their patience, good humour, excellent analyses and timely contributions on their areas of expertise. I also thank the thousands of middle and senior managers and policy-makers in Australia, India, Singapore, Thailand, Vietnam and the USA, and from around the world, who provided feedback and helped me to refine my ideas.

Several of the articles in this book originated from four special issues on strategic management and organizational change in the Asia Pacific that I guest edited for *Management Decision* (*MD*) and the *Journal of Organizational Change Management* (*JOCM*) from 1996 to 1998. I greatly appreciate the unstinting co-operation of MCB University Press, publishers of the journals, in granting me permission to republish these articles. At MCB, I owe special thanks to Jonathan Barker, Jenny Pickles and Chris Perry. John Peters (Editor of *MD*) and David Boje (Editor of *JOCM*) rendered friendship, support and guidance through this book project.

Others contributed to developing and to polishing this book. Rod Davies gave opportunities to discuss several ideas on the Asia Pacific Management Forum. My little kittens, Comet and Marmalade, made their suggestions and kept me company through the writing.

Finally, I appreciate the forbearance and support of my publisher, Butterworth-Heinemann: Jonathan Glasspool (who has since left Butterworth-Heinemann to join an MBA programme), Kathryn Grant, Catherine Clarke and Margaret Denley (at Oxford) and Katherine Greig (at Boston), who fielded many calls and queries, even after hours, and offered suggestions with grace and calm in the flurry of activity.

I dedicate this book to my parents, Dr C. Venkatesan and Nandini Venkatesan, and my grandparents, Vasudev N. Bellare and Indira (Kutta) Bellare, for their love, support and intellectual stimulation through this life's journey.

Usha C. V. Haley
October 1999
E-mail: uhaley@asia-pacific.com

Section A

Introduction and overview

Chapter 1

Why the Asia Pacific still matters

■ Usha C. V. Haley ■

■ Introduction

Tokyo, 1989. The Nikkei Index hits 39 000. Japanese newspapers hail a new era, predicting when Japan's gross domestic product (GDP) will overtake the USA's. Japan's revered bureaucrats send missions to teach others in the Asia Pacific how to replicate the Japanese model of capitalism. The country's enormous banks, flush with cash, extend their global reach with huge loans abroad. Restaurants sprinkle sushi with gold leaf. Japanese leaders sternly warn the USA that its lazy workers and huge deficits threaten the world's economy.

New York, 1999. The Dow Index hits 11 000. The *Wall Street Journal*'s Op-Ed Page hails a new era as old measures of market risk no longer apply. Alan Greenspan, the Federal Reserve Bank's Chairman, says the Japanese model of capitalism is dead. Citicorp and Travelers work on a megamerger to extend their global reach. Manhattan restaurants charge $4000 for a $1500 bottle of wine. President Clinton sternly warns Japan that its political paralysis and inadequate economic initiatives threaten the world's economy. *The more things change, the more they remain the same ...*

In the throes of the Asian financial crisis, a book on strategic management in the Asia Pacific may appear ill-timed. The interconnected Asia Pacific economies are faring badly. Since 1990, Asia accounted for two-thirds of global GDP growth; in 1999, because of the crisis, most estimates have the Asian economies experiencing a recession, perhaps even a depression. Japan, which exports about 4.4 per cent of its GDP within Asia, is already in recession. Australia and New Zealand, with Indonesia and Japan as major trading partners, and which export about 12 per cent of their GDP to Asia generally, will probably dip into recession.

Researchers and policy-makers no longer talk glowingly about Japanese management or Asian values; and no one is alluding to the Pacific Century as this millennium was going to be called. Now, the Asia Pacific limps to the twenty-first century with weak banks, beleaguered currencies and looming national deficits; while, in the West, the traditionally dominant economies stride buoyant, strong and confident. The USA, in particular, is experiencing a seven-year boom, with its first budgetary surplus in a generation, unemployment at its lowest in over two decades, a very strong currency, and more citizens expressing hope for the future than in the last forty years. No wonder Western analysts and journalists have labelled the Asian financial markets' collapses as the Asian Contagion and they now sneeringly refer to a once vibrant Asia Pacific region as Asia Pathetic. The West can indulge in this emotional gratification for one moment – but, not unscathed, for two.

The Asia Pacific remains central to the West for three primary reasons: the sources of self-renewing growth and market potential that Asia offers Western manufacturers, and the alternative models of development and change that the Asia Pacific presents for global competition. The recent, much-publicized economic and organizational failures do not alter these fundamentals for strategic decision-making and investment.

- *Sources of growth* In recent years, the Asian developing countries have been net consumers, making them the only parts of the world, besides the USA, to run trade deficits. Asia fuelled global GDP growth by providing markets for foreign manufacturers' products. In Asia, competition between US and Japanese multinational corporations (MNCs) fanned regional growth and provided avenues for many corporate innovations and changes, and Asia's emerging markets provided channels for corporate investments when growth prospects looked bleak in developed markets. Increasing Asian demand concurrently increased production and investments in several foreign countries including the USA, Japan, New Zealand and Australia. However, this situation will probably change as the Asian economies try to export their way out of trouble. For example, after the Mexican peso's devaluation in 1995, cheap Mexican exports jumped by 30 per cent in most industries, turning Mexico from a net consumer to a net exporter. As financial issues resolve, cheap Southeast Asian exports will probably flood the USA's and Europe's markets.

- *Market potential* The West accounts for around 45 per cent of the world's GDP with 13 per cent of the population. Successful changes in the Asia Pacific, within open, market-based economies, will probably reduce the West's share of GDP in three decades to around 30 per cent, while Asia's may rise to around 58 per cent. These predictions rest on the reasonable assumption that three of the four most populous countries in the world – China, India and Indonesia, with about 41 per cent of the world's population – achieve per capita average growth of 5 per cent or more for the next thirty years. Growth rates tend to fall as developing countries close income gaps with the USA (at about US$27 000 per capita). While all of the Asia Pacific has continued room for significant growth, the high-income East Asian countries, as well as Australia and New Zealand with developed economies, will grow much more slowly in the next thirty years because of capital deepening and ageing populations. Through institutional and political changes, managerial training and policy reforms, Indonesia and China, with low incomes and young populations, should continue to grow by at least 5 per cent. With policy reforms, India should surpass its previous growth rates as demographic changes favour higher savings and greater consumption.

- *Alternative models of development and change* Many of the Asia Pacific's countries lack the West's corporate structures and sophisticated markets. For example, much of

Asia's human capital lay in its governments and, so, state planners led the way in developmental efforts. These alternative models of change and capitalism resulted in enormous, unthinkable successes. With the leapfrogging of technological and developmental cycles, Singapore, Hong Kong and Taiwan blazed an array of changes to approximate developed country status in a little over two decades. The Asian high-flying economies achieved rapid export growth, followed wise fiscal policies, controlled population growth, encouraged savings, education and basic literacy, and continued to support agriculture. These Asian achievements often drew on alliances between local governments and foreign MNCs. Something went very right in the Asia Pacific: No region sustained such high growth rates for that long – providing some validity to these models of development and change.

Something also went very wrong in the Asia Pacific. Wee Chow Hou, the dean at my former business school, the National University of Singapore, once told me that at his university, and in the Asia Pacific's organizations generally, process (or how one gets along within the system) assumes more importance than the bottom line (or what one actually achieves). Singapore remains one of the least corrupt countries in the world. Yet, in the Asia Pacific generally, without public scrutiny, the iron triangle of the three *b*s, businessmen, bureaucrats and bankers, led to the insidious three *c*s of complacency, corruption and cronyism. Private bankers and organizations neglected global standards when assessing investments; the investors relied instead on personal judgements or on personal connections. Spectacular regional growth and churning regional change obfuscated most bad business decisions; yet, these decision-making models had disturbing repercussions. In financially troubled Korea, for example, of the thirty top industrial corporations, twenty-five carried debt to equity ratios of between 3:1 and 8:1; 1:1 serves as the norm in Western economies. None of Korea's major trading partners (such as Singapore) or business partners (such as the Australian or US MNCs with joint ventures) knew of these business decisions. Similarly, by some estimates, East Asian banks' bad loans now account for about 20 per cent of their total loans in contrast with 1 per cent for US banks. The present Asian financial and economic crisis consequently provides many opportunities for harnessing regional change to decrease or control these debilitating regional characteristics.

The changes in the Asia Pacific have realigned coalitions and redistributed benefits and costs among stakeholders. The Asian crisis constitutes a propitious time to re-evaluate the region, to shed light on foreign investors' concerns and on local stakeholders' attempts to navigate and to harness regional change. Indeed, the regional countries' currency devaluations in the last year against the US dollar, from over 20 per cent (for the Australian and Singaporean dollars) to over 90 per cent (for the Indonesian rupiah), have whetted Western investors' efforts to snap up bargains. Daniel Schwartz, the publisher of *Asian Venture Capital Journal* which is published in Hong Kong, indicated that in the first four and half months of 1998, his company had tracked 479 merger and acquisition deals in Asia worth more than US$35 billion: These figures surge well ahead of the 711 such deals worth nearly US$59 billion for the whole of 1997 and the 627 deals worth US$45 billion in 1996 (Richardson, 1998). Multinational corporations, banks and money managers mainly from the USA and Europe, but also from some cash-rich companies in Australia, Singapore, Taiwan and Hong Kong, dominated this buying. "No matter how bad it is over here, this is a part of the world you can't ignore,' said Michael Koeneke, chairman of Global Mergers and

Acquisitions for Merrill Lynch securities. 'If you do not have a position in the Asia-Pacific region, you're behind the curve' (Richardson, 1998).

Foreign MNCs appear to incorporate perceptions of political and economic risks, as well as market potential considerations, into their acquisition decisions in the Asia Pacific. For example, in 1998, foreign MNCs appeared extremely cautious about making acquisitions in Indonesia because of the country's political and economic instability. Similarly, foreign acquisitions in Malaysia during the second half of 1998 approximated only around US$250 million. The IFR Securities Data's Robert Babbish argued that, 'This lack of enthusiasm by foreign buyers can perhaps be attributed to a large degree to the Malaysian government's vigilant attitude towards foreign acquirers as manifested by the government's stringent limitation on foreign ownership of local companies' (Behrmann, 1998). According to KPMG Corporate Finance, in 1998, Asian high-risk countries experiencing big drops in foreign direct investments (FDI) included China (down to US$2.53 billion from US$6.5 billion in 1997), India (down to US$209 million from US$1.26 billion in 1997) and Indonesia (down to US$1 billion from US$2.2 billion in 1997). The Philippines appeared hardest hit with almost no FDI in 1998 compared with US$2.4 billion previously (Behrmann, 1998). The MNCs' nervousness spread to Australia, said KPMG, where FDI crumbled to US$2 billion in the first six months of 1998 from US$6.2 billion a year ago. However, as this book indicates, some perceptions of risk by MNCs may revolve around superficial indicators. Theory development is desperately needed in this agitated region to guide future investment and to influence present business operations. Section B explores some of the influences of the regional changes on foreign investors, local stakeholders and local governments.

The regional changes over the last decade have also demanded and received correspondingly great changes from organizations operating in the Asia Pacific. Some of the major forthcoming organizational changes will derive from changed ownership: corporate ownership in Asia is shifting from local companies and governments to foreign MNCs. Countries hit hardest by the crisis, including Thailand, Indonesia, South Korea, Malaysia and the Philippines, are relaxing restrictions on foreign ownership in areas such as financial services, property and retailing where they previously barred or tightly controlled foreign investors. The economic and financial crisis is also forcing many East Asian companies to sell loss-making and non-core assets to pay off loans and to stay in business; similarly, local debt-laden banks, finance companies and securities houses are seeking large injections of foreign money to stay afloat. For example, in 1998 South Korea's heavily indebted Hanwha Energy Company Ltd sold its power-generation business to the USA's AES Corporation for US$874 million; Thailand's largest company, the Charoen Pokphand group, sold a 75 per cent stake in its Lotus supermarket chain to the British supermarket giant Tesco PLC for £200 million (US$320 million); and Merrill Lynch said it would pay up to US$68 million to take majority control of Phatra Securities Company, one of Thailand's largest brokerage firms, in a bet on the eventual turnaround of the battered Thai stock market. Similarly, Commerzbank AG of Germany announced in mid-1998 that it would invest US$250 million to buy 30 per cent of Korea Exchange Bank in South Korea. Earlier in 1998, two of Thailand's largest banks, Bangkok Bank Ltd. and Thai Farmers Bank Ltd., raised about US$2 billion between them in private sales to foreign institutional investors. As much as half of Thailand's banking system will fall into the large foreign banks' hands, said Aswin

Kongsiri, chairman of the board of executive directors at Bangkok Bank of Commerce (Richardson, 1998). These foreign MNCs will have to learn how to do business in Asia and against traditionally dominant competitors who know the local markets.

According to IFR, since the Asian crisis began, foreign MNCs have aggressively stepped up acquisitions in six key Northeast and Southeast Asian countries that have experienced a collapse in currencies and markets – notably Japan, South Korea, Hong Kong, Malaysia, Thailand and Indonesia (Behrmann, 1998). The IFR's data, based on announced public and private deals, show that the foreign MNCs' acquisitions slumped to US$1.7 billion in the third quarter of 1997 from US$3.9 billion in the second quarter and US$2 billion in the first. After the financial and economic crisis hit full stride, the foreign MNCs' acquisitions jumped to US$3.4 billion in the fourth quarter of 1997 and, in 1998, purchases of select depressed Asian businesses soared to US$6.3 billion in the first quarter and to US$7.6 billion in the second. The IFR's latest data from July 1998 reveal that acquisition deals have already reached US$1.04 billion. US MNCs undertook 59 per cent of the total acquisitions in the past four quarters, followed by the UK with 11 per cent and Germany with 9 per cent. Japanese and South Korean companies formed more than 60 per cent of the acquisitions. In Japan, Merrill Lynch, Travelers Group and others are repositioning themselves in anticipation of the Big Bang reforms, said Robert Babbish from IFR. In South Korea, conversely, the list of sellers constitutes debt ridden companies struggling to recapitalize and to refocus their businesses by shedding non-core assets amassed from free-spending yesteryears (Behrmann, 1998). While Hong Kong sold notably less than Japan and Korea to non-Asian MNCs, its sell-off volume none the less increased to about US$825 million in the first half of 1998 from US$351 million in the same 1997 period. Purchases in Thailand also rose noticeably in the first half of 1998 from the corresponding period in 1997. Purchases in the Asian financial services sector, mainly Japan, paralleling the development of universal banking globally, accounted for about a quarter or more than US$5 billion of the deals from mid-1997 to mid-1998 (Behrmann, 1998; Richardson, 1998).

The Asian financial crisis has dramatically accelerated the process of change among local companies and governments. Asia has experienced severe crises in the past, like the oil crisis of 1973–74; yet, these crises constituted external shocks. In contrast, the present crisis seems more of a collapse from within, especially with Japan's long stagnation since 1990. Consequently, the Asian crisis raises fundamental questions about structural changes in the Asia Pacific and whether new strategies appear necessary for locals. In the wake of the Asian financial crisis, many governmental policy-makers and managers regard capitalism's Eastern versions, particularly the variety that Japan developed and South Korea adopted, as creating problems rather than providing solutions. While many aspects of East Asia's community ethos will remain, Asian officials and scholars suggest that the region's organizations may emerge from the financial crisis looking more like those of the USA. As Lee Hong-koo, a member of the South Korean National Assembly and a former Prime Minister, said,

> The model is now clear. It's not Japan. It's the West. The current crisis has convinced almost all people that that the old style doesn't work. We will adjust ourselves rapidly to the new requirements, which means we will fashion ourselves more like the West, like the U.S. and European model. (*New York Times*, 1998)

Although organizational changes appear inevitable, MNCs and local companies face looming questions about which organizational characteristics and practices they plan to retain and which they hope to change for long-term competitive advantage. Section C explores some of the strategies for change undertaken by MNCs, local companies and local governments.

Generally, through the Asian crisis's froth and spray, some trends seem to be affecting the Asia Pacific region and organizational operations, portending major changes for stakeholders. The trends include:

- *Japan's relative decline*   The fight for corporate advantage in the Asia Pacific constitutes part of an intensifying global competitive fight in many key industries. Of the three groups of MNCs, US, Japanese and European, most prominent in the struggle, analysts perceive that the Japanese now lie in the underdog position in the Asia Pacific because of their economy's, banking system's and currency's weaknesses. Consequently, Japan and Japanese MNCs greatly risk losing their previous commercial dominance in the region. Concomitantly, the US and European economies and MNCs will hold greater sway in the Asia Pacific and probably dominate the Asia Pacific's economies and cultures.

- *Nationalistic backlashes*   Some East Asian officials and other critics of foreign takeovers in Malaysia, Thailand and South Korea have already voiced concerns about Asia losing control of its economic destiny. This nationalist backlash will probably grow shriller and stronger as the region's economic pains increase in the months ahead. In mid-1998, Prime Minister Mahathir bin Mohamad of Malaysia repeatedly lambasted attempts by foreign 'robbers' to take over major Malaysian companies. Mahathir warned that the foreign MNCs' takeovers of devalued assets in East Asia threatened regional governments' independence and created a new form of colonial exploitation similar to that of the US-controlled Latin American 'banana republics'. Increased control and scrutiny of MNCs' local operations form natural corollaries to this nationalistic backlash – as do steadily-increasing, potentially explosive local outrage and animosity over some of the MNCs' ostensibly exploitative activities.

- *Less local governmental control*   Governments may control economies less than before. The Korean Finance Ministry no longer chooses borrowers for banks; and the Japanese Finance Ministry has lost its capacity to determine banks' and securities houses' fates. Consequently, despite official Japanese assurances that no big bank would fail, some did. Less governmental control would constitute a major shift for many of the government-led economies of East and Southeast Asia, and allow for the mushrooming of other local forms of enterpreneurship and capital.

- *More labour market flexibility*   As the financial crisis churns economic futures for countries and companies, labour markets in the Asia Pacific may display more flexibility, and unemployment rates will rise. Lifetime employment and rigid seniority systems will assume less importance and lay-offs will increase. South Korea's unemployment rate may quadruple by 1999 to over 10 per cent. Similarly, Singapore and Hong Kong, for the first time in nearly two decades, are experiencing significant unemployment and lay-offs.

- *More open systems*   Generally, relationships in the Asia Pacific may assume less importance. A more open system may replace the traditional system of linked companies, called *keiretsu* in Japan and *chaebol* in South Korea, that conduct business with each other on a basis of loyalty rather than price. For the first time, business groups in both countries are allowing affiliates to collapse; similarly, Hong Kong's home-grown champion of relationship finance, Peregrine Securities, collapsed in early 1998.

• *Global imperatives and logic*   Globalization, and global, rather than national, logic and imperatives are changing the manners in which local companies work and perceive their environments, managers interact with stakeholders and governmental policies affect local citizens. Local companies may focus more on making money and less on building market share. Local governments and foreign investors are demanding that Japanese banks and South Korean *chaebol* disclose more accurate and useful financial information. Everyone is paying more attention to credit-worthiness.

• *More privatization and governmental restructuring*   East Asian governments, under pressure to cut costs and to raise revenues, are selling substantial stakes in state-owned and state-controlled industries to foreign investors to access extra cash, management expertise, technology and new markets. In mid-1998, the Indonesian government named nine investment banks to manage the sale of substantial stakes in twelve state-controlled companies spanning telecommunications, cement, steel, airports, mining, toll roads and plantations. Regional governments are concomitantly facing the dilemma of raising the maximum amount of money while giving away the least amount of management control.

The remainder of this book explores in greater detail these trends' facets and their influences on stakeholders. The next section provides an overview of the book's contents.

■ Overview

This book about strategic management in the Asia Pacific draws on varied levels of analysis to explore strategies of change, and responses to new and diverse pressures, in the rapidly changing Asia Pacific. The mission engaged authors and topics across Asia, Australia, New Zealand, Europe and the USA over three years spanning some of the most momentous changes in the region's history. Many of the chapters in this book come from four special issues on that topic for journals that I guest edited from 1996 to 1998. The chapters form a documentary of the events that led to the Asian financial and economic crisis, precipitated it and are now shaping the global future. Consequently, the crisis serves as a watershed to observe continuity and discontinuity in theories and understandings about the Asia Pacific and the organizations in the region. I explicitly requested the contributors, acknowledged experts in their fields, to find patterns in the Asia Pacific's economic, political and social environments, both before and after the Asian crisis, to bridge discontinuities and to use their renewed comprehension to guide MNCs, local companies and local governments to manage strategically through and beyond the present crisis.

The chapters focus on the Asia Pacific's major markets and organizations: the contributors discuss the effects of some of the large-scale changes in the Asia Pacific on regional and organizational stakeholders, propose implications for successful and effective regional and organizational restructuring, and thereby have implications for management and research. The chapters in Section B, Regional Change, centre on regional trends, long-lasting patterns, and stochastic changes and their influences on investors, local stakeholders and local governments. The chapters in Section C, Organizational Change, focus on the corresponding strategic changes for organizations and include implications for MNCs, local companies and local governments. Each chapter has an accompanying mini-chapter applying the theoretical findings to the present-day crisis in the Asia Pacific and exploring implications for effective strategic management. As further changes appear inevitable, Sections B and C include some of the best World Wide Web (WWW) resources for managers, academics and policy-makers to continue to research the topics and to keep current on developments. An outline follows.

Outline

Section B, Regional Change

- *Part One: Foreign Investors' Concerns*   *Chapter 2*, by Llewellyn D. Howell and Donald Xie, and *Chapter 2.1*, by Llewellyn D. Howell, address the problems of predicting the region's political and economic risks in the period surrounding the Asian crisis and propose strategies for reducing errors. In *Chapter 3*, Kong-Yam Tan, Singapore's former chief economist, provides a historical perspective on East Asia's growth and elaborates on how this new economic order is shaping competitive environments. In *Chapter 3.1*, Kong-Yam Tan continues with an analysis of Asia's economic and financial crises, incorporates the explanations into Asia's historical evolution and provides scenarios to help foreign investors' planning. *Chapter 4*, by Anthony Saunders and Ingo Walter, explores costs and benefits of universal banking for investors, extrapolating from the largest financial market in the world, the USA, to the restructuring financial markets in the Asia Pacific. In *Chapter 4.1*, Usha C. V. Haley specifically analyses Dutch Bank's, ABN Amro's, counter-intuitive universal banking strategy in the post-crisis Asia Pacific. *Chapter 5*, by Mike Hobday, spotlights the competitive problems and opportunities, especially for the European Union, regarding technological innovation by MNCs in Malaysia. In *Chapter 5.1*, Mike Hobday focuses on the effects of the Asian crisis on innovation opportunities and lessons for MNCs operating in the Asia Pacific. *Chapter 6*, by Ian Marsh, generally addresses Australia's regionalization drive and the lack of qualified managers who know the Asia Pacific. In *Chapter 6.1*, Ian Marsh elaborates on the specific effects of the Asian financial and economic crisis on Australian investments in Asia.

- *Part Two: Local Stakeholders' Concerns*   *Chapter 7*, by Kam-hon Lee, highlights the Chinese ethics, values and morals that permeate local managers' and policy-makers' behaviours and expectations. In *Chapter 7.1*, Kam-hon Lee analyses some moral considerations and strategic moves in post-crisis Asia. In *Chapter 8*, George T. Haley and Chin-Tiong Tan survey the lack of data in the Asia Pacific to make market-related decisions and explain how the dearth stemmed from local business groups' efforts to compete against often superior foreign technologies. In *Chapter 8.1*, George T. Haley focuses on the effects of the Asian crisis on transparency and directness in local business groups' business practices. In *Chapter 9*, Usha C. V. Haley, Linda Low and Mun-Heng Toh expand on the ramifications for local stakeholders of the metaphor they coined, Singapore Incorporated, subsequently used by the govern-

ment to market itself locally and globally, as well as to address Singapore's government-led development. In *Chapter 9.1*, Usha C. V. Haley indicates the symbolic significance of Singapore Incorporated's official WWW site. In *Chapters 10* and *10.1*,
Sam K. Steffensen sketches how Japanese information networks are jerkily restructuring themselves and local managers are reevaluating traditional work practices in
response to new information technologies. *Chapter 11*, by André M. Everett, elaborates on how sweeping structural reforms have affected New Zealand's business
environments. In *Chapter 11.1*, André M. Everett explores the effects of the Asian
crisis on New Zealand's companies and other local stakeholders.

- *Part Three: Local Governments' Concerns* In *Chapter 12*, Usha C. V. Haley and
Linda Low weigh the benefits and costs of the Singaporean government's deliberate crafting of a Singaporean culture to respond to MNCs' needs. *Chapter 12.1*,
by Usha C. V. Haley, focuses on INSEAD's first international campus in
Singapore as a governmental effort to heighten local creativity and research. In
Chapter 13, Usha C. V. Haley elaborates on Singapore's self-perceived role as
intermediary to the world through industrial parks and focused investments in
emerging Asian economies. *Chapter 13.1*, by Usha C. V. Haley, homes in on the
Vietnamese and Singaporean governments' efforts concerning the Vietnam-
Singapore Industrial Park. In *Chapter 14*, Usha C. V. Haley and George T. Haley
indicate how foreign investment in tourism is shaping Vietnam's future, and how
governmental policy can control this country's trajectory of development. In
Chapter 14.1, Usha C. V. Haley elaborates on the Vietnamese government's concerns in post-crisis Asia.

- *Part Four: World Wide Web Resources on Regional Change* Chapter 15, by Usha C. V.
Haley, includes carefully-chosen WWW sites generally to track regional change in
the Asia Pacific and specifically for up-to-date information on the topics covered by
individual chapters in Section B.

Section C: Organizational Change
- *Part Five: Foreign Multinational Corporations' Strategies* In *Chapter 16*, Gary Fontaine
elaborates on problems encountered when transferring foreign employees to, from
and within the Asia Pacific and offers practical suggestions for MNCs' human
resource practices. In *Chapter 16.1*, Usha C. V. Haley specifically identifies some
MNCs' strategies to retain expatriate employees in the Asia Pacific. In *Chapter 17*,
George T. Haley and Usha C. V. Haley profile the powerful local business networks,
the Overseas Chinese and Overseas Indians, against whom foreign MNCs have to
compete in Southeast Asia, and offer suggestions for effective strategies. *Chapter
17.1*, by George T. Haley, highlights possible modifications in foreign MNCs' strategies when dealing with these business networks in crisis torn Asia and for long-
lasting regional dominance. *Chapter 18*, by Terence Jackson and Mette Bak,
examines Western MNCs' human resource practices in China, identifies probable
reasons for failures to inculcate desired work values in Chinese employees and
suggests successful strategies. In *Chapter 18.1*, Terence Jackson and Mette Bak place
MNCs' human resource practices and investments in the broader context of China
in the wake of the Asian crisis. In *Chapter 19*, Truong Quang, Fredric William
Swierczek and Dang Thi Kim Chi indicate why most foreign MNCs' joint ventures
with Vietnamese companies fail, and spotlight avenues for successful strategies.
Chapter 19.1, by Truong Quang and Fredric William Swierczek, explores the impli-

cations of the Asian crisis for official ideology and MNCs' joint ventures in Vietnam.

- *Part Six: Local Companies' Strategies*   In *Chapters 20* and *20.1*, George T. Haley describes how the dominant business force in Asia, the Overseas Chinese business networks, engage in strategic planning and indicates how they are reacting to the crisis. In *Chapters 21* and *21.1*, R. I. Westwood and P. S. Kirkbride narrate how one Hong Kong company imitates Western business practices for symbolic reassurances to local stakeholders, and analyse Western symbols' relevance for local companies in financially-troubled Asia. Ho-Ching Wei and Chris Christodolou in *Chapters 22* and *22.1* analyse how small and medium sized Taiwanese companies make decisions to invest in the Asia Pacific and how the Asian crisis has affected these practices. *Chapters 23* and *23.1*, by Peter Ping Li, examines innovative restructuring strategies, historically and in crisis torn Asia, undertaken by Taiwan's Acer, the third largest computer manufacturer in the world, whose founder, Stan Shih, used the metaphor of fast-food preparation to change his company's operations. *Chapter 24* and *24.1*, by Ranjan Das, indicate how MNCs emanating from India formulate strategies to compete effectively with foreign investment at home, and how India's post-crisis business environments have affected these strategies.

- *Part Seven: Local Government' Strategies*   In *Chapters 25* and *25.1*, Lindsay Nelson and Peter J. Dowling explore the Australian government's privatization of the electricity industry in Tasmania and general Australian concerns about privatization programmes. In *Chapter 26* and *26.1*, Siew Kien Sia and Boon Siong Neo sketch restructuring efforts by a Singaporean governmental organization, the Inland Revenue Authority, in response to deregulation and global efficiency requirements, and the Singaporean government's drive for bureaucratic efficiency.

- *Part Eight: World Wide Web Resources on Organizational Change*   *Chapter 27*, by Usha C. V. Haley, includes carefully chosen WWW sites with which, generally, to track organizational change in the Asia Pacific and, specifically, to obtain up-to-date information on the topics covered by individual chapters in Section C.

For countries and organizations, long-lasting prosperity relies on analysing historical factors for successes, and in controlling them for effective change, rather than in wholesale condemning or abandoning of the past. Some analysts mistakenly equated the Asia Pacific economies' past successes with their models' and values' absolute superiority; analogously, the West should avoid mistakenly equating the Asia Pacific economies' present troubles with their models' and values' absolute inferiority. Unlike the Mexican case, the Asian crisis reveals that private organizations and banks, rather than solely governments, made large-scale faulty investments and strategic decisions that cast a shadow over Western investments. However, in the Chinese alphabet, the character for crisis also serves as the character for opportunity. This book aims to contribute to perceiving and harnessing opportunities for strategic change in the midst of crisis. With effective intervention, the millennium will yet prove to be the Pacific Century.

■ References

Behrmann, N. (1998). Foreign acquisitions in six key Asian nations soar. *Business Times* (Singapore), 27 July.

New York Times (1998). 17 January.

Richardson, M. (1998). West snaps up Asian businesses, *International Herald Tribune*, 20 June.

Section B

Regional change

Part One

Foreign investors' concerns

Chapter 2

Asia at risk: the impact of methodology in forecasting[1]

■ Llewellyn D. Howell and Donald Xie ■

■ Assessing risk for foreign investors

As foreign investors have clamoured into Asia in the 1990s hoping to tap into the spectacular economic growth, the importance of the concept of 'international political economy' has struck nearly all. Investing firms have found that they must deal with governments in gaining access, with cultural attributes in human resource management, with local politics in developing and maintaining operations, with social attributes in marketing. In the rush to capitalize on the opportunities of emerging and developing markets, many investors are stepping into the unknown. But no one likes the unknown. Every investor wants to narrow the odds. Some steps are inevitably taken to shape the odds of winning the foreign investment game. Shaping the odds with respect to the social and political context means reducing political risk. To reduce future risk, it first has to be projected or forecast.

There are a number of models which underlie the projections of political risk. The projections are employed today by numerous firms planning risk management or protection for foreign investors. The large majority of these models are constructed by using a set of variables which represent the complexity of social and political phenomena found in the environment of the foreign investor. The forecasting concept is that certain societal characteristics today (such as the existence of an authoritarian government) will be followed within a specified period by damaging actions against the foreign investor (such as expropriation). More extreme characteristics would be followed by more extreme actions. The responsibility of the risk analyst is to examine today's attributes and project tomorrow's damage. Sets of indicative societal characteristics are assembled into configurations which are referred to as 'models'.

Most of the models are linear; that is, they project on the basis that the more the neg-

[1] This chapter has been published previously by MCB University Press Limited: Howell, L. D. and Xie, D. (1996). Asia at risk: the impact of methodology in forecasting. *Management Decision*, **34** (9), 6–16.

ative characteristic, the more damage. Among the linear models there are two basic categories. Widely available and accessible are 'editorial' models created by business magazines and publications such as *The Economist* and *Fortune*. There are also professionally constructed models which emanate from the academic communities and commerce-oriented research organizations. A number of political risk services (PRS) exist which provide forecasts for foreign investors based on these models. Among these are BERI (Business Environment Risk Intelligence), ICRG (the International Country Risk Guide), the Economist Intelligence Unit (EIU), S. J. Rundt and Associates, and others (Coplin and O'Leary, 1994).

In this assessment we have examined two models, one from each category. From the business magazine category, we will examine *The Economist* model. From the professional services, we will look at the BERI model. The two models are representative of their categories and they are both influential and come with a reputable standing. Used appropriately, each can be of significant use to the investing firm.

■ Socio-political risk

Before a forecast of political losses (an assessment of 'risk') can be undertaken, a definitional description of political risk is required. A solution to this definitional problem is to start with the practitioners. 'Risk' clearly raises a probabilistic question. Probability of what? Insurers against political risk have indicated what they will pay for. The common categories are expropriation, inconvertibility, war damage, civil strife damage, and breach of contract by a government or by reason of government interference. Political risk can initially be defined and described as the probability that a firm will suffer a loss due to expropriation or one of the other insured types of damage.

The US government's Overseas Private Investment Corporation (OPIC) insures US businesses against political risk but only for losses occurring in the first four categories mentioned above. Other types of politically-related losses exist as well and certainly are borne by firms other than those which are foreign based. In 1989 the government of China abruptly ended the agreed allocation of foreign exchange to a Chinese-American joint venture. The decision was political and arbitrary from the perspective of the foreign (US) investor. The Chinese government action could be seen as falling within the broad range of losses characterized by the Multilateral Investment Guarantee Agency (MIGA) of the World Bank and such private insurers as the American International Group (AIG) as 'breach of contract'. For this loss to be considered 'political', the contract must be repudiated in some way that can be described as having its origin in governmental decision-making or subject to political processes.

The insurance-based definition of political risk, however, does not address the wider list of politically-based damage to investing firms such as that due to arbitrary interference in personnel decisions or corruption. A broader definition and measure of political losses is therefore needed. For example, in November of 1991, four engineers who had been kidnapped in Colombia were freed after their company reportedly paid between $800 000 and $1 million. Such costs, while entirely due to the political situation in the country, are not recoverable from OPIC and therefore are not tabulated under this one existing loss tabulation system. Another example: because of the deteriorating political and military situation in Burma, Thai Airlines flights to Rangoon have flown only minimally occupied. Considerable revenue has been lost, similarly without compensation. These, too, are political losses to investors but do not fall into the standard insurable categories.

Close examination of political and social damage to foreign investors generates long lists of actions that business people wish they could have anticipated. A few of these that are easily identifiable from readings of the *New York Times* or the *Financial Times* are: damage to property; actions against personnel (such as kidnapping); limits on remittances; government interference with terms of a contract; discriminatory taxation; politically based regulations on operations; and loss of copyright protection.

These types of identifications are derived from observations or complaints by foreign investors. William Coplin and Michael O'Leary have developed a distinctive model for using a modified Delphi technique with expert predictions to project political risk. The variables employed in the PRS analysis represent a different stage in the process than those used by the linear models we are discussing here. While the former examine societal and system attributes, PRS – with one exception – examines direct government actions or economic functions that are likely to occur under potential political regimes in the country under study. Individually these constitute other acts that may be termed politically sourced losses. The events or actions that PRS includes in its analysis are: equity restrictions; personnel/procurement interference; taxation discrimination; repatriation restrictions; exchange controls; tariff imposition; non-tariff barrier imposition; payment delays; fiscal/monetary expansion; labour cost expansion.

These government actions constitute the 'taking' of profits from investors by a government and are therefore politically based losses. If we add these to the definition of what constitutes a politically based loss for OPIC or MIGA, we have an inclusive range that incorporates the more obvious (war damage or expropriation) as well as the more subtle (interference in personnel decisions by political personages or because of government social policy). Political risk is therefore the probability that damage emanating from a variety of political or social actions will damage the firm, some of which are insurable and some of which are not.

The problem remains of projecting the damaging actions. In the development of forecasting techniques, the task is to link theoretically the act resulting in loss (e.g. civil strife damage) to the causes of the act (an ethnic dispute dissolving into open conflict) or predictors of the cause or the event (such as the existence of ethnic tension). Based on historical memory, the argument is made that the presence of ethnic tension has a good probability of resulting in civil strife, and civil strife in turn directly resulting in a loss to the investor. Similarly, a rapid urbanization pace could result in a deterioration in health standards that takes a toll in the labour market, which in turn results in high absenteeism or poor performance. A modeller would presumably start with a list of acts having political or social manifestations that result in losses to an investor and look for predictors that can be observed in society. Since not all social and political circumstances would necessarily have the same influence on loss outcomes, variable impact should be differentiated, i.e. weighted.

Beginning with a list like that from OPIC and PRS, the modeller would try to envision the circumstances under which these events will occur. Political risk thus includes the existence of observable circumstances that could lead to damage. Political risk is not just the likelihood of losses but also the presence of threatening conditions. Assessment of political risk is the answer to the question: 'Based on the presence of threatening circumstances, what is the probability of damage?'

In projecting or forecasting, of course, the damage events are out in the future somewhere. The risk analyst must be able to project the events playing out at some point (say five years) and/or must also be able to forecast how the predictors will look in that somewhat distant future. The first assignment of the modeller, however, is simply to judge what circumstances lead to losses. Exactly what are the threatening conditions? *The Economist* and BERI Political Risk Index (PRI) methods are two such efforts to project from social and political attributes to subsequent losses to foreign firms investing in a country.

■ *The Economist* model

The Economist method (*The Economist*, 1986) is what might be termed an 'editorial' model, a creation of the editorial staff of a respected and widely distributed publication. It contains the basic elements a business user would expect to have included. An index of risk was created based on 100 points. Of those 100, thirty-three were attributed to economic factors, fifty to politics, and seventeen to 'society'. Each individual variable was assigned a weight the writers felt reflected the importance to the forecast of the particular variable. How these divisions between sets of variables were made or how weights were determined is not explained in the text but reportedly were contributions by editors and reporters.

For each of the three areas, specific variables (or 'threatening conditions') were selected which the writers felt reflected that particular domain. Among economic factors, *The Economist* selected 'Falling GDP per person', 'High inflation', 'Capital flight', 'High and rising foreign debt', 'Decline in food production per person', and 'Raw materials as a high percentage of exports'. While no explanation was provided of why these variables were selected or others (such as level of employment) were not, the variables chosen make sense from both a business and common-sense perspective. This is a point, however, where underlying theory should have directed choices but apparently did not.

In addition to the economic variables listed above, *The Economist* chose six political variables and four social variables that were felt to reflect threatening conditions. Each was weighted according to its presumed importance. They are:

1 *Political variables*:
   (a) Bad neighbours (three negative points) – regional conflicts and potential super-power intrusions.
   (b) Authoritarianism (seven points) – the absence of democratic practices and popular government.
   (c) Staleness (five points) – government too long in power, political sluggishness.
   (d) Illegitimacy (nine points) – lack of acceptance by the population.
   (e) Generals in power (six points) – the rigidity of military approaches to rule.
   (f) War/armed insurrection (twenty points) – open domestic or international conflict.

2 *Social variables*:

   (a) Urbanization pace (three points) – too rapid rural to urban shift, with associated ills.

   (b) Islamic Fundamentalism (four points) – an impact of Islamic extremists.

   (c) Corruption (six points) – the absence of contract law and regulated business practices.

   (d) Ethnic tension (four points) – ethnic division and disputes.

The Economist's results were widely distributed to business people and governments throughout the world. Their scores for Asia for the political and societal variables – which fall together under the category of 'political risk' – are presented in Table 2.1 (Howell, 1992). Table 2.1 lists the ten variables as mentioned above, in the same order, plus a total of the combined weights assigned to each Asian country. The total constitutes an index of political risk. The Asian countries in the Table 2.1 list are ranked from lowest risk score (best) to highest (worst). The economic variables are not included in this analysis. Our focus here is only on the political and social variables and the losses that stem from them. In this list based on 1986 data[2], Hong Kong, China, Singapore and Malaysia have the lowest political risk – the lowest in projected losses to foreign investors. Pakistan, Vietnam and Indonesia have the most risk and greatest projected losses in the period following the forecast (presumably about five years).

The Economist approach has appropriate qualities of clarity and simplicity. The variables have scope and meet common sense standards. They are weighted and thus differentiated. The resulting index meets important communications standards. But how good is that index? Before answering that question, let us examine another approach.

■ The BERI model

The BERI PRI was originated under the leadership of F. Ted Haner in the mid-1970s. The BERI index is based on scores assigned to ten 'political' variables by experts. These variables are conditions under which or following which losses occur. The BERI PRI variables are clearly identified as being 'socio-political'. The ten variables are divided into three categories: 'Internal causes of political risk', 'External causes of political risk' and 'Symptoms of political risk':

1 *Internal causes*:

   (a) Fractionalization of the political spectrum and the power of these factions.

   (b) Fractionalization by language, ethnic and/or religious groups and the power of these factions.

   (c) Restrictive (coercive) measures required to retain power.

   (d) Mentality, including xenophobia, nationalism, corruption, nepotism, willingness to compromise.

   (e) Social conditions including population density and wealth distribution.

   (f) Organization and strength of forces for a radical left government.

---

[2] As will become evident later, 1986 data are being used to forecast investor losses in the 1987–92 period as a means of establishing the historical adequacy of the model.

Table 2.1 *The Economist* 1986 political risk evaluations for Asia

Country	NEIGH	AUTHN	STAL	ILLE	GENLS	WAR	URBAN	ISLAM	CORR	ETHNC	Total	
Hong Kong	3	2	0	5	0	1	3	0	1	0	15	Best
China	3	3	1	2	1	4	0	0	2	1	17	
Singapore	0	5	5	3	0	0	3	0	0	2	18	
Malaysia	1	4	0	4	0	5	1	1	3	4	23	
South Korea	3	3	0	4	5	6	1	0	1	0	23	
Taiwan	3	4	4	2	2	3	0	0	1	3	24	
India	2	2	3	2	0	7	0	0	5	4	25	
Sri Lanka	0	3	0	6	2	15	0	0	1	4	31	
Bangladesh	0	5	3	5	5	5	1	1	6	2	33	
Burma	1	5	3	3	3	10	0	0	4	2	33	
Thailand	3	3	2	3	6	10	2	0	3	1	33	
Philippines	0	3	4	4	3	10	1	2	4	3	34	
Pakistan	3	4	3	4	4	7	0	4	5	3	37	
Vietnam	3	4	5	4	6	15	0	0	3	2	42	
Indonesia	1	6	5	5	5	8	0	3	6	3	42	Worst

Key:
NEIGH = Bad neighbours
AUTHN = Authoritarianism
STAL = Staleness
ILLE = Illegitimacy
GENLS = Generals in power
WAR = War/armed insurrection
URBAN = Urbanization pace
ISLAM = Islamic Fundamentalism
CORR = Corruption
ETHNC = Ethnic tension

2 *External causes*:

   (a) Dependence on and/or importance to a hostile major power.

   (b) Negative influences of regional political forces.

3 *Symptoms*:

   (a) Societal conflict involving demonstrations, strikes and street violence.

   (b) Instability as perceived by non-constitutional changes, assassinations and guerrilla wars.

These variables cover a range of social, cultural and political characteristics of societies. Those most knowledgeable about them will obviously be trained sociologists or political scientists who are steady observers. It is they who help establish the link between the investor's success and knowledge of societal conditions.

How does the BERI system work? In an initial run at assessment, BERI's experts grade a country's political risk climate by variable. Each of the ten can be assigned as many as seven points. A seven represents the optimal circumstance, the least amount of risk. A perfect, without risk situation would be represented by 70. However, an additional value may be assigned to any of the internal or external variables if the condition reflected by the variable is notably favourable for business operations. The total of these bonus points may range as high as thirty, making a maximum of 100 points possible if the risk conditions were absolutely perfect. However, this is never the case. If the bonus points score is more or less ten, this is moderate risk. If there are no bonus points, this by itself would be an indication of a high-risk circumstance.

The total of the variable scores, plus the bonus points, becomes the BERI index for the circumstance cited. Employed here is the BERI 1986 five-year forecast. It is important to understand that separate ratings are done for 'Present conditions' and '+ ten years conditions' as well as for the five-years conditions.

Table 2.2 presents the 1986 BERI data for the Asian countries that it covers. The ten variables are listed in the order that they are presented in the description above. As with *The Economist* model, a total or index (PRI) is created by combining the individual variables additively. In this evaluation, Japan and Singapore stand out as the best risks and Pakistan, India and the Philippines as the worst. There are several variances between the two evaluations of risk, apart from countries that are included or not included. India and Malaysia fare notably worse in the BERI model while Indonesia is somewhat better. If an investor is intending to enter one of these three countries, which model (advice) should be accepted, if either? It is this question that is pursued in the analysis below.

We will look at *The Economist* and BERI models in turn, first examining their portrayal of risks across the countries they cover in Asia. We will then assess retrospectively the abilities of the models to forecast business losses that are due to political causes. This assessment is dependent on being able to regress loss data on the series of variables that the models employ as their indicators of future trouble.

The definition of political risk, the definition of politically sourced losses, the measure of losses, and the measures of the variables are, of course, all integral parts of establishing utility.

Table 2.2 BERI 1986 five-year political risk index for Asia

Country	HSTLP	REGNL	POLFAC	ETHFR	RESTR	MENTAL	SOCCD	RADCL	CONF	NCNST	Total	
Japan	6	6	7	13	11	4	10	6	5	7	75	Best
Singapore	7	7	10	9	5	9	7	8	6	7	75	
Australia	7	9	7	9	9	4	9	4	3	7	68	
Taiwan	2	4	10	7	6	5	8	10	6	7	65	
South Korea	7	2	9	9	3	2	3	11	5	5	56	
Malaysia	7	6	7	0	9	4	6	6	3	6	54	
Thailand	7	3	5	10	5	2	2	5	5	5	49	
Indonesia	7	7	8	5	1	0	1	7	5	6	47	
Pakistan	3	2	8	2	5	4	0	6	4	5	39	
India	6	5	4	0	5	3	0	5	3	3	34	
Philippines	7	7	5	3	3	0	0	3	2	1	31	Worst

Key:
HSTLP = Hostile major power
REGNL = Negative regional forces
POLFAC= Political fractionalization
ETHFR = Ethnic fractionalization
RESTR = Restrictive/coercive measure
MENTAL = Mentality
SOCCD = Social conditions
RADCL = Radical left forces
CONF = Social conflict
NCNST = Non-constitutional changes

■ Method and outcomes

The core of the analysis in this study lies in an assessment of how well the 1986 *Economist* and BERI forecasts actually foretold the levels of loss in the subsequent five-year period (mid-1987 to mid-1992 was used). The method employed in the development of the loss data which are the applied objective of this study is relatively simple and straightforward. It has also been discussed, for the most part, elsewhere (Howell and Chaddick, 1994).

Researchers explored media reports, US government statistics, and OPIC claim reports for instances, by country, of losses which could be termed politically based and then documented and assembled that data. The researchers then assigned a value of zero to ten to the country for the period, with the continuum being zero for no politically sourced losses of any kind and ten being a loss of all foreign investment. The process was repeated with a separate set of researchers. In each case the group of researchers discussed the scores to adjust them comparatively and some adjustments were made when discrepancies were found between the two groups (Howell and Chaddick, 1994).

This loss index constitutes the dependent variable for the underlying analysis in this study. The forecast data are the focus of this assessment. The questions addressed here are:

- How well did the 1986 data, as presented to the users, forecast politically sourced losses?

- If the models are improved by reselection of variables (elimination of statistically insignificant variables), how well do they forecast losses?

- If the models are restructured by reweighting, how does this change the forecasts?

- What are the implications for investors examining Asian investment sites and markets?

The basic forecast data from the two models have been presented in Tables 2.1 and 2.2. Combining them with the loss index, we can address the question of how good were the two forecasts. For all countries for which there were loss data (*The Economist* N = 35, BERI N = 28), the respective political risk indices from 1986 were correlated with the loss index for 1987–92. For *The Economist* the result was r = 0.33 (significance 0.053). This translates into an explanation of variance in the dependent variable (loss index) of 11 per cent. For the BERI PRI, the correlation was r = 0.51 (significance 0.01), an explanation of 26 per cent. *The Economist* index is particularly weak as an indicator of actual risk but both can be improved on.

Let us take the next step and see if the data from the two studies can be reconfigured to provide more useful forecasts. Table 2.3 provides the results of two regression applications. In each case, the variables ('threatening conditions') were regressed on the same dependent variable, the 1987–92 loss index. The table lists the independent variables in the order that they were entered into the equation by an SPSS regression program, with entry order being determined by the added contribution to the equation. Provided are the multiple correlation coefficient (MltR), the coefficient of determination (R^2) or 'explained variance', and the added contribution to the equation (ADDED). The latter is used in subsequent analysis as the weight that should be accorded each variable. Both sets of results are statistically significant at the 0.05 level or better.

Table 2.3 Multiple regression results dependent variable = politically-based losses

| The Economist *model* | | | | BERI *model* | | | |
Independent variable	*Multiple correlation coefficient*	R^2	*Added*	*Independent variable*	*Multiple correlation coefficient*	R^2	*Added*
NEIGH	0.36	0.13	0.13	REGNL	0.45	0.20	0.20
ISLAM	0.44	0.20	0.07	RADCL	0.59	0.35	0.15
AUTHN	0.56	0.31	0.11	RESTR	0.65	0.42	0.07
WAR	0.59	0.35	0.04	ETHFR	0.68	0.47	0.05
ETHNC	0.63	0.39	0.04	HSTLP	0.71	0.50	0.03
URBAN	0.66	0.44	0.05	NCNST	0.72	0.52	0.02
GENLS	0.67	0.45	0.01	CONF	0.72	0.53	0.01
				SOCCD	0.73	0.53	0.01

Key:

NEIGH = Bad neighbours

ISLAM = Islamic Fundamentalism

AUTHN = Authoritarianism

WAR = War/armed insurrection

ETHNC = Ethnic tension

URBAN = Urbanization pace

GENLS = Generals in power

REGNL = Negative regional forces

RADCL = Radical left forces

RESTR = Restrictive/coercive measures

ETHFR = Ethnic fractionalization

HSTLP = Hostile major power

NCNST = Non-constitutional change

CONF = Societal conflict

SOCCD = Social conditions

The regression results in Table 2.3 each provide three salient outcomes. The first is the number of variables that are remaining in each equation. Variables are no longer added to the equation by the SPSS routine if statistical significance exceeds 0.05. This means that for *The Economist* data, Corruption, Illegitimacy, and Staleness do not tell us anything new about the likely losses to businesses. This does not mean that they are not useful predictors by themselves but rather that the future damage that they reflect is already forecast by one of the included variables. To include them all in a risk index would mean that we would be counting a phenomenon twice and therefore distorting the warning that the risk index is providing. For the BERI data, Political fractionalization and Mentality are excluded on these same grounds. Here, then, is some preliminary advice for the user: both risk indices contain some variables that do not relate to investor losses or are a duplication of information. Beware!

The second salient outcome is the variance explained by the combined set of included variables ($R^2 = 0.45$ for the seven usable *Economist* variables, $R^2 = 0.53$ for the eight usable BERI variables). This constitutes more advice. After eliminating duplicative variables, *The Economist* information can help us in explaining 45 per cent of the variance in investor losses while the BERI information helps us explain 53 per cent of those same losses. Simply put, the BERI information, employed properly, is more useful than *The Economist* information. Note also that by reconfiguring the data provided, we have improved the forecasting capability of *The Economist* model from 11 per cent for the original index to 45 per cent for the revised model and that of the BERI model from 26 per cent to 53 per cent.

The third salient outcome is the list of added contributions. If these are used as indicators of importance in comparing the various threatening conditions, we would note from *The Economist* results that the presence of 'bad neighbours' is the most powerful indicator that there is danger for investors (weight = 13). This is followed by an indication that an authoritarian government is an important sign of danger to investors (weight = 11). Similarly, the BERI results tell us that threatening regional forces (similar to *The Economist*'s 'bad neighbours') is the most powerful indicator of danger (weight = 20), and that the power of the radical left is the second most useful variable in projecting investor losses (weight = 15). A synthesis of the two forecasts, incorporating the order and weight of variable contributions, tells the foreign investor one more thing: it is at least just as important to examine the external environment – the international environment – of an investment location as it is to examine what is going on inside the country. The regional forces and superpower activity tend to be the sources of ultimate war damage (covered specifically by both OPIC and MIGA) and of a host of ethnic and racial disputes that ultimately turn into civil strife and further war.

We now have information that will allow us to take another important step in providing political risk advice to the outside investor. If we take the demonstrably significant combination of variables for the two models, and also reweight them using the added contributions as weights, a new risk index will reflect what we have discovered about the weaknesses of the two original models and incorporate these as improvements. The new political risk index is reflective of what should have been forecast in 1986.

Tables 2.4 and 2.5 contain recalculated scores and totals, including for the two models only those variables that were shown to have some statistically significant role in forecasting politically based losses and the incorporated variables reweighted according to their contributions to their respective equations. That is, if a variable's addition to the regression equation resulted in an increase of 15 per cent in the total coefficient of determination (R^2), that variable was given a weight of 15. The new weights are listed across the top of the tables. As with Tables 2.1 and 2.2, they are ranked from the best risk countries to the worst. At the right in each table is a comparison with the original ranking. Where ranks are different by more than two between the original and reformatted, the new rank is marked with [a]. The two rank differential is, of course, a subjective criterion for reflecting error and the reader may wish to reinterpret these outcomes. But the principle of attempting to improve forecasts based on an analysis of historical adequacy and accuracy is demonstrated either way (Howell and Xie, 1995).

If we consider the rank differential to be an indication of misleading information about levels of political risk, it is clear that the outcome from *The Economist* model is inadequate and even mistaken. There is a rank difference of greater than two in ten of the possible fifteen Asian cases. For BERI, there is a rank difference of greater than two in only one case out of eleven. If we accommodate the smaller number of BERI cases by counting the differences of two or greater, there are still only three 'errors' in the original index. Either way, the original BERI index of political risk is considerably more useful than that of *The Economist*. Conclusion? The professionally constructed risk model is clearly more reliable than that generated from a journalistic source, despite the stature of that source for other types of information. Other specifics of the differences of forecasts for individual countries are also interesting but let us address these in a moment in the context of more current forecasts from BERI.

Table 2.4 Revised *Economist* impact variables weighted by contribution percentage

Weight Country	13 NEIGH	7 ISLAM	11 AUTHN	4 WAR	4 ETHNC	5 URBAN	1 GENLS	45 Total	Revised rank	Original rank
Sri Lanka	0.0	0.0	0.5	0.3	0.4	0.0	0.0	1.20	1[a]	8
Singapore	0.0	0.0	0.8	0.0	0.2	0.5	0.0	1.49	2	3
Bangladesh	0.0	0.2	0.8	0.1	0.2	0.2	0.1	1.51	3[a]	9
Philippines	0.0	0.4	0.5	0.2	0.3	0.2	0.1	1.54	4[a]	12
Burma	0.4	0.0	0.8	0.2	0.2	0.0	0.1	1.67	5[a]	10
India	0.9	0.0	0.3	0.1	0.4	0.0	0.0	1.72	6	7
Malaysia	0.4	0.2	0.6	0.1	0.4	0.2	0.0	1.90	7[a]	4
China	1.3	0.0	0.5	0.1	0.1	0.0	0.0	1.97	8[a]	2
Hong Kong	1.3	0.0	0.3	0.0	0.0	0.5	0.0	2.13	9[a]	1
South Korea	1.3	0.0	0.5	0.1	0.0	0.2	0.1	2.14	10[a]	5
Taiwan	1.3	0.0	0.6	0.1	0.3	0.0	0.0	2.32	11[a]	6
Indonesia	0.4	0.5	0.9	0.2	0.3	0.0	0.1	2.44	12[a]	15
Thailand	1.3	0.0	0.5	0.2	0.1	0.3	0.1	2.50	13	11
Vietnam	1.3	0.0	0.6	0.3	0.2	0.0	0.1	2.53	14	14
Pakistan	1.3	0.7	0.6	0.1	0.3	0.0	0.1	3.14	15	13

Note: [a] Ranks are different by more than two between the original and reformatted ranking

Key:
NEIGH = Bad neighbours
AUTHN = Authoritarianism
GENLS = Generals in power

WAR = War/armed insurrection
URBAN = Urbanization pace
ISLAM = Islamic fundamentalism
ETHNC = Ethnic tension

Table 2.5 Revised BERI impact variables weighted by contribution percentage

Weight Country	3 HSTLP	20 REGNL	5 ETHFR	7 RESTR	0.5 SOCCD	15 RADCL	0.5 CONF	2 NCNST	53 Total	Revised rank	Original rank
Japan	0.14	0.92	0.50	0.59	0.04	0.69	0.04	0.20	3.12	1	1
Singapore	0.16	1.38	0.35	0.48	0.03	0.46	0.02	0.20	3.09	2	2
Australia	0.16	1.08	0.35	0.27	0.03	0.92	0.04	0.20	3.05	3	3
Taiwan	0.05	0.62	0.27	0.32	0.03	1.15	0.04	0.20	2.68	4	4
Indonesia	0.16	1.08	0.19	0.05	0.00	0.81	0.04	0.17	2.50	x5[a]	8
Malaysia	0.16	0.92	0.00	0.48	0.02	0.69	0.02	0.17	2.48	6	6
South Korea	0.16	0.31	0.35	0.16	0.01	1.27	0.04	0.14	2.44	x7	5
Thailand	0.16	0.46	0.38	0.27	0.01	0.58	0.04	0.14	2.04	8	7
Philippines	0.16	1.08	0.12	0.16	0.00	0.35	0.01	0.03	1.90	x9	11
Pakistan	0.14	0.77	0.00	0.27	0.00	0.58	0.02	0.09	1.86	10	9
India	0.07	0.31	0.08	0.27	0.00	0.69	0.03	0.14	1.59	11	10

Note: [a] Ranks are different by more than two between the original and reformatted ranking

Key:

HSTLP = Hostile major power
REGNL = Negative regional forces
ETHFR = Ethnic fractionalization
RESTR = Restrictive/coercive measures
SOCCD = Social conditions
RADCL = Radical left forces
CONF = Societal conflict
NCNST = Non-constitutional changes

▪ Application for business

Firms interested or already involved in investing in Asia can find several useful pieces of information in the outcomes of this study. Some of these have to do with the quality of the information on risk that is accessible to them, some with the specifics of the Asian forecasts. These include:

1 *The Economist* method explains only 45 per cent of the variance in the loss index (see Table 2.3). While this number may seem small (and is smaller than that for BERI), it should not be interpreted as being the same as flipping a coin. Given the complexity of the variable structure, a guessing game approach by the investor would probably not result in more than 10 per cent predictability.

2 Only seven of the ten *Economist* sociopolitical variables are useful in forecasting losses (impact variables). Staleness, illegitimacy and corruption variables provide no new information to that contributed by the other seven (Table 2.3). As noted above, this does not necessarily mean that they are not important, only that the information they have provided here is covered already by another variable in the model. Corruption, for example, correlates highly and significantly with the degree of authoritarianism. If a government is authoritarian, the investor can also expect to find bribery and corruption in the system. The more authoritarian a system is, the more corrupt one can expect it to be. An authoritarian system of government would therefore be doubly problematic for American investors who must abide by the Foreign Corrupt Practices Act.

3 Bad neighbours (that is, regional conflicts and superpower influences) and the extent of authoritarianism in the country are the best indicators, 13 per cent and 11 per cent respectively, of whether there will be losses to foreign investors (Table 2.3). Foreign affairs, the foreign policy of the country, and international relations generally are very impactful in the area of foreign investment. The investor looking at prospects for a particular country needs to look at its environment as well as at its internal situation.

4 When corrected weights are employed along with only the critical variables, the forecast risks were actually less for Sri Lanka, Bangladesh, Burma, the Philippines and Indonesia than indicated in the original model, and more for Hong Kong, China, South Korea, Taiwan and Malaysia (Table 2.4). Countries which change position by more than two ranks as a result of applying the adjusted model for *The Economist* data include:

(a) Less risk (i.e. users of the original 1986 index were made overly cautious about investment in these countries):

    (i)   Sri Lanka – up seven ranks in the revised model

    (ii) Bangladesh – up six

    (iii) the Philippines – up eight

    (iv) Burma (Myanmar) – up five

    (v) Indonesia – up three.

(b) More risk (i.e. users of the original 1986 index were not sufficiently warned about possible dangers):

(i)   Hong Kong – down eight ranks in the revised model

(ii) China – down six

(iii) Malaysia – down three

(iv) South Korea – down five

(v) Taiwan – down five.

Remembering that these were 1986 projections, some of these still seem counter-intuitive unless the user is aware of the strong roles played in political risk by negative regional forces and threats (high for Hong Kong, China, South Korea and Taiwan, low for Sri Lanka, Bangladesh, the Philippines, Burma and Indonesia) and by authoritarianism (high for Malaysia and Taiwan, but also for Burma, Bangladesh, and Indonesia); low for the Philippines and Sri Lanka.

• The inconsistency in the forecasts by *The Economist* model demonstrates, at minimum, that the raw index generated should not be taken at face value. Some of the individual *Economist* variables can be valuable for investment advice if the data source is readily accessible and the investor can make the appropriate variable selections.

• The BERI method explains 53 per cent of the variance in the loss index, an improvement of 8 per cent over *The Economist* model (Table 2.3). In social science analysis, this is a reasonably substantial improvement. The advantage of the BERI model over that of *The Economist* is even greater when the original summary risk indices are compared (26 per cent over 11 per cent). Both would support the argument that the theoretical foundations of the BERI model are substantially stronger than those of *The Economist* model and that political risk forecasting has a theoretical element that cannot be ignored.

• The most impactful variables in forecasting risk in the BERI model are Negative influence of regional forces (20 per cent) and Power of the radical left (15 per cent) (Table 2.3). These are essentially the same two variables that were found to be the most impactful in *The Economist* method.

• After eliminating the two variables from the BERI model, there were no significant differences in the rankings of risk for Asian countries (Table 2.5). Having got over the hurdle of correct variable inclusion, BERI is at least consistent in its portrayal of risk, as well as more accurate than *The Economist* model. Of eleven countries in the study, only three are changed by two ranks or more; Indonesia and the Philippines are comparatively less risky by three and two ranks, respectively, and South Korea is more risky by two ranks. None of these is a dramatic change that would have significantly misled the investor moving into the Asian market, although Indonesia might claim that investors were unnecessarily deterred.

On all counts of comparison, the BERI model for political risk forecasting shows up as superior to *The Economist* model as advice for the foreign investor. In terms of specific advice, however, the variation in index scores needs to be considered in addition to the rank differences. How would this bear on advice to investors in Asia today?

■ Reconfigured advice

Tables 2.6 and 2.7 provide recent data from the more reliable BERI system. Table 2.6 is the Asia data from early 1995, Table 2.7 is that for the reweighted and selective model. Table 2.6 gives the actual scores or raw data submitted by BERI's experts on the ten variables included in their analysis.

For BERI 1995 data, only two of the Asian countries have risk differentials of two ranks or greater: Indonesia is less risky (three ranks) and South Korea is more risky (four ranks) than portrayed in the raw data (Table 2.7). The reason for South Korea's relatively poorer risk rating in both of the reconstructed 1986 models was its score on the critical variables, Bad neighbours (*Economist*) and Negative regional forces (BERI). The problem remains the same in the 1995 BERI forecast. The source of concern about South Korea's investment environment in both timeframes is the threat from North Korea. A renewed conflict between North and South would devastate both domestic and foreign investors and the possibility of such conflict never seems to be remote. Reflecting this circumstance, Professor Lee Seo Hang of the Korean Institute of Foreign Affairs and National Security notes that 'With the prevailing uncertainties over the future of North Korea and the continuing row over the nuclear issue, the Korean Peninsula is probably entering a most dangerous period of uncertainty' (*International Herald Tribune*, 1995). The revised BERI model seems to confirm this qualitative observation.

Indonesia's relative strength (between the original and revised models) can be seen in a lower level of threat from regional conflict and exhibited control of the forces of the radical left, the two most important of BERI's political risk variables. The weights for these two variables play up Indonesia's strengths in these areas. They then more than offset the Indonesian government's use of restrictive measures, which provides them with the worst rating on that variable among the Asian countries covered by BERI. Restrictive measures bear a weight of only seven compared to twenty for Regional environment and fifteen for Power of the radical left.

A translation for the future: our point here is not to advise investors about South Korea or Indonesia; instead it is to provide the following recommendations:

- Professional advice about political risk is valuable. Area specialists might be very capable of indicating how much corruption or political fractionalization there is in an investment environment but they often cannot assess the relative role of those characteristics in determining how they fit into the context of business operations.

- BERI is a more valuable source of political risk advice than *The Economist* or other journalistic sources.

- Either with BERI data or with data from other sources, the investor should use a check list of indicators that have been shown to be precursors of business losses historically. These specifically include negative regional forces and superpower involvement in the area, the power of the radical left, restrictive measures taken by the government, and ethnic fractionalization in the society.

- Either in one's personal assessment or with some computerized help (Lotus or Excel will do), the factors considered to be threatening should be weighted and not treated equally. The weights provided in Table 2.3 will provide a reasonably reliable start.

- Most importantly, do not walk into the unknown. This might sound simplistic or a

Table 2.6 BERI 1995 five-year forecast with ten variables for Asian countries

Country	HSTLP	REGNL	POLFAC	ETHFR	RESTR	MENTAL	SOCCD	RADCL	CONF	NCNST	Total	
Singapore	7	8	9	9	5	9	7	8	6	7	75	Best
Taiwan	6	5	8	8	7	7	8	10	6	7	72	
Australia	7	9	7	9	9	4	9	4	3	7	68	
Japan	6	6	3	12	9	3	8	6	5	6	64	
South Korea	7	3	6	7	5	3	6	7	6	5	55	
Malaysia	7	6	7	0	8	4	6	7	3	6	54	
Thailand	7	5	4	8	5	2	3	5	5	4	48	
Philippines	6	7	5	5	6	2	1	5	4	6	47	
Indonesia	6	7	7	5	2	1	1	7	4	6	46	
Pakistan	4	4	5	3	5	4	0	6	4	4	39	
India	6	4	4	3	4	4	0	5	3	4	37	Worst

Key:
HSTLP = Hostile major power
REGNL = Negative regional forces
POLFAC = Political fractionalization
ETHFR = Ethnic fractionalization
RESTR = Restrictive/coercive measures
MENTAL = Mentality
SOCCD = Social conditions
RADCL = Radical left forces
CONF = Societal conflict
NCNST = Non-constitutional changes

Table 2.7 Revised BERI 1995 impact variables weighted by contribution percentage

Weight Country	3 HSTLP	20 REGNL	5 ETHFR	7 RESTR	0.5 SOCCD	15 RADCL	0.5 CONF	2 NCNST	53 Total	Revised rank	Original rank
Singapore	0.18	1.33	0.38	0.29	0.03	1.00	0.04	0.20	3.45	1	1
Australia	0.18	1.50	0.38	0.53	0.04	0.50	0.02	0.20	3.33	2	3
Taiwan	0.15	0.83	0.33	0.41	0.03	1.25	0.04	0.20	3.25	3	2
Japan	0.15	1.00	0.50	0.53	0.03	0.75	0.04	0.17	3.17	4	4
Malaysia	0.18	1.00	0.00	0.47	0.03	0.88	0.02	0.17	2.73	5	6
Indonesia	0.15	1.17	0.21	0.12	0.00	0.88	0.03	0.17	2.72	6[a]	9
Philippines	0.15	1.17	0.21	0.35	0.00	0.63	0.03	0.17	2.70	7	8
Thailand	0.18	0.83	0.33	0.29	0.01	0.63	0.04	0.11	2.42	8	7
South Korea	0.18	0.50	0.29	0.29	0.03	0.88	0.04	0.14	2.34	9[a]	5
Pakistan	0.10	0.67	0.13	0.29	0.00	0.75	0.03	0.11	2.08	10	10
India	0.15	0.67	0.13	0.23	0.00	0.63	0.02	0.11	1.94	11	11

Note: [a] Ranks are different by more than two between the original and reformatted ranking

Key:
HSTLP = Hostile major power
REGNL = Negative regional forces
ETHFR = Ethnic fractionalization
RESTR = Restrictive/coercive measures
SOCCD = Social conditions
RADCL = Radical left forces
CONF = Societal conflict
NCNST = Non-constitutional changes

belabouring of the obvious but enough major catastrophes have befallen unknowing foreign investors in recent years that the obvious may need repeating. Whether the consequence is a high seas confrontation between oil exploration vessels and warships or the imposition of specific taxation on a foreign investor, being forewarned is being forearmed.

Needless to say, there are issues involved in risk forecasting that must be explored further. But the conclusions provided above can assist the foreign investor in Asia now. Both models discussed have merits, although one more than the other. The investment advice from BERI is consistent and seems to be grounded well in theory. The investor who understands the models can work selectively within them to garner more useful information than is provided in a summary index. There are, it is important to add, political and social pitfalls throughout the investment markets of Asia and the investor who ignores them, and the methodology to assess them, does so with considerable peril.

■ References

Coplin, D. W. and O'Leary, M. K. (eds) (1994) *The Handbook of Country and Political Risk Analysis*, Political Risk Services.

The Economist (1986). Countries in trouble: who's on the skids? **301**, 20 December, 60–72.

Haner, F. T. and Ewing, J. S. (1985) *Country Risk Assessment: Theory and World-wide Practice*, Praeger.

Howell, L. D. (1992) Political risk and political loss for foreign investment, *The International Executive* **34** (6), November–December, 485–98.

Howell, L. D. and Chaddick, B. (1994) Models of political risk for foreign investment and trade: an assessment of three approaches, *Columbia Journal of World Business*, **XXIX** (3), 70–91.

Howell, L. D. and Xie, D. (1995) Asia at risk: critical issues in forecasting, paper presented at the Annual Meeting of the Academy of International Business, Seoul, Korea, November.

International Herald Tribune (1995) 13 November, p. 4.

Chapter 2.1

Forecasting Asian risk: a follow-up study

■ Llewellyn D. Howell ■

In a follow-up to the original study of political risk as portrayed by BERI and *The Economist* method (Chapter 2), the two sets of forecasts were compared for two time frames with the objective of determining which models are more successful in providing useful forecasts over time.

In the first analysis, forecast data from 1986 were correlated with a loss index reflecting politically sourced losses to business in the years 1987 to 1992, the five-year period following the forecast. In the second analysis, late 1991 or early 1992, risk forecasts were compared with a loss index for the years 1992 to 1997. In each case the single index that was created through the model was correlated with the loss index from the following five-year period. Then, using regression, a multiple correlation coefficient was also generated employing the individual indicators as independent variables and the loss index for the subsequent five-year period as the dependent variable. Analytical results stem from comparisons of the correlations (either the simple r against the multiple *R*, one model as compared to another, or individual models across time periods) (Howell, 1998). The number of cases for both time periods has been expanded over the original study.

The outcomes are stated as propositions below:

1 Of the two models as employed in 1986, the BERI PRI provides the best indication of where business losses will occur (r = 0.50) in the following five years but only accounts for 25 per cent of the variance in the loss variable.

2 Of the models as employed in 1991–92, the BERI PRI again provides the best indication of losses, although the level of projection is considerably lower, explaining less than 10 per cent of the variance in the loss index.

3 As contributing variables in explaining losses through *The Economist* model, 'Urbanization' is the most explanatory variable, followed by 'Islamic fundamentalism', 'Bad neighbours', and 'Generals in power'.

4 *The Economist* variables were individually much more predictive in 1992 than they were in 1986 but the index was less useful.

5 From the BERI model with 1986 data, 'Restrictive measures' used by the government and the presence of 'Radical forces' provide most of the explanation of losses in 1987–92, followed by the presence of a 'Hostile major power'. In 1992, the most useful variables are 'Social conflict' and 'Mentality' (which includes corruption, nepotism, xenophobia, and nationalism), followed again by 'Hostile major power'.

6 For both models, the individual variables that provide the strongest explanatory contribution to variance in future losses (risk) *have changed between the two periods.* This means that an index with a set of variables and assigned weights created in one timeframe may not be applicable in another timeframe. As the sources of loss change (e.g. the shift from 'Inconvertibility' in the late 1980s to 'Civil strife damage' in the early 1990s), so must the choices of variables that are used to forecast those losses.

7 Risk indices created in the 1980s (or earlier) indicate some utility in 1986 but have a vastly reduced predictive quality in 1992, strongly suggesting a need for restructuring of the variable choices and their interrelationships. Most existing political risk models were developed to fit the circumstances of the Cold War. With the end of the Cold War, the relative importance of risk variables has changed – some dramatically – calling for a restructuring and a rethinking of the way risk is measured.

■ Reference

Howell, L. D. (1998) Forecasting Political Risk in International Investment And Trade: Toward an Integrated Model, Paper prepared for the Annual Meeting of the International Studies Association, March 21, Minneapolis, Minnesota.

Chapter 3

A historical perspective on East Asia as an independent engine of growth: prospects and implications for managers[1]

■ Kong-Yam Tan ■

■ Introduction

After the Second World War ended in 1945, the General Agreement on Tariffs and Trade (GATT) was established to create an open and free trading system. Together with the system of fixed currency exchange established under the International Monetary Fund (IMF) agreement at Bretton Woods, a stable global trading and monetary system was instituted. These two key post-war institutions, sustained by the hegemonic power of the USA – based on her technological, economic and military superiority – ushered in an unprecedented period of steady expansion in world output and trade, and closer economic interdependence in the non-communist free world. World trade in volume terms expanded at an average annual rate of 5.6 per cent between 1953 and 1963 and 8.5 per cent between 1963 and 1973, much higher than the average rate of 3.5 per cent between 1873 and 1913 and the 0.9 per cent in the interwar period of 1919 to 1939.

This unprecedented expansion in world output and trade in the post-war era provided the Asia Pacific economies like Japan and the four newly industrializing economies (NIEs) South Korea, Taiwan, Hong Kong and Singapore, with a conducive and stable environment for export-led growth. They were lucky to set sail on the path of industrial catching-up when the gust of wind was strongest. Consequently, during the past three decades, the four East Asian NIEs became the most dynamic middle-income economies in the world. Their annual growth rates in gross national product (GNP) per capita between 1965 and 1995 averaged 6 to 8 per cent, triple the average rate of 2.3 per cent for middle-income economies of the world and almost double the 4.0 per cent average for countries in the Association of South East Asian Nations (ASEAN), excluding Singapore.

The pattern of industrialization and exports of the NIEs has been rather similar. After

[1] This chapter has been published previously by MCB University Press Limited: Tan, K-Y. (1997). East Asia as an independent engine of growth: prospects and implications for managers. *Management Decision*, **35** (8), 574–86.

a short period of protectionist import-substitution policy in the 1950s and early 1960s, they soon turned to an export-oriented strategy for growth. During the early stage of the outward-oriented development strategy in the 1960s, the emphasis was on the production and export of traditional labour-intensive products such as textiles, clothing, footwear, toys, leather goods and other light manufactured goods. Technology for these products was standard and the main competitive factor in the world market was low labour cost relative to labour productivity. Their major markets were the OECD countries, particularly the USA which had a major interest in nurturing these market economies through generous foreign aid, capital inflow, technology transfer, market access and special tariff preferences against the ideological challenge of the socialist countries of East Asia like China, North Korea and North Vietnam. Consequently, manufacturing exports of the four NIEs were able to grow between 20 per cent to 50 per cent per year for the period 1965–73 and even after the first and second oil shock, at an annual rate of 13–21 per cent between 1973 and 1985. Gradually, with rising income and savings, together with a higher educational level and better infrastructural facilities, the NIEs, like Japan before them, were able to invest in and upgrade to more capital, skill and technology-intensive industries like steel, shipbuilding, chemicals, machinery, electrical machinery, telecommunication and office automation equipment (Amsden, 1992; Chen, 1979; Low et al., 1993; OECD, 1988).

Thus, with the benefits of latecomers in the process of industrialization and taking full advantage of the conducive world trading system as well as the ideological imperatives of the free world, the NIEs have been able to telescope an industrialization process that took the OECD countries 100 to 150 years to complete in the nineteenth and early twentieth centuries into 25 to 30 years in the post-war era. However, unlike Japan, they have industrialized with a greater degree of dependence on direct foreign investment (FDI), particularly for Singapore. Throughout the 1980s, foreign firm exports accounted for about 80 per cent of total exports for Singapore, 25 per cent for Korea, 15 per cent for Taiwan and 20 per cent for Hong Kong (Galenson, 1985; Hughes, 1988; Noland, 1990).

By the beginning of the 1980s, the success of the NIEs had begun to have a significant demonstrable effect on policy-makers in ASEAN and China. They have increasingly looked on a liberal trading regime, as well as the inflow of FDI, as a quick way to jump-start the process of industrialization.

▪ Competitive unilateral liberalization and regionalism in East Asia

Until the early 1980s, many ASEAN countries, particularly Indonesia, Malaysia and Thailand, clung on to import-substituting industrialization strategy and remained restrictive in trade and foreign investment policies. Protection of domestic industries under this strategy has made possible the proliferation of inefficient public enterprises. The role of market forces and the potential role of direct foreign investments in fostering dynamic economic growth and development were substantially circumscribed.

The substantial decline in oil and commodity prices between 1982 and 1986, resulted in a significant deterioration in the terms of trade for the ASEAN countries. Prices (in current US dollars) of non-fuel primary products like rubber, tin and palm oil fell by 25–60 per cent between 1981 and 1986. In addition, petroleum prices fell steadily from about US$39.0/barrel in 1981 to reach a low of US$14.8/barrel in 1986. This resulted in the Malaysian terms-of-trade index falling by about 24 per cent from 1980 to 1986. These external shocks on the economy were severe for the commodity-based ASEAN economies. The World Bank estimated that due to external disturbances over the period 1983–88, Indonesia suffered an income loss equivalent of some 9 per cent of its annual GDP. The financial and budget burdens of the inefficient state-owned enterprises, which were masked during the commodity boom period in the 1970s, were starkly revealed. This dramatic decline in the terms of trade and consequent pressure on the budget gave the impetus to the political will for liberalization and assault against vested interests and inefficiencies.

These economic and financial liberalization policies in ASEAN were aimed at directing economies towards a system of regulation based on the competitive markets of the private sector. The basic paradigm is the preeminence of competition, whether domestic or international. The key areas of liberalization are international trade in goods and services, including tariff, quota and licensing structures; internal and external capital movement including abandonment of financial repression, deregulation of interest rates, easing of restrictions on foreign banks and other financial institutions; competitive goods and factors markets, including suppression of domestic rent seekers, elimination of subsidies and significant revision and liberalization of the foreign investment regulations, including equity rules on foreign investment, business fields open to foreign investors and local content regulations (Ng and Wagner, 1991; Sopiee, 1989).

More significantly, the period of the mid-1980s when these ASEAN countries had begun to learn and absorb the lessons of the NIEs' success of the outward-oriented development strategy and were keen to liberalize and deregulate their economies to welcome inflow of foreign capital and technology, coincided with the outflow of direct foreign investments from the NIEs and Japan. These capital outflows from Northeast Asia, under the pressure of US, and Economic Community (EC) protectionism, rising domestic wages and other business costs as well as the strengthening of currencies, were searching for cheaper offshore production bases to sustain their international export competitiveness and profitability. They found them in the ASEAN countries. In particular, the significant appreciation of the Japanese yen, Taiwan dollar, Korean won and Singapore dollar against the depreciating Indonesian rupiah, Malaysian ringgit, Thai baht and Chinese yuan acted as the key push and pull factors in attracting direct foreign investments from Japan and the NIEs into ASEAN and China since 1986.

Consequently, since the mid-1980s, the outflows of FDI from Japan and the NIEs to ASEAN have been very rapid. Between 1986 and 1990, direct foreign investment in Malaysia rose by twelve times to US$6.2 billion, by twenty-four times in Thailand to US$14.1 billion and by eleven times in Indonesia to US$8.8 billion (see Table 3.1). By 1990, the major foreign investors in the ASEAN countries like Malaysia, Indonesia and Thailand were Taiwan, Japan, Korea, Hong Kong and Singapore, displacing the USA and Europe. For example, Hong Kong was the largest investor in Thailand, accounting for 50.7 per cent of the world total, followed by Japan (19.2 per cent). In Malaysia, the top investor in 1990 was Taiwan (36.3 per cent), followed by Japan (23.9 per cent) while in Indonesia, Japan (25.6 per cent) was the largest investor, followed by Hong Kong (11.4 per cent). The NIEs as a group constituted the largest investors in all the three major ASEAN countries. In all these three ASEAN countries, investments by the NIEs accounted for the lion's share, being 62.2 per cent in Thailand, 47.2 per cent in Malaysia and 29.8 per cent in Indonesia.

Table 3.1 FDI in manufacturing in selected Asian countries (million US$)

| | *Malaysia* | *Thailand* | *Indonesia* | *China* | |
				Contracted	*Actual*
1986	525	579	800	3 330	1 874
1987	750	1 949	1 240	4 319	2 314
1988	2 011	6 249	4 409	6 191	3 194
1989	3 401	7 995	4 719	6 294	3 392
1990	6 228	14 128	8 750	6 986	3 487
1991	5 554	4 988	8 778	12 422	4 366
1992	7 036	10 792	10 180	58 736	11 007
1993	2 297	4 294	8 100	110 000	27 514
1994	4 277	5 950	23 700	81 406	33 787
1995	3 660	16 346	39 915	90 288	37 736
1996	6 800	15 200	29 900	73 200	40 100

Sources: Malaysian Industrial Development Authority, Malaysia; Board of Investment, Thailand; Capital Investment Co-ordinating Board (BKPM), Indonesia; *Statistical Yearbook of China.*

In Malaysia, the bulk of these upsurges in Northeast Asian foreign investments was concentrated in electrical and electronics products, chemicals and chemical products, food manufacturing, textiles and textile products, wood and wood products, and basic metal products. In Indonesia, the concentration was in chemicals, paper and paper products, textiles and, increasingly, metal products. In Thailand, the bulk of direct foreign investments was concentrated in electrical and electronic products, chemicals, textiles, and machinery and transport equipment (Lim and Pang, 1991).

This surge of foreign investment inflows from Northeast Asia into ASEAN, together with the dynamic effect of the liberalizing and deregulatory measures undertaken domestically, resulted in an ASEAN economic boom between 1987 and 1995. The average annual real GDP growth during the period 1987–95 was 8.8 per cent for Singapore, 9.5 per cent for Thailand, 8.5 per cent for Malaysia, 6.6 per cent for Indonesia, significantly higher than the 5.5 per cent, 5.4 per cent, 4.5 per cent and 4.9 per cent achieved respectively during the period 1981–86 (Table 3.2).

In the mean time, in a sharp break with previous policies, China in 1978 began actively to pursue foreign capital, as part of the programme for opening up the economy. Such investment was also viewed as an effective means of transferring technology and managerial expertise to China. In 1978, it was announced that China would welcome FDI, and legislation governing such investment was adopted in the following year. In line with this approach, special economic zones (SEZs) were established in 1980 as the principal areas for direct investment. Special economic zones were set up along the southeastern coast of China at Shenzhen (near Hong Kong), Shantou (north of Hong Kong), Zhuhai (near Macao), and Xiamen, positioned to attract investments from overseas Chinese. One crucial difference between SEZs and other areas in China was the administrative decentralization that permitted SEZ authorities to operate largely outside the state plan. They were allowed to attract foreign investors through prefer-

Table 3.2 Growth rate of GDP in ASEAN countries (percentage)

	Singapore	Malaysia	Thailand	Indonesia	Philippines
1981	9.6	6.9	6.3	7.9	3.9
1982	6.9	5.9	4.1	2.2	2.9
1983	8.2	6.3	7.3	4.2	0.9
1984	8.3	7.8	7.1	6.	−6.0
1985	−1.6	−1.0	3.5	2.5	−4.3
1986	1.8	1.2	4.5	5.9	1.4
Average1981–86	5.5	4.5	5.4	4.9	−0.2
1987	9.4	5.2	9.5	4.9	4.7
1988	11.1	8.9	13.2	5.7	6.3
1989	9.2	8.8	12.0	7.4	5.6
1990	8.3	9.8	10.0	7.4	2.4
1991	6.7	8.8	8.2	6.6	−0.9
1992	5.8	8.0	7.4	6.1	0.3
1993	9.8	8.6	8.2	6.6	1.0
1994	10.1	8.7	8.4	6.9	4.3
1995	8.9	9.5	8.7	7.5	5.3
1996	7.0	8.8	6.7	7.8	5.5
Average 1987–96	8.7	8.5	9.3	6.7	3.3

Source: Asian Development Outlook 1996; National Statistics

ential policies and undertake their own infrastructural development by raising their own funds. In 1984, it was decided to promote foreign investment on a wider geographic basis. To this end, fourteen coastal cities and Hainan Island were permitted to offer tax incentives for such investment similar to those offered by the SEZs. In these areas, imports by foreign investors of machinery, equipment and other inputs were exempt from import licences and customs duties and a special 15 per cent preferential income tax was applied to foreign investment enterprises (Wei, 1993).

Direct foreign investments began to pick up in 1984, reaching US$2.9 billion in contracted value and US$1.4 billion in utilized value. The extensive liberalization and the opening of the fourteen coastal cities led to an upsurge in 1985, reaching an unprecedented contracted amount of US$6.3 billion (see Table 3.1) (Ball et al., 1993).

Although China had considerable success in attracting foreign investment, objectives in this area did not appear to have been completely fulfilled between 1980 and 1990. There were increasing complaints from foreign investors, particularly non-Chinese foreign investors, that the business environment in China was not favourable. In particular, they cited the artificially high costs of key inputs (such as land, office space, and labour), inadequacies of infrastructure (especially transportation and energy), unclear rules, punitive charges and problems in dealing with the government bureaucracy. More significantly, the initial requirement that foreign investment enterprises had to balance their foreign exchange earnings was a major impediment to the expansion of foreign investment, in part because this requirement made it difficult for these enterprises to repatriate profits. It also severely restrained investment in projects designed to produce for the domestic market, the key attraction in investing in China for non-overseas Chinese investors. These problems, as well as the cyclical swing in the macroeconomics cycle, resulted in the contracted amount of direct foreign investments declining to about US$3–4 billion between 1986 and 1987, while the ASEAN countries attracted away the bulk of the outflows of direct foreign investments from Japan and NIEs during this period.

To address the problems that had emerged, the State Council issued draft regulations on direct investment in October 1986. The regulations provided for reductions in land use fees, taxes, costs of certain inputs, and labour costs. Improved access was promised for important inputs under state control, particularly for transportation and energy. Approval and licensing procedures for foreign investment enterprises were streamlined, and greater autonomy of these enterprises over production plans, imports and exports, wages, and terms of employment was guaranteed. In addition, to address the problem of balancing foreign exchange accounts, the foreign exchange adjustment centres were established. In 1988, local authorities in a number of areas established 'one-stop' offices to speed up the processing of permits needed by foreign investment enterprises to begin or expand operations. Direct investment picked up to about US$6 billion in 1988–89 but stagnated in 1990 due to the Tiananmen event on 4 June 1989 (see Table 3.1) (Ball et al., 1993).

The Tiananmen effect of June 1989 introduced a significant level of uncertainty into the business and investment climate in China. Consequently, in 1989 and 1990, the outflows of investments from Japan and the NIEs were substantially diverted from China to ASEAN. While FDI stagnated at US$6.9 billion in China in 1990, it doubled to a total of US$29.3 billion in Malaysia, Indonesia and Thailand (see Table 3.1).

In late January 1992, Deng Xiaoping made a historic tour to South China, calling for faster economic growth and deeper economic reform. This speech was later circulated as 'Internal Party Document No 2' for senior cadres to 'study'. This call for greater economic reforms sparked off an unprecedented investment boom in South China, which soon spread to other cities. Direct foreign investments contracted, which almost doubled from US$6.6 billion in 1990 to US$12.0 billion in 1991, skyrocketed to reach US$58.7 billion in 1992. Foreign capital actually utilized also rose substantially, from US$3.5 billion in 1990 to US$4.4 billion in 1991 and more than doubled again to US$11.0 billion in 1992. The momentum continued unabated to reach US$26 billion in 1993, US$34 billion in 1994 and US$38 billion in 1995.

The acceleration of economic reform and the open-door policy since early 1992 have led to the re-evaluation of China as a destination for direct investment by foreign companies. The Chinese government has expanded the list of industries permitted for investment by foreigners to include service industries like commerce, retailing as well as infrastructural development like power generation, telecommunication, transportation and real estate. At the same time, regions open to foreign investment have been extended beyond the coastal regions to major cities along the border regions and the Yangtze River.

This upsurge of direct foreign investments into China since early 1992 had been increasingly at the expense of ASEAN. The surge of Northeast Asian investments into Southeast Asia between 1986 and 1990 has moderated (see Table 3.1). While the ASEAN-3 (Indonesia, Malaysia and Thailand) managed to capture 80 per cent of total direct foreign investments contracted flowing into Southeast Asia and China in 1990, their share declined steadily to 59 per cent in 1991. By 1992, it had fallen to only 40 per cent, with China accounting for 58 per cent and Vietnam's share rising to about 3 per cent.

The competitive pressure from China exerted tremendous impact on the process of trade and investment liberalization in Southeast Asia, particularly Indonesia. The various reform packages announced by the Indonesian government since 1992 had largely the Chinese competition in mind. The main objectives were to further ease foreign investment requirements, reduce import protection, ease bureaucratic impediments, and streamline the duty drawback scheme for exporters.

An important step in deregulation was taken in July 1992, when 100 per cent foreign ownership was permitted for projects worth at least $50 million or located in any one of fourteen less-developed provinces. In October 1993, the Indonesian government further addressed the principal concerns of foreign investors on the bottlenecks in infrastructure (physical infrastructure, electricity, and communication), long and complex licensing procedures, complications in obtaining land titles, ownership limitations, and the lack of transparent rules for business dealings.

These liberalization reform measures, particularly the easing of restrictions on foreign ownership and forced divestment, have had significant effect in sharpening Indonesia's competitiveness in attracting FDI compared to China, Vietnam and South Asia. While FDI fell from US$10.3 billion in 1992 to US$8.1 billion in 1993, with particularly severe declines from Japan, Hong Kong, Taiwan and the USA, FDI rose to a record of US$23.7 billion in 1994 and an estimated US$36 billion in 1995 (see Table 3.1). Major infrastructural projects like power plants and refineries have substantially boosted the approved FDI.

It is clear that since the mid-1980s, competitive unilateral liberalization among the ASEAN countries and China, as well as the pressure of exchange rates and wage costs in Japan and the NIEs, have resulted in an investment-driven regionalism in East Asia. While rapidly rising intraregional trade reflected greater intra-firm trade regionally with final demand continuing to be in the USA and European Union (EU) in the 1980s, increasing empirical evidence points to rapidly rising consumption expenditure and investment demand as well as independent growth momentum within East Asia since the early 1990s.

Thus, the empirical evidence indicates that the rise in intra-regional trade in East Asia was largely economically driven. The fundamental forces were the forces of economic expansion, geographical proximity, web of business networks, lower transportation and transaction costs, a higher level of information flows, intra-firm trade and increasing policy convergence in trade and investment regimes among countries in the region.

■ East Asia as an independent engine of growth

Since the early 1990s, it became increasingly clear that East Asian (NIEs, ASEAN and China) growth managed to maintain its momentum despite the economic slowdown in the USA, Europe and Japan. For example, while the major OECD economies were in recession between 1990 and 1992, the East Asian countries were still chalking up growth rates of 6–12 per cent during this period (see Table 3.3). The empirical evidence appears to support the fact that until the mid to late 1980s, East Asia was basically a wagon. Now it has increasingly become an independent locomotive.

Table 3.3 Sustained East Asian growth momentum – real GDP growth

	1990	1991	1992	1993
Industrial countries				
USA	0.8	–1.2	1.9	2.7
Germany	4.5	0.9	1.8	–1.3
United Kingdom	1.0	–2.2	–0.8	1.8
Japan	5.2	4.4	2.0	0.1
ASEAN (3)[a]	9.5	7.7	7.2	7.8
China	5.2	7.0	12.8	12.0
NIEs	5.8	6.6	6.5	6.6

Note: [a] ASEAN (3) refers to Indonesia, Malaysia and Thailand
Sources: OECD; National Statistics

Figure 3.1 shows that during the period 1971–81, East Asian growth (consisting of the NIEs and ASEAN but excluding Japan) tracks the US growth very closely. Simple regression analysis indicates that about 85 per cent of the variation in East Asian growth during this period can be attributed to variation in US growth. During this

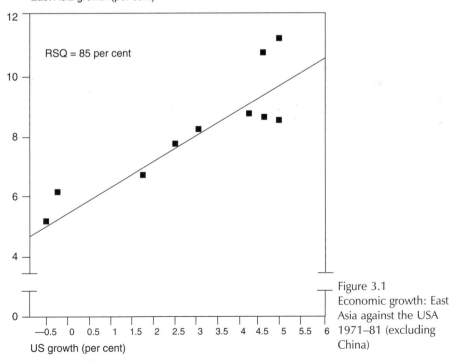

Figure 3.1 Economic growth: East Asia against the USA 1971–81 (excluding China)

period, a 1 percentage point increase in the US growth led to an about 0.8 percentage point increase in East Asian growth. This was a period of asymmetrical relationship between the locomotive and the wagon.

Figure 3.2 shows that remarkable structural changes transpired between the earlier period and the period 1983–94. East Asian growth no longer tracks the US growth closely, particularly when China is added.[2] In fact, it appears from the chart that East Asian growth has consistently clustered around 6 per cent to 10 per cent whether the US economy is in recession at 0 per cent or booming at 4 per cent. Econometric estimates show that only 36 per cent of the variation in East Asian growth can now be attributed to variation in US growth, with the other two-thirds driven by variables like their own domestic private consumption and investment. This is the period of gradual transformation of the wagon into an independent locomotive.

Major reasons for the rise of East Asian independent momentum of growth in the global economy include massive infrastructural development projects like highways, power plants, telecommunication facilities, housing, construction of commercial and retail space as well as industrial estate expansion that generates substantial independent domestic growth momentum; rising domestic purchasing power as a result of employment expansion and wage increases as well as a rapidly expanding middle-class; substantial expansion in private investment, rising interdependence in direct foreign investment; and intra-industry trade flows among the regional economies.

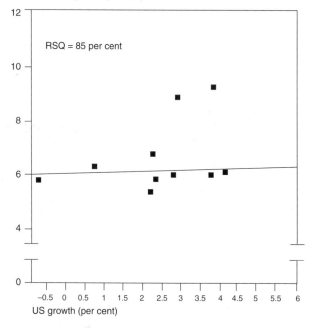

Figure 3.2
Economic growth: East Asia against the USA 1983–94 (including China).

---

[2] A Chow test on the stability of the coefficients during the two periods confirmed that we could reject the hypothesis that the relationship was stable at the 5 per cent level.

▌ Implications for managers

What are the major implications of East Asia as an independent centre of growth in the global economy for managers?

East Asia as an expanding consumer market

The substantial expansion in private consumption expenditure was the main engine driving the East Asian independent momentum of growth. With sustained economic growth and rising income and educational levels, the rapid emergence of the middle class in East Asia was having significant economic, social and political impact on the region and beyond. The region was no longer merely a low-cost production base. It was becoming a considerable consumer market. Japan and the NIEs have reached per capita income ranging from US$10 000 to US$30 000. In addition, the ASEAN countries of 320 million people, with income levels of US$2000 to US$9000, passed the subsistence level and were generating a vast demand for manufactured goods and many high ticket consumer durables like cars, home appliances and electronics. More significantly, due to the demographic and income distribution structure for the East Asian countries, a modest 25 per cent rise in average income over five years could lead to a doubling of the size of the middle income group and hence create more potential consumers. Based on existing trends of growth in output and consumption expenditure, by the year 2000 the East Asian market was projected to be comparable in size to that of Western Europe. More significantly, the OECD estimated that, if China, India and Indonesia were to grow at 6 per cent per year in the next fifteen years, by 2010, there will be 700 million Asian consumers equal to Spain's present income level of US$13 000. This 700 million consumer market is equivalent to the size of the present market of USA, EU and Japan combined. Japanese big names in the retail industry, like Yaohan, Takashimaya, Daimaru and Sogo, geared up by expanding their operations in the region.

Segments of consumer markets became important. In Japan and the other NIEs, single women in their early to mid-twenties were fast becoming important consumers in the tourist markets of Singapore and Hong Kong. Equally affluent and willing to spend was a new generation of young, dual income families. As the proportion of women in the labour force increased from about 25 per cent to 30 per cent in the early 1980s, to over 45 per cent in the 1990s, East Asian working women were buying convenience foods, microwave ovens and disposable nappies. They were also buying more cosmetics and a wide range of branded products. Rising middle-class affluence was also reflected in a greater market for natural and health foods like low fat fruit yogurt and milk, non-dairy creamer and cholesterol-free products.

McKinsey and Company estimated that by the year 2000, some 260 million people in China will attain the income level to afford packaged food products like biscuits, beer, soft drinks, as well as skin-care products. Consequently, a number of global consumer goods companies significantly expanded their presence and long-term strategic commitment in the China market. They included Procter and Gamble, Unilever, Nestlé, Coca-Cola, Pepsi Cola, as well as less well known, mid-sized Asian food manufacturers like Lam Soon and Yeo Hiap Seng of Singapore, as well as President Food of Taiwan. Facing the poor transportation infrastructure, the underdeveloped and highly fragmented distribution channels, counterfeiting and arbitrary pricing, major food companies are improving distribution control, helping to upgrade and train major wholesalers and installing systems for monitoring inventories and performance. In the case of a company with large volumes like Coca-Cola, it can afford to bypass wholesalers by trucking and selling directly to tens of thousands of retailers, giving it a significant competitive edge in controlling product positioning and promotions across over eighty cities. Taiwan's President Food, on the other hand, has aggressively built sales teams to promote and merchandise its products in thousands of smaller outlets across the country. As rapid expansion tends to stretch resources, non-competing multinationals with lower volume such as Colgate-Palmolive and Johnson and Johnson are banding together to share warehousing and distribution facilities. Confronting the dearth of local managers, all these companies are also spending considerable time training and developing key local managers, especially sales supervisors.

The rising consumer market in China also led to the rise of direct marketing. Avon has relied on its 70 000 lady distributors in China to rack up sales increases of over 50 per cent for its cosmetics in the last three years. Michigan-based Amway set up its $100 million plant in Guangzhou, China to produce detergent, washing liquids and household cleaners. Its long-term plan is to set up an extensive direct marketing network in China (*Far Eastern Economic Review*, 27 April 1995).

Strategic alliances between Western and Asian firms

More significantly, the lure of the East Asian market was leading to increasing numbers of strategic alliances between Western corporations and local East Asian firms. This is because a significant number of the East Asian regional conglomerates have been built up behind protective walls of tariff and non-tariff barriers in the past. They have been strong in political networking, which helps gain approval for projects or win concessions, extensive in their regional business links and contacts as well as relationships with suppliers and customers, but weak in technology, brand name, marketing know-how and managerial expertise. As the regional economies liberalized, partly driven by the conclusion of the Uruguay Round, partly by the liberalization programme of the Asia-Pacific Economic Cooperation Conference (APEC) and the ASEAN Free Trade Area, regional conglomerates were increasingly under intense pressure to seek strategic alliances with Western firms to rise up to the new environment of intense regional and global competition. Their pressure to upgrade in technology, marketing and managerial expertise found natural strategic partners in Western companies attracted by the regional expanding market but somewhat perplexed by the confusing business networks, political and cultural environment in the region. Significant strategic alliances between regional conglomerates and OECD multinationals looking at the expanding regional markets abound. For example, Lippo, one of the largest Indonesian firms formed ventures with car-maker Chrysler, retailers Wal-Mart and J. C. Penney, power-plant builders Mission Energy and Entergy and financial services company First Union (*Far Eastern Economic Review*, 28 September 1995). Similarly Bakrie Brothers, Indonesia's largest *pribumi* (native Indonesian) conglomerate, linked up with Hughes Network Systems, a unit of GM Hughes Electronics, to set up a fixed wireless communications system. YTL Corporation of Malaysia linked up with Siemens to move to the power generation business in Malaysia. The CP Group of Thailand formed ventures with Wal-Mart into retailing, PepsiCo into the beverage industry, Oscar Mayer into processed meat. Cheung Kong of Hong Kong linked up with Cable and Wireless and ATT into telecommunication.

Coca-Cola facilitated its entry into China by linking up with Kerry Beverages to set up bottling plants. Kerry Beverages, part of the conglomerate led by Malaysian tycoon Robert Kuok, has impeccable *guanxi* (connections) throughout Asia, especially in China. The relationship allowed Coca-Cola to rapidly establish its bottling plants in key Chinese cities and this speed proved pivotal in its rivalry with Pepsi in the rapidly expanding market. By 1996, Coca-Cola had sixteen bottling plants and 8000 employees across the country and its 23 per cent share of the soft drink market was about double that of Pepsi, even though both companies entered China at about the same time in the early 1980s.

Like Coca-Cola, US telecoms group Nynex has been using its technological capabilities, managerial skills, global brand name and network as a bargaining chip to enter the Asian market. Nynex formed Telecom Asia with the CP Group, an Overseas Chinese conglomerate based in Thailand. Besides being a major financial success, Telecom Asia allowed Nynex an opening into the relationship web that could bring further opportunities in other parts of Asia.

These relationships can prove critical in securing a business licence. In the early 1990s, the German car-maker, Daimler-Benz had been struggling to obtain investment approval for a car and light truck plant in Ho Chi Minh City, Vietnam. Despite several rounds of application and fee payments, no business licence had been approved. However, when the Singapore government took a 22 per cent stake in the $80 million plant and approached the Vietnamese authority directly, the project was approved within two weeks, indicating the importance of relationships in the Asian context.

The rising significance of the Asian market was featuring more and more prominently in the strategic plan of most global MNCs. The spokesman of Ford Motor in Bangkok, commenting on competition with Japanese car companies for market share in Asia put it graphically, 'The strategy for us is basic. If five to ten years from now, we only have 1 per cent to 2 per cent of the Asian market, we won't be No. 2 in the world in the car industry anymore. We are not about to let that happen' (*Far Eastern Economic Review*, 13 June 1996).

Expanding business in infrastructural development

Between 1995 and 2004, investment requirement in infrastructure in East Asia was estimated by the World Bank to amount to US$1509 billion. Out of these, US$607 billion would be in transport infrastructure like road, bridges, tunnels, etc., US$493 billion in power plant and energy production, US$256 billion in telecommunication infrastructure and US$153 in water and sanitation infrastructure. The lion's share of these projects will be in China, which would account for US$743 billion or almost half of the total infrastructural investment, followed by South Korea (US$268 billion), Indonesia (US$192 billion), Malaysia (US$192 billion) and Thailand (US$145 billion) (see Table 3.4) (World Bank, 1995).

As a result of the substantial funding needed for these infrastructural development projects, infrastructural privatization as well as private sector financing became the key financing features. In this win-win model, private investors achieved attractive

Table 3.4 East Asia's investment requirements in infrastructure, 1995–2004

	Power $bn	Telecoms $bn	Transport $bn	Water saturation ($bn)	Total as per cent of GDP
China	200	141	302	101	7.4
Indonesia	82	23	62	25	6.8
South Korea	101	32	132	4	5.6
Malaysia	17	6	22	4	4.8
Philippines	19	7	18	4	6.8
Thailand	49	29	57	10	7.2
Other[a]	25	18	14	4	7.5
Total East Asia	493	256	607	153	6.8

Note: [a]Cambodia, Fiji, Kiribati, Laos, Maldives, Mongolia, Myanmar, Solomon Islands, Tonga, Vanuatu, Vietnam and Western Samoa
Source: World Bank

rates of returns by participating in the financing and structuring of these infrastructural development projects to accelerate the country's economic development. The government assisted by creating a conducive legal and regulatory framework for the private sector to attain an attractive return and to manage the risks of operating power generation and distribution, sea ports and airports, telecommunications, railways, roads and bridges.

These infrastructural projects have begun to substantially benefit European and US firms. Major power projects include the 1,400-megawatt, coal-fired power plant in Prachuab Khiri Khan province, South of Bangkok. It is to be built by the Thai company Sahaviriya in a joint venture with Ansaldo Energie of Italy. In Indonesia, the $1.7 billion Jawa Power project is a joint venture project between Germany's Siemens Power Ventures, which holds a 50 per cent stake, the UK's PowerGen, with 35 per cent and an unlisted company controlled by Bambang Trihatmodjo, the second son of ex-President Suharto, with 15 per cent. Construction of the twin 610-megawatt coal-fired power plant was to begin in late 1996 and is scheduled for completion in 1999. In Malaysia, ABB Asea Brown Boveri AG has been awarded a power plant and transmission contract from Ekran Bhd, a Malaysian publicly listed company. The Bakun Dam project in Sarawak is valued at $5 billion. ABB will lead a consortium to build a 2,400-megawatt hydroelectric power generation plant and transmission system, be responsible for overall project management and supply all electrical equipment for the project, including six 420-megawatt hydrogenerators and a complete 500-kilovolt high voltage direct current transmission system to connect the power plant in Sarawak to population centres in the Malaysian peninsula 1,300 kilometres away, via three submarine cables under the South China Sea (*Asian Wall Street Journal*, 18 June 1996).

As a result of the rapid expansion of infra-structural projects in East Asia, an increasing share of total revenue for major firms was derived from the Asian countries. For example, ABB's global power generation business has increasingly depended on three large Asian countries, Indonesia, China and India. In 1995, ABB's power generation revenue totalled about US$10 billion, out of which 35–40 per cent came from Asia.

The rapid opening of the telecoms markets in East Asia has also spawned start-ups hungry for technical expertise as well as capital to build local, international and cellular networks. In 1995, Deutsche Telekom paid $586 million for 25 per cent of Indonesia's Satelindo, a new telecom operator which is one of only two companies allowed to provide international services in Indonesia until the year 2005. In May 1996, Deutsche Telekom signed a letter of intent to take a stake in Technology Resources Industries (TRI), a Malaysian firm headed by Tajudin Ramli. The German company agreed to pay $570 million for a 21 per cent stake in TRI. In the same month, Deutsche Telekom clinched a 25-year, $190 million deal to build and operate a phone system in Tianjin in Northeast China (*Far Eastern Economic Review*, 6 June 1996).

Part of the boost in infrastructural expansion came from the privatization programme in the regional economies. The most extensive and successful case was the programme in Malaysia. Malaysia's privatization programme involved not only full and partial sales but also extensive build-operate-transfer schemes like the M$3.4 billion North South Highway, as well as contracting schemes like municipal garbage disposal. For example, in the island of Pangkor, United Engineers Malaysia and Arab-Malaysia Development, together with three Danish firms, I. Kruger Engineering, Chemcontrol and Enviroplan, have formed a joint venture to handle the waste management facility along the build-own-operate scheme. The M$353 million facility will be an integrated complex with four types of treatment facilities: incineration, physical or chemical treatment, solidification and landfill (*Far Eastern Economic Review*, 19 January 1996; Ng and Wagner, 1989).

In particular, dependence on the private sector for infrastructural projects was estimated to have saved the Malaysian government M$41 billion by 1996, leading to a healthier government budgetary position and improved external debt service ratio. More significantly, businesses and consumers have benefited substantially from greater efficiency. For instance, the North South Highway has reduced the six-hour trip between Singapore and Kuala Lumpur to four and a half hours. Average turnaround time at the Kelang Container Terminal has dropped to less than three days from the eight it previously took to clear cargo.

A major project launched by the Malaysian Government in 1996 was the so-called multimedia super corridor (MSC). The 750 sq km MSC was set up to attract information technology firms and content providers in areas ranging from tele-medicine and distance learning via satellite, to software engineering, electronic publishing, multimedia entertainment and Internet providers. To jump-start itself as a regional multimedia hub, Malaysia was offering generous tax incentives to pioneering companies by providing tax exemption on multimedia equipment, special concessions on foreign currency loans and transactions, unrestricted ownership and employment rights, as well as preferential treatment in the award of infrastructure-development contracts. In addition, laws that guaranteed the free flow of information and protected intellectual property were drafted. To kick-start the MSC, the government invested US$2 billion on basic infrastructure and to build an 'intelligent city'. In 1996, the MSC attracted investment commitments from more than 100 companies, including the major IT companies from Japan and the USA.

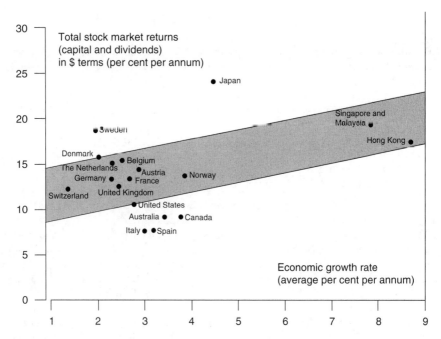

Figure 3.3 Relation between economic growth and stock market total returns 1970–89

Portfolio investment

With East Asia emerging as an independent growth centre in the global economy, fund managers from the USA and EU were increasingly looking to the region for asset diversification and higher returns. Over the long term, there is a close relationship between average economic growth rate and total stock market returns (capital + dividends). Between the period 1970 and 1989, annual GDP growth averaged 8 per cent in Singapore, Malaysia and Hong Kong and the total stock market returns were about 18–20 per cent per annum. On the other hand, for most of the European and North American countries, GDP growth during the same period averaged around 3 per cent, while the total stock market returns were around 10–15 per cent (see Figure 3.3) (Greenwood, 1993).

Traditionally, most of the US pool of savings under management, about $7.5 trillion at the end of 1994, held by insurance, pension funds and mutual funds, were invested in the USA. For example, an IMF survey in 1991 of 100 leading funds in the USA and Europe showed that only 3.4 per cent of US assets ($4.5 trillion) were invested in foreign equities, while the European funds ($3.7 trillion) invested 9.7 per cent abroad. As the US investors caught up with higher foreign stock returns, particularly in Asia, the net purchase of US investors of foreign stocks rose steadily from around $10 billion in 1990 to $33 billion in 1992 and further to about $50 billion per year in 1993-95. As US funds move into Asia, they helped to broaden and deepen the market in the region. Being from a more highly regulated and sophisticated home market, these investors also helped to bring Asian stock markets faster into line with international standards for disclosure and force investment practices to be based more on economic fundamentals than on gossip and speculation.

More significantly, now that the East Asian business cycle was no longer an adjunct of the US cycle, there was greater scope for geographical diversification. This has important implications, as it implies that the higher rate of returns to capital in the East Asian economy would benefit future US retirees whose pension funds are now increasingly being invested in companies or projects in the region. There was no better way to ensure improved market access and cordial economic relations between the USA, EU and East Asia than linking the future retirement income of citizens (voters) in the former to the economic prosperity in the latter. From this perspective, a win-win situation could be fostered and East Asian countries could do well by gradually liberalizing their capital markets and allowing the OECD funds to benefit from the growth of the region, thus deepening the industrialized West's interests in the region's peace and prosperity.

Rising intra-regional trade

The integration of the regional economies through a web of intraregional investment, trade, business networks and procurement patterns is indicated in a case study at the firm level in Figure 3.4.

The disk drive plant in Singapore imports various components like magnetic heads, metal parts, disk media, integrated circuits, and motors from different parts of the Asia Pacific. The final product is then exported to the USA, Europe and other Asian countries. A significant point to note is that the market for final output has shifted substantially. In 1987, the USA absorbed 57 per cent of the output, while Western Europe took in 25 per cent, Japan 3 per cent and Asia 15 per cent. By 1994, the US share had declined to 35 per cent, and the Asian share risen to 40 per cent with Europe and Japan's shares being somewhat stable at 21 per cent and 4 per cent (Economic Development Board).

Increasingly, the export markets of East Asian countries had become less dependent on the USA and EU and more among themselves. Table 3.5 shows that by 1994, most of

Table 3.5 Export markets of East Asia, 1994 (percentage)

	USA	EU	Japan	Dev. Asia[a]
Korea	21	11	14	32
Hong Kong	23	14	6	46
Singapore	19	13	7	51
Indonesia	17	17	31	25
Malaysia	21	14	12	44
Thailand	23	16	18	29
Philippines	39	17	15	23
China	18	12	18	40
Vietnam	1	20	26	28

Note: [a] Dev. Asia refers to developing Asia or Asia excluding Japan
Source: International Financial Statistical Yearbook, IMF

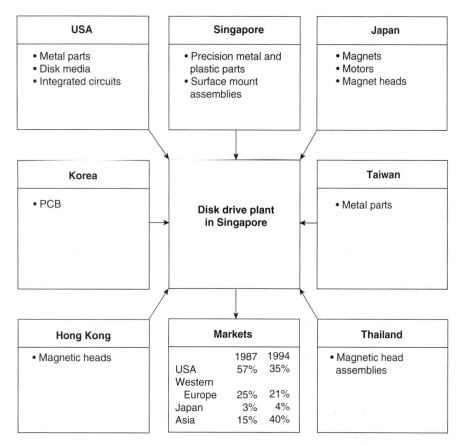

Figure 3.4 Intra-regional trade (disk drive plant)
Source: Economic Development Board, Singapore, *Census of Industrial Production*.

the countries in East Asia depended on the USA for 17–23 per cent of their exports (except for the Philippines at 39 per cent and Vietnam at 1 per cent due to trade embargoes) while their dependence on other Asian countries (excluding Japan) had risen to 25–51 per cent. Compared to the East Asian countries' dependence level of 20–42 per cent on the US market in 1985, the shift had been significant.

▓ Conclusion

In the long term, the emergence of East Asia as an independent engine of growth will substantially enhance East Asian bargaining power in a global environment with a rapid slide towards regionalism. As North America and Europe decline as important markets for East Asian products, EU and North American Free Trade Agreement members (NAFTA), even if increasingly protectionistic, will look less threatening. On the other hand, the lure of the East Asian market for North American and EU firms, both as a destination for direct exports and direct investment targeting local/regional sales, will increasingly emerge as an important countervailing force against protectionistic impulses in these regional groupings.

While East Asian growth has been impressive over the past three decades, considerable concern exists on its future as well as the political risks associated with the region. While the earlier generation of countries that took off, like Japan, Korea and Taiwan have evolved into more mature economies with increasingly stable democratic institutions, late-comers like Indonesia, Thailand, China and Vietnam have yet to develop stable political institutions to facilitate leadership transition. In particular, ageing leaders dominate in Indonesia, Vietnam and China. With rapid economic liberalization, rising foreign investment, and extensive contacts with the outside world, an emerging urban middle class increasingly feels constricted by the ossified political institutions and authoritarian control. While Korea and Taiwan proved capable to transit from authoritarian political structures to more democratic institutions to accommodate this inevitable demand of the educated middle class without major instability, it is not clear that the other countries, particularly China and Vietnam, with Leninist party tradition, can transit smoothly and peacefully.

In particular, the post-Deng leadership in China has yet to consolidate its control and feel secure about its power. While it is likely that the open-door policy and further integration with the global economy are likely to continue, the major problems unleashed by Deng's liberalization policies in the past two decades could prove difficult for the new leadership to manage. This included the increasing inequality between the booming coastal region and the poor interior provinces, especially when compounded by the restiveness and grievances of minority groups in Xinjiang, Tibet and the interior provinces. The extensive problems of the inefficient state-owned enterprises have also resulted in increasing unemployment, largely disguised in the urban cities. Moreover, the corroding effect of widespread corruption of party and government officials has created extensive cynicism among the populace. In the event of an economic downturn, the combination of rising urban unemployment, cynicism with the party and government officials as well as grievances in the interior provinces could prove to be destabilizing.

Partly as a result of the collapse of semiconductor prices and the weakening of the global electronic industries in 1996, growth in several East Asian countries moderated considerably. In 1996, the export growth of East Asia had fallen to 5 per cent, a significant decline from over 20 per cent growth in the previous two years. In addition, the stock markets of Thailand and South Korea plunged and their financial system witnessed several cases of collapse. This weakening in growth rekindled the discussion on the sustainability of East Asian growth in the future.

Various economists, including Paul Krugman and Alwyn Young, used growth theory and accounting to show that growth in East Asia could be largely attributed to sheer increase in the inputs of labour and capital and very little to total factor productivity or more productive use of these inputs (see Krugman, 1994; Young, 1994). Recent evaluation of the empirical evidence, however, has indicated that Young's numbers were subject to large measurement errors. Studies by the Union Bank of Switzerland and International Monetary Fund, have shown stronger total factor productivity gains, amounting to about 2–2.5 per cent between 1978 and 1996, compared with a weaker 0.3 per cent for the USA (see Sarel (IMF), 1996; Union Bank of Switzerland, 1996).

On the other hand, in 1996, while East Asian growth looked likely to be sustained for some period, the rates of growth were likely to decline as the economies matured. This has already happened to Korea, Taiwan and Hong Kong, whose growth rate declined from 9–10 per cent in the 1970s to 7–8 per cent in the 1980s and have further fallen to 5–7 per cent in the 1990s. More significantly, East Asian countries are still in the income range of US$3000–13 000 (excluding city states like Singapore and Hong Kong) compared with the industrial economies' US$20 000. It is unclear whether East Asian countries, whose culture and value systems of hard work and discipline have been conducive for rapid catching up with the Western economies, will also prove to be conducive for creative thinking, and innovation in sustaining growth when they reach the technology frontier in their development. If East Asian societies prove incapable of being more creative and innovative, their growth could stagnate before they could catch up with the Western industrial economies.

■ References

Amsden, A. (1992) *Asia's Next Giant: South Korea and Late Industrialization*. Oxford.

Asian Wall Street Journal, 18 June 1996.

Ball, M. W., Khor, H. E. and Kochhar, K. (1993). *China at the Threshold of a Market Economy*. International Monetary Fund.

Chen, E. K. Y. (1979). *Hyper-Growth in Asian Economies: A Comparative Study of Hong Kong, Japan, Korea, Singapore and Taiwan*. London.

Economic Development Board, *Census of Industrial Production*, Institute of SouthEast Asian Studies, Singapore, various issues.

Far Eastern Economic Review, 27 April 1995; 28 September 1995; 19 January 1996; 6 June 1996; 13 June 1996.

Galenson, W. (1985). *Foreign Trade and Investment: Economic Growth in the Newly Industrializing Asian Countries*. University of Wisconsin Press.

Greenwood, J. G. (1993). Portfolio investment in Asian and Pacific economies: trends and prospects. *Asian Development Review*, **11** (1).

Hughes, H. (ed.) (1988). *Achieving Industrialization in East Asia*. Cambridge University Press.

Imada, P., Montes, M. and Naya, S. (1991). *A Free Trade Area*. Institute of Southeast Asian Studies.

Krugman, P. (1994). The myth of the Asian miracle. *Foreign Affairs*, **73** (6).

Lim, L. Y. C. and Pang, E. F. (1991). *Foreign Investment and Industrialization in Malaysia, Singapore, Taiwan and Thailand*. OECD.

Low, L., Toh, M. H., Soon, T. W. and Tan, K. Y., with special contribution from Hughes, H. (1993), *Challenges and Response: Thirty Years of the Economic Development Board*. Times Academic Press.

Ng, C. Y. and Wagner, N. (1989). Privatization and deregulation in ASEAN. *ASEAN Economic Bulletin*.

Ng, C. Y. and Wagner, N. (1991). *Marketization in ASEAN*. Singapore.

Noland, M. (1990). *Pacific Basin Developing Countries: Prospects for the Future*. Institute for International Economics.

Noordin, S., See, C. L. and Jin, L. S. (eds) (1990). *ASEAN at the Crossroads*, Institute of Strategic and International Studies.

OECD (1988). *The Newly Industrializing Countries: Challenges and Opportunity for OECD Industries*. OECD Publications and Information Center.

Sarel, M. (IMF) (1996). Growth and productivity in ASEAN economies. *IMF Economic Issues*, (1).

Sopiee, N. (1989) *Crisis and Response: The Challenge to South–South Economic Co-operation*. Viking Penguin.

Tan, K.-Y., Toh, M. H. and Low, L. (1992). *ASEAN at the Crossroads*, Institute of Strategic and International Studies.

Union Bank of Switzerland (1996). The Asian economic miracle. *UBS International Finance*, (29), Autumn.

Wei, S.-J. (1993). The open door policy and China's rapid growth: evidence from city level data. National Bureau of Economic Research Working Paper No. 4602, December.

World Bank (1995). *Infrastructural Development in East Asian and Pacific*. Oxford University Press.

Young, A. (1994). The tyranny of numbers: confronting the statistical realities of the East Asian growth experience. National Bureau of Economic Research Working Paper No. 4680, March.

Chapter 3.1

Perspectives on East Asia since the financial crisis in July 1997

Kong-Yam Tan

Since July 1997 when the Thai baht was floated, the East Asian financial crisis has resulted in massive collapses in the stock markets, exchange rates as well as the property markets in the region. Asset-market collapses in the second half of 1997 have led to major declines in wealth, significant increases in non-performing loans in the banking system, and to a substantial reduction in consumption expenditure and investment spending. By September 1998, over a year after the triggering event in Bangkok, the financial crisis had already resulted in an economic meltdown, with falling output and rising unemployment leading to severe stress on the social and political stability in the afflicted countries. In addition, the contagion effect from Asia had led to the spread of the financial crisis to Russia and Latin America.

Overborrowing and the dynamics of financial turmoil

The root cause of the financial crisis is the over-borrowing and rapid accumulation of foreign debts, especially by Thailand and Indonesia. Figure 3.1.1 shows that external debts owed to foreign banks more than quadrupled in Thailand between 1990 and 1997. Despite the underestimation of foreign debts in Indonesia due to poor coverage and supervision, foreign debts almost doubled during the same period. More significantly, these rising foreign debts have become increasingly short-term in nature, especially when measured against available foreign reserves in these countries. As indicated in Table 3.1.1, by the end of 1996, short-term liabilities towards banks in industrial countries had risen to 181 per cent of foreign reserves in Indonesia, and 169 per cent in Thailand. On the other hand, partly due to lower interest rate differentials between foreign and domestic interest rates as well as more-stringent supervision over foreign borrowings, Malaysia has not built up foreign debts as rapidly. Philippines, under the supervision of the IMF, with a less robust economy and a restructured independent central bank, has also been prudent in incurring foreign borrowing. Consequently, the foreign debt ratio was more modest for Malaysia (47 per cent) and Philippines (77 per cent). Overall, Japanese banks accounted for 40–60 per cent of the total lending, with European (10–20 per cent) and American (8–10 per cent) banks somewhat smaller in exposure.

Table 3.1.1 Short-term liabilities towards Bank of International Settlements banks, end of 1996 (as percentage of foreign reserves)

Country	Percentage
Korea	213
Indonesia	181
Malaysia	47
Philippines	77
Thailand	169

Source: Bank of International Settlements

In addition, the corporate sectors in Malaysia and Thailand had also over-borrowed domestically, resulting in rapid domestic debt accumulation. As indicated in Figure 3.1.2, by the end of 1997, domestic credit to the private sectors as a share of GDP had reached 160 per cent in Malaysia and over 150 per cent in Thailand. The over-leveraging of the domestic corporate sectors made them very vulnerable to sudden interest rate increases and falling domestic demand. As a large share of these borrowing went into real estate investment, and stock market speculation, the economy and banking system became vulnerable to sudden collapses of the stock markets and property markets. The overinvestment was particularly serious in Malaysia where the investment share of GDP rose from 35.2 per cent in 1987-92 to 42.6 per cent in 1993–96. The corresponding increase for Thailand was from 37.9 per cent to 41.6 per cent. For Indonesia and Philippines, over-investments were not as serious.

These over-investments exerted a serious cost on the economy as they led to lower efficiency for capital. The incremental capital output ratio (ICOR) for Malaysia, or the amount of capital needed to produce one dollar of output, rose from 3.8 in 1987–92 to 4.8 by 1993–96, a serious deterioration of capital efficiency. Similarly ICOR increased from 3.3 to 5.1 for Thailand in the corresponding period. The over-borrowings had been used by the private sectors in over-investments, particularly in real estate, stock market speculation, over-expansion in specific industries, like petrochemicals, power plants, telecommunication facilities and other infrastructural projects (see Figure 3.1.3). By mid-1997, the share of bank lending to the property sectors had reached 30–40 per cent in Malaysia and Thailand, 25–30 per cent in Indonesia and 15–20 per cent in the Philippines (*J. P Morgan Asian Financial Market*, 1998). Thus, excessive bank lending following a period of rapid financial market and capital account liberalization, particularly in foreign bank lending, is a key contributing factor to the Asian financial crisis. Deregulation and privatization of banks with appropriate regulatory measures allowed them much greater latitude to borrow from abroad. With domestic interest rates much higher than foreign interest rates in Thailand and Indonesia as well as a stable peg (Thailand) and limited depreciation of about 5 per cent per year against the US dollar (Indonesia), the private corporate sectors in these countries, confident of limited exchange rate risks, borrowed massively in the cheaper foreign currencies (McKinnon and Pill, 1996). Consequently, banks and near-banks – such as Thailand's finance companies, became intermediaries for channelling foreign capital into the domestic economy. These under-capitalized banks and finance companies operated under highly distorted incentives, borrowed abroad and invested domestically with

US$ Billion

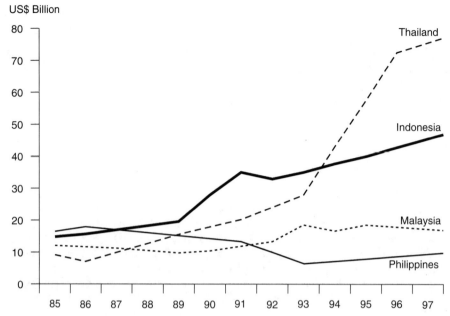

Figure 3.1.1 ASEAN 4: External debt owed to foreign banks
Source: Bank of International Settlements, annual reports

% of GDP

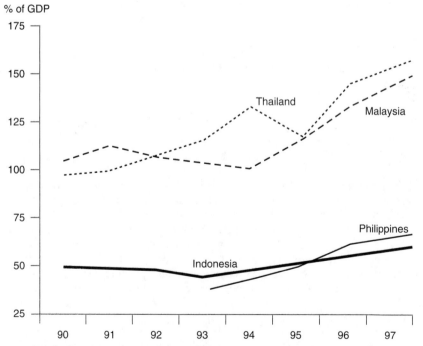

Figure 3.1.2 Domestic credit to private sector
Source: IFS, National Central Banks

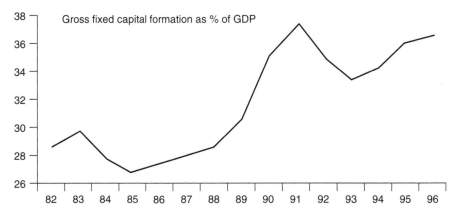

Figure 3.1.3 Overinvestment in Asia: gross fixed capital formation as percentage of GDP
Note: Asia refers to Thailand, Malaysia, Indonesia, Philippines and Korea
Source: IFS

reckless abandon. For these banks, even if the lending failed, while the depositors and creditors stood to lose money, the banks' owners shouldered little risk themselves because they had little capital tied up in the banks. Even the depositors and the foreign creditors would be secure from risk, if the governments bailed them out in the case of bank failures.

Thus, the moral hazard problem derived from the implicit promise of government bailouts in case things went wrong led to over-foreign-borrowing by the domestic banking systems as well as the corporate sectors. More significantly, the moral hazard problem was compounded by the fact that many banks were directly or indirectly controlled by the governments or politically favoured groups, substantially lending to politically favoured firms, individuals or investment projects. International banks thus lent vast sum of money to the domestic banks and corporate groups, assuming similar implicit bail-out commitments from the governments or the IMF (Krugman 1998, Sachs 1997).

It is clear that by the end of 1996, the Asian countries were highly vulnerable to a turn-around in foreign investor confidence and consequent capital outflows or the cessation in the rollovers of short-term foreign loans. Thus, rapid liberalization of the financial systems, internationalization of the capital markets, privatization of the banking systems, moral hazard problems arising from the implicit government guarantees, politically privileged groups' access to capital as well as weak regulation of the financial systems, led to domestic banks borrowing substantially from foreign banks and loaning the monies to the domestic companies. The higher domestic interest rates as well as the pegging of the currencies distorted incentives towards foreign borrowings that became increasingly short term and mostly unhedged. When these loans to domestic firms became non-performing due to poor investments or collapses of the real-estate market, domestic banks were saddled with large non-performing loans and substantial short-term foreign currency liabilities to the foreign banks. As exports declined and current account deficits became unsustainable, foreign reserves started to fall and foreign banks and investors began to lose confidence on the sustainability of the currency pegs. Foreign funds began to withdraw from the equity markets, foreign banks became less willing to roll over short-term loans, stock markets started to plummet and currencies depreciated drastically. Domestic costs of foreign debt sky-rocketed, foreign banks became even less willing to roll over loans to domestic banks, leading to a liquidity squeeze, bankruptcy of domestic financial institutions and the private corporate sectors.

As indicated in Figure 3.1.4, the foreign capital outflows led to significant currency depreciations, substantially increasing the domestic costs of foreign debt for the domestic banks and corporate sector. In addition, rising risk premiums and eventual monetary contractions to support the exchange rates led to higher interest rates and aggravated the debt-servicing problems of the corporate sectors, further depressing the property markets and the equity markets. Demand for the US dollar rose substantially due to sudden hedging of the US dollar debt by the corporate sectors, exporters' tendencies to hoard the US dollar and the bringing forward of demand for the US dollar by worried importers. These demands for the US dollar further aggravated the exchange rate declines. Eventually, domestic residents also lost confidence, resulting in domestic-capital flights and the shifts of domestic currency into foreign currencies. Loss of confidence, capital flights, declining exchange rates, higher interest rates, col-lapsing property and stock markets, ballooning foreign-debt services, rising non-per-forming loans, weakening capital adequacy ratios and further liquidity crunch then reinforced each other in a vicious cycle of downward spiral.

This sudden turnaround of foreign capital was substantial and drastic. As indicated in Table 3.1.2, Thailand enjoyed a net private-capital inflow amounting to 9.3 per cent of GDP in 1996. The collapse of investors' confidence and subsequent capital outflows

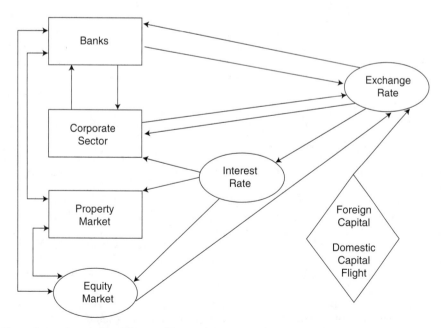

Figure 3.1.4 Dynamics of financial turmoil

led to net private capital outflows amounting to 10.9 per cent of GDP in 1997, a net turnaround of 20.2 per cent of GDP! The impact of such capital outflows was less drastic in the other countries, but still substantial in the Philippines, Indonesia and Malaysia.

Table 3.1.2 Net private capital flows (percentage of GDP)

	Thailand	*Indonesia*	*Malaysia*	*Philippines*
1996	9.3	6.3	9.6	9.8
1997	−10.9	1.6	4.7	0.5

Source: Institute for International Finance

The collapse of investors' confidence was partly triggered by the increasing doubts of the markets over the sustainability of the exchange rates as well as the declines in export growth beginning in early 1996. The pegging of the Southeast Asian currencies to the US dollar resulted in significant over-valuation of their currencies, especially after the US dollar strengthened substantially against all the major currencies since early 1995. Taking 1990 as the base year, the J. P. Morgan real exchange rate index indicated that by mid-1997, the real exchange rate had appreciated by 19 per cent in Malaysia, 24 per cent in the Philippines, 14 per cent in Thailand and 8 per cent in Indonesia. It is likely that a real exchange rate index based more on competitive currencies like the Chinese Rmb, Mexico peso etc. would indicate a much larger over-valuation.

▓ Key lessons

A painful lesson learned in this financial crisis is that over-hasty financial and capital markets' liberalization, before proper institution building and regulatory frameworks, could be disastrous. In particular, political influence in the allocation of credit as well as implicit or explicit government guarantees against losses distorted incentives and encouraged risky lending. For example, the genesis of the financial crisis in Thailand could be traced back to the last tenure of the Chuan government during 1992–95. It created the Bangkok International Banking Facility (BIBF), the channel through which Thai banks and companies, driven by substantial interest-rate differentials between domestic and US interest rates as well as the promised pegged exchange rate, borrowed funds heavily from abroad. These BIBF loans were used for over expansion and speculation in the real estate sector as well as over-investments in industrial capacities in steel, petrochemicals and oil refineries. Similarly, the proliferation of private banks owned by politically well-connected groups, under poor regulatory frameworks, as well as the weak supervision of foreign borrowings by the corporate sector, led to the Indonesian financial crisis.

As Alan Blinder, a former Federal Reserve Deputy Chairman, noted, financial markets tend to run in herds: they tend to over-react to almost everything, are susceptible to speculative bubbles and often behave as if they have ludicrously short time horizons. Jagdish Bhagwati (1998) argued that the Wall Street Treasury Complex in the US has a vested interest to promote unfettered global capital flows. Consequently, there is a need for developing countries to ensure a more cautious and measured approach to capital account liberalization, especially for short-term capital flows. A pace of liberalization more commensurate with the institutional and regulatory capabilities of the countries concerned is critical for financial stability and long-term sustainable development.

The Asian financial crisis and collapses revealed starkly a significant power shift in the global capital-market and financial systems. Over the past two decades, significant deregulation of domestic financial markets, substantial liberalization of international capital flows, rapid financial innovations as well as stupendous progress in information technology and telecommunications have occurred. These developments in the global capital markets resulted in substantial erosion of government controls over interest rates, exchange rates, capital flows, credit control, taxes and spending. There is now the harsh punishment of global capital, on actual or perceived misbehaviour of the macro policies of countries. The sudden withdrawal of foreign capital from Asia precipitated the financial crisis and collapses. This phenomenon also represented a power shift from elected governments to speculators, bond traders and fund managers. It represented a significant power shift from newly independent developing countries, still insecure about their newly won independent political sovereignty, towards powerful Western financial capital. The visceral reaction of Prime Minister Mahathir towards George Soros epitomized this painful power shift. There are bound to be significant geopolitical implications falling out of the present Asian financial crisis.

The regional financial crisis has taken a heavy toll on the Southeast Asia economies. While assets' market prices, like exchange rates, stock prices and interest rates, have stabilized somewhat, the full effects of the financial collapse on the real sectors of the economy have yet to work their way through. For 1998 through to 2000, there will be declining outputs, falling investments and consumption, corporate retrenchments, banking crises, rising unemployment, increasing inflation, falling standards of living and social and political instability.

The key lessons for Southeast Asia and other emerging markets include:

1 Real exchange-rate over-valuations in the face of large current-account deficits could lead to serious questions of sustainability of the exchange rates and invite speculative attacks. There is a need for Southeast Asian countries to manage their exchange rates with an eye on export competitiveness, particularly against China and Latin America.

2 Pegged exchange rates and free capital movements can lead to excessive foreign currency borrowings especially when foreign interest rates are lower than domestic interest rates. Exchange-rate flexibility and uncertainty can keep borrowers in domestic markets and prevent excessive short-term foreign currency borrowings.

3 Excessive bank lending and the bursting of property-price bubbles have been a feature of many banking crises in both industrial and developing countries. Bank lending booms, arising from excessive domestic lending as well as large, net private-capital inflows are precursors to bubbles built on euphoria and over-optimism. Consequently, governments should be extremely careful about rapid growth in bank liabilities relative to the sizes of the economies or the stocks of international reserves. Significant mismatches between bank assets and liabilities with respect to

liquidity, maturity and currencies of denomination are risky. This is particularly important as advances in information technology, and financial and capital market liberalization have made it much easier for corporations and banks to borrow in foreign currencies. In particular, when domestic interest rates are high, the temptation for corporations and banks to resort to short-term foreign currency borrowings in the interbank market to fund longer-term bank loans is high. This strategy can become unstuck when substantial devaluations occur.

4 Rapid financial liberalization without adequate regulatory and institutional preparations can be risky. Easier access to offshore markets may allow banks to engage in riskier activities, without proper ceilings on banks' foreign-currency exposures.

5 Political interference and loose controls on connected lending played an important role in generating the banking crisis by intruding into all aspects of banking operations and distorting credit-allocation decisions.

6 Weakness in accounting systems, disclosure practices and legal frameworks can hinder the operation of market discipline, and prevent effective banking supervision. Financial markets need timely and reliable information to work efficiently.

7 Sudden withdrawals of foreign capital can be highly destabilizing. Limits on short-term foreign borrowing through an implicit tax like the Chilean system, could prevent the surge of capital inflows resulting from excessive optimism.

8 Proper sequencing is important. Countries should liberalize their domestic financial systems before opening up to foreign capital. Southeast Asian countries, particularly Thailand and Indonesia, failed to do so. Interest rate ceilings, government-directed lendings, etc. distorted the surge of foreign capital, leading to excessive investments in unproductive and speculative sectors.

▓ Future trends

In order for the Asian economy to have a sustained recovery, it is crucial to regain investors' confidence. With the return of foreign and local capital, the exchange rates would be stabilized and gradually appreciate, the stock markets would recover, allowing the central banks to ease domestic interest rates and the property markets would stabilize. These developments would ease the foreign and domestic debt burdens of the banks and corporate sectors and help to repair their tattered balance sheets. To achieve that, there need to be improvements in the current account deficits through export increases and import declines. More significantly, serious financial-sector restructurings and the political wills to implement the tough IMF programme become the litmus test on the authorities' seriousness to regain market confidence. In addition, by mid-1998, an increased easing in the IMF programme to foster growth has become more significant in helping the recovery processes.

As of September 1998, there are emerging signs that the financial markets and economies of Thailand and Korea have stabilized. Export volumes have risen, exchange rates have stabilized or even appreciated, domestic interest rates have declined and trade balances have improved significantly. On the other hand, the Indonesian economy has continued to collapse and Malaysia has embarked on a highly risky policy of implementing capital control in order to facilitate the pump-priming of the collapsing economy through interest rate reduction and an easing of fiscal policy. China and Taiwan, however, have been much less affected by the financial contagion and have continued to sustain growth rates of 5–7 per cent.

Overall, East Asia will eventually continue to be a major market for consumer products and infrastructural development. In particular, China and Taiwan have been much less affected by the financial turmoil, partly due to the existence of capital controls and the lack of short-term foreign borrowings. In addition, the collapses in asset prices have resulted in greater opportunities for Western firms to engage in acquisitions and expansions in the region. More significantly, the strong fundamentals in East Asia that led to the past three decades of high growth, like high savings rates, rising educational and skill levels, strong infrastructural foundations, increasing technological levels as well as integration and openness to the global economy, are likely to be sustained. Once the painful process of bank recapitalization and private-sector debt restructuring are progressively addressed, the gradual process of recovery is likely to gather momentum. Overall, the financial crisis and the collapse of the banking system will set East Asia back about five years. After the deep recession in 1998 and 1999, weak growth could resume in 2000. For Southeast Asia and Korea, growth rates are expected to recover to 2 to 4 per cent by the year 2000, increasing steadily to reach 5–6 per cent by the year 2002. Indonesia, however, could take eight to ten years to recover to a stable growth of around 5 per cent due to the significant social and political problems. On the other hand, China and Taiwan are projected to sustain growth of 6–8 per cent over the next five years (see Table 3.1.3).

Table 3.1.3 Projected GDP growth

	1997	1998	1999	2000	2001	2005
Singapore	7.8	1.0	1.5	3.5	5.0	5.0
Philippines	5.1	1.5	2.5	4.0	5.5	5.5
Korea	5.5	–6.2	1.0	3.0	5.0	6.0
Thailand	–0.3	–7.0	–1.0	2.0	4.0	5.5
Malaysia	7.8	–5.0	–0.5	2.5	4.5	6.0
Indonesia	4.6	–20.0	–3.0	0.5	1.5	2.5
Hong Kong	5.3	–4.5	1.0	3.0	4.5	4.5
China	8.8	6.5	7.0	7.5	8.0	8.0
Taiwan	6.8	5.0	5.5	6.0	6.0	6.0

References

Bank of International Settlements. Annual report, various issues.
Bhagwati, J. (1998). The capital myth, *Foreign Affairs*, May/June, 7–12.
Krugman, P. (1998) What happened to Asia? Mimeo, MIT.
McKinnon R. and Pill, H. (1996). Credible liberalizations and international capital flows: the overborrowing syndrome. In *Financial Deregulation and Integration in East Asia* (T. Ito and A. O. Krueger, eds), Chicago University Press.
J. P Morgan Asian Financial Market, various issues.
Sachs, J. (1997). Personal view. *Financial Times*

Chapter 4

Financial system design in the Asia Pacific context: costs and benefits of universal banking[1]

⬛ Anthony Saunders and Ingo Walter ⬛

⬛ Introduction

There are a number of forces which today make the issue of financial system design extremely timely in economies such as those of the Asia Pacific region.

First, academics have focused increasingly on the issue of which financial architecture is best for the long-term performance of national economies – a universal bank-based financial system or a financial market-based system. A universal-banking system is characterized by a set of dominant banks with equity and debt stakes in other financial and non-financial firms. In this type of system, corporate control is exercised largely through bank monitoring (including presence on supervisory boards) rather than through an active – and often hostile – market for corporate mergers and acquisitions (M&A) transactions, and firms tend to be highly leveraged with bank debt. By contrast, in a market-based financial system ownership and control of enterprises is diffused among many investors, who compete for control rights in an open and contestable market, the stock market. In general, bank-firm links are weaker in such a system, with small (if any) bank equity stakes in non-financial firms and a lesser reliance on bank debt in the capital structure of corporations (Walter, 1994). Papers by Allen and Gale (1995), and Saunders (1994) among others, have reviewed the costs and benefits of these two systems, and these will be considered below.

Second, many emerging market countries such as those in the Asia Pacific region are undergoing periods of financial system deregulation and redesign. So the issue of which system is best, universal bank or financial market based, has been at the core of the debate over the optimum architecture of national financial systems. In most Asia Pacific countries, there also has been considerable debate on the degree to which banks

[1] This chapter has been published previously by MCB University Press Limited: Saunders, A. and Walter I. , (1996). Financial system design in the Asia Pacific context: costs and benefits of universal banking. *Management Decision*, **34** (9), 29–36.

should be allowed to undertake a universal set of financial services activities. For example, in Korea there appear to be few explicit restrictions on banks moving into other lines of financial services such as securities underwriting and leasing. In addition the Big-5 *chaebols* have extensive cross-equity links with a number of financial service firms. A key issue in Korea has been whether it is a good idea to allow banks into life insurance activities – that is, what are the benefits of greater universality with respect to bank-life insurance linkages?

Third, whether regulators like it or not, there is currently a massive wave of consolidation among banks and other financial services firms taking place worldwide. This consolidation is not just bank to bank, but involves almost every conceivable universal financial services combination imaginable. We will describe below the consolidation process, presenting new evidence as to its dimensions and offer some explanations as to why it is occurring.

■ The nature of universal banking

Although the concept of universal banking is very clear – extensive ownership/control links extending from a bank to other financial services and real sector firms – real-world financial systems have developed numerous variants of this concept. On the first level are financial sector universal banks with little or no equity stakes/links with non-financial firms. Examples of this might be Canada and Great Britain, where banks engage in other financial service activities such as securities underwriting and insurance through separate subsidiaries of the bank itself. The USA might also be viewed as part of this set of countries, allowing banks access to other financial sector activities (subject to safety-and-soundness firewalls and other restrictions) through a bank holding company structure.

On the second level are the 'main bank' universal banking systems typified by Japan and Korea. Here there are extensive equity cross-holding links among banks and real-sector firms, usually via a *keiretsu* or *chaebol* structure. In addition, banks are allowed to engage in various other financial service activities such as securities underwriting (although this has been limited in Japan). Most Asia Pacific financial systems fit this model.

On the third level are the 'full' universal banks characterized by the German and Swiss systems, for example. Here there is a far greater integration of financial services within the universal bank – e.g. securities underwriting activities taking place in a department of the universal bank, as well as more extensive control over non-financial firms. This control emanates from a number of sources including: large bank-debt stakes in firms; large bank-equity stakes in firms; control over nominee equity votes; and bank membership on corporate boards of directors (Saunders and Walter, 1994).

Because of the many varieties of universal banking systems we will analyse costs and benefits in the context of relatively extreme forms of the basic models.

■ Universal banking: benefits and costs for whom?

In analysing the benefits and costs of universal banking, we need to recognize that defining the social welfare function one wishes to maximize is extremely difficult. That is, what weights should one give to the preferences of households versus non-financial firms versus banks? Without knowing how governments rank the welfare of different interest groups, it is impossible to design a first-best financial system. All the academic observer can do is to lay out the costs and benefits to each group associated with the different systems, and let the regulator (policy-maker) assign weights to these costs and benefits according to prevailing politically-driven perceptions of the national interest.

Benefits and costs for banks themselves

The first issue involves the perceived benefits and costs of universal banking from the perspective of a more efficient and safer banking system. The benefits include:

- economies of scale
- economies of scope
- increased revenue generation (cross-selling)
- increased revenue diversification
- new sources of bank equity funds.

The costs centre on:

- greater market concentration (potential reduction in competition)
- greater potential for conflicts of interest
- increased threat to the regulatory safety net (deposit insurance, lender of last resort role of the central bank)
- reduced incentives for financial innovation
- reduced degree of financial and real sector openness to the international economy.

Benefits and costs for non-financial firms

The benefits and costs of universal banking from the perspective of firms that have developed close equity and/or debt links with a 'main bank' or a universal bank concentrate on the following benefits:

- enhanced leverage (in the form of tax benefits)
- support in times of restructuring or economic downturns because of long-term lender relationships
- ability to borrow more for long-term project purposes rather than short-term working capital needs
- increases in investment efficiency (bank monitoring and equity stakes limit firms' incentives to 'overinvest').

On the other hand, the costs comprise:

- managers who are subject to weaker corporate control and discipline, thereby exacerbating agency problems
- small firms which are more likely to be credit rationed by large universal banks

• lack of diversity of opinion and information production regarding the future prospects of the firm.

Benefits and costs for consumers

The benefits of universal banking from the perspective of households who are end users of the financial services generated by the financial system include the following:

• one-stop shopping involving savings in transaction and information costs

• greater opportunity for inter-generational risk sharing

• suppression of 'noisy' information.

The costs focus on:

• the potential for market concentration and monopoly pricing

• conflicts of interest

• reduction in opportunities for cross sectional risk sharing as compared to market-based financial systems.

This enumeration suggests that there are a wide array of benefits and costs impacting the three groups of agents (other than government) that are most directly affected by a financial system design based on the universal banking model. As noted earlier, all the academic can do is to point to the relevant benefits and costs and leave it to the regulators and politicians to weight them in evaluating society in preference for one system over another.

■ Illustration: banks and insurance

One aspect of the debate over universal banking is the degree to which banks should be allowed to penetrate the life insurance industry (and insurance companies into banking). For example, this issue is at the centre of the ongoing debate over the deregulation of the US financial system, while in Asia Pacific countries like Korea a number of banks appear poised to acquire life insurance firms. There are, of course, different degrees of bank–insurance connections.

On the first and lowest level, a bank could simply sell insurance products on behalf of a life insurance subsidiary as an agent. In this case the risks are minimal.
Alternatively, a bank could hold an insurance company (or a stake in an insurance company) as a portfolio investment without exercising control.

On the second, higher level, banking and insurance activities may be integrated more closely, with banks underwriting insurance policies and having a more direct (principal) stake in the insurance company's operations. When banks have a direct stake in an insurance company and its activities, the question arises – especially for regulators – whether the bank understands and can manage these risks in an appropriate fashion. In particular, how similar is writing a life insurance policy to writing (making) a loan to a customer? The greater the degree of similarity among product characteristics and the associated risks, the more comfortable a regulator might feel about letting banks engage directly in life insurance activities such as underwriting as principals.

In life insurance, the profitability of a policy that a company writes depends on the size of premiums collected relative to loss rates on that policy plus expenses. In banking, the return on a loan depends on the interest rate on the loan relative to the expected loss rate plus operating expenses. The similarities between underwriting life insurance and making a loan can be taken further by examining the similarity of risks (to the writer) that impact the net return on an insurance policy and the net return (to a bank) on a loan. Specifically:

- Insurance policies are subject to mortality risk, which is similar to credit risk over large population samples (e.g. the application of 'mortality analysis' to loan default rates).

- Life insurance investment returns depend on interest rate and credit quality changes in a similar manner to bank loan returns.

- Both life insurance and loans involve operating expenses, although distribution costs via agents tend to be unique to life insurance.

- Both life insurance and lending face adverse selection risks.

- Life insurance risks can be reduced by reinsuring them with third parties, while loan risk can similarly be reduced by selling loans or loan participations to third parties.

- Both life insurance and lending are exposed to liquidity risk – that is, while banks face the risk of bank deposit runs, life insurers face the risk of non-renewal of policies and a drop in premiums.

In fact the similarities between making a life insurance decision and making a lending decision are arguably greater than between the decision to underwrite corporate securities or to make a loan. Thus, there appears to be a reasonably strong case – based on risk analysis – to allow banks into life insurance activities. Note, however, that a different analysis would be required in the case of property casualty insurance, since these risks are far less predictable and often more severe than those incurred in life insurance. Moreover, property and casualty insurance contracts tend to be much shorter than life insurance contracts.

▪ Patterns of financial services industry restructuring through mergers and acquisitions

As noted in the introduction, there is currently a worldwide wave of financial services consolidation. A significant part of this activity is intended, via mergers or acquisitions, to create universal financial institutions. Here, we first describe a framework within which this M&A activity can be described. Second, we analyse the empirical evidence. Third, we offer some explanations for the continuing merger wave in the financial services industry.

Financial sector M&A activity

Restructuring via M&A activity in the financial services industry can involve at least twelve types of transactions, depicted in the matrix in Table 4.1. The permutations are clear.

Table 4.1 Taxonomy of mergers and acquisitions in financial services

	Domestic bank	Foreign bank	Target institution			
			Domestic securities firm	Foreign securities firm	Domestic insurance company	Foreign insurance company
Domestic bank	Type 1-B	Type 2-B	Type 3-BS	Type 4-BS	Type 3-BI	Type 4-BI
Foreign bank	Type 2-B	X	Type 4-BS	X	Type 4-BS	X
Domestic securities firm	Type 3-SB	Type 4-SB	Type 1-S	Type 2-S	Type 3-SI	Type 4-SI
Foreign securities firm	Type 4-SB	X	Type 2-S	X	Type 4-SI	X
Domestic insurance company	Type 3-IB	Type 4-IB	Type 3-IS	Type 4-IS	Type 1-I	Type 2-I
Foreign insurance company	Type 4-IB	X	Type 4-IS	X	Type 2-II	X

First, domestic banks may acquire other domestic banks (Type 1-B) – such as Chemical Bank's acquisition (technically a merger) of Manufacturers Hanover Trust Company in the USA, or Swiss Bank Corporation's acquisition of Banca Svizzera Italiana – or foreign banks through cross-border M&A deals such as the Hong Kong and Shanghai Banking Corporation's acquisition of Midland Bank of Great Britain (Type 2-B).

The same intrasector domestic or cross-border acquisitions may occur in insurance (Types 1-I and 2-I), such as the French insurance group AXA's acquisition of Metropolitan Life in the USA, or in the securities industry, as occurred domestically in a major way after deregulation in the 1970s in the USA and 1980s in the UK (Type 1-S), and more recently on a cross-border basis in the case of Merrill Lynch's 1995 takeover of Smith New Court in London (Type 2-S).

Finally cross-sector domestic (Type 3) or foreign (Type 4) acquisitions may take place bidirectionally between banks and insurance companies, banks and securities firms, or securities firms and insurance companies. Recent examples include Swiss Bank Corporation's 1995 cquisition of S. G. Warburg and Co., Internationale Nederlanden Groep's 1995 acquisition of Barings plc, and Travelers Group's 1993 divestiture of Dillon Read, the American Express 1993 divestiture of Lehman Brothers, and the General Electric Capital Services 1994 divestiture of Kidder Peabody and Co. Transactions not involving the reference country are denoted by X in Table 4.1. Available data shed some light on these developments on a global basis during the ten-year 1985–94 period.

As Table 4.2 indicates, there were 7280 completed, announced M&A transactions in the financial services industry worldwide valued at over $400 billion. Well over half the total represented banks acquiring other banks, followed by insurance companies acquiring other insurance companies. The volumes presumably reflect the relative size of the two sectors and the number of institutions in existence.

Table 4.2 Financial services M&A deal flow, 1985–94 (millions of US dollars and number of transactions)

| Acquiring institution | Banks | Target institution | | Total |
		Securities	Insurance	
Banks	248 435	12 121	13 722	274 278
	(4 854)	(298)	(110)	(5 262)
Securities firms	7 664	14 714	5 138	27 516
	(128)	(565)	(40)	(733)
Insurance companies	16 125	4 177	95 199	115 501
	(125)	(85)	(1 075)	(1 285)
Total seller	272 224	31 012	114 059	417 295
	(5 107)	(948)	(1 225)	(7 280)

Source: Compiled from Securities Data Corporation online M&A dataset

Presumably for the same reason, transactions among securities broker-dealers are small by comparison. In terms of intersector transactions, the largest transactions volume was between banks and insurance companies. Surprisingly, there were more insurance company purchases of banks (125 deals valued at $16 billion) than banks purchasing insurance companies (110 transactions valued at $14 billion). There were 298 bank purchases of securities firms, mostly in advanced countries, and 128 transactions representing securities firms buying banks, mostly in emerging market countries and often involving control groups acquiring state-owned banks that have been privatized.

Geographically, the majority of intra-banking sector transactions (almost 60 per cent by value) were within the USA. During the 1985–94 period the number of US banks declined from about 12 000 to about 8 000 mainly by acquisition. Transactions in the insurance industry were concentrated in the USA and the EU, including significant acquisitions of US insurance firms by European players. Almost 70 per cent of the value of transactions within the securities industry occurred in the USA and the UK, the only OECD financial systems with significant numbers of independent broker-dealers, and in emerging market countries such as Hong Kong, Singapore, Chile and Brazil. Cross-border intrasector transactions were concentrated in foreign acquisitions of US and UK banks, German and British acquisitions of insurance companies abroad, and foreign purchases of UK merchant banks. Banks acquiring foreign insurance companies occurred mainly in emerging market countries, which was also true of banks acquiring foreign securities firms, especially as part of the debt-for-equity swap transactions that occurred in the 1980s.

There are several other interesting aspects to M&A data in the financial services sector. For example, almost 40 per cent of the intra-banking sector deals shown in Table 4.2 were done on a hostile basis (defined as deals completed after initial rejection by the board of the target bank), predominantly in the USA, while about 19 per cent of the deal-flow involved partial ownership stakes as opposed to 100 per cent control, the latter mainly in emerging market countries. The share of hostile transactions in the insurance sector was only 18 per cent, but over 42 per cent of that deal-flow involved partial ownership positions. In the securities industry, 16 per cent of the deals were hostile and 40 per cent involved partial ownership positions.

The same pattern emerges in intersector deals, with the incidence of hostile transactions much lower in the insurance sector than in the banking and securities sectors, no matter what kind of firm does the acquiring. At the same time, 68 per cent of the deals involved banks acquiring stakes in insurance companies and 53 per cent involved banks acquiring stakes in securities firms with partial control. Partial stakes in the case of securities firms acquiring banks were 70 per cent of the deal-flow.

It appears that in the financial services sector the role of hostile transactions is for the most part quite limited, while the role of partial stakes is relatively high, as compared with global M&A transactions in the non-financial sector. This may be explained partially by the role of regulatory approvals in this sector, the importance of staff who may well leave in the event of a hostile takeover, and the perceived value of strategic alliances cemented by stakeholdings in achieving management objectives without attaining full control. Finally, although comparable data are not available for non-US deals, the price-to-book-value ratio for intrabanking sector transactions in the USA during the 1985–94 period varied widely, from 3.24 to 1.1 times book.

◼ The dynamics of M&A activity in financial services

A useful way to visualize the competitive opportunity set that faces a bank (or an insurance company or securities broker-dealer) combines three principal dimensions in the delivery of financial services in terms of the clients served (C), the geographic arenas where business is done (A) and the products supplied (P) (Walter, 1988). Figure 4.1 depicts these dimensions in the form of a matrix of C-A-P cells. Individual cells represent a more or less distinct 'market' in which a financial services firm either is already active or might become active. The characteristics of each potential market can be analysed in terms of conventional competitive structure criteria.

The competitive structure of each C-A-P cell is an important determinant of the excess returns a financial institution may be able to obtain. Competitive structure is measured conventionally using concentration ratios based on the number of vendors, distribution of market share among vendors, and similar criteria. To the extent that competition takes place on the basis of price, prospective returns are transferred to clients. The inherent attractiveness of each cell clearly depends on the size of the prospective risk-adjusted returns that can be extracted from it. The durability of these returns will depend on the ability of new players to enter the cell, as well as the development of substitute products over time. But beyond this, the economics of supplying financial services is subject jointly to economies of scale and economies of scope.

Economies of scale suggest an emphasis on deepening the activities of individual firms within a cell, or across cells in the product dimension. Economies of scope suggest an emphasis on broadening activities across cells – that is, a player can produce a given level of output in a given cell more cheaply or market it more effectively than institutions that are less active across multiple cells. This depends importantly on the benefits and costs of linking cells together in a coherent web.

The gains from linkages among C-A-P cells depend on the possibility that a firm competing in one cell can move into another cell and perform in that second cell more effectively than a competitor lacking a presence in the first cell. The existence of economies of scope and scale is a critical factor driving financial institutions' M&A strategies. Where scale economies dominate, the drive will be to maximize throughput of the product within a given C-A-P cell configuration, driving for market penetration.

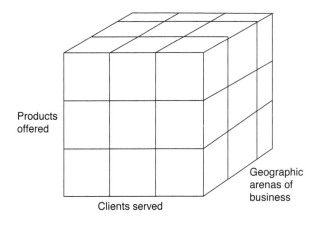

Products
offered

Geographic
arenas of
business

Clients served

Figure 4.1
The competitive
opportunity set

Where scope economies dominate, the drive will be towards aggressive cell proliferation, often through acquisitions.

There is an important risk dimension in the clustering of cells in the C-A-P matrix as well. Transactions volumes and earnings among the clusters of cells in which a financial services firm operates are unlikely to be perfectly correlated, so that a firm's overall earnings stream may be more stable with a broader range of activities. Normally, the addition of vendors to a particular C-A-P cell would be expected to reduce market concentration, increase the degree of competition, lead to an erosion of margins and trigger a more rapid pace of financial innovation. If the new vendors are from the same basic strategic groups as existing players (e.g. one more bank joining a number of others competing in a given cell), then the expected outcome would be along conventional lines of intensified competition. But if the new player comes from a completely different strategic perspective (e.g. banks offering insurance services), the competitive outcome may be quite different. Cell penetration by a player from a different strategic group may lead to a greater increase in competition than an incremental player from the same strategic group. This is because of potential diversification benefits, scope for cross-subsidization and staying power, and incremental horizontal or vertical integration gains that the player from a 'foreign' strategic group may be able to capture.

The higher the barriers to entry, the lower the threat of new entrants' reducing the level of returns available in each C-A-P cell. Natural barriers to entry include the need for capital investment, human resources, technology, and the importance of economies of scale. They also include the role of contracting costs avoided by a close relationship between the vendor and its client, which in turn is related to the avoidance of opportunistic behaviour by either party. These barriers may be overcome most easily in many cases by means of an acquisition.

Not least, the competitive structure of each cell depends on the degree of potential competition. This represents an application of the 'contestable markets' concept, which suggests that the existence of potential entrants causes existing players to act as if those entrants were already active in the market. Consequently pricing margins, product quality and the degree of innovation in a given cell may exhibit characteristics of intense competition even though the degree of market concentration is in fact quite high.

In penetrating a particular cell or set of cells, it may be to the advantage of a particular player to 'buy into' a potential market by cross-subsidizing financial services supplied in that cell from returns derived in other cells or by paying an excessively high price for an acquisition. This may make sense if the assessed horizontal, vertical or lateral linkages – either now or in the future – are sufficiently attractive to justify such pricing. It may also make sense if the cell characteristics are expected to change in future periods, so that an unprofitable presence today is expected to lead to a profitable presence tomorrow. And it may make sense if a player's behaviour in buying market share has the potential to drive out competitors and alter fundamentally the structure of the cell in his or her favour.

The latter can be termed predatory behaviour, and is no different from predation in the markets for goods. The institution 'dumps' (or threatens to dump) financial services into the cell, forcing out competitors either as a result of the direct effects of the dumping in the face of more limited staying power or because of the indirect effects, working through expectations. Once competitors have been driven from the market, the institution takes advantage of the reduced degree of competition to widen margins and achieve excess returns. However, it is important to note that the predatory behaviour is not consistent with the view of market contestability. The greater contestability and the credibility of prospective market entry, the less will be the scope for price discrimination and predation.

Conversely, it may also be possible for an institution with significant market power to keep potential competitors out of attractive cells through explicit or implied threats of predatory behaviour. It can make it clear to new entrants that it will respond very aggressively to incursions, and that they face a long and difficult road to profitability. In this way, new competitors may be discouraged and the cell characteristics kept more monopolistic than would otherwise be the case.

Clearly, regulatory issues have an important bearing in terms of accessibility of geographical cells in the matrix. Besides applying entry and operating restrictions to foreign-based players, regulators may tolerate a certain amount of anti-competitive, cartel-like behaviour on the part of domestic institutions. Economies of scope and scale may be restrained significantly by entry and operating restrictions in a particular market, indicating the importance of the impact of competitive distortions on horizontal integration. Within this context, various motivations have been identified as to why financial services firms engage in M&A transactions (Hawawini and Swary, 1990). These include:

- access information and proprietary technologies (know-how) possessed by the target firm

- increase market power by raising market share to widen cost-price margins, including the ability to carry out large transactions that otherwise would require participation by other firms

- reduce unit costs and increase operating efficiency by eliminating redundant facilities and personnel, as well as improve the quality of management, including hostile takeovers to improve incumbent under-performing management

- achieve diversification and greater earnings stability

- achieve certain tax benefits

- management hubris and self-aggrandizement, driven by management's utility function that may be quite different from the shareholder's utility function

- achieve economies of scale by creating a combined institution of larger size

- achieve economies of scope, or synergies with the target firm.

While all of these motivations are likely to be at work in the M&A deal flow identified in Table 4.2 most important are the presumed exploitation of economies of scale and scope.

An example of growth through M&A activity in the USA is provided in Figure 4.2, which shows the development through time of America's largest banks as of mid-1995. Clearly, these developments represent a search for attractive market positioning

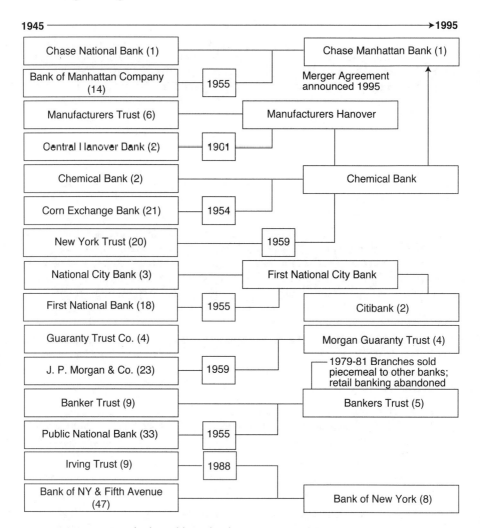

Figure 4.2 Dynamics of selected large bank mergers, 1945–95
Sources: American Bankers; company reports; Hoover's *Handbook of American Corporations*

in terms of Figure 4.1, as well as the elimination of redundant costs and the search for economies of scale and scope. If such economies in fact exist, these banks should be well positioned to exploit them once US regulatory barriers are removed and they are able to penetrate fully the insurance and securities markets from a very large commercial banking platform. Again, this may well occur – as it has in Europe – through cross-functional M&A activity, with some of these banks acquiring fund managers, securities broker-dealers and insurance companies.

▣ Conclusions

There is a clearly consistent pattern that has developed in mergers and acquisitions in the financial services sector over the last decade or so. The underlying motivations involve accessing new markets, offering superior risk-adjusted returns over reasonable periods of time, as well as exploitation of available economies of scale and scope – although there is contradictory evidence as to how prevalent these economies actually are – as well as earnings stabilization through diversification of lines of business. There are less defensible reasons for M&A transactions as well, some of which may eventually place financial firms in conflict with shareholders, antitrust authorities and bank regulators. In each case, countervailing regulatory or corporate governance actions may well develop. As financial markets become still more 'seamless', the M&A data presented here may well be just the beginning. Furthermore, some of the evidence from the past, such as limited hostile transactions and extensive minority stakeholdings, are likely to evolve rather differently in the future and portend exciting times ahead in international banking and in many domestic financial markets.

Finally, the growth and consolidation of banks and financial firms worldwide may have very adverse consequences for one particular group of agents – small firms. As financial services firms grow bigger and decisions become more centralized, they are likely to be less willing to invest time and resources in monitoring and lending to small business firms. That is, consolidation of the industry, while bringing efficiency gains overall, may well imply greater credit rationing of small firms. This issue has raised much interest in the USA, where there is at least some anecdotal evidence that such an effect is already taking place with the fall in the number of banks by approximately one-third over the last decade. Most of the banks which have disappeared have been small with prospects of full interstate banking to come (in 1997) along with prospective deregulation and elimination of the Glass-Steagall Act. In one study, Berger et al. (1995) using a survey of 1.7 million individual loans to domestic businesses by US banks, estimated that there was 39.2 per cent real contraction in loans to borrowers with bank credit of less than $250 000 over the first half of the 1990s. Moreover, the authors found that large banking organizations lend almost exclusively to large borrowers. In 1994, an estimated $90 billion out of $92 billion in commercial and industrial loans by the largest US banks were to borrowers with bank credit of more than $1 million. Meanwhile, small banks lend almost exclusively to small borrowers. Given their very limited access to capital markets and their heavy reliance on bank loans, consolidation in the banking system has potentially severe adverse implications for small firms.

In the Asia Pacific region, governments and financial regulators will have to think carefully about the costs and benefits of universal financial services firms from the perspective of several quite distinct interest groups. M&A activity patterns in this sector suggest aggressive efforts to exploit the benefits of scale and scope that presumably derive from universal structures. Governments in the region need to create a level regulatory playing field in which the structure of the dominant competitors is dictated not by bureaucratic whim but by market forces distinguishing the winners from the losers. Letting financial structures be driven by the forces of competition alone will assure the emergence of performance financial systems in the region that promise to equal the global competitive performance of its manufacturing sector.

■ References

Allen, F. and Gale, D.(1995). A welfare comparison of intermediaries and financial markets in Germany with the US. *European Economic Review*, 179–209.

Berger, A. et al. (1995). *The Transformation of the US Banking Industry: What a Long Strange Trip It's Been*. Brookings Panel Report, September.

Hawawini, G. and Swary, I. (1990). *Mergers and Acquisitions in the US Banking Industry*. North Holland.

Saunders, A. (1994). Banking and commerce: an overview of the public policy issues. *Journal of Banking and Finance*, March, 225–31.

Saunders, A. and Walter, I. (1994). *Universal Banking in the United States*, Oxford University Press.

Walter, I. (1988). *Global Competition in Financial Services*, Ballinger-Harper and Row.

Walter, I. (1994). *The Battle of the Systems*. Institut für Weltwirtschaft.

Chapter 4.1

ABN Amro's counter-intuitive universal-banking strategy

■ Usha C. V. Haley ■

In mid-1998, in a small room at the Shangri-La Mactan Island resort in the central Philippines, about thirty, senior, ABN Amro executives watched Sergio Rial, the Dutch bank's new Asia Pacific head from Brazil, hand a farewell present to the man he was replacing, Ton de Boer. The gift, a framed caricature of de Boer steering a ship through the Asian waters, recalled the region's early Dutch explorers. The bank's green and yellow logo adorned the ship's bow (Granitsas, 1998). The symbolic significance resonated: As captain of Asian operations, de Boer had surveyed and charted a daring course – to turn ABN Amro into one of Asia's three leading banks, alongside Citibank and HSBC, and among the biggest in the world. In 1997, Asia accounted for about 7 per cent (US$1.8 billion) of ABN Amro's worldwide revenues. By contrast, in 1997, Citibank earned more than US$4.3 billion in Asia, roughly 20 per cent of its worldwide revenues. HSBC – the only one of the three that began life in Asia – earned US$7.4 billion in Asia, or 39 per cent of its worldwide revenues.

ABN Amro's changes in Asia form part of the towering transformations taking place in the world's banking industry as indicated by Anthony Saunders and Ingo Walter (Chapter 4). Size matters so ABN Amro aims to create a universal bank by expanding geographically, developing new products, and providing each of the three separate strands of banking – commercial, investment and retail – at branches across the world. The exclusive club of six, global, full-service banks competing as world leaders include Citibank, Chase Manhattan, Bank of America, HSBC, Deutsche Bank and ABN Amro. Of this club, Citibank and Bank of America have announced separate merger plans with other entities (Sapsford, 1998; Weiner, 1998). In Asia, while domestic banks fight for survival, ABN Amro constitutes one of the few foreign banks making acquisitions. 'Our overall aspiration is that we should be one of the top three universal banks in Asia,' said Mathew Welch, the bank's Senior Vice-president for Strategy and Acquisitions (Granitsas, 1998). By the end of its current five-year plan, in 2002, ABN Amro plans to generate at least 10 per cent – and more likely 15 per cent – of the bank's worldwide revenues from Asia, roughly double its current ratio.

ABN Amro's Asian strategy mirrors its worldwide strategy. For example, since 1996,

ABN Amro has acquired four banks in the USA, and now constitutes the largest foreign bank. For its Asian growth, ABN Amro has identified five key markets in Asia – although it will not publicly identify them. 'Organic growth will not take us to the level we have set for ourselves,' said Rial, the new Asia Pacific head. 'The key thing is we are ready to acquire' (Granitsas, 1998). In banking, as in other businesses, the crisis constitutes a good time to buy cheaply in Asia (Weiner, 1998). Indeed, ABN Amro has been acquiring since the Asian financial crisis hit full throttle in December 1997. In December, it bought the Australia and New Zealand operations of Barclays de Zoete Wedd, Barclays Bank's investment banking division. Subsequently, in May 1998, it made a deal to acquire 75 per cent of Bank of Asia, Thailand's eleventh largest bank, which has a network of 110 branches; the acquisition instantly transformed ABN Amro into the country's largest foreign bank.

Despite its global consistency, ABN Amro's Asian strategy seems counterintuitive. First, it is expanding regionally as many rivals are treading more cautiously (Goad, 1998; Sapsford, 1998). Deutsche Bank, for example, badly stung by the regional crisis, is calling in Asian loans. Similarly, HSBC has slowed down its Asian retail-banking network's planned expansion. However, ABN Amro has doubled its Asian employees since 1996 to more than 4100, and has budgeted for another 10 per cent increase for 1998; this increase excludes employees at the bank's separately managed Hong Kong-headquartered investment bank (formerly HG Asia) or at any of the bank's new acquisitions. Second, ABN Amro's new strategy represents a huge shift in mind-set. For years, the bank had some impressive regional fragments such as a strong Indonesian retail-banking business and a sizeable Singaporean treasury operation; but, it never managed the businesses as a consolidated whole. For example, until 1996, Hong Kong and Singapore both hosted ABN Amro's regional headquarters. Along with its new focus, ABN Amro now has a new, unified, regional headquarters building in Singapore.

ABN Amro's greatest assets include its roughly 5000 blue-chip borrowers in Asia – a mix of European multinational corporations, such as Philips and Ericsson, and big local groups. Slowly, the bank is expanding its bank-client relationships through cross-selling or offering additional services such as cash management for commercial clients and mutual funds for retail clients. Citibank, and others in retail banking, have engaged in cross-selling for years. 'Citibank is light years ahead of them,' said a senior official at a European bank that's also expanding in Asia. 'And Citibank is big enough to offer everything.' ABN Amro also lags in cash-management services such as handling corporate clients' cash and currency transaction needs. In the past few years, Citibank, HSBC, Deutsche Bank, Chase Manhattan and Standard Chartered have carved out hefty shares of the cash-management market, one of the fastest-growing areas in commercial banking.

In investment banking, ABN Amro has very successfully actualized its abilities, both in Asia and worldwide. Investment banking – the business of raising debt and equity financing for companies – has accounted for roughly 40 per cent on average of the bank's Asian annual revenue. ABN Amro Rothschild, the bank's equity capital markets venture with Rothschild, has proven a notable performer. Since 1996, the venture has led several high-profile issues, including the Australian telecoms company's, Telstra's, huge initial public offer. ABN Amro Rothschild now ranks as one of the Asia Pacific's top three equity houses. By contrast, Deutsche Bank, which acquired London-based investment bank Morgan Grenfell nearly 10 years ago, has struggled with the acquisition.

In retail banking, the gap between ABN Amro's hopes and the reality appears widest. The bank has modestly successful retail businesses in several countries – Hong Kong, Indonesia, India, Pakistan and Taiwan – but has never considered itself a retail bank. For example, at the end of 1997, ABN Amro had just seven branches in Hong Kong, compared with 220 for the local powerhouse HSBC. However, strong retail profiles form crucial considerations for universal banks in Hong Kong. Global retail banking is also experiencing an enormous transformation that calls for a new creed, cutting-edge technology and money. In many ways, retail banking appears more like selling consumer products, such as soap and dishwashers, than like making loans and deposits. The credit card business has proven enormously successful for Citibank and HSBC is developing it enthusiastically. Yet, hampered by daunting up-front costs for marketing, distribution, back office technology and staff, ABN Amro has pursued the credit card business aggressively only in Taiwan. Start-up costs vary from market to market, but they approximate US$50 million, with a breakeven date of two or three years. For banks that earn profits within weeks of making a loan, the credit card business' break-even points can conjure scary scenarios.

In the Asia Pacific, ABN Amro has the ingredients to seriously challenge Citibank and HSBC: ample size and money, and a presence in the region since 1826. But, its two competitors pose formidable threats. As one ABN Amro senior executive admitted, 'I think Citibank and HSBC are here to stay'; he saw the Dutch bank as the third member of a triumvirate. Citibank's Asian brand business, technology base and productivity appear unmatched making it the bank to beat. In Singapore, for example, Citibank has cornered 25 per cent of the credit card business, even though it can legally operate from only three local branches. Citibank has about 10 000 private banking clients, more than four times as many as ABN Amro does. In global foreign-currency transactions, too, Citibank towers above all other banks; the Citicorp–Travelers merger will make it even larger.

ABN Amro is counting on its European connections and the Euro, the new European currency introduced in January 1999, to tow it successfully in global finance's choppy waters. '[The Euro] is an initiative that is taking place in our own backyard. We should be able to take advantage of that. If we haven't, then we're doing something wrong,' said John Bubrik, ABN Amro's coordinator on the Euro in Asia (Granitsas, 1998). ABN Amro is issuing bank statements quoted in Euros and has launched several Euro-denominated mutual funds in Asia. Back in Amsterdam, 1000 computer experts have worked for months to ensure Euro-compliancy for the bank's internal software and for free programs for clients.

A three-way competition in Asia between ABN Amro, Citibank and HSBC has a satisfying symmetry: one European, one American and one Asian-origin bank. Each has its own distinct corporate culture: ABN Amro has a reputation for consensus management, Citibank for fierce internal politics, and HSBC for top-down management. All three have the same ambition – to be the best and biggest in Asia, and to remain that way. ABN Amro aims to give Citibank and HSBC tough competition and admits that the charted course appears daunting. However, as the new regional head, Rial, confidently asserted, 'Over the next five years the landscape will have been reordered, and we will be up there' (Granitsas, 1998).

■ References

Goad, G. P. (1998). Calls to reform global system resonate beyond Asian region. *Wall Street Journal*, 5 October.

Granitsas, A. (1998). On the move. *Far Eastern Economic Review*, 18 June.

Sapsford, J. (1998). Citibank credit line for Sumitomo reflects new role for foreign banks. *Wall Street Journal*, 2 October.

Weiner, E. (1998). Opportunity knocks world-wide for merger and acquisitions deals. *Wall Street Journal*, 5 October.

Chapter 5

Innovation in Southeast Asia: lessons for Europe?[1]

■ Mike Hobday ■

■ Introduction: the role of transnational corporations in industrial development

Previous research on innovation in South Korea, Taiwan and Hong Kong, shows how locally owned (or 'latecomer') firms such as Samsung of South Korea and ACER of Taiwan narrowed the technological gap with the West and Japan and learned to innovate (Hobday, 1995). However, in the Southeast Asian economies (including Malaysia, Singapore and Thailand) industrial export growth has been led by transnational corporations (TNCs), rather than local firms. The role of TNCs in growth and innovation raises questions of vital importance, not only for Southeast Asia but also for the UK and the EU which depend on inward investment from TNCs. Britain, which attracted £7 billion of foreign investment in 1994 (more than any other European country), is especially dependent on TNCs for its industrial and export growth, not only in semiconductors and automobiles, but also in finished electronic equipment such as colour televisions and personal computers (*Independent*, 1995).

The aim of this chapter is to examine one example of TNC-led growth in Southeast Asia (the case of the Malaysian electronics industry), focusing on innovation and technological progress. On the basis of the evidence, the chapter then raises key issues for the EU and, in particular, the UK.

The chapter illustrates the importance of electronics to Malaysian economic growth and then analyses innovation within the TNC subsidiaries, using case evidence based

[1] This chapter was a paper written as part of the UK Economic and Social Research Council (ESRC) Pacific Asia search Programme (project reference: L32453023 – Technological Dynamism in Pacific Asia: Implications for Europe). The author would like to thank Martin Bell, Norlela Ariffin and Sanjaya Lall for helpful comments and advice. The author is also grateful to Viswanathan Selvaratnam and William Rees for their help and guidance during the field research. The normal disclaimers apply. This chapter has been published previously by MCB University Press Limited: Hobday, M. (1996). Innovation in South-East Asia: lessons for Europe? *Management Decision*, **34** (9), 71–81.

on an innovation audit of a number of electronics producers. The aim is to explore the meaning of 'innovation' in the TNC subsidiary context and to examine TNC strategies towards technology and innovation. Motivations for local plant upgrading are looked at and the importance of innovation to export growth is assessed. Following this, a single case example is used to highlight the historical path of innovation of a large Japanese silicon wafer producer, called Shin-Etsu Handotai. The chapter then raises key questions for Europe and the UK by developing a simple model to show how innovation in Malaysia fits within global technology strategies of the TNCs, comparing Malaysia with other locations such as Scotland and China.

◼ Do TNC subsidiaries innovate in Southeast Asia?

In general our knowledge of the nature and extent of innovation in Southeast Asia is very poor. The astonishing pre-crisis growth performance of countries such as Malaysia, Singapore and Thailand is well known. Malaysian GDP, for example, grew at an average of 6.7 per cent per annum during the period 1971 to 1990 and just under 9 per cent per annum in 1994 and 1995 (Malaysia survey, *Financial Times*, 1995). However, despite these rates of growth we have yet to gain satisfactory answers to the following basic questions:

- Has industrial growth been accompanied by innovation and technological change within the TNCs?

- If so, what kind of innovation has occurred?

- How important has innovation been to industrial success?

- What would motivate (or prevent) foreign TNCs to transfer skills and technology?

- Did the subsidiaries (or the Government) encourage headquarters to transfer technology and, if so, how?

- Is TNC-based growth likely to continue in the future?

The conclusion returns to the above questions to provide answers based on the specific case of Malaysia. This is important because the general lack of knowledge in this area acts as a barrier to understanding growth in Southeast Asia and prevents other regions such as the UK and the EU from learning the lessons (if there are any) from the economies of Southeast Asia.

If we turn to existing literatures, they provide little guidance on innovation in TNC subsidiaries. According to traditional innovation study (Utterback and Abernathy, 1995), TNC product life cycle theory (Vernon, 1996, 1975), TNC location theory (Dunning, 1975), and theories of industrial clustering (Porter, 1990), innovation is not 'supposed' to occur in the developing countries. After all, the advanced countries of the USA, Japan and Europe are the source of most research and development (R&D) and they alone enjoy the 'technology pull' of highly advanced markets (Lundvall, 1988; Schmookler, 1966).

Mainstream explanations of East Asian growth tend to ignore innovation and technological change (Riedel, 1988; World Bank, 1993). Single country studies tend to focus on government policies as explanations for development (Amsden, 1989; Wade, 1990). The most revealing studies illustrate the general processes of technological change, but these tend to focus on the industry level rather than the firm or the TNC subsidiary level (Dahlman et al., 1985; Lall, 1982, 1992; Westphal et al., 1985). Overall, with few exceptions (Capannelli, 1994; Rasiah, 1994) the existing literature has not much to say about innovation in Malaysia or more generally in Southeast Asia. More often than not, when the issue is raised, the TNC subsidiaries are criticized as 'screwdriver' plants or 'merely assemblers' of goods for export. However, research on TNCs in developed countries shows the critical importance of innovation on the part of subsidiaries for enhancing competitiveness (Bartlett and Ghoshal, 1987a, 1987b).

The importance of electronics to Malaysia's growth

Malaysia, with a population of around 19.5 million people, was one of the fastest growing economies in the world. Its GDP has exceeded 8 per cent in each of the past seven years before 1996 and doubled since 1987. In 1994 and 1995 growth was 9 per cent as discussed above (Malaysia survey, *Financial Times*, 1995).

As with Singapore and Thailand, Malaysia's economic growth over the past two decades or so has been led by manufactured exports. Within the manufacturing sector, electronics has played a large part in Malaysia's growth. It is the most dynamic industrial sector in the country, accounting for around 45 per cent of total exports and 61 per cent of manufactured exports and, as noted earlier, almost all electronics exports are conducted through TNCs. As an example, Malaysia is the world's largest exporter of semiconductors, which account for 21 per cent of total manufactured exports. This compares with other major exports such as textiles and clothing at 6.2 per cent and rubber products at 2.7 per cent (MITI, 1994).

The electronics industry (which includes domestic electrical appliances) in Malaysia began in the 1960s and took off during the 1970s. During the 1980s, mirroring the growth in other East Asian economies, there was a sixfold increase in the volume of electronic exports. By 1994 electronics exports exceeded US$22 billion. The industry became the single largest export industry in 1986, at which time semiconductor testing and assembly dominated, accounting for 82 per cent of electronics exports.

Since the late 1980s further rapid growth was accompanied by a healthy diversification and upgrading of the industry. By 1993 semiconductors had declined to 46 per cent of electronics exports while consumer goods had risen to 26 per cent and industrial electronics to 28 per cent. One major boost to the industry was the shift of Japanese colour TV manufacturing to Malaysia. New US investments took place in disk drives and computing, while Taiwanese producers entered to supply calculators, telephone handsets and so on.

Strategic groupings of companies in Malaysian electronics

Unlike Singapore and other major electronics exporters, very little systematic data in Malaysia appear to be collected on the industry. Therefore in order to construct a sample for study it was necessary to gain a picture of the industrial structure of the industry and the types of companies involved. Figure 5.1 describes the main strategic groupings of firms, based on preliminary interviews with industrialists and policy-makers and existing academic studies of the industry (Kam, 1992; Ngoh, 1994; O'Connor, 1993).

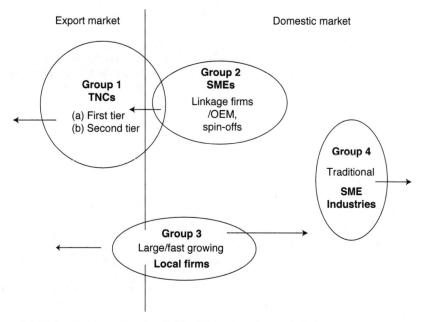

Figure 5.1 Major strategic groupings in the Malaysian electronic industry

The four major groups of electronics firms overlap to some extent, but by far the largest segment in terms of output is Group 1 TNC exporting firms (including Motorola and Sony). This group can be subdivided into: direct exporters of semiconductors, disk drives, other components and a variety of goods and systems; and second-tier TNC suppliers of subsystems, components and OEM (original equipment manufacture) services to the first-tier companies.

Closely tied to the TNCs is Group 2, SME linkage firms. This group includes new start-ups which have spun-off from the TNCs forming their own operations (e.g. Globetronix), often supplying (in the first instance) their former employees.

Group 3 includes the relatively new, fast-growing large local firms (e.g. Sapura, Likom, HIL and UNISEM). These firms supply both the domestic and export markets. They are nationally owned companies which are high technology in practice and aspiration. Each has forged technological partnerships with major companies abroad.

Group 4 represents the large number of traditional low technology SMEs in Malaysia. Largely oriented towards the domestic market, Group 4 firms focus on low quality, low value-added goods and activities. Management practices are poor, technology lags behind the other groups and investments in training are low. The majority of Group 4 firms supply low technology indirect materials and services, such as packaging supplies, freight services, brackets, TV cabinets, power cords and cables.

A sample was constructed from three of the four strategic groups for in-depth interviews and factory visits. Table 5.1 shows the list of twenty firms, which included: twelve TNCs (Group 1); five linkage firms (Group 2); and three large local companies (Group 3). An analysis of Group 4 companies is provided by Kam (Kam, 1992).

Around forty-two interviews were carried out with managing and R&D directors, engineers and factory managers, using open-ended questionnaires. A further twenty or so interviews took place with government and research institutions to verify findings and to gather further data and reports on the industry. Information was collected on company histories, spending on technology, technical employment, specific examples of innovation, training schemes, patterns of technological change, motivations for innovation, key business and technological milestones, and technological strengths, weakness, problems and plans.

The sample covered most electronics subsectors, most product groups, large firms, small firms and US, Japanese, European, Taiwanese and Malaysian owned companies. The total sample amounted to around US$7.3 billion production (approximately 30 per cent of total electronics exports in 1995). Two research visits to Malaysia were carried out in late 1994 and early 1995, involving about five weeks in the field. A further visit was arranged to present the findings to a Malaysian policy and industrial audience as part of the World Bank's review of Malaysia's 2020 programme (Bell et al., 1995). This helped further verify the findings, obtain feedback from key individuals and allowed for a few more interviews.

◾ TNC innovation survey: key findings

Table 5.2 presents some of the findings of the research and illustrates a small sample of recent innovations from each firm interviewed. The main findings from the survey area are as follows.

R&D departments were very small by the international standards of leading firms. Most technological activities were carried out by technicians and engineers, rather than researchers or scientists. Most firms had larger budgets for training and skills than they did for R&D. In no cases were long-term or basic research (e.g. into new materials, novel designs or artificial intelligence) undertaken (i.e. the 'R' of R&D), although some TNCs carried out significant product design work, focusing on incremental design changes and new models of existing product lines.

The TNCs could not be described as merely assemblers (or screwdriver plants). A great deal of innovative activity was carried out, centred on improvements to products and processes and the introduction and development of organizational methods (e.g. total quality management and statistical process control). Substantial design-for-manufacture (sometimes called product-process interfacing) was conducted in order to ensure the efficient mass production of electronic goods. This involved learning about core product design, software engineering, automation technologies, manufacturing materials planning and so on. Another point worth noting is that production-led innovations occurred not only in TNCs but in all groups of firms interviewed.

Extensive improvements and modifications to capital equipment were carried out by almost all firms, in a few cases leading to patents and own-brand sales abroad. In the increasingly complex area of semiconductor assembly and testing, Malaysia is now a world technology centre, with a cluster of leading firms in Penang (e.g. Intel). Substantial technical support was carried out for production and other near-term technological needs in most firms (e.g. at Sony there were 1300 technically trained people amounting to 16.2 per cent of the workforce).

Table 5.1 Sample profile: electronics, components, electrical and supporting industries

Firm	Product area (principal)	Principal activities	Ownership	Start-up Malaysia	Employment turnover (1994) (US$ millions)
Strategic group 1:					
TNCs, first- and second tier					
Intel, Penang	Semiconductors	Assembly, test	USA	1972	2600/na
Motorola, Penang	Mobile communications	Manufacture, design	USA	1974	2600[a]/na
Matsushita	Air conditioners	Manufacture	Japanese	1972	24 700[b]/2500[c]
SEH (Shin-Etsu)	Semiconductors	Wafer manufacture and preparation	Japanese	1973	1350/196
Sony Electronics	CD player, radio, cassette, hi-fi	Manufacture and design	Japanese	1987	8000/1059
Sony Mechatronics	Floppy disk drives (3.5 in.)	Manufacture	Japanese	1989	2900/830
Centronix	Audio and telecommunications	Assembly OEM/ODM[d]	Taiwanese	1988	700/29.5
Inventec	Telephones, calculators, pocket organizers	Manufacture design	Taiwanese	1987	3000/240
Grundig	Audio, hi-fi, cassette recorders	Manufacture and design	German	1988	900/90
MEMC	Semiconductors	Wafer manufacture and preparation	German	1972	640/86.8[e]
Siemens	Optoelectronic components	Manufacture and design	German	1972	1560/128
Philips/JVC	VCR, TV, audio electrical appliance	Manufacture and design	Dutch/ Japanese joint venture	1988	3190/400
Strategic group 2:					
SME linkage firms/spin offs					
LS Technology	Semiconductors	Electro-plating	Local	1990	200/3.0
Globetronix	Semiconductors	Assembly, test burn-in	Local	1991	800/na
Oris (Orisystems)	Semiconductors	Wire bonding	Local	1994	15/0.23
Sanda Plastics	Plastic housings and components	Injection moulding	Local	1974	360/0.98
LSBS (Leong Bee	Semiconductors	Cutting/grinding tools for wafer	Local	1921	150/7.8

Large/fast-growing independent local firms

Likom	Electronics (micro-computers, disk-drives)	OEM/ODM	Local	1992	3300/500
Sapura	Telecommunications handsets/ payphones	Manufacture, design	Local	1975	4500/392[f]
UNISEM	Semiconductors	Assembly and testing	Local	1991	1100/na

Notes: [a] Total Motorola employment in Malaysia amounted to 13 000 in five separate factories in 1994. Total investment in Malaysia exceeds RM1 billion (roughly US$400 million).

[b] Based on current exchange rate of US$1.0 = RM$2.55.

[c] Includes all five Malaysian plants.

[d] Original equipment manufacturer/own design and manufacture (i.e. the company produces for brand-name purchasers according to general design specifications).

[e] Estimated from data on MEMC corporate turnover per employee.

[f] Includes total group turnover (1994) of Uniphone, Sapura Telecom and other companies.

Table 5.2 Engineering, technical support, R&D and recent innovations

Company	Total employment	Engineers/ technicians	Percentage of employment	R&D[a] dept/staff	Recent innovation examples
Intel Penang	2600	n/a	–	40	Reliability analysis breakthrough; development of new jigs, fixtures, machinery; new SPC[b] techniques
Motorola Penang	2600	300[c]	11.5	130	Cordless phone design (CT2); changes to advanced manufacturing simple ASIC designs; new product design for manufacture
Matsushita	24 700	n/a	–	40	Numerous split air-conditioner design changes (e.g. voltage, style); die and mould development; design for manufacture
SEH (Shin-Etsu)	1350	50/100	9.0	10	Capital goods (e.g. new automated etching and slicing machines (patented); total quality management modification
Sony Electronics	8000	500/800	16.2	30[d]	Design specifications for Sony Discman (portable CD) development of capital goods; prototypes for new hi-fi systems
Sony Mechantronics	2900	80/150	7.9	n/a	Continuous improvements to processes; minor changes to locally purchased inputs
Centronix	700	30/58	12.6	10	Telephone handset designs; new tooling specifications; design for manufacture
Inventec	3000	130/134	8.8	10	Calculator model designs (including LSI chip); manufacturing specifications for telephone handset
Grundig	900	54/35	9.9	38	Product designs for hi-fi, cassette recorders design for manufacture
MEMC	640	60/60	18.8	–[e]	Re-engineering of production lines into cellular form, including integration of R&D into production; improvements to wafer saw and other equipment
Siemens	1560	50/110	10.3	8	World centre for Siemens opto production and design; applied new approach to TQM[f]; development of new bonding machines with foreign suppliers
Philips/JVC	3190	32/40[g]	2.3	11	Design for manufacture; continuous improvements to production processes
LS Technology	200	2/6	4.0	–	Unique mini-rack plating machine (exported); chemical process improvements; changes to capital goods
Oris (Orisystems)	15	4[c]	27.0	–	Developed new low-cost gold wire bonding machine; substantial refurbishment and re-engineering of depreciated

to under own-brand name; refurbishment of depreciated equipment

					Recent innovations
Sanda Plastics	360	2/20	6.1	–	Continuous line process improvements; just in time production; re-engineering of material flow system
LBSB	150	6/5	7.3	–	Design and development of saws and grinders for wafers; redesign of production processes for simplification
Likom	3300	270/700	29.4	45[h]	Own-design PC for local schools (Atom projects); design and specification of computer parts for buyers (ODM); improvements to production processes
Sapura	4,500	1500[c]	33.0	40[i]	New software platform licensed out to foreign TNCs; early development of precision engineered goods; many new telecommunication products
UNISEM	1100	20/80	9.1	–	Designed assembly plant (layout equipment etc.) from scratch in six months (a world record); substantial equipment re-engineering; advanced SPC application

Notes: Here 'recent innovations' is not exhaustive (illustrative examples only); innovations are defined as commercially exploited ideas, new to the firm and or to the country (not necessarily to the market or to the world); technological and organizational innovations are included.

a R&D refers to technical staff; note that R&D, engineers and technicians are not strictly comparable across firms, as company definitions differed.

b SPC = statistical process control.

c Total engineers and technicians combined (separate details not available).

d Planned to expand to 70 by 1997.

e R&D activities integrated into production under new cellular approach to production.

f TQM = total quality management.

g This firm applied a very strict definition of 'engineer' (a bachelors degree holder) and also to 'technician' (diploma holder); therefore technical support staff are probably understated, relative to other firms in sample.

h Plus a further 90 R&D staff in overseas acquisitions.

i Data for Sapura Research Sdn. Bhd (SRSB), a wholly owned subsidiary of Sapura (reported in *Malaysian Business*, 1–15 July 1993, pp. 14–15).

Sources: (unless otherwise stated), company interviews, annual reports and miscellaneous published material

In some leading cases significant design work was beginning to be carried out. For example, Motorola Penang had been designated a corporate design centre for cordless telephones for Motorola worldwide. Sony Electronics was designated a corporate centre for the Sony Discman and had developed new model designs and prototypes for hi-fi systems. As discussed below, SEH from Japan had developed and patented several capital goods.

Innovation in Malaysia involved not only technological activities but also managerial and organizational improvements (sometimes called 'soft' innovations). Soft innovations had resulted in impressive records of continuous improvement and productivity gains at Siemens, MEMC and SEH. MEMC (the German wafer manufacturer) had developed its own version of a modular manufacturing system involving worker empowerment, leading to substantial productivity gains. Siemens Penang also had applied and modified a total quality management system to suit its own needs. This plant received regular visits from German headquarters, from managers keen to learn about the techniques used. Siemens Penang was also a designated design centre for optoelectronics.

Why should the TNCs transfer technology? In analysing the motives for technological upgrading most TNCs pointed out that parent companies were commercially motivated to transfer technology and that plant expansions and export growth depended on the upgrading of local plants. Specific TNC motives for capability building included the need to: reduce plant start-up times; control and reduce operating costs of plant, once set up; shorten production lead-times; minimize equipment down-times; bring about continuous improvements; and raise productivity.

Overall, the efforts to innovate had improved the efficiency of the TNC subsidiaries through time, enabling the rapid export expansion witnessed in Malaysia. Equally, success in capability building allowed Malaysian managers to argue for more TNC investment, adding a strategic motive for the subsidiary to demonstrate innovative capacity.

During the 1980s one of the most important triggers for technology transfer was the influx of automation and semi-automation equipment into manufacturing plants in Malaysia. Automation demanded substantial new skills and technical services. Machinery had to be set up, adapted, improved and maintained for competitiveness. In the interviews, numerous specific examples of incremental innovations to equipment were identified, including improvements to semiconductor (chip) handlers, chip tapers, markers, burn-in ovens, solder plating processes, die bonding materials, simple jigs, automated assemblers, specialized tooling, stamping dies for lead frames, and cutting tools for trimming lead frames.

The TNC subsidiaries had also transferred skills and subcontracted out work to local firms. Some engineers left the TNCs to set up their own companies (often to supply the subsidiary with components or some kind of technical service). Other local suppliers to the TNCs had emerged from the base of existing SMEs.

Although significant innovation advances had been made it is important to recognize that problems and weaknesses were evident in the electronics industry and that progress was not without its difficulties. One major problem was that the number of backward linkages, Group 2 (new suppliers to the TNCs), was viewed as too low for the needs of the TNCs. This is an important problem as a key feature of successful industrial growth (e.g. in Taiwan and Hong Kong) is the amount of local firm interactions with TNCs. The latter can lead to growth and job creation and technological change. Healthy backward linkages can also help integrate foreign TNCs into a local economy and reduce the risk of them pulling out.

Overall, despite some subcontracting, linkage forming was weak, involving too few local firms. Most major suppliers were other TNCs (e.g. from Taiwan). The majority of locally owned firms were low value-added (Group 4) producers. Partly as a result of weak backward linkages and their exclusive export orientation, the TNCs were largely insulated from the local economy. This is a serious cause for concern for the continued rapid growth of the industry and the further upgrading of technology.

Several other significant problems were also identified, which can only be mentioned here. The first was widespread skill shortages of skilled operators, technicians and engineers. At the skilled operator level, staff turnover rates were frequently in the order of 25 per cent. A second problem, related to the first, was rising wages. In order to recruit skilled workers some firms had entered a spiral of continuously increasing wages, leading to higher operating cost structures for all firms. This was due partly to general rapid growth (or overheating) of the industry. The problem was particularly worrying given the lower cost competition emerging from China, Vietnam and other parts of the region. A third problem was the weakness of vocational and technical education at both the school and university level. Most firms were concerned that they might find it difficult to move to higher technology operations if this problem was not resolved in the short to medium term.

To sum up, despite the difficulties, the evidence illustrates the general nature and direction of innovation in the TNC subsidiaries in Malaysia. Innovation was incremental rather than radical in character. Indeed, almost all the examples derived from the needs of production and competition, not from blue sky research or laboratory ideas. At the heart of Malaysian innovation was improvement to manufacturing processes and this had led to substantial engineering and technical investments among the subsidiaries. From basic manufacturing, many firms had progressed to product-process innovations, incremental product designs, prototyping and in a few cases some longer-term development work.

▩ The case of Shin-Etsu Handotai

Shin-Etsu Handotai (SEH) is a Japanese firm with more than two decades of experience in Malaysia. According to received wisdom, Japanese firms are more reluctant to transfer technology than US and European firms (Guyton, 1994). By contrast, the case of SEH is one of vigorous technology transfer and local development. The case also emphasizes: the long-term gradual nature of technological development; the surprising extent of local capability in some cases; and the complexity of (apparently) simple, production technologies.

Although no single case can truly be representative, another feature of SEH common among early entrants was the painstakingly difficult process of technological learning. Rather than a 'leapfrog', learning to innovate involved a 'hard slog' of effort and investment.

SEH is the subsidiary of a major Japanese silicon wafer manufacturer. Wafers are one of the key raw materials used by chip manufacturers worldwide to produce integrated circuits, such as dynamic random access memories (DRAMs). SEH started up in Malaysia in 1973. By 1994, local sales had reached US$185 million (all for export) and the subsidiary employed 1350 staff. Worldwide the SEH group had thirty-one subsidiaries and affiliates. Its main activities were in chemicals and related products, plastics and silicon materials (the group boasted a 30 to 40 per cent world market share in wafer supply). In 1995, the Malaysian plant was the largest producer of wafers worldwide, claiming between 8 per cent and 9 per cent of world consumption of wafers. In addition, a new advanced plant was under construction.

An apparently simple production task, wafer manufacture involves a series of complex activities, involving very high quality silicon and a knowledge of several chemical processes. Wafer preparation is made up of a series of process steps including cutting (or 'slicing'), flattening (called 'lapping'), chemically etching, cleaning and polishing. The technology involves precision engineering and a skill-intensive work force. Of the 1000 staff in the main plant, around 100 were technicians and thirty were development engineers. A further thirty or so engineers worked in an R&D department to co-ordinate the process technology and prepare for future needs.

Basic research into crystals and new materials was carried out in the parent factory in Japan and in the main US plant. However, quite a number of Malaysian engineers were involved in working with clients on new requirements. For example, the latest 64M bit DRAM wafers demanded not only a deep knowledge of the process steps and capital equipment, but also an understanding of the special parameters set by individual customers. In 1995 most of the engineers and technical staff were Malaysian. However, there were thirteen Japanese working in the plant, carrying out various activities.

The case of SEH illustrates a progressive history of local innovation, not uncommon among the early investors in Malaysia (Intel, Motorola and Siemens had similar stories to tell). The SEH subsidiary had made several significant innovations over the years, involving a number of US patents and exports of new capital equipment from Malaysia. In 1978–79 after five years of operating, minor improvements were made to the slicing process and, in 1981, the lapping machines were retooled by local engineers. These were later transferred to SEH plants in the USA and Japan as they added to productivity.

During the 1980s several other capital goods improvements were made, including an automated etching machine and a new type of jig (both of which were patented). According to the company, soft as well as hard innovations were important to growth and productivity. For example, the plant had introduced its own version of statistical process control (SPC) linked to employee incentives.

An R&D department was set up in 1981 (with just three people) to co-ordinate process improvements and, later on, to carry out development work. In retrospect, this was one of the first TNC R&D units in Malaysia. By 1994 thirty or so engineers worked in the R&D laboratory including one physics PhD and three masters degree holders. The innovative efforts of the company culminated in 1994–95 with a world first 'wax free' polishing system for wafers, which was being patented at the time of the research. This was considered to be a major breakthrough in the process technology.

Innovation in SEH was a difficult and demanding task, involving learning, education, the hiring and training of specialist engineers, educational links, new training schemes, visits to Japan by Malaysian workers and vice versa. Over the years, substantial engineering competencies had been built up through formalized training programmes. Operator training was conducted mainly on the job, while engineers and R&D staff received formal training, often requiring a year or so in Japan. Training programmes had also been designed for engineers to learn soft technologies (e.g. SPC and TQM).

At the time of the study, the company was training new engineers in computer sciences, factory automation, software engineering and production management. However, as with other TNCs in the sample, SEH found it very hard to recruit and to keep staff due to wage rises and 'job hopping'.

Two final points are worth stressing regarding innovation in SEH which are also confirmed by evidence from most other large companies in the study. First, innovation was (and had to be) accompanied by competence building in other related areas, including finance, management and human resources. Innovation and technological advance cannot occur in isolation from other competencies and responsibilities. For instance, for product design to be effective, a subsidiary probably needs marketing competencies to understand customer needs and the financial ability to invest in the necessary equipment and training.

Second, innovation capabilities (sometimes called new skills, improvements, modifications or changes by interviewees) helped subsidiary managers bargain with their parent headquarters for more investments in Malaysia, sometimes in competition with other TNC locations. The demonstration of new capabilities helped firms persuade headquarters that the benefits already shown (e.g. rapid production cycle times, efficiency gains and flexibility of response to new demands) would be also gained from future investments. In the case of SEH, this confidence had resulted in an ambitious plan for the company to set up the most advanced (and largest) wafer plant worldwide under the control of the SEH subsidiary.

■ A simple TNC technology positioning model

In order to identify key questions for the EU and the UK, it is helpful to develop a simple technological positioning model to show how TNC subsidiaries fit into the overall structure of global TNC activities, given that the latter are usually determined by decisions at corporate headquarters.

To capture the complex structure of the technological activities of the TNCs in relation to their subsidiaries, Figure 5.2 provides a rough technology profile of a typical large electronics TNC and, within it, the positioning of the Malaysian subsidiaries. The triangle represents an approximation of global technological activity, as measured say by the proportion of technology staff or technology expenditure for each activity.

The simple model helps to highlight several important points regarding TNC global strategies and Malaysia. The first is that R&D is a small proportion of total technological activity of the global company. Defined strictly, R&D amounts to the tip of the iceberg in Figure 5.2, principally areas 1, 2 and 3. The bulk of technological activity is a variety of engineering and operating tasks, essential for the competing firm (areas 4 to 7). Continuous improvements in areas 4 to 7 are key to TNC competitive performance. Indeed, the requirements of 4 to 7 usually drive much of the corporate R&D

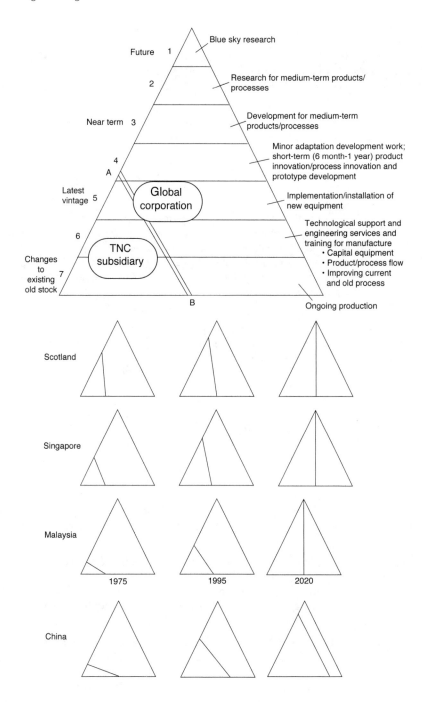

Figure 5.2 Technology positioning of Malaysian electronics TNCs

investment strategy. Put another way areas 4 to 7 provide much of the demand for R&D in areas 1, 2 and 3. Rather than blue sky, experimental research, most corporate R&D is carried out in response to competitive needs and near-term products and processes. In addition, core R&D activities tend to be located in the headquarters of the parent company, as already emphasized.

Regarding the technology positioning of the TNC subsidiaries in Malaysia, these constitute one part of the overall TNC operation. Usually, major investments are determined by corporate-level strategy, taking into account the costs and benefits of competing investment locations and likely future changes. A typical technological profile of a TNC subsidiary in Malaysia, circa 1995, is shown in the area A to B. This profile has shifted substantially over the past two decades or so and by 2020 the government hopes that the TNCs will be fully integrated within Malaysia. As shown earlier, since the 1970s the subsidiaries have progressively integrated upwards (or 'verticalized') into higher stages of technological activity, especially early entrants such as Motorola, SEH and Intel.

Verticalization can be facilitated or hampered by government policies, especially those towards the macro economy, industry, technology and education. For example, in Singapore, TNCs were encouraged to verticalize by vocational education policies, macroeconomic stability, rapid economic growth, rising wage and land costs and highly competent government. TNC subsidiaries are far less likely to verticalize under conditions of high inflation, economic instability and inefficient government.

Verticalization often, if not always, requires that the domestic TNC management gains greater control over local operations, including manufacturing process technology. Verticalization also requires an upgrading of other essential, related capabilities, especially marketing, management and finance. Progress to higher value-added activities requires the integration of technology with other important skills and resources.

As Figure 5.2 shows, Malaysian electronics operations tend to be situated between higher technology operations in countries such as Scotland and Singapore and lower cost countries such as China. While early entrants tended to verticalize gradually, recent entrants have tended to enter at more or less the current profile, reflecting the general level of technological development and the cost structure of the economy.

One of the key implications of the positioning model is that to verticalize upwards in the future the TNC subsidiaries and their suppliers in Malaysia will need to build up further technological capabilities, especially in precision engineering, prototype building, and product design and development. Although this is already taking place to some extent as firms move to higher value-added production, several major difficulties confront the industry as discussed earlier.

■ Issues raised for the UK and Europe

With the evidence of Malaysia's innovation and the above positioning model, it is possible to raise key questions for the EU and, in particular, the UK which depends heavily on TNC investment. Although it is not possible to answer the following questions without more evidence, the case of Malaysia raises a series of vitally important issues for the UK's future industrial growth.

As noted in the introduction, Britain is now a major location for TNC investments within the EU. More than 3500 US firms have invested in Britain and more than 40 per cent of Japanese European investment is based in Britain. The largest 2500 foreign-owned companies employ a total of two million people. Following the lead of the USA and Japan, companies from the four dragons are also investing in Britain, with a new Samsung (South Korea) investment of US$400 million in 1994 and the Tatung (Taiwan) subsidiary, Chunghwa, building a US$1.4 billion plant in Tyneside to produce colour TV picture tubes. So far there are only eleven South Korean and nine Taiwanese companies in the UK (compared with 221 Japanese) but the total investment is larger than all of the rest of the EU put together. Scotland is especially dependent on FDI. Scotland's so-called Silicon Glen today boasts one of the largest clusters of electronics operations in the EU, due largely to US and Japanese FDI (*Independent*, 1995).

Regarding the TNC subsidiaries, the evidence from Malaysia shows that: TNCs will transfer technology if the business conditions are conducive; and the TNCs are important channels for learning, training and best practice. Are the TNCs playing a similar role in the UK and other parts of Europe? If so, how can we encourage even more TNCs into the economy? How can countries like the UK ensure the benefits of FDI, in particular, those associated with verticalization? Has sufficient verticalization occurred, or do the TNCs lag behind in innovative capacity building? Is value-added high enough (e.g. in Scotland)? Are there enough backward linkage firms to create further growth and technological synergy? Can government policies help more in these respects, or is policy sufficiently 'tuned in' to the needs of the TNCs? For example, are training and education policies focused on firms' real technological needs, according to their verticalization position?

Questions are also raised concerning UK and EU technology policies. The Malaysian evidence clearly shows the importance of innovation at the subsidiary level. The message is that it is not just R&D that is important. On the contrary, there appears to be great scope for behind-the-frontier innovation. Is the UK and the EU taking non-R&D, technical and engineering activities seriously enough in their policies? Historically, many of the major programmes (e.g. Alvey, ESPRIT and Eureka) have concentrated on R&D, the tip of the technology triangle.

If the TNCs do have such a positive role to play in the UK and EU, then should we invite them into our national and EU programmes? Are they already present in sufficient numbers? If not, would they join in? How could we persuade them to join programmes such as ESPRIT in greater numbers?

One final matter of particular concern for the UK is that in the investigation into Malaysia (also previous work in Singapore) no major UK-owned firms could be found. Does this matter? The UK is better represented in other industrial sectors, so this may not be a major worry. Also, the EU as a whole is surprisingly well represented in electronics with firms such as Thomson/SGS, Philips, Siemens, MEMC, Grundig, Ericsson and Alcatel operating not just in Malaysia but in other parts of Southeast Asia.

■ Conclusions

In conclusion, it is helpful to return directly to the key questions concerning innovation in Malaysia raised in the opening sections.

First, has growth been accompanied by innovation within the Malaysian TNC subsidiaries? The answer to this question is definitely yes. Substantial innovation has occurred, particularly during the 1980s, as automation proceeded apace. In fact, the rapid company growth witnessed probably could not have occurred without a substantial degree of innovative capability on the part of the subsidiaries.

Second, what kind of innovation has occurred? Clearly, innovation was not radical or R&D based, but was incremental – driven by the needs of competitive manufacturing. Innovation was of the continuous improvement variety, including technical process innovations and soft or organizational/managerial innovations. At the heart of Malaysian innovation was improvements to mass manufacturing processes. In some cases this had led on to design for manufacturability, prototype development and incremental product design.

Third, how important has innovation been to industrial export success? The evidence suggests that innovation was central to export success. Indeed, it is difficult to imagine how such rapid plant expansion could occur effectively and efficiently without local capabilities for innovation.

Fourth, what would motivate foreign TNCs to transfer skills and technology? The chief motivations for technology transfer were commercial. Technology transfer allowed for the rapid and efficient expansion of capacity and helped meet the need for higher productivity, operating cost reductions and flexibility of response to market changes. For technology transfer to occur substantial local capabilities needed to be in place. Therefore, local innovation and overseas technology transfer were mutually dependent and inextricably linked in Malaysia.

Fifth, did the subsidiaries (or the government) encourage headquarters to transfer technology and, if so, how? In the case of Malaysia, the subsidiaries directly encouraged technology transfer by demonstrating their skills, competencies and abilities. Chief among these skills was the ability to innovate – to actually improve on processes and practices. At the same time, government played its part by providing the necessary infrastructure as well as allowing the freedom for TNCs to grow within the country. The low-cost labour force and tax incentives also played their part, especially in the early stages of development.

Finally, is growth likely to continue in the future? Although it is impossible to predict the future and surprises often happen in industrial development the answer to this question is 'probably yes'. However, as the chapter showed, several important problems face the electronics industry. More backward linkages to local suppliers are badly needed if the TNCs are to continue on their path of expansion and technological progress. The technical vocational education system lags behind the needs of manufacturing firms, resulting in the widespread shortage of skilled workers, technicians and engineers. As wages spiral due to shortages, not only does the overall cost of operating in Malaysia rise but also competing locations such as China and Vietnam become more attractive to the TNCs who may begin to question their future investments in Malaysia.

Such challenges are not insurmountable and programmes are already in place in Malaysia to address some of the problems. In some areas, the TNCs are collaborating to form their own centres for training and skills development (e.g. the Penang Skills Development Centre). The government's 2020 Programme is also addressing the question of the industrial demand for technology. Therefore, although Malaysia cannot take its growth in electronics for granted, there is every chance that innovation and industrial progress will continue.

References

Amsden, A. (1989). *Asia's Next Giant: South Korea and Late Industrialization*. Oxford University Press.

Bartlett, C. and Ghoshal, S. (1987a). Managing across borders: new strategic requirements. *Sloan Management Review*, **28** (4), Summer, 7–17.

Bartlett, C. and Ghoshal, S. (1987b). Managing across borders: new organisational requirements. *Sloan Management Review*, **29**)(1), Fall, 43–53.

Bell, M., Hobday, M., Abdullah, S., et al. (1985). *Aiming for 2020: A Demand Driven Perspective on Industrial Technology Policy in Malaysia*. Final Report for the World Bank and the Ministry of Science, Technology and the Environment, SPRU, Malaysia, October.

Capannelli, G. (1994). Technology transfer and industrial development in Malaysia: subcontracting linkages between Japanese multinationals and local suppliers in the colour television industry. Unpublished Master Course dissertation, Hitotsubashi University, Japan.

Dahlman, C. J., Ross-Larson, B. and Westphal, L. E. (1985). *Managing Technological Development: Lessons from the Newly Industrialising Countries*. World Bank

Dunning, J. H. (1975). Explaining changing patterns of international production: in defence of the eclectic theory. *Oxford Bulletin of Economics and Statistics*, **41**, 269–95.

Guyton, L. E. (1994). *Japanese FDI and the Transfer of Japanese Consumer Electronics Production to Malaysia*. Report prepared for the United Nations Development Programme (UNDP).

Hobday, M. G. (1995). *Innovation in East Asia: The Challenge to Japan*. Edward Elgar.

Independent, 15 November, p. 19.

Kam, L. V. (1992). *The Role of Subcontracting in Development of Entrepreneurship in SMIs*. Likom.

Lall, S. (1982). *Developing Countries as Exporters of Technology*. Macmillan.

Lall, S. (1992). Technological capabilities and industrialisation. *World Development*, **20** (2), 165–86

Lundvall, B. (1988). Innovation as an interactive process: from user-producer interaction to the national system of innovation. In *Technical Change and Economic Theory* (G. Dosi, C. Freeman, R. Nelson, et al., eds) Frances Pinter.

Financial Times (1995). 19 September, p. 3.

Malaysian Business (1993). 1–15 July, pp.14–15.

MITI (1994). *Malaysia International Trade and Industry Report 1994*, Ministry of International Trade and Industry, Malaysia.

Ngoh, C. L. (1994). *Motorola Globalisation: The Penang Journey*. Lee and Sons.

O'Connor, D. (1993). Electronics and industrialisation: approaching the 21st century. In *Industrialising Malaysia: Policy, Performance, Prospects* (K. S. Jomo, ed.), Routledge.

Porter M. E. (1990). *The Competitive Advantage of Nations*. Macmillan.

Rasiah, R. (1994). Flexible production systems and local machine-tool sub-contracting: electronics components transnationals in Malaysia. *Cambridge Journal of Economics*, **18**, 279–98.

Riedel, J. (1988). Economic development in East Asia: doing what comes naturally? In *Achieving Industrialisation in East Asia* (H. Hughes, ed.), Cambridge University Press.

Schmookler, J. (1966*). Invention and Economic Growth*. Harvard University Press.
Utterback, J. M. and Abernathy, W. J. (1995). A dynamic model of process and product innovation. *OMEGA, The International Journal of Management Science*, **3** (6), 639–56.
Vernon, R. (1975). The product life cycle hypothesis in a new international environment. *Oxford Bulletin of Economics and Statistics*, **41**, 255–67.
Vernon, R. (1996). International investment and international trade in the product life cycle. *Quarterly Journal of Economics*, **80** (2), 190–207
Wade, R. (1990). *Governing the Market: Economic Theory and the Role of Government in East Asian Industrialisation*. Princeton University Press.
Westphal, L. E., Kim, L. and Dahlman, C. J. (1985). Reflections on the Republic of Korea's acquisition of technological capability. In *International Transfer of Technology: Concepts, Measures, and Comparisons* (N. Rosenberg and C. Frischtak, eds) Praeger Press.
World Bank (1993). *The East Asian Miracle: Economic Growth and Public Policy*. World Bank and Oxford University Press.

Chapter 5.1

Do the lessons still stand?

■ Mike Hobday ■

Since doing the research for Chapter 5 in 1996, a severe economic crisis has engulfed many parts of East and Southeast Asia. While Chapter 5 looked at the learning and innovation progress of TNCs, it is important to ask: do these firm-level results and lessons still hold, given the dramatic financial and macroeconomic problems confronting the region? To consider this basic question it is helpful to assess three issues:

1 The causes of the crisis.

2 How the crisis relates to TNCs and vice versa.

3 What bearing TNC learning and innovation have on the current crisis and possible future recovery.

First, it appears that the fundamental causes of the crisis relate to financial and macroeconomic management (and institutions) rather than the production and technological activities of exporting firms (also see Chapter 3.1). Macroeconomic instability, monetary mismanagement and protected financial institutions have all been cited as the cause of exchange rate depreciations, the lack of confidence in local currencies and ongoing economic disruption.

Second, the impact on TNCs has been to challenge the very foundations of long-term corporate investment confidence from which Southeast Asia has benefited for thirty years or so (see Chapter 5). Economic instability, exchange rate fluctuations and, in some cases, social and political unrest undermine confidence and threaten to reduce the region's share of global FDI. (East and Southeast Asian investments together accounted for around 60 per cent of developing country FDI in 1995.)

Third, if the planned reforms are implemented and stability returns in the short term, paradoxically, this could improve the conditions for investments by TNCs. Indeed, the lowering of costs and exchange rates would make exporting firms (TNCs and local) more competitive and improve their scope for expansion, learning and innovation. In this positive scenario, the TNCs could play a part in assisting recovery through increasing export competitiveness, building upon the traditional strength of the region. By contrast, if reforms are delayed or fail to restore stability, the history (and benefits) of learning and innovation could easily be wiped out as firms withdraw or scale back operations. Such a negative scenario would further worsen the economic crisis by damaging the productive export base of the region.

To conclude, while it is impossible to predict the future, the fundamental lessons of learning, innovation and export-led growth apply as much today as they did in the past. The history of learning and innovation described in the 1996 article (Chapter 5) remain a positive aspect of Southeast Asia's past and something from which all other regions, including Europe, can learn. If the current economic crisis can be overcome quickly, then the TNCs could well lead a new wave of Southeast Asian export-led growth.

Chapter 6

Australia's Asian business orientation: investor and intermediary[1]

■ Ian Marsh ■

Offshore investment by Australian owned or based firms is a relatively recent development – part of the more general, government led effort to internationalize Australia's economy. Its specific encouragement can perhaps best be dated from the relaxation of exchange controls in 1983. Since that time the number of major firms active in Australia has grown progressively and these firms have established offshore operations. More recently, there is evidence of similar activity by growing numbers of small and medium enterprises and a range of service providers.

For reasons to be explored later, the first wave of offshore investment – roughly in the decade to 1992 – was concentrated in the familiar markets of the USA, UK and New Zealand. Since 1992 there is strong evidence of a marked switch of focus to Asia – particularly to the 'open' economies of Indonesia, Malaysia, Singapore, China and Vietnam. The intended direction of offshore investment, future investment plans and the approach and orientation of firms in a wide range of sectors all suggest that Australia's internationalization has culminated in the emergence of the Asian region as a primary focus of business interest.

This chapter offers an overview of this emerging regional orientation, reviews the explanations that have been offered for its timing and pattern and assesses its significance for business and public policy. First, the general political and economic context is explored. Then the growth of offshore investment is described, its major phases identified and explanations for these phases discussed. Third, the importance of this change in orientation both for the approach and perspectives of individual firms as well as for the general business and investment climate within Australia is examined and its significance in historical, regional and comparative contexts assessed. The chapter concludes by identifying some remaining challenges both in consolidating developments and in capitalizing on the wider national opportunities opened up by this new business orientation to Asia.

---

[1] This chapter has been published previously by MCB University Press Limited: Marsh, I. (1996). Australia's Asian business orientation: investor and intermediary. *Management Decision,* **34** (9), 49–64.

◼ The context

Individual firms make investment decisions. But they do so in a context. In the past fifteen years, at least three developments have framed the strategic context in which offshore investment has entered the calculations of Australian enterprises. These are: the pattern of economic development in Asia; the Australian domestic policy environment; and expansion of the number of Australian enterprises and institutions able or motivated to operate offshore. These are explored in turn.

The pattern of economic development in Asia is the first contextual factor. The emergence of the Asian region as a leading force in the global economy has been documented thoroughly (The World Bank, 1993). Because of their dynamic growth, their burgeoning cadre of middle-income consumers and the emerging tastes and preferences of these consumers, regional states provided progressively expanding economic opportunities (Tan, 1992). Yet the policy framework and the timing of development varied between regional states. This particularly affected the environment for foreign investors. Of the early industrializers – initially Japan, and then progressively Korea, Taiwan, Hong Kong and Singapore – only the latter two offered relatively 'liberal' investment environments. The other states based development on high levels of domestic saving, and a policy framework of, in Wade's (Wade, 1990) term, 'governed markets'. Governments sought to build local strong firms capable of competing in global markets – an objective that has been achieved with spectacular success (Wade, 1990; Weiss and Hobson, 1995). Foreign investment in these countries, while not precluded, was impeded by explicit and tacit restrictions.

The other Asian states – including Thailand, Malaysia and Indonesia – adopted export-led growth strategies. However, they grounded their economic development on investment by foreign firms. This approach was inaugurated in Thailand in 1980 and in Malaysia and Indonesia in 1986 (The World Bank, 1993, pp. 134–49). A similar approach was later adopted by Vietnam and China. All these states gained particular impetus from Japanese investment after the Plaza Accords of 1987 (Abbeglen, 1994). Initial investment in export-oriented sectors has had wide-ranging multiplier effects and thus enhanced their attractiveness to further categories of investors (e.g. service firms, consumer goods producers, infrastructure providers). The significance of this difference in the pattern and timing of development between North and Southeast Asia will be further considered later. In general, however, the investment environment in the Asian region can roughly be conceived to consist of at least two phases – before and after 1987.

The second contextual influence encouraging Australian direct investment offshore was a historic change in the domestic Australian political and economic environment (Marsh, 1995, Chapter 5). Australian governments have progressively altered national economic strategy from an inward to a more outward-looking stance. They have done so on the presumption that the standard of living hitherto accomplished, and now taken for granted, by Australians, can no longer be sustained on primary and resource-based exports alone. Other sectors of Australia's economy need to participate in international trade if living standards and expectations are to be maintained, at least for the overwhelming majority. The decisive shift from the perspective of foreign investment occurred in 1983 when exchange controls were lifted. Since that date, policy frameworks and settings, affecting almost all areas of the economy, have been progressively recast (see, for example, Marsh, 1995, Chapter 3; Edwards, et al., 1996). This has included a progressive tariff rollback, reworked corporate taxation arrangements, labour practices, training, the commercialization of public utilities, competition policy and so forth. One can trace through a series of official reports growing recognition of the importance of foreign investment as a key element in wider processes of internationalization. These reports establish its generally positive consequences for the national economy (see, for example, Bureau of Industry Economics, 1995a, especially Chapter 8). Further, policy has deliberately encouraged offshore firms to base operations in Australia not, as in the past, to serve protected domestic markets, but rather to take advantage of Australia's potential as a springboard to Asia (Department of Industry, Science and Technology, 1995a; Price Waterhouse, 1995a).

A third contextual element was the changed structure of Australian industry. At the outset of the 1980s, Australia's established corporate sector was distinctive both in terms of organizational size and product market areas. One legacy of the inward looking strategy of economic development was an industry structure composed of a few large firms and many small- and medium-sized enterprises (SMEs). A variety of studies have demonstrated the correlation between firm size and propensity to invest offshore (Yetton et al., 1992). In Australia's case, large firms have traditionally existed in the mining and resource sector. These firms have traditionally exhibited a strong international orientation (Blainey, 1993). By contrast, in the manufacturing sector, in 1990, only approximately twenty firms had an annual turnover in excess of $1billion (Pappas et al., 1990). These large firms were concentrated in distinct product/market segments. They offered products that were not internationally tradeable and that served mature consumer markets (Yetton et al., 1992, p.18). We will see later these features decisively influenced their internationalization strategies.

The 1980s also witnessed the growth in the number of major enterprises in Australia capable of investing offshore. This has occurred as hitherto non-commercial public utilities have been progressively commercialized and, in some cases, privatized. Major enterprises have been created in areas like telecommunications, power supply, water supply, banking, insurance and aviation. These enterprises have progressively acquired greater freedom in commercial decision making and, in the early 1990s, some appear to have emerged as major regional investors (Cornell, 1994; Lewis, 1995). For example, Australia's former telecommunications public utility, now commercialized as Telstra, has an annual turnover in excess of $14 billion and has become an active regional investor (Brewster, 1995). There have been other new quasi-commercial entrants to the trade and investment market. For example, a number of Australian universities have invested in regional campuses.[2]

Finally, in the internationalized climate of the late 1980s and with growing market opportunities for high-tech products and services, a number of new Australian SMEs have been established which, in the words of one analysis, were 'born global'(McKinsey and Co, 1993). Other established SMEs have begun to extend operations offshore. As SME exports develop, so their propensity to establish offshore operations grows. Survey evidence suggests Asian states are their preferred location

[2] See, for example, Education Agreement between Australia and Malaysia, statement by Minister for Employment, Education and Training, 16 January 1995, Parliament Home, Canberra. This statement notes the agreement between Monash University (Melbourne) and the Sungeiway Group to establish a branch campus. Three other Australian universities are recorded as interested in Branch Campus Licenses – Sydney University, Adelaide University and Royal Melbourne Institute of Technology.

(McKinsey and Co, 1993, pp.30–31). Together these developments imply the number of firms potentially available or motivated to invest in regional markets has expanded spectacularly in the late 1980s.

There has been limited, piecemeal analysis of the fit between the pattern of Australian industry and emerging trade and investment opportunities in Asian markets. Most detailed analysis has hitherto focused on the major manufacturing enterprises. Information on the SME sector is much less comprehensive (Department of Foreign Affairs and Trade, 1995; McKinsey and Co, 1993). Government targeting is rudimentary. Sectors such as processed foods, information technology, pharmaceuticals and scientific instruments have been nominated as presenting particular opportunities (Australian Agri-Food Industries, 1992; Button, 1988; Griffiths, 1992). However, no detailed targets or implementing strategies have been formulated. Without such measures performance and outcomes cannot be benchmarked.

■ Direct investment: an overview

There are a number of sources for data on past and likely patterns of offshore investment by Australian-based firms. These include official statistics and reports, special purpose surveys and surveys of investment intentions.

The major source of data is the Australian Bureau of Statistics which routinely collects information on direct equity investment by Australian firms offshore. This data has a number of limitations (discussed in Sturgiss, 1995). First, it is subject to marked fluctuations, for example because of asset revaluations or withdrawals. Second, the use of intermediaries can mask the final destination of investment. This is particularly the case in Asia where Singapore and Hong Kong have demonstrably played such a role. Third, a variety of other forms of investment are not included – for example, debt, foreign partner contributions or capital raisings on offshore markets. Thus investments may be significantly understated. As we will see later, equity may also so lag corporate activity as to be a misleading guide to current management preoccupations.

Aggregate data on offshore investment by Australian firms has been collected and analysed in a series of official reports. These point to the strong growth of foreign direct investment (FDI) outflows in the 1980s. Figure 6.1 compares FDI outflows with selected economic aggregates in the period from 1969–70 to 1993–94. The spurt of growth after 1983 followed the relaxation of exchange controls that year. Before this date the growth of FDI outflows was lower than that of exports and gross domestic product (GDP). After this date, it exceeded both these measures by a significant margin until the divestment associated with the recession of 1990–91. Strong growth resumed in 1992.

Over this period, FDI stocks grew from $534 million (1970) to $47 575 million (1994). This represents an annual average growth rate of 20.5 per cent (Table 6.1). As a share of GDP, FDI stocks grew from 1.7 per cent to 11.2 per cent.

International comparisons suggest that Australia ranked low (with Japan and Italy) in the proportion of its GDP accounted for by FDI stocks in 1980 but that its growth since that date has been among the world's fastest (Figure 6.2).

The data on FDI stocks in different regions shows an increase in the absolute level of investment in ASEAN states but a far greater growth in the more distant markets of

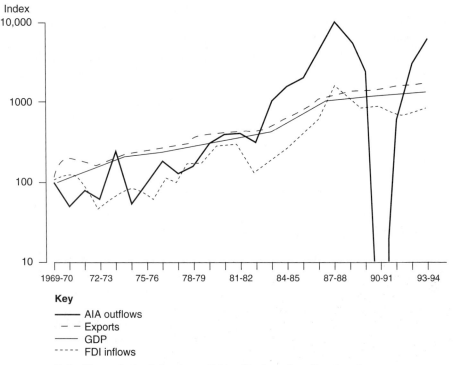

Note: The vertical axis is a base 10 logarithmic scale, with values for 1969-1970 set equal to 100

Figure 6.1 Comparison of foreign direct investment outflows with selected economic aggregates, 1969–1970 to 1993–1994
Sources: Australian Bureau of Statistics (Cat. No. 5206. 0, various issues); Australian Bureau of Statistics (Cat. No. 5203. 0, various issues); Bureau of Industry Economics (1995a)

the USA and the UK. This resulted in a vastly diminished proportionate engagement with regional states through the period of the 1980s (Table 6.2). Investment in ASEAN dominated up to 1983. It was rapidly displaced up to 1988 by investment in the UK, USA and New Zealand. Thereafter it has gradually expanded (Figure 6.3).

Looked at comparatively however, by 1993, Australia's share of investment (and exports) into Asia exceeded that of all other OECD states except Japan (Table 6.3).

A progressive switch in focus to states in Asia in recent years is suggested in three data sources. First, a study of the investment intentions of 35 major manufacturing firms and ten major service firms sought to establish their expected distribution of total assets in the period 1994 to 1999 (Bureau of Industry Economics, 1995a, p. 33). The results for the manufacturing group indicate some twenty of the firms surveyed expected to increase their assets in Asia by 20 per cent or more. By contrast some twenty-seven firms expected no change in their level of UK assets and fifteen no

Table 6.1 Australian investment abroad stocks: current price values and as a share of GDP, selected years

Year	Value (US$)	Share of GDP (per cent)
1970	534	1.7
1975	882	1.4
1980	4 219	3.4
1985	9 771	4.5
1990	39 484	10.8
1994	47 575	11.2

Note: Data are at 30 June of each year
Source: Bureau of Industry Economics (1995a) p.13; Australian Bureau of Statistics (Cat. No. 5205. 0, various issues); Australian Bureau of Statistics (Cat. No. 5353. 0, various issues); Australian Bureau of Statistics unpublished data.

Table 6.2 Australian investment abroad stocks: by location in current prices and as a share of the total, 1980 and 1994, and average annual growth rate, 1980–94

	1980 value (US$)	Share (per cent)	1994 value (US$)	Share (per cent)	1980–94 growth rate (per cent)
UK	499	11.8	18 675	39.3	29.5
USA	553	13.1	10 403	21.8	23.3
New Zealand	340	8.1	7 017	14.7	24.1
ASEAN	1 193	28.3	2 797	5.9	6.3
Papua New Guinea	244	5.8	2 145	4.5	16.8
Hong Kong	742	17.6	1 326	2.8	4.2
Other	648	15.4	5 212	11.0	16.1
Total	4 219	100.0	47 575	100.0	18.9

Note: The growth rates are average annual figures derived from the end points.
Source: Bureau of Industry Economics (1995a) p. 22.

Table 6.3 Share of investment and exports into (non-Japan) Asia by OECD countries, 1993

Country	Investment share (%)	Export share (%)
Australia	10	38
USA	7	18
UK	7	8
Japan	16	38
Canada	6	4
France	2	6
Switzerland	3	10

Source: Sturgiss (1995)

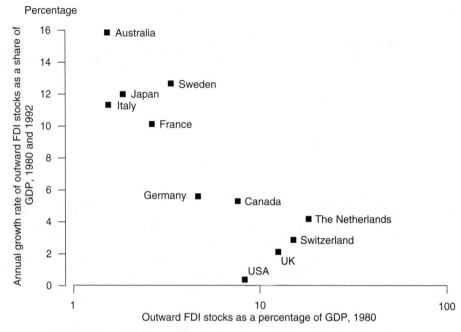

Figure 6.2 Annual growth rate of outward FDI stocks as a share of GDP between 1980 and 1992, and outward FDI stocks as a share of GDP, 1980
Source: Bureau of Industry Economics (1995)

change in their US assets (Figure 6.4). Similar results were derived from the much smaller sample of service firms (Figure 6.5). The report however cautions: 'As Asia currently accounts for a relatively low percentage of the sample's total assets, the flow of investment to Asia is expected to remain small relative to flows to other countries/regions.'

Other evidence however suggests this cautionary note may be inappropriate. A survey of investment intentions by the accounting firm Price Waterhouse confirms a switch to a regional focus. This covered the investment intentions of the top 500 listed companies excluding mining enterprises (Price Waterhouse, 1995b). It attracted a 23 per cent response. More than 56 per cent of respondents saw the greatest potential for offshore expansion to be in Asia with the next preferred site North America and Europe at 14 per cent each. Within Asia, the report shows most interest was concentrated on Indonesia (26 per cent) followed by China (16 per cent) and Malaysia (14 per cent). Figure 6.6 sketches the reasons for these decisions.

Perhaps the most powerful source of evidence of a marked shift to the Asian region is in a survey of overseas projects undertaken routinely since 1993 by the commercial

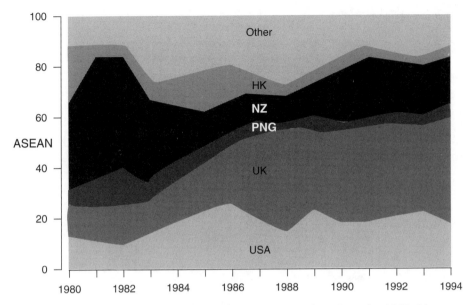

Figure 6.3 Distribution by country of Australian investment abroad: stocks, 1980–94
Note: Stocks data on a comparable basis are not available for earlier years due to corporate equities being valued at paid-up value and the other components such as borrowing and branch liabilities to head office, being valued at market value. From 1980 corporate equities are valued at market value. Data are as at 30 June of each year
Sources: Bureau of Industry Economics (1995a) p. 33; Australian Bureau of Statistics (Cat. No. 5205. 0, various issues).

consulting firm Access Economics (1996). Indeed this survey suggests the analysis, reported above, on the investment plans of thirty-five manufactures and ten service firms may seriously underestimate the dynamics. The Access Economics data cover all major new investment projects by Australian companies, excluding takeovers. Investment plans are documented in four categories – under construction, committed, under consideration and possible; and in four sectors – manufacturing, mining, power and water and other (e.g. telecommunications, leisure, transport, health). The value is for the total project, not the share specifically subscribed by the Australian firm. Takeovers are not included. This survey covers projects reported to Australia's stock exchanges or announced by commercialized public utilities – that is, activities which might be expected to show up in equity values only after a considerable lag. While the absolute amounts do not isolate the capital contribution of the Australian participant, the direction and relative magnitudes between regions are a strong indicator of corporate preoccupations.

Table 6.4 shows total overseas projects by region. The predominant interest in Asia is clear. More then 60 per cent of projects committed or under construction in the calendar years covered were in the region. A very high proportion of foreshadowed projects were also regionally based. The 1994 proportion is distorted by a very large mining

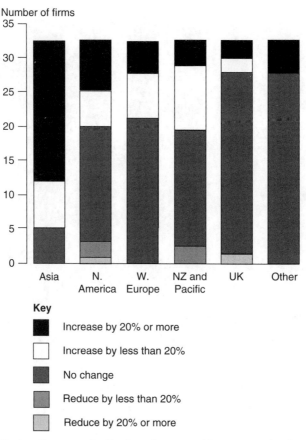

Figure 6.4 Regional/country distribution of proposed investments by the sample manufacturing multinational enterprises, 1 July 1994–30 June 1999
Source: Bureau of Industry Economics (1994).

project in South America. Equally the turn away from North America and Europe is equally clear – the share of these regions averages under 10 per cent. This is a marked change from the regional pattern of existing Australian direct offshore investment. This survey may underestimate investments in Europe and the USA by excluding takeovers – although the proportions are consistent with the findings of the Bureau of Industry Economics (BIE) survey (Bureau of Industry Economics, 1995a).

Tables 6.5 and 6.6 separate projects committed and under construction (Table 6.5) and total projects (Table 6.6) and then detail the proportions between regions in the various industry categories – manufacturing, mining, power and water, and other. This separation was made to isolate investments that will spill into assets and equities from investments that reflect management attention and preoccupations. A strong switch of focus to the Asian region is evident among manufacturers (compared with the data reported earlier on equity shares) and an overwhelming regional focus is clear for firms involved

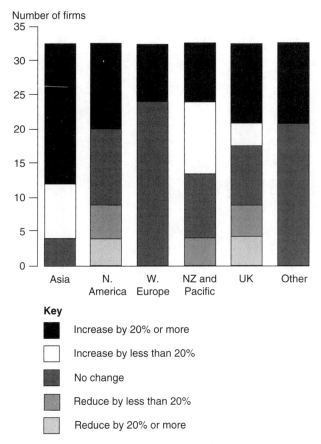

Figure 6.5 Regional/country distribution of proposed investments by the sample service multinational enterprises, 1 July 1994–30 June 1999
Source: Bureau of Industry Economics (1994).

in infrastructure provision (power and water investment) and for firms in the 'other' category – telecommunications, leisure, education, transport, services, etc.

As Table 6.5 shows, North America also continues as a focus for manufacturing with 41 per cent of projects under construction and committed in 1994 (compared to 40 per cent in Asia) and 43 per cent in 1995 (33 per cent in Asia). However when all manufacturing projects are taken into account, the Asian region again predominates – regional states were sites for 76 per cent of projects reported in 1993, 71 per cent in 1994 and 50 per cent in 1995 (Table 6.5). This suggests a regional focus is now at the centre of manufacturing firms' preoccupations – and this will presumably be reflected in subsequent moves in investment commitments and, even later, assets. Finally, mining companies are clearly operating with a global focus.

Table 6.7 provides a listing of projects by number and value for individual countries in the Asian region for the year to September 1995. By both categories China was the major focus of Australian interest with 43 per cent of the number of projects and 21 per

Table 6.4 Committed and foreshadowed Australian investments by region (excluding Papua New Guinea)

	Under construction/committed						Total[a]					
	1993		1994		1995		1993		1994		1995	
	$	%	$	%	$	%	$	%	$	%	$	%
Asia	7 615	66	8 195	60	13 121	65	14 453	48	22 389	28	45 108	62
Europe	2 780	24	2 255	16.5	1 304	6.5	2 798	9	4 351	5	2 988	4
North America	125	1	1 059	8	1 558	8	979	3	2 324	3	3 690	5
South America	–	–	–	–	3 020	15	–	–	–	–	12 172	17
Africa	–	–	–	–	522	3	–	–	–	–	2 378	7
Other	947	8	2 150	16	436	2	11 689	39	50 629	64	6 508	9
Total	11 467		13 659		19 961		29 919		76 693		72 843	

Note: [a] Covers reported projects in four categories: under construction, committed, under consideration and possible
Source: Access Economics (1996).

Table 6.5 Investment projects committed or under construction by regions and sector (percentage)

	1993			1994				1995			
	Manufacturing	Mining	Other	Manufacturing	Mining	Power and water	Other	Manufacturing	Mining	Power and water	Other
Asia	63.5	46	83	40	36	83	88	33	36	84.5	98
Europe	22	33	–	6	23	17	12	7	–	–	–
North America	13	–	–	41	–	–	–	43	55	–	–
South America	–	–	–	–	–	–	–	4	10	–	–
Africa	–	–	–	–	–	–	–	–	–	–	–
Other	1	20	17	12.5	40	–	–	12	–	–	–

Source: Access Economics (1996).

Table 6.6 All investment projects by regions and sector (percentage)

	1993			1994				1995			
	Manufacturing	*Mining*	*Other*	*Manufacturing*	*Mining*	*Power and water*	*Other*	*Manufacturing*	*Mining*	*Power and water*	*Other*
Asia	76	16	90	71	15	89	75	50	37	88	100
Europe	7	10	–	3	–	–	–	–	5	–	–
North America	8	5	–	19	–	–	–	33	–	–	–
South America	–	–	–	–	–	–	–	14	30	–	–
Africa	–	–	–	–	–	–	–	–	7	–	–
Other	9	70	10	–	70	–	22	–	18	–	–

Note: All investment projects cover reported projects in four categories: under construction, committed, under consideration and possible.
Source: Access Economics (1996).

Reasons[a] for starting off shore production

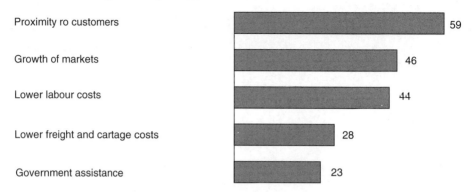

Proximity ro customers — 59

Growth of markets — 46

Lower labour costs — 44

Lower freight and cartage costs — 28

Government assistance — 23

Note:[a] Top three reasons were asked for in survey

Figure 6.6 A number of factors lead manufacturers to produce offshore: percentage of 39 respondents
Source: McKinsey and Co. (1993), p. 32.

cent of the value. Indonesia was next with 11 per cent of the number and 16 per cent of the value.

Table 6.7 Projects in regional states by number and value and relative share (nine months to September 1995)

	Number	*%*	*Value ($m)*	*%*
China	68	43	15 062	21
Indonesia	33	11	11 408	16
India	15	5	6 185	9
Vietnam	18	6	2 962	4
Thailand	9	3	2 677	4
Philippines	12	4	1 269	2
Malaysia	11	4	216	4
UK	9	3	2 352	3
USA	12	4	1 850	3
Total	291	100	70 895	100

Source: Access Economics (1995).

Comparative data on the volume and relative ranking of Australian investment in Asian states provide further confirmation of this switch in focus (Table 6.8). These data are sourced from the investment boards in individual states. The survey covered the top fifteen investors by country of origin in each state. The year covered varied between calendar 1992 (Singapore), 1993 (Hong Kong), 1994 (Taiwan, Vietnam,

Thailand and, Malaysia) and April 1994 to March 1995 (Indonesia and Japan). Australian firms were the second biggest investors in Indonesia in the year covered and the eighth biggest investors in Malaysia, Singapore and Taiwan. Australian firms did not rank in the top fifteen in South Korea, the Philippines or China.

Table 6.8 Australian investment volume and ranking in regional states mainly calendar 1994

	($m)	*Rank (of top 14)*
Hong Kong	79	10
Indonesia	3469	2
Japan	30	14
Malaysia	70	8
Singapore	2190	8
Taiwan	25	8
Vietnam	50	4
Thailand	11	10

Source: Far Eastern Economic Review (1995a), pp. 45–118.

These numbers are extremely volatile. For example in Indonesia, in 1991, investment approvals for projects by Australian-based firms equalled just $41 million. This surged to $1.6 billion in 1994 (*Far Eastern Economic Review*, 1995a, pp. 45–124). The 1995 total is swollen by a single oil refinery project. Yet the breadth and variety of Australian investors reflects the depth of corporate interest in that market (Table 6.9). Similarly for Vietnam, the survey reported above placed Australian based firms as fourteenth in the overseas investor league table with $50 million project approvals in 1994. Another survey covering approvals in 1993 ranked Australia as third biggest investor with 48 approved projects for a total value of $1.13 billion (*Australian Financial Review*, 1994).

Generally, Australian foreign investment in the period roughly from 1983 to 1992 concentrated on the USA, UK and New Zealand. After 1992 the Asian region has become the predominant focus of corporate interest. Most new investment will be focused here. No calculations have been made estimating the impact of this investment boom on likely shares of investment stocks between the regions by say, 2000. But the information reported above on investment intentions points to a marked shift in focus – on such a scale that a major shift in regional shares might be expected to emerge. This is further confirmed by the Bureau of Industry Economics (BIE) survey of selected manufacturing and service firms that reported no expected change of asset levels in the UK and only limited likely asset increase in the USA. The evidence thus suggests a reorientation to the Asian region by Australia's corporate sector is well under way. It is to explanations of this development that we now turn.

■ Explanations

The data reviewed above suggests offshore investments might be categorized into three broad phases: the period up to the lifting of exchange controls in 1983, 1983–92 and beyond 1992. These are explored in turn in the following paragraphs.

Table 6.9 Australian investment in Indonesia

Company	Estimated investment ($M)	Project	Business	Stake (%)	Main partner
CRA	560	Kaltim Prime	Coal mine	50	BP
		Kelian Equatorial	Gold mine	90	Harita
BHP	250	Cilegon	Steel coating	65	Krakatua Steel
		BHP Building	Metal products	40	Various
		Arutmin/Utah	Coal	80	Bakrie/Mitsui
New Hope	200[a]	Adaro	Coal	50	Tirtamas
		Multi Harapan	Coal	50	Risjad
		IBT	Port facilities	50	Tirtamas
		Grafen Invesindo	Finance	40	Swabara
CC Amatil	200[a]	Franchises	Coca-Cola	90	Pan Java
Telstra	150	MitraGlobal	Phones	20	Indosat
		Justrindo	Mobile radio	75	Various
AMP	100	AMP Panin Life	Life insurance	65	Panin
Aurora	90	Indo Muro	Gold	90	Local
P&O Australia	70	Alatief/P&O	Port facilities	50	Alatief
		P&O Spice Island	Cruises	50	Widjaya
BOC Australia	65	IGI	Industrial gas	70	Aneka
Rothmans	60	Rothmans	Cigarettes	100	n/a
Boral	60	Petro Jaya	Plasterboard	42	Pembangunan
		Jaya Readymix	Concrete	50	Pembangunan
Clough	50	Petrosea	Engineering	66	Public
Good. Fielder	40	Sinar Meadow	Cooking oil	50	Sinar Mas
		Smartindo Kencana	Snack food	50	Sinar Mas
Leighton	37	Thiess Contractors	Engineering	80	Mintek Indo
ANZ	32	ANZ Panin Bank	Banking	85	Panin
BTR Nylex	30	BTR Perkasa	Automotive	50	Texmaco
		Kangar (ACI)	Glass containers	50	Bob Hasan
CSR	30	Prima Karya	Plasterboard	85	Napitupulu
		Sun Bradford	Glasswool	50	
John Holland	20	John Holland Asia	Construction	50	Hume
Transfield	20	Trans-Bakrie	Construction	49	Bakrie
Pacific BBA	18	Webforge	Building products	100	n/a
		Dynaplast	Moulding	10	Hambali
Amcor	18	Indopak Pratama	Cardboard	55	Pakerin
Pac Dunlop	18	Olex	Cable	60	Various
Matrix	12	Telematrixindo	Paging	50	Various
Lend Lease	10	LL Graha Indonesia	Construction	50	Sinar Mas
		Bill LL Investments	Funds	50	Sinar Mas
		Sinar Mas LL Life	Insurance	50	Sinar Mas
Southcorp	8	Rheem	Cans	40	DKI
Pacific Mag.	6	Kharisma	Printing	50	Portamina

Note: [a] More than 50 per cent still to be invested.
Source: *Australian Financial Review* (1995a).

Business investment before 1983

Capital controls prior to 1983 and the preservation of a domestic tariff regime both worked to restrain direct Australian investment. The relatively small total stock of Australian offshore investment ($4.2 billion) was relatively heavily concentrated in ASEAN states and Hong Kong (approximately 46 per cent of total investment). Survey data suggest the principal motive for establishing offshore operations was import substitution in small domestic markets. Many investments were reportedly unsuccessful (Bureau of Industry Economics, 1984; East Asia Analytical Unit, 1994).

Business investment 1983–92

The relaxation of exchange controls in 1983 was a decisive event. As noted above, foreign direct investment surged thereafter. Yet the share of Australia's direct foreign investment in Asia declined significantly during the 1980s – although the absolute stock increased. Yetton, Davis and Swan (1992) suggested this outcome resulted from the strategy adopted by Australian manufacturing firms in their first move to international markets. Australia's first wave of international investment was focused on the USA and the UK. They ascribed this to a collection of factors including low cultural differences, similar legal and business structures, and similar or higher living standards and patterns of consumption. Yetton, Davis and Swan (1992) termed this a strategy of 'one risk at a time'. Based on research undertaken in 1991 they reported

> the majority of (Australia's) successful MNEs see investment in the (dynamic Asian region) as entailing more than one risk … Investments in Asia may give rise not only to market risk (differences in language, in legal systems and in modes of behaviour) but also control risks (requirements for minority share holding or joint venture structures.

They also observed: 'Several senior managers pointed to the lack of fit between their firm's particular area of expertise and local consumption patterns in South East Asia as for example in residential housing and packaging requirements'. (Yetton, Davis and Swan, 1992, p.20)

The mode of entry could be by greenfield investment or acquisition. They concluded the preferred mode depended on the particular firm's competitive advantage – those with proprietary manufacturing technologies typically established new facilities. These firms only used acquisitions to augment their marketing capacity. By contrast, firms with mature technologies sought local acquisitions where suitable candidates were available.

The 1987 stock market crash and a subsequent domestically induced recession in Australia halted offshore investment activity and indeed precipitated a withdrawal of funds in 1990 and 1991. With domestic recovery in early 1992, investment growth resumed at its earlier rate – that is, in excess of other indicators of domestic activity. We have noted the UK and the USA continued to attract most interest through to 1991. Thereafter there appears to be a distinct shift in focus to the Asian region.

Business investment beyond 1992

The switch in corporate focus to Asia in the early 1990s requires explanation. Yetton, Davis and Swan (1992), cite management prudence as the primary ground for the approach of manufacturers. Ron Edwards suggests higher transport costs for exporting to more distant markets might have encouraged manufacturing firms to set up earlier in North America and Europe then in Asia (Tower, 1995). Alternative explanations might look to changing market conditions in regional states, to the requirements for successful market entry and to changes in the Australian domestic market. In relation to market conditions in regional states, two distinct, but complementary, developments occurred in the middle to late 1980s which might have made them vary markedly in their attractiveness as investment environments.

Following the Plaza Accords and the yen revaluation in 1985, Japanese investment to regional countries, particularly Thailand and later Malaysia and Indonesia, moved forward rapidly. Subsequently, cost-driven investment also flowed to China. This was later reinforced by Korean and Taiwanese investment as rising exchange rates pushed low-skill activities progressively offshore. Much of this investment was for the production of consumer goods bound for US and other global markets. However, this investment was a major stimulus to development in these three states in the late 1980s. The demand for capital goods and infrastructure grew rapidly. Similarly, a burgeoning middle class rapidly developed tastes and consumption patterns in some respects analogous to those familiar in Western states (Goodman and Robison, 1995).

That Australian manufacturing and service firms may have responded to these changes both in the regional regulatory climate and in capital and consumer goods market development is suggested in the above data on investment plans beyond 1991 (Tables 6.5 and 6.6). The earliest systematic work (Yetton, Davis and Swan, 1992) focused on the twenty major firms with total sales in excess of $1billion. There the evidence is overwhelming that, in the first instance at least, these firms favoured the mature European and American markets. We have already noted this was based at least partly on their perceptions of opportunities and risks in regional markets.

For individual firms, a variety of strategic and domestic market considerations may have been relevant. For some firms facing a mature domestic market, growth could only be pursued offshore and exports were not a real alternative. This would affect such sectors as telecommunications, power and water, beer, banks and construction. Prior to 1983 such firms could only diversify within Australia – after the relaxation of exchange controls they could specialize internationally. For their part, mining enterprises want deposits at the bottom of the cost curve, wherever they are. This might explain the shift in focus to Latin America. Some manufacturers were looking for lower cost sourcing following the relaxation of tariffs in Australia (e.g. some of Pacific Dunlop's investment). Others may want 'insider' status as the best path to realize sales goals. And some service companies may be following their own domestic customers (e.g. mining contractors).[3]

Other research suggests offshore activity is not confined to large enterprises. Although relatively few SMEs have internationalized, of those which have a significant number are investing offshore. Asia appears to be their preferred first port of call. A 1993 study of 700 elaborately transformed manufacturing (ETMs) exporters in the SME category found that 13 per cent had already set up offshore operations in the Asian region and interviews indicated 50 per cent were considering this step. Figure 6.6 analyses the reasons for establishing offshore operations. Proximity to customers and market

[3] I am indebted to Dr Ed Shann of Access Economics for these points. See, for example, Shann, E. (1994). Our industry pushes out to the world. *Business Review Weekly*, 14 February.

How much of function stays in Australia when
firm establishes some offshore production?

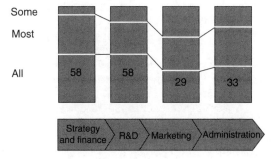

Note: Based on 39 respondents who produce off-shore

Figure 6.7 Strategy and R&D is often retained in Australia when some production goes offshore (percentage)
Source: McKinsey and Co. (1993), p. 33.

growth were the principal factors. This study also established that strategy, finance and research and development were the activities most likely to remain in the home company after the move offshore (Figure 6.7) (McKinsey and Co., 1993).

These findings were confirmed in a subsequent study of internationalizing small and medium enterprises. Of the respondents, 25 per cent had established offshore operations as part of their internationalizing strategy. Confirming other findings, the establishment of offshore operations was correlated with scale. Of the larger enterprises, (between 101 and 500 employees) 50 per cent had offshore operations versus 20 per cent of smaller operations (with up to 100 employees). Service sector MNEs were much less likely than manufacturers to establish operations offshore and advanced technology enterprises were most likely to go offshore. Southeast Asia and New Zealand were the most favoured locations (Department of Foreign Affairs and Trade, 1995).

In sum, there is clear evidence of increasing attention to regional opportunities by a wide range of enterprises in most size categories. So far as the multidomestics are concerned, recent evidence suggests a strong switch in focus to Asia (Bureau of Industry Economics, 1984). The extent to which declared investment intentions and actual investments will translate into a significant shift in the proportion of assets held in each region is unclear. Such data as are available suggest a shift is in progress. However, its precise impact on relative magnitudes has yet to be estimated.

Nevertheless the absolute magnitude of the investment amounts and their direction is strong evidence of a major shift in focus. This is reinforced by the scope of activities covered which extends across mining and resource projects, manufacturing, power and water, telecommunications, leisure and health sectors. In other words most sectors of the Australian economy have now at least some firms with considerable engagement in regional activity.

■ Australia as a regional headquarters

One other contributor to this change in focus might be noted. This is the government-led effort to have Australia adopted as a regional headquarters (RHQs) location. A variety of factors have stimulated this development. There are considerable cost advantages by comparison with other major regional cities. Australia's ethnic mix is unique in the region. For example, Sydney has 127 distinct ethnic groups represented in its population. People of Asian origin constitute the biggest immigrant group in Australia. Lifestyle and service facilities are highly developed. Although physical distances remain large, Australia is advantageously placed for regional time zones. Australia's management pay scales are also lower than for other major centres. Finally, Australia's federal and state governments have crafted packages of incentive measures (*Australian Financial Review*, 1995b; *Far Eastern Economic Review*, 1995b).

Reflecting Australia's socially and politically constructed advantages, firms adopting Australia appear to come from distinct sectors. By 1995, some 150 firms had been identified as establishing RHQs in Australia, thirty-one during the preceding twelve months (*Telegraph-Mirror*, 1995). Of these, approximately twenty were international Information Technology (IT) companies and a further twenty were involved in aspects of telecommunications. This reflects the size of the Australian domestic market relative to other regional states. For example, the Australian market is eight times as large as Singapore and the region's second largest after Japan. Further, Australia has the region's most deregulated telecommunications environment. Also, unlike Singapore and Hong Kong, all telecommunications providers can take advantage of the Pacific Rim east-west fibre optic cables.

The enterprises attracted include both Western and Asian firms. For example, the Hong Kong Jockey Club has selected Australia as the regional centre for its computer based data and support services. Guangzhou Television has established its international headquarters in Melbourne. Equally, for Western firms, the availability of Asian speakers has been cited as an advantage. For example, the US software firm Novell found Sydney to be one of the few centres where it could hire staff fluent in the eleven languages used in its operations in seventeen regional countries. The government has also used its own substantial IT procurement as an incentive to draw firms to Australia. For example, Olivetti established a regional headquarters under this scheme (Department of Industry, Science and Technology, 1995b).

Other examples of regional firms selecting to base key activities in Australia for reasons of costs or availability of skilled labour include the *Straits Times* (Singapore) which established a subediting department in Sydney at the end of 1994 (Harris, 1995).

In the processed foods area, Campbell Soup, Cadbury-Schweppes and Sara Lee have adopted Australia as a regional headquarters. Yet research in 1994 suggested Australia had a considerable distance to match Singapore and Hong Kong in the regional headquarters competition. These locations had attracted respectively 254 and 500 international firms (The Allen Consulting Group, 1994).

■ Regional business strategies

For business, a new orientation to Asia has presumably involved the development of new skills, organizational arrangements and strategic perspectives. There is clear evidence of the adoption of distinct regional strategies by major firms and of top management commitment to those strategies (Dalton, 1994). This is reflected, for example, in the growing practice of major firms convening board meetings at regional locations (Pheasant, 1995).

There has been no systematic research on firm level strategies beyond limited survey and case study work. Despite Australia's thirty-five business schools and at least seventeen university-based research centres focused on Asia, no scholarly studies by Australian business academics on any major organization, strategy, market entry or other issue affecting Australian companies operating in the Asian region could be identified.[4] Only one paper could be identified analysing the experience in a particular sector – this was an analysis of the causes of the relative lack of success of banks in their regional strategies (Cornell, 1994).

Evidence gathered in the various official reports suggests some of the strategic scenarios that might underlay investment in regional states (see, for example, Figure 6.6). So far as large manufacturers are concerned, the study by Yetton, Davis and Swan (1992) classifies most of Australia's firms as multi-domestics – that is they produce products for consumer markets that are not traded internationally, usually because of transport costs. As consumer markets have emerged in regional states, these firms have established a regional presence. This explains the strategies adopted by, for example, the steel group BHP Co. Ltd or the building products groups CSR and Boral. Boral, for example, has segmented regional opportunities into four categories: frontier countries reliant on world aid and without the necessary economic growth to be self-sustaining; industrializing countries; mature countries; and those that are compelling because of size (Figure 6.8). It has developed distinct strategies for its desired segments. For example, Boral is market leader in concrete in Indonesia. With an annual rate of growth of 25 per cent there are substantial capital implications. To stay market leader Boral estimated further investment of $100 to $150 million would be required over five years. The operational implications are also considerable covering the development of staff to operate equipment, run accounting systems and so forth (Boyd, 1995).

The need to be close to customers also governs investment in many service sectors. For example, the health-care division of Mayne Nickless has formulated a regional strategy whose initial elements include the establishment of several private hospitals in Indonesia and Malaysia. Lend Lease, an insurance, financial services and construction conglomerate, has signed a $70 million design and construction contract in Jakarta, is planning to market information services in China and plans a joint venture to enter Indonesia's emerging pensions sector. Other major Australian or Australian-based insurance firms, AMP, Legal and General, GIO, QBE and National Mutual, have already established joint ventures in Indonesia (Condon, 1994; Porter, 1995).

The food processing sector has been identified as a major opportunity in official reports (Australian Agri-Food Industries, 1992; Button, 1988; Griffiths, 1992). Here distinctive consumer tastes often require the establishment of facilities to serve local markets. For example, firms such as Burns Philp and Goodman Fielder have well-developed regional strategies, involving investment in yeast and bread-making facilities. The former company has established operations in China and Malaysia and is

---

[4] This conclusion is based on a survey of the Australian Public Affairs Information Services database.

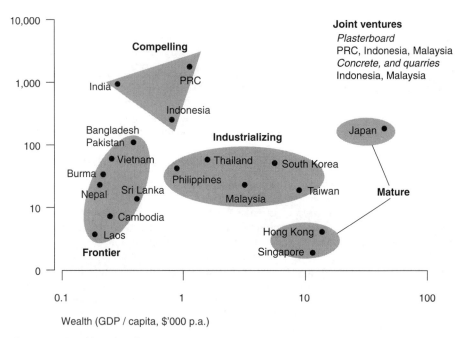

Figure 6.8 Boral's regional strategy
Source: Boral Ltd, Corporate Office, Sydney.

considering India, Vietnam, Thailand and the Philippines. Goodman Fielder has established baking and milling operations in Singapore and Malaysia. Coca-Cola-Amatil, a snack food producer and franchise bottler, has extensive operations in Indonesia. However, the Australian share of the processed foods markets in Asia declined in the six years from 1986–87 to 1992–93. The relationship between establishing offshore operations and processed food exports has not systematically been explored (Armitage, 1994).

There is now a considerable management community focused on, and preoccupied by, markets and operations in regional states. The primary engine of regional economic development – participation in world trade in manufactures – is not an area in which Australian firms figure. As noted earlier, they are typically oriented to consumer and industrial markets in individual regions or countries. The burgeoning requirements for telecommunications and other infrastructure by regional states and the growth of 'secondary' markets (e.g. building products, processed foods, services) will ensure the continued attractiveness of the region to Australian based firms. Their progressively deeper engagement will be driven by the key success factor – the need to stay close to customers.

▨ Policy implications

This new orientation by Australian firms has a number of implications for both business and government. From a public policy perspective, this development vindicates government's judgement that the Asian region is the sector of major opportunity (see, for example, Keating, 1995). The Australian government has been active in an array of regional multilateral and bilateral forums, most visibly in APEC, and that effort is demonstrably consistent with the concerns of Australian business.

Yet the speed with which business interest has developed and the pace of investment are not reflected in conclusions of the officially sponsored reports reviewing Australia's economic relations with the region. This raises an immediate issue about the scanning processes adopted by the official research bureaus. Since they are the source of strategic policy advice, their failure to incorporate available data in recent reports is a cause for concern.

While there is clear evidence of a switch in focus by business, the absence of benchmarks for market or country shares, or even routine comparative data, makes tracking relative performance very difficult. There is no routine comparative data on investment shares of particular product/market segments. There is not even systematic data on export performance in particular segments. Most published data compare present developments to historic performance. In this perspective, growth rates are invariably favourable. The more telling tests – comparative performance or performance against targets – remain to be applied. That these numbers may be less congenial is clear in earlier discussion of regional processed foods markets. In another example, the Construction Industry Development Association determined Australia's market share of the estimated $1.4 billion Asian infrastructure market was significantly lower than that of Japan, US and EU-based firms when taking into account the comparative size of each country's construction sector (Williams, 1994).

The processes through which government seeks to promote internationalization in general, and regional opportunities in particular, may also merit more attention. At least in the late 1980s, there appeared to be a marked lag between general corporate expectations and attitudes about regional opportunities and impediments, and the experience of firms actually so engaged. One key issue concerned the relative profitability of operations in different regions. Some firms investing in the USA and UK suggested they did so because they anticipated lower profitability from regional operations. These perceptions were not matched by outcomes. Published data on Australia's top 1000 companies for 1991 showed subsidiaries in Asia earning higher returns than those in any other region (Bureau of Industry Economics, 1995a, pp. 24–25; Port Jackson Partners Limited, 1992). Similarly, perceptions of the difficulties of dealing in Asia were not shared by those actually engaged in both Asian and non-Asian locations. According to a 1992 survey, only 14 per cent of companies actually involved in Southeast Asian markets felt they were more difficult than other international markets in which they had experience (East Asia Analytical Unit, 1994).

Such attitudes are, at least in part, politically constructed. This occurs through the process I have described elsewhere as 'political learning'. (On the idea of political learning, the role of the state in constructing expectations and attitudes at the level of a policy community and mobilizing its members for action see Marsh, 1995, especially Chapter 9.) In the present case, the 'learning' is at the policy community level – but it is a very large and diverse policy community embracing most business sectors and, at least in the first instance, potentially perhaps most firms. For example, both the McKinsey report on SME exporters and the LEK report on services exporters note the large number of firms who might be mobilized to engage in international activities.[5] There are some remarkable success stories – but successful firms constitute only a small proportion of the potential pool. The conditions and requirements for such learning and mobilization are complex and cover both the generation of relevant information and, no less important, modes of dissemination and mobilization. One recent official report also attributes key importance to such activities. These are cited as key elements in 'constructing' corporate attitudes and expectations (East Asia Analytical Unit, 1994, p.2). It remains to be seen if the government's own currently preferred strategy, networking, will prove adequate to the task (Bureau of Industry Economics, 1995b).

In trade relations it remains to be seen if the new conservative government will continue to emphasize multilateralism in trade negotiations. John Ravenhill has explored the very great obstacles to sustaining APEC momentum (see, for example, Bernard and Ravenhill, 1995; Ravenhill, 1996). One potential area of regional trade tension involves technology. For those states anxious to increase their technological autonomy (Taiwan, Singapore, Korea), tension can be anticipated between the interventions and restrictions involved in the development of domestic capacity and external pressures for market liberalization; similarly, the states reliant on foreign investment (Malaysia, Thailand and Indonesia, for example) may trade greater commitment to increased domestic research and development against market liberalization. In general, APEC's rhetoric has been conducted, and its agenda fabricated, from the perspective of neo-classical economic orthodoxy. Yet a different model of economic development has guided the practice of most regional states. Further, the more complex relationships between states and firms that characterize contemporary economic life have also to be accommodated (see, for example, Strange, 1992). All these factors inhibit the prospects for trade liberalization. They may also create opportunities for bilateral linkage. For example, there may be scope to extend Australia's security relationship with Indonesia to an economic front, perhaps on the model of the Closer Economic Relations (CER) treaty with New Zealand.

This new orientation to regional countries by Australian-based firms also has considerable implications for managers. Four reports have surveyed management experience (Port Jackson Partners Limited, 1992; McKinsey and Co., 1993; LEK Partnership, 1994; Department of Foreign Affairs and Trade, 1995). They identified a number of success requirements. The strongest common finding concerned the need for chief executive commitment. This was true irrespective of whether the firm was an exporter or investor, or whether it was a multidomestic or an SME. Of chief executives of SMEs which grew faster than 15 per cent per annum, 35 per cent spent more than 40 per cent of their time on regional matters compared with 13 per cent of the leaders of firms growing at less than 15 per cent (McKinsey and Co., 1993, p.18). Multidomestics faced additional organizational issues. Most had adopted a 'line of business' structure. Managers were assigned global responsibilities for business development. For regional activity, a geographic dimension was then added. For example, Pacific Dunlop, a conglomerate, obliged its line of business managers to draw on the help of a sixty-person (in 1992) services group based in Hong Kong. This group embodied accumulated regional experience in structuring joint ventures, taxation and finance. Others created regional divisions – for example, Boral: a concrete and plasterboard manufacturer.

[5] Only 10 per cent of manufacturing firms and just over 1 per cent of service firms are exporters (McKinsey and Co., 1993, p. 38; LEK Partnership, 1994, p. 42).

Other steps taken by larger organizations to build regional experience included establishing local advisory boards. Successful firms also stressed the need to select staff carefully – typically, they posted only volunteers and ensured expatriate managers possessed appropriate personal qualities, such as flexibility, openness and a relaxed style. A number of larger firms also attached importance to their ability to develop local staff by progressively bringing groups to Australia to gain operational experience. For example, both ICI Explosives and the Mars group followed this practice (Port Jackson Partners Limited, 1992, pp.44-45). The reports also trace the major phases in progressively deeper regional business engagement – for example, in the transition from an opportunistic to strategic exporting and then to 'insider' status. Differences in corporate culture are noted as potential points of tension if insider status is achieved through a joint venture. For example, in the pyramid structure of Chinese enterprises, profits are typically taken in the privately owned entities and losses, if they occur, apportioned to its publicly listed components (Port Jackson Partners Limited, 1992, pp. 45). In general, where joint venture was selected as the entry strategy, respondents stressed the need to retain control of key elements, such as brands and technology. Based on major company experience, one report recommends adopting what it termed 'an iterative phased approach to unfold a business over a long time frame' with joint venture as a step on the way to a wholly owned subsidiary. Both this report, and a later study of internationalized SMEs, stress the need to gain control of customers as the key success factor. For example, in one survey over 70 per cent of respondents identified attention to customer needs as the most important source of sustained success. Management skills scored next (35 per cent), followed by knowledge of competitors (28 per cent) (Department of Foreign Affairs and Trade, 1995, p. 42).

The reorientation of Australian business to the region is a another reflection of the historic change of focus progressively occurring at many levels of Australian society, away from Europe and America towards a more independent stance and in closer association with neighbouring states in Asia. The increasingly intimate engagement of Australian business with neighbouring states is very important in its own right, and a very important harbinger of broader national aspirations and interests. National borders are of decreasing significance for economic activity and the links being forged between Australia's economic destiny and that of her neighbours are consonant with her wider economic and political interests and social realities. The significance of this development is as great, if not greater, on the political and security, as on the economic, level. The regional security outlook is very uncertain, to say the least (Dibb, 1995). In this context, Australia's economic presence attests to her regional bona fides and adds weight and credibility to her more complex political and security engagements.

■ Conclusions

One notable omission from the above list of economic engagements by Australian business is Japan. Yet one seasoned observer, James Abbeglen, suggests a Japan strategy as the centrepiece of a regional strategy. This is because of the size and maturity of this market and the liberalizing developments that ever so slowly are occurring (Abbeglen, 1994, p. 45). Australian firms have yet to enter this consumer market on any scale. The causes of their reluctance would seem to invite further analysis.

There is a variety of operational issues of shared concern between companies – for example, recruitment, training, technology transfer, alliances, requirements for expatriate staff, accounting standards and other protocols, experience with labour relations. The absence of routine, systematic comparative data is surely to be regretted. Similarly, the articulation of business trade, political and security concerns and their linkage to official negotiations seems underdeveloped.

In particular, the apparent lack of attention to issues of business strategy, human resource management, organization and operations from a business perspective by any of Australia's management academics is surely of concern. The research community seems to be operating at some remove from its primary constituency. Yet the emerging Asian business environment is one of the few areas where Australian scholarly research might enjoy comparative advantage. For example, in a more plural world, the two most dynamic, but non-Anglo-American, varieties of capitalism – Japanese and Chinese – have been sired by regional cultures (see, for example, Imae and Komiya, 1994; Reading, 1990). There are novel, emerging patterns of regional, sub-regional and national markets. Complex managerial challenges embracing such areas as strategy, networking, production, logistics, distribution, organization, marketing, human resource development, and information management are associated with regional activity. At the level of the implications for management training and development, particularly in Master of Business Administration (MBA) programmes, there also appears to be a marked divergence between reputable commentators (Carter, 1995; Yetton and Craig, 1995).

The lack of comparative data at a product/market or country level has already been referred to. While the scale of Australia's switch is great in historic terms, it is not yet clear that it is sufficient to meet national needs for foreign earnings. In this context, the failure to monitor the public policies which have delivered such spectacular success to regional states seems a major omission. Taiwan for example has an industry structure somewhat similar to Australia's. Where is the analysis of the strategies used by the Taiwanese government to mobilize its SME sector for export – a process at which it has been demonstrably successful? The derision accompanying discussion of industrial policies in regional states in some official quarters is surely to be regretted.

There is another reason to more fully document and monitor the reorientation of Australian business to Asia. The 2000 Olympics in Sydney will produce a unique level of international publicity. What image of economic capacity and business performance will be projected to the world? The evidence assembled here suggests there is a new story to be told about Australia's emerging regional orientation, with the activities of business buttressed by, and complementing, other trends in Australian politics and society. There is also a new story to be told about Australia's potential as a 'bridge' between East and West, in both directions. Yet if these messages are to be communicated, they must first be adequately documented. So much appears to be happening, at such a fast rate, on so many fronts, that a more sustained monitoring and research effort would seem to be required.

References

Abbeglen, J. (1994). *Sea Change: Pacific Asia as the New World Industrial Centre*, The Free Press.
Access Economics (1996). *Quarterly Investment Monitor*, February. Access Economics, Melbourne.
Armitage, C. (1994). Let them eat bread – and lamingtons. *Sydney Morning Herald*, 28 February.

Australian Agri-Food Industries (1992). Joint Statement by Ministers for Industry, Technology and Commerce and Primary Industries and Energy, 19 July.

Australian Financial Review (1994). Australia is No. 3 investor in Vietnam, 24 November 1994.

Australian Financial Review (1995a). 16 August 1995.

Australian Financial Review (1995b). Australia top choice for IT regional bases, 4 January 1995, p.3

Bernard, M. and Ravenhill, J. (1995). Beyond product cycles and flying geese. *World Politics*, January, 171–209.

Blainey, G. (1993). *The Rush that Never Ended: A History of Australian Mining* (4th edn). Melbourne University Press.

Boyd, T. (1995). Boral cemented its Asian future. *Australian Financial Review*, 8 August.

Brewster, D. (1995). Despite the risks, Telstra sees big rewards offshore. *The Australian*, 1 August, p. 61.

Bureau of Industry Economics (1984). *Australian Direct Investment Abroad: Effects on the Australian Economy*. Research Report 14, Canberra.

Bureau of Industry Economics (1994) *Australian Investment Abroad Survey*. Australian Government Publishing Service.

Bureau of Industry Economics (1995a). *Investment Abroad by Australian Companies: Issues and Implications*. Report 95/19, October. Australian Government Publishing Service.

Bureau of Industry Economics (1995b). Beyond the firm: an assessment of business linkages and networks in Australia., *Research Report No. 67*, Australian Government Publishing Service.

Button, J. (1988). Information Industries Strategy. Ministerial Statement, 27 September, Department of Industry, Technology and Commerce.

Carter, C. (1995). The Australian manager of the twenty-first century. *Enterprising Nation, Renewing Australia's Managers to Meet the Challenges of the Asia-Pacific Century*, vol. 2, pp. 1223–89. Research Report, Australian Government Publishing Service.

Condon, T. (1994). Lend lease opens duplicate front in Asia. *Australian Financial Review*, 3 August.

Cornell, A. (1994). Australian success in Asia limited by inexperience. *Australian Financial Review*, 7 January.

Cornell, A. (1994). CBA revs up its Asian advance. *Australian Financial Review*, 23 February.

Dalton, T. (1994). *Building a Successful Strategy for Asia, Lessons from Leading Australian Companies*. International Market Assessments.

Department of Foreign Affairs and Trade (1995). *Winning Enterprises: How Australia's Small and Medium Enterprises Compete in Global Markets*. Australian Government Publishing Service.

Department of Industry, Science and Technology (1995a). *Australia: Your Strategic Investment Location*, Department of Industry, Science and Technology.

Department of Industry, Science and Technology (1995b). Olivetti in Canberra agreement. *Australian Financial Review*, 14 September.

Dibb, P. (1995). *Towards a New Balance of Power in Asia*. Oxford University Press.

East Asia Analytical Unit (1994). *Changing Tack: Australian Investment in South East Asia*, p. 17. Department of Foreign Affairs and Trade.

Edwards, J. (1996). *Paul Keating*. Penguin Books.

Far Eastern Economic Review (1995a). Rags to riches, 12 October, 45–124.

Far Eastern Economic Review (1995b). Australia beckons as a regional headquarters, 5 January, p. 92.

Goodman, D. and Robison, R. (eds) (1995*). The New Rich in Asia: Mobile Phones, McDonald's and Middle Class Revolution.* Asia Research Centre, Murdoch University.

Griffiths, A. (1992). Tourism: Australia's passport to growth, a national tourism strategy. Ministerial Statement, 5 June.

Harris, M. (1995). Australia's middle class sweat shop. *Sydney Morning Herald,* 18 November.

Imae, K. and Komiya, R. (1994). *Business Enterprise in Japan: Views of Leading Economists* (R. Dore and H. Whittaker, trans. and intro.). The MIT Press.

Keating, P. J., Hon., MP (1995). Australia, Asia and the New Regionalism, The Singapore Lecture, 17 January.

LEK Parternship (1994). *Intelligent Exports,* Australian Trade Commission, p. 42.

Lewis, S. (1995). Telstra in $460m Indonesian venture. *Australian Financial Review,* 18 December.

Marsh, I. (1995). *Beyond the Two Party System: Political Representation, Economic Competitiveness and Australian Politics,* Cambridge University Press.

McKinsey and Co. (1993). *Emerging Exporters: Australia's High Value-added Manufacturing Exporters.* Australian Manufacturing Council.

Pappas, Carter, Evans and Koop/Telesis (1990). *The Global Challenge,* p. 133. Australian Manufacturing Council.

Pheasant, B. (1995). Boards go on the overseas trail to track their assets. *Australian Financial Review,* 26 June.

Port Jackson Partners Limited (1992). *Australian Business in Asia: Climbing the Mountains,* p. 19. Business Council of Australia.

Porter, I. (1995). Health care invests in Indonesia hospitals. *Australian Financial Review,* 31 July.

Price Waterhouse (1995a). *Locating Your Regional Headquarters in Australia: Government Incentives.*

Price Waterhouse (1995b). *Survey of Investment Intentions,* Melbourne, May.

Ravenhill, J. (1996). Trade policy options beyond APEC. *Australian Quarterly,* **68** (2), 1–17.

Reading, S. G. (1990). *The Spirit of Chinese Capitalism.* De Gruyter.

Shann, E. (1994). Our industry pushes out to the world. *Business Review Weekly,* 14 February.

Strange, S. (1992). States, firms and diplomacy. *International Affairs,* **68** (1), 1–15.

Sturgiss, R. (1995). Australian Investment in Asia. *International Trade Papers.* Department of Foreign Affairs and Trade.

Tan, Y. K. (1992). Emerging economic and social realities in East Asia: some implications for Australian business and public policy. *Australian Journal of Management,* **17** (1), June.

Telegraph-Mirror (1995). Sydney is top foreign dollar lure, 6 November 1995.

The Allen Consulting Group (1994). *The Benefits of Regional Headquarters and Factors Influencing Location in Australia.* A report to the Department of Industry, Science and Technology and the National Investment Committee, Melbourne, March.

The World Bank (1993). *The East Asian Miracle, Economic Growth and Public Policy.* Oxford University Press.

Tower, G. (ed.) (1995). Australian business in the United Kingdom, Thailand and Malaysia: a comparative study. *Asian Pacific International Business: Regional Integration and Global Competitiveness*. Proceedings of Academy of International Business Conference, 20–23 June, pp. 405–10.

Wade, R. (1990). *Governing the Market: The Role of the State in East Asian Industrialisation*. Princeton University Press.

Weiss, L. and Hobson, J. (1995). *States and Economic Development: A Comparative, Historical Analysis*. Polity Press.

Williams, L.(1994). The need for a competitive edge. *Sydney Morning Herald*, 3 March.

Yetton, P. and Craig, J. (1995). Skills for international operations: a uniquely Australian perspective *Enterprising Nation, Renewing Australia's Managers to Meet the Challenges of the Asia-Pacific Century*, vol. 2, pp. 1349–95. Research Report, Australian Government Publishing Service.

Yetton, P., Davis, J. and Swan, P. (1992). *Going International: Export Myths and Strategic Realities*, Australian Manufacturing Council.

Characteristics of Australia's post-crisis orientation towards Asia

■ Ian Marsh ■

The data and analysis reported in Chapter 6 relate to the period up to 1996. The financial crisis of 1997 has supervened. The full implications of this development have yet to unfold (eg. Dibb, Hale and Prince, 1998; Grenville, 1998; Wade, forthcoming 1999). But available data already provide evidence of (natural) investor caution and uncertainty. This is clear in data concerning investor plans (Access Economics, 1998). In the twelve months to 30 June 1998, the total of new overseas investment projects reported by Australian-based firms was $104 billion. This covered projects in four categories: under construction, committed, under consideration and possible.

The Asian region remained the major focus of interest with 45 per cent of the funds destined for this geographic area. Further, infrastructure, which accounted for 47 per cent of funds, remained the major area of activity. Mining, which accounted for 30 per cent of funds, was the next largest category. Transport and communications (15 per cent) was third and manufacturing (8 per cent) fourth. The reduction in manufacturing investment was at least partly a response to the decline of regional consumer and construction markets.

The impact of the financial crisis was even clearer in the phases assigned to investment plans: 79 per cent of the funds allocated to the Asian region were for projects classified as under consideration or possible. The long lead times associated with infrastructure and mining projects are clearly one relevant consideration. But caution arising from the crisis is also a factor. Only approximately 10 per cent of projects were under construction, with a further 10 per cent classified as committed. Nevertheless, of the total of projects under construction in 1997–98, 31 per cent remained in the Asian region.

In sum, the evidence suggests the orientation to Asia continues. But the crisis has naturally had a significant impact on the immediate commitment of investment funds. Early stabilization would doubtless result in the renewal of investment flows and the transition of projects from planning to implementation phases. Other circumstances might produce other outcomes. For example, scenarios for the future anticipate a variety of possible reverses (e.g. a second round of competitive devaluations triggered by a drop in the yuan, an Indonesian implosion or, in the worst case, a Japanese deflation). Any of these developments could be expected to delay new investment still further; indeed, in the worst case they might begin to reverse at least some of the orientations seeded so strongly this past decade.

■ References

Access Economics (1998). *Investment Monitor*, (34), June

Dibb, P., Hale, D. and Prince, P. (1998). The strategic implications of Asia's economic crisis. *Survival*, **40** (2), Summer, 5–27

Grenville, S. (1998). The Asia crisis, capital flows and the international financial architecture. *Occasional Paper*, Reserve Bank of Australia, Sydney May

Wade, R. (forthcoming 1999). Gestalt shift: from 'miracle' to 'cronyism' in the Asian crisis. *Cambridge Journal of Economics*

Part Two
Local stakeholders' concerns

Chapter 7

Moral consideration and strategic management moves: the Chinese case[1]

■ Kam-hon Lee ■

■ Business and business ethics

The Chinese constitute a formidable economic force in the Asia Pacific region. (Hong Kong and Taiwan are Chinese societies as is, of course, the moving giant, China.) Although Japan has been widely recognized as the economic power house in Asia, according to the latest available statistics in August 1995, in terms of purchasing power parity, per capita gross domestic product (GDP) of Hong Kong (US$22 527) was already greater than that of Japan (US$21 328). Again, in terms of purchasing power parity, GDP of China (US$3172 billion) was already greater than that of Japan (US$2662 billion) (*Asiaweek*, 1995). In addition, the ethnic Chinese in other Asian countries are also influential economically. This includes the economic strength of Singapore, Malaysia, Philippines, Indonesia and Thailand. The key players in the economic activities in these countries have also been ethnic Chinese. According to an Australian Government study of Overseas Chinese entrepreneurs, ethnic Chinese had replaced Japan as Asia's prime source of capital (East Asia Analytical Unit, 1995). Thus, in order to manage business operations effectively in the Asia Pacific region, it is imperative to understand the Chinese way to run business.

This chapter first affirms the nature of business and the importance of ethics in business transactions. Then, this chapter attempts to point out that moral considerations in China have evolved along a unique path, which carries a significant impact on the Chinese way to conduct business.

Ethics is the study of standards of conduct and moral judgement. According to the Chinese philosophical tradition, truth cannot be obtained based purely on detached and objective studies. Rather, truth has to be experienced and learned through one's

[1] This project is supported by the Research Grants Council Earmarked Grant CUHK 142/94H, University Grants Committee, Hong Kong. The author would like to thank Dr Usha Haley, the guest editor, and two anonymous reviewers for their helpful comments on an earlier draft of this article. This chapter has been published previously by MCB University Press Limited: Lee, K.-H. (1996). Moral consideration and strategic management moves: the Chinese case. *Management Decision*, **34** (9), 65–70.

life. Thus, for the Chinese, ethics refers to the proper way to relate to one another (Chen, 1994). This contention has support from China's business history and current business practices in China and overseas. Finally, this chapter suggests advice that business executives can use to understand doing business better in China.

In business, the fundamental external strategic management move is to make a business deal. The fundamental internal strategic management move is to hire business associates. In business, the buyer gets the goods and gives up the money, and the seller gives up the goods and gets the money. To the buyer, the goods are more treasured than the money. To the seller, the money is more treasured than the goods. Thus, every transaction, when properly done, brings blessing to the buyer and to the seller. The seller has the profit and the buyer has consumer surplus. When the buyer and the seller are both better off, and when others in the society are not affected, the whole society is better off. This justifies the existence of the buyer–seller relationship. When one is talking about buying and selling in the labour market, one may draw a similar conclusion for the employer–employee relationship.

Business itself is something ethical because it is meant to bring blessing to both the buyer and the seller. People may make mistakes, and they may not be able to benefit from a particular business transaction. However, these are the exceptions rather than the rule. In the mean time, when people involved in business transactions are ethical, it is likely that the transactions will become more cost-effective, and thus more profitable. Thus, good ethics means good business.

However, it is also true that in business, it is more likely that people will become less ethical. The temptation there is just much greater.

In business, it is generally agreed that we should create a bigger pie. The bigger, the better. However, the first ethical difficulty is that there is no general agreement with respect to the way to divide the pie. In theory, both parties can have a legitimate claim to have a bigger share at the expense of the other party, depending on the persuasion to which one subscribes. A second difficulty arises because the business situation is very dynamic. A practice which is proper in one situation can be totally improper in another situation. One good example is infant-formula selling in the Third World, which is regarded as signing the death certificate for the infant. A third difficulty arises from the fact that not all parties are equally powerful. The more knowledgeable and financially powerful giants usually can negotiate more effectively and get better deals. It is tempting for the more powerful to rationalize and claim that he is making a greater contribution and thus deserves more. A fourth difficulty is that, in the course of time, unconsciously and subconsciously one may absorb and adopt in life a money orientation. One can become cool and cold towards others. One may inherit the face of a miser rather than a steward. Thus, ethics is inherent in business deals. In a way, business can be regarded as a moral phenomenon (Donaldson, 1989).

■ Chinese emphasis on moral considerations

The Chinese tradition is to depend on moral considerations to conclude a profitable business deal and to ensure that the business deal will be enforced. One can find support in China's history, Overseas Chinese management practices and business practices in China nowadays.

A macro-historical review

A proper starting point is to take a macro-historical review (Lee, 1983) to understand the rationale behind the regulatory environment of today. For China, the policies the emperors adopted in different dynasties did matter. In reviewing the chronological development, one would conclude that back in ancient times the significance of business activities was duly recognized. It seems that in the Age of Five Rulers, all people would participate in production activities, and would be involved in the exchange process and gain in commercial activities. The situation changed when people started to specialize in commercial activities. In general, one could observe that merchants carried several significant characteristics in comparison with peasants. These were: merchants could get rich much more quickly; they were mobile; they were influential because of their wealth; they were much smaller in number in the total population; it was much more difficult to ensure a proper conduct in the commercial activities.

During the Warring States Period, the Ch'in Dynasty rewarded the peasants and penalized the merchants because peasants could serve as soldiers and agricultural produce was an important food supply for survival during the warring period. Peasants could not move, and they would be loyal. Merchants, on the contrary, were rich and hesitant to join fighting. Also, they could easily leave the country because they were mobile. Thus, it was understandable that Ch'in would promote the peasant and suppress the merchant. Finally, Ch'in won the war.

The concerns of Han and all subsequent dynasties basically centred on achieving 'equality' among all groups of people, and on counterbalancing power so that government would not be threatened. This analysis basically was applicable in all periods where there were no civil wars. On the one hand, government recognized that commercial activities were significant in economic affairs and they tried to preserve the best operating environment for them. They prevented government officials from taking bribes and from intervening in the commercial activities. They also tried to establish a sound monitoring system to regulate commercial malpractice. On the other hand, government tried to ensure two things: there was a sense of 'equality' between the merchants and the peasants; and the merchants would not be so influential as to threaten the government.

Since merchants were already wealthy, materially powerful and enviable, they should be deprived of privileges of some other kind, so that a sense of 'equality' would be in the people's mind. If it were successful, peasants would be willing to stay as peasants, and would not want to become merchants. If there were too many merchants, and there were very few peasants, there would be economic turmoil. The Han Dynasty and subsequent dynasties basically adopted the following two measures:

1 Merchants were not allowed to wear silk, and they were not allowed to ride on carts. This measure might also have a function of inflation control, since silk may have been in short supply and the merchants were so rich that their strong demand might raise the market price sky high and cause inflation. However, whether or not this measure carried the function of inflation control, this measure was certainly important in according social status.

2 Merchants, their children and their grandchildren were not allowed to become government officials. This measure would have prevented the merchants from having both economic and political power. On the one hand, the government would not be

threatened. On the other hand, it opened up a channel for the peasants to have upward social mobility. This hope could sustain the peasants so that they would not mind suffering materially.

Basically, these measures would strike a delicate balance among all groups of people in the society. Since the image of businessmen remained low, business people throughout the centuries had the aspiration to become scholars. There was also an urge to conduct business in a scholarly way.

The ten great merchant guilds in China

Business became quite well developed in China during the Ming and Ching Dynasties. Chung Hwa Book Publisher published in 1995 ten volumes on ten respective merchant guilds in China in the Ming and Ching Dynasties (Chang and Chang, 1995), and a total of twenty-one historians participated in this project.

Although they were called merchants, they were involved in all kinds of business activities, including manufacturing, retailing and financing. They became, in fact, the middleman who was the captain of the marketing channel. The captain directed and shaped all business activities from manufacturing to retailing. The captain took part directly in the most strategic business activities (e.g. in the old days, wholesaling), and indirectly influenced others in those which were less strategic ones (e.g. in the old days, manufacturing and retailing).

In six of the ten volumes, there are extensive descriptions about how much these merchants treasured business ethics. For Ninbao merchants, the leading trait in business operation was to 'use sincerity to gain trust'. For Shandong merchants and Shanxi merchants, the common trait in business operation was to treasure Shun Yung (credibility). Zhangxi merchants were famous for their business conduct and their sense of justice. Lungyao merchants treasured fair deals, even for children and old people. In addition, they constantly improved their own cultural and moral development.

Among the ten great merchant guilds, two were especially outstanding. They were the Feizhou merchants and Shanxi merchants. These two groups were most thorough in the pursuit of business ethics. Feizhou is the county of Chu Xi, a great Confucian scholar in the late Sung Dynasty where Confucian thought had been quite influential. For Feizhou inhabitants, some engaged in business first and later became scholars. Others were first scholars and later became merchants. Still others were scholars who were at the same time involved in business. The motivation to become a merchant was profit. The motivation to become a scholar was to have fame. In general, for Feizhou inhabitants, their first love was to become a scholar and have fame. Only when they could not make it would they become merchants. After they had accumulated wealth, they would make use of it to advocate scholarship advancement. Their ultimate motive was to study hard and become a government official in order to bring honour and fame to themselves and their families. The Feizhou merchants had the concepts of Yu Ku (a merchant with the spirit of a Confucian scholar) and Ku Yu (a Confucian scholar with a merchant orientation). They would rather have become Yu Ku than Ku Yu. The Confucian ethical stand manifests in:

- being sincere towards others (i.e. no deception and always seeking for mutual benefits)

- being trustworthy in handling transactions (i.e. treasuring one's credibility)

- taking righteousness as profits (i.e. treasuring righteousness more than profitability)

- being grounded on kindness (i.e. being kind to others and not taking advantages when others are having crises).

For Shanxi merchants, since they were running financial operations, they treasured even more the conduct of their employees. They used different methods to try their workers. They wanted to find out their subordinates' qualities along nine dimensions. These included: being truthful; being respectful; being competent; being intelligent; being trustworthy; being honest; having integrity; being disciplined; and staying away from sexual affairs.

They would give different assignments to try out their workers' qualities. When one was far away, one could easily deceive the superior. Thus, the superior would ask the subordinate to take up an assignment far away in order to see whether the subordinate would remain truthful. When the subordinate and the superior were close, it would be easy for the subordinate to feel intimate and become impolite. Thus, the superior would create opportunities to allow the subordinate to become close in order to see whether the subordinate would remain respectful. When things were complicated they would be difficult to handle. Thus, it became appropriate to assign complicated, tough tasks to find out whether the subordinate was competent. When there were situations where there was no way out, they would be difficult to defend and find a solution. Thus, it became prudent to ask the subordinate to find a solution in such a situation and find out whether the subordinate was intelligent. When one had to complete a task in a short period of time, it would be difficult to keep one's promise. Thus, the superior could give an assignment with a short notice and see if the subordinate remained trustworthy. When one was entrusted a lot of money, one would easily become greedy. Thus, the superior could entrust to the subordinate a lot of money to find out whether the subordinate was honest. When one was facing a crisis situation, one would be tempted to make a change and leave. Thus, the superior could put the subordinate in a crisis situation and see if the subordinate still had integrity. When one stayed with a job for too long, it would be easy to become lazy. Thus, the superior could assign the subordinate to a post and ask him to stay there for two years. By so doing, one could see whether the subordinate was disciplined. When one was mixing with people from different social backgrounds, one would easily become entrenched in adultery. Thus, the superior could send the subordinate to a prosperous city and see if the subordinate could stay away from sexual temptation. Out of nine dimensions, seven are related to the subordinates' ethical stands.

Overseas Chinese business practice

In the Overseas Chinese society, businessmen take the verbal promise seriously. Even if there are no legal documents, they respect and honour the verbal promise. If somebody does not respect and honour the promise, word spreads around and nobody wants to have any more business deals with him. This becomes an effective measure to ensure that business transactions can be done in a highly cost-effective manner. This is one secret of success in the Overseas Chinese business community. Let me cite one example. Cheng Yu-tung was a world-class entrepreneur and a business leader in Hong Kong. According to Cheng, his secret of success can be summarized in twenty-three Chinese characters. The English translation reads as follows: 'Preserve your credibility. Keep your promise. Be diligent. Be cautious. Honour those who have helped you before. Do not sell righteousness for profits'. One can see the importance of ethics in his wisdom and advice (Cheng, 1993). When one reviews the development of Chinese banking in Southeast Asia, one can also see the importance of ethics in business dealings. The foreign and international banks depended on professional management and a system approach to identify potential customers and screen customers for bank loans and other business transactions. There were a lot of personnel changes there, and they did not bother Chinese bankers who, on the other hand, depended on their long-time participation in the local communities to know and identify clients. Their relationships also enabled them to assess whether the people they encountered were dependable and good clients. The emphasis on personal connection and personal assessment of others as a person, becomes a unique feature of running one's business (Nyaw and Chang, 1989). This emphasis quite naturally also leads to an inclination to have family organization and management, and ethnic ties in business transactions.

China business

China is now eye-catching. China is a giant moving. When one reviews business dealings in China, one can see similar emphasis on personal relationship and ethical consideration. The most important source of foreign investment for China is Hong Kong. Most of the Hong Kong investment goes to the Pearl River Delta. When one listens to the investment stories, many times, people go back to their counties, and they have a good working relationship. There are many rules and regulations which are not fully comprehended. There may be new rules and regulations coming up from time to time. The assurance of prudent investment comes from an assessment of personal connection. The investors can trust the integrity as well as the competence and influence of the partners in China. When they feel comfortable with the connection, they can put their factories there (Radio Television Hong Kong TV Programme, 23 January 1994).

The same is true for the multinational corporations (MNCs). Strictly speaking, most of them did not have a serious start until three years ago. In order to do it successfully, MNCs had to make use of the Chinese connections. According to a survey among global executives reported in November 1994, Hong Kong was chosen as the world's best city for business. The major reason for Hong Kong's ranking was that Hong Kong was recognized as the business gateway to China. In Hong Kong, there were a large number of people who could open a variety of doors for China business for different business partners in the world (Saporito, 1994). For those who team up with a Hong Kong conglomerate, they depend on the Hong Kong partner to provide personal connections to open the doors in China. P&G had tremendous success in their China operations (Kahn, 1995). They had as their partner Hutchison Whampoa Ltd, which Li Ka-shing owned. For those who do it on their own, they still have to identify the old China hands who have dependable and powerful connections. Basically, it goes back to the same mode of assessing one's competence and integrity (for example, Coca-Cola and Pepsi-Cola can represent these two modes: see Seet and Yoffee, 1995).

While Chinese put a lot of emphasis on personal integrity, China today is routinely classified as one of the most corrupt countries in Asia (Political and Economic Risk Consultancy Ltd, 1996). These two phenomona, although seemingly contradictory, can coexist. Corruption refers to an act which violates the formal rules of a public office for the sake of private gain. The source of power comes from the absolute authority of the government office. The opportunity to corrupt grows together with economic prosperity and business opportunities. When the renumeration package for government officials remains low and rigid, corruption becomes more likely. Personal integrity refers to the way people relate to one another. For the sake of making a distinction, it may be appropriate to cite one extreme example. While two corrupt officials both receive bribes, one may deliver the 'convenience' as promised, and the other may just receive money and do nothing. The former can be regarded as ethical while the latter is not.

■ Management implications for foreign investors

It becomes clear that moral consideration is crucial in making business deals in China. It is only right for foreign investors to appreciate and treasure the Chinese emphasis on ethics. When one is skilful in handling and nurturing the relationship from an ethical perspective, one will be able to conclude more profitable business deals.

In response to Chinese ethics

One effective way to conceptualize the Chinese ethical perspective is to make use of Confucianism's five relationships. They include: loving relationships between parents and children; loyal relationships between emperor and officials; different roles played by husband and wife; orderly relationships between seniors and juniors; and trusting relationships between friends.

One can group these five relationships into three settings, i.e. the dynasty (emperor–officials), the family (parent–children, husband–wife, and seniors–juniors), and friends.

For business encounters, the first test is whether two persons, originally as strangers, are willing to become friends. Friends are supposed to help each other, and not to exploit and/or betray each other. The strength of friendship is measured by the degree of trust in the relationship. When a company is regarded as an old friend, it means that the relationship has been cordial and trustworthy for a long time. There are at least three implications:

1 The first implication is that the foreign investor has to be friendly and willing to help. It was reported that Toyota was perceived by the Shanghai Automobile Group as unfriendly and insincere. Toyota was perceived as not willing to transfer technology, and not sympathetic towards China's difficulty in managing the foreign exchange situation. Thus, the China side ended up choosing to talk to General Motors and Ford, although they knew that Toyota was superior in manufacturing technology (Cheung, 1996).

2 The second implication is that it pays to have a long track record. When the foreign investor is friendly and helpful, even on rainy days, the foreign investor is likely to continue to enjoy the first-mover advantage because he has passed the moral test.

Motorola started their China operations earlier than others. They chose to stay on despite the 4 June event in 1989. They even put up bigger stakes there. Thus, Motorola managed to continue to dominate the China electronic market as it was growing (Schoenberger, 1996).

3   The third implication is that the foreign investor has to subscribe to the concept that a relationship is more important than a contract. Friendship is supposed to be long lasting. Thus, friendship transcends an individual contract, which can be renegotiated in case of need. Because of this assumption, the China side has often not been afraid of signing contracts, despite inadequate knowledge of the industry. They assume that as long as the friendship is there, it is appropriate for both parties to renegotiate the arrangement. This of course will generate surprises and complaints from the foreign investor, who, as a rule, thinks that the contract is binding in a legalistic manner. If all things go as well as expected, the contract of course will be as binding as those contracts signed in the Western world. However, when things do not go well, friends are supposed to understand one another's difficulty. Thus, a contract can be renegotiated to smooth out the difficulties for the troubled party. The foreign investor should not take this as an additional risk factor in China business. Rather, it only represents a different style of business dealing. This understanding can work both ways, and it can be beneficial to the foreign investor. A Hong Kong developer went to Beijing in the late 1980s and signed a big development project. After the 4 June event, the original market forecast was no longer valid. Although the China side could force the Hong Kong developer to complete the real estate development project according to contract stipulation, the China side understood and was willing to renegotiate the whole arrangement so that the Hong Kong developer could minimize the loss.

Trusting, long-term friendship is important in Chinese business. Moreover, one has the option to convert 'friendship' into 'family relationship' in due course. This may be done formally through marriage. This may also be done through carefully engineered social interaction. For example, children of the chief executive officers (CEOs) from two companies may attend the same school. Because the children are schoolmates, there may be more frequent social gatherings. In the course of interaction, they may ask their children to address the business counterparts as uncles. Over time, the 'uncles' might behave as if they were real uncles. For example, they would advise their 'nephews' on career development. They give personal counselling which one would only give to members of one's own family. Attempts like this are moves to intensify the relationship and bring it up to a higher level of bondage.

An even higher level of relationship is one similar to the loyal relationship in a dynasty. This can be seen in Overseas Chinese business empires. One may find several generations of employees working for several generations of employers in the same business empire. In the interaction between a dominant business firm (the flagship company in a business network) and the subcontracting firms, one can see the loyalty between firms. The subcontracting firm may do extra things (e.g. work without pay) for the dominant firm so that the latter can survive during turbulent time. The dominant firm may continue to run not-so-profitable business operations so that the subcontracting firms still have orders and jobs.

Beyond business ethics

As we can see, throughout the history of China, and to some extent for most Overseas Chinese businessmen, the governing environment has not been encouraging and friendly. Nationalization and indigenization hurt the economies and Chinese business firms (Chang, 1989). Yet, because of profit-making motives and persistent attempts to overcome the difficulties, somehow Chinese businessmen managed to develop an ethical tradition which would be able to sustain a certain level of business development.

The emphasis on personal relationships and personal integrity, when properly sustained, can promote business prosperity. In fact, as deliberated earlier, it has nurtured a unique style of doing business among the Chinese. However, this does not mean that institutional development is not important. When the legal framework is in place, institutional development can facilitate a lot of impersonal business dealing.

In the mean time, it is important to make it clear that personal assessment and institutional development are not mutually exclusive. In fact, they are complementary.

Many MNCs and foreign investors complain that the regulatory framework in China is less than desirable. While it is true that there is a need for China to develop further along the legal dimension, it is equally important for the MNCs to appreciate and treasure the emphasis on ethics in the Chinese tradition, which also facilitates business deals in a cost-effective way. Some MNCs which are unfamiliar with the Chinese way of doing business may choose to conclude business deals with China and sign contracts in Hong Kong. This will enable the MNCs to enjoy the benefits of the legal framework. It is an acceptable arrangement for a limited scope of business operation. However, if business operations expand, MNCs have to learn to conclude business deals with China in a Chinese way. Of course, as the legal framework in China continues to mature, one day, foreign investors may find that the China business environment becomes very much like the Hong Kong business environment where both legal framework and personal relationship are important and treasured.

■ References

Asiaweek, 4 August 1995, pp. 63–4.

Chang, C.-Y. (1989). Localization and Chinese banking in Southeast Asia. In *Global Business, Asia-Pacific Dimensions* (E. Kaynak and K.-H. Lee, eds), pp. 351–67, Routledge.

Chang, H.-P. and Chang, H.-Y. (eds) (1995). *Ten Greatest Merchant Guilds in China*. Chung Hwa Book Publisher (in Chinese).

Chen, T. (1994). *Ethics: An Exposition*. Tung Da Book Publisher (in Chinese).

Cheng, Y.-T. (1993). Entrepreneur on entrepreneurship. An address delivered to the Chinese University of Hong Kong MBA Alumni, 10 June (in Chinese).

Cheung, I.-F. (1996). A report on Toyota's failure in China market. *Hong Kong Economic Journal*, 7 May, 27 (in Chinese).

Donaldson, T. (1989) *The Ethics of International Business*, Oxford University Press.

East Asia Analytical Unit (1995). *Overseas Chinese Business Network in Asia*, pp. 6–7. Parkes, ACT, Department of Foreign Affairs and Trade, Australia.

Kahn, J. (1995). P&G marketing army conquers China. *Asian Wall Street Journal*, 13 September, 1 and 5.

Lee, K.-H. (1983). History for theory building in marketing – a study note on businessmen's image in China. *American Marketing Association Proceedings of Historical Research in Marketing*, pp. 152–9. Michigan State University.

Nyaw, M.-K. and Chang, C.-Y. (eds) (1989). *Chinese Banking in Asia's Market Economies*. Overseas Chinese Archives, The Chinese University of Hong Kong.

Political and Economic Risk Consultancy Ltd (1996). Corruption in Asia. *Asian Intelligence* (458), 3 April

Radio Television Hong Kong (1994). *The Common Sense: Part II of a Four Part Series on Pearl River Delta*. Television programme broadcast on 23 January.

Saporito, B. (1994). The world's best cities for business. *Fortune*, 14 November, 69–91.

Seet, R. and Yoffee, D. (1995). *Internationalizing the Cola Wars (A): The Battle for China and Asian Markets*, Harvard Business School Case 9-795-186 (Rev. 21 July 1995).

Schoenberger, K. (1996). Motorola bets big on China. *Fortune*, 27 May, 42–50.

Chapter 7.1

Post-crisis consideration and moves

■ Kam-hon Lee ■

The recent Asian crisis is painting a very different picture for the Asia Pacific region. Some people who sang the song of the Pacific Century two years ago may think that after all, Asia Pacific countries are not that outstanding. Many Asian countries are suffering. Hong Kong Special Administrative Region (Hong Kong SAR) and China have also been affected (see Chapter 18.1). However, as the following examples note, in handling this crisis and making strategic moves, the decision-makers in Hong Kong SAR and China have been paying full attention to moral consideration.

When Jiang Zemin and Zhu Rongji initially announced that there would be no devaluation for the renminbi, the primary justification they gave was China's moral obligation towards Hong Kong SAR and the Asian countries. When Donald Tsang and Joseph Yam announced that the Hong Kong government would intervene, defend the exchange rate and the stock market, and drive out the international manipulators who engaged in double-market play in Hong Kong, the primary justification they gave was the government's moral obligation towards Hong Kong citizens. When Li Ka-Shing announced that he and other tycoons should not sell their companies' stocks to cooperate with the Hong Kong government, his rationale again, was moral consideration. Subsequently, many investors sent letters to their fund managers and demanded to know if the fund managers had lent the investors' entrusted shares to international manipulators. If their fund managers could not deny these suspicions, these investors then withdrew their money and switched their investments to fund managers who could guarantee that their money would not be used by international manipulators. All these actions demonstrate vividly the importance of moral consideration for Chinese decision-makers when they make their strategic moves.

Chapter 8

The black hole of Southeast Asia: strategic decision-making in an informational void[1]

George T. Haley and Chin-Tiong Tan

An old adage posits that the quality of one's decisions depends on the quality of one's information. The more complex the situation, the more important that one has appropriate data to analyse, to understand the situation better, and to make an optimal decision. Few organizations demonstrate more complexity than multinational corporations (MNCs), and few environments show more complexity than Southeast Asia. Yet, with respect to the information necessary for sound strategic decision-making, Southeast Asia represents an informational black hole. This situation has led to a decision-making and strategic management style that differs from that practised in the West.

In addressing the development of strategic management in the Asia Pacific, Nakamura argued (Nakamura, 1992) that strategic management in the newly industrializing economies of the region, including five of the Association of Southeast Asian Nations (ASEAN) countries of Southeast Asia, is developing in the same fashion as strategic management did in Japan. However, Nakamura (1992) ignored some of the basic environmental differences between Japan during its post-Second World War developmental period and today's Southeast Asian countries.

Though both the Japanese government then, and the Southeast Asian governments more recently, chose the path of managed, export-oriented economic growth, differences emerge in the direction of their economic ties. Much is now being made of the Asiafication of Japanese trade; however, when the Japanese economy was at the different stages of development at which Nakamura (1992) places the Southeast Asian economies, it was almost entirely oriented towards exports to the West in general, and to the USA in particular. Although the Southeast Asian economies depend heavily on trade with the industrial West, they have sought to emphasize a regional thrust to their developmental and trade ties – especially since their larger firms have grown large enough and their economies advanced enough to expand internationally. For example,

[1] The authors thank the guest editor, Dr Usha C. V. Haley, two anonymous reviewers, and Comet, for their excellent comments and suggestions. This chapter has been published previously by MCB University Press Limited: Haley, G. T. and Tan, C.-T. (1996). The black hole of South-East Asia: strategic decision-making in an informational void. *Management Decision*, **34** (9), 37–48.

Singapore has negotiated economic growth triangles, or areas of focused investment, with its closest neighbours, Malaysia and Indonesia. Moreover, most of the region's exports to the West have occurred through foreign MNCs rather than local firms. Consequently, Southeast Asian firms have the same informational advantages when investing in the West's industrialized, information-rich economies as their Japanese counterparts did; however, they have to deal with the informational vacuum of their own region when investing in what they consider their primary markets.

The lack of information, especially information on the external environments of firms operating in the region, poses a serious challenge to traditional forms of strategic planning and management. This lack of information has contributed to a unique, strategic management style for the region's major firms. Consequently, Western MNCs entering the region cannot base their expectations of their local competitors and potential strategic partners on their prior experiences with Japanese firms. The region also presents Western MNCs with substantial challenges to their traditional, information-rich, strategic management techniques. In the balance of the chapter, we will first consider what information Western theorists generally consider desirable for strategic decisions. We will then present evidence of the Southeast Asian informational black hole and compare the available information with that available in the USA. We will subsequently discuss the strategic management and decision-making styles of Southeast Asian managers and, finally, we will propose some implications for Western MNCs doing business in the region.

■ Traditionally desired information

To understand the lack of environmental information in the region, we will first consider what strategic-planning theorists regard as information desirable for effective strategic planning and management. We will then compare it with the information that Southeast Asian firms use. Finally, we will contrast the availability of information in the region with that available in the USA to sketch how much and what kind of secondary information and analysis strategic planners and managers can expect.

Wheelen and Hunger (1992, p.13) define strategy formulation as, 'the development of long-range plans for the effective manipulation of environmental opportunities and threats, in light of corporate strengths and weaknesses'. To formulate strategies, management must scan external environments, both societal and task, and also scan internal environments. Wheelen and Hunger identify several key variables to scan: in the societal environment – sociocultural, economic, technological and politico-legal forces; in the task environment – suppliers, competitors, employees and/or labour unions, customers, special interest groups and communities, among others; and in the internal environment – structure, corporate culture and resources (Wheelan and Hunger, 1992). Hofer and Schendel (1978) include a much more detailed set of factors and variables to consider, broadly grouping them under: opportunities and threats that identify market, industry and supply factors; environmental variables that highlight demographic trends, technological changes, sociocultural trends and political-legal factors; the different functional activities within the firm.

In his strategic marketing text, Jain also includes a two-page list of 'possible strategic factors in business' (Jain, 1995) for strategic planners to consider in their decision-making. He classifies the factors under the subheadings: General managerial;

Financial; Marketing; Engineering and production; Products; Personnel; and Materials.

■ The black hole

Tables 8.1 and 8.2 present the results of a literature search of the ABI-Inform database – probably, the most commonly available database, worldwide, of published articles. The topical keywords we used in the search do not constitute a comprehensive list; however, the keywords do represent many of the different kinds of information that strategic planners and executives seek to understand new environments into which they, and their firms, are entering.

Three things should be noted. First, the topic titles in the tables frequently represent more keywords than those the titles indicate: for example, 'Market research' represents searches we conducted using the keywords marketing research, market research, market data and marketing data. Second, we screened the results of the search presented in Tables 8.1 and 8.2 to eliminate spurious hits unrelated to management issues and to ensure that the articles addressed the subject matter, or its application, in the countries we searched. Probably the most common problem of this sort related to Vietnam where many articles profiling particular executives or firms mentioned the executives being Vietnam War veterans or the firm's Vietnam War related activities; however, as authors researching and/or writing about the business environments in any of the Southeast Asian countries rarely consider this focus important, we eliminated it from our search. Finally, for the purposes of this study, the term Southeast Asia refers only to the seven ASEAN countries, Myanmar (Burma), Laos and Cambodia, as indicated in Table 8.3.

Ironically, researchers have focused most intensively on Singapore, the smallest state geographically in the region, with the second smallest population. Singapore also has an advanced economy and domestic market, with one of the most homogenized and Westernized business communities and environments in Southeast Asia. This focus approximates the drunk looking for his keys under the lamp-post, because he finds light there, rather than searching for them on his unlit doorstep where he dropped them.

To contrast the available information from Southeast Asia and the USA, we use some data to show how the region compares to the USA in terms of population and economic size. In Table 8.3, we can see that the gross domestic product (GDP) of Southeast Asia, at US$1424 billion, represents 22.3 per cent of the US economy's, US$6380 billion. Southeast Asia also has a significantly smaller land mass, representing only 45.3 per cent of the US land mass. Although investing firms often consider such broad data, an economy's market segments, various corporate and societal cultures, and myriad environments, economic, competitive, political and legal, form the foci for firms' strategic planning. When we look at population figures, we find that Southeast Asia has a significantly larger population – almost 497 million to the USA's 264 million, or about 188 per cent of the US population. With its melting-pot population, the USA arguably constitutes the most culturally diverse single nation in the world; however, it lives under, basically, the same set of business, economic, competitive, political and legal environments. One cannot assume this of Southeast Asia's populations that do not form one nation. Each country has its own rich historical, cultural, economic, legal and ethnic backgrounds that, with the exception of Thailand, have been mixed with

Table 8.1 Academic business articles on Southeast Asia

Topic	Brunei A	B	C	Burma A	B	C	Cambodia A	B	C	Indonesia A	B	C	Laos A	B	C	Malaysia A	B	C	Philippines A	B	C	Singapore A	B	C	Thailand A	B	C	Vietnam A	B	C
Marketing	0	0	0	0	0	0	0	1	0	1	8	2	0	1	0	3	5	9	0	1	0	9	13	11	3	11	5	0	1	0
Pricing	0	0	0	0	0	0	0	0	0	0	3	1	0	0	0	2	2	1	0	0	0	2	1	0	0	0	1	0	0	0
Promotion	0	0	0	0	0	0	0	0	0	1	1	0	0	0	0	2	2	3	0	0	0	2	2	3	0	0	0	0	0	1
Distribution	0	1	0	0	0	0	0	1	0	1	1	2	0	1	0	2	2	5	0	0	0	1	10	1	1	2	2	0	1	1
Product development	0	0	0	0	0	0	0	0	0	0	0	1	0	0	0	0	0	0	0	0	0	1	0	1	0	1	0	0	0	0
Channels of distribution	0	0	0	0	0	0	0	0	0	0	0	1	0	0	0	0	0	0	0	0	0	0	1	0	0	1	0	0	0	0
Buyer behaviour	0	0	0	0	0	0	0	0	0	0	0	0	0	0	0	0	0	0	0	0	0	0	0	0	0	0	0	0	0	0
Consumer behaviour	0	0	0	0	0	0	0	0	0	0	2	0	0	0	0	1	0	0	0	0	0	2	3	2	0	4	1	0	0	0
Demographics	0	0	0	0	0	0	0	0	0	1	1	0	0	0	0	7	2	3	0	0	0	4	2	2	2	2	1	0	0	0
Advertising	0	0	0	0	0	0	0	0	0	0	2	0	0	0	0	1	3	2	0	0	0	2	2	5	0	2	1	0	0	0
Product management	0	0	0	0	0	0	0	0	0	0	0	0	0	0	0	0	0	0	0	0	0	0	0	0	0	0	0	0	0	0
Sales management	0	0	0	0	0	0	0	0	0	0	0	0	0	0	0	0	0	2	0	0	0	0	0	0	0	0	0	0	0	0
In-store	0	0	0	0	0	0	0	0	0	0	0	0	0	0	0	0	0	0	0	0	0	0	0	0	0	0	0	0	0	0
Business research	0	0	0	0	0	0	0	0	0	0	0	0	0	0	0	0	0	0	0	0	0	0	0	0	0	1	1	0	0	0
Management research	0	0	0	0	0	0	0	0	0	0	0	0	0	0	0	0	0	0	0	0	0	0	0	0	0	0	1	0	0	0
Marketing research	0	0	0	0	0	0	0	0	0	0	0	1	0	0	0	0	0	2	0	0	0	5	1	4	0	0	1	0	0	0
Consumer research	0	0	0	0	0	0	0	0	0	0	0	0	0	0	0	0	0	0	0	0	0	1	1	0	0	1	0	0	0	0
Industrial marketing	0	0	0	0	0	0	0	0	0	0	2	0	0	0	0	0	0	0	0	0	0	0	0	0	0	0	0	0	0	1
Transport/logistics	0	0	0	0	0	0	0	0	0	2	0	1	0	0	0	3	1	0	0	0	0	5	3	1	2	1	2	0	0	0
Strategic management	0	0	0	0	0	0	0	0	0	0	1	0	0	0	0	0	0	0	0	0	0	0	3	0	0	1	0	0	0	0
Management decision-making	0	0	0	0	0	0	0	0	0	0	1	0	0	0	0	0	1	0	0	0	0	0	3	0	0	1	0	0	0	0
Culture	1	1	0	0	0	0	0	0	0	1	4	1	0	0	0	1	2	2	0	0	0	5	11	9	2	6	7	0	0	1
Media habits	0	0	0	0	0	0	0	0	0	0	0	0	0	0	0	0	0	0	0	0	0	0	0	1	0	0	0	0	0	0
Mass media/communications	0	0	0	0	0	0	0	0	0	0	2	0	0	0	0	0	0	0	0	0	0	0	0	1	0	0	0	0	1	0
Strategic planning	0	0	0	0	0	0	0	0	0	0	2	0	0	0	0	1	3	1	0	0	0	0	7	9	0	3	0	0	0	1
Total articles	1	2	0	0	0	0	0	2	0	6	26	9	0	2	0	21	21	25	0	1	0	39	60	49	9	36	20	0	3	4

Notes:
Period A = 1987–89
Period B = 1990–93
Period C = 1994–mid-1995

Table 8.2 Business articles on Southeast Asia

Topic	Brunei			Burma			Cambodia			Indonesia			Laos			Malaysia			Philippines			Singapore			Thailand			Vietnam		
	A	B	C	A	B	C	A	B	C	A	B	C	A	B	C	A	B	C	A	B	C	A	B	C	A	B	C	A	B	C
Marketing	0	0	0	0	1	0	0	1	0	3	39	36	0	2	0	16	61	32	0	1	0	20	21	16	6	23	12	0	10	17
Pricing	0	0	0	1	0	0	0	0	1	1	4	1	0	0	2	5	7	5	0	0	0	3	2	1	1	6	1	0	2	1
Promotion	0	0	0	0	0	0	0	0	0	0	2	0	0	0	0	0	1	8	0	0	0	4	5	3	2	1	0	0	0	1
Distribution	1	2	0	0	0	0	0	1	1	2	20	11	0	1	1	8	22	9	0	0	0	5	18	3	6	8	6	0	1	6
Product development	0	0	0	0	0	0	0	0	0	0	5	3	0	0	0	2	5	0	0	0	0	1	3	5	0	2	0	0	1	0
Channels of distribution	0	0	0	0	0	0	0	0	0	0	0	0	0	0	0	0	0	0	0	0	0	0	0	0	1	2	0	0	1	0
Buyer behaviour	0	0	0	0	0	0	0	0	1	1	4	0	0	0	0	1	2	0	0	0	0	0	0	0	0	0	0	0	0	0
Consumer behaviour	0	0	0	0	1	1	0	0	0	2	6	0	0	0	1	7	4	3	0	0	0	2	4	3	0	7	2	0	1	1
Demographics	0	0	1	0	1	2	0	0	1	0	15	5	0	2	1	5	11	6	0	0	0	5	6	2	2	6	2	0	1	1
Advertising	0	0	0	0	0	0	0	0	0	0	0	0	0	0	0	0	1	0	0	0	0	5	10	16	2	12	5	0	7	10
Product management	0	0	0	0	0	0	0	0	0	0	0	0	0	0	0	0	0	0	0	0	0	0	0	0	0	0	0	0	0	0
Sales management	0	0	0	0	0	0	0	0	0	0	0	0	0	0	0	0	0	1	0	0	0	0	0	0	0	0	0	0	0	0
In-store	0	0	0	0	0	0	0	0	0	0	0	0	0	0	0	0	0	0	0	0	0	0	0	0	0	0	0	0	1	0
Business research	0	0	0	0	0	0	0	0	0	1	0	0	0	0	0	0	0	0	0	0	0	0	0	0	0	1	1	0	0	0
Management research	0	0	0	0	0	0	0	0	0	0	1	0	0	0	0	0	0	2	0	0	0	5	2	4	0	1	1	0	0	0
Marketing research	0	0	0	0	0	0	0	0	0	0	1	1	0	0	0	0	0	0	0	0	0	1	1	0	0	1	0	0	0	0
Consumer research	0	0	0	0	0	0	0	0	0	0	0	0	0	0	0	0	0	0	0	0	0	0	0	0	0	0	0	0	0	0
Industrial marketing	0	0	0	0	0	0	0	1	0	0	3	0	0	1	2	0	0	0	0	0	1	1	1	0	0	0	0	0	2	2
Transport/logistics	0	0	0	0	0	0	0	1	0	5	19	10	0	1	2	6	5	9	0	0	1	10	21	7	5	10	9	1	4	14
Strategic management	0	0	0	0	0	0	0	0	0	0	1	0	0	0	2	0	1	0	0	0	0	0	4	0	0	1	0	0	0	0
Management decision-making	0	0	0	0	0	0	0	0	0	0	0	0	0	0	0	0	1	0	0	0	0	0	1	0	0	0	0	0	0	0
Culture	1	1	1	0	1	0	0	0	0	1	9	6	0	4	1	2	9	9	0	0	0	5	17	13	5	12	13	0	3	4
Media habits	0	0	0	0	0	0	0	0	0	0	0	0	0	0	0	0	0	0	0	0	0	0	0	0	0	0	0	0	0	0
Mass media/communications	0	1	0	0	1	0	0	0	0	0	0	0	0	1	0	0	1	0	0	0	0	0	0	1	0	1	1	0	2	0
Strategic planning	0	1	0	0	0	0	0	0	0	0	8	1	0	0	0	1	6	7	0	0	0	1	17	9	3	11	3	0	1	4
Total articles	2	4	2	1	5	3	0	3	4	16	136	74	11	11	10	53	136	90	0	1	1	67	126	83	33	105	56	1	36	61

Notes:
Period A = 1987–89
Period B = 1990–93
Period C = 1994–mid-1995

the corresponding backgrounds of the various colonial powers that controlled segments of Southeast Asia.

Table 8.3 A comparison of Southeast Asia and the USA

	Population[a]	*GDP*[b] *(billions $)*	*Area* *(square miles)*
Brunei	292 266	2.5 [c]	2 226
Burma	45 103 809	41.0 [d]	261 228
Cambodia	10 561 373	6.0 [d]	70 238
Indonesia	203 583 886	571.0 [d]	741 052
Laos	4 837 237	4.1 [d]	91 429
Malaysia	19 723 587	141.0 [d]	127 584
Philippines	75 265 584	171.0 [d]	115 860
Singapore	2 890 468	42.4 [d]	247
Thailand	60 271 300	323.0 [d]	198 115
Vietnam	74 393 324	72.0 [d]	127 246
Total	496 922 834	1 424.0 [d]	1 665 057
USA	263 814 032	6 380.0 [d]	3 679 192

Notes: a = Derived from US Census Bureau (1995). *World Population Profile.*
b = International Monetary Fund, purchasing power equivalents unless otherwise noted.
c = 1991 figure.
d = 1993 figure.

This mix of native and foreign backgrounds gives the region a complexity that can challenge even the most culturally adept corporate management. Given the region's inherent complexity, the amount of research and publication on the region seems exceedingly small. The comparison of research and publication between the nations of the region and the USA, presented in Tables 8.4, 8.5, 8.6 and 8.7, seems to indicate a profound void where the few articles on the region's various competitive and business environments spiral into a black hole of ignorance about the region's markets.

Tables 8.4–8.7 indicate the significant imbalance in the relative amount of published knowledge about the USA and Southeast Asia. When we look from Table 8.4 to 8.5 and 8.6, we notice the increase in publications on Southeast Asia from one time period to the next. However, total publications and publications on the USA also increase substantially.[2] The combined increases confound our ability to determine whether the increased numbers of publications on Southeast Asia represent an actual increase in the proportion of articles covering the region. Such a proportional increase would reflect the increasing importance of the region economically and politically. If the increase merely demonstrates an increase in the numbers of publications, without an actual increase in the proportion of total publications, the increase probably only reflects an increase in total articles published, and/or an increase in publications

---

[2] The base of information in Tables 8.4–8.7 is different than in Tables 8.1 and 8.2. The number of publications on the USA for some topic areas is so large that it was impossible to screen them as we did for Tables 8.1 and 8.2. To ensure comparability, the publications for Southeast Asia are also the unscreened totals.

Table 8.4 Southeast Asia business publications trends, period A: 1987–89

Topic	Number	Southeast Asia Percentage of USA	Percentage of total	USA Number	Total on topic
Marketing	79	2.9	0.56	2 681	14 012
Pricing	16	2.6	0.48	612	3 367
Promotion	20	3.4	0.66	585	3 037
Distribution	37	2.6	0.55	1 416	6 710
Product development	5	0.9	0.22	505	2 306
Channels of distribution	4	3.1	0.64	130	626
Buyer behaviour	0	0.0	0.00	1	13
Consumer behaviour	3	1.5	0.23	196	1 280
Demographics	15	2.4	0.76	629	1 983
Advertising	22	1.6	0.36	1 390	6 070
Product management	0	0.0	0.00	29	226
Sales management	0	0.0	0.00	15	222
Point-of-purchase	1	1.8	0.27	56	370
Business research data	2	3.7	0.64	54	311
Management research data	0	0.0	0.00	16	288
Market research data	11	13.1	0.35	84	3 183
Consumer research data	1	4.3	0.44	23	228
Business-to-business	1	1.1	0.14	87	697
Transport/logistics	31	4.4	1.14	698	2 715
Strategic management	1	2.5	0.28	40	357
Management decision-making	0	0.0	0.00	13	118
Culture	30	4.7	1.14	645	2 642
Media habits	0	0.0	0.00	4	13
Mass media/communications	1	4.2	0.86	24	116
Strategic planning	15	2.4	0.43	632	3 528
Total on region	1 391	4.9		28 443	

tracked by ABI-Inform. By taking the percentages of publications listed in Tables 8.4, 8.5, and 8.4, and subtracting them from the percentages in Tables 8.5, 8.6 and 8.6, respectively, one gets a series of positive (+), negative (–), or no change (/) results. A signs test can then be used to determine if actual increases in publications have occurred relative to the USA and to total publications. If publications on Southeast Asia have continued to increase significantly, relative to the USA or to total publications, plus (positive) signs should dominate; if not, minus (negative) signs or slash (no change) signs should dominate. Perfect chance would be represented by equal numbers of plus and minus signs. A Z-score can then be developed to determine if the variance from chance is significant.

In considering Table 8.7, we see that plus signs do not dominate; most signs emerge negative when comparing publications on Southeast Asia with publications on the USA. In testing the Z-score for plus signs, we found that the negative trend runs extensively and deeply. Even after the widespread drop in publications from period A to period B, the drop between period B and period C remains significant at the 0.06 level.

Table 8.5 Southeast Asia business publications trends, period B: 1990–93

Topic	Number	Southeast Asia Percentage of USA	Percentage of total	USA Number	Total on topic
Marketing	219	1.0	0.75	21 174	29 297
Pricing	41	0.9	0.63	4 661	6 530
Promotion	76	1.9	1.35	4 100	5 648
Distribution	117	1.3	0.88	8 739	13 271
Product development	32	0.6	0.47	5 321	6 852
Channels of distribution	10	1.4	1.00	725	999
Buyer behaviour	0	0.0	0.00	21	31
Consumer behaviour	17	1.2	0.71	1 474	2 387
Demographics	25	0.9	0.73	2 789	3 422
Advertising	73	0.6	0.46	13 164	15 984
Product management	1	0.5	0.34	186	298
Sales management	0	0.0	0.00	195	260
Point-of-purchase	2	0.3	0.25	685	812
Business research data	1	0.2	0.13	442	787
Management research data	0	0.0	0.00	212	491
Market research data	19	0.7	0.39	2 789	4 828
Consumer research data	19	10.4	5.54	183	343
Business-to-business	8	1.1	0.78	721	1 021
Transport/logistics	83	1.8	1.12	4 726	7 406
Strategic management	5	1.0	0.61	482	826
Management decision-making	1	1.2	0.65	83	154
Culture	111	3.0	1.81	3 707	6 142
Media habits	0	0.0	0.00	20	30
Mass media/communications	2	0.9	0.68	226	296
Strategic planning	162	2.4	1.57	6 784	10 320
Total on region	5 444	2.5		216 016	

Though the second score does not provide the strongest endorsement, considering the drop in the number of plus signs between the first two periods, it remains significant. As plus and minus are not mutually exclusive, and as a substantial number of no changes occur in our middle column, we conducted a second signs test for minus signs. Here we found that changes between periods A and B are significant only at the 0.06 level, and that changes between periods B and C are not significant at all. Changes between the beginning and end of the time period studied showed that the negative trend in coverage is highly significant.

When comparing publications on Southeast Asia with total publications on the topics, the region fares better. Overall, a trend of increased coverage on Southeast Asia has occurred relative to total publications. Interestingly, both the overall increase, as measured by the number of pluses, and the increase between period A and period B, as measured by the number of pluses, are significant only at the 0.08 level, and virtually all of the overall increase comes in the first period (B-A). In comparing the change in publications between periods B and C, we find that the number of pluses is signifi-

Table 8.6 Southeast Asia business publications trends, period C: 1994–mid 1995

Topic	Number	Southeast Asia Percentage of USA	Percentage of total	USA Number	Total on topic
Marketing	155	1.0	0.65	15 739	23 766
Pricing	29	1.0	0.77	2 894	3 750
Promotion	60	2.3	1.63	2 647	3 672
Distribution	63	1.0	0.73	6 472	8 683
Product development	17	0.3	0.34	4 974	4 974
Channels of distribution	4	0.5	0.42	845	958
Buyer behaviour	0	0.0	0.00	11	14
Consumer behaviour	9	1.0	0.70	867	1 292
Demographics	10	0.6	0.55	1 573	1 826
Advertising	60	0.5	0.36	11 461	16 490
Product management	0	0.0	0.00	109	153
Sales management	0	0.0	0.00	254	280
Point-of-purchase	2	0.4	0.37	457	545
Business research data	3	1.1	0.76	262	393
Management research data	1	0.6	0.29	179	350
Market research data	11	0.7	0.44	1 512	2 483
Consumer research data	0	0.0	0.00	108	156
Business-to-business	7	1.4	1.13	483	620
Transport/logistics	64	1.9	1.29	3 361	4 978
Strategic management	1	0.3	0.21	324	477
Management decision-making	0	0.0	0.00	32	53
Culture	91	3.6	2.39	2 521	3 808
Media habits	0	0.0	0.00	8	11
Mass media/communications	2	1.5	0.89	134	225
Strategic planning	83	1.3	1.02	6 197	8 126
Total on region	4 430	2.3		189 610	

cantly (at the 0.02 level) below chance. Although none of the analyses show the number of minuses above the chance level (12.5 in this instance), they would seem to indicate that the 1990s has seen a leveling off, or perhaps even some reduction, in the relative number of articles published on Southeast Asia. This trend occurred regardless of the much greater interest the private sector has shown in the area through its investments in the region. With increasing foreign investment in the region aimed at serving local markets, rather than markets in the industrialized countries, the overall trend in research and publication is puzzling.

Operating in the black hole

The analyses indicate that Southeast Asia as a region does indeed constitute an informational black hole. The tables also show that the more industrially developed nations in the region received better coverage than less industrially developed ones; however, as expected, the amount of information on any country does not quite correspond with its stage of economic development. For example, Singapore, ranked ninth in per capita

Table 8.7 The signs test

Topic	Compared to USA			Compared to total		
	B-A	C-B	C-A	B-A	C-B	C-A
Marketing	–	/	–	+	–	+
Pricing	–	+	–	+	+	+
Promotion	–	+	–	+	+	+
Distribution	–	–	–	+	–	+
Product development	–	–	–	+	–	+
Channels of distribution	–	–	–	+	–	–
Buyer behaviour	/	/	/	/	/	/
Consumer behaviour	–	–	–	+	–	+
Demographics	–	–	–	–	–	–
Advertising	–	–	–	+	–	/
Product management	+	–	/	+	–	/
Sales management	/	/	/	/	/	/
Point-of-purchase	–	+	–	–	+	+
Business research data	–	+	+	–	+	∣
Management research data	/	+	–	/	+	+
Market research data	–	/	–	+	+	+
Consumer research data	+	–	+	–	–	–
Business-to-business	/	+	–	+	+	+
Transport/logistics	–	+	–	–	+	+
Strategic management	–	–	/	+	–	–
Management decision-making	+	–	–	+	–	/
Culture	–	+	/	+	+	+
Media habits	/	/	–	/	/	/
Mass media/communications	–	+	–	–	/	+
Strategic planning	/	–	–	+	–	+
Total on region	–	–	–			
Number of plus signs	3	9	2	15	9	15
Z-scores for plus signs	–3.92	–1.57	–4.31	1.41	–1.98	1.41
Probability	0.000	0.058	0.000	0.079	0.024	0.079
Number of minus signs	17	12	19	6	12	4
Z-scores for plus signs	1.57	–0.39	2.35	–3.68	–0.28	–5.72
Probability	0.058	0.348	0.009	0.000	0.390	0.000

Notes: + = positive change; – = negative change; / = no change

gross national product (GNP) worldwide (higher than the UK, Australia and New Zealand), has a significantly lower level of information published about it than New Zealand, which has about the same population.

One can understand better the black hole phenomenon by examining the history of business development in the region. Southeast Asia has had three major clusters of large businesses: the state-owned or government-linked corporations (GLCs), the overseas Chinese family businesses, and MNCs. All three groups have prospered despite the lack of local business and market information. Historically, these clusters have not advocated for more and better information; given their primary markets and situations, they adjusted their strategies and management accordingly, and coped quite adequately with their environments.

The first cluster of businesses, the state-owned corporations or GLCs, played a major economic role in many industries in their respective home countries. Many GLCs started as suppliers of products or services in protected, if not monopolistic, domestic market environments. With strong domestic demand, and lack of serious competition, many of these businesses flourished. For such businesses, strategic planning and management were often patterned after the countries' plans for economic growth and development; market information and industry data never formed critical success factors. Hence, information has not historically assumed a top priority for the businesses.

The next cluster of businesses, the Overseas Chinese family businesses, probably constitutes the single, most-dominant, private, business grouping in Southeast Asia. Figure 8.1 indicates the Overseas Chinese as respective percentages of their local populations, and their respective degrees of participation in the local economies of several Southeast Asian countries. As can be seen, in virtually every country in Southeast Asia, the degree of the Overseas Chinese participation in the economy far outstrips their numbers in the population. Today, they have used their various networks to extend their reach to many parts of the world.

Historically, many Overseas Chinese started their businesses as merchants and traders. They quickly moved into property-related businesses, and before long, diversified into almost any business deemed profitable. These businesses were characterized by an intuitive, entrepreneurial and fast decision-making style, and paternalistic management. Due to their low level of education, especially of business education, founders of these businesses made decisions to invest, grow and compete almost solely on the basis of business sense, experience and their individual propensity to take risks. The requirements of business information and detailed analyses of business

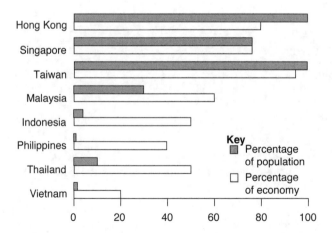

Figure 8.1 The Overseas Chinese
Source: Kohut, J. and Cheng, A. T. (1996)

ventures rarely occurred, if at all. On occasions when truly difficult decisions had to be made, and additional information was considered necessary, the Chinese business-men usually depended on their network of friends and/or well-connected govern-ment officials to supply them with the relevant information. Trust and loyalty formed central concerns: they still do. Desired information need not have included hard data, but frequently involved subjective views or beliefs that the businessmen used to increase confidence levels in their decisions.

This somewhat holistic, yet intuitive, decision-making style corresponded well to an information-scarce environment; it also served to exclude effectively new entrants who lacked the Overseas Chinese business community's experience and network. For instance, many Southeast Asian banks have historically had community bases – that is, they serve particular groups, or networks, of people, not groups of people who live within specific geographic areas; these community bases continue today. Consequently, individuals who apply for business loans from banks in Indonesia often find that all the information included in their applications has been transferred to the banks' related companies in the same business as the applicants'; and, that the related companies have not only moved into the business, but have even implemented the business plans submitted with the application! (East Asia Analytical Unit, 1995). Observers have attributed the rapid growth of many Overseas Chinese family busi-nesses in the region to their amazing speed of decision-making (Chu and MacMurray, 1993); this speed and ability to dominate access to information made the ability to seize major business opportunities possible.

The third cluster, foreign MNCs, arrived in the region much later. In Southeast Asia, European trading houses have existed for decades. However, the trading houses have not contributed as much to the region's economic growth and activity as the manu-facturing-based MNCs that entered the region in large numbers much more recently. Manufacturing-based MNCs, unlike the trading houses, originated from all the indus-trialized regions and have served as key contributors to the export-led economic growth of many of the region's countries. Since the Second World War, when MNCs were rationalizing their low-cost manufacturing policies worldwide, many found Southeast Asia an attractive option. With attractive tax incentives, investment benefits, and cheap labour offered by host countries, many MNCs transferred some of their manufacturing operations to the region.

The MNCs' managers seldom found decisions to relocate to Southeast Asia difficult to make; in many instances, the host governments compiled and offered to the MNCs information relevant to such decisions. The MNCs did not design their manufacturing operations to serve local markets, but rather to obtain production cost advantages in their worldwide operations. The products manufactured were generally intended for export markets. Hence, the MNCs' managers either did not encounter the unavail-ability of information on Southeast Asian markets; or, they did not consider the infor-mational void important. Their decisions to relocate manufacturing operations constituted internal decisions to maximize operational efficiency rather than decisions to serve local markets; decisions regarding the latter require much greater under-standings of the local environments.

In sum, the informational black hole in Southeast Asia appears tangible. It exists because of the manner in which business has historically been conducted and because of participants' goals. As the key decision-makers have not actively sought out more objective, empirical data and information in the past, the region has remained an informational void.

▉ Lack of knowledge and its effects

This lack of available knowledge has led to major differences in the manner in which strategic decisions are made and undertaken in Southeast Asia. The significant contrasts in available knowledge between Southeast Asia's and Japan's primary export and domestic markets also create serious doubt about Nakamura's conclusion that strategic planning in Southeast Asia is developing as it did in Japan (Nakamura, 1992). The limited published information on Southeast Asia, along with much of the general literature on international management, lends support to our argument.

Hofstede (1994) provides interesting insights into the variations in strategic management by describing some of the cultural and ethnic differences in the practices of strategic management worldwide. In doing so, Hofstede differentiates between Japanese and other Asian management practices (primarily the Chinese), and also between the mainland and the Overseas Chinese who exercise such great influence in the Southeast Asian economies. Haley and Stumpf (1989) have shown that managers of differing personality types favour different decision-making styles. Haley (1997) also found evidence that different countries' managerial cadres may consist of significantly different proportions of the various personality types.

Ghosh and Chan (1994) conducted a study on strategic-planning behaviours among emergent firms in Singapore and Malaysia. Although not MNCs, some of the firms had international operations, Ghosh and Chan concluded that planning activities in these firms generally appeared *ad hoc* and reactive. If one considers the data collected from the managers involved in the study, the only factor that addresses the issue of environmental scanning, market research, or any other kind of research, is 'CEO's personal knowledge of market', that ranks as the fourth most important factor in contributing to the success of planning. While a CEO's experience is important in any situation, one must consider how many failures must occur before the CEO attains that experience. If the CEO's personal knowledge of the market forms the sole source of market or environmental knowledge, one must also wonder how a firm could expand beyond its local or domestic market.

In their study of strategic planning of franchising in Singapore, Chan, Soon and Quek (1994) ignored all market or environment-related factors. This lack of importance given to environmental scanning may have been understandable when the world was frozen into two opposing economic, political and military camps striving for domination – though nothing was ever as static as this position would seem to indicate; however, it seems incomprehensible when these studies occurred. With the fall of the Soviet Communist Bloc, and the economic liberalization that has occurred among the Chinese Communists, the economic and business environments are experiencing such high rates of change that environmental scanning and marketing research have become more crucial than ever (Stanat, 1992). This seems especially true of a Southeast Asia that includes the fastest-growing world economies; and where the major economic powers, the USA, Europe and Japan are vying for influence and market share with the economically resurgent, geographically closer, and in many instances, culturally closer, People's Republic of China and Asian tigers.

■ Implications for international managers

A typical MNC forms a complex network of structures, systems, processes and stake-holders. Its normal work routines are analytical, procedural and systematic. On an average day, elaborate compilation of data, sophisticated analyses of data, and systematic approaches to problem-solving constitute the norm.

A young executive joining such an environment, to be successful, must learn his or her company's corporate business procedures and practices. By the time the executive has obtained sufficient seniority to merit an overseas posting, he or she will have acquired great competence in the firm's corporate approach to business management. The executive will likely appear a highly analytical, rational decision-maker, prone to rely on relatively dependable and abundant information. Such a manager is likely to be most effective when competitive dynamics and environments are fairly stable and relatively transparent due to the abundance of reliable data and data analysis on which to base decision-making.

Although numbers of MNCs from newly industrializing and developing economies are increasing, the bulk of MNCs originate from industrially developed, mature economies. Mature economies provide abundant data, and often the time in which to collect and to analyse the data before developing business strategies and taking action. When sent overseas, executives from such environments are expected to deliver the same top performance as they did in their home markets. However, their training and experience provide them only with the same skills with which they have obtained their previous successes. Unfortunately, if their assignment is to a region like Southeast Asia where the market dynamics are in constant flux, business opportunities move quickly, and environmental information seems generally unavailable, their previous training and experience will not reflect the requirements for success in the region.

Such experiences appear common among MNCs' executives newly assigned to Southeast Asia. Consequently, inquiries assume critical importance into how international managers can acclimatize themselves to such situations rapidly; and how MNCs can better obtain the skills to function more effectively in regions that form informational voids.

Judging from Southeast Asia's rapid growth, and the recent aggressive international expansion of many firms from the region, one may attribute success in the region to ability in making fast decisions and seizing business opportunities (Wada, 1992). Southeast Asian executives' swift darting in and out of businesses, their quick execution of strategies, and their constantly doing new things in an environment where little or no information seems available often puzzles professionally trained managers; the latter often express disbelief and shock that decisions appear to be made in such haphazard fashions. Undoubtedly, many successful Southeast Asian executives' decision styles do not correspond to the conventional, corporate analytic model taught in business schools and used so successfully in more mature economic and informational environments. The Southeast Asian style approximates an experience-based, intuitive, idiosyncratic model, well suited to an uncertain environment with little information.

To be effective in Southeast Asia, Western managers need to study holistic/intuitive decision-making, and to learn it fast. Although social psychologists and popular gurus have studied differences between Eastern and Western thought processes, learning capabilities, and decision-making styles, little knowledge exists of Southeast Asia's holistic/intuitive decision-making styles. In part, this stems from the lack of management research in the region. Drawing on our observations and study of Asian executives in consulting and executive development seminars, we propose that several salient characteristics are common to such an experience-based holistic/intuitive approach to decision-making. They are hands-on experience, transfer of knowledge, qualitative information, holistic information processing and action-driven decision-making.

Hands-on experience

To make quick decisions comfortably, without detailed analyses of hard data, a manager needs extensive knowledge and experience in the strategic environment. The manager must almost be a hands-on, line manager who has gone through the firm's work routines and processes, and knows first hand the product, market, business environment and industry. If he or she forms staff, without sufficient exposure to the detailed workings of the trade, the manager will have difficulty putting things in perspective quickly enough to make timely decisions. Consequently, and quite commonly, many senior Chinese businessmen running huge companies remain active in all aspects of their businesses. This level of involvement appears necessary for an executive to make comfortably the right decisions without data support. Wada (1992) gives an example where a Chinese businessman in Hong Kong responded within fifteen minutes to an offer by Mr Li Ka Shen, chairman of the Hutchinson/Cheung Kong conglomerate, to enter into a joint venture. The businessman's confidence in Mr Li's judgement, his ability to trust Mr Li's word, and importantly, his in-depth knowledge of the business and markets under consideration allowed him to make such a rapid decision.

Transfer of knowledge

Managers often have difficulties making new decisions within new environmental contexts. However, in Southeast Asia, companies often diversify successfully into new businesses, which are totally different and considered non-core. This runs contrary to conventional business wisdom of staying within one's core business and pursuing related diversification.

For an executive to function and to succeed in a completely new industry in which he or she has no prior experience, the executive must have the ability to make generalizations from past experience. The executive must also be able to transfer those generalizations into the new context. The dexterity to extract knowledge and the perspective to help one to tackle new problems in different situations involves conceptualization skills different from analytical skills. Successful Southeast Asian executives have the ability to see the big picture and to sense intuitively winners from losers. Whether one believes or not in the continuation of this characteristic decision-making style, it forms an accepted part of business activity in the region (Chu and MacMurray, 1993). Chu and MacMurray believe that this aspect of business in Southeast Asia must change; yet, many businessmen in the region feel it contributes importantly to their firms' growth. For example, Thailand's Charoen Pokphand (CP Group), owned by the

Chearavanont family started in poultry farming, and has since branched out into property investments and telecommunications in order to continue its rapid growth rates. It has done so while maintaining levels of profitability almost unheard of in the West.

Qualitative information

Southeast Asian executives appear to take unnecessary risks by not undertaking sufficient research or analysis before acting; however this appearance may prove misleading. The executives often process myriad bits of information and consider several alternatives in depth before they take action. They differ from their Western counterparts in that for the Southeast Asian executives the process may occur, almost completely, internally. Although their decision-making may contain high degrees of articulation, the Southeast Asian executives may not present the results in detailed, written, analytical forms.

The executives almost always use external sources of information when making strategic decisions. Our experience indicates that executives will actively seek out information and search for the critical pieces that will impact their final decisions. However, executives are less likely to refer to documented evidence or data in published forms. They refer to sources of often qualitative, even subjective information, such as friends, business associates, government officials, and other people in whose judgement they trust, and in whom they personally trust. They may often travel to local scenes to check personally on the reliability of local information, rather than rely on secondary information. Their contacts and connections among local sources often consist of people who can supply up-to-date, accurate information that may not be published. Such firsthand information from original sources may prove superior to any other available alternatives. Consequently, with hindsight, many of the decisions that the Southeast Asian executives make appear correct.

Network building goes beyond linking oneself to some senior government official or great industrialist. Southeast Asian businessmen, while criticized for not building their firm's internal base of managerial talent, often seek out promising individuals who they feel will prove valuable contacts in the future. For example, several years ago, Mr Liem Sioe Liong of the Salim Group, the largest, and probably the most successful of the Overseas Chinese conglomerates, met a young army lieutenant he thought showed promise. He maintained contact with the lieutenant, and offered him his support during his military, and subsequent political, career. The promising young lieutenant was President Suharto of Indonesia and remains Mr Liem's close friend.

Holistic information processing

Conventional analytical problem solving, as taught in business schools and universities, tends to stress sequential, systematic and step-by-step approaches to solving problems and making decisions. This approach proves most effective when, at each step, managers can obtain the proper inputs for use. The approach may be optimal in situations where managers can readily generate or purchase needed data. In an informational void situation, managers may find the approach unworkable.

Alternatively, the experience-based intuitive model views the problem in totality; managers take a general approach to problems, define parameters intuitively, and explore solutions in holistic manners. Such an approach appears to resemble Asian thinking and learning processes. It forms an alternative mode of decision-making that works well in many situations, especially in those environments in which it has developed.

Action-driven decision-making

Speed constitutes one key characteristic of decision-making in the Southeast Asian business context. Executives often make key decisions without consulting anyone. Their preference appears to revolve around action. Several stories exist of well-known Southeast Asian executives who decided on important matters in minutes and implemented the results almost immediately. The quickness also reflects the empowerment and accountability of the executives' actions. Executives often have great latitude in deciding matters. Long debates and committee meetings rarely occur.

The Southeast Asian decision-making model does reflect an authoritative management style. However, when one person has responsibility in a situation, and the authority to make final judgement, a little authoritativeness can move things more quickly and get work done faster. This formed Mr Kazuo Wada's conclusion also, and was the main reason why he moved the headquarters for his firm, Yaohan, from Japan to Hong Kong, and the international headquarters for all operations outside of Hong Kong and China, to Singapore; the domestic Japanese operations remain the only ones with headquarters still in Japan.

■ MNCs' options

Can MNCs learn new skills and equip their staff with them to make more effective international managers in Southeast Asia? The answer forms a definite 'Yes!' Managers can embark on several courses of action:

- When necessary, managers must change the traditional analytical model of management development training to a more experience-based method. Training can assist a manager in learning and practising a holistic way of processing information, and in making decisions in situations where informational vacuums exist. Action learning programmes are increasingly available.

- As fast decision-making is critical, managers must have close links on the ground in each country to accelerate decision-making. Using more locals, having strong connections in the local community, and building trust-based relationships constitute some of the ways to establish stronger links to local information. Managers should also learn to recognize the evolution of relationships. Unlike many other networks in different cultures around the world, an individual's acceptance within a Chinese network is flexible, and can vary based on developments on which the individual has no influence; acceptance does not depend totally on the individual's actions alone, but also depends on the actions of others who influence the situation(s) in which the individual interacts with the network. Executives of Western MNCs do not have total freedom to undertake some of the behaviours that will help to cement their position with a network. (This has nothing to do with bribery, but more to do with freedom to act independently and to involve their families in the business relationship as completely as ethnic Chinese networks often do.)

- Managers must encourage staff to develop different skills that fit different environments. More importantly, management may need to change its preference for an analytical approach to a more flexible methodology. In situations where a less analytical approach may prove beneficial, managers must agree to it and appreciate it. In the event of failures, which will occur when decisions are made in uncontrollable environments, managers must refrain from meting out severe punishment. The culture must encourage more intuitive decision-making when necessary.

Finally, this lack of information has influenced Chinese business culture: the culture draws on superstitious learning, symbolism and luck. For example, Feng Shui forms a common practice in Hong Kong and Singapore: it consists of the art of proper positioning of buildings, entrances and furniture in daily business and life; rituals and custom determine the objects' precise locations. Many Chinese also feel they can generate good luck by having successful first negotiations of the day. Hence, Western businessmen may have more successful dealings by scheduling important appointments for early morning hours: their Chinese associates may strive for successful conclusions to the negotiations, and may even surrender more than usual for the purpose. Chinese business communities also frequently associate numbers, including price tags, car plates and office addresses with homonyms' characteristics: For example, two is associated with the word 'easy', four with 'death', and eight with 'money' as they sound the same in Cantonese. An office address of 28 may prove very desirable with an association of 'easy money'; with an office address of 24, however, one may wish to get a Post Office Box!

References

Chan, P. S., Soon, J. F. K. and Quek, G. (1994). An investigation of the strategic and competitive aspects of franchising in Singapore. *International Journal of Management,* **11** (3), 778–85.

Chu, T. C. and MacMurray, T. (1993). The road ahead for Asia's leading conglomerates. *McKinsey Quarterly,* (3), 117–26.

East Asia Analytical Unit (1995). *Overseas Chinese Business Networks.* AGPS Press, Dept of Foreign Trade and Affairs, Canberra.

Ghosh, B. C., and Chan, C.-O. (1994) A study of strategic planning behavior among emergent businesses in Singapore and Malaysia. *International Journal of Management,* **11** (2), 697–706.

Haley, U. C. V. (1997). The Myers-Briggs type indicator and decision-making styles: identifying and managing cognitive trails in strategic decision-making. In *Developing Leaders. Research and Applications in Psychological Type and Leadership Development* (C. Fitzgerald and L. Kirby, eds), Consulting Psychologists Press, pp. 187–223.

Haley, U. C. V. and Stumpf, S. A. (1989). Cognitive trails in strategic decision-making: linking theories of personalities and cognitions. *Journal of Management Studies,* **26** (5), 477–97.

Hofer, C. W. and Schendel, D. (1978). *Strategy Formulation: Analytical Concepts,* West.

Hofstede, G. (1994). Cultural constraints in management theories. In *International Review of Strategic Management,* vol. 5 (D. E. Hussey, ed.), pp. 27–47, John Wiley.

Jain, S. C. (1995). *Marketing Planning and Strategy*, 4th edn, pp. 64–5. South-Western.

Kohut, J. and Cheng, A. T. (1996). Return of the merchant mandarins. *Asia Inc.*, March, pp. 22–31.

Nakamura, G.-I. (1992). Development of strategic management in the Asia Pacific region. In *International Review of Strategic Management* (D. E. Hussey, ed.), vol. 3, pp. 3–18. John Wiley.

Stanat, R. (1992). Trends in data collection and analysis: a new approach to the collection of global information. In *International Review of Strategic Management*, vol. 3 (D. E. Hussey, ed.), pp. 99–132, John Wiley.

US Census Bureau (1995). World Population Profile.

Wada, K. (1992). *Yaohan's Global Strategy, the 21st Century is the Era of Asia*, Capital Communications Corporation, Hong Kong.

Wheelen, T. L. and Hunger, J. D. (1992). *Strategic Management and Business Policy*, 4th edn, p. 13. Addison Wesley.

Chapter 8.1

Fool me once ...

■ George T. Haley ■

With Asia's growing economic depression has come growing disillusionment with Asian management practices. A growing chorus of crony capitalism is already rising in the West. To some extent, the accusations ring true, especially in Indonesia; but crony capitalism exists in all countries. The Savings and Loan scandal manifested the US variety not long ago.

This growing chorus of accusations appears largely emotional. Asia had the golden touch – the source of all economic growth. Yet, Asia constituted an informational void for the hard data that Western investors traditionally use to judge investments. Most investors and analysts made their Asian decisions with passion and blind faith, not reasoned analysis.

Asian leaders seemed equally passionate. Seeing Asia's growing economic success and influence, and its people's growing wealth and prosperity, hardly a week passed without Prime Minister Mahathir of Malaysia or Senior Minister Lee of Singapore, or any number of other Asian leaders, trumpeting the superiority of Asian values – generally, hard work, loyalty and an emphasis on society's needs (see Haley, 1997). These Asian values' similarities to Western values, such as the Protestant work ethic, appeared immaterial to these leaders.

Then, on 7 July 1997, the Thai government indicated it would no longer support the Thai baht; suddenly dreams of wealth and prosperity became nightmares of poverty and bankruptcy. The present difficulties arose when two other closely held values, extreme privacy and circumspection, made their presence known. It took the Thai Ministry of Finance six months and a change of ministers to discover from the Thai National Bank's governors just how low Thailand's currency reserves had sunk (Haley, Tan and Haley, 1998). The primary, negative, economic manifestation of these values appears as a lack of transparency.

The lack of transparency permeates Asian business and government. For example, with the deregulation of their financial services industry, the Japanese government cannot raise Japanese interest rates to keep Japanese citizens from transferring their investments to foreign accounts; if the government raised interest rates, the increased payments on government debts not officially carried on government books would drive it into default on its payments. Eleven of South Korea's forty largest *chaebol* have reached bankruptcy because Korean accounting rules did not require declaration in companies' books of debts owed to companies within the same *chaebol*. Hence debt to equity ratios reached 5:1 and more: neither the *chaebol*'s business partners, nor South Korea's trading partners, had the slightest knowledge of the problem's scale (Haley, 1997). Similarly, the Peregrine Fund plunged into bankruptcy because an Indonesian client, Steady Safe, could not repay a bridging loan of $260 million after Indonesia's currency collapsed. Indonesia's extremely poor currency, accounting and financial controls prevented Hong Kong's governmental investigators from tracing a single penny of Peregrine's funds, much less getting any of it back (Haley, Tan and Haley, 1998).

The lack of transparency creates uncertainty in Asian markets at the worst possible time for all parties. Asian institutions and businesses need capital. For the first time in over a decade, there are true bargains for foreign investors in non-Japanese Asia. Yet, foreign investors have no way of truly knowing what they will get for their money.

Researchers, managers and policy-makers have made endless comparisons between Mexico's crisis and Asia's in formulating Asian rescue plans – and later in explaining why what worked so well in Mexico failed in Asia. Part of the explanation, not yet debated, concerns transparency. Mexico always had a more transparent economy and accounting and management practices than Asia has. When Mexico desperately needed capital, foreign investors had a fair degree of knowledge of what they were getting; this statement does not hold true for Asia.

Researchers and managers have largely misunderstood Asian management practices as they required trust-based relationships at the highest corporate levels; fortunately, the management practices are surrendering to analyses such as those presented in *New Asian Emperors* (Haley, Tan and Haley, 1998). Unfortunately, Asia has made little headway in increasing transparency of accounting standards for either government or private reporting: hence, understandably, investors are following Benjamin Franklin's old adage: 'Fool me once, shame on you. Fool me twice, shame on me.'

■ References

Haley, G. T. (1997). The values Asia needs. *Business Times* (Singapore), Editorial and Opinion section, 24 December, p. 6.
Haley, G. T., Tan, C. T. and Haley, U. C. V. (1998). *New Asian Emperors: The Overseas Chinese, their Strategies and Competitive Advantages*, Butterworth-Heinemann.

Chapter 9

Singapore Incorporated: reinterpreting Singapore's business environments through a corporate metaphor[1]

■ Usha C. V. Haley, Linda Low and Mun-Heng Toh ■

■ Introduction

> We market Singapore as a 'product'. To stay ahead of the competition we have to constantly innovate and enhance the Singapore product.
>
> Philip Yeo, Chairman, Economic Development Board[2]

In April 1994, in a high-powered London forum, the Economic Development Board (EDB), Singapore's main governmental institution for attracting foreign investment, inaugurated Singapore Unlimited – formally acknowledging the corporate metaphor with which Singapore identifies. In a highly symbolic meeting, Singaporean Prime Minister, Mr Goh Chok Tong, two other ministers, several government-linked corporations' (GLCs') and statutory boards' chairmen, and Singaporean multinational corporations' (MNCs) chief executive officers addressed over 400 European businessmen: they urged the European businessmen to tap the Asia Pacific boom through Singapore Unlimited (Economic Development Board, 1994).

This chapter uses a corporate metaphor, Singapore Incorporated, to reframe Singapore's growth and to explain Singapore's government-led development. The corporate metaphor encapsulates sets of relationships between stakeholders; as they do for organizations (March and Simon, 1958), the relationships provide both goals and constraints for Singapore. Thus, the corporate metaphor provides a tool to reinterpret Singapore's business environments and strategic destiny. First, we translate

[1] The authors thank George T. Haley and Kong-Yam Tan for helpful comments and suggestions. An earlier version of this chapter was presented at the 1995 Academy of International Business Annual Conference in Seoul, South Korea in November. This chapter has been published previously by MCB University Press Limited: Haley, U. C. V., Low, L. and Toh, M.-H. (1996). Singapore Incorporated: reinterpreting Singapore's business environments through a corporate metaphor. *Management Decision*, **34** (9), 17–28.
[2] Quoted in Economic Development Board (1994).

Singapore's growth and development into behavioural components; we highlight strategic alliances with stakeholders. Next, we focus on Singapore's enacted economic, political and social environments. Finally, we explore the corporate metaphor's implications for Singapore's destiny; we also discuss its relevance for theory and policy.

■ Nurturing Singapore Incorporated

We use the term Singapore to denote the city-state, and the term Singapore Incorporated to describe strategic alliances between the Singapore government and key stakeholders to promote business. Logical incrementalism (Lindblom, 1959) has marked Singapore Incorporated's evolution. Since its independence in 1965, Singapore has espoused only one formal plan (Low, 1991; Toh and Low, 1993). Indeed, behaviours such as adaptive rationality and learning, the quasi-resolution of conflict, problemistic search and uncertainty avoidance (Cyert and March, 1963), all seem evident in Singapore's growth and development. This section examines stakeholders' influences and evolving roles through Singapore Incorporated's growth and development.

Government-linked and multinational corporations in the 1960s

Unconsciously, Singapore Incorporated began in the 1960s: the United Nations Survey Mission, led by Dr Albert Winsemius, recommended an industrialization programme (Low et al., 1993). Singapore's Economic Planning Unit used Dr Winsemius's unpublished document to prepare the First State Development Plan. Singapore's need for funds from the World Bank, and a demonstration of rationality and legitmacy from this newly independent state, prompted the plan. The First State Development Plan covered the years from 1960 to 1964; after the plan proved successful, the government extended it. This comprises the only plan that Singapore has had. The result of a problemistic search, the plan provided the blueprint for industrialization with the EDB as the central player. The plan also paved the way for the government's central and dominant roles as agenda setter and agenda achiever (Low and Toh, 1992).

In 1968, the EDB spun off the Development Bank of Singapore (DBS) and the Jurong Town Corporation (JTC) for industrial development and management; these governmental institutions concentrated on financing, allowing the EDB to concentrate on promoting investments. That same year, the government intensified the use of the Central Provident Fund (CPF), a social security scheme begun in 1955, to garner domestic savings and to finance capital formation. The government extended the CPF into a macroeconomic stabilization tool by tying CPF contribution rates to wage policies, to an account for purchases of property, and to an investment account for approved investments. Through the CPF, Singaporeans increased their stakes in the economy. Also in 1968, the government founded the International Trading Company (Intraco) to trade with centrally-planned economies; and the Education Ministry's Technical Education Department to provide a continual stream of much-needed technical manpower in the government's industrialization drive. These institutions also sowed the seed for the government-led development that characterizes Singapore (Low et al., 1993).

Singapore's merger with Malaysia terminated in 1965. Economic crises aborted the second development plan for 1966 to 1970. The ruling People's Action Party (PAP) lacked faith in formal planning and felt no further necessity to approach the World Bank for funds; consequently the PAP deemed *ad hoc* planning, and public-sector planning, as more practical for the small, open, government-dominated state. Besides the First State Development Plan, Singapore's only other plan carries the label indicative (Low and Toh, 1992; Toh and Low, 1993). However, tight government controls continue over resources and policy decisions.

In the 1960s, problemistic search also led to government-owned enterprises in ship building and ship repair, metal engineering, chemical and electrical equipment and appliances. As local capital and entrepreneurs appeared scarce, such minority share participation granted the government the role of catalyst. However, conversely, the government's participation also stifled entrepreneurship and local initiative. With private enterprises still nascent, government-owned enterprises engaged in alliances with MNCs to promote export-oriented industrialization; this alliance forms the crucible of Singapore Incorporated. When Indonesia opened for oil exploration, the Singaporean government formed several joint ventures to construct oil rigs, and to build and to repair ships. To woo MNCs' capital, the government offered fiscal incentives. In 1968, the government also amended the Employment Act and the Industrial Relations (Amendment) Act to confer increased power to employers (Low et al., 1992).

Labour in the 1970s

With rapid growth, supply-side bottlenecks emerged more strongly in labour and land. Preindependence experiences involving disruptive disputes with unions, and work stoppages, influenced possible governmental solutions to these bottlenecks. The government favoured co-operation with the labour unions and forged strong alliances with them. In 1972, Singapore Incorporated moved into wage settlements: it established a tripartite National Wages Council (NWC) to ensure that wages and labour's shares grow to maintain Singapore's competitive edge. After the first oil-induced crisis in 1973, the government delayed economic restructuring to obviate high unemployment by giving less sustainable industries some reprieve. This compromise caused a loss of 6 per cent in productivity increase. The tight labour market attracted more low-skilled foreign labour, perpetuating low value-added activities and attaining only horizontal expansion.

In 1979, the government adopted a corrective, high-wage policy to orchestrate belated economic restructuring. Labour costs rose by as much as 10.1 per cent between 1979 and 1984 compared to productivity growth of 4.4 per cent. The Skills Development Fund (SDF) levy and other fiscal incentives encouraged automation, mechanization and robotics to emphasize efficient labour utilization and productivity. In 1982, the introduction of levies for foreign workers dampened the demand for unskilled foreign labour relieving some of the economy's heavy dependence on this labour source (Lee and Low, 1989; Low, 1993).

Local, private firms in the 1980s

Foreign direct investments (FDIs) came to Singapore in electronics, computer peripherals, aerospace and biotechnology. Singapore Incorporated responded with a ten-year indicative economic plan for the 1980s. This indicative plan aimed to develop Singapore into a modern industrial economy based on science, technology, skills and knowledge (Low et al., 1993).

The 1985 recession disrupted the indicative plan; however, the Economic Committee to contain the recession preserved the indicative plan's aims for greater participation by private firms. It reviewed macroeconomic polices that impinge on operating business costs: the Economic Committee reviewed high-saving policies, high wage and labour costs, the payroll tax, foreign worker levies, CPF contributions and statutory boards' excessive fees and charges. It re-examined the contractionary effects generated through the public sector's surpluses and growing size. These contractionary effects threatened to crowd out the private sector. However, timely policy adjustments helped economic recovery and forged alliances with local firms. The Economic Planning Committee, established in 1989 under the Ministry of Trade and Industry, also formulated the Strategic Economic Plan. This mission statement aspires to make Singapore a developed state in 2020 by Dutch standards or 2030 by US standards (Ministry of Trade and Industry, 1991).

Knowledge-intensive firms in the 1990s

The 1980s left industrial restructuring in its wake. The government concluded that the next lap required daring, innovative and qualitative thinking in a more competitive international environment and more resource-constrained domestic environment; consequently, Singapore Incorporated expanded its regional and global horizons (Economic Development Board, 1994). To maintain competitiveness, Singapore Incorporated aims to promote alliances with knowledge intensive firms and institutions; as Starbuck (1992) identified, these constitute firms and institutions in which knowledge has more importance than other inputs of capital or labour.

The EDB appears to follow a corporate approach. The current Chairman, a Harvard MBA, Mr Philip Yeo, expects EDB officers to have a 'can do' attitude, energy and an understanding of clients' needs (Economic Development Board, 1994). He keeps the EDB lean and agile to move fast and to maintain an entrepreneurial spirit. The EDB's current vision includes Manufacturing 2000 to develop and to strengthen Singapore's industry clusters; International Business Hub 2000 to make Singapore an international node between Asia and the rest of the world, adding value with skills, capital and knowledge; Regionalization 2000 in which the EDB acts as business architect to identify opportunities and partners to participate in the Asia Pacific; and Promising Local Enterprises 2000 to build Singaporean firms into MNCs and industry leaders of tomorrow.

This section outlined how Singapore Incorporated grew and developed incrementally; and how stakeholders provide both goals and constraints. As with other organizations (Normann, 1971; Weick, 1979), the Singaporean government only examined environmental choices when external pressures raised doubts about the present environment's viability; and, it only re-evaluated those segments under attack. The next section details the economic, political and social environments that Singapore Incorporated chose and created.

■ Enacting business environments

Just as in organizations (Starbuck, 1976; Weick, 1979), the unconscious assumptions and values implicit in Singapore Incorporated's decision making resulted in its enacting several environments. This section explores the environments that Singapore

Incorporated directly engaged or enacted. Thus, Singapore Incorporated forged economic, political and social environments with which businesses have to contend.

Economic environment

With 2.87 million people in 1995, and a land area of 641.4 sq km, Singapore cannot influence world trade, employment or interest rates. Yet, one can gauge Singapore's vital role in the global economy by indicators of its efficiency and productivity: for example, Singapore accounts for some 40 per cent of global output for disk drives; and, its communication and information highways help it to play a strategically important role in the Asia Pacific. Singapore Incorporated has met with astounding success: the first trade policy review by the General Agreement on Trade and Tariffs ranked Singapore's economy as among the world's most dynamic. Similarly the Swiss-based International Institute for Management Development (IMD) ranked Singapore as the second most competitive economy, two years in a row, after the USA, in their *World Competitiveness Report* (International Institute for Management Development, 1996), with a highly effective government (ranked first), sound financial structure (third) and good performance in management (fourth); and, the World Economic Forum that prepares the *Global Competitiveness Report* (World Economic Forum, 1996) ranked Singapore as the most competitive economy in the world, up from second place in the previous year, with strengths in finance, trading and as a multinational hub (Serrill, 1996). The US-based Business Environment Risk Intelligence Inc. (BERI) in 1996, similarly granted Singapore top rankings on its government-proficiency measure.

Through deliberately *ad hoc* government planning, Singapore Incorporated's competitive advantages shifted from labour intensive to service oriented. As Table 9.1 shows, over the last three decades, the Singaporean economy has grown at an average rate of 9.1 per cent per annum. Percentages of gross domestic product (GDP) by agricultural and quarrying fell from 3.4 per cent in the 1960s to 0.9 per cent in the 1980s and 0.3 per cent in 1994 and 1995; these shifts, and others such as employment, growth in services and declines in manufacturing, reflect the changes in and labour-saving forces operating on Singapore's industrial structure.

International trade constitutes Singapore Incorporated's primary thrust. Singapore has the world's highest trade to GDP ratio: in 1995, exports constituted about 190 per cent of GDP; about 18 per cent of Singapore's exports went to Malaysia, which surpassed by about 1 per cent, the USA, Singapore's other largest export market. Singapore's seaport has consistently been ranked as among the two busiest in the world; and the 1994 *World Competitiveness Report* ranked it as the best globally for access infrastructure. FDI has continued to pour into Singapore Incorporated: since independence, the USA and Japan have constituted the largest investors. In 1995, the EDB revealed that the USA remained Singapore's largest investor, although its share of total investment fell from 41.9 per cent in 1994 to 30.5 per cent in 1995. Europe increased its share from 17.3 per cent to 22.4 per cent in 1995 – as did Japan, whose investment share rose to 17 per cent from 15.3 per cent in 1994 (*Straits Times*, 1996a). Table 9.2 details manufacturing investments by country. Table 9.3 shows manufacturing investments by industry; currently, electronic and electrical equipment draws the most investment, reflecting industrial shifts. Tables 9.4 and 9.5 detail service investments by country and by industry; the USA ranks as the top investor in services; and

Table 9.1 Real GDP, industrial structure and employment

	1960–69	1970–79	1980–89	1994	1995
Average growth (%)					
Real GDP	9.4	9.8	8.2	10.1	8.9
Employment	2.9	5.0	2.1	3.6	3.1
Industry contribution as % of GDP					
Agriculture and quarrying	3.4	1.9	0.9	0.3	0.3
Industry[a]	29.6	36.9	35.1	37.4	39.2
Construction	8.2	8.1	7.8	7.1	7.5
Manufacturing	19.6	26.9	25.4	28.2	29.7
Services[b]	67.0	61.2	64.0	62.3	60.5
Real average industry growth (%)					
Agriculture and quarrying	4.5	3.1	–3.3	2.6	7.9
Industry[a]	13.3	11.0	7.0	13.2	9.8
Construction	15.7	10.8	6.0	15.7	8.5
Manufacturing	13.0	12.2	7.4	9.1	10.3
Services[b]	8.0	9.4	9.1	8.9	7.9
Employment as % of total (%)					
Agriculture and quarrying	7.1[c]	2.5	0.9	0.3	0.3
Industry[a]	23.1[c]	33.0	35.9	32.7	24.0
Construction	5.7[c]	5.4	7.2	6.6	6.6
Manufacturing	16.1[c]	26.4	28.0	25.6	30.9
Services[b]	69.8[c]	64.5	63.2	67.0	69.3
Average employment growth (%)					
Agriculture and quarrying	–11.7[c]	–4.4	–14.4	23.8	–11.5
Industry[a]	8.1[c]	6.9	1.6	0.1	–2.5
Construction	6.7[c]	2.6	1.3	6.5	3.4
Manufacturing	9.0[c]	8.0	1.7	–1.6	–3.4
Services[b]	2.5[c]	4.5	2.6	5.3	5.8

Notes: [a] Comprises utilities, construction and manufacturing.
[b] Comprises commerce, financial and business services, transport and communications and other services.
[c] Data for 1960–66 only.
Sources: Department of Statistics (1987) *Singapore National Accounts*; Ministry of Trade and Industry (1994) *Economic Survey of Singapore*.

information technology and communications form the top industrial recipients of investments in services. Table 9.5 also indicates the prominent role played by overseas headquarters (OHQs) in Singapore Incorporated. The EDB hopes to attract 200 companies to set up headquarters in Singapore by the year 2000, more than double the eighty OHQs in 1996.

Singapore still engages in very little outward FDI as a proportion of GDP; however as Figure 9.1 details, this percentage is growing. Singapore Incorporated's resolve to go international appears in the sharp rise in FDI after 1988. Figure 9.2 reveals the desti-

Table 9.2 Manufacturing investment commitments (gross fixed assets, S$million)

	1986	1987	1988	1989	1990	1991	1992	1993	1994
USA	443.4	543.5	586.6	520.2	1054.8	969.2	1201.4	1452.2	2451.7
Japan	493.8	601.1	691.3	541.2	708.2	713.2	858.0	779.4	913.8
Europe	218.8	285.8	358.1	517.3	435.3	684.2	618.8	881.9	907.0
EC	204.8	241.0	345.1	498.4	395.5	615.9	536.4	795.7	893.0
UK	93.4	42.4	56.6	174.6	89.9	186.5	305.5	357.8	525.1
The Netherlands	57.1	70.9	82.9	147.0	72.6	216.2	43.1	7.7	175.6
Germany	16.7	90.3	46.7	26.4	165.7	60.2	106.4	204.6	91.8
France	27.8	15.2	86.0	106.0	60.4	75.2	34.1	124.9	54.0
Italy	5.1	22.0	68.0	32.8	0.0	70.1	26.7	43.3	38.9
Other EC	4.7	0.2	4.9	11.6	6.9	7.7	20.6	57.4	7.6
Sweden	5.4	8.7	0.0	0.0	7.1	1.2	19.3	5.0	0.0
Switzerland	7.7	27.8	10.1	0.9	32.7	12.6	63.1	66.3	11.4
Other Europe	0.9	8.3	2.9	18.0	0.0	54.5	0.0	14.9	2.7
Others	34.6	17.6	21.7	19.8	19.6	94.5	55.0	63.5	54.9
Foreign	1190.6	1448.0	1657.7	1598.5	2217.9	2461.1	2733.2	3177.0	4327.4
Local	259.4	295.0	349.6	333.3	269.5	472.9	748.0	748.0	1437.2
Total	1450.0	1743.0	2007.3	1931.8	2487.4	2934.0	3481.2	3925.0	5764.6

Source: Department of Statistics (1994) *Yearbook of Statistics.*

Table 9.3 Manufacturing investment commitments (gross fixed assets, S$million)

	1986	1987	1988	1989	1990	1991	1992	1993	1994
Light									
Food, beverages	83.3	156.6	168.4	34.1	43.8	39.8	76.5	92.9	36.3
Textiles	5.6	3.0	10.6	2.0	2.8	11.2	5.2	0.0	0.0
Wearing apparel	0.0	6.8	0.9	0.4	0.2	5.7	10.0	2.4	0.0
Leather, rubber	0.4	8.5	5.6	0.0	10.0	4.4	2.8	1.7	2.6
Wood	11.4	14.7	0.0	2.1	8.6	2.8	4.6	24.7	0.0
Paper, printing	36.2	25.1	72.0	93.8	76.2	109.4	89.5	92.2	268.4
Others	0.0	11.8	0.7	14.3	0.0	35.7	10.5	1.8	11.9
Service/engineering	19.9	8.4	15.9	9.8	24.3	0.0	0.0	0.0	0.0
Chemical									
Industrial	78.0	32.9	124.7	213.5	265.9	322.0	294.3	783.5	1192.8
Others	111.5	11.0	25.7	21.7	35.0	243.4	248.4	340.4	113.9
Petrol	116.0	122.4	0.0	290.0	381.0	99.5	454.2	84.6	1180.3
Plastic	42.6	115.9	53.5	37.8	8.9	87.2	110.8	48.3	26.9
Non-metallic products	9.3	6.2	133.8	0.0	9.0	47.9	63.1	126.1	206.8
Engineering									
Basic metals	8.3	5.2	15.3	86.6	0.0	2.8	34.3	69.4	6.6
Transportation equipment	64.0	61.7	110.4	50.8	114.1	124.3	167.1	341.2	555.4
Manufacturing systems									
Fabricated metals	82.0	104.3	109.9	101.0	103.1	127.1	152.5	150.3	324.5
Machinery	205.6	93.5	180.5	131.0	186.2	376.5	343.7	330.8	276.5
Electronic/electrical									
Electronics	522.0	838.4	935.6	776.9	1197.1	1260.4	1275.2	1321.0	1542.2
Precision	53.8	116.6	44.0	93.0	21.2	34.0	138.3	113.7	19.6
Foreign	1190.5	1448.0	1657.9	1625.5	2217.9	2461.2	2733.0	3177.0	4327.2
Local	259.4	295.0	349.6	333.3	269.5	472.9	748.0	748.0	1437.2
Total	1449.9	1743.0	2007.5	1958.8	2487.4	2934.1	3481.0	3925.0	5764.6

Source: Economic Development Board (1994).

Table 9.4 Services investment commitments by country (total business spending, S$million)

	1987	1988	1989	1990	1991	1992	1993	1994
USA	66.24	55.58	55.57	64.42	89.70	204.90	168.00	224.1
Europe	33.29	69.50	37.04	87.00	97.91	93.35	70.60	186.7
Japan	26.65	18.66	45.46	96.25	146.80	98.10	121.50	16.0
Asia Pacific	2.34	43.36	45.89	33.50	22.50	27.42	25.20	53.9
Singapore	72.33	72.32	116.47	89.63	89.34	83.20	84.40	101.9
Total	200.85	259.42	300.43	370.80	446.25	506.97	469.70	582.5

Source: Economic Development Board (1994).

Table 9.5 Services investment commitments by industry (total business spending, S$million)

	1987	1988	1989	1990	1991	1992	1993
Overseas headquarters	63.91	67.60	105.46	173.78	207.00	274.32	270.50
IT/communications	74.56	61.93	71.15	66.72	70.40	105.20	105.10
Transportation/distribution	23.65	21.60	2.30	64.20	84.20	44.90	12.70
Exhibition/leisure	12.87	43.36	20.00	28.45	34.50	34.50	7.20
Medical	21.58	32.09	62.21	21.05	27.49	12.00	7.50
Engineering/testing	2.62	2.60	10.38	9.65	10.16	11.55	25.00
Education	0.07	22.30	18.05	0.00	4.50	2.00	5.20
Others	1.59	7.90	10.88	6.95	8.00	22.50	36.40
Total	200.85	259.42	300.43	370.80	446.25	506.97	469.60

Source: Economic Development Board (1994).

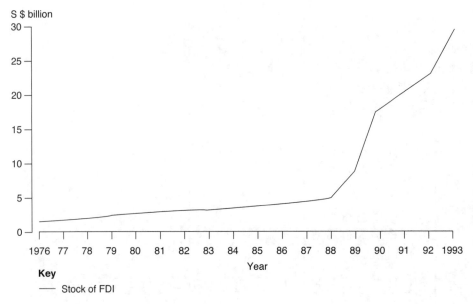

Figure 9.1 Singapore's foreign direct investment
Source: Economic Development Board (1994).

nation of this FDI by region in 1993 – Asia draws the bulk of Singapore's FDI; and in Asia, the ASEAN countries form the biggest recipients. In 1994, Singapore's stock of FDI rose to S$28.16 billion, with about S$4.7 billion or 22 per cent in Malaysia, about S$4 billion or 19 per cent in Hong Kong and China, and smaller amounts of S$1.8 billion in the USA, S$1.5 billion in New Zealand and S$0.5 billion in Indonesia. In 1996, Singapore formed one of the largest investors in Malaysia, China, Vietnam, Cambodia, Myanmar and Indonesia. Singapore Incorporated's financial and manufacturing sectors made most of the FDI.

Political environment

The political environment displays strong tints of democratic corporatism. Other theorists have indicated how states deal with economic change; for example, Katzenstein (1985) elaborated on state capitalism as corporatism. Democratic corporatism paints Japan as a big business firm or the USA as run by Wall Street; it emphasizes both giant corporations' domination of economic life and integration of businesses into governmental and bureaucratic decision making. It also emphasizes pursuits of international interdependence through trade and investment. However, democratic capitalism fosters the relative exclusion of unions and leftist parties from centres of power. On the other hand, organized capitalism, as in post-war West Germany, includes politically all business unions and conservative and progressive parties. These models of small states in world markets provide the basis for our understandings of the redistribution of resources in Singapore.

First, like other small states, Singapore espouses an ideology of social alliances. These alliances on questions of economic and social policy permeate everyday economic and

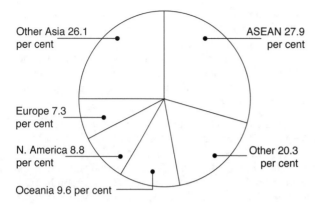

Other Asia 26.1 per cent

ASEAN 27.9 per cent

Europe 7.3 per cent

N. America 8.8 per cent

Other 20.3 per cent

Oceania 9.6 per cent

Figure 9.2
Singapore's foreign direct
investment by region in
1993
Source: Economic
Development Board (1994).

social decisions. The ideology mitigates class conflicts between business, corporations and unions; and it integrates differing concepts of group interest with vaguely but firmly held notions of the public interest. Even casual visitors notice the self-dramatizations and ritual invocation of Singapore's smallness as explanations for actions. A culture of compromise pervades Singapore Incorporated that manages to couple narrowly conceived group interests with shared interpretations of the collective good (Haley, 1991; Low, 1993).

Second, like other small states, relatively centralized and concentrated stakeholder groups distinguish Singapore. As the previous section indicated, influential stakeholders include MNCs, labour, local firms, linked economies, and knowledge-intensive firms and institutions. Tight hierarchical controls exist in the formulation of policy: the government forms the most influential stakeholder by far, constituting agenda setter and agenda achiever; to control, it also forms a major stockholder in the major corporations.

For a migrant society with 140 years of British rule, the building of social cohesion and national values prompted the government's initial welfare policies. Public housing served more than infrastructural needs. When Singapore separated from Malaysia in 1965, poverty and mass discontent hovered amid threats of unemployment and Communist-inspired industrial unrest. Consequently, home ownership formed a political means to implant long-term stakes and security. The government started the Home Ownership Scheme (HOS) using CPF funds to purchase public housing in 1968; the government extended this scheme to private and non-residential properties in 1981.

Singapore's compactness and unitary government allows an expedience in political control and policy implementation many governments would envy. Policies in public housing (Low, Toh and Soon, 1991), education, health and wealth accumulation have made home owners and asset owners, shareholders, owners of corporations and others who depend on Singapore's prosperity and progress into Singapore Incorporated's stakeholders. Financing merit goods rather than cash payments reflects the government's paternalism and faith in human capital theories. The government's schemes include upgrading public housing and the small family scheme to help pay for housing and children's education.

Robin Hood style policies to redistribute income have hampered growth in some countries; however, Singapore's government has promoted high growth by maintaining low taxes on successful individuals and businesses, and by avoiding incentive-dampening distortions. Instead, the budget has a happy problem of surpluses that the government reduces to lower contractionary impacts. In the last few budgets, the Finance Minister has used accumulated surpluses to enhance human resource development, to improve low-income families and to upgrade public housing. Again, the government's intervention has taken a softer focus.

Not many governments have served as benevolent providers using resources commandeered from the private sector. The government forms the largest landlord, backed by the Land Acquisition Act that liberal democracies may deem unconstitutional. The government justifies such rent-seeking behaviour by indicating that its efforts in infrastructure enhance land values. The government's very entrepreneurial approach under the state enterprise system, and via land sales, has increased budgetary surpluses.

The PAP's economic successes have prompted electoral victories in every general election since independence. However, in the 1984 general election, two opposition members broke the hegemony of an all-PAP house; the majority fell from 75.5 per cent to 62.9 per cent. Then Prime Minister, Mr Lee Kuan Yew had noted that his job consisted of making an opposition possible, not of building one (*The Economist*, 1986). But, when popular fancy for an opposition produced only populist versions, an alarmed government created the nominated Member of Parliament (NMP) as a halfway house.

Social environment

Singapore's corporatism differs significantly from states like Japan, USA or West Germany. Singapore tempers democratic corporatism with its own ideological brand of Confucianism. Traditional Confucianism despises business; Singapore revels in it. Government looms as patriarch and patron; yet, government encourages free trade. Strange paradoxes result. For example, although deregulation extends over 90 per cent of trade in Singapore, the Singapore government will intrude into social and business policy if it feels that the business environment and Singapore Incorporated's future could be affected. Hence, recent government campaigns on everything from speaking Mandarin, to having more children, to demonstrating punctuality and courteousness.

The first Prime Minister, Mr Lee Kuan Yew recalled that when he realized that Hong Kong had leaner and keener workers than Singapore, he resolved to reverse the welfare policies inherited or copied from the British Labour Party (Lee, 1992). He scaled back subsidies except where they enhanced productivity through better education, better health and better housing. However, probably because of the government's patronage, Singaporean workers still demonstrate more dependence on the government, and less independence than Hong Kong's workers (Low et al., 1993).

Drawing on Confucian beliefs of governmental paternalism and omnipresence, the government also sees itself as the only agenda setter in the business environment. For example, in numerous statements from 1994 to 1996, published in the *Straits Times* (Singapore), Prime Minister Goh Chok Tong indicated that if citizens express views that criticize government policies, the government will view them as entrants to the political arena. Similarly, Mr Lee Kuan Yew argued that thirty years ago, Singapore would have failed if the English-educated middle class had dominated the population.

'If we had an English educated middle class to begin with in the 1960s – querulous, arguing, writing letters to the press, nit-picking, chattering away – we would have failed' (*Straits Times,* 1996b). Fortunately, he said, Chinese-speaking, Malay-speaking and Tamil-speaking Singaporeans dominated the population then, and now: these groups maintained traditional, down-to-earth and realistic views of government and society (*Straits Times,* 1996b).

Arguing that a society's right to survive precedes individuals' rights, the government confers on itself a veritable fistful of sanctions to deal with social problems. Despite the government's extraordinary control, one sometimes hears rumblings. For example, a Singaporean journalist made the charge of 'one government, two styles'; this journalist implied that Prime Minister Goh Chok Tong, backtracked from his aspirations of making Singapore a more refined, more compassionate, kinder and gentler society (*Sunday Times,* 1994). Mr Goh promised this five months before he became Prime Minister. But, as Senior Minister Lee commented after the charge, Mr Goh's becoming kinder and gentler after becoming Prime Minister, may reduce his ability to govern Singapore (*Straits Times,* 1995).

One vestige of Singapore Incorporated's social philosophy emerges in a stark acceptance of a hierarchical, often unfair, society and its top managers' sole prerogatives in setting policies. A vivid display occurred in a parliamentary debate in May 1996 regarding an inquiry into Mr Lee Kuan Yew's personal finances. In the debate, Senior Minister Lee revealed that he earned nearly S$1.3 million annually; his son, Deputy Prime Minister Lee Hsien Loong earned about S$1 million; while his daughter-in-law, also director of the GLC, Singapore Technologies, earned 'peanuts' or around half a million Singapore dollars. Consequently, Mr Lee argued he could pay cash of around S$10 million for two condominiums – even after discounts. The news sparked an impassioned nationwide debate over the rising costs of private housing, its unattainability for most, and its correspondence to the Singapore dream.

At its crudest, the Singapore dream comprises the Five Cs : cash, credit card, car, condominium and country club. Yet, the dream may appear elusive for most in this nation with an average income of S$25 032 in 1994. For example, in 1992, about 31 per cent of Singaporean households had cars.[3] New cars average S$100 000 because of governmental policies to control the numbers of cars. Similarly, the Housing Development Board's (HDB's) government-subsidized public housing, in which 85 per cent of Singaporeans live, can cost more than half a million Singapore dollars at the upper end. Private condominiums and houses generally cost at least twice as much and have risen steeply in price over the last five years; in 1994, private residential property prices increased by 44 per cent over the previous year.[4]

'Let's grow up!', scolded Mr Lee in Parliament. 'It is an unfair and unequal world. If you want an equal world you end up with a Communist world with Mao's salaries.' However, a nineteen-year-old intern's plaintive letter to the *Straits Times* echoed average sentiments in Singapore.

> I am not asking for an emperor's condo and stables of Benzes, just a small place I can belong to and that can belong to me. Already I have friends who are drawing up blue-

---

[3] Data released by the Department of Statistics, Singapore.
[4] Data released by the Department of Statistics, Singapore.

prints of their futures in Australia and America, where they believe they can stretch their income much further. (Mydans, 1996)

Mr Lee was 'puzzled' and 'sad[dened]' by the letter (*Straits Times*, 1996c). In May 1996, the government announced measures to curb speculation in residential property thereby dampening rising property costs.

The next section explores the corporate metaphor's implications for Singapore Incorporated's destiny. It also discusses the limitations and opportunities afforded by this metaphor for Singapore and other states.

■ Implications

The Merlion, an improbable creature, half lion and half fish, serves as the closest approximation that Singapore Incorporated has to a logo. About thirty years ago, the Singapore Tourist Promotion Board created the Merlion as its corporate logo. Yet, rather than the Merlion, the corporation provides the guiding metaphor and symbolic denotation of Singapore, with attendant ramifications (Haley, 1991; Meyer and Rowan, 1978).

Singapore's self-image of a corporation has tremendous policy implications (Lee and Naya, 1988). The symbolic resonance of Singapore Incorporated ripples through the land: the government goes though periodic public justifications and interpretations of its stances *vis-à-vis* the corporate metaphor, thereby confirming its symbolic importance (Haley, 1990); it informs key stakeholders of its performance and status using the language of the metaphor; it evaluates policies using the standards set by the metaphor; and it plots future courses using the guiding light of the metaphor. For example, official statements in 1995 on raising Singapore's ministerial salaries, already the highest worldwide, emphasized that the government had to compete with corporations for qualified people: consequently, ministerial salaries had to synchronize with corporate salaries for top managers who earned over one million Singapore dollars annually. These salaries would then also appropriately reveal the levels of influence, discretion and managerial skill exercised by ministers.

Similarly, Singapore Incorporated guards its name and reputation like a corporation would. Recently, the *Straits Times* (Tan, 1994) reported that the government has tightened up on the use of the name 'Singapore' for industrial park projects in China; 'the move, observers say, will help protect the reputation of Singapore investors and the Republic itself ... . Singapore's Ministry of Trade and Industry said: "The Chinese government has brought to our attention that some of our private sector companies are applying the Singapore name on their industrial parks in China, and in the process would give the wrong impression that the Singapore Government is directly involved in these projects"' (Tan, 1994).

If Singapore views itself as a corporation, it must see itself as a MNC. With very few natural resources, Singapore has emphasized successfully the intangible assets that make MNCs powerful: product and engineering design, technical services support, information technology and communication, marketing and distribution, infrastructure, human resources and financial and treasury management. Total trade constitutes four times GDP; exports comprise about twice GDP, making Singapore vulnerable to trade wars: consequently, the government follows a policy of continuous diversifica-

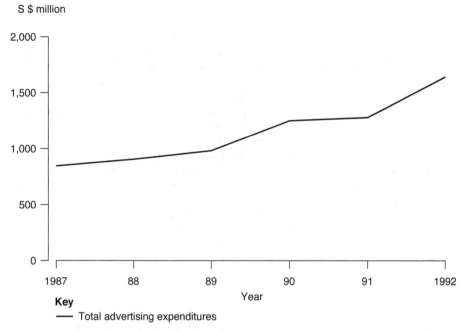

S $ million

Figure 9.3 Advertising receipts by industry for Singapore (S$million)
Source: Data released by the Department of Statistics, Singapore.

tion. FDI forms a small proportion of total GDP: the government has advocated a stringent policy of encouraging FDI – especially in the region. Rising investments in intangible assets that grant MNCs competitive advantages (Hennart, 1982) like information technology (Table 9.5) and advertising services (Figure 9.3) testify to the environment that Singapore Incorporated is enacting.

Unlike other countries, Singapore actively encourages its companies to invest abroad. In 1991, government-led regionalization started with a pilot project: labour-intensive, lower-skilled and technology-intensive industries moved from Singapore to the Riau Islands in Indonesia and to Johore in Malaysia; by 1993, this area had evolved into the Indonesia–Malaysia–Singapore growth triangle, an area of focused investment, expanded in 1995 to include West Sumatra, Malacca, Negri Sembilan and Pahang. The Singapore dollar's real appreciation since 1985 also caused domestic costs to escalate. Consequently, the EDB and the Committee to Promote Enterprises Overseas (Ministry of Finance, 1993) began to implement incentives for companies to regionalize. Economies in transition, such as China, Indo-China or India, allow Singapore Incorporated to build its external economy. However, Singapore has less capital and people to spread in the region than other Asian newly industrialized economies. Therefore, Singapore Incorporated has drawn together its old coalition of statutory boards, GLCs and MNCs to blaze the trail. When MNCs and GLCs move abroad, the government extends the Local Industry Upgrading Program to enable MNCs and GLCs to upgrade local contractors' technologies. Through many assistance schemes, the EDB gives local companies a total business development package which caters for them from cradle to maturity.

Singapore Incorporated's regionalization drive has also resulted in ambitious projects to create subsidiaries, or Virtual Singapores, in labour and land-rich developing countries. The Virtual Singapores form industrial parks that Singapore Incorporated is erecting in China, India, Indonesia and Vietnam. Most of these projects constitute clusters of factories, roads and power plants for which Singapore Incorporated serves as landlord to MNCs; but, in Suzhou, China, Singapore Incorporated is also embarking on an ambitious experiment in social development. The China–Singapore Suzhou Industrial Park constitutes a twenty-one company consortium, dominated by local, private firms, GLCs and Singaporean government agencies, including the EDB. With a completion time of twenty years, an estimated size of 70 sq km and 600 000 people, Suzhou forms an experimental base for Singapore Incorporated to serve as middleman to the world; through Suzhou, Singapore Incorporated also hopes to perpetuate its influence and stakeholder base by advocating an alternative model for developing China (Kraal, 1996). The consortium will funnel to China the transfer of Singaporean software and culture, as well as methodologies ranging from urban planning and fire fighting to the CPF. Faced domestically with increasingly non-competitive labour rates, land shortages and impending competition from ports in Thailand and Malaysia, Singapore Incorporated is trying to retain regional economic dominance by transmitting unique cultural and political values, as well as key technologies, through its industrial parks.

Singapore's self-image as a corporation carries some structural implications as well. Structurally, like Tokugawa Ieyasu three centuries before in Japan, first Prime Minister Lee Kuan Yew argued for a hierarchical, stabilizing society in Singapore of mandarin bureaucrats on top, hardworking, disciplined, blue collars on the bottom, and leading businessmen and a closely watched professional class in between (Krause, 1988; Pye, 1988; Redding, 1990). The internalizing of markets through hierarchies, as a MNC would, carries both its costs and benefits: its benefits translate to increased efficiency and strategic speed; its costs contribute to a relative lack of initiative, entrepreneurship and creativity, and a rigid bureaucracy.

Despite its astounding success, in some respects Singapore Incorporated appears eerily sterile. No one passionately chronicles its development. Singapore Incorporated has no renowned poets, short story writers, musicians or bards to interpret events. Despite its great economic progress, Singapore also appears limited in intangible assets like research and development (R&D), a key asset for MNCs. A National Science and Technology Board survey revealed that in 1993, Singapore spent about 1.2 per cent of its GDP on R&D – as opposed to the USA's 2.72 per cent, Japan's 2.72 per cent, Germany's 2.53 per cent, Taiwan's 1.73 per cent and South Korea's 2.17 per cent (Mok, 1995). As Figures 9.4 and 9.5 demonstrate, Singapore's expenditures on R&D, and its number of scientists and engineers appear woefully small, reflecting its limited population. Despite governmental support for R&D, the *World Competitiveness Report* (International Institute for Management Development, 1996) revealed that as other nations progressed, Singapore slipped in relative ranking from the previous year on the availability and qualification of human resources (from fifth to eighth), on science and technology (from seventh to twelfth) and on infra-structure (from twenty-ninth to thirty-third). The report indicated that Singapore's challenge would lie in finding its next dimension of economic development, making a discontinuous change from one plateau to another (Teo, 1996).

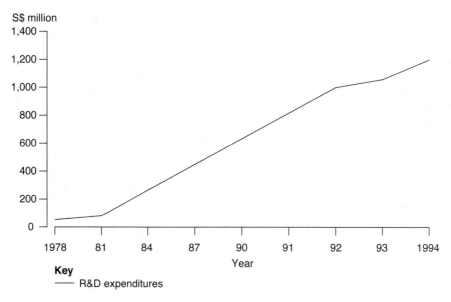

Figure 9.4 Singapore's R&D expenditures
Source: Data released by the National Science and Technology Board, Singapore.

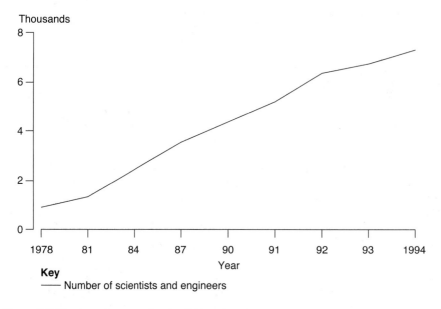

Figure 9.5 Singapore's research scientists and engineers
Source: Data released by the National Science and Technology Board, Singapore.

Unlike leaders of other countries, Singapore Incorporated's leaders unhesitatingly accept it as an artificial creation with a purpose and a finite life span. In an interview with the *New York Times* on 3 August 1995, Mr Lee Kuan Yew called Singapore 'man-made'. He argued, 'It's very contrived to fit the needs of the modern world and it has to be amended all the time as the needs change'. In the interview, Mr Lee gave a sober reading of Singapore's chances of survival. 'This is 1995. Can it go on for another 50 years? I'm not sure. Can it go on for another 20 years? Maybe. Can it go on for another 10 years? I would say most probably' (Chuang, 1995). In balance, Mr Lee suggested a one in five chance that Singapore would go the way of the great city states of the past – down (Chuang, 1995). In another recent talk, Mr Lee presented a scenario in which Singapore would eventually rejoin Malaysia. 'Let us assume that whatever we do, the Malaysians do as well … Let's say they go the whole road, meritocracy, no "Malayism"; then I say "Let us rejoin them and stay in the federation. Because that's what we fought before to achieve".' (Ong, 1996)

For management and international business theorists, Singapore Incorporated provides a unique opportunity to observe and to analyse an almost textbook application of theories and concepts about corporate behaviours. This chapter has elaborated how Singapore Incorporated diversifies, maintains flexibility, moulds culture, invests in intangible assets, and strives for competitive advantages. If the metaphor of Singapore Incorporated has provided Singapore with opportunities and great successes, it has also provided Singapore with constraints. Singapore Incorporated has excluded many environments from consideration, unreflectingly or unconsciously. Singapore seems to imitate some of the strategies and policies of what Evans (1966) labelled the 'organization set': for Singapore, MNCs seem to set perceptions of prices, costs and available resources and strategies. Yet, ultimately, states do not form corporations; and corporate concepts, values and cultures may have only limited effects on states' survival and prosperity: Singapore Incorporated's final transformation may involve some realization of this.

In conclusion, Singapore's economic success flows as much from conventional comparative and competitive advantages as from history and accident. Singapore Incorporated's gradual evolution holds testimony to this process as the government, with the aid of strategic alliances, innovatively takes on national and international development. The unapologetically authoritarian government emphasizes discipline and strategic thinking; it sees liberal democracy as a luxury good that helps to mobilize resources for Singapore Incorporated. The many crises in the 1960s gave the PAP government legitimacy and rationales for its style. This style has matured with rising affluence, civic culture and a younger, better educated but more demanding electorate. Social and technology issues have joined traditional economics and political dimensions of governance and development. All Singapore Incorporated's major stakeholders do not have commitment to these new developments. Thus, extending Singapore Incorporated internationally, and drawing in local enterprises, forms a strategy to overcome potential conflicts.

Singapore Incorporated demonstrates an obsession with competitiveness such as few states do: ministers and the media often discuss in length the implications of the various surveys that rank nations on competitiveness. Krugman (1994) argued that competitiveness can prove a dangerous obsession for states; and, comparing states' behaviours with corporate behaviours can lead to poor economic policies that hamper and confuse development. Yet, measures of competitiveness do not constitute complete nonsense. Any country's future prosperity depends on its growth in productivity – which government policies can influence. Nations compete in that they choose policies to promote higher standards of living. So far, Singapore Incorporated has proven Krugman (1994) wrong by achieving high growth and maintaining competitiveness. Yet, Singapore also provides a living laboratory to observe the limits and potential of management and international business theories; future research could extend these observations, as well as lessons from Singapore Incorporated's success, across other states.

■ References

Chuang, P. M. (1995). S'pore has a 1-in-5 chance of failing. *Business Times*, 16 August, p. 1.

Cyert, R. M. and March, J. G. (1963). *A Behavioral Theory of the Firm*. Prentice-Hall.

Economic Development Board (1994) *Economic Development Board Yearbook*. EDB, Singapore.

Evans, W. M. (1966). The organizational set: towards a theory of inter-organizational relations. In *Approaches to Organizational Design* (J. D. Thompson, ed.) pp. 174–91, University of Pittsburgh Press.

Haley, U. C. V. (1990). From catalysts to chameleons: multinational firms as participants in political environments. PhD dissertation, Stern School of Business, New York University.

Haley, U. C. V. (1991). Corporate contributions as managerial masques: reframing corporate contributions as strategies to influence society. *Journal of Management Studies*, **28** (5), 486–509.

Hennart, J. F. (1982). *A Theory of Multinational Enterprise*. University of Michigan Press.

International Herald Tribune, 6 June, p. 1.

International Institute for Management Development (1996). *World Competitiveness Report*. IMD.

Katzenstein, P. J. (1985). *Small States in World Markets, Industrial Policy in Europe*. Cornell University Press.

Kraal, L. (1996). The Singapore connection. *Fortune*, 4 March, 86–93.

Krause, L. B. (1988).Hong Kong and Singapore: twins or kissing cousins? *Economic Development and Cultural Change*, s45–s66.

Krugman, P. (1994). Competitiveness: a dangerous obsession. *Foreign Affairs*, March/April, 28–44.

Lee K. Y. (1992). A tale of two cities – twenty years on. Li Ka Shing Lecture at the University of Hong Kong, 14 December.

Lee T. Y. and Low, L. (1989). *Local Entrepreneurship in Singapore: Private and State*. Times Academic Press for Institute of Policy Studies.

Lee, C. H. and Naya, S. (1988). Trade in East Asian development with comparative reference to Southeast Asian experiences. *Economic Development and Cultural Change*, s123–s152.

Lindblom, C. E. (1959). The science of muddling through. *Public Administration Review*, **19**, 79–88.

Low, L. (1991). *The Political Economy of Privatization in Singapore: Analysis, Interpretation and Issues*. McGraw-Hill.

Strategic Management in the Asia Pacific

Low, L. (1993). The public sector in contemporary Singapore: in retreat? In *Singapore Changes Guard: Social, Political and Economic Directions in the 1990s* (G. Rodan, ed.), pp 168–83, St Martin's Press.

Low, L. and Toh M.-H. (1992). *Public Policies in Singapore: Changes in 1980s and Future Signposts*. Times Academic Press.

Low, L., Toh, M.-H. and Soon, T. W. (1991). *The Economics of Education and Manpower: Issues and Policies in Singapore*. McGraw-Hill.

Low, L., Toh, M.-H., Soon, T. W. and Tan, K. Y. with special contribution from Hughes, H. (1993). *Challenge and Response: Thirty Years of the Economic Development Board*. Times Academic Press.

March, J. G. and Simon, H. A. (1958). *Organizations*, John Wiley.

Meyer, J. W. and Rowan B. (1978). Institutionalized organization: formal structure as myth and ceremony. *American Journal of Sociology*, **83**, 340–63.

Ministry of Finance (1993). *Report of the Committee to Promote Enterprise Overseas*. Interim, May and Final, August, Singapore National Printers.

Ministry of Trade and Industry (1991). *The Strategic Economic Plan: Towards a Developed Nation*. Singapore National Printers.

Mok, D. (1995). Local R&D spending close to $1b mark, survey shows. *Business Times*, 12 April, p. 2.

Mydans, S. (1996). Singapore dream: to reach the upper end of the playing field.

Normann, R. (1971). Organizational innovativeness: product variation and reorientation. *Administrative Science Quarterly*, **16**, 203–15

Ong, C. (1996). Will Singapore be reabsorbed into Malaysia? *Business Times*, 8–9 June, p. 1.

Pye, L. W. (1988) The new Asian capitalism: a political portrait. In *In Search of an East Asian Development Model* (P. L. Berger and H. H. M Kaoe eds), pp. 81–98, Transaction Book.

Redding, S. G. (1990). *The Spirit of Chinese Capitalism*. Walter de Gruyter.

Serrill, M. S. (1996). Unlock the shackles. *Time*, 10 June, p. 39.

Starbuck, W. H. (1976). Organizations and their environments. In *Handbook of Industrial and Organizational Psychology* (M. D. Dunnette, ed.), pp. 1069–123, Rand McNally.

Starbuck, W. H. (1992). Learning by knowledge-intensive firms. *Journal of Management Studies*, **29** (6), 713–40.

Straits Times (1995). 3 February 1995, p. 1.

Straits Times (1996a). 31 January 1996, p. 36.

Straits Times (1996b). 9 June 1996, p. 1.

Straits Times (1996c). 8 June 1996, p. 1.

Sunday Times (1994). 20 November 1994.

Tan, C. (1994). Use of 'Singapore' name restricted. *Straits Times*, 27 July, p. 40.

Teo, A. (1996). S'pore still 2nd in competitiveness. *Business Times*, 27 May, p, 1.

The Economist (1986). 22 November 1986.

Toh M.-H. and Low, L. (1993). Development planning in Singapore. In *Development Planning in Asia* (S. Tambunlertchai and S. P. Gupta, eds), pp. 223–54, Asian and Pacific Development Centre.

Weick, K. E. (1979). *The Social Psychology of Organizing*. Addison Wesley.

World Economic Forum (1996) *Global Competitiveness Report*. World Economic Forum.

Chapter 9.1

Singapore Inc.'s official World Wide Web site

■ Usha C. V. Haley ■

The metaphor 'Singapore Incorporated' (Chapter 9) that I developed in 1996 with my co-authors attracted the Singaporean government's attention. The government subsequently used the metaphor to market Singapore regionally and globally, to address Singapore's governmental-led development and to emphasize the government's efficacious design of business environments (see also Chapters 12, 12.1, 13 and 13.1).

The official Singapore Inc. WWW site (at http://www.singapore-inc.com) constitutes one way in which the Singaporean government imaginatively plays to a global audience. Tony Tan, then Deputy Prime Minister and Minister for Defense, officially launched the WWW site on 11 March 1997.

Singapore-inc.com echoes with corporate symbols. An initial banner announces, 'In Asia we make it happen'. As one clicks to enter, the site swirls with the names of the alliance's dominant partners – all governmental agencies. Singapore Inc.'s emblazoned official communiqué appears like a corporate annual report's introduction:

Singapore aims to be a global city with linkages to key centers of the world, and a home base to leading international corporations and international talents. With the world as its arena, Singapore's open economic policies, willingness to learn and adapt to global trends, and the country's partnerships with business and foreign governments have allowed it to tap resources beyond itself. Singapore has innovatively overcome its limitations to growth. This philosophy has enabled it to progress, transforming Singapore into Singapore Unlimited. The Singapore Unlimited vision articulates Singapore's aspirations to become a first league developed nation and its strategies to enhance its economic activities in an integrated, holistic manner, using a total systems approach. Through the co-operation and support of all parties – political leaders and government, institutions and academia, chambers of commerce and trade associations, industrialists and labor, foreign investors and local companies, the people, and all who have identified themselves to be the nation's stakeholders – the vision for Singapore will be achieved in harmony and with measurable success for each party. Together, these stakeholders form Singapore INC, working together like entities in a large corporation. Each responsible for a specific aspect of Singapore's value chain. Each working as a team to support and add value to our business partners. The Singapore INC spirit has contributed to the nation's present success. It believes that by borrowing strengths from one another, Singapore and its partners will realize the promises of a new age. Singapore believes that through sharing, it will be empowered to achieve a whole new Singapore Unlimited with unlimited opportunities and potential wealth. Singapore invites you to discover how it can help you soar to greater heights. Together, we will realize an unlimited tomorrow.

A list of partners and their self-descriptions from the WWW site indicate Singapore Inc.'s formal structure:

- Singapore Economic Development Board (EDB): The lead agency for industrial planning, development and promotion of investments in manufacturing, services and local businesses. Within a strategic and economic framework, the EDB will assist investors in setting up operations speedily.
- National Computer Board (NCB): The national Information Technology (IT) authority dedicated to the development of IT in Singapore. The NCB spearheads the implementation of Singapore's IT2000 master plan.
- National Science and Technology Board (NSTB): The national agency for the promotion of R&D activities in the industrial and services sectors. The NSTB spurs R&D efforts and capability development in niche areas of science and technology through its fourteen research institutes and centers for R&D activities.
- Singapore Productivity and Standards Board (PSB): The national agency for productivity and standards. The PSB's key thrusts are productivity promotion, manpower development, technology application, industry development, standards and quality development and incentive management.
- Singapore Trade Development Board (TDB): The national trade-promotion agency. The TDB secures international market access for Singaporean goods and services; attracts international traders to base in Singapore; facilitates and protects the nation's external trade interests.
- Singapore Tourism Board (STB): The agency that develops and promotes tourism and related facilities and services in Singapore. The STB promotes Singapore as a venue for conventions, exhibitions, sporting events, incentive travel and other tourism businesses.
- Jurong Town Corporation (JTC): The agency that serves as principal developer and manager of industrial estates and related facilities. The JTC offers manufacturers a wide range of facilities from industrial land, high and low rise factories to R&D and Business Park facilities.
- Port of Singapore Authority (PSA): The agency responsible for the provision and maintenance of efficient port facilities and services. The PSA operates 6 port terminals for all types of vessels including container ship, cargo freighters, coasters, lighters and passenger lines.

The site includes links to the partners' home pages, sources of data, interviews with agency heads elaborating on their visions for Singapore Inc., contact addresses, performance reports and press releases. The Singapore government spent about US$250 000 to market this brand name on other top WWW sites such as Alta Vista, C|NET, the PointCast Network, Wall Street Journal Interactive and Yahoo.

Chapter 10

Informational network industrialization and Japanese business management[1]

■ Sam K. Steffensen ■

■ Introduction

The co-occurrence of a protracted domestic economic recession and an epidemic financial crisis in Asia have hit most Japanese industries as a double punch. Strikingly, the extent and speed of the markets' meltdown in Asia was not foreshadowed, let alone suggested, by economists. Furthermore, the recent events in Asia have left an almost anachronistic image of the whimsy 'cottage industry' (Wade, 1994) of state capacity propositions which emerged in the slipstream of the Japanese government-sponsored World Bank East Asia miracle study in the early 1990s. Somehow, the happenings in Asia may now be interpreted as a momentous appending factor of the Japanese recession. Meanwhile, Japanese industries and their organizational practices are challenged by new developments common to the entire international business community. These developments, to which Japanese industries, as well, have to change and to adapt, are primarily propelled by the revolutionary progress in digitized network-system technologies and volatile, globalizing, competition dynamics. Hence, the strategic agenda facing Japanese change management is very complex. Figure 10.1 provides a rough framework outlining some of the main issues contained in the restructuring agenda of Japanese firms.

In Japan, it is widely perceived that the advent of a genuine information economy is a major cause behind the industrial revival in the USA and, conversely, the recession domestically. This chapter concentrates on informational network industrialization and the primary influence factors embodying this process with respect to Japanese business organization and management. It is argued that, rather than political and market driven forces, technological progress appears to be a firsthand driving force

---

[1] This chapter has been published previously by MCB University Press Limited: Steffensen, S. K. (1998). Informational network industrialization and Japanese business management. *Journal of Organizational Change Management*, **11** (6), 515–529.

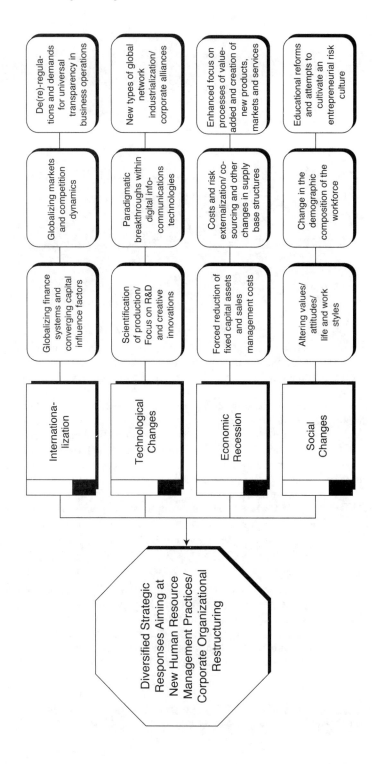

Figure 10.1 Major issues challenging Japanese-style management and organization
Source: Steffensen and Dirks (1997).

behind the opening and transformation of Japanese production networks. The technology push entails several facets, for instance:

- international economic transactions, production networks and alliances are premised on, and impelled by, secure and reliable info-com technologies and digitized communication systems

- constant technological upgrading occurs of all sourcing layers and the general scientification of production requires open, flexible and speedy innovation processes, real-time co-operation and research and development (R&D) alliances

- progress arises in converging info-com and media technologies, and the scope-oriented interlinking structures of network economics are carriers of open systems logic.

These facets define informational network industrialization.

The chapter is divided into three main sections: The first deals with the commonplace concept of Japanese business networks and the challenges facing these from informational network industrialization. The second section, concentrates on challenges imposed on Japanese organizational management by ongoing globalization trends. The final section, discusses the organizational change aspects of Japanese production networks in Asia with specific respect to the current economic recession in the Asia-Pacific region.

▉ Japanese business networks versus informational network industrialization

Networking has in multifarious ways become a keyword for the ongoing arrangement of the next generation of socioeconomic infrastructures and business structures. Surely, Japan is no exemption. Japanese academics well known to the Western public, such as Imai (1990; 1992), Aizu (1994) and Kumon (1992; 1994), have been among the theoretic forerunners in highlighting the network qualities of Japanese industrial organizations. As a product of complex interfirm networks, specialization, flexible production management, and constant process innovations, Japanese firms have long been conceived as the precursors of a strategy that marks a renunciation of vertical integration. Numerous studies have demonstrated how the Japanese-type industrial organization has produced great results in efficient supply chain management, flexible production designs, organizational learning and strenuous R&D activities. In fact, Japanese multilateral interfirm networks, including *keiretsu* structures, industrial groupings and the networks' wide-reaching institutional characteristics, have been one of the most central research subjects in studies on Japanese business economics in recent years. Particularly, organizational features such as bank and trading houses in long-term internalized transactions, financial and personal entanglements, and cross-industry co-operation are features associated with these networks. All tend to agree that the prevailing Japanese-style interorganizational structures have come into shape on the basis of a strong reliance on human networks and social exchange dynamics. This has further inspired many scholars to establish instructive theoretical links between Japanese industrial organization patterns and production capacities, R&D practices, markets' formation, management environment, corporate governance and investment behaviours (e.g. Fruin, 1992; Gerlach, 1992; 1997). During economic growth periods the internalized group structure served as dynamo behind a distinct enterprise expansion strategy leading to the rapid growth of subsidiary business ventures raised with almost free capital. During the recession, this structure converted into a handy means of adjusting surplus workforce and escalating wage spending. Despite admirable efforts, this practice has, however, reached its limits in terms of capacity and cost structure. By early 1998, for example, a company such as Nippon Steel had one-third of its official labour force on transfer, while another large manufacturer such as Hitachi had more than 10 000 workers on transfer (based on personal interview data).

Meanwhile, corporate Japan increasingly acknowledges that new speedy types of flexibly organized networking capabilities are an essential requirement to sustain its international competitiveness. Also, Japanese industrial researchers are increasingly paying attention to the dynamics and role of new types of networked industries, externalities, and the economics of transactions (e.g. Hayashi, 1998; Kokuryô, 1995; Nanbu, Itô, and Kimata, 1994). Embedded in the imperatives of international competition and technological advances, industrial networks are strategies to realize production cost reductions, lead time shortenings, quality improvement, product innovation and market adaptation/entry. Corporate network theories today cannot be separated from the generic progress taking place in digital technologies, communication devices and information infrastructures. Technological breakthroughs in such areas sustain the dynamic development of information networks. Besides being remarkable processors and calculators, computers (including integrated devices) are playing a core function as co-ordination technology (Malone and Rockart, 1993), linked into extending networks ordering and co-ordinating activities and information flows. Electronic information technology (IT) network systems, such as EDI, LAN, CALS, Intranets and GroupWare, are now state-of-the-art solutions to cost-efficient co-ordination of large supplier networks, services, and business ventures. This kind of networking in corporate activities actually alters existing organizations and the outlines of industries (Steffensen, 1998). Advanced information networks, in their widest sense, constitute a new type of volatile globalizing economic activity space. In organizational terms the informational space constitutes a new non-territorial, and therefore erratic, dimension hard to control, predict, and incorporate into rigidly internalized company structures. Additionally, the convergence taking place in info-com technologies demand new organizational structures in order to realize the emerging new business potential. For example, Hitachi managers, interviewed in their Tokyo headquarter in 1998, admit that they face major difficulties just in getting the established television division and computer division to work together, despite the fact that everyone involved knows that an exiting convergence is taking place here. According to these managers, strong guidelines from the top, followed by new types of project-oriented reorganization, are required. Actually such evidence is not rare, particularly among Japan's old establishment of 'full-set' manufacturers, and reports about the challenges facing their traditional divisionalized structure, including the closed community-type innovation practices.

As Antonelli (1992) has pointed out, the economics of information networks, as part of a broader economic theory of information production and use, has, so far, primarily emerged in six major areas: a) the economics of the generation of technological innovations; b) the economics of diffusion of technological innovation; c) regional economics; d) the economics of market competition; e) the theory of industrial organization; and f) the theory of the firm. Here, however, it is argued that the dynamic features of these new types of network, and the intangible economic activity space they constitute, question such divisions in practice. For instance, inquiries targeted at global competitive forces, interfirm organization, and theories of the firm are factually intertwined and inseparable. Likewise, radical innovations in digital technologies and related areas are constantly breaking new ground, e.g. in markets and spaces, in information economics. Simultaneously these innovation processes are redefining the universe of organization and management principles. Put roughly, what is commonly perceived as paradigmatic shifts taking place in the info-communication industries may be boiled down to four major interrelated processes:

1 Downsizing/ system shrinking.

2 Networking/interconnecting.

3 (System/standard) opening/converging.

4 Software and contents creating.

Consequently, informational network industrialization is dynamically entangled in logic emanating from paradigmatic (predominantly techno-scientific) processes advancing synchronously.

Actually, the organizational change challenges facing the Japanese business networks and their transforming information systems architecture have several commonalties. Japanese company groups have for years built up complex, costly, proprietary and customized information systems and software solutions. Simultaneously, a striking computerization discrepancy between large manufacturers and small lower-level subcontractors has come into existence (for data: InfoCom Research Inc., 1997; SMEA, 1998; Steffensen, 1998). Indeed, the stable hierarchical transaction patterns facilitated by the distinct diversification process of the Japanese industrial system have, so far, reduced the need for open computer networking. Actually, top-efficient proprietary electronic communication systems between parent manufacturers and their intimate elite suppliers have existed for long and supported the fine-tuned logistics. A comparatively high ratio of production subcontracted to elite component suppliers on a stable long-term basis has facilitated parent manufacturer's efforts to deal directly (online) only with these first-level business partners. While it is not unusual for a large Western manufacturer to link directly to some thousand suppliers, the number in Japan is normally only a quarter to a third of this. Obviously, this organizational transaction structure is also reflected in the comparatively limited size of the parent firms. In fact, some Japanese parent companies now see changes in opening and rationalizing their procurement structure by cutting directly linked suppliers and decentralizing business competencies (Nissan being an example). Moreover, not only has the post-war supply-base system been stable and exclusive, but it has also to a high degree been conditioned on geographical proximity. Stability, closeness and industrial policies impelled the build-up of costly proprietary wired infostructures and customized software solutions. However, neither closed-system stability, nor spatial proximity are weighty concerns contained in the dictates of informational networks.

Ikeda (1997), for example, in his prize-winning study, deals with paradigm shifts in the info-communication industries and Japanese-style organization. According to his findings, Japanese companies find difficulties in accommodating themselves to new trends emerging in these industries and attendant techno-economic dynamics. First, based on field observations he argues that Japanese-style organizations tend to pay too much attention to internal consensus in a present-day business environment stressing individual creativity less than (internal) co-ordination. Along with software standardization, integration, and open flexible network systems becoming the norm, many of the social, co-ordination skills of complex Japanese organizations are growing less important. Along with developments in IT, market-based co-ordination is becoming more attractive while flexible project teams cutting across organizational boundaries are indispensable driving forces for innovation. Confronting an increasingly streamlined business environment that demands more creativity, bottom-line results, and speedy alliances across companies than internal co-ordination, the Japanese-style organization needs to reduce its attention to its inveterate consensus and internal management features. Evidently, internal consensus features and company cultures sustained each other during the many years of successful efforts by Japanese companies to co-ordinate interrelated (or complementary) production processes in constantly changing socioeconomic environments. The strength of these co-ordination efforts probably showed itself most distinctly in the later half of the 1970s. However, a momentous break in continuity is now on the agenda: Interrelationships are increasingly being extended beyond company frameworks, while the domestic socio-economic setting is transforming in largely unknown directions. Simultaneously, the dictates of global capitalism in a rejuvenated raw and explicit form is present more than ever. In short, it appears to be the case that while classical, market-directed organizations emphasized open, concentrated networks, closed, decentralized networks largely characterized Japanese enterprise culture. Now, dynamics inherent in the informational network age require the strategic formation of open decentralized networks.

■ Japanese business management versus globalization trends

The international firm of the information network age must be conceived as an entity that commands an expanding variety of simultaneously managed network relations over time. The spread of digital information networks gives rise to a visionary virtual corporation concept and provokes a range of new theories of the firm (e.g. Casson, 1997; Dosi, Teece and Chytry, 1998; Wigand, Picot and Reichwald, 1997). Of particular interest to traditional stakeholders, virtual business activities are constituting transaction and innovation systems beyond large companies', unions' and governmental controls. Also, what is understood as 'the extended enterprise' is essentially about extending operations and alliances beyond organizational frameworks through extended, flexible, network structures. Another tendency is the expanding – both in scope and complexity – of industrial production networks. These networks involve constant rationalization of the parts-supply system, for instance, in the case of joint use and development of parts among competing companies (co-sourcing), severe technological-capacity demands on all subcontracting tiers, and increased, open procurement on a global scale. Behind such new extraorganizational transaction dynamics stands primarily the Internet. In fact, it is argued that the Internet in itself constitutes an open innovation system, which cannot be ignored by any enterprise, as shown in Figure 10.2.

Thus, in a series of interviews with Japanese managers, almost all point to the Internet boom from the mid-1990s as a mind-changing event with respect to their business

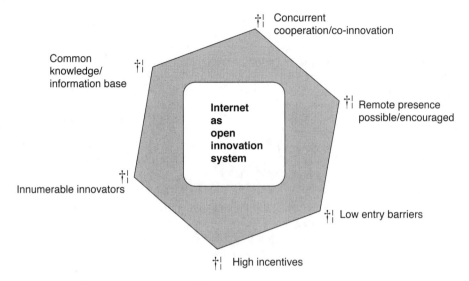

Figure 10.2 The Internet: an open innovation system

practices and organizations. This is further sustained by recent survey data (SMEA, 1998) that show a jump in Internet use in Japanese firms from 11.7 per cent in fiscal 1995 to 50.4 per cent in fiscal 1996. The jump was extraordinary for large companies from 34.3 per cent to 74.8 per cent. Business Internet is today, by far, the most frequently used network in communication exceeding the company framework.

Seen from the viewpoint of a typical, networked Japanese firm, increased, open, strategic transaction patterns beyond the company represent almost a third dimension in the organizational texture. Intrafirm reforms, diversified organizational externalizing patterns, and genuine outsourcing strategies are now often forming part of the same managerial agenda.[2] Interviews conducted among high-ranking executives at large Japanese companies during 1997 and 1998 by the author and his team, reveal considerable similarities in envisioned restructuring, although speed of execution, competence and ambition vary significantly. The major restructuring directions highlighted by Japanese managers can roughly be summed up in four points:

- Slimming internal hierarchies; raising task-oriented group leaders; decentralizing departmental decision-making and management responsibility both in administration and line manufacturing. Typically, at least, one layer of each organizational hierarchy is to be eliminated accompanied by more fluid authority spaces. For example, Nippon Steel has subsequently eliminated one layer, while Sony has constructed team structures which compete internally for project financing and recruits.

[2] Usually in Japan the term 'outsourcing' signifies that some internalized company (semi-core) functions are being externalized to a more transparent, formalized, contractual basis for economic exchange. Consequently, a higher supplier-switching ratio is implied as well. Simultaneously, the growing importance of information processing activities implies that outsourcing strategies go in two directions: One aims at the flexible use of specialized information services, and the other aims at scale to increase and refine competence (Steffensen, 1997).

- More focus on company core competencies; merging, transforming, or cutting off fringe activities both domestically and overseas; comprehensive human resource mapping; more organizational support and space for venture-type projects and increasing use of external sources (including contract workers). For example, this feature is strongly recognized by the traditional trading houses, such as Mitsui Bussan, that are drawing less than 50 per cent of their earnings from ordinary trade activities.

- More formal corporate diversification along the lines of a (string configured) holding-company structure, in the wake of commercial law amendments and corporate tax code changes; increased focus on bottom-line results and managerial vision and skills. For example, this is an obvious organizational change strategy for the major general electronics companies such as Toshiba, Hitachi and Mitsubishi.

- Rationalization of component sourcing and product portfolios, and stricter policies towards loss-producing activities, especially in manufacturing; shedding economically troubled divisions, either through organizational splits (Hitachi air conditioners) or through external joint-venture activities (Toshiba air conditioners).

Although, there exists a certain consensus regarding the directions, companies are struggling with their various organizational peculiarities. Just to give one example: an interview with head of personnel at Mitsui Bussan revealed that all regular workers are given a company number (*sebangô*) when they enter the company. The number reveals with which division you started, in what year, and so on. In short, the number reveals which internal community you belong(ed) to. This old system has for many years sustained the company spirit, but makes it now a very difficult task for leading managers to go back to their old areas, as 'traitor', and promote rationalization and restructuring measures. Obviously, such systems also run counter to the teamwork structure and logic of the information-network age (e.g. Lipnack and Stamps, 1997).

Symptomatically, Japanese management studies in the 1990s tend to emphasize that tie-ups are evolving into firm level networks and making open strategic collaboration between firms desirable (Hanaoka et al., 1995; Iwasawa et al., 1995). Increasingly, these studies pay attention to 'the economics of interconnections' with particular respect to international-business strategy issues (Iwasawa et al., 1995). Takagi (1995) even argues in favour of viewing the concept of 'poly-agent systems' as a leading organizational paradigm of 'the multimedia age'. These systems, according to him, constitute the 'poly-agent society' where individual agents in networks, are bound to construct their own internal models to link up effectively with external systems and to enter client-server types of market transactions. These enhanced concerns with relational aspects of open-style managed networks and the networks' economic effects on information and communication logic have been underestimated for some time in corporate Japan. This applies, for instance, with respect to the diffusion of technical *de facto* standards, in an environment where industrial product cycles are shortening and time to market has gained a crucial role in the competition race.[3]

Globalization in business is basically signified by expanding market interconnections, and multiplicity of and competition among corporate and national strategies (BRIE,

---

[3] However, any possible comparative delay to market among Japanese manufacturers is not likely to be rooted in the parts-production flow or the assembly process but, rather, in the upstream management decision-making processes, and a target for organizational change.

1996). The formation of regional architectures may be considered as well. However, its is doubtful if one can speak of an internal regional architecture in the case of Asia, as assessed by the Berkeley Roundtable on the International Economy (BRIE) study. More precisely, the growth of various types of alliances on a global scale in recent years is probably, together with financial market dynamics, one of the best indicators of an ongoing globalization trend. Our interviews at Sony revealed that for a top-ranking manager at Sony's headquarters in Tokyo, globalization proves itself by the fact that the company has only one-fourth of its sales and less than half of its production in Japan. However, more important to him, and to Sony's corporate strategy, is the evolving human-resource globalization, particularly with regards to cross-national teamwork for technical experts and software engineers. Sony is, at the same time, convinced about the importance of operating self-contained regional headquarters and facilitating a sense of belonging. Evidently, globalization heralds open interconnectivity (Castells, 1996), as well as new competencies and forms of co-operation (alliances) facilitated by the progress of info-communication technology. Particularly, diversified corporate alliances have shown a conspicuous growth both in number and scope for more than a decade. According to Mody (1993) an alliance can be understood as a flexible organizational mode that allows firms to bring complementary strengths together in order to experiment with new technologies and organizational ideas.

Alliance's roles as strategic learning devices need great attention. Data (from Japan External Trade Organization – JETRO) confirm that Japanese firms increasingly enter into international alliances, including partnerships through mergers and acquisitions (with a recent increase also in in-in and out-in types), as a part of their restructuring, competence-building and expansion strategies. Domestically, flexible alliances, as a strategic approach to organizational learning and change management, have been an effective part of Japanese innovation and business systems. Japanese firms show a clear and skilful preference for such an approach also when extending their business activities internationally. In conclusion, growing cross-national collaboration agreements and R&D-intensive corporate alliances involving Japanese manufacturers compel these to diversify their networks and supply linkages. Rearrangements are often prompted by international business developments and bound to influence the evolutionary development patterns of overseas production networks.

▪ Transformational perspectives of Japanese production networks in Asia

As also underlined by the Economic Planning Agency (EPA, 1996), the growing use of IT is increasingly placing limits on the traditional practice of fostering internal supplier–manufacturer relationships in technological-development processes. Globalizing techno-economic competitive principles cause Japanese companies to open their supplier networks. Accordingly, the design of open and flexible extended networks is required to upgrade fast-product-cycle industrial management, take advantage of value-adding synergy effects, and make increased strategic use of external resources on a global scale. The indispensable specialist-oriented team dynamics behind continuous R&D-based innovation processes and influx of new technologies constitute major push factors (Steffensen, 1997). Increasingly, Japanese manufacturers are incited to extend their hitherto transactional relations, such as original equipment manufacturer (OEM) contracts, to outsourcing strategic R&D collaboration agreements with foreign manufacturing partners. Corporate information systems increase the ability to co-ordinate and manage internal and external relations flexibly. Evidently, just judged narrowly from an ordinary economics of transactions perspective, an intensified use of IT interchange incites Japanese companies to make increasing use of the organizations' external sources of production and specialist services. Decisive, however, is the technical fact that companies concurrently are capable of imposing their minutely systematized supply and quality control standards. The elaborate manufacturer (procurer)–supplier relationships and logistics in the complex Japanese industrial network formations are rooted in technical perfection and interlinked activity spin-offs.

In fact, Japanese companies, for example in the general assembly and electronics industry, are all in the process of rethinking existing introverted parts procurement systems and other structures in conjunction with open networking. It is common knowledge that the strength of the yen was prompting a shift away from technology exchanges in favour of direct local production and procurement, and displacement of facilities overseas, particularly in Asia in the early 1990s. The yen's appreciation, however, only partly explains this shift. It is worth keeping in mind, that for the last decade, international production has been growing significantly faster than international trade. Moreover, recent years have shown a dramatic increase in strategic alliances in Asia involving Japanese firms, often in the shape of joint ventures.[4] In response to this situation, the scope of Japanese industrial network studies has broadened accordingly. Not surprisingly, some of the same spirited considerations as put forward in this chapter, in relation to technology-based network management, also echo from some of these recent studies (BRIE, 1996; Ernst, 1997). Most studies observe that centralized management processes have predominantly characterized Japanese affiliates in Asia and closed governance structures. One measure of relevance in a network perspective is the conspicuous high ratio of intrafirm trade, a factor, however, hard to grasp. In a timely study, Hatch and Yamamura (1996) demonstrate how Japanese companies actually have transplanted many essentials of their organizational structure to Asia, and this transplantation process relates closely to the macrodevelopment strategies for the region. Evidently, Japanese business activities in Asia display some noteworthy characteristics, which have impact on current organizational change management strategies. For instance, on a worldwide scale, manufacturing and non-manufacturing Japanese business activities have almost equal shares. However, a very large share of manufacturing activities among the total number of Japanese foreign affiliates is concentrated in Asia. Moreover, this development took speed in the 1990s. In particular, a high level of start-ups could be observed in the mid-1990s (MITI, 1997).

As concerns intrafirm trade, a major point is that the Japanese strive to achieve a high local-sourcing ratio, that in many cases translates into a high ratio of component sourcing from locally present Japanese suppliers. This feature testifies to the fact, that the Japanese manufacturers to a large extent have aimed to establish a copy of their domestic production network, including their internalized information network and governance system. Even in cases where a potential local supplier may have been

---

[4] JETRO's data show that China, as destination country, accounted for 37 per cent (almost similar to the US share) in Asia. Some of the joint ventures in Asia are, however, likely to have certain, obviously strategically impelled, pro forma characteristics. Nevertheless, the co-operation approach to Asia may be more obvious to Japanese firms as this strategic conduct is strongly prevailing in their home base. The highest levels of independent investments (as percentage of total) are to be found in countries such as Thailand, Malaysia, the Philippines and Singapore.

present and economic incentives, such as currency devaluation, may have been manifest, this may not have been seriously considered. As Streeten (1996: 361) remarks,

> Firms are reluctant to drop their own subsidiaries as suppliers in favor of a domestic rival, unless the devaluation is large and sustained. In any case, the allocation of shown profits between countries will be quite different for intrafirm trade than arms-length trade. It will be guided by taxation, of trade union pressures, of price controls, of insistence on joint ventures, on public image, and all other considerations that give rise to price transfer.

Adding to this, Japanese manufactures show a remarkable, and so far greatly justified, confidence in Japanese technical production quality, diligence, and supply standards. Not accidentally, the features in question are mostly rooted in national institutional settings that cannot easily be replaced. However, the face value of such confidence may be dwindling along with the spread of new informational production modes, as spelled out above. In any event, the institutional settings are confronting fundamental organizational and human resource management (HRM) strategic challenges, as shown in Figure 10.1 and explained elsewhere (Steffensen and Dirks, 1997).

Furthermore, the current economic crisis in Asia provokes delicate managerial strategic options and action patterns among industrial stakeholders. For example, as most Japanese industry has already establish localized production networks and informal relationships, they may, on the one hand, actually welcome the prevalence of some protectionist measures such as local content requirements, upheld by national governments. In certain strategically important sectors, Japanese industry (and supporting institutions) can actually back up protectionist measures taken – or sustained – by national governments. On the other hand, the omnipresent sales slump and bleak investment mood may force many lower-tier Japanese suppliers out of the markets. When large manufacturers, such as Matsushita, announce that they are considering an increase in local sourcing, it is therefore questionable whether this primarily is considered as a rescue operation for Japanese SMEs or a real localization improvement. For one thing, data show (MITI, 1997) that withdrawals increase typically after three years from start-up, so far with the highest ratio in Europe. Next, the withdrawal ratio is far highest among SMEs. Finally, most withdrawals happen due to problems in 'sales-related issues'. Now, considering 1) the location spurt in Asia in the mid-1990s (under extremely different conditions), 2) the high ratio of manufacturing Japanese SMEs in Asia, 3) the recession in Asian markets (including Japan), and 4) the long-time existing excess production capacity and investments, it is clear that forced rearrangements are impending.

Largely resembling the situation at home, the closed and Japan-centred features of Japanese production networks in Asia increasingly are inappropriate and leading them into a set of competitive dilemmas. Based on observations so far, there is no doubt that the extensive restructuring taking place in Japanese corporations, of which much is still on the drawing board, will immediately ramify into the Asian production networks. Many tasks will be outsourced on open contract basis, while pressure and rationalizations will be even tougher on the supplier tiers. Likewise, many of the redundancy structures associated with Japanese firms and their innovativeness and knowledge creation and welfare, will, in many cases, be eliminated as they will be found too slow and costly. Moreover, temporary employment will increase and larger differences in company membership status will emerge, just to line up the basic directions. As Japanese business is a major employer in Asia, the restructuring will contribute to destabilize the labour market in the Asian countries, not much different from what is happening in Japan. For instance, the introduction of upgraded information technological environments, particularly among labour-absorbing SME suppliers, will deepen the workforce–skill mismatch problem and create tension and frictions. But surely, this will all take place under the 'a Japanese economic recovery is the way out of the dark for Asia' headline attempted to uphold a communal stakeholder perception.

The rapidly dwindling profits and earnings, deriving from the sales slump, while advantages in cost structures largely remain, of Japanese manufacturers in Asia, will speed up inevitable rationalization measures and open inter-regional sourcing strategies of the Japanese production networks in Asia. Whether a dramatic setback in reinvestments in Asia is going to take place is uncertain, but hardly politico-economically desirable by any of the partners. It is, however, clear that the recession in Asia is putting a brake on Japan's capital-goods export strategies for the region and putting considerable constraints on Japanese direct investment profits. The adjustment of excessive manufacturing capacity in the Asia-Pacific region hurts Japanese high-end production technology exports, among other things, and effects the domestic economy negatively. Exports of intermediate products to overseas activity bases make up about one quarter of the total Japanese exports and are particularly significant in Asia. Hence, intercompany, intermediate product exports have by far exceeded reverse imports. Consequently, the current recession in Japan and Asia forces Japanese manufacturers to speed up their restructuring plans, also with respect to rethinking and integrating their Asian production networks much more into international production complexes in compliance with the advancing informational network industrialization. Evidently, this process is going to be very uneasy, but may, in the longer run, offer more potential for real industrial upgrading and national innovation system building in the Asia Pacific region.

■ Concluding summary

Divided into three main sections, this chapter has, accordingly, investigated the challenges facing Japanese-style industrial organization and management from three major change factors, namely:

- informational network industrialization
- ongoing globalization trends
- the sudden economic recession in the Asia Pacific region.

First, it has been argued and demonstrated that while closed decentralized networks have largely characterized Japanese enterprise culture, dynamics inherent in the informational network require strategic formation of open decentralized network structures, a trend to which Japanese industry has to accommodate. Second, growing cross-national collaboration agreements and flexible R&D intensive corporate alliances compel Japanese companies to decentralize competencies, and diversify networks and supply linkages. Rearrangements are usually prompted by international business developments and are affecting the evolution and operation strategies of overseas production networks. Finally, the economic recession in Japan and Asia forces, for better or worse, Japanese manufacturers to speed up their restructuring plans at home and abroad. As the Japanese Asian production networks are structured on much the same principles as their domestic production, significant parts of the domestic restructuring strategies are likely to be extended in much the same way to these. For one thing, organizational change strategies will seek to integrate the Asian production networks much more into international production complexes in compliance with the advancing informational network industrialization.

■ References

Aizu, I. (1994). *Shinka suru nettowa-ku (Hyper Network Society)*. NTT.

Antonelli, C. (ed.) (1992). *The Economics of Information Networks*. Elsevier.

BRIE (1996). Briefing book for the policy conference on East Asian Networks. Copenhagen, October.

Casson, M. (1997). *Information and Organizations – A New Perspective on the Theory of the Firm*. Clarendon Press.

Castells, M. (1996). *The Rise of the Network Society*. Blackwell.

Dosi G., Teece, D. and Chytry, J. (eds) (1998). *Technology, Organization, and Competitiveness*. Oxford University Press.

EPA(1996). *Nihon keizaihakusho heisei 8 nen (The Japan Economic Whitebook)*. Ministry of Finance Publishers.

Ernst, D. (1997). Partners for the China circle? The Asian production networks of Japanese electronics firms. In *The China Circle* (B. Naughton, ed.), The Brookings Institute.

Fruin, M. W. (1992). *The Japanese Enterprise System*. Oxford University Press.

Gerlach, M. L. (1992). *Alliance Capitalism*. California University Press.

Gerlach, M. L. (1997). The organizational logic of business groups: evidence from the zaibatsu. In *Beyond the Firm* (T. Shiba and M. Shimotani, eds), Oxford University Press.

Hanaoka, S., Takarabe, J., Shimada, T. and Yoshida, M. (1995). *Keiei kakushin to jôhôgijutsu (Information Technology and Management Innovations)*. Nikagiren.

Hatch, W. and Yamamura, K. (1996). *Asia in Japan's Embrace – Building a Regional Production Alliance*. Cambridge University Press.

Hayashi, K. (1998). *Nettowa-kingu jôhôshakai no keizaigaku (Economics of the Networking Information Society)*. NTT.

Ikeda, N. (1997). *Jôhôts shinkakumei to nihonkigyô (The Digital Revolution and Japanese Firms)*. NTT.

Imai, K.-I. (1990). *Nettowa-ku shakai no tenkai (The Information Network Society 1990)*. Chikuma shobô.

Imai, K.-I. (1992). Japan's corporate networks. In *The Political Economy of Japan, Vol. 3: Cultural and Social Dynamics* (S. Kumon and H. Rosovsky, eds) Stanford University Press.

InfoCom Research Inc. (eds) (1997). *Jôhôtsûshin handobukku '98 nenban (Info-Communications Handbook '98 edition)*. InfoCom/NTT.

Iwasawa, T., Miyazawa, M., Nabeta, H. and Arakawa, T. (1995). *Keiei kakushin to sangyô nettowa-ku (Industrial Networks and Management Innovations)*. Nikagiren.

JETRO: http://www.jetro.go.jp

Kokuryô, J. (1995). *O-pen nettowa-ku keiei (Open Network Management)*, Nihon Keizai Shimbunsha.

Kumon, S. (1992). Japan as a network society. In *The Political Economy of Japan, Vol. 3: Cultural and Social Dynamics* (S. Kumon and H. Rosovsky, eds) Stanford University Press.

Kumon, S. (1994). *Jôhô bunmei ron (Information Civilization Theories)*, NTT.

Lipnack, J. and Stamps, J. (1997). *Virtual Teams: Reaching Across Space, Time, and Organization with Technology*. John Wiley.

Malone, T. and Rockart, J. (1993). How will information technology reshape organizations? Computers as coordination technology. In *Globalization, Technology and Competition – The Fusion of Computers and Telecommunications in the 1990s* (S. P. Bradley, J. A. Hausman, and R. L. Nolan, eds) Harvard Business School Press.

MITI (1997). *Overseas Business Activities of Japanese Companies*. Definite Report, International Business Affairs Division of Industrial Policy Bureau, November.

Mody, A. (1993). Learning through alliances. *Journal of Economic Behavior and Organization*, **20**, 151–170.

Nanbu, T., Itô, N. and Kimata, N. (eds) (1994). *Nettowa-ku sangyô no tenbô (The Prospects of Network Industries)*. Nihon Hyôronsha.

SMEA (MITI) (1998), *Chûshôkigyô hakusho heisei 10nenban (White Paper on Small and Medium-sized Enterprises, 1998 edition)*. Ministry of Finance Publishers.

Steffensen, S. K. (1997). *Post-bubble Corporate Restructuring in Japan: The Case of Outsourcing and Venturing in Japanese Society*, vol. 2. pp. 118–40. Japanese Society Research Institute.

Steffensen, S. K. (1998). IT and organizational design perspectives in Japanese firms. In *Business Information Technology Management: Closing the International Divide* (P. Banerjee, R. Hackney, G. Dhillon and R. Jain, eds), Har Anand.

Steffensen, S. K. and Dirks, D. (1997). *Between Efficiency and Effectiveness: Technological Change, Restructuring, and Human Resource Management in Japanese Firm*. In Proceedings of the 14th Annual EAMSA Conference 'Asian Firms Looking Towards the Global Market', Metz (France), 23–25 October, pp. 191–218.

Streeten, P. (1996). Free and managed trade. In *National Diversity and Global Capitalism* (S. Berger and R. Dore, eds) Cornell University Press.

Takagi, H. (1995). *Nettowa-ku ri-da-shippu (Network Leadership)*. Nikagiren.

Wade, R. (1994). Selective industrial policies in East Asia: is the East Asian miracle right? In *Miracle or Design? – Lessons from the East Asian Experience* (G. Fishlow, R. Haggard and R. Wade, eds), Policy Essay No. 11, ODC, Washington, DC.

Wigand, R., Picot, A. and Reichwald, R. (1997). *Information, Organization and Management: Expanding Markets and Corporate Boundaries*. John Wiley.

Chapter 10.1

Japanese organizational change in an era of information network industrialization

■ Sam K. Steffensen ■

Despite rapid and radical transformations in their operational environments, the logic of supplementary adjustments rather than drastic, substitutionary interventions have driven Japanese corporate change and expansion strategies during the last decades. The intra- and inter-organizational effects have been noteworthy. Now, along with the advent of informational network industrialization and globalization, the limits and shortcomings of supplementary adjustments have become increasingly clear.

The supplementary approach is, for instance, reflected by the fact that information management studies in Japan have predominantly displayed an information-processing view of organizations. Organizations are understood as information-processing systems. When uncertainties increase, organizational processing capabilities are assumed to grow accordingly in a somewhat organic, task-group centred manner. Social dimensions are ignored. Rather, the so-called 'J-firm' corporate-network organizations, with their distinct complex information systems and accompanying indigenous information, co-ordination and processing skills are almost assumed. Actually, this feature can be traced socio-structurally by looking at comparative, information-related employment figures and formal job classifications for Japan. The figures substantiate that Japanese information-processing tasks to a great extent have been functionally embedded in production processes. Organizations have tended to integrate information processing into their production flows. Hence, the social dimensions of organizations have primarily been discussed with respect to company/sector managerial cultures, either constraining or facilitating the introduction of particular IT networks and multimedia systems. The tables are now turning, however, as many processing and co-ordination tasks are undertaken by computer networks; open network management and diversified team structures beyond organizational frameworks are becoming the norm, and organizations are forced to transform accordingly.

Until recently, Japanese firms have shown some reluctance in making use of comprehensive organizational computing and open-computer networking. An especially striking discrepancy exists in this respect between large manufacturers and small lower-level subcontractors. In a large 1997 MITI survey, in terms of internal on line setups, 42 per cent of small-scale manufacturers (fewer than twenty employees) reported 'not on line', while 46.3 per cent responded 'no relevance' as they operated only one computer. For middle-sized manufacturers (between 20 and 299 employees) the figures were 25.2 per cent and 46.5 per cent, while the figures for larger manufacturers were stated as 3.2 per cent and 6.4 per cent, respectively.

Learning and management practices of most Japanese small- and medium-sized enterprises (SMEs) facilitate close face-to-face contact between top-managers and workers, as well as among workers. Because of these face-to-face contacts, internal on-lining of computers has rarely been judged as urgent. In fact, same data sources reveal that internal on-lining of computers is comparatively far more widespread in SMEs in which managers practise indirect control of work and business processes. Also the hitherto stable and internalized hierarchical transactions have reduced the need for open-computer networks. Efficient, proprietary electronic communication systems between large parent manufacturers and their élite suppliers have depended on expensive customized software solutions. In an era of packaged software, however, Japanese firms are now embracing more standardized solutions. Such solutions not only save considerable costs and time, but also provide access to precious updates and innovations, thereby assisting firms to address changing markets. Hesitant to embark on total switching strategies, though, Japanese firms search for technologically feasible designs to combine their strengths (thereby leading the demand for new types of flexibly packaged mix-and-match products, e.g. SAP R/3 ERP). Many transactional structures must undergo transformations, wholly or partly, in conjunction with open digital networking and business restructuring trends. As informational network industrialization in several respects creates new opportunities for smaller organizations, any informational backwardness of small-scale manufacturers is a serious issue in the present socioeconomic environment of Japan.

The Japanese strategic approach to organizational change management may be evaluated from two opposite positions: one emphasizing the importance of the prevalence of internal consensus and of not inflicting setbacks in self-perceived organizational strengths underpinning human resource development, innovation, and knowledge creation; another interpreting the supplementary strategies as only half-finished solutions, primarily due to organizational constraints and lack of clear leadership. The second position sees the need for a break in organizational continuity and a renewal led by new players. For example, just the fact that old-established organizations in Japan dominate moves into new industrial growth sectors is remarkably different from the US, and even neighbouring Taiwan. So far, Japanese firms have tended to affiliate themselves with the first position, while the latter position is gaining more universal cogency in the current era of information network industrialization. Change management strategies more oriented towards discontinuous organizational designs demand, however, stronger proactive vision at firm levels, and much more entrepreneurial freedom in the entire environment than presently can be observed.

Chapter 11

Strategic management of international business relationships with New Zealand: a primer for executives and investors[1]

■ André M. Everett ■

■ Introduction to New Zealand

New Zealand consists of two large (and several small) islands in the South Pacific, about 1500 km southeast of Australia and 7500 km south of Hawaii. In area it is comparable to the British Isles, Honshu or Colorado, while its population is similar to that of Singapore, Ireland, Colorado or Yokohama. The climate is generally mild, with few days over 30 °C and few frosts in urban areas. The North Island is smaller, warmer, more fertile, and three times as populated as the South Island. Auckland, the largest city with nigh on 1 million people, is more populous than the entire South Island. While the North Island features rolling hills and geothermal activity, the South Island offers more hills, the Southern Alps with numerous peaks and glaciers, and a fiord-laced rain forest coastline.

Famous for historically bearing over twenty sheep per person and a 'clean, green, nuclear free' environment with fantastic scenery, the islands were untouched by humans until just 1200 years ago. Lacking mammals (other than bats and seals), large flightless birds developed; one of these, the kiwi, has become the symbol of the country and the nickname for its people. Settled by the Maori, arriving in canoes from their island home of Hawaiiki, the islands were named Aotearoa, or 'Land of the Long White Cloud'. The Dutch name Nieeuw Zealand originated with Abel Tasman, the first European explorer to sight the islands, in 1642. British settlement, based on the exploratory claims of Captain James Cook, commenced in earnest in 1840 with the signing of the Treaty of Waitangi, in which the Maori ceded sovereignty to the British crown in exchange for inalienable rights (which were not fully respected). New

[1] This chapter has been published previously by MCB University Press Limited: Everett, A. M. (1996). Strategic management of international business relationships with New Zealand: a primer for executives and investors. *Management Decision*, **34** (9), 82–104.

Zealand is now an independent parliamentary monarchy in the British Commonwealth (with the Queen also Queen of New Zealand), and an active participant in international organizations ranging from the United Nations to Greenpeace.

The 3.6 million population is principally European in origin, with nearly 80 per cent claiming European-only descent. The New Zealand Maori population reached 9.7 per cent of the total in the 1991 census, with a further 3.2 per cent mixed Maori and other ethnic groups, rising both in numbers and as a percentage of the total from the previous (1986) census. Pacific Islanders accounted for 3.9 per cent, Chinese 1.1 per cent, Indians 0.8 per cent, and other 0.8 per cent. The groups posting the largest increases were mixed Chinese/Indian/other, Indian, other, Tongan, and Chinese (*New Zealand Official Yearbook 95*, 1995, p. 150), evidencing the widely touted shift in New Zealand's orientation from Europe to Asia Pacific. During the twentieth century, New Zealand experienced a faster population growth rate than Asia as a whole, due to both large families and active immigration.

Following its declaration as one of the two official languages of New Zealand in 1987 (English being the principal), Maori has experienced a resurgence, with more speakers now than 100 years ago. Official encouragement, language teaching in some preschools, and bilingual printing of some publications have given the tongue new life. Closely related to Hawaiian and Tahitian, Maori is the first language of about 50000 adults, or 12 per cent of the Maori population (*New Zealand Official Yearbook 95*, 1995, pp. 161–162). Despite the constant greenness of the environment, the country is not as cultivated or forested as popularly perceived. Forest cover, estimated at 78 per cent before Maori settlement, now stands at 27.4 per cent (by contrast, Japan is 66.5 per cent forest; the USA 31.3 per cent) (*Japan, 1994*, p. 6). Pastoral and arable land constitutes 50.7 per cent (*New Zealand Official Yearbook 95*, 1995, p.361), but horticulture occurs on only 0.5 per cent, whereas non-native timber plantations cover 8 per cent (*New Zealand Official Yearbook 95*, 1995, p.408). The economy remains heavily based on agriculture and primary processing, although the number of sheep is declining (48 million at latest count, doubling following the lambing season – just in time to cover the landscape during the peak tourist season). Dairy and beef cattle are at record highs (four and five million, respectively) but so are possums (75 million) and rabbits (15 million), both notorious imported pests that are inflicting serious damage on the landscape.

The legal system is based on British common law, with an added emphasis on business cost reduction to promote healthy competition (*New Zealand Investment*, 1994, pp.25, 27). Company and security laws are being harmonized with those of Australia to facilitate trans-Tasman commerce (Perera and Rahman, 1995; Rahman et al., 1994). The Companies Act 1955 enables relatively simple company formation, while the Commerce Act 1986 prohibits anti-competitive conduct. The Securities Commission monitors public information disclosure and compliance with the Securities Act 1978, with insider trading a civilly remediable offence. The Fair Trading Act 1986 protects consumers by prohibiting false, misleading or deceptive conduct or representations. Intellectual property such as patents, designs, trademarks and publications is protected. The Resource Management Act 1991 promotes sustainable management through planning for land use, subdivision, water use, discharges into water, air or land, and coastal effects. Statutory liability for violations of various Acts applies to directors, managers and employees as well as businesses; conviction can result in fines or imprisonment (Lawlink, 1995). The Privacy Act 1993 directly affects human resource managers, particularly in hiring decisions, as information collection, release and disposal are governed with an eye towards elimination of discrimination and false statements (Story and McManus, 1995).

■ Recent economic reforms and their impact on business

In 1950, New Zealand boasted the third highest standard of living in the world; by 1987, this had fallen to twenty-third, with the worst employee productivity trend and one of the lowest outputs per employee in the OECD (Crocombe et al., 1991). The socialist paradise in the Pacific had deteriorated into a state-protected, inefficient, isolationist economic backwater.

Rejuvenation commenced with the election of a Labour government in 1984. Reform was inevitable; the degree, speed and sequence, however, were (and remain) hotly debated. The Finance Minister at the time, Roger Douglas, pushed through radical changes; by the time his political party was ousted in the next election, with reform only partially achieved, much of the 'pain' inherent in reform had been spread, without much 'gain' in exchange. Reform continued with some modifications under the following National Party government, still in power in 1996 and naturally claiming much of the credit for the economic advances over the interim. (Douglas in 1996 campaigned for Parliament as the key player in the new ACT party, vowing to complete his reform agenda by eliminating income tax and ending state-sector control of education, health and retirement security.)

Critical points in New Zealand's revitalization over the past decade include substantial income tax reductions (1986) to levels resembling those in the USA; the State Owned Enterprises Act (1986), which triggered privatization of government operating assets including Telecom and the Railways (whose principal owners are now US corporations); the Labour Relations Act (1987) defining the legality of strikes and lockouts; the State Sector Act (1988), which made state sector chief executives accountable for effective and efficient management; the Public Finance Act (1989), which shifted focus from inputs to outputs and outcomes; the Reserve Bank Act (1989), which mandated price stability as the sole objective of monetary policy, with stability defined as 0–2 per cent underlying inflation; local government reorganization (1989); and the Fiscal Responsibility Act (1994), requiring public reporting of independently audited government finances. The former head of the OECD's Economics and Statistics Department, David Henderson, stated that although New Zealand was not alone in reforming its economy, 'if one looks across all the different areas of policy ... New Zealand emerges as a leading reformer in all. No other OECD country has such a portfolio of liberalising measures to show' (*Otago Daily Times*, 1996a).

Today's New Zealand economy is starkly different from what it was ten years ago. The rewards for the wrenching reforms include gross domestic product (GDP) growth of 7.9 per cent, business profit increases of 8.6 per cent, a 26 per cent increase in national savings, and a 17.3 per cent rise in fixed asset investment (all for the year ended March 1995) (*Otago Daily Times*, 1995a). Public debt peaked at 51 per cent of GDP in 1992 and has since been falling sharply, to an estimated 30 per cent in mid-1996, while the OECD average has continued to climb. Per capita public debt dropped to approximately NZ$8600 at the start of 1996, compared to NZ$28 900 for the USA (*Otago Daily*

Times, 1996b). Despite two promised personal income tax cuts in 1996 and 1997, the government surplus was expected to grow, net debt to shrink, and inflation to remain under 2 per cent) (*Otago Daily Times*, 1995b). The *Economic Freedom of the World* report, published in 1995 by eleven leading international economic institutes, ranked New Zealand third of 102 countries in economic freedom, behind Hong Kong and Singapore (Gwartney et al., 1996); *The Economist* conducted its own confirmatory international study, resulting in New Zealand rated first (Singapore seventh, Hong Kong not included, twenty countries total) (*The Economist*, 1996).

The annual *World Competitiveness Report* raised New Zealand's rank from eighteenth (of twenty-four countries) overall in 1991 to eighth (of forty-eight) in 1995, while its 'Executive opinion survey' component ranked New Zealand second for 1995, behind only Singapore. Among the twenty-four OECD countries, New Zealand was rated first in 1992, 1993, 1994 and 1995 on the 'extent to which government policies are conducive to competitiveness' (only Singapore and Hong Kong, non-members of the OECD, rated higher). In the four most recent annual reports, New Zealand was placed first among all countries on what is regarded as the critical issue: 'The domestic economy is well-adapted for long-term competitiveness.' On this crucial point, New Zealand was far in front at 8.48 (out of ten); Singapore came second, at 7.25, and the USA third, at 5.82 (*The World Competitiveness Report*, 1995). In other results of substantial interest to business, New Zealand ranked first in the world:

- lowest likelihood to be in recession in the next two years (*The World Competitiveness Report*, 1995, item 1.26)

- freest from government intervention in investment (Ibid., item 3.10)

- least affected by government price controls (Ibid., item 3.20)

- greatest independence for local authorities (Ibid., item 3.28)

- having the least prevalence of improper practices (bribing and corruption) in the public sphere (Ibid., item 3.32)

- most equitable in fiscal policy treatment of enterprises (Ibid., item 3.49)

- most equitable in access to both local and foreign capital for domestic and foreign companies (Ibid., items 4.09, 4.10)

- highest in price/quality ratio of domestic products relative to foreign competition (Ibid., item 6.14)

- fastest to bring new products to market (Ibid., item 6.19).

Impacts of the Reserve Bank Act, 1989

According to Rudi Dornbusch of MIT, 'The worst enemy of the transition to a free market is a central bank staging fights against inflation or unduly concerned with maintaining a hard currency' (Dornbusch, 1995) – precisely what the Reserve Bank Act requires, and what the Bank (with Dr Don Brash at the helm) is accomplishing with alacrity by holding interest rates at high real levels. In January 1996, underlying inflation for the previous year was reported as 2.0 per cent, while the freely floating New Zealand dollar's trade-weighted index reached eight-year highs. The latest government finance report, through 30 November 1995, indicated an operating surplus exceeding expectations by 32 per cent, at NZ$2.618 billion, leaving little room for loosening of fiscal restraints (*Otago Daily Times*, 1996c).

In response to ongoing increases in the value of the New Zealand dollar relative to the Australian dollar, the Manufacturers Federation, whose exporting members are strongly affected by the exchange rate for their biggest market, noted that costs, and possibly jobs, would have to be cut (*Otago Daily Times*, 1996d). The position of the government's Investment Promotion Unit is that while a strong currency does 'make it harder for the exportable sector to compete', it simultaneously 'enhance[s] the attractiveness of New Zealand as an investment destination and secure[s] the asset valuation of the original investment' (Economic Development Unit, 1994, p.23). The Minister for Industry, Philip Burdon, noted manufacturers' concerned, but counted that raw materials and other input imports will cost less, and reduced inflation and interest rates would provide further compensation (Burdon, 1995). Don Brash, the governor of the Reserve Bank, emphasized that 'the Reserve Bank does not have an exchange rate target. We do have an inflation target implying that ... we have to form a view about what exchange rate range is consistent with the inflation target' (Brash, 1995).

The Fiscal Responsibility Act (1994) requires the government to publish independently audited accounting statements – balance sheet and accrual-based operating income statement – covering government finances. As its name implies, the Act is a motivator towards responsible fiscal management; it imposes neither targets nor penalties, but induces more complete disclosure of more accurate information. With the combination of the Reserve Bank Act and the Fiscal Responsibility Act, *The Economist* proclaimed that 'New Zealand now probably boasts the best framework for monetary and fiscal policies of anywhere in the world' (*The Economist*, 1995a).

Business impacts of the reforms

The transition from a statist economy to a free market redistributes opportunities and wealth, often leaving higher unemployment and resentment in its wake (Dornbusch, 1995). New Zealand was not spared these consequences, with unemployment shooting up from negligible to 10.9 per cent in September 1991 (Marshall, 1995; OECD, 1994), since dropping below 6 per cent and still falling, given credit by *The Economist* as the lowest real unemployment rate in the OECD as of July 1995.

Perhaps the greatest degree of reform occurred in the labour relations sector, promulgated as the Employment Contracts Act (ECA, 1991). By permitting labour-management co-operation, labour-flexibility, performance-based pay, and other relaxations of the power of erstwhile dominant unions, the ECA facilitated the establishment of new international philosophies of operations management, including just in time (JIT) and total quality management (TQM). Praised by some as the liberator of the New Zealand economy, the ECA has also been cursed as the greatest inequality inducer in the country's history.

Industry did not escape government reforms; all export subsidies and import restrictions were abandoned, although some tariffs remain. Capital gains tax was removed, spurring an investment boom that occasionally gives New Zealand an unfavourable trade balance praised by local analysts. Some sectors of the economy lost nearly all their producers and employees; those firms which survive learned to target high quality, high-price niche markets, as the local market scale precluded head-on competition with imports from foreign mass producers. The textile and footwear industries exemplify this trend: Tamahine, a former contract manufacturer of undershirts and generic woollen goods, reformulated its strategy to target fashion wool and tourists, switching from $2 T-shirts to $200 own-brand sweaters; in the interim, it has acquired the assets of over thirty failed competitors. The Last Footwear Company, on a philosophy of design and customization, rose to international fame for quality, durability and style, while most other shoemakers disappeared in a flood of cheap imports.

The effects of a protected market should not be underestimated. In the early 1980s, the quality of many local goods had deteriorated to unacceptable levels, yet import substitution guidelines decreed that no foreign competitors were allowed in. A case in point is Toyota, which has long operated an assembly plant at Thames near Auckland. In 1984, it found itself the target of a consumer rights television show, *Fair Go*, with a nearly new but rusting Corolla ignominiously paraded during prime time. The plant was given an ultimatum from Japan: shape up or be shut down. Adapting Toyota's famous production system to New Zealand conditions did not prove easy, but once appreciated by the workers, it was embraced wholeheartedly. The Thames plant is now Toyota's highest quality plant outside Japan, typically matching the defect rate of the previous year in Toyota's mother plant. The aim, naturally, is to beat the main plant as soon as possible. Comparative defect rates for mid-1994 in faults per vehicle were Japan 0.9 (1.5 in 1993), New Zealand 1.6 (2.3), USA 4.9, Australia 6.2, and South Africa 12.5. Toyota has designated the Thames plant as the only one outside Japan allowed to provide international training for other Toyota sites (*Made in New Zealand*, 1994; *Expressing the Values*, 1995).

Services were also held back by protection, particularly in the communications sector. Prior to privatization, the telephone system was sluggish at best; now, service is prompt (guaranteed), competition is blatant, Telecom NZ is both highly profitable and respected, and prices are tumbling. In the 1995 *World Competitiveness Report*, New Zealand ranked first in telecommunications infrastructure as supportive of business (*The World Competitiveness Report*, 1995, item 5.32), a result underscored by international industry opinion, especially on convergence of telecommunications, computers and entertainment (Wallis, 1995). The postal system has not yet been privatized, but some sectors have been opened for competition, resulting in an explosion in courier and package delivery services. Anticipating a promised open letter-delivery market, highly profitable NZ Post recently slashed the prime letter rate, which last rose almost nine years ago. Even before the reduction, it was the only letter rate in the Western economies lower than that in the USA (26 US cents for up to seven ounces nationwide). NZ Post, Telecom NZ, and several other communications specialists now export their knowledge and technology, installing systems and providing advice from the Czech Republic to Vietnam.

Knowledge-sector industries which simply did not exist a few years ago represent the vanguard of New Zealand's modern export drive. Firms based on advanced technical skills and intellectual property have succeeded in software, electronics, cinema and consulting, among others. For example, UNISYS' Link network management software was written by Aoraki in Christchurch; United Airline's award-winning Mileage Plus commercial featuring a membership card was crafted by Animation Research in Dunedin; and Cannes film festival winner *The Piano* was produced in New Zealand. New Zealand consultants are managing oil exploration in China, salmon farming in

Chile and port construction in the Maldives. Advanced physical goods targeted at specific niches have achieved international recognition; these include laser chip-making equipment used by every memory chip maker in the world (Buckley Systems) (*New Zealand Manufacturer*, 1995) and a revolutionary direct-drive plastic motor-washing machine exported to over eighty countries (Fisher and Paykel Industries Ltd, 1995). The 1994 New Zealand Supreme Export Award went to Tait Electronics, which exported over US$70 million of mobile radio equipment (Sullivan, 1995a). Rakon, a small Auckland firm, is the world's leading maker of quartz crystals for use in global positioning equipment, including that produced by Rockwell International for the US military (Sullivan, 1995a). The universities have not fared poorly either, with numerous patents, discoveries and international awards, particularly in medical, engineering and agritech research (Hunter, 1995; *NZ Business*, 1995a). Internet use is booming; according to the Internet Society, New Zealand experienced by far the world's highest growth rate in servers per head during 1994, at 441 per cent, placing it third in number of installed servers per person behind Finland and the USA, tied with Australia (*The Economist*, 1995b).

In 1990, Dutch researchers Bolwijn and Kumpe (1990) proposed a hierarchy of manufacturing goals: efficiency, quality, flexibility, and innovation. Innovation was judged both the indicator of an industry's currency and the ultimate challenge to all enterprises. Due to its isolation and dispersed population, New Zealand has often been left to its own devices; the result is an inherently innovative populace, ranging from the traditional farmer's claim of being able to fix anything with a bit of number eight wire through to the world champion Britten motorcycle, devised and constructed by a tinkering engineer in his home garage. Flexibility, long suppressed by labour regulation, resurfaced with the ECA; the small size of New Zealand firms has proved an advantage through flatter organizational structures. Quality, long believed more a matter of natural inputs than processing, has improved to world standards through open international competition and wholesale adoption of quality management techniques and standards. Efficiency, once deemed unattainable due to small scale, has led to a refocusing on niche markets that can be suitably addressed, combined with process innovation and a continuous focus on cost reduction. Efficiency enhancement has been spurred by the strength of the New Zealand dollar, which has held or climbed against all major currencies over the recent past, rising to eight-year highs on the trade-weighted index by early 1996. Thus, all four aspects of Bolwijn and Kumpe's progression are in ready evidence, with the prevailing mentality among manufacturers and exporters being that efficiency and quality have been established but require continuous improvement, while flexibility and innovation are more elusive, yet are the vital factors necessary for firms to succeed internationally.

▓ The business environment

With 192 871 enterprises and 1 262 974 full-time equivalent persons engaged in February 1995, New Zealand features one business for every six workers (*Business Activity Statistics*, 1994). The breakdown of these firms by industrial sector is shown in Tables 11.1 and 11.2; key points are the preponderance of very small businesses; the concentration of firms in trade, community/social/personal services, construction, and manufacturing; and high employment in community/social/personal services, trade, and manufacturing.

The top 200 firms achieved a 1995 turnover of NZ$79.6 billion, with after-tax profit of $5.2 billion, on total assets of $91.3 billion and shareholders' funds of $43.5 billion, while employing 183 730 (on average 1015 each, adjusted for missing data) (*Management (NZ)*, 1995). The largest firm in 1995, by substantial margins, was construction, energy and forest products conglomerate Fletcher Challenge, with sales of NZ$8.5 billion, assets of $13.2 billion, $4.7 billion in shareholders' funds, and an estimated 23 000 employees (Goulter, 1995; *Management (NZ)*, 1995). Telecom earned the greatest profit after tax, $620 million, on sales of $2.9 billion (*Management (NZ)*, 1995). Information about individual New Zealand companies, including financial and contact details, can be found in the *New Zealand Investment Year-book* by Datex, the *New Zealand Export Year-book*, and *The New Zealand Business Who's Who*; popular rankings include the annual *Management (NZ)* magazine Top 200 and *NZ Business* magazine's annual list of The NZ 500.

Table 11.1 Number of enterprises by industrial classification and size, February 1995

	Persons engaged (FTEs)					
Industrial classification	*0–5*	*6–9*	*10–49*	*50–99*	*100+*	*Total*
Agricultural services[a], hunting, forestry and fishing	7 833	638	528	21	9	9 029
Mining and quarrying	366	47	56	6	8	483
Manufacturing	13 359	2 372	3 083	382	365	19 561
Electricity, gas and water	50	3	11	16	28	108
Construction	25 660	1 440	1 131	62	28	28 321
Wholesale and retail trade, restaurants and hotels	41 608	5 441	4 262	322	237	51 870
Transport, storage and communication	10 733	719	749	86	76	12 363
Business and financial services	37 652	1 824	1 689	136	137	41 438
Community, social and personal services	23 234	2 649	3 200	313	302	29 698
Total	160 495	15 133	14 709	1 344	1 190	192 871

Notes: [a] Economically significant enterprises (excluding farms) with over NZ$30 000 in tax-reported expenses (or sales if tax-exempt).
FTEs = full-time equivalent people engaged.
Source: Annual Business Directory Update (ABDU) database (1996).

Agriculture

Agriculture is structured entirely differently from other industries. Production occurs on privately owned or leased farms, with sales principally to or through co-operatives owned by the farmers. Processing is performed by numerous firms, but a few tend to dominate each product type. Subsidies have been completely removed, although research and development funding remains and some advisory services assist the sector. From an international perspective, the most notable feature of the key agricultural trades is the legal export monopoly granted to the producer boards: the New

Zealand Dairy Board, the Meat Producers Board, Wools of New Zealand, the Apple and Pear Marketing, and the Kiwifruit Marketing Board. With the domestic market effectively deregulated and production far greater than consumption, highly attractive export markets are inducing legal challenges to the board monopolies by both individual and corporate farmers, backed by the reform-minded Business Roundtable (Rotherham; 1995; Macfie, 1996a; *Otago Daily Times*, 1996e). Exports take 60 per cent of meat, 40 per cent of forestry and 80 per cent of fish production; New Zealand is the world's second largest wool producer and exporter. The Dairy Board's 1995 sales of NZ$5.1 billion retained its status as the country's second largest business as well as the leading exporter (*Management (NZ)*, 1995). The board monopolies pose a quandary for multinationals investing in New Zealand, as in a limited number of areas production may occur (e.g. cheese by Kraft), but exporting must occur through one of the monolithic boards, either limiting sales to the domestic market or imposing unwanted intrusions on corporate strategy.

Table 11.2 Number of employees by industrial classification and size, February 1995

Industrial classification	Persons engaged (FTEs)					
	0–5	6–9	10–49	50–99	100+	Total
Agricultural services[a], hunting, forestry and fishing	12 419	4 452	9 046	1 511	2 331	29 759
Mining and quarrying	579	320	1 062	396	1 981	4 338
Manufacturing	28 098	16 504	60 163	26 057	120 611	251 433
Electricity, gas and water	52	19	311	1 146	8 580	10 108
Construction	43 429	9 764	19 554	4 316	8 364	85 427
Wholesale and retail trade, restaurants and hotels	90 765	37 376	75 311	21 806	77 030	302 288
Transport, storage and communication	17 524	4 984	14 127	6 039	44 276	86 950
Business and financial services	46 815	12 578	29 964	9 072	59 256	157 685
Community, social and personal services	46 018	18 296	61 373	21 928	187 415	335 030
Total	285 691	104 286	270 904	92 262	509 835	1 262 974

Notes: [a] Does not include farm workers, who total approximately 120 000.
FTEs = full-time equivalent people engaged.
Columns do not sum exactly due to calculations to determine FTEs.
Source: Annual Business Directory Update (ABDU) database (1996).

Agriculture was an early target of major governmental reforms, which included the elimination of nearly all forms of state subsidy of private agricultural or industrial activity. Following a worrisome start, family farms have proved not only able to survive without protection and subsidy, but to thrive, as farmers have switched from sheep to dairy, deer, vineyards, forestry, and even exotics such as emus and llamas. Research breakthroughs include the first cultivation of black truffles outside France and development of new strains of apples tailored for specific Asian markets. New Zealand dairy producers now claim cost efficiencies, attained through both advanced technological and natural factors, of up to three to one over those in the USA and five to one over those in Europe. When the expected benefits of the Uruguay Round of GATT (Harrison, 1995) are examined on a per person basis, New Zealand achieves the second highest benefit from this trade liberalization, trailing only Singapore, with the European Union (EU) third. However, whereas Europe will achieve its benefit by reducing internal subsidies (and the accompanying taxation), New Zealand will gain by lowered barriers in its (principally agricultural) export markets, emphasizing its enhanced competitiveness.

State of management practice development

Management practices in New Zealand, as in many other nations, cover the gamut from antiquated to world class (Australian Manufacturing Council, 1994). Expecting that geographical isolation would have stunted management development, international observers have been surprised to find that the latest international 'best practices' often take hold in New Zealand far faster than in most other settings (Mendzela, 1995). Culture and geography have played a role, necessitating small organizations, flexible approaches, multiskilled workers, broadly based management, international orientation, and minimal hierarchy (Mitchell, 1995). Project and matrix structures, with staff regrouping as fully or partially autonomous teams to complete customer assignments, are prevalent in some industries (Bell, 1995), while teams in general are pervasive in both society and business (Moloney, 1995) and worker empowerment is common (in 55 per cent of firms in a 1994 study (Sullivan, 1995b). None the less, surveyed managers recently expressed dissatisfaction with their achievements in implementing human resource management practices, notably in employee performance management (Lyons, 1995; *Otago Daily Times*, 1995c). One explanation for this phenomenon is that New Zealanders hear of a new foreign managerial advance or fad, believe that it is actually widespread overseas, and immediately try to apply it themselves – even when it is no more than bluster, goals or exaggeration at its source (Moloney, 1995; Wallis, 1995). Despite foreign reports to the contrary, New Zealand organizations implementing TQM reported substantial success in improving labour productivity (up by 20 per cent or more in 69 per cent of firms studied), equipment productivity, profit, suggestions, customer complaints, stock volumes and absenteeism (Sullivan, 1995b).

New Zealand perpetually looks abroad for its standards, adopting and adapting 'best practice' wherever it may be found. The NZ National Quality Award is an unabashed copy of the US Malcolm Baldrige award; Toyota's Thames assembly plant won the inaugural competition in 1993, and Telecom Directories in 1995. Regional awards in various industries have been added, and further awards are promulgated by trade associations, government departments and large firms. Realizing that it would open market doors, despite being a poor second cousin of true quality management, the ISO 9000 standards were adopted wholesale as the corresponding New Zealand standards (e.g. ISO 9001:1994 is NZS 9001:1994) (Sullivan, 1995b). Tradenz, the government's export promotion board, pushed ISO 9000 heavily, particularly in the food and beverage industry, realizing certification rates among the highest in the world. On a per population basis, New Zealand rates fourth, behind the UK, where the ISO standards originated (and where about half of the world's issued certificates reside), tiny Liechtenstein, and Ireland (*Q-NewZ*, 1995). Recognizing the small business nature of the local economy, the national accreditation authority Telarc developed Q-Base, an entry-level quality systems standard targeted at smaller firms; this too is being exported. Once an acceptably high level of ISO 9000 certification was achieved, Tradenz shifted focus to promoting ISO 14000, the standard for environmental management systems.

Both the country and individual firms are eager to compare themselves with international benchmarks. To this end, Michael Porter was called in to repeat his 'Competitive advantage of nations' analysis in New Zealand, publishing in 1989 a report that stimulated substantial debate about the status and direction of the nation (Cocombe et al., 1991). Many of the recommendations were taken to heart; as a result, local competitors are judged by their international performance. For example, the public testing of the pleasure boat building industry, including its advanced computer simulation capabilities and sail-making innovations, was resolved favourably in winning the America's Cup yacht race in San Diego in 1995 and the Whitbread Round the World yacht race in 1994. (The obvious emphasis on teamwork in both sailing and construction was not lost to the international media (MacAlister, 1995).) Solely to demonstrate its multimedia documentation expertise, Cardinal Professional Services published two CD-ROMs in the US market (prior to release in New Zealand): one is an encyclopedia of Antarctica, included in *PC Magazine*'s (USA) 'Top 100 CD-ROMs' for 1995 (Ulanoff, 1995), the other is a children's educational self-directed pirate story named Mungo (US accents were used to enhance acceptability in the primary target market). Over the past five years, teams from the University of Otago alone have won seven international computer programming, marketing and MBA case competitions; partly in consequence, foreign student enrolments are booming.

More to the point, the Australian Manufacturing Council was joined by the New Zealand Manufacturing Advisory Group in examining application of best manufacturing practices in the two countries in 1994. The findings demonstrated that leading practices are being implemented (and more rapidly than in Australia); some firms are equivalent to 'world class' or the best anywhere (Australian Manufacturing Council, 1994). (One example is New Zealand Breweries, which in 1995 became only the fourth firm in the world to be awarded the Oliver Wight Class A operating system rating in all five business disciplines (Mackenzie, 1995).) Similarly positive results arose in academic research by teams investigating manufacturing strategy and quality (Adam et al., 1993; Batley, 1994a), manufacturing/accounting systems linkages (Adler et al., 1995; Adler et al., 1996), service quality (Batley, 1994b), advanced manufacturing technology implementation (Croke, 1994), accounting education (McClelland, 1993), and education and use of quality control statistical methods (McAlevey et al., 1995). The gurus of quality, strategy, and other management disciplines attract attentive audiences at their lectures in New Zealand; they include W. Edwards Deming, Michael Porter, James Brian Quinn, Peter Scholtes, Peter Senge and numerous others.

National associations such as the New Zealand Institute of Management (NZIM), the New Zealand Organisation for Quality (NZOQ), the Institute of Directors in New Zealand (IOD), the New Zealand Manufacturers Federation, the Total Quality Management Institute (TQMI), and the Institute of Personnel Management New Zealand (IPMNZ) actively originate and promote courses designed to bring local standards even with or ahead of international best practice. For instance, the Certificate in

Quality Assurance, developed by the NZOQ, compares favourably with similar courses worldwide; it balances and merges approaches from Japan and the USA to respond to local requirements (Everett, 1995). Companies frequently send their executives for overseas short courses or degrees, favouring the leading North American and European programmes. Foreign corporate role models are often emulated; for example, New Zealand's largest grocery store operator, Progressive Enterprises, sought advice from Wal-Mart and subsequently attained profitability in all of its 133 outlets within two years.

Labour and management

The New Zealand labour market is the most deregulated in the OECD, permitting flexibility in work practices and wages (*The Economist*, 1993). Despite popular press complaints of unemployment and conditions disputes, the labour scene is relatively quiet. Union membership, once mandatory, is now voluntary; in December 1985, 259 unions with 683 006 members represented 43.5 per cent of the labour force; by December 1994 this had dropped to 82 unions, 375 906 members, and 23.4 per cent, with further falls likely as unions become increasingly superfluous (Marshall, 1995; *Otago Daily Times*, 1996f). According to Steve Marshall, chief executive of the NZ Employers' Federation, 'the distinction between industrial relations and human resources is disappearing. ... Industrial negotiations for employee contracts, be they individual or collective ... are mutual discussions based on agreed objectives with identified roles and responsibilities' (Marshall, 1995, p.11). Work stoppages (including strikes, lockouts and go-slows) have returned to the low levels of the early 1960s in absolute numbers, and below that in terms of percentage of hours lost. From a peak of 562 stoppages in 1977, a steady decline resulted in 54 stoppages in 1992 and 58 in 1993. The year ending June 1995 saw a slight increase, to 64 stoppages. The peak number of working days lost (1 329 054) occurred in 1986, an unprecedented spike due to workers reacting to labour law reform, particularly as it affected union membership. In contrast, 1993 experienced only 23 771 lost days; the average time lost per striking worker was just over one day (*New Zealand Official Yearbook 95*, 1995, p.339; 66).

Under the Human Rights Act 1993 (and secondarily the ECA), employment discrimination affecting hiring, firing, training and promotion is illegal in terms of sex, marital status, religious or ethical belief, colour, race, ethnic or national origins, disability, age, political opinion, employment status, family status, or sexual orientation (*New Zealand Official Yearbook 95*, 1995, p.338). The government promotes equal employment opportunities (EEO), but 'considers that EEO will be achieved most effectively by voluntary promotion of progressive EEO management policies' orientation (*New Zealand Official Yearbook 95*, 1995, p.338). In essence, the government promotes EEO as good management policy, and funds EEO programmes and practices in the private sector. EEO has received substantial positive publicity through media reports of successful efforts by Maori groups, such as advance training of candidates for the new Harrah's Sky City Casino in Auckland, where approximately half of the gaming employees hired are Maori; the casino spokesperson stated that 'only the best candidates were hired' and that a quota was not even considered (TV 3 Evening News, 1996). Such successes are particularly meaningful given the substantially higher unemployment rates experienced by Maori and Pacific Islander groups, roughly triple that of the European (or Pakeha) group (*New Zealand Official Yearbook 95*, 1995, p.324).

New Zealand historically has experienced low, even negligible, unemployment. A common tale from the 'good old days' exemplifies the popular perception of unemployment in the 1950s, 1960s and early 1970s: a foreign diplomat asked the Prime Minister what he was doing for the unemployed; he replied, 'I took them both to lunch last week to ask when they wanted to start working again'. Admittedly due in major part to governmental full-employment practices, unemployment remained near zero until 1978. Unemployment peaked at 10.9 per cent in September 1991 (Marshall, 1995; OECD, 1995, p. 96), it is currently below 6 per cent. Employment growth topped the OECD in 1994, following second place in 1993 (OECD, 1995, p. A23).

Wage rates are low by Western standards, although high compared with some Asian levels. The 1993 average hourly manufacturing labour cost in New Zealand was the lowest of nineteen industrial countries compared by *The Economist*, at US$8.01; Spain, next lowest, cost $11.55/hour; Australia $12.00; the USA $16.75; Japan $19.50; and Western Germany $25.59 (*The Economist*, 1994). According to the Director of the Investment Promotion Unit of the Ministry of Foreign Affairs and Trade, 'on a skills basis our labour costs are lower than those throughout most of Asia, which gives excellent value for money' (Hall, 1994a). The Minimum Wage Act 1983 and subsequent rates statements set an adult minimum wage of NZ$6.25 per hour, and a youth (age 16–19) rate at 60 per cent, or $3.75, effective in March 1995 (*New Zealand Official Yearbook 95*, 1995, p.337). Wage inflation has been minimal over the recent past, with private surveys showing 1–2 per cent increases for 1995 (Price Waterhouse, 1995) and government statistics indicating a 1.5 per cent overall salary and wage rate increase for the year through September 1995 (*The Prices Report for September 1995 Quarter*, 1996, p.12). Labour cost increases varied by industry, ranging from a low of 1.7 per cent for agriculture, basic metals and mining to a high of 2.8 per cent for paper, printing, and publishing (*The Prices Report for September 1995 Quarter*, 1996, p.12). The OECD predicted 1996 unit labour cost increases of 1.8 per cent, easing to 1.2 per cent in 1997 (OECD, 1995, p.A16).

Compensation for executives in New Zealand is overridingly in the form of base salary or wages, although performance pay is becoming an increasingly important part of packages for all levels of employees (Table 11.3). This includes all state-owned enterprise chief executives, who are on fixed-term contracts linked to performance. Non-cash benefits, such as company cars, insurance and retirement fund contributions, appear to be reverting to cash payments, but still apply to the greater portion of executives (Table 11.4). Managerial base salaries inflated by only 3.1 per cent to 6.5 per cent, and total packages by 3.3 per cent to 5.3 per cent, during 1995 (Table 11.5); however, incentives grew as shortages of some skills worsened (Story, 1996), with the

Table 11.3 Structure of executive compensation (percentage of total)

Compensation category	1989	1990	1991	1992	1993	1994	1995
Base salary	72	73	74	75	76	76	79
Performance pay	2	3	3	4	4	7	7
Credit and deferred	26	24	23	21	20	17	14

Sources: Watson Wyatt survey of senior executives, published November 1995; data from Story (1996).

highest jobs and best performers rising fastest (Yarwood, 1995). Sample rates of executive remuneration are shown in Table 11.6.

Table 11.4 Benefits as a component of executive compensation

Benefit	Sheffield	Wyatt
Bonus or profit share	51	48/55[a]
Company vehicle	80+	79
Vehicle allowance[b]	10	46
Retirement fund contribution (superannuation)	60	86
Health (medical) insurance	63	54
Professional or club fees	n/a	61
Home telephone	68	68
Low interest loans	5.5	4
Salary continuous insurance	n/a	4
Accident, death and disability insurance	49	n/a
Employee share (stock) scheme	17.8	n/a
Cellular telephone	29	n/a
Entertainment allowance	n/a	29
Non-business travel	4.7	n/a
Liquor/merchandise allowance	8	n/a
Staff discounts	n/a	29
Partner allowance	1.5	n/a

Notes: Values are the percentage of executives reporting receipt of given benefit during 1995; categories which do not match are denoted as 'n/a'.
[a] 48 per cent of companies employing waged staff, and 55 per cent of those employing salaried staff, were eligible for a bonus scheme in 1995.
[b] Sheffield's vehicle allowance is instead of a company vehicle; Wyatt's is most often in addition to it.
Source: Sheffield Consulting Group survey of 450 general managers and managing directors, Watson Wyatt survey of senior executives; data from Story (1996).

Table 11.5 Salary inflation in 1995

	Base salary	Total cash	Fixed remuneration	Total remuneration
Operational staff	3.1	3.9	2.3	3.3
Middle management	3.8	3.9	2.7	3.4
CEO, mid-sized company	5.6	5.8	3.0	3.3
CEO, large company	6.5	8.7	4.0	5.3

Note: Values are the percentage increase from September 1994 to September 1995.
Sources: Price Waterhouse *Remuneration Report*; data from Story (1996).

Table 11.6 Chief executive remuneration, mid-1994

Typical chief executive (salary only)	110 000
Typical chief executive (package)	169 863
CEO remuneration for company with under $5million revenues	113 869
CEO remuneration for company with revenues of $50–100 million	195 394
CEO remuneration for company with over $500million revenues	344 243

Source: Yarwood, V. (1994).

Executive surveys conducted by leading consulting firms late in 1995 offer the following key indicators:

- 51 per cent of general managers and managing directors received a bonus and/or profit share payment (and rising) (Sheffield Consulting Group, 1994)

- bonuses or profit sharing were most prevalent in engineering and contracting, insurance, communications, retailing and professional services (Sheffield Consulting Group, 1994)

- executive salary increases in 1995 surpassed expectations; this was primarily due to larger performance-based bonuses (PA Consulting Group, 1995)

- the mean bonus/profit share rewards for general managers and managing directors was NZ$28 864; the maximum was NZ$497 000 (Sheffield Consulting Group, 1994)

- 83 per cent of organizations have a formal bonus policy; of these, 42 per cent cover all staff levels (Watson Wyatt, 1995)

- about half of top executive compensation packages were between NZ$100 000 and $200 000; 6.5 per cent exceeded that amount (PA Consulting Group, 1995)

- over 80 per cent of CEOs were given a company car; 10 per cent received a vehicle allowance averaging NZ$15 000 (Sheffield Consulting Group, 1994)

- remuneration package increases varied between 2 per cent and 12 per cent across nine industry sectors (Price Waterhouse, 1996)

- average increases for 1996 are expected to be moderate, with estimates of 2.8–3.7 per cent (Price Waterhouse, 1995) and 3.1–4.7 per cent (PA Consulting Group, 1995); but

- industry and function specialization will continue, enhancing pay differentials based on value-adding skills, notably for logistics, human resources, and operations personnel (Price Waterhouse, 1996).

Operations aspects other than labour and management

Costs other than management and labour are relatively lower in New Zealand than in other OECD locations. Inner city office rentals in Auckland are less than half those in Los Angeles or Sydney, and one-fifth to one-twentieth those of Hong Kong, Singapore and Tokyo. Industrial property rentals in Auckland are also substantially below those for all of the above cities (Knight Frank Baillieu Research, 1992). Energy prices, particularly for electricity and diesel oil, are very low by world standards (*New Zealand Investment*, 1994, p.14). In the highly competitive and efficient transport and utilities sector, air transport, railroads, port access, telecommunications and power supply rank higher than those of the USA in the *World Competitiveness Report* 1995; in telecommunications infrastructure, New Zealand was rated best in the world (*The World Competitiveness Report*, 1995, items 5.27, 5.28, 5.29, 5.32, 5.45, 5.46).

The New Zealand dollar floats freely on world markets. There are no foreign exchange controls; investments and profits may be repatriated at will. Income tax applies to all income earned by New Zealand residents, and to all profits earned in New Zealand by domestic or foreign companies. In 1994, New Zealand had the lowest maximum personal income tax rate in the OECD, at 33 per cent, in conjunction with a low company tax rate of 33 per cent (38 per cent for branches of foreign companies, which are not liable for withholding tax on repatriated dividends). Two personal income tax cuts were announced, to take effect in 1996 and 1997. There is no land or property tax, although municipal services are charged annually as a rate based on assessed value of land and improvements. Goods and services tax (GST), at 12.5 per cent, is a comprehensive value-added tax applied to all goods and services supplied in New Zealand. Double taxation is avoided through tax treaties with Australia, Belgium, Canada, China, Denmark, Fiji, Finland, France, Germany, India, Indonesia, Ireland, Italy, Japan, Korea, Malaysia, The Netherlands, Norway, the Philippines, Singapore, Sweden, Switzerland, the UK, and the USA (*New Zealand Investment*, 1994, p.26). Overall, *The Economist* praised New Zealand's tax system: it 'now produces fewer market distortions than that of any other industrial country' (*The Economist*, 1993).

Professional service fees, including legal, financial, and medical, are reasonable to low, with many international groups present (e.g. all six of the major US accounting firms); standards are high and competition keen. Raw materials vary in availability, with many (e.g. timber, pulp, wool, meat) exported in vast quantities in a relatively unprocessed state, while others are imported with the specific purpose of taking advantage of lower costs for processing in New Zealand (e.g. bauxite imported by Comalco to produce aluminium for export, effectively exporting inexpensive New Zealand electricity and technical labour).

■ International trade and investment

Reversing export dependency

The impact of the UK on the New Zealand economy until the 1970s was equivalent to that of the Soviet Union on the economies of Eastern Europe, albeit from a much more voluntary and amicable origin. New Zealand proudly produced what Britain wanted, not only in range, quantity and features, but also in terms of limits, focusing on those primary products where nature had endowed it with comparative advantage, including the hemispheric reversal of seasons. The economy depended on Britain to absorb two-thirds of its exports, and to provide over half its immigrants and its inward investment funds.

The economic upheavals resulting from Great Britain's accession to the European Community (EC) in 1974 induced the New Zealand government to adopt a policy of export market diversification. Bulk frozen mutton and raw wool are fading symbols of the past rather than the future. From the UK's erstwhile 'Pacific garden', generating top-quality produce customized to the British palate, New Zealand has realigned itself economically, balancing exports around the world and across the spectrum (Tables

11.7 and 11.8). Success has been achieved in markets as diverse as the first foreign ice cream sold in Siberia (Head, 1995), through sonar components for the US Navy. The export role of non-primary manufactured goods has risen dramatically, from 2.7 per cent in 1966 to 33.1 per cent in 1993–94 (Manufacturing Advisory Group, 1994; *New Zealand Investment*, 1994). Primary products which were once exported only raw increasingly receive further processing at home, and now constitute 26.8 per cent of exports; raw primary goods are down to 18.7 per cent, while services are 21.4 per cent of exports (*New Zealand Investment*, 1994). In broad terms, Asia is now New Zealand's largest export market, taking over 42 per cent of exports in 1995. Australia was the largest individual importer, with 19.8 per cent; followed by Japan with 16.8 per cent, the European Community (EC) at 16.3 per cent, and the USA with 9.7 per cent. Given its rapid growth in export purchases, Korea (5.3 per cent) is expected to pass the UK (6.2 per cent) during 1996. Other important EC markets are Germany, Italy, Belgium and France, while further key Asian markets are Hong Kong, Taiwan, China, Malaysia, Indonesia, Singapore, Thailand and the Philippines (all over NZ$200 million or 1 per cent of exports) (*Export News*, 1996).

Table 11.7 New Zealand's twenty largest export markets

	Year ended October 1995	%	Year ended October 1994	%	% change
Australia	4 044.5	19.9	3 995.0	20.5	1.24
Japan	3 512.5	17.2	2 948.0	15.1	19.15
EC	3 282.8	16.1	3 224.0	16.5	1.82
USA	2 036.9	10.0	2 107.8	10.8	−3.36
South Korea	1 059.8	5.2	949.3	4.9	11.64
Taiwan	616.3	3.0	538.3	2.8	14.49
Hong Kong	600.9	3.0	506.5	2.6	18.63
China	505.1	2.5	569.9	2.9	−11.38
Malaysia	408.0	2.0	386.5	2.0	5.55
Indonesia	308.6	1.5	228.0	1.2	35.37
Canada	300.4	1.5	340.9	1.7	−11.87
Singapore	275.7	1.4	254.6	1.3	8.26
Thailand	259.0	1.3	212.2	1.1	22.05
Philippines	197.3	1.0	189.5	1.0	−4.12
Russia	193.5	1.0	122.0	0.6	58.63
Fiji	159.7	0.8	183.9	0.9	−13.16
Saudi Arabia	157.5	0.8	217.9	1.1	−27.71
Turkey	142.3	0.7	132.5	0.7	7.39
India	124.6	0.6	143.4	0.7	−13.13
Mexico	118.0	0.6	230.5	1.2	−48.79
Total of above	18 303.4	90.1	17 480.7	89.6	4.71
Estimated total	20 315		19 510		4.13

Note: Values are in NZ$ millions; % of total exports.
Source: *Export News* (1996).

Table 11.8 New Zealand's exports by category

	1995	1994	% change
Dairy produce	2723.2	2794.9	–2.6
Meat and edible offal	2668.1	2799.0	–4.8
Wood and wood articles	1616.6	1683.3	–4.0
Wool	1176.8	1180.4	–0.3
Fish, crustaceans and molluscs	1146.1	1073.9	+6.7
Fruit and nuts	928.4	753.7	+23.2
Mechanical machinery	845.3	837.2	+1.0
Unwrought aluminum	716.8	551.3	+30.0
Raw hides, skins, leather	683.2	678.3	+0.7
Electrical machinery	541.1	495.6	+9.2
Wood pulp	536.1	400.8	+33.8
Casein and caseinates	517.2	575.3	–10.1
Textiles and textile articles	338.1	317.1	+6.6
Pearls, stones, jewellery etc.	336.5	304.1	+10.7
Iron and steel	281.5	257.9	+9.2

Notes: NZ$ million; year ended December; 1995 provisional Free on Board (FOB).
Source: Department of Statistics (1996) *Overseas trade: December 1995.*

Special relationship with Australia

No one nation now dominates the New Zealand economy, but Australia clearly deserves an honourable mention. Physically and culturally the closest nation to New Zealand, Australia absorbs one-fifth of its exports, the largest share of any single country. In turn, New Zealand is Australia's largest market for manufactured goods (*New Zealand Official Yearbook 95*, 1995, p.88). New Zealand was heavily influenced by Australia in its developmental years, and is specifically named as a potential 'State' of the Commonwealth of Australia in its Constitution Act (*The Constitution*, 1986, p. 6). The original NAFTA, or New Zealand Australia Free Trade Agreement, in 1965, linked the two countries into an ever-tightening trade embrace; the pact was recast as CER (Closer Economic Relations, short for ANZCERTA or Australia-New Zealand Closer Economic Relations Trade Agreement) in 1983 (Ministry of External Relations and Trade, 1990). Prior to NAFTA, in 1964–65, Australia purchased 4.8 per cent of New Zealand's exports; by 1990, this had risen to 20 per cent, where it remains today. Throughout these years, Australia provided on average 20 per cent of New Zealand's imports (see Figure 11.1). NAFTA/CER thus assisted New Zealand in developing a more balanced trade pattern with Australia, producing benefits for both economies in terms of expanded, liberalized trade through lower tariffs and less regulation. The core of CER is full free trade in all goods (achieved 1 July 1990), with application to the services trade, business law, customs and quarantine procedures, standards, and industry assistance (Ministry of External Relations and Trade, 1990).

Recently, CER has grown into a political thorn for the Australian government, with worries that the benefits have become too lopsided (Australian perspective) (*The Economist*, 1995c) or that the structural and attitudinal reforms in New Zealand have engendered superior competitive performance (New Zealand perspective). The most

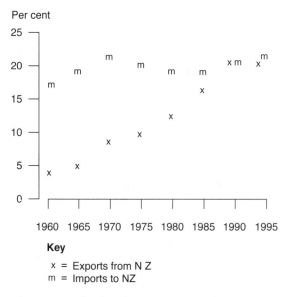

Per cent

Figure 11.1 Australia–New Zealand trade, 1960–1995 (values are percentage of total New Zealand trade)
Source: *The Constitution, as Altered to 31 October 1986* (1986); Ministry of External Relations and Trade (1990), p. 8.

visible sign of the increased tension was the Australian government's decision to delay implementation of an agreement to open its domestic air travel market to Air New Zealand (and potentially other Kiwi competitors) until Qantas, the Australian national airline, was floated successfully and operating more competitively (*The Economist*, 1995c). However, CER is likely to proceed, having already eliminated tariffs on all Australia-New Zealand trade in goods. The triennial review in late 1995 advised facilitation of trade in services and professional registration, potentially taking effect on 1 January 1997 (*Export News* (Tradenz), 1995a). The announcement on 31 January 1996 that the international credit rating service Standard and Poors had raised New Zealand's long-term foreign currency credit rating to AA+, above Australia's AA, was greeted with a sense of glee in New Zealand business circles (*Otago Daily Times*, 1996g). A leading Australian commentator noted earlier that New Zealand's success was threatening Australia's feeling of relative superiority, given that 'New Zealand is the only country in the world which thinks Australia is big and important' (McGuiness, 1994). In essence, there is a friendly rivalry between the two countries that recognizes their interdependence, particularly from the smaller New Zealand towards the larger Australia, in a manner paralleling the relationship between Canada and the USA.

The links with Australia are perceived abroad as being sufficiently tight to associate the New Zealand dollar with the Australian dollar on world currency markets. As the economic performance disparity between the two nations grows, the relative value of the New Zealand dollar has risen, threatening to reach parity early in 1995 before slipping back. The New Zealand currency has also risen against the US dollar, gaining about 35 per cent from early 1993 through early 1996.

Foreign direct investment

The third country with a major influence on the New Zealand economy is the USA, which has at times provided by far the largest share of investment (56.7 per cent of the total foreign investment between 1984 and 1991; for related data, see Table 11.9). The US investment presence is felt most dramatically in large purchases of government privatizations (e.g. Telecom NZ and NZ Rail, now renamed Tranz Rail) and corporate acquisitions (e.g. Wattie's by Heinz, Carter Holt Harvey (CHH) (1995), by International Paper, and Arnott's by Campbell); in periods without such major acquisitions, the US share of net investment inflows shrinks dramatically: from 56.7 per cent in the years ending March 1984–91 to net disinvestment in 1991–93. The Wattie's, CHH, and Arnott's purchases produced a rebound in 1993–95 statistics, bringing in 40.5 per cent of foreign direct investment (FDI) from North America during those two years (see Table 11.9). Cultural influences from the USA have been especially noticeable during the 1860s gold rush, the stationing of US troops during the Second World War, and the present era of Hollywood-originated films and television (which has most recently transplanted the American holiday of Halloween, complete with costumes and trick-or-treating).

Table 11.9 Flows of foreign direct investment into New Zealand by origin

Year ended March (NZ$ millions)	European Union	USA and Canada	Japan	Australia	Asia and Oceania	Other	Total
1989–90	751	271	379	1 237	110	76	2 824
1990–91	–387	3 716	107	–728	160	64	2 932
1991–92	928	–796	11	879	894	110	2 026
1992–93	545	144	–46	3 127	323	–24	4 069
1993–94	1 554	1 556	54	903	651	–8	4 710
1994–95	438	1 885	75	510	619	254	3 781
Six-year total 1989–95	3 829	6 776	580	5 928	2 757	472	20 342
	18.8%	33.3%	2.9%	29.1%	13.6%	2.3%	100
Preceding five-year total 1984–89	1 006	871	–65	749	254[a]		2 815
	35.7%	30.9%	–2.3%	26.6%	9.0%		100

Note: [a] Asia, Oceania and other
Source: Regional Direct Investment Statistics database, Statistics New Zealand, reported in *Export News*, 22 January 1996.

Major acquisitions also affect the investment values for other sources and destinations of funds. For example, in the ongoing Australia-New Zealand rivalry, National Australia Bank bought the government-privatized Bank of New Zealand, the largest bank in the land, in 1992 for NZ$850 million; 'in response', Lion Nathan (New Zealand's premier brewers) purchased Bond Brewing, the largest source of beer in Australia.

Japanese investment is an entirely different story from its popular perception. In Australia, 90 per cent of Japanese investment is in tourism and real estate; a similar figure is probable for New Zealand, where Japanese purchases have focused on forests and tourism facilities such as ski resorts and golf clubs – high profile targets which have generated more animosity than the manufacturing and service takeovers performed by other foreigners. Exceptions are due to remaining tariffs which encourage local assembly, in particular of automobiles and trucks; such investments are popularly valued for the jobs they provide. Whether or not the Japanese perceive opportunities in an entirely different manner, Japan remains one of the smaller players on the New Zealand foreign investment scene, providing 4.9 per cent of inbound investment between 1984 and 1991, shrinking to a negligible 0.06 per cent for 1991–95; in turn, New Zealand invested negligible amounts in Japan (Tables 11.9 and 11.10). In 1990, the Japan-New Zealand Business Council advised that attention should be directed to why New Zealand was unsuccessful in attracting more Japanese investment, rather than worrying about the effects of what little was occurring (Japan–New Zealand Business Council, 1990). Prime Minister Bolger echoed this sentiment on a trip to Japan in May 1996: 'We would welcome a greater level of interest by Japanese investors.' (*Otago Daily Times*, 1996h).

Table 11.10 Flows of New Zealand direct investment abroad

Year ended March (NZ% millions)	European Union	USA and Canada	Japan	Australia	Asia and Oceania	Other	Total
1989–90	–449	445	16	3 402	689	–142	3 961
1990–91	3 361	–260	5	–539	624	–645	2 546
1991–92	664	78	–6	305	–1 379	1 066	728
1992–93	554	–407	24	–253	–2 701	249	–2 534
1993–94	850	1 839	–25	1 151	707	–1 084	3 438
1994–95	1 179	–891	2	715	814	176	1 995
Six-year total	6 159	804	16	4 781	–1 246	–380	10 134
1989–95	60.8%	7.9%	0.2%	47.2%	–12.3%	–3.8%	100

Source: Regional Direct Investment Statistics database.

Popular reaction to FDI in general has been one of suspicion, with accusations that ownership of the country was shifting overseas, or that excessive amounts of profit were being repatriated, rather than accruing to New Zealanders. One poll in early 1995 found 51 per cent supporting a hypothetical law to ban foreign investment (*Otago Daily Times*, 1995d), while another found rapidly rising support for Asian investment in the country, with 34 per cent in favour, 35 per cent mixed and 31 per cent opposed (*Otago Daily Times*, 1995e). A 1995 study of major FDI companies in New Zealand led to an opposite conclusion, that 'foreign investors were found to bring in a broad set of skills and assets to the economy, including capital, technology, management practices and access to global networks', the latter being deemed critical to New Zealand businesses' competitive advantage (Enderwick, 1995).

The actual foreign ownership of New Zealand non-farm businesses is small in terms of percentage of enterprises, but substantial in its employment impact, due to the heavy concentration of foreign ownership in larger enterprises (Tables 11.11 and 11.12).

Of the nearly 200 000 businesses in New Zealand in February 1995, only 2.8 per cent had foreign ownership of at least 1 per cent; this contrasts with 38 per cent of firms with 100+ employees, and 23 per cent of firms with fifty to ninety-nine employees. Most tellingly, 29 per cent of all firms with 100 or more employees are majority-owned overseas firms (Table 11.11); 20 per cent of all non-farm employees work in enterprises with at least 1 per cent foreign ownership; 16 per cent work in majority foreign-owned firms, which provide nearly 200 000 full-time equivalent jobs (Table 11.12). Strictly by count, the typical foreign choice of a New Zealand investment remains a small business; of the nearly 4000 majority foreign-owned firms in New Zealand, 58 per cent employ five or fewer people (Table 11.13). However, majority ownership of a larger organization is the principal destination of investment funds and of employment impact, providing 63.5 per cent of jobs in firms with 1 per cent or more foreign ownership and over 80 per cent of the total employment in majority foreign-owned businesses (Table 11.14). Of the *Management (NZ)* magazine Top 200 companies, nearly 40 per cent have majority overseas owners (*Management NZ*, 1995).

Table 11.11 Percentage of enterprises by degree of overseas equity and size, February 1995

Percentage of overseas equity	Persons engaged					Total %	Enterprises
	0–5	*6–9*	*10–49*	*50–99*	*100+*		
< 1	98.0	97.2	93.0	77.2	62.0	97.2	187 523
1 to < 25	0.4	0.5	1.1	4.2	5.0	0.5	973
25 to < 50	0.2	0.3	0.6	1.6	3.9	0.3	491
50 or more	1.4	2.0	5.2	17.1	29.0	2.0	3 884
1 to 100	2.0	2.8	7.0	22.8	38.0	2.8	5 348
Total enterprises	160 495	15 133	14 709	1 344	1 190		192 871

Notes: Economically significant enterprises (excluding farms) with over NZ$30 000 in tax-reported expenses (or sales if tax-exempt); full-time equivalent persons engaged.
Source: Annual Business Directory Update (ABDU) database (1996), Tables 1.8a–1.8d.

Foreign investment funds have found banking and finance, manufacturing, and property most attractive (Table 11.15). The largest percentage of foreign ownership involvement is in mining, where 23 per cent of enterprises have at least 1 per cent foreign ownership (8 per cent are majority foreign-owned); business and financial services; and trade (wholesale, retail, restaurants, and hotels). In every industry, foreign ownership percentage rises with firm size. In three of the nine major economic sectors, over 25 per cent of workers are engaged by firms with majority foreign ownership (manufacturing; transport, storage, and communication; and business and financial services). The trade sector, notable for its large proportion of small businesses, is dominated by the 94 foreign majority-owned firms, which account for over 60 per cent of employment in the largest size category (100 or more employees).

New Zealand's inward and outward FDI flows exhibit a rather dramatic shift commencing in the year ended 31 March 1990; prior to this date, inward and outward flows each remained under $1 billion annually, whereas in that year and subsequently the average has been well over $2 billion in each direction annually (see Table 11.16).

Table 11.12 Percentage of employment by degree of overseas equity and size, February 1995

Percentage of overseas equity	*Persons engaged (FTEs)*[a]						
	0–5	*6–9*	*10–49*	*50–99*	*100+*	*Total %*	*Enterprises*
< 1	98.7	97.1	91.4	76.7	60.6	80.0	1 010 453
1 to < 25	0.2	0.5	1.4	4.2	3.7	2.2	27 518
25 to < 50	0.1	0.3	0.8	1.5	4.3	2.0	25 842
50 or more	1.0	2.1	6.4	17.6	31.5	15.8	199 161
1 to 100	1.3	2.9	8.6	23.3	39.4	20.0	252 521
Total enterprises	285 691	104 286	270 904	92 262	509 835		1 262 974

Notes: Economically significant enterprises (excluding farms) with over NZ$30 000 in tax-reported expenses (or sales if tax-exempt).
[a] Full-time equivalent persons engaged.
Source: Annual Business Directory Update (ABDU) database (1996), Tables 1.8a–1.8d

Table 11.13 Enterprises by degree of overseas equity and size, February 1995

Percentage of overseas equity	*Persons engaged*					
	0–5	*6–9*	*10–49*	*50–99*	*100+*	*Total*
< 1	157 356	14 710	13 682	1 037	738	187 523
1 to < 25	612	77	168	56	60	973
25 to < 50	290	42	91	21	47	491
50 or more	2 237	304	768	230	345	3 884
Total 1 to 100	3 139	423	1 027	307	452	5 348
Total enterprises	160 495	15 133	14 709	1 344	1,190	192 871

Notes: Economically significant enterprises (excluding farms) with over NZ$30 000 in tax-reported expenses (or sales if tax-exempt); full-time equivalent persons engaged
Source: Annual Business Directory Update (ABDU) database (1996), Tables 1.8a–1.8d.

Table 11.14 Employment by degree of overseas equity and size, February 1995

Percentage of overseas equity	*Persons engaged (FTEs)*[a]					
	0–5	*6–9*	*10–49*	*50–99*	*100+*	*Total*
< 1	281 868	101 261	247 570	70 778	308 978	1 010 453
1 to < 25	585	544	3 740	3 885	18 765	27 518
25 to < 50	331	296	2 128	1 388	21 700	25 842
50 or more	2 907	2 185	17 466	16 211	160 392	199 161
Total FTEs	285 691	104 286	270 904	92 262	509 835	1 262 974
Total FTEs, 1 to 100	3 823	3 025	23 334	21 484	200 857	252 521

Notes: Economically significant enterprises (excluding farms) with over NZ$30 000 in tax-reported expenses (or sales if tax-exempt)
[a] Full-time equivalent persons engaged.
Rows and columns do not sum exactly due to calculations used to determine FTEs
Source: Annual Business Directory Update (ABDU) database (1996), Tables 1.8a–1.8d.

Table 11.15 Applications to the Overseas Investment Commission, 1991–94

Industry	NZ$ (000)	%
Agriculture	288 266	1.0
Forestry	1 620 387	5.8
Fishing	25 510	0.1
Mining	480 533	1.7
Manufacturing	5 658 919	20.3
Electricity	616 342	2.2
Wholesale and retail	2 524 419	9.0
Transport	1 317 337	4.7
Communications	2 659 673	9.5
Banking and finance	6 282 227	22.5
Property	5 494 184	19.7
Other	948 925	3.4
Total	27 916 722	100.0

Source: KPMG (1996).

Cumulative investment position figures from Statistics New Zealand show New Zealand investments abroad totalling NZ$23 443 million at the end of March 1995, while foreign investment totals NZ$96 726 million – a net foreign investment base of NZ$73 billion, roughly 86 per cent of GDP.

The official position on FDI, official being that of the National Party government as expressed by Finance Minister Bill Birch, is that overseas investment is a fundamental necessity for continuing economic and job growth (*Otago Daily Times*, 1995f). The Governor of the Reserve Bank, Don Brash, reversed his earlier criticism of FDI during 1995, proclaiming that 'almost all foreign investment will be of benefit to New Zealand and New Zealanders' (*Otago Daily Times*, 1995g). The Ministry of Foreign Affairs and Trade has also issued statements strongly supporting FDI, calling it 'a key contributor to a dynamic economy' (Ministry of Foreign Affairs and Trade, 1994). Government immigration policy strongly supports FDI, including it among criteria useful in gaining a residence permit (to be discussed in the section on Immigration and citizenship).

Despite being eager to attract FDI, the government will 'not offer investment incentives. Rather we regard them at best as compensating for distortions elsewhere in the economy. We have relied instead on the economic reform process to transform New Zealand into an attractive destination in its own right,' according to the Director of the Investment Promotion Unit of the Ministry of Foreign Affairs and Trade, Christopher Butler. The resulting 'advantage is not one artificially maintained by supports and subsidies. It is a genuine international competitive advantage arising from an economy with most of its fundamentals in balance' (Economic Development Unit, 1994).

Table 11.16 New Zealand foreign direct investment, 1982–95

Year ended March (NZ$ million)	FDI into New Zealand	New Zealand outward FDI	Difference (into NZ)
1982–83	364	604	−240
1983–84	205	54	151
1984–85	456	349	107
1985–86	745	166	579
1986–87	402	949	−547
1987–88	238	938	−700
1988–89	725	226	499
1989–90	2 824	3 961	−1 137
1990–91	2 932	2 546	386
1991–92	2 026	728	1 298
1992–93	4 069	−2 534	6 603
1993–94	4 710	3 438	1 272
1994–95	3 781	1 995	1 786
13-year total 1982–95	23 477	13 420	10 057

Source: *New Zealand Official Yearbook 95*, p. 398. *European Union News* (1995).

■ Opportunities for MNCs and other overseas businesses

New Zealand should interest multinational firms from several perspectives: specifically as a manufacturing or service provision base from which to supply Asia, as a source of raw or processed materials, as a pool of talent and innovation that is readily transferred abroad, as a market for both imports and domestic goods and services, and as a potential joint venture partner anywhere in the world. Smaller overseas businesses, particularly those in developing or reforming economies, should spot opportunities for co-operation in setting up joint ventures; obtaining product, process and management expertise; and finding suppliers who are enthusiastic at providing small runs of customized goods which larger firms might avoid. New Zealand is an outstanding business partner or venue; as *Business Week* captioned its feature on the leader among ten 'global hot spots', 'The Kiwis are open for business' (Nakarmi, 1995).

Invest for export and domestic sales

As a production base, New Zealand offers inexpensive, flexible, skilled labour, an abundance of raw materials and energy, and an amenable organizational climate that fosters teamwork, innovation and international orientation. Government policy and promotional efforts have redirected the economy from a monolithic focus on the UK to a balanced world perspective, with special emphasis on expanding and refining contacts with the growing, proximate Asian markets. Numerous multinationals employ New Zealand as a production base from which to supply Asia, with noticeable recent growth in their numbers and business volume:

- When HJ Heinz purchased food processor Watties in 1993, the single largest investment it ever made, it stated that this was to be its gateway to the vast, rapidly growing Asian market. Heinz's intention is to expand Watties' exports from under NZ$100 million to over $500 million by the end of the decade (*Otago Daily Times*, 1995g). Chairman and Chief Executive Tony O'Reilly highlighted a 26 per cent competitive cost advantage over Australia (where Heinz already operated, including exporting to New Zealand), low inflation, low interest rates, favourable labour market conditions, tariff reforms, New Zealand's encouragement of free trade, attractive transport costs, and low raw materials costs as the key factors in Heinz's decision. 'New Zealand is probably the best equipped low cost operator base to approach the entire Asian market. We think New Zealand is, of all places, the right place to be' (*New Zealand Investment*, 1994, p.11).

- Sumitomo Forestry, the dominant forest-based company in Japan, built the largest medium density fibreboard (MDF) plant in the world in 1986, doubling capacity in 1991, at a cost of NZ$200 million. A newly announced third production line (costing $100 million) will nearly double capacity again, to 375 000m triannually. This one plant currently supplies 20 per cent of Japan's entire MDF requirements, with additional production sold to Australia, Southeast Asia, and China. Expansion will allow exporting to the USA and growth in China (Hall, 1994a; *Otago Daily Times*, 1996i).

- International Paper, the world's largest forest products company, increased its shareholding in CHH, New Zealand's largest forest owner (24 per cent) and sawn timber and paperboard manufacturer, from 23.8 per cent to 50.3 per cent on 31 March 1995. CHH continues to be owner or joint-venture partner in forestry processing, plastic packaging, glass wool, paper distribution, and related industries in Latin America and Australia with exports of lumber, building materials, foils, pulp, paper, tissue, and packaging to Asia, Australia, and the USA (Carter Holt Harvey, 1995; New Zealand Forest Owners Association, 1995).

- Gillette supplies its aerosol markets in Australia, Singapore, Korea and Taiwan from New Zealand (Hall, 1994a).

- Kraft General Foods produces jams, beans, cheeses and other processed foods for export and domestic sales (Hall, 1994a).

- Shiseido Corporation manufactures makeup for the Asian market (Hall, 1994a).

- Many East Asian fishing firms have invested large sums in fish catching and processing, with major sales to Japan, Korea and Taiwan (Hall, 1994a).

Invest for domestic sales

The relatively small size of the New Zealand market, with only 3.6 million consumers and no physically attached neighbouring markets, is both a bane and a blessing. In the words of JETRO, 'the largest problem is the market size … Japanese manufacturing representatives in Sydney … often complain about the small size of the Australian market which means they cannot enjoy the scale of economy in production. … New Zealand has the same problem but it is even bigger' (*Otago Daily Times*, 1995h). The predictable effect of this perception on Japanese direct investment in New Zealand is borne out by the bidirectional FDI values, discussed previously.

The domestic market may be small, but it is a discerning, growing market eager for new goods and services. The OECD, in its December 1995 *Economic Outlook*, forecast that real domestic demand will grow faster in New Zealand by 1997 than anywhere else in the OECD; imports were expected to grow even faster than demand, following 16 per cent growth in 1994 (OECD, 1995, pp. A11, A13, A43). Although New Zealanders are amenable to purchasing competitive foreign-made goods, it sometimes helps to have locally made products on the shelves. The persuasive factors range from psychology and nationalism (the 'Buy NZ Made' campaign) to tariffs, such as those affecting motor vehicle imports. Although these tariffs are being phased out, they retain a noticeable impact on costs. Toyota, Nissan, Mitsubishi and Honda have long-established automobile and truck assembly plants, supplying 40 per cent of the domestic market. Toyota in particular has attained success, with the top-selling car and truck for eight consecutive years, and a level of quality unprecedented outside Japan.

Due to their nature, services often must be provided domestically for a foreign parent to profit from the New Zealand market. Much foreign investment has targeted the leisure sector, where growth is rapid (e.g. the number of tourists is expected to double from 1.5 million in 1995 to 3.0 million in 2000). For example, the largest hotel operator in New Zealand, CDL Hotels, is owned in Hong Kong and Singapore (Hall, 1994a). The top-selling magazine in the country is *TV Guide*; in third place is the New Zealand edition of *Reader's Digest* (*Facts New Zealand*, 1995). One of the three national television networks is primarily foreign owned: profitable and popular TV3 has three major stakeholders, CanWest Global Communications Corporation of Canada, Westpac Bank of Australia and TV3 Network Holdings Ltd (*Facts New Zealand*, 1995, p.125). Sky Network, the first subscriber television company in New Zealand, is 51 per cent overseas owned (*Facts New Zealand*, 1995, p.126). On all three networks as well as Sky's five channels, foreign programming dominates, with the lion's share belonging to the USA, UK and Australia. The most popular restaurant chain in the country is McDonald's, with a per person outlet ratio second only to the USA. Pizza Hut and Kentucky Fried Chicken are also dominant in their sectors, and Subway Sandwiches announced market entry for 1996.

Government privatization sales have turned many former public services and manufacturers into foreign assets. Chief among these is Telecom NZ, sold for NZ$4.25 billion to Bell Atlantic and Ameritech; the sale agreement required that the two US owners subsequently reduce their stake to 49.9 per cent (the remaining Telecom shares are now traded on the New York and New Zealand stock exchanges). The two principal competitors for Telecom, Clear Communications Ltd (1991) with 22 per cent of domestic and international toll calls, and BellSouth digital cellular network, are also majority foreign-owned (*Facts New Zealand*, 1995, p. 180). The Bank of New Zealand was sold to the National Bank of Australia for NZ$1.4 billion, while the second biggest (and most profitable) bank, National, is now owned in the UK, and Countrywide Bank belongs to Scotland. The Railways Corporation (renamed Tranz Rail, from NZ Rail, in October 1995) was sold to a Wisconsin Central-led consortium for NZ$330 million. Air New Zealand, sold for NZ$660 million, saw 19.9 per cent of its shares go to arch-rival Qantas, and 7.5 per cent each to Japan Air Lines and American Airlines (Hall, 1994b).

Sourcing products available only from New Zealand

Vast distances to all markets forced early innovation, resulting in the world's first shipment of frozen meat, from Dunedin to the UK in 1882. Today, numerous patented and/or unique goods are available only from New Zealand. Opportunities for multinationals and strictly domestic firms abound in importation, licensing, distribution, and assembly incorporation of these products or components. Three examples suffice to illustrate this type of relationship, and the range of unique goods on offer:

- Taura Natural Foods' industrial food ingredient concentrates, exported to major food processors (Nestlé, Kraft, Cadbury, Uncle Toby, and others) in Australia, Europe, Asia and North America, employ a closely-guarded Ultra Rapid Concentration process developed in New Zealand. Ultra Rapid Concentration retains natural flavours and colours to an unprecedented degree, such that the concentrate magnifies rather than degrades the flavour. Its original plant has been shifted to Australia, from which exports will flow to Asia, Europe and the USA until Taura builds factories in those markets. In a strategic partnership, McDonald's sources ketchup for its New Zealand and Asia/Pacific markets from Taura, along with other products primarily for the New Zealand market (e.g. caramels, chocolate fudge). Taura is McDonald's sole supplier of orange juice for Indonesia and New Zealand, as well as supplying chocolate sauce to KFC in China. Originally a citrus growers' juicing co-operative, Taura Natural Foods is now 80 per cent owned by Berryvale Orchards Ltd, the largest fruit juice firm in Australia (Economic Development Unit, 1994; *NZ Business*, 1995b).

- Vega Industries has relentlessly sought breakthroughs and continuous improvement, co-operated closely with its suppliers, tackled problems no one else wanted, and insisted on world-class quality and on-time delivery. Developing and manufacturing lighthouse beacons, the eleven-person company won a contract to supply the US Coast Guard with rotating medium-range beacons to specifications that could not be achieved by any existing light. The new product is so dramatically superior that the Coast Guard committed to replacing all 120 of its medium-range beacons, regardless of condition. An earlier unique beacon, indicating direction by sharp colour changes, established markets in Australia, Britain, Europe, Asia and Canada, while a second innovative product brought the initial breakthrough with the US Coast Guard. The beacon uses 150 watts of power for a 26 nautical mile range, operates from –24 °C to +65 °C, replaces blown lamps automatically, switches on and off automatically, monitors itself continuously, operates for 12 months without inspection, and is solar powered. Purchasers of other speciality beacons and traffic control lights include Australia, Canada, Hong Kong and Japan (Fletcher, 1995; *NZ Business*, 1995c).

- Buckley Systems Ltd is the world's leading supplier of ion beam instrumentation used in the manufacture of silicon chips. Already installed at every computer chip maker in the world, Buckley's ion beam implanters have recently been superseded by a newer generation that enhances transmission quality while extending portable battery life tenfold (*New Zealand Manufacturer*, 1995).

Co-operating with New Zealand businesses overseas

Once strictly homebodies, New Zealand firms are reaching out to the world, forming joint ventures and setting up processing and distribution facilities. Their actions both anticipated and responded to the urgings of the 1994 *World Competitiveness Report*, which gave 'internationalization' (foreign trade, partnerships with foreign firms and FDI) as the key area demanding attention (New Zealand ranked twenty-fifth of forty-one countries, creeping up to twenty-third of forty-eight in the 1995 report). Examples of New Zealand firms with foreign partners overseas include:

- Swichtec Power Systems, designer and manufacturer of standby power equipment for telecommunications and computer equipment; 90 per cent of its NZ$50 million production is exported. Swichtec fabricates high-tech rectifiers and microprocessor modules in New Zealand, and through a manufacturing agreement with the Railways Ministry in China produces the low-tech, bulkier components in Beijing. A joint venture with telecoms firm Qiao Sing in Hangzhou has also been established. The firm also exports to the UK, Hungary, the UAE, Saudi Arabia, Southeast Asia, Latin America and Australia, operating a technical support centre in Kuala Lumpur and 20 sales agencies from Cyprus to Jakarta, Vancouver and Buenos Aires (Macfie, 1996b; Swichtec Power Systems, 1995).

- Nu-Con Ltd designs and manufactures pneumatic systems which convey bulk solids in processing plants. Its first major overseas success in the US dairy industry resulted in a joint venture manufacturing operation in Minneapolis, which supplies specialized systems for handling 'instantized' products such as infant formula, coffee and cream. With a strong Asian focus, the company exports almost 70 per cent of its production (a third going to China); staff in the Auckland home office speak five Asian languages.

- Fisher and Paykel Industries Ltd (F&P) manufactures (in New Zealand and Australia) and distributes (to over eighty countries) kitchen and laundry appliances and electronic health care products. Speciality products range from programmable state controllers to computer-aided yacht keel machining. Overseas sales account for 44 per cent of revenue; within the health care range, 90 per cent. F&P also annually distributes on the domestic market NZ$100 million of Panasonic consumer electronics for Matsushita, with which it has a particularly supportive relationship. In 1995, F&P's Production Machinery division shipped a mixed-model refrigeration production line to Atlas Electrica SA in Costa Rica, the largest appliance maker in Central America. F&P's largest shareholder is Morgan Stanley Asset Management, at 11 per cent. Test marketing of F&P's Smart Drive clothes washing machines in the USA, bearing the GE brand, commenced in 1996 (Fisher and Paykel Industries Ltd, 1995).

Purchasing services for delivery abroad

New Zealand is establishing an international reputation for consultancy and research and development, with innovative processes, speed, and practicality among the leading characteristics of local firms. The range of expertise provided abroad includes sheep and cattle ranch management in Argentina, apple orchard establishment in China, dairy industry development in India, telecommunications infrastructure advising in Vietnam, forestry and salmon farming consultation (with investment) in Chile, and civic management to Australia.

- The winner of the 1995 Tradenz Export Excellence Award for an Exporter of Services is UniServices Ltd, owned by the University of Auckland with the goal of marketing the university's skills and resources. The principal product is research and development contract management; 45 per cent of 1994 sales were exported to twenty countries. Key clients include the National Cancer Institute (USA), a French company for whom UniServices is managing a NZ$26.1 million clinical trial, and Walt Disney Imagineering, for which a batteryless electric car was designed (Hunter, 1995; *NZ Business*, 1995c).

- New Zealand Post Ltd, corporatized in 1987, is profitable, efficient and respected. Profit after tax for the year ended 31 March 1995 was 11 per cent on sales of NZ$644 million (Goulter, 1995). The regular letter rate, which last increased in 1987, was lowered by over 10 per cent in October 1995, remaining one of the lowest in the world. Given its dramatic successes, NZ Post has become an active international adviser on the restructuring and modernization of postal services, with projects in South Africa, Malaysia, Vietnam, the Czech Republic, Thailand, Namibia, Western Samoa, Pakistan, Laos, Vanuatu and Papua New Guinea. Study tours and visits have been conducted by numerous others *(Export News* (Tradenz), 1995b).

- Aircraft maintenance training for two private Indian airlines, ELBEE and NEPC, was conducted in Madras (India) and Christchurch (New Zealand) by Air New Zealand Engineering Training Services (Overseas Investment Commission, 1994).

■ Regulation of foreign direct investment

Principal concerns for foreign investors, both firms and individuals, include two key areas: governmental regulation of investment, and restrictions on immigration and citizenship. In the case of funds, the government actively encourages FDI, but has some preferences (detailed below). Immigration, once fairly open, has become more restricted as the number of applicants surged in response to immigration law reform, approval increases and economic success.

Overseas Investment Commission

The Overseas Investment Commission (OIC), established in 1973, considers applications for investment by overseas individuals or organizations when the intended investments are 'significant' or involve a 'specified business'. A 'significant' investment is defined as one exceeding NZ$10 million, when:

- 25 per cent of any class of shares or voting power is acquired or controlled

- a new business is set up

- business assets are acquired or

- cumulative shares issued or allotted to an overseas person exceed this amount.

There are two sorts of 'specified business': commercial fishing and the purchase of rural land. Under such circumstances, the OIC is required to apply the following criteria, which should collectively provide a net economic benefit to New Zealand (Overseas Investment Commission, 1994):

- added market competition, lower prices, greater efficiency and enhanced consumer services

- the introduction of new technology, managerial and/or technical skills

- the development of new export markets or increased market access

- the creation of new job opportunities or the retention of existing jobs

- the relative opportunities for current owners to realize their investment to the best advantage and flow-on effects that will accrue from that realization.

The intention of the OIC is to guide and evaluate, not prevent, significant foreign investment. This is evidenced by its extraordinarily high approval rate of 99.8 per cent for all applications presented to it between 1985 and 1990, and 100 per cent from 1991 through 1995 (Overseas Investment Commission, 1996). In 1994, the OIC considered 362 applications, valued at NZ$5 billion; all were approved (the last two refusals occurred in 1990). Of the applications, 30 per cent by value and 14 per cent by number originated in Australia. Hong Kong provided 18 per cent by value and 11 per cent by number; the pattern of US applications differed, with 13 per cent by value but 23 per cent by number. Canada, Singapore and the UK also each originated over 5 per cent of OIC applications by value. While applications from Hong Kong, China and Singapore have been increasing, those from Japan and the UK have decreased over the past four years (Overseas Investment Commission, 1995). Standard conditions are that: the investment actually takes place within twelve months; and any consent-requiring activities outside the original consent scope require a new consent. The OIC has the authority to specify conditions for investment, including continued access rights, prior to approving overseas rural land sales (Overseas Investment Commission, 1994), however, typically no specific conditions or restrictions are attached (Overseas Investment Commission, 1996).

All overseas investors, whether subject to the OIC assessment or not, are officially advised by the OIC to consider the following legislation and regulations, as well as engage legal counsel (Overseas Investment Commission, 1994):

- Customs Department requirements

- Immigration requirements

- The Commerce Act, 1986

- The Companies Act, 1955

- The Resource Management Act, 1991

- The Crown Minerals Act, 1991

- Land Settlement Promotion and Land Acquisition Act, 1952 and Amendments

- Reserve Bank requirements for banking licence

- Fish Packhouse and Export Licenses.

Immigration and citizenship

Since 1945, the percentage of New Zealand residents born outside the country has hovered around 15 per cent. Significant trends over the past ten years include a dramatic rise in the number of Asian-born residents, with numbers more than doubling between the 1986 and 1991 censuses. By 1991, 2.0 per cent of New Zealand residents were born in Asia; significant increases in immigration were recorded from China,

Hong Kong, Malaysia, the Philippines, Taiwan, Thailand and India (*New Zealand Official Yearbook 95*, 1995, p.151). During 1995, over 20 per cent of immigrants originated in Taiwan, followed by Great Britain, China and South Korea (Table 11.17). A points system for general immigrants was introduced in late 1991, rating candidates on factors deemed contributory to the economic and social well-being of current residents (namely, employability, age and settlement factors). Despite an increase in the number of permanent residence approvals from 10 313 in 1991 to 54 811 in 1995, the points threshold rose from 20 to 31, which the government regards as evidence of 'the success of the system in attracting quality migrants' (New Zealand Immigration Service, 1995a; *New Zealand Official Yearbook 95*, 1995, p.153). Revision of the points system resulted in the General Skills category, effective in January 1996, with altered scales and floating 'pass marks', adjusted weekly 'in order to manage migrant numbers' (New Zealand Immigration Service, 1996, p.2).

Table 11.17 Immigration sources, January–December 1995 (number of people approved for permanent residency)

Country	Immigrants	%
Taiwan	12 263	22.4
Great Britain	6 345	11.6
China	4 881	8.9
South Korea	3 635	6.6
India	3 232	5.9
Hong Kong	3 114	5.7
Iraq	2 310	4.2
Western Samoa	1 942	3.5
South Africa	1 849	3.4
Sri Lanka	1 327	2.4
All others	13 913	25.4
Total	54 811	100.0

Source: New Zealand Immigration Service (1996), p. 3.

Of greater utility for potential business investors is the Business Investor category of immigration, established in January 1996. The intention of this category is 'to ensure that high quality migrants with proven business skills and experience gain entry to New Zealand' (New Zealand Immigration Service, 1995b, p.13). Points are awarded for business experience, formal qualifications, accumulated earnings, direct investment funds, age and settlement factors. As for General Skills category immigrants, health, character and English language requirements must also be passed. Investments by immigrants in the two investment categories effective in 1995 (but discontinued in January 1996) are shown in Table 11.18; it is apparent that the principal source of immigrant capital inflows is North Asia, which includes Taiwan, China and Hong Kong.

Overseas firms intending to assign managers or other employees to positions in New Zealand should seek legal advice on each person's immigration status and possibilities, as unexpected difficulties can arise, notably with timing and points totals in the General Skills category.

New Zealand citizenship can be obtained through birth, descent (parents), or grant. Introduction of the Citizenship Act 1977 resulted in a surge in citizenship grants, which averaged 2000 annually during the 1960s and early 1970s, to nearly 18 000 in 1978. In the year ended 30 June 1994, 18 010 people were granted New Zealand citizenship. Dual citizenship is permitted, and eligibility criteria are not unusual, with minimum legal residence prior to application being three years (*New Zealand Official Yearbook 95*, 1995, p.152).

Table 11.18 Investments by immigrants by category and source, January–December 1995 (amounts in NZ$)

	Investment category	
Source	Business (000s)	General (000s)
North Asia	326 000	285 500
Europe	33 000	16 400
Southeast Asia	14 250	13 400
Americas	14 250	4 400
Middle East/Africa	3 500	4 100
South Asia	500	4 200
Pacific	1 750	
Other	750	600
Total	394 000	328 600

Source: New Zealand Immigration Service (1995b)

In a survey conducted by the American Chamber of Commerce in New Zealand in 1995, immigration conditions for key overseas personnel were seen as a difficult hurdle, but not as restrictive as the Resource Management Act: 53 per cent of the 100 primarily US-owned firms indicated that their decisions were influenced by the detailed information requirements of applications under the Resource Management Act; 52 per cent also felt the OIC consent requirement was too restrictive, while 43 per cent indicated it was beneficial; 58 per cent believed the absence of takeover rules impeded foreign investment, while 35 per cent thought it benefited them. However, respondents gave strong support to the Reserve Bank Act (81 per cent) and the Employment Contracts Act (90 per cent) (*Otago Daily Times*, 1995i).

■ Conclusions

New Zealand's radical reform experiment completed its first decade in 1996, with a mixed verdict: 'superb' from economic and business commentators (*The Economist*, 1993; *The Economist*, 1995c), 'dismal' from social equity and compassion adherents (Kelsey, 1995). The key current question is to what degree the reforms will stick. The first election under the new mixed-member proportional voting system, held in October 1996, may result in moderation of some policies, notably social welfare, health and education spending. The general populace is now accruing benefits from the revamped economy, but a feeling of palpable loss remains; a system based on individuality, competition and innovation is inherently less comforting than the previous collective, caring and (enforced) sharing society. Some relish the opportunities of the new New Zealand; others yearn for the security and nurture of the old. Continuation without backsliding on the reforms will increase proportional personal disparities, particularly in income and access to goods and services. Civil society had its say for nearly a century, and showed it could not balance the books; business is now being saddled with the opportunity to prove it can run a caring economy profitably.

The world of strategic management has set a new course, favouring flexibility, innovation, co-operation and 'small is beautiful'. These are inherent characteristics of the New Zealand culture and, increasingly, of its businesses. The kiwi, long flightless under benevolent government restraint, is now exercising its newly granted wings of economic liberty. For both inbound foreign firms and domestic enterprises eyeing world markets, these are indeed exciting times of unprecedented opportunity.

■ Appendix: Government advisory assistance to foreign investors

Investment Promotion Unit, Ministry of Foreign Affairs and Trade, Private Bag 18901, Wellington; Tel: 64 4 472 8877; Fax: 64 4 473 7416. (Provides general information on New Zealand as an investment destination, and co-ordinates government promotion activities.)

Investment Services, New Zealand Trade Development Board (Tradenz), PO Box 10341, Wellington; Tel: 64 4 499 2244; Fax: 64 4 473 3193. Promotes inward investment and exporting through numerous domestic and overseas offices, providing sector information and company contact details.

The Secretary, Overseas Investment Commission, PO Box 2498, Wellington; Tel: 64 4 472 2029; Fax: 64 4 472 3262. Approves investment applications involving 'significant investment' (NZ$10 000 000 or more) and 'specified business' (commercial fishing and rural land).

New Zealand Immigration Service, PO Box 3705, Wellington; Tel: 64 4 473 9100; Fax: 64 4 495 4242. Furnishes forms, advises on criteria, and assesses immigration and visa applications.

Further information and assistance is available at any overseas post of the New Zealand government.

■ References

Adam, E. E. Jr, Corbett, L. M. and Rho, B. H. (1993). A comparison of quality improvement practices in Korea, New Zealand and the United States of America. *Proceedings of the 2nd International Conference of the Decision Sciences Institute*, Seoul, 14–16 June, pp. 914–16.
Adler, R. W., Everett, A. M. and Waldron, M. A. (1995). The impact of costing techniques and practices on manufacturing performance in New Zealand. *Proceedings of Pan-Pacific Conference XII*, Dunedin/Queenstown, 29 May–1 June, pp. 310–12.
Adler, R. W., Everett, A. M. and Waldron, M. A. (1996) *Advanced Management Accounting Techniques in Manufacturing: Utilisation and Benefits*. Working paper, University of Otago.

Annual Business Directory Update (ABDU) Database (1996) Statistics New Zealand, January.

Australian Manufacturing Council (1994) *Leading the Way: A Study of Best Manufacturing Practices in Australia and New Zealand,* 2nd edn, November.

Batley, T. W. (1994a) Applying total quality principles as an operations management strategy in New Zealand companies. In *Operations Strategy and Performance, Manufacturing Engineering Group* (K. W. Platts, M. J. Gregory and A. D. Neely, eds) Cambridge University Press.

Batley, T. W. (1994b) Service quality in New Zealand: the new competitive edge. *Total Quality Management,* **5** (4), 139–49.

Bell, S. (1995). Kiwis leaders in flexibility. *The Independent,* Auckland, 10 November, p. 31.

Bolwijn, P. T. and Kumpe, T. (1990) Manufacturing in the 1990s – productivity, flexibility and innovation. *Long Range Planning,* **23** (4), August, 44–57.

Brash, D. (1995). Why monetary policy can't please all the people all the time. *The Independent,* Auckland, 10 November, pp. 11, 40.

Burdon, P. (1995). Digging deep on the exchange rate. *New Zealand Manufacturer,* April, 6.

Business Activity Statistics 1994 (1995), May. Statistics New Zealand (updates obtained direct).

Carter Holt Harvey (1995) *Interim Report for the Six Months Ended 30 September 1995.* 8 December.

Crocombe, G. T., Enright, M. J. and Porter, M. E. (1991) *Upgrading New Zealand's Competitive Advantage.* Oxford University Press.

Croke, N. (1994) *Information Technology and Organisational Integration in New Zealand Manufacturing.* Working paper No. 2/94, University of Canterbury, Christchurch.

Department of Statistics (1996) *Overseas trade: December 1995,* Department of Statistics, January.

Dornbusch, R. (1995). Free markets work best – but they need a little tweaking. *Business Week,* international edn, no. 3439–769, 18 December, 8.

Economic Development Unit (1994). *The Competitive Economy,* September, Ministry of Foreign Affairs and Trade.

Enderwick, P. (1995). Cited in Foreign investment has positive impact – study. *Otago Daily Times,* 23 October, p. 10.

European Union News (1995) EU/NZ investment flows, **13** (4), May–June 1995, p. 3, data from Statistics New Zealand.

Everett, A. M. (1995). Statistical awareness: a necessary condition for quality. Presentation at the 3rd International Conference of the Decision Sciences Institute, Puebla, Mexico, 12–14 June.

Export News (1996) 15 April, p.12, data from Statistics New Zealand.

Export News (Tradenz) (1995a) New phase highlighted in 1995, 13 November 1995, p. 14.

Export News (Tradenz) (1995b) New Zealand Post knowhow sought worldwide, 2 October, p. 12.

Export News (Tradenz) (1995c) Air New Zealand conducts training for two airlines, 30 October, p. 13.

Expressing the Values (1995) New Zealand National Quality Awards Foundation, Auckland.

Facts New Zealand (1995). 2nd edn, p. 124. Statistics New Zealand.

Fisher and Paykel Industries Ltd (1995) *Annual Report* 1995, 29 May.

Fletcher, R. (1995) Reef the spur for Vega industries' sector lights. *Export News* (Tradenz), 30 October, p.5.

Goulter, J. (1995). NZ's first 500 companies. *NZ Business*, **9** (10), November, 13–37.

Gwartney, J., Lawson, R. and Block, W. (1995). *Economic Freedom of the World: 1975–1995*. Institute of Economic Affairs; summarized in *The Economist*, 13 January 1996, pp. 19–21.

Hall, T. (1994a). Politics stalls more asset sales. *Asiamoney*, April.

Hall, T. (1994b). The benefit works two ways. *Asiamoney*, April.

Harrison, G.W. (1995). Recent developments in world trade. *Decision Line*, **26** (2), March, 5–7.

Head, W. (1995). Tip Top scoops top 1995 export award. *Export News* (Tradenz), 30 October, 1–2.

Hunter, A. (1995). Academia slips into commerce with great success. *Export News* (Tradenz), 30 October, p.4

Japan 1994: An International Comparison (1994) Keizai Koho Centre, Tokyo.

Japan–New Zealand Business Council (1990) *Japanese Direct Investment in New Zealand*, Japan–New Zealand Business Council, Auckland.

Kelsey, J. (1995) Economic Fundamentalism: The New Zealand Experiment – A World Model for Structural Adjustment, Pluto Press.

Knight Frank Baillieu Research (1992). *Pacific Rim Property Report*, 13th edn, 3rd Quarter.

KPMG (1996) *KPMG Survey of Foreign Direct Investment in New Zealand*, KPMG, Table reproduced in *Export News*, 4 March 1996, p. 1. Data from Overseas Investment Commission.

Lawlink (1995). Personal liability for corporate directors and officers – and what you can do about it. *The Independent*, Auckland, 10 November, p. 17.

Lyons, K. (1995). Top people strategies for 1995. *Management (NZ)*, **42** (2), March, 60–70.

MacAlister, P. (1995) The management skills behind black magic. *Management (NZ)*, **42** (10), November, 18–22.

Macfie, R. (1996a) Rebel apple growers to head for high court. *The Independent*, Auckland, 2 February, p. 3.

Macfie, R. (1996b). Research, development prove their worth for Swichtec. *The Independent*, Auckland, 2 February, p. 21.

Mackenzie, D. (1995) Speights' role in 'A' accreditation. *Otago Daily Times*, 25 October, p. 13.

Made in New Zealand (1994) Television series, episode aired 31 October featuring Toyota Thames

Major, R. (1995) Revolutionary technology puts Taura on world stage. *Export News* (Tradenz), 30 October, p.4.

Management (NZ) (1995) Management 1995 Top 200: solid foundations for the future, **42** (11), December, 63–127.

Manufacturing Advisory Group (1994) *Manufacturing for Growth 1995*, November.

Marshall, S. (1995) Employers, employees enter an era of greater inter-dependence. *The Independent*, Auckland, 27 October, p. 11

McAlevey, L., Everett, A. M. and Sullivan, C. (1995). The changing relevance of quality in business statistics courses: an international comparison. *Asia Pacific Journal of*

Quality Management, **4** (3), 4–15.

McClelland, L. A., Everett, A. M. and Walker, K. B. (1993) Accounting education in New Zealand: a model for reforming the American system? *Proceedings of Pan-Pacific Conference X*, Beijing, 10–12 June, pp. 655–7.

McGuinness, P. P. (1994). Australian superiority threatened; NZ could rival Singapore success. *Sydney Morning Herald*, 6 December.

Mendzela, J. (1995). Down under on top when it comes to management practice. *Management (NZ)*, **42** (11), December, 44–5.

Ministry of External Relations and Trade (1990) *Closer Economic Relations*, Information Bulletin 33, December, Wellington.

Ministry of Foreign Affairs and Trade (1994). Foreign direct investment: a key contributor to a dynamic economy. *Business*, **1** (3), October, p. 1.

Mitchell, I. (1995). Teamwork gives kiwis competitive edge. *The Dominion*, 4 December, IT19.

Moloney, D. (1995). World Quality Day speech, New Zealand Organisation for Quality, Dunedin, 9 November.

Nakarmi, L. (1995). The Kiwis are open for business. *Business Week*, international edn (3429-759), 9 October, 47–8.

New Zealand Forest Owners Association (1995) *Forestry Facts and Figures 1995*, New Zealand Forest Owners Association, Wellington, p. 5.

New Zealand Immigration Service (1995a) *Fact Pack*, Issue 3, New Zealand Immigration Service, July.

New Zealand Immigration Service (1995b) *Self Assessment Guide for Residence in New Zealand*, New Zealand Immigration Service, November.

New Zealand Immigration Service (1996) *Fact Pack*, Issue 4, New Zealand Immigration Service, February.

New Zealand Investment (1994) Ministry of Foreign Affairs and Trade, Wellington.

New Zealand Manufacturer (1995) Prototype implanter shipped. NZ Manufacturers Federation, April, p. 1.

New Zealand Official Yearbook 95 (1995) 98th edn, Statistics New Zealand.

NZ Business (1995a) Matching academic skills with R&D, **9** (10), November 1995, 17–18.

NZ Business (1995b) 'Agony' while awaiting bigger plant, New Zealand Export Award Winners. *NZ Business* **9** (10), November, 14–15.

NZ Business (1995c) Kiwi beacons for US Coast Guard. 1995 New Zealand Export Award Winners. *NZ Business*, **9** (10), November 1995, 19–20.

OECD (1994) *OECD Economic Surveys 1993–1994: New Zealand*. Organization for Economic Co-operation and Development.

OECD (1995) *OECD Economic Outlook*, 58th edn, December, p. 96. Organisation for Economic Co-Operation and Development.

Otago Daily Times (1995a) Economy growing strongly, 1 November, p. 13.

Otago Daily Times (1995b) $3B tax cut and giveaway greeted as conservative, 14 December 1995, p. 19.

Otago Daily Times (1995c) Managerial aims not realised, 25 October.

Otago Daily Times (1995d) Half of NZ opposes foreign landlords – poll, 27 May, p. 13.

Otago Daily Times (1995e) More favour Asian investment in NZ, survey shows, 11 September, p. 10.

Otago Daily Times (1995f) Overseas investors 'key to economic strength', 30 August, p. 18.

Otago Daily Times (1995g) Brash does about-face to back foreign investment, 21 November, p. 10.

Otago Daily Times (1995h) NZ 'too small' to attract Japanese investors, 1 November, p. 14.

Otago Daily Times (1995i) US Chamber pleads for easier investing rules, 30 September, p. 15.

Otago Daily Times (1996a) NZ economic reform portfolio beats most, 11 January, p. 3.

Otago Daily Times (1996b) Conditional funding offer by republicans, 23 January, p. 9.

Otago Daily Times (1996c) Improvement in surplus unwelcome event for RB, 20 January, p. 16.

Otago Daily Times (1996d) Exporters concerned by rising NZ dollar, 30 January 1996, p. 10.

Otago Daily Times (1996e) Boards slated, 6 February 1996, p. 22.

Otago Daily Times (1996f) Pressured unions planning mergers, 3 January, p. 16.

Otago Daily Times (1996g) NZ pips Australia on credit rating, 1 February, p. 13.

Otago Daily Times (1996h) NZ would welcome more Japanese investment, Bolger says in Tokyo, 11 May, p. 11.

Otago Daily Times (1996i) Nelson pine plans $100m line at fibreboard plant, 23 January, p. 9.

Overseas Investment Commission (1994) *Investment Application: A Guide to Making an Application under the Overseas Investment Regulations 1985*, April. Overseas Investment Commission.

Overseas Investment Commission (1995) *Origin of Investment, 1991–94*, July.

Overseas Investment Commission (1996) Personal communication, 26–30 January.

PA Consulting Group, *1995 Salary Survey*, reported in Story, M. (1996). Salaries and incentives: what '96 holds in store. *The Independent*, Auckland, 26 January, pp. 19–21.

Perera, M. H. B. and Rahman, A. R. (1995) Conceptual foundation of accounting and financial reporting: emerging commonality of purpose between Australia and New Zealand. *PacificAccounting Review*, **7** (1), June, 1–23.

Price Waterhouse (1996). *Remuneration Report through September 1995*, reported in M. Story, Salaries and incentives: what '96 holds in store. *The Independent*, Auckland, 26 January, pp. 19–21.

Q-NewZ (1995) The Mobil survey of ISO 9000 certificates awarded worldwide, February 1995, 6–9.

Rahman, A. R., Perera, M. H. B. and Tower, G. D. (1994). Accounting harmonisation between Australia and New Zealand: towards a regulatory union. *International Journal of Accounting*, **29** (4), 316–33.

Regional Direct Investment Statistics database (1996) Statistics New Zealand, reported in *Export News*, 22 January 1996.

Rotherham, F. (1995) Growers vote for kiwifruit monopoly. *The Independent*, Auckland, 19 January, p. 6.

Sheffield Consulting Group (1994). *Chief Executive Survey*, reported in Hall, T. (1994). The benefit works two ways. *Asia-money*, April.

Story,. M. (1996) Salaries and incentives: what '96 holds in store. *The Independent*, Auckland, 26 January, pp. 19–21.

Story, M. and McManus, J. (1995). The good, the bad and the ugly side of the privacy act. *The Independent*, Auckland, 3 November, pp. 20–1.

Success! (1995) Television series, episode aired 24 July 1995, featuring Taura Natural Foods.

Sullivan, M. (1995a) Wired for growth. *NZ Business*, **9** (6), July, 22–9.

Sullivan, M. (1995b). Quality management: not a short term cure all. *NZ Business*, **9** (10), November, 46–50.

Swichtec Power Systems (1995) *Company Profile*. April.

The Constitution, as Altered to 31 October 1986 (1986). Australian Government Publishing Service.

The Economist (1993) The mother of all reformers, **329** (7833), 16 October, p. 18.

The Economist (1994) Manufacturing wage comparisons, 27 August, p. 82.

The Economist (1995a) The great escape? **335** (7908), 1 April, p.70.

The Economist (1995b) The accidental superhighway: a survey of the Internet, **336** (7921), 1 July, S1–S20.

The Economist (1995c) Smaller is more beautiful, **334** (7907), 25 March, p. 33.

The Economist (1996) In the eye of the beholder, 13 January, p. 21.

The Independent (1995) Auckland, 3 November, p. 30.

The Prices Report for September 1995 Quarter (1996), Statistics New Zealand, January, p. 12.

The World Competitiveness Report 1995 (1995) 15th edn, September, item 1.29. World Economic Forum.

TV 3 *Evening News* (1996) New Zealand, 29 January.

Ulanoff, L. (1995) The top 100 CD-ROMs. *PC Magazine*, 27 June, 102–65.

Wallis, A. (1995). Convergence – New Zealand meets with overseas approval. *TUANZ Topics*, **5** (11), December, 8–9.

Watson Wyatt (1995). *Redbook Top Executive Survey*, November, reported in Story, M. (1996). Salaries and incentives: what '96 holds in store. *The Independent*, Auckland, 26 January, pp. 19–21.

Yarwood, V. (1994). Are you paid what you're worth? *Management (NZ)*, **41** (9), October, 30–5.

Yarwood, V. (1995). The salary split. *Management (NZ)*, **42** (9), October, 52–60.

Chapter 11.1

Characteristics of post-crisis New Zealand

■ André M. Everett ■

The confident exuberance of New Zealand in 1996 in no way presaged the roller-coaster ride of the two subsequent years, carrying the national and international economies into the unprecedented 'Asian' financial crisis. A referendum strongly approved conversion of the parliamentary election system to mixed member proportional, which gave the country its first coalition government in October 1996. Before collapsing in August 1998, the coalition bore the brunt of accusations of broken promises from left and right. Reversing prior policy, the coalition ramped up government social spending and delayed the second of the promised income tax cuts (from 1997 to July 1998). Partially in response to domestic policies and partially through global pressures, including the current Asian woes, economic growth was put on hold; unemployment increased, the currency and stock markets dropped, and interest rates rose.

Foreign direct investment has continued to boom, with two-thirds of New Zealand stocks held overseas, including majority ownership of nearly every large firm. 1998 investments featured the purchase by Kirin Brewery (Japan) of Lion Nathan, New Zealand's largest brewer (also an important player in both Australia and China), while 1997 saw the opening of Rayonier's (USA) ultramodern medium-density fibreboard plant; the debate about the relative value of investments in new productive assets versus acquisition of existing companies continued. Direct investment in 1997 topped 50 per cent of GDP, over double the figures for Australia and Canada; majority investors continued to be Australia, the USA, and the UK.

New Zealand–Asian commerce dropped noticeably in 1998, with Southeast Asian sales down by 30 per cent and Asian tourist arrivals down by 37 per cent. However, the fallen New Zealand dollar resulted in dramatically increased sales to the USA (up 27 per cent in the year to July 1998) and Australia, with accompanying increases in tourist numbers. The net impact, in New Zealand dollars, was a slight increase in total exports.

Two landmarks in politico-economic reform were reached in mid-1998, with the early removal of all tariffs on passenger cars (effectively closing down the domestic auto assembly industry) and approval of parallel importing (earning threats of sanctions from the US for over-liberalizing international trade).

Immigration reforms saw a sharp decline in Asian arrivals, largely due to introduction of an English language requirement. Taiwan tumbled from its top spot (22.4 per cent in 1995) to 1.6 per cent, while South Africa rose from 3.4 per cent to 12.7 per cent; total residence approvals fell from 54 811 to 29 805, approximating the government's target for that year. Great Britain regained its traditional first rank, albeit with only 5033 immigrants – far short of 1995's Taiwan tally of 12 263, and below its own total of 6345 for that year (see Table 11.17). China, with 4201 approvals, came second. While we're at it, let's revise history as well – recent research fairly well proves that both the Portuguese (1525) and Spanish (1576) 'discovered' New Zealand, and its Maori inhabitants, long before the Dutch (1642).

Innovation continues as the critical strength of the economy, overcoming hurdles of distance and small scale. For US consumers, the first noticeable New Zealand product to hit the American shelves since kiwifruit will be the DishDrawer, a radically redesigned plastics-based dishwasher that conserves energy, water, detergent and space; two full, independent units fit into a standard dishwasher cabinet slot, yet the total number of parts was drastically reduced, resulting in manufacturing efficiencies. Such products represent the 'new way of thinking' that now pervades New Zealand – innovative, focused and ready to take on the world. But, in the mean time, let us worry about the Asian financial crisis, domestic political squabbles, the need for more management education, a fluctuating currency, and hordes of Australian tourists.

Part Three

Local governments' concerns

Chapter 12

Crafted culture: governmental sculpting of modern Singapore and effects on business environments[1]

Usha C. V. Haley and Linda Low

These [major state institutions] are institutions unique to Singapore, institutions created in response to the huge problems of the 1960s and the 1970s. At the national level, the act of creation has been largely accomplished and this is now internalized in the Singapore soul. But below the level of the state, at the level of civic life, the Singapore soul is still evolving. Yes, the state is strong. The family is also strong. But civic society, which is the stratum of social life between the state and the family is still weak. Without a strong civic society the Singapore soul will be incomplete. (Brigadier-General George Yeo, then Acting Minister for Information and the Arts, in a 1991 speech at the National University of Singapore)

Since the 1970s, policy-makers and academics have touted Singapore as a regional model for its economic growth; economic zones; public housing and town planning; technological upgrading; public transportation; traffic and environmental management; successful demographic transition; cleanliness; absence of corruption; efficiency, bureaucratic transparency and freedom of red tape; magnificent airport and national airlines; and strategic direction (Haley, 1998). Since its independence in 1965, the government has steadfastly and actively encouraged multinational corporations (MNCs) to invest within Singapore. Government-led development in Singapore has involved crafting a culture that will adapt to MNCs' needs and to fast-changing global environments in a restructured economy. Indeed, Singapore constitutes a crafted construct: Despite some innate geographical and sociocultural characteristics, the government has tried through policy measures, regulation, planning, propaganda and information to forge a Singaporean soul that will satisfy Singapore's *raison d'être*, currently economic growth and welfare. This chapter explores the crafting of the Singaporean culture and its ramifications for business and cultural change.

[1] The first author thanks the Managing Business in Asia program at The Australian National University for the facilities and support to conduct this research. Please address all queries regarding this chapter to the first author at alamo@compuserve.com. This chapter has been published previously by MCB University Press Limited: Haley, U. C. V. and Low, L. (1998). Crafted culture: governmental sculpting of modern Singapore and effects on business environments. *Journal of Organizational Change Management*, **11** (6), 530–553.

The Singaporean government has enjoyed an astounding record of success based on its ability to attract MNCs and corresponding capital to a country that aims to consti- tute an international hub. The World Economic Forum's *World Competitiveness Report* and the US-based Business Environment Risk Intelligence (BERI) report have repeat- edly cited Singapore as one of the best places in the world to do business (Haley, 1998; Haley, Low and Toh, 1996). In a rapidly churning and developing region, Singapore provides good infrastructure and a graft-free business environment, with transparent and consistent regulations. Consequently, in 1997, about 5000 MNCs operated in Singapore and about half maintained regional headquarters there (Economic Development Board, 1997). BERI has once again rated Singapore's labour force as the best in the world. Additionally, Singaporean citizens enjoy the highest average regional income (higher than the UK's at S$25 000). Today, Singapore's crafted culture appears hierarchical, disciplined, repressed and materially successful – a show house of technocratic, authoritarian, dependent capitalism. Tiny Singapore's viable combi- nation of high growth, top-down management, social development and authoritarian policy offers a cultural model that giant China is trying explicitly to emulate (Haley, 1998). Yet, questions remain about whether the government can continue to change Singaporean culture effectively for a knowledge economy; and whether the costs of such social re-engineering will outweigh its benefits.

The genealogy of Singaporean culture reveals that no one imagined such a project before it happened; economic success has buttressed the project and subsequently shaped it. The material focus for social re-engineering and cultural change entailed demobilizing Singapore's ethnic aspects; promoting the idea of national interest; pri- oritizing the economic (at state and individual levels); fashioning a suitable social order (through language, discipline and education); and restructuring the community (from ethnic based to a mixed population). As indicated earlier, the government has been astoundingly successful and economic prosperity has resulted along with many welfare benefits, particularly in housing. In return, Singaporean citizens have incurred many costs: in cultural, social and political terms they have lost many of their pre- independence patterns and have emerged depoliticized, docile and consumerist.

Patterns of economic activities provide the key to understanding Singaporean culture. Crafted Singapore corresponds ideally to dependent capitalism's manpower resources. The premier set of ideals celebrates technocratic efficiency and obedience and a sec- ondary set identifies what citizens must avoid. The government perpetually and pub- licly addresses the question: does action or social arrangement facilitate or hinder the pursuit of growth? It dismisses all other decision criteria as subjective, irrelevant and emotive. The public's recognition of the government's extraordinary performance record provides the foundation for the government's claim to moral authority and tan- gible proof of the ruling élite's effectiveness (Haley, Low and Toh, 1996; Khong, 1995).

In Singapore, governmental policies have produced great economic successes; yet, paradoxically, the government's ideology and action, and even its undoubted success, entail apparent failure. As Singapore ever more successfully achieves the ruling People's Action Party's (PAP's) goal of effective nationhood, it becomes more deeply enmeshed within the global capitalist system. As Singapore becomes more techno- cratic, its citizens appear to lose the creativity and entrepreneurship it needs to prosper in a rapidly changing, global context. Further crafting of the Singaporean culture in line with traditional ideologies seems to have resulted in a diminishing ability to produce creative, innovative and productive workers for the knowledge economy and the MNCs that dominate it.

In the first section of this chapter, we sketch the ideological bases for Singapore's crafted culture. Next, we explore Singapore's distinctive characteristics, as well as governmental policies that have moulded this culture. In the ensuing section, we highlight specific governmental policies that are designing Singapore for the restructured, globalizing and fast-changing knowledge economy; we also discuss the competing model offered by Taiwan in this regard. Finally, we concisely propose some implications for civic society and cultural change in Singapore.

▓ Ideological bases of Singapore's crafted culture

Many researchers have chronicled and analysed Singapore's growth and development (see Castells, 1988; Low, 1994; Low and Toh, 1992; Low et al., 1993; Rodan 1989 and 1993; Sandhu and Wheatley, 1989; Young, 1991) as well as the government's role in particular (see Cho, 1994; Chua, 1995; Haley, 1998; Haley, Low and Toh, 1996; Low, 1991 and 1998; Toh and Tan, 1998; Vinod and Wang, 1993). This section distils many of those studies' findings to concentrate on governmental attempts to define rationally an ideology, or sets of interrelated beliefs and values on which to re-engineer Singaporean society (Clammer, 1985).

The government dominates Singapore and all external links by providing infrastructure (such as utilities, telephone and post, port and airports, industrial estates, television, sanitation, all education, three-quarters of the housing and medical services); engaging in production (through government-linked corporations or GLCs, state airlines, state shipping lines, shipyards, banking and many joint ventures); holding an estimated 75 per cent of Singaporean land with mandates to acquire the rest if necessary; directing the capital markets (via the Central Provident Fund or CPF's compulsory savings, and the POSBank's, the Development Bank of Singapore's and the Monetary Authority of Singapore's holdings); offering various incentives to guide private investment (Haley, 1998; Haley and Haley, 1997); and shaping labour markets through extensive regulation of work conditions and labour. From its dominant position, the government actively constructs Singapore through identifying desirable and undesirable values; defining ethnicity and its relationships; stressing the use of language (English plus one's mother tongue); enforcing housing policy (through the Housing Development Board or HDB's extensive social, economic and political role); requiring compulsory national service in the Singapore Armed Forces (of all male citizens); emphasizing education (which it often portrays as social engineering); improving health; affecting the position of women (through family policies); increasing savings and pensions (through the CPF); forging workplace and labour laws (via regulation and co-opted unions); supporting community centres; constraining political and social campaigns; and press controls.

A technocratic ideology permeates Singaporean culture. Williamson (1993) identified technocrats as economists who use professional and technical skills in government to create and to manage economic systems that will further the general good. Technopols include the burgeoning breed of economic technocrats who assume positions of political responsibility (Feinberg, 1992). Thus, technopols constitute civil servants or technocrats with political appointments and attendant responsibilities. Because of the extent and magnitude of state-owned enterprises in Singapore, technopols wield great influence and control. However, by many measures, these economically trained professionals appear highly motivated, rather than rent seeking, in a relatively clean and efficient administrative system (Vennewald, 1994). Singapore's Economic Development Board or EDB, in particular, has achieved a global reputation for outstanding and creative technopols and technocrats (Schein, 1996).

The technocratic élite that manages the Singaporean government and political system regards political debate as dysfunctional and an obstacle to achieving rational solutions. Consequently, the government presents economic growth as a rational, non-ideological, pragmatic course of action requiring a disciplined population: Only economic growth can bolster Singapore's fragile and exposed position. Concomitantly, the pursuit of economic growth constitutes a technical matter. For this end, the government has designed social institutions to express and to channel growth through schools, urban planning, ethnic identities, language policies and industrial planning. The government has also taken extreme care to control incoming cultural messages through direct control of the media, to exclude unwanted material and to disseminate desired material. Additionally, the government has deployed state campaigns for clean streets, against cigarettes, for politeness, and even to smile (*Asia Inc.*, 1996b) to maintain the population's mobilization for growth.

Some scholars have highlighted the institutional environment of cultural control in Singapore. Tremewan (1994) analysed four institutions that dominate the culture and the interactions between them: public housing through the HDB housing estates that appear as working-class barracks; education that seems a tool for the citizens' submission; Parliament; and the law. Tremewan (1994) identified an alliance between Singapore's productive sector (dominated by foreign MNCs) and the government that controls the workers. Deyo (1981) also argued that the government uses social controls to pressure Singaporeans to conform to the alliance's needs. Low (1994) indicated how the government wields housing and education to socialize the masses and to engender belonging and stakeholders' interest. Later, Haley, Low and Toh (1996) explicitly identified the evolving stakeholder alliance between the government, MNCs, labour, local, private firms and knowledge-intensive firms that forms the bases for Singapore Incorporated. The government justifies its ubiquitousness and intervention at every level of life as necessary for political stability and economic growth (Clammer, 1985: 160; Haley, Low and Toh, 1996).

Other scholars have also noted that the PAP government exercises power not by suspending ideology and legitimizing coercion but through ideological efficacy (Chua, 1995). Survival and pragmatism underpin ideological efficacy: The first concept creates a state of uncertainty and operational room for the second concept that the government interprets as doing whatever necessary to survive. Other studies emphasize heritage and Chinese culture in Singapore's cultural development (like Chen, 1971; Clammer, 1985; Mahizhnan, 1993; Ong, Chan and Chew, 1995; Suryadinata, 1995; Willard, 1973). Yet, in Singapore, these factors while affecting some behaviors and choices, appear less tangible and less direct than the government's direct and deliberate policies and actions.

The PAP government enjoys a very successful record. The government has invited the MNCs and, via labour laws, welfare and educational programmes, made the Singaporean population available to the MNCs. Initially, the government promulgated a survival ideology that emphasized discipline and organization. Concern that citizens would imbibe values from abroad that the élites could not monitor or control led to officially-sponsored debates over Asian values (good) versus Western values (bad). The Asian values constitute the Chinese culture's alleged values although they bear a striking resemblance to Weber's Protestant work ethic; the Western values include many that most would have no hesitation in rejecting although they also include some such as individualism that could prove inimical to a disciplined, compliant and orga-nized labour force.

In early 1989, the Singaporean government approached the Institute of Policy Studies (IPS) to identify officially those national values that would help to unite all Singaporeans and to provide a blueprint for the development of a national ideology to which all Singaporeans could subscribe. The national ideology would sculpt a Singaporean identity by incorporating the relevant parts of various cultural heritages as well as the attitudes and values that have helped Singapore to survive as a nation. The ideology would also help safeguard against undesirable values permeating from more developed countries that could undermine Singapore's social fabric. A multidis-ciplinary team of scholars and practitioners guided by an eminent advisory panel began by identifying national values and national ideology for nation building. At the outset, the team quoted the then First Deputy Prime Minister and Minister for Defence, Goh Chok Tong, as noting in 1988 the clear shift in values from communitar-ianism to individualism especially among younger Singaporeans (Quah, 1990).

The IPS study generally endorsed the four core values already identified in President Wee Kim Wee's address at the Seventh Parliament on 9 January, 1989; the then Minister for Trade and Industry, Brigadier-General Lee Hsien Loong also amplified these values in a speech to the Alumni International in Singapore on 11 January, 1989. Synchronizing with these governmental leaders' views, the IPS study found four core values compatible with all the ethnic cultures and religions in Singapore:

1 Community over self.

2 Upholding the family as the basic building block of society.

3 Resolving major issues through consensus instead of contention.

4 Stressing racial and religious tolerance and harmony.

Brigadier-General Lee also exhorted that the resulting national ideology should contain certain properties. First, he emphasized that the ideology should distinguish Singapore from other countries. Second, he identified the national values as non-polit-ical and non-religious. Third, he cautioned for a conservative though not unquestion-ing approach to preserve Singaporean heritages. Fourth, he advocated universal and not particularistic national values to reflect Singapore's special circumstances. Finally, he advised the IPS team to focus on a few key values. Accordingly, the IPS team added only two other additional values:

5 Honest government.

6 Compassion for the less fortunate.

The final recommended list of national values for Singapore from the IPS study in descending order of importance comprises:

1 Enhancing racial and religious tolerance and harmony.

2 Preserving and maintaining the tradition of honest government.

3 Harmonizing individual interests with the interests of the community at large.

4 Upholding the family as a basic institution of society.

5 Showing compassion for the less fortunate in society.

6 Resolving major issues through consensus as far as possible.

The government identified the national ideology as shared values. In January 1991, during his first New Year's Day address as Prime Minister, Goh Chok Tong announced that the White Paper on shared values was to be mooted in Parliament, together with the Elected President Bill, to articulate the government's long-term plans for Singapore. The government revealed its official position on shared values in a White Paper released on 5 January 1991. A nationwide debate ensued. A feedback unit suggested rephrasing the third and fourth values. Parliament debated the issue from 14 to 15 January. On 15 January 1993, the government made two amendments to the third and fourth values before the House adopted five statements as the nation's Shared Values. The values now appear as:

1 Nation before community and society above self.

2 Family as the basic unit of society.

3 Community support and respect for the individual.

4 Consensus, not conflict.

5 Racial and religious harmony

The next section traces the influences that have shaped Singaporean culture including Singapore's distinctive characteristics, as well as governmental policies.

■ Influences on Singapore's crafted culture

Singapore's crafted culture appears to have resulted from both innate characteristics as well as deliberate policies. This section elaborates on the clay or Singapore's unique characteristics that have contributed to its culture; as well as specific actions by the craftsmen or governmental policy-makers that have moulded the culture.

The clay: Singapore's natural and acquired characteristics

Figure 12.1 portrays the web of unique characteristics that have provided the raw material for Singapore's crafted culture. As in most social systems, these characteristics also influence each other through mutually reinforcing mechanisms; and, over time, the Singaporean culture has influenced and shaped these characteristics through self-selection and interpretation. This subsection focuses on how the five characteristics, external dependency, migrant stock, environmental cross-fertilization, the PAP government and global competition have contributed to the Singaporean culture's clay or make-up.

1 *External dependency.* The country's and the economy's survival stem from Singapore's small, open economy. Singapore approximates the size of Chicago (641.4 sq km) with about the same population (3 million). This smallness provides

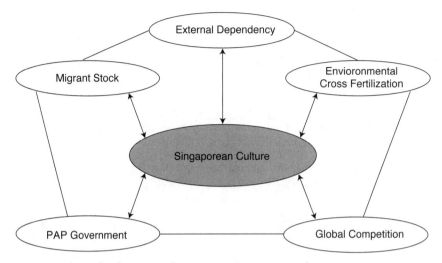

Figure 12.1 The web of unique influences on Singaporean culture

inherent advantages and disadvantages. For example, Singapore's physical size appears as a weakness in terms of natural resources resulting in dependencies and vulnerabilities. Conquest and political domination by larger entities also pose threats. However, Singapore's smallness serves as a strength by contributing to its resilience and nimbleness in policy responses and to the PAP government's ability to control the implementation of its policies.

2 *Migrant stock.* Singapore forms a multiethnic society criss-crossed with inter-racial marriages. The migrant stock of people consists of Chinese, Indians and native Malays. The Chinese form the great majority or about 78 per cent of the population comprising four dialect groups – the Hokkiens, Teochews, Cantonese and Hakkas. The Indians form about 7.1 per cent of the population, most originating from Madras. Singapore's official languages, Mandarin, Tamil, Bahasa Malay and English reflect its population's multiethnicity. Because of Singapore's small size and the business-minded migrants' proclivities, the multiethnic society displays urban demographical features and growing materialism. These demographic features satisfy the government's security and proprietary interests.

3 *Environmental cross-fertilization.* By virtue of history and trade, Singapore enjoys very close relations with the Association of South East Nations (ASEAN) in which it plays a central role. This pivotal relationship requires that Singapore live harmoniously with the rest of ASEAN, itself a pot-pourri of many cultures. One common denominator comprises the Overseas Chinese and Chinese heritage (Haley, Tan and Haley, 1998). However, the enormous concentration of MNCs also grants Singapore a cosmopolitan culture not found in the rest of ASEAN. This cosmopolitan culture, together with science-based, mostly Western, technology acquisition, adds another environmental blend to counteract cultural, historical and mythical bonds with ASEAN.

4 *PAP government.* The PAP has uninterruptedly governed Singapore since independence in 1965. The leadership in the PAP appears to follow a crisis mentality – a government knows best attitude of paternalism, efficiency, authoritarianism,

meritocracy and some élitism on the stage of Singapore's vulnerabilities (Chua, 1995). This extremely important predilection has characteristically imprinted the population that reacts in response to governmental policies involving both carrots and sticks. The PAP's crisis mentality stands in contrast to the mandate mentality where the government may introduce reforms if it campaigned on a program of reforms (Grindle and Thomas, 1991: 105).

5 *Global competition.* Sociopolitical revolutions and technological changes propel attendant changes in industrial structures and competition. Singapore, enmeshed in a global economy, greatly experiences the ramifications and changes of attendant rules in industrial organization, regionalization and competition. As a small player, and as one striving to maintain its relative competitive position, Singapore has to play by these rules and has done so by restructuring its economy from labour intensive to service oriented (Haley, 1998; Haley, Low and Toh, 1996).

Within the web portrayed in Figure 12.1, Singapore's external dependency, migrant stock and environmental cross-fertilization seem more as natural characteristics forged by geography and historical circumstances. The PAP government's make-up appears grafted for economic success and national survival (Low, 1998). Singapore has in part chosen the avenue of global competition and in part has had this influence thrust upon it: although governmental strategies have moved Singapore in the direction of global competition, it cannot revert to the fishing village, Singapura, that Sir Stamford Raffles proclaimed as a British conquest in 1819.

The craftsmen: policy trends and motivations

The PAP government's post-independence record in Singapore reveals a series of phases: 1965–67 when hostile neighbors endangered the newly independent state's viability; 1967–79 when accelerated outward-directed industrialization succeeded; 1979–81 when the government attempted to shift the economy into a higher value-added posture; 1985–86 when recession set in and invoked the government's aggressive response; and finally, 1987 to date when the pursuit of high-tech industry, regional service centre and shifting of low-wage production into the surrounding region has continued (Preston, 1994). Governmental polices in each phase contributed to crafting the Singaporean culture.

The crafted nature of Singaporean culture may originate with its heritage as a British colony since 1819. The migrant and multiethnic society resulted as much from British efforts to make the small fishing village its eyes and ears in the Far East as a consequence of upheavals in China (Huff, 1994). Chinese and Indian migrants swelled the labour pools that fuelled the staple port: Singaporean growth relied on three staples, tin, rubber and petroleum, from the 1880s to the end of the 1920s.

After the Second World War, though Singapore comprised an economic part of the Malayan region, its administrative incompatibility with the rest of the region grew as it developed into an international port and a Chinese metropolis. Consequently, in 1948, and again when Malaya attained its independence in 1957, British administrators omitted Singapore but not the other Straits Settlements of Penang and Malacca from the Malayan Union and then from the Federation of Malaya. As part of efforts to wind up British Malaya, the colony of Singapore became the internally self-governing state of Singapore in 1959 (Castells, 1988; Sandhu and Wheatley, 1989; Soon and

Tan,1993). But the PAP, created in 1954, and that made up the government in 1959, concurred that Singapore formed politically an accidental creation and not in any real sense a country, constituting a geographic and economic part of Malaya (Purcell, 1965). Thus, the PAP saw Singapore and Malaysia's union as a historical necessity, but clearly argued for the preservation of the free port that provided the foundation for Singapore's economy (PAP, 1959).

However, Malaysian political wrangling resulted in Singapore's expulsion from the union in August 1965 and incurred a confrontation with Indonesia that ended only in June 1966. The union's dissolution resulted as much from over a century of divergent development as from personality conflicts between Singaporean and Malaysian leaders. The PAP's single-minded drive for economic success probably resulted from the union's bitter failure, and the forced realization of an independent Singapore, isolated and excessively dependent on Malaysia (even for its water).

Without Malaysia and a promised common market, import-substituting industrialization had to turn export oriented as Singapore designed itself as a global, city state (Low et al, 1993). However, the MNCs that provided capital, markets, technology and know-how that all developing countries desire, also demanded a cosmopolitan culture with efficient and productive business environments. The MNCs' global logic, in contrast to nationalistic logic, imposed an economic culture entailing industrialization and modernization, and leaving the *kampong* or village life behind (Deyo, 1981).

The government's ideological stance rapidly evolved with successive crises since the separation including the Indonesian confrontation, the pound devaluation in 1967 (that cost Singapore some 15 per cent in official reserves) and the announcement in 1968 of the British withdrawal of its military bases east of the Suez (Low, 1998). The reluctant and newly independent nation had to grapple suddenly with an economic and security vacuum. An economic recession appeared imminent as the British bases had accounted for about 20 per cent of employment and gross domestic product (GDP). Almost overnight, too, the government had to construct a defence force from scratch. To prevent Singapore's collapse, the PAP took an immutable and almost messianic path with strong doses of paternalism and a government knows best mentality (Goh, 1972). Goh Keng Swee, the first Finance Minister and later first Defence Minister, mused that in the early years, the PAP leaders were like Moses leading the children of Israel through the wilderness in search of the Promised Land, 'having to exhort the faithful, encourage the faint-hearted and ensure the ungodly' (Goh, 1972). Singapore Incorporated progressed to Singapore International as an outward orientation appeared the only way for the manufacturing and services sectors' expansion given Singapore's very small domestic market (Haley, 1998; Haley, Low and Toh, 1996). Its global city-state strategy required an outward orientation in industrial practices and technology acquisition along with the preservation of cultural roots as reflected in educational policies. The crises, and the PAP's policy initiatives, provided for the economic success that Singapore enjoyed with other East Asian economies till the present day (Leipziger and Thomas, 1993; Petri, 1993; World Bank, 1993). The PAP, that has become synonymous with the government, has used every subsequent crisis, including the present regional financial crisis, as the inspiration to drive Singaporeans harder, resulting in ever-more interventionist and paternalistic policies.

Initially, after converting the British bases into the nucleus of the shipbuilding, repair and maritime industry, the government used policies and institutions to restructure the economy towards manufacturing and services. As the PAP government created a public enterprise system and used GLCs for the industrial transformation from an entrepôt economy to an industrialized base, Singapore Incorporated materialized (Haley, Low and Toh, 1996; Low, 1991). Singapore Incorporated implies that the government manages the country as a corporation with technocracy in the government sector spilling over to the GLCs, as exemplified in the EDB (Schein, 1996). Through successful and successive stages of industrial restructuring, technocrats and technopols have constructed an immense public enterprise system with an overall healthy and large public sector surplus that has become a point of contention since the economic recession in 1985 (Ministry of Trade and Industry, 1986). Conversely, any crowding out or contractionary effects have been counteracted by generous spending, especially for human-resource development and welfare programs as in Medifund and Edusave and those to help small, poor families (Low, 1994). The PAP government has therefore reaped economic rents on a national scale from infrastructural and investment efforts and ploughed them back to promote national welfare and quality of life.

Essentially, the technocratic subculture, alluded to in the earlier section, enables the PAP government's effective manipulation of public enterprises. Politicians and civil servants receive extremely high wages and bonuses for their efforts and consequently do not have to resort to corruption. Indeed Singaporean ministers and top officials are the highest paid in the world (Haley, Low and Toh, 1996). Additionally, the system of checks and controls institutionalized in the Corrupt Practices Investigation Bureau (CPIB) makes corruption extremely difficult or very painful through fines and imprisonment.

The buoyant economic conditions in the 1970s also helped the government to garner budget surpluses and economic rents for massive public investments. The resultant public sector surpluses and reserves became important as they give resources to Singapore and latitude to the PAP to pursue policies for a matured economy in a more competitive environment. In truth, they reflected the success and legitimate use of seemingly interfering and interventionist policies into sacrosanct areas such as marriage and childbearing. Lee Kuan Yew, Prime Minister from 1959 to 1990, in his National Day rally speech in 1986 authoritatively said:

> I am often accused of interfering in the private lives of citizens. Yet, if I did not, had I not done that, we wouldn't be here today. And I say without the slightest remorse that we wouldn't be here, would not have made the economy progress, if we had not intervened on very personal matters – who your neighbor is, how you live, the noise you make, how you spit (or where you spit) or what language you use. Never mind what the People think – that's another problem ... It was fundamental social and cultural changes that brought us here (*The Economist*, 1986; *Straits Times*, 1987).

Deputy Prime Minister, Brigadier-General Lee reiterated that a hardheaded approach forms the best way to help progress (Lee, 1992; *Straits Times*, 1992). While Prime Minister Goh Chok Tong has appeared more consultative and people-oriented, fundamental policy issues and ideological stances remain unquestionably non-negotiable. Skirmishes with local reporter, Catherine Lim, who wrote on the 'great affective divide' between the government and Singaporeans (Lim, 1994a) and later coined the phrase 'one government, two styles' (Lim, 1994b), as well as a court case against the *International Herald Tribune* that alleged the practice of dynastic politics in Singapore

(*Straits Times*, 1995), constitute only two instances of the government's determined defence of its two pillars, integrity and meritocracy. The government has often taken the Western media to court (and won) in defence of these virtues.

As the ASEAN economies and other Southeast and East Asian economies began industrialization and market reforms, the concept of Singapore Unlimited took shape. The concept drew on regionalization policy in 1993, heralded by the growth triangle in 1991 that capitalized on the trinity of capital, land and labour from Singapore, Johor in Malaysia and the Riau Islands in Indonesia (Haley, 1998). As the Asia Pacific region, stimulated by China's awakening and the Indochinese countries' reforms, assumed economic prominence, the government saw Singapore as a useful bridge between the East and the West (Haley, 1998). This bridging function would assure Singapore a continuing critical economic role between the Malay-dominated ASEAN, the Confucian-based East Asian economies and the Western countries. Domestically, the regionalization policy proved timely as local enterprises needed nurturing to expand outwards in response to limited supplies of factors of production and very limited market demand for products and services.

Paralleling the Singapore Unlimited effort, the government maintained the aspiration of Singapore becoming a developed nation by 2020 or 2030 depending on Dutch or American standards. The Strategic Economic Plan enshrined this governmental vision in its next lap (Ministry of Trade and Industry, 1991). As globalization and regionalization emerged, worldwide trends further transcended ethnic cultures but global tribalism still appears relevant: Haley, Tan and Haley (1998) indicated the Singaporean government's cultural efforts to forge tribal networks and to build ethnic ties over the Internet through the World Chinese Business Network. Over the decades, from raw nation building and economic survival to the more matured economy and mellow society in the 1990s, crises still recur in Singapore; yet, they constitute less of the do or die genre as Singapore has attained a certain level of GDP per capita, housing, health and other social amenities.

Lee Kuan Yew has reasoned that the exuberance of democracy leads to undisciplined and disorderly conditions that prove inimical to development (see also Barro, 1994). The ultimate test of a political system concerns if it helps society to establish the conditions for improving standards of living. Thus, he stated: '[that he] does not believe that democracy necessarily leads to development ... believes what a country needs to develop is discipline more than democracy' (Lee, 1992a).

When success begets further success, the government is emboldened and legitimized to charge more rapidly and deeply into certain areas. The ease that the government enjoys in terms of governability and responsiveness to policies and campaigns may have accounted for the growth and prosperity paid back to a supportive and docile electorate. But the price includes an addiction to a government-led society with pockets of dissent, especially among the younger, better-educated and English-educated segments, that may create more instability than is warranted.

Generally, the economic culture for sustainable and rapid success has generated a very practical and materialistic mentality among Singaporeans (Haley, Low and Toh, 1996). GDP distributed as income and wealth has transformed into the best bottom line or measure of success and attainment. The government encourages the acquisition of properties and assets to ensure that stakeholders will defend Singapore's economic and political survival. The formula appears flawless with a double coincidence of wants as people want homes, cars and other material goods as well. But, the materialistic orientation may have gone too far in directing people towards economic and social objectives. Lee Kuan Yew realized that Hong Kong people seem leaner and keener than Singaporeans: he resolved to reverse welfare policies that the PAP had inherited or copied from the British Labour Party's policies, scaling back subsidies except where they made people more productive through better education, better health and better housing (Lee, 1992b). Singaporean workers, according to Lee, do not appear psychologically geared to be as independent minded and resilient as Hong Kong workers; the Singaporean workers appear relatively government-dependent compared to their Hong Kong counterparts who accept responsibility for lives and livelihoods. As we note in the next section, these cultural traits among Singaporean workers may adversely affect Singapore's place in the knowledge economy.

▓ Singapore in the knowledge economy

In his 1998 National Day message, Prime Minister Goh Chok Tong said that Singapore needs to do more to foster an environment where creativity and enterprise can flourish. The 'new buzzword is knowledge economy', he said (*Business Times*, 1998). The Singaporean government is currently crafting Singaporean culture to deal with the fast-changing knowledge economy. A modern telecommunications network and a computer-literate workforce has since the 1970s been considered a wellspring of economic development. 'It was an act of faith that technology would swamp us if we didn't get ahead of it,' said Minister for Information and the Arts, Brigadier-General George Yeo (*Asia Inc.*, 1996a). This national obsession inspired a 1990 television documentary by the British Broadcasting Corporation that dubbed Singapore the 'intelligent island' – a tag that local boosters have used as a promotional slogan ever since. Singaporeans comprise the world's most computer-literate people; nearly one in every two households owns a personal computer (PC). This section explores the government's consistent and highly rational investments and policies, as well as their relative successes and failures in modifying Singaporean culture for a restructured, global economy. First, we outline the government's key strategic thrusts for the knowledge economy; next, we compare a competitive model offered by Taiwan.

The government, which has been spending some $400 million a year on information technology, recently rolled out the centrepiece for what it calls its broadband multimedia initiative: a national communications network, among the most advanced in the world. Called Singapore ONE, the network by the end of 1998 will reach almost all of Singapore's 900 000 households, as well as schools and government offices. The fibre-optic network backbone, linked to homes through telephone lines and cable television connections, provides extremely speedy data delivery: for example, through advanced computer modems, users can download Moby Dick's text from the Internet in three seconds; conventional hardware can fetch just one page per second. In addition to high-speed Internet access, Singapore ONE offers films, interactive games, tutorials in Mandarin, workout videos, on-line shopping, governmental services, even travel insurance. In a few months, users can log in to check traffic conditions on local highways. The Singapore ONE network extends what few other cities can – a broadband system with an entire population as potential laboratory rats for application. With the network as test-bed, governmental officials reason that MNCs will migrate to the city-state, bolstering a growing, domestic, technology industry and preventing talented workers from migrating to Silicon Valley. Towards that end, Singapore already makes computer literacy a priority in the schools. By 2002, every school will have one PC for every two students; roughly one-third of the curriculum will include a computer-based component. As for the technology-challenged adult population, well, 'they'll have to learn to get used to it,' said Brigadier-General Yeo; in some cases, such as automated toll roads, they have no other options. The government is responding to those reluctant to switch to services such as online banking with financial incentives or penalties: for example, policymakers are considering a surcharge on check-writing over electronic debits (*Asia Inc.*, 1996b).

Singapore also hopes to become a hub for electronic transactions. US-based research group IDC predicts electronic-commerce activity in Singapore will jump from a minuscule $5 million in 1998 to more than $800 million by 2001. Yet, few governments appear as keen as Singapore to regulate Internet use. For example, the government can prosecute senders of electronic messages for defamation; the Singapore Broadcasting Authority can deny public access to any World Wide Web (WWW) site it deems morally offensive or a threat to public order; and local residents need a licence to create religious and political home pages on the WWW. Singapore's Minister of Information and the Arts, Brigadier-General Yeo, recently said, 'Our goal is to position ourselves as a hub city. So we have to be at the center of the exchange of information. Everything we do has to promote that. But when we promote the Internet it does not mean that we subscribe to the idea that it has to be anarchic' (*Asia Inc.*, 1996a).

Key strategic thrusts

In a recent policy speech, Deputy Prime Minister Brigadier-General Lee clarified the government's strategic stance in the knowledge economy. The government has been pursuing three strategic thrusts to develop Singapore as a vibrant and robust global hub of knowledge-driven industries: Building capabilities through science, technology and innovation; managing manpower resources; and, nurturing local enterprises (Lee, 1998).

1 *Building capabilities through science, technology and innovation*: The government has sketched out a long-term vision for Research and Development (R&D) in the National Science and Technology Plan (NSTP 2000). It has instituted incentives such as the Research Incentive Scheme for Companies (RISC), the Research and Development Assistance Scheme (RDAS) and the Innovation Development Scheme (IDS), to help companies to undertake R&D and to develop capabilities in product and process innovation. Commercializable products and services, and not the R&D activities *per se*, provide the focus. 'However, bricks and mortar and financial incentives are only one part of the solution. We also need to create an environment that nurtures creativity, where rules and regulations are not beyond what is necessary. An environment that is conducive to calculated risk taking, and is tolerant of "intelligent" failure', Brigadier-General Lee (1998) indicated. Over time, Lee continued, Singapore hopes to develop a thriving community where flows of ideas and people produce innovative products and services that give the economy a competitive edge.

2 *Managing manpower resources*: As Singapore progresses towards a knowledge-based

economy, the nature of manufacturing and manufacturing services will change. Companies will need even more knowledge and skilled workers, especially those from the science and engineering disciplines. Singaporean universities and polytechnics still do not produce enough engineering graduates to meet industry demands, even though they have expanded their intakes for science and engineering courses enormously over the years. Consequently, the government is allowing more foreign talent into Singapore to augment local talent. Simultaneously, it is tightening up the widespread use of unskilled foreign labour. For example, the government is raising the levy for unskilled construction workers, while reducing the levy for skilled workers who pass trade tests or possess relevant qualifications. In this fashion, the government can facilitate continued restructuring of the economy by encouraging companies to use more skilled workers without burdening them with higher costs.

3 *Nurturing local enterprises*: The EDB has been helping local companies to build core competencies and niche capabilities through the Promising Local Enterprise (PLE) programme. The statutory boards survey networking opportunities to help smaller local enterprises keep in touch with the latest technological and market developments. Simultaneously, the government is promoting the venture capital industry and developing programmes to encourage technopreneurs to establish themselves in Singapore. In the 1998 Budget, the Minister for Finance extended the tax incentives enjoyed by venture capital funds, to encourage them to take a longer-term perspective of their investments. The government is also exploring ways to assist start-ups.

To position Singapore as a regional hub for the global knowledge economy, the government has embarked on an extremely ambitious program of retraining and re-educating the Singaporean work force (Haley, 1998; Haley, Low and Toh, 1996). Reflecting the government's key priorities, despite the current economic crisis, governmental spending on education rose by a hefty 30 per cent to $5.7 billion in 1998. This increase will bring educational expenditures to 3.6 per cent of GDP, up from 3 per cent, and nearer the medium-term target of 4 per cent. The government also supports product and process innovations through policies such as the National Innovation Framework for Action (NIFA) launched during the National Innovation Forum in 1998. Singapore has generally lagged behind other industrialized and industrializing countries on indicators such as patents. For example, between 1990 and 1994, 148 patents were filed in Singapore compared to 2150 in Australia, 9812 in Canada, 142 612 in France, 36 223 in Germany, 279 in Hong Kong, 1603 in Israel, 107 152 in Japan, 2889 in South Korea, 6110 in Switzerland, 5268 in Taiwan, 12 539 in the UK, and 260 130 in the USA (Loh, 1998). The NIFA announced the government's intention to place innovation as a priority in Singapore's economic development in the twenty-first century.

The NIFA constitutes a collaboration among the EDB, National Science and Technology Board, and Productivity and Standards Board. The Construction Industry Development Board, National Computer Board, Singapore Tourism Board, Trade Development Board and the manufacturing industry also support the framework. The goals for attainment by the end of 2008 include (Economic Development Board, 1998):

• To have new and innovative products and services contribute at least 15 per cent to the revenue of manufacturing companies.

- To reach the Swiss standard (1993) of 237 patents secured per 100 000 inhabitants.

- To have at least fifty successful new seed venture capital-type start-ups per year.

The NIFA programmes, outlined by EDB's Managing Director Ho Meng Kit, aim to:

- *Enhance innovation education*: Include innovation training in the education system to make the future workforce well versed in innovation's ways and methods.

- *Strengthen innovation training*: Institute proper training and practice in innovation for the existing workforce, with 10 per cent of worker training to include creativity building and innovation.

- *Strengthen market/technology linkages*: Establish Singapore Centre in Silicon Valley to enable Singaporean companies to gain access to the latest market and technology information. Encourage companies to use industry-specific consultants to assess market opportunities and to explore innovative applications of technology. Use the Idea Bank programme to match innovative ideas with interested parties to help commercialize the ideas or inventions. Build flagship projects, similar to Singapore ONE, to encourage the application of new technologies.

- *Improve the innovation environment*: Establish a mentorship programme, where experienced consultants and entrepreneurs can give valuable advice and assistance to aspiring innovators and new start-ups. Enhance linkages between local research institutes and overseas centres, like TNO (a Dutch government-funded research institute) and the Illinois Institute of Technology.

- *Build awareness*: Carry out regular awareness drives to give exposure and mind-share to innovative practices. Introduce the certification of innovative companies by establishing a benchmarking standard similar to ISO 9000.

- *Provide government support*: Review government rules and practices to foster greater entrepreneurship and risk taking. Examples include those governing investment, bankruptcy protection and financial loans. Extend the Skills Development Fund and the EDB's manpower training grant scheme to support innovation training for all levels of workers.

- *Strengthen infrastructure support*: Set up industry-specific technology application competence centers, much like the Industrial Design and Product Development Centre, and the Precision Engineering and Application Centre. Build pilot experimentation plants for food and specialty chemicals to help research institutes, universities and small companies test new technologies and processes.

The EDB's Chairman Philip Yeo stressed: 'NIFA's programs should enable Singapore to harness innovation for sharper competitiveness and greater economic growth. Our government is fully committed to innovation as a key competitive tool for Singapore to move aggressively up the high value-added growth ladder' (Economic Development Board, 1998).

Competing models

Even Asia's model economy may need new models these days. Disquieting signs indicate that despite enormous governmental expenditure, and careful governmental planning, the Singaporean workforce lacks creativity and entrepreneurship abilities to exploit global environments. For example, the Political and Economic Risk Consultancy's (PERC's) 1998 annual survey ranked Singapore last among thirteen Asian economies on labour quality, cost and availability (Tan, 1998). Evaluations on labour from over 400 executives in the region ranged from top-ranked India, through the Philippines, China, Vietnam, Thailand, Malaysia, Australia, Indonesia, Taiwan, South Korea, Japan, Hong Kong, and bottom-ranked Singapore. Singapore placed ninth, tenth and twelfth respectively on unskilled labour's quality, cost and availability; and sixth, eleventh and ninth on that for skilled labour. The executives generally perceived Singaporean skilled workers as lacking imagination and adaptability when compared with skilled workers from the other countries (Tan, 1998).

Settled mostly by ethnic-Chinese immigrants, Singapore attracted small entrepreneurs carving out the trading niches the British colonial authorities allowed them to fill (Haley and Haley, 1998; Haley, Tan and Haley, 1998). Since Lee Kuan Yew consolidated power in the late 1950s, the government has taken huge risks, like the massive early-1960s plan to fill in swamps on the island's Western side and to build a new industrial zone. That high-risk plan, initially ridiculed as a pie-in-the-sky scheme, probably constituted Singapore's most successful industrial policy (Haley, 1998). But, as the government assumed the lead in economic development, Singaporean entrepreneurs became scarcer. The public sector skims off talent with its high salaries, prestige and security. 'The environment discourages entrepreneurialism,' said Friedrich Wu, vice-president at the Development Bank of Singapore. 'The careers offered by the government and multinationals are just too good to miss' (Dolven, 1998).

Yet, as their strategic plans and investments reveal, the Singaporean government is working hard to identify and to harness components for creativity. In late August 1998, a group from Taiwan's government came to Singapore to offer Singaporeans suggestions on promoting business innovation. Then in October, Singaporean government officials lead a group of small businesses to Taiwan to visit and to learn from successful companies on the high-tech island (Dolven, 1998). Singapore does have some world-class entrepreneurs such as Sim Wong Hoo of leading sound-card maker Creative Technology. But Taiwan, despite serious shortcomings including inefficient infrastructure and rampant corruption, has proven a much more effective incubator for entrepreneurs whose bright new ideas form essential ingredients for economic growth. Despite the regional crisis, Taiwan's home-grown companies continue to push technical boundaries and to fight for more dominance in the high-tech markets they have already captured. Taiwan constitutes a leading supplier of computer monitors, motherboards, scanners, desktop and portable computers. 'They've been very successful in coming out with their own companies and their own products,' said Chow Tat Kong, a director at Singapore's EDB, 'and we need to look at how we can learn from them' (Dolven, 1998).

The two island economies have followed very different formulas. Taiwan's democratic government has relinquished an industrial policy that tries to pick winners. Indeed, a convoluted bargaining process between elected officials and interest groups hampers governmental efforts even to set initiatives. Instead, Taiwanese firms compete for funding in the island's vibrant capital markets. Taiwan boasts a dynamic local manufacturing sector, full of globally competitive companies such as Acer, Asustek and Taiwan Semiconductor Manufacturing. 'Instead of multinationals coming to Taiwan, I think we can look at Taiwan companies becoming multinationals,' said Steve Hsieh, vice-chairman of Taiwan's National Science Council (Dolven, 1998). There lies the key difference between Taiwan and Singapore.

Singapore steers its own best and brightest into government, offering not only high salaries, but also hundreds of lucrative scholarships that require students to serve obligatory terms in the public sector. These policies create highly skilled technocrats and technopols that maintain the port's efficiency, the traffic's free flow, and the MNCs' continued investments (Toh and Tan, 1998). But, very few Singaporean companies take risks through succeeding or failing on their own merits. Without them, Singapore will have to continue to rely on MNCs – whose profits flow to foreign head offices.

Several factors hamper would-be Singaporean entrepreneurs. First, the MNCs and large GLCs that dominate the economy have the clout and connections to squeeze out potential competitors. Prospective start-ups have difficulties accessing the capital they need to grow: risk-averse banks and investors have long preferred safe property to uncertain enterprising ideas. Second, Taiwan's exuberant and emerging democracy encourages free expression of ideas, however incongruous, an environment under which entrepreneurship thrives. By contrast, Singaporeans grow up in a culture that encourages them to follow the government's lead, not to strike out on their own.

Between 1994 and 1997, Taiwanese firms raised $27.6 billion through rights issues and initial public offerings, top in Asia outside Japan. Additionally, Taiwan's grey market, (an unregulated exchange run by local brokerages) trades around 400 stocks; and, in 1997, its growing venture-capital industry pumped $563 million into local start-ups. Taiwanese firms also get some governmental help: Publicly funded bodies like the Industrial Technology Research Institute (ITRI) engage in large amounts of R&D in commercial areas such as information technology. ITRI has spun off numerous firms, including TSMC, the republic's largest chip-maker. 'They've been very good at identifying what Taiwan is good for,' said Pindar Wong, Managing Director of Hong Kong-based Internet service provider Vertex. 'But the actual deployment is free-market, survival of the fittest, which is perfect for hi-tech where you've got to be on your toes.' In contrast, the Singaporean government sits on huge fiscal reserves, primarily from its mandatory public savings plan, the CPF. The fiscal reserves provide the government with the resources to develop infrastructure and to take care of the public's needs – and the economic record shows that the government has done a consistently good job. 'Singapore has really created true institutional capital and put it to use for the public good,' said Gregg Gibb, senior consultant at McKinsey and Co. However, as the world gets more and more complex, Gibb asked, can the Singapore government continue consistently to make the right decisions? Overall, he answered, the odds favour Taiwan (Dolven, 1998).

Of course, Singapore and Taiwan differ greatly on more than entrepreneurial culture. Taiwan has a broadly diversified electronics industry that dwarfs Singapore's, while Singapore has built itself into a financial and service hub for Southeast Asia. Unlike Taiwan's economy that relies heavily on small and medium-sized local firms, Singapore's appears highly centralized. According to a 1997 report from the US embassy, the government and GLCs create about 60 per cent of Singapore's GDP. Meanwhile, over the past twenty years, MNCs have provided about 80 per cent of the manufacturing investment in Singapore (Haley, Low and Toh, 1996). Most importantly for Singaporean leaders, Taiwan expected to grow at around 5 per cent in 1998, while Singapore looked for just 0.5 per cent to 1.5 per cent expansion.

For business people in Singapore, the government sets the tone. For example, Singaporean government leaders have advocated that GLCs must lead Singapore Inc. overseas (Haley, 1998; Haley and Haley, 1997). As a result, most of Singapore's outward foreign direct investment goes into real estate projects and industrial parks rather than small, manufacturing footholds as in Taiwan. Indeed, the GLCs while providing solutions may also create major problems. The government owns a controlling stake in each GLC, and both civil servants and professional managers run them. Many GLCs operate in capital-intensive industries that nobody else in Singapore had the money to tackle such as telecommunications, ship repair and airlines (Haley, Low and Toh, 1996). Recently, the GLCs have tried to restructure themselves into sprawling commercial ventures spanning everything from banking to property to cappuccino chains. The GLCs' activities leave little room for small businesses. 'The Singapore government has been very effective in eradicating entrepreneurs,' said Jeffrey Goh, who in 1998 started a company called Lightspeed Technologies to provide inexpensive intracompany e-mail services for small firms. 'The government is the single biggest economic actor here, and by virtue of being there it squeezes out the opportunities. All the things that make Singapore so successful today,' particularly its ability to marshal talent and resources into government, Goh said, 'will make it unsuccessful in the 21st century' (Dolven, 1998). The next section proposes some implications of governmental domination for civic society and cultural change in Singapore.

■ Implications

In the middle of Asia's financial crisis, 200 Singaporeans, including governmental leaders, met in a luxury hotel to ponder its culture and civic society (Koh, 1998). The future-oriented Singapore government which ensures that economic imperatives drive every state policy from education and family planning, to marriage patterns and the arts must continue to manage every area of national life to remain effective. However, governmental leaders know that they cannot manage a complex, increasingly cosmopolitan society, with globalization's contradictions and social costs, through the authoritarianism that worked in a simpler past. Singapore's Minister for Information and the Arts, Brigadier-General Yeo, concluded his keynote speech by hoping that the conference on civic society in Singapore would define more precisely the Singaporean ideal and find new and better ways to bind state and society together.

Community Development Councils form among the most recent efforts to bind state and society even more closely; Brigadier-General Yeo aptly described these councils as government-sponsored civic organizations that elicit the government's support, either tacitly or explicitly, by co-operating with it. He envisaged that the trend would continue as many governmental committees have become civic committees (among them, environmental, anti-smoking, National Courtesy and Speak Mandarin campaign committees) with a non-political, harmonious emphasis on community development. Not coincidentally, sponsorship of civic bodies steadily extends the government's reach, fuses the society, state, party, government and nation, and sustains the political status quo via a mutually beneficial network of associations. For example, the government-sponsored People's Association for HDB public-housing estates recently extended its extensive patronage to include autonomous, spontaneously-formed residents' associations in private housing estates through neighbourhood committees; the committees would provide one more bridge between Singaporeans and the government. The private associations were ably promoting neighborliness, harmony and cohesiveness. Yet, the members argued that governmental protection would grant them a louder voice and ease pest control and upgrading (*Straits Times*, 1998).

Koh (1998) indicated that in Singapore, autonomous groups (such as the Nature Society and the Society Against Family Violence) as well as autonomous individuals, find that their views and ideas disappear into a black hole or that the government takes them without acknowledgement. Consequently, the government gains in stature and authority as the sole provider of good ideas and plans while autonomous groups gain neither credibility nor influence. Brigadier-General Yeo has argued that Asian exceptionalism justifies this governmental appropriation and control: 'Without top-down direction, many civic organizations are plagued by internal disputes' because 'the separation of powers is not a tradition in Asian society. Without central leadership, many Asian societies do not hold together naturally. Singapore society is half-Asian and half-Western. We have to strike our own balance' (quoted in Koh, 1998).

The poet Dennis Enright concluded about Singapore almost thirty years ago:

> The free exchange of ideas? The freedom of the press? People thinking for themselves? ...
>
> These amenities are expensive ...
>
> Who really appreciates these luxury goods, but the spoilt liberal?
>
> We shall settle for peace and prosperity, and death only in bed or on the roads. Happy the country that needs no heroes. Happy the times that are tidy ...
>
> ... the children are better for it, The cow milk's cream an inch thick'
>
> (quoted in Koh, 1998)

Yet, despite governmental efforts at retraining and fostering creativity, Singapore's crafted culture may not breed the creative entrepreneurial labour force that Singapore needs for the knowledge economy, MNCs' continued involvement and unceasing prosperity. Globalization, and increasing needs for creativity, entrepreneurship and individuality, may force Singapore to re-evaluate its carefully crafted cultural balance of governmental-led development and consensus for continued economic success.

References

Asia Inc. (1996a). Wired but not wild. July.
Asia Inc. (1996b). Briefing: News in brief. December.
Barro, R. J. (1994). Democracy and growth. National Bureau of Economic Research, Working Paper No. 4909, October.
Business Times (1998). Be efficient and smart to retain our edge. 24 August.
Castells, M. (1988). The developmental city state in an open economy: the Singapore experience. University of California, Berkeley Roundtable on the International Economy.

Chen, P. S. J. (1971). *Development Complexity: East and Southeast Asia*. University Education Press.

Cho, S. (1994). Government and market in economic development. *Asian Development Review*, **12** (2),144–65.

Chua B. H. (1995). *Communitarian Ideology and Democracy in Singapore*. Routledge.

Clammer, J. (1985) *Singapore, Ideology. Society, Culture*. Chopmen Enterprises.

Deyo, F. (ed.) (1981). *Dependent Development and Industrial Order: An Asian Case Study*. Praeger.

Dolven, B. (1998). Taiwan's trump. *Far Eastern Economic Review*, 6 August.

Economic Development Board (1997). *EDB Yearbook 1996/97*. EDB.

Economic Development Board (1998) Press release, February.

The Economist (1986). 22 November.

Feinberg, R. (1992). Latin America: back on the screen. *International Economic Insights*, **3** (4), July–August, 52–6.

Goh K. S. (1972). *The Economics of Modernization and Other Essays*. Asia Pacific Press.

Grindle, M. S. and Thomas, J. W. (1991). *Public Choices and Policy Change*. Johns Hopkins University Press.

Haley, G. T. and Haley, U. C. V. (1998). Boxing with shadows: competing effectively with Overseas Chinese and Overseas Indian networks in the Asian arena. *Journal of Organizational Change Management*, special issue on Strategic management in the Asia Pacific: strategies for foreign investors, **11** (4), 301–20.

Haley, G. T., Tan , C. T. and Haley, U. C. V. (1998). *The New Asian Emperors: The Overseas Chinese their Strategies and Competitive Advantages*. Butterworth-Heinemann.

Haley, U. C. V. (1998). Virtual Singapores: shaping international competitive environments through business-government partnerships. *Journal of Organizational Change Management*, special issue on Strategic management in the Asia Pacific: strategies for foreign investors, **11** (4), 338–56.

Haley, U. C. V. and Haley, G. T. (1997). When the tourists flew in: strategic implications of foreign direct investment in Vietnam's tourism industry. *Management Decision*, special issue on Strategic management in the Asia Pacific: perspectives from the region, **35** (8), 595–604.

Haley, U. C. V., Low, L. and Toh, M. H. (1996). Singapore Incorporated: reinterpreting Singapore's business environments through a corporate metaphor. *Management Decision*, special issue on Strategic management in the Asia Pacific, **34** (9), 17–28.

Huff, W. G. (1994). *The Economic Growth of Singapore: Trade and Development in the Twentieth Century*. Cambridge University Press.

Khong, C. O. (1995). Singapore. Political legitimacy through managing conformity. In *Political Legitimacy in Southeast Asia. The Quest for Moral Authority* (M. Alagappa, ed.) pp.108–35, Stanford University Press.

Koh, T. A. (1998). Civil or civic society? The S'pore ideal. *Business Times*, 30 May.

Lee, H. L. (1992). Core principles of government. Speech delivered during the parliamentary debate on the Presidential Address, 15 January, Ministry of Information and the Arts.

Lee, H. L (1998). Speech at the official opening of Hitachi-Nippon Steel Semiconductors DRAM Wafer Fabrication Plant, 14 April.

Lee, K. Y. (1992a). Speech at the Philippine Business Conference, 18 November, Manila.

Lee, K. Y. (1992b). A tale of two cities – twenty years on. Li Ka Shing Lecture at the University of Hong Kong, 14 December.

Leipziger, D. M, and Thomas, V. (1993). *An Overview of Country Experience*. D. M.

Leipziger (series ed.), *The Lessons of East Asia*. World Bank.

Lim, C. (1994a). Great affective divide. *Straits Times*, 22 September.

Lim, C. (1994b). One government, two styles. *Sunday Times*, 20 November.

Loh, L. (1998) Technology policy and national competitiveness. In *Competitiveness of the Singapore Economy. A Strategic Perspective* (M. H. Toh and K. Y. Tan, eds) pp. 40–80, Singapore University Press and World Scientific.

Low, L. (1991). *The Political Economy of Privatization in Singapore: Analysis. Interpretation and Issues*. McGraw-Hill.

Low, L. (1993), The public sector in contemporary Singapore: In retreat? In *Singapore Changes Guard: Social, Political and Economic Directions in the 1990s* (G. Rodan, ed.) pp. 168–83, St Martin's Press, Longman Cheshire.

Low, L. (1994). A market system with Singapore characteristics. Master in Public Policy Working Paper Series, Center for Advanced Studies, National University of Singapore, November.

Low, L. (1998). *Political Economy of a City State: Government-made Singapore*. Oxford University Press.

Low, L. and Toh, M. H. (eds.) (1992). *Public Policies in Singapore: Changes in 1980s and Future Signposts*. Times Academic Press.

Low, L., Toh, M. H., Soon, T. W. and Tan, K. Y. with special contribution from Hughes, H. (1993). *Challenge and Response: Thirty Years of the Economic Development Board*. Times Academic Press.

Mahizhnan, A. (ed.) (1993). *Heritage and Contemporary Values*. Times Academic Press.

Ministry of Trade and Industry (1986). *The Singapore Economy: New Directions*. Report of the Economic Committee, February. Singapore National Printers.

Ministry of Trade and Industry (1991). *The Strategic Economic Plan: Towards a Developed Nation*. Singapore National Printers.

Ong, J. H., Chan, K. B. and Chew, S. B. (eds.) (1995). *Crossing Borders: Transmigration in Asia Pacific*. Simon Schuster.

PAP (1959). *The Tasks Ahead: PAP's Five Year Plan*.

Petri, P. A. (1993). *Common Foundations of East Asian Societies*. D. M. Leipziger (series ed.), *The Lessons of East Asia*. World Bank.

Preston, P. W. (1994). *Discourses of Development. State, Market and Polity in the Analysis of Complex Change*. Avebury.

Purcell, V. (1965). *The Chinese in Southeast Asia*, 2nd edn. Oxford University Press.

Quah, J. S. T. (ed.) (1990). *In Search of Singapore's National Values*. Times Academic Press.

Rodan, G. (1989). *The Political Economy of Singapore's Industrialization: National, State and International Capital*. Macmillan.

Rodan, G. (ed.) (1993). *Singapore Changes Guard: Social, Political and Economic Directions in the 1990s*. St Martin's Press, Longman Cheshire.

Sandhu, K. S. and Wheatley, P. (eds) (1989). *Management of Success: The Moulding of Modern Singapore*. Institute of Southeast Asian Studies.

Schein, E. H. (1996). *Strategic Pragmatism: The Culture of Singapore's Economic Development Board*. MIT Press.

Soon, T. W. and Tan, C. S. (1993). *Singapore: Public Policy and Economic Development*. D. M. Leipziger (series ed.), *The Lessons of East Asia*.World Bank.

Straits Times (1987). 20 April.

Straits Times (1992). 16 January.

Straits Times (1995). 14 June.

Straits Times (1998). 2 May.

Suryadinata, L. (1995). *Southeast Asian Chinese: The Socio-cultural Dimension*. Times Academic Press.

Tan, A. (1998). Singapore last in PERC labor survey but this may attract investors. *Business Times*, 8 September.

Toh, M. H. and Tan, K. Y. (Eds) (1998). *Competitiveness of the Singapore Economy. A Strategic Perspective*. Singapore University Press and World Scientific

Tremewan, C. (1994). *The Political Economy of Social Control in Singapore*. St Martin's Press.

Vennewald, W. (1994). Technocrats in the state enterprise system of Singapore. Asia Research Center, Murdoch University, Western Australia, Working Paper No 32, November.

Vinod, T. and Wang, Y. (1993). *Government Policy and Productivity Growth: Is East Asia an Exception?* D. M. Leipziger (series ed.), *The Lessons of East Asia*.World Bank.

Willard, H. A, (1973). Culture, yellow culture, counterculture and polyculture in culture-poor Singapore. American Universities Field Staff, Reports Service, Southeast Asian Series, **21** (2).

Williamson, J. (1993). In search of a manual for technopols. In *The Political Economy of Policy Reform* (J. Williamson, ed.) pp 1–34, Institute for International Economics, January.

World Bank (1993). *The East Asian Miracle*. Oxford University Press.

Young, A. (1991). A tale of two cities: Factor accumulation and technical change in Hong Kong and Singapore. Sloan School of Management, Massachusetts Institute of Technology, February, mimeo.

Chapter 12.1

International education and crafted culture in Singapore

■ Usha C. V. Haley ■

French business school, the European Institute of Business Administration (INSEAD), constituted the first international business school to set up a campus in Singapore. INSEAD started building its first overseas campus in Singapore by the end of 1998. The S$60 million campus in the Science Hub in Buona Vista will accept its first students in January 2000. The Economic Development Board (EDB) of Singapore is marketing INSEAD's campus in Singapore as 'another Singapore Inc Effort' (Economic Development Board, 1998; see also Chapters 9 and 13). This project forms part of the EDB's strategic intent to position Singapore as a global and intellectual hub in the knowledge economy. The project also attempts to craft Singaporean culture by responding to the continued criticism (expounded in Chapter 12) that Singaporean workers lack creativity, imagination and adaptability. Additionally, the project provides a source for continued inputs of imported talent and ideas into Singapore Inc.

Singapore has three national universities, the National University of Singapore, the Nanyang Technological University and the Singapore Management University. Yet, to complement the foreign multinational corporations around whose needs the Singaporean government has crafted a culture, the EDB is wooing ten world-class universities to set up branch campuses in Singapore. These foreign universities will provide postgraduate education and research in a spectrum of disciplines – from business and management to engineering, medicine and applied sciences. Besides INSEAD, the American medical school, the Johns Hopkins University, has also agreed to construct a campus in Singapore. The EDB will seek out the other eight in the next ten years (Davies, 1998).

Liew Heng San, the EDB's Managing Director, highlighted that these 'brand-name institutions' (Economic Development Board, 1998) will continue the governmental crafting of Singaporean culture by:

1 *Enhancing educational standards*: Besides adding diversity and widening the choice for students ... these world-class institutions will uplift tertiary educational standards. In

addition, they can play a significant role in manpower development. Professionals can acquire world-class capabilities, stay at the cutting edge and remain relevant in tomorrow's fast-changing world of knowledge-driven industries. These institutions will also train researchers, scientists and engineers to undertake leading edge R&D activities.

2 *Building research depth and capabilities*: Other brand-name institutions will also be encouraged to set up research centres in Singapore. By broadening our knowledge base, we can build up additional capabilities. With strong linkages to industry, world-class research standards, and good access to funding, these research institutes will further raise the potential to commercialize their R&D globally. In addition, the presence of ten world-class research institutes in close proximity will help create a hotbed of ideas, encourage innovation and creativity, and boost the engines of economic growth.

3 *Strengthening capabilities and technology development for industries*: Strong collaboration between these institutions and industry will speed up the building of world-class capabilities and advanced technologies. Institutions and industry can develop win-win relationships. By undertaking collaborative projects with leading industry players, educational institutions will be more closely aligned to industry developments and trends. Only then will the graduates of these institutions retain their value. Similarly, the knowledge base and brain power that these institutions will bring will greatly help companies in their continual search for better products and services, more efficient processes, new management methods or technologies and breakthrough solutions to existing problems.

4 *Attracting talent*: The strong brand names of these educational institutions will be a tremendous boost to our efforts to attract talent. World-class faculty and researchers will want to work here. Top students and executives from Asia will have another option of getting world class education here. Students and executives from the West can also come to Singapore for Asia-related studies, and stay on to work after graduation. Even those who choose to return to their home country can remain connected to our global network through links with their alma mater in Singapore.

5 *Conclusion*: This pool of world-class educational institutions will strengthen our research base, enhance tertiary educational standards, boost our talent attraction efforts, and help us build world-class capabilities for our industries. All these efforts will help us transit to a knowledge-based economy. INSEAD's announcement today will help develop Singapore faster into a global intellectual hub (Liew, 1998).

■ References

Davies, S. (1998). Work starts on Insead's S'pore campus this year, *Straits Times*, 29 September.
Economic Development Board (1998). Top business school, INSEAD builds $60m Singapore Campus. Press release, 28 September.
Liew, H. S. (1998) Remarks at INSEAD Press Conference, 28 September.

Chapter 13

Virtual Singapores: shaping international competitive environments through business–government partnerships[1]

■ Usha C.V. Haley ■

> In governing the people, the sage empties their minds but fills their bellies, weakens their wills, but strengthens their bones. He always keeps them innocent of knowledge and free from desire, and ensures that the clever never dare to act (Lao Tzu, contributor to Taoism and Confucianism, quoted in Lau, 1963: 59).

In early 1996, the German auto maker, Daimler-Benz, had been trying for a year for permission to build a car and light-truck factory in Ho Chi Minh City, Vietnam: like other manufacturers, the multinational corporations (MNCs) believed that most of its future growth would come from Asia's developing countries. Several Vietnamese officials had collected Daimler-Benz's application fees – always in cash and in US bills of small denomination; however, the officials would not grant the MNC a business licence. Frustrated, Daimler-Benz turned to Singapore for a surprising kind of government-to-business aid. At Daimler's invitation, two Singaporean government-linked corporations (GLCs) bought a 22 percent stake in the proposed Vietnam project. Then, Lee Kuan Yew, Singapore's Senior Minister, visited Vietnam's capitol, Hanoi, and pressed Daimler-Benz's case. Within two weeks the Vietnamese government approved Daimler-Benz's application. The MNC planned to invest about US$80 million in Vietnam over the next five years and to turn out 11 000 vehicles a year by 2005 (Kraar, 1996). Once again, Singapore Incorporated had effectively managed business-government relations in Asia.

Haley, Low and Toh (1996) first described Singapore Incorporated, the potent, regional, strategic alliance primarily between the Singaporean government, foreign

[1] Earlier versions of this chapter were presented at the Academy of International Business annual conference (Seoul, 1995) and at the Strategic Management Society's annual meetings (Phoenix, 1996). The author thanks the Economic Development Board of Singapore for prompt, helpful information; and the Managing Business in Asia Program at the Australian National University for supporting this research. This chapter has been published previously by MCB University Press Limited: Haley, U.C.V. (1998). Virtual Singapores: shaping international competitive environments through business–government partnerships. *Journal of Organizational Change Management*, **11** (4), 338–56.

MNCs and Singaporean GLCs (later extended to include other stakeholders including labour, local private firms and knowledge-intensive firms): Haley, Low and Toh (1996) argued that the corporate metaphor, rather than governmental plans, served to guide Singaporean policy and its regional destiny. Singapore Incorporated now provides the label that local governmental and business leaders candidly use to describe the way private businesses and the government work together to advance mutual interests. Since the late 1980s, the primary stakeholders in Singapore Incorporated have started regionally diversifying their assets (Haley, Low and Toh, 1996): the stakeholders are parlaying their potent alliance into an imaginative, unprecedented, ambitious, and potentially lucrative international enterprise that projects Singapore's merchant history into a controlled future trajectory of regional change.

Foreigners doing business in Southeast and East Asia have long relied on Overseas Chinese and Overseas Indian middlemen to cut through red tape, to connect with the right people, to get deals done, and to take a small piece of the action. These middlemen have generally consisted of well-connected individuals. However, with Singapore Incorporated, a country is willing to serve as middleman for foreign MNCs across Asia. In the most ambitious, and perhaps the most imaginative, part of its new role, Singapore is creating Virtual Singapores across Asia. The Virtual Singapores form industrial parks that this tiny country (about the size of Chicago, 641.4 sq km) with 3 million people and the highest average regional income (higher than the UK's at S$25 000) is erecting inside Asia's big, developing countries – China, India, Indonesia and Vietnam so far. Most of these industrial parks consist of clusters of factories, roads, and power plants; but in Suzhou, China, Singapore is engaging in a social experiment of structural change on a grand scale (Haley, 1996).

This chapter explores the ramifications of the Virtual Singapores, Singapore's industrial parks in Asia's developing countries. The first section elaborates on Singapore's regionalization drive and describes the Virtual Singapores. The ensuing section identifies the strategic goals for internationalizing Singapore Incorporated. The final section discusses the implications of the Virtual Singapores for competitive environments, organizational and structural changes in the Asia Pacific.

■ Singapore Incorporated's regionalization drive

The World Economic Forum's *World Competitiveness Report* and the US-based Business Environment Risk Intelligence (BERI) report have repeatedly cited Singapore as one of the best places in the world to do business (Aggarwal, 1997; Economic Development Board of Singapore, 1995; 1996a; 1997b; Fernandez, 1998; *Straits Times Weekly Edition*, 1997). In a rapidly churning and developing region, Singapore provides good infrastructure and a graft-free business environment with transparent and consistent regulations. Singapore's labour force has once again been rated the best in the world by BERI. The republic also retains its position as the second most profitable country in which companies can invest, after Switzerland (*Straits Times Weekly Edition*, 1997). Additionally, since its independence in 1965, the government has steadfastly and actively encouraged MNCs to invest within Singapore. Consequently, in 1997, about 5000 MNCs operated in Singapore and about half maintained regional headquarters there (Economic Development Board of Singapore, 1997b).

As Table 13.1 shows, Singapore has also become a major investor in Asia. Characteristically, in 1997, following a trend of incrementally increasing regional investments since the late 1980s (Haley, Low and Toh, 1996), Singapore emerged as Vietnam's biggest investor, primarily because of the Vietnam Singapore Industrial Park (Haley and Haley, 1997). Inside the industrial parks or Virtual Singapores, MNCs can operate as they do in Singapore. Consequently, though still under construction, the Virtual Singapores have already attracted more than US$4 billion of investments from over 280 MNCs, including US-based Advanced MicroDevices, France-based L'Oreal, and British Oxygen. The US-based computer disk-drive maker Seagate Technology has set up a US$30 million plant in the Wuxi-Singapore Industrial Park in China – though in 1998, because of high operating costs, this second-largest private employer in Singapore laid off 11 per cent of its Singaporean workforce. The German-based electronics giant, Siemens, is erecting factories in every Virtual Singapore to make devices ranging from hearing aids to semiconductors. 'We're comfortable wherever they sell the Singaporean way of doing business', said Harmut Lueck, managing director of Siemens Components in Singapore (Kraar, 1996).

Table 13.1 Approved Singaporean foreign direct investment into regional countries in 1995 and 1996

Country	1995 (US$m)	Rank	1996 (US$m)	Rank
Indonesia	1469	6	3100 (Jan–Dec)	3
Thailand	1514	6	1061 (Jan–Sept)	4
Malaysia	403.5	4	1324 (Jan–Aug)	1
Philippines	3.6	–	18.6 (Jan–Sept)	6
China	1,860	5	987 (Jan–Jun)	5
Vietnam	455.57	5	952.5 (Jan–Dec)	2
Myanmar	287.38	1	554.74 (Apr–Nov)	–
India	300.04	10	63.7 (Jan–Aug)	12

Source: Economic Development Board of Singapore (1996a, b)

This section traces the regionalization programs undertaken by Singapore including the Singapore, Johore (Malaysia), Riau Islands (Indonesia) growth triangle, an area of focused investment for the three countries; and the Virtual Singapores or industrial parks that Singapore has constructed in Asia's developing countries. Although both advance Singapore's regionalization drive, differences exist between the growth triangle and the industrial parks: the former serves as a physical fusion of Singapore's economic infrastructure with its neighbors'; the latter form virtual enclaves of Singapore's business environment in other countries. Singapore Incorporated has transferred labour-intensive and spatially-driven manufacturing from Singapore to the geographically contiguous growth triangle; and set up subsidiaries or Virtual Singapores for operation in Asia's more geographically-dispersed areas.

Expanding economic space

Unlike other countries, Singapore Incorporated has actively encouraged its stakeholders – local, private firms and foreign MNCs – to invest in the region's developing and liberalizing economies. Lee (1991) and Peebles and Wilson (1996) described the concentrated governmental efforts to create the economy's second wing and in Prime Minister Goh Chok Tong's words, 'to expand Singapore's economic space' (Peebles and Wilson, 1996).

In 1991, government-led regionalization started with a pilot project: labour-intensive, lower-skilled and technology-intensive industries moved from Singapore to the Riau Islands in Indonesia and to Johore in Malaysia; by 1993, this 20 000 sq km area evolved into the Indonesia–Malaysia–Singapore growth triangle, and in 1995 expanded to include West Sumatra, Malacca, Negri Sembilan and Pahang. The first Virtual Singapore, Batamindo Industrial Park in Indonesia, also took form in the early 1990s. Foreign MNCs' initial doubts about investing in Indonesia (with historically unfavourable laws regarding foreign ownership and generally hostile governmental attitudes towards foreign investment) evaporated when many MNCs perceived the Economic Development Board (EDB), Singapore's main institution for channelling inward and outward investments, and the GLCs, as developing Batam and Bintan. This important signal bolstered foreign MNCs' confidence and provided for the Singapore government as the key interface for them with the Indonesian bureaucracy. Yet, Singapore retained importance for the MNCs because of its business environment, its trained and specialized workforce, and its global connections.

The regionalization policies to create scale and scope economies for Singapore have fanned some local concerns about the economy's hollowing out. Hollowing out refers to the possibility that Singaporean manufacturing firms might relocate to cheaper neighboring countries, thus exporting jobs and reducing the economy's manufacturing core. Local concerns also include the sandwich problem of Singapore's losing its comparative advantage in the production of low-skill, labour-intensive goods, and some capital-intensive goods, to other newly industrializing and emerging countries – before competing effectively with advanced industrialized countries in technology and skill-intensive goods. Since the 1980s, Singapore's economy has restructured to become more high-tech and service oriented (Haley Low and Toh, 1996). Consequently, so long as the service sector grows through regionalization to absorb the growing and retrenched labour force, Singapore can continue to provide conference facilities, to encourage tourism, as well as to service the high value-added manufacturing MNCs that would remain in Singapore.

Many MNCs are incorporating Singapore's infrastructure into their regional strategies. For example, Becton Dickinson, a US-based manufacturer of hypodermic syringes and other health-care products, uses its Singapore plant to supply managers and to train workers for its factory in Suzhou's Virtual Singapore. Eugenio Naschold, president of the company's Asia Pacific medical division, said, 'Having Singapore managers who speak Chinese is our best means for crossing the culture gap' (Kraar, 1996). Indeed, with a multiracial population of 3 million Chinese, Indians and Malays, most of whom have mastered Western ways, including the English language, Singapore seems well positioned to serve as a middleman between foreign MNCs and Asia's major frontier economies.

The next subsection elaborates on Singapore Incorporated's ambitious projects to create subsidiaries, or Virtual Singapores, in labour and land-rich Asian developing countries. Faced domestically with increasingly non-competitive labour rates, land shortages and impending competition from ports in Thailand and Malaysia, Singapore Incorporated is trying to retain regional economic dominance by transmitting key technologies, as well as unique cultural and political values, through these industrial parks.

Orchestrating change

The Virtual Singapores, or industrial parks created and maintained by Singapore and hosted by Asia's developing countries, serve as tools to help Singapore to co-ordinate and to manage change to its advantage. For the most part, the hosts, China, India, Indonesia and Vietnam, present mirror-image vistas of Singapore with plenty of land, cheap labour, and low credibility among foreign MNCs. Table 13.2 indicates the Virtual Singapores and some of their tenants.

In India, Vietnam and Indonesia, the Singapore government uses its local contacts to play familiar host to foreign MNCs. For example, to replicate itself in India, Singapore relied heavily on the personal relationships that feature prominently in Asian business. Philip Yeo, the EDB's Harvard-educated chairman, contacted his old friend, Ratan Tata, chairman of the Tata Group, a leading Indian conglomerate. Tata quickly agreed to join forces with Singapore Incorporated – and brought along two blue-chip tenants, IBM and AT&T. In forty-eight hours, Yeo sold the idea to the Karnataka state government, a minority investor in the International Technology Park in Bangalore. Built to Singaporean standards, the initial phase of the US$480 million complex opened in 1997. A consortium of six Singaporean companies backing the park also won a deal, along with Tata and US-based Raytheon, to build a US$535 million international airport in Bangalore.

In China, Singapore's flagship social-engineering project in the city of Suzhou constitutes its most ambitious undertaking by far. China's leader, Deng Xiao Ping, paved the way by suggesting that the People's Republic could learn a lot from the island Republic. As Deng said in 1992, 'Singapore enjoys good social order and is well managed. We could tap on their expertise and learn how to manage better than them' (Kraar, 1996). Taking those remarks as an invitation, Singapore's government leaders offered to bring their expertise into China – if they could get a free hand to demonstrate it. The China-Singapore Suzhou Industrial Park provides the Singaporean model for China's development. Suzhou's Mayor Zhang Xin Sheng, an exceptionally pro-business Chinese official, acknowledged that Suzhou is borrowing Singapore's credibility with MNCs, its capital, and its management skills 'so that a latecomer can catch up'. Many Chinese mainlanders share Singapore's self-perception of itself as middleman: 'Westerners find it relatively easy to accept Singapore compared with China', said Li Juchuan, a Chinese official from the park's administration, 'and we find it easier to accept Singaporeans than Westerners. So Singapore stands right in the middle' (Kraar, 1996).

Table 13.2 Virtual Singapores and some tenants

China	China-Singapore Suzhou Industrial Park
	Area: 70 sq km
	Employees: 360 000[a]
	Investment: US$2.86 billion
	Some tenants: RJR Nabisco, Eli Lilly
	Wuxi-Singapore Industrial Park
	Area: 1000 hectares
	Employees: 150 000[a]
	Investment: US$585 million
	Some tenants: Seagate Technology, Sumitomo Electric
India	International Technology Park, Bangalore
	Area: 27.2 hectares
	Employees: 15 000[a]
	Investment: US$480 million
	Some tenants: Owens-Corning Fiberglas, Sony
Indonesia	Batamindo Industrial Park
	Area: 500 hectares
	Employees: 54 046
	Investment: US$725 million
	Some tenants: AT&T, Siemens
	Bintan Industrial Estate
	Area: 4000 hectares
	Employees: 2679
	Investment: US$161.3 million
	Some tenants: Poly-Allied Knitwear, Sumitomo Metal Mining
	Bintan Beach International Resort
	Area: 23 000 hectares
	Employees: 1400
	Investment: US$128.6 million
	Some tenants: Banyan Tree, Club Med
	Karimun Marine Industrial Complex
	Area: 1050 hectares
	Employees: 300
	Investment: US$100 million
	Managers: SembCorp Industries, Bangun Cipta Group
Vietnam	Vietnam Singapore Industrial Park, Ho Chi Minh City
	Area: 500 hectares (with option for another 500)
	Employees: 50 000[a]
	Investment: US$312 million
	Some tenants: New Toyo, Alcamax

Note: [a] Projected.
Source: Economic Development Board of Singapore (1996a; 1996b; 1998).

The China-Singapore Suzhou Industrial Park constitutes a twenty-one company consortium, dominated by local, private firms, GLCs and Singaporean government agencies, including the EDB. With a completion time of twenty years, an estimated size of 70 sq km and 600 000 people, Suzhou forms an experimental base for Singapore Incorporated to serve as middleman between China and the world; through Suzhou, Singapore Incorporated also hopes to perpetuate its influence and stakeholder base by advocating an alternative model for developing China (Kraar, 1996). The consortium will funnel to China the transfer of Singaporean software (or values and culture), covering methodologies ranging from urban planning and fire fighting to the Central Provident Fund (CPF).

The China–Singapore Suzhou Industrial Park has already drawn over US$2 billion of investment commitments from fifty-six manufacturers including Samsung Electronics with a semiconductor factory; RJR Nabisco with a prefabricated factory from Australia to manufacture Ritz crackers; and Eli Lilly with a US$28 million factory to make the antidepressant Prozac. Multinational corporations usually cannot maintain construction schedules in China, yet Suzhou appears different. As Lee Dong Sup, Samsung's construction manager in Suzhou said, 'NEC of Japan took almost two years to build a semiconductor factory in Beijing. Everything is much easier here' (Kraar, 1996). Besides comfort and familiarity, Suzhou's Virtual Singapore offers major savings in labour costs. A factory worker in Suzhou costs about US$71 a month or one-tenth of a Singaporean worker. However, productivity poses serious problems in Suzhou. As Clifton Hong, Rexton Hearing System's general manager, noticed, the Chinese workers 'thought this was like a state corporation that would pay them no matter how many pieces were made' (Law, 1996).

Suzhou's hard, brown, flat land also provides the opening scene of China's biggest attempt at social engineering since Mao Zedong launched the Cultural Revolution in the 1960s: the Singapore Software Project Office (SSPO) is trying to teach new skills and to change attitudes in the Virtual Singapore based there. In the past four years, the SSPO has trained more than 280 Chinese officials; about 180 travel annually to Singapore for courses in financial management, provident fund operations and public housing administration. The Suzhou Industrial Park Administrative Committee's (SIPAC's) executives are also studying Singaporean regulations for implementation in the new township. Beijing's central government has granted administrative powers to SIPAC beyond those wielded by provincial governments. 'But the new rules will not undermine China's sovereignty', said SIPAC's official Zhao Dazheng. 'Everything will have to be approved by the central government' (Law, 1996).

The next section elaborates on what Singapore Incorporated hopes to achieve through its regionalization projects.

▪ Singapore Incorporated's goals for going international

Singapore Incorporated's goals for going international involve harnessing structural changes in Asia to ride them out for Singapore's advantage; alternatively, the governmental policy-makers have argued that successive waves of structural changes could overwhelm tiny Singapore. This section elaborates on how Singapore aims to control regional structural changes through transferring what the government labels as software (or culture and values) and hardware (or manufacturing facilities and personnel). The transfers of software include presenting Singapore as a model, thereby ensuring its psychological centrality in the region; the transfers of hardware include using Singapore as a regional hub, thereby ensuring its economic centrality.

Transfers of software

Software transfers of culture and values comprise offering Singapore as a positive regional model. Singapore offers an unusual and atypical positive model. First, Singapore is a tiny country, a city-state, with a small population, no rural hinterland, and almost no natural resources; indeed, it depends on Malaysia for most of its water supply. Second, no economy has such a presence of MNCs. Additionally, as with Seagate Technology (the major manufacturer of computer disk drives in Singapore), MNCs' production in Singapore contributes importantly to global production and to the MNCs' export strategies (about 40 per cent of the world's disk drives are manufactured in Singapore). Third, Singapore's prosperity derives closely from its port, one of the two busiest and among the most modern in the world. Singapore enjoys the highest trade to gross domestic product (GDP) ratio in the world – total trade approximates four times GDP; and exports constitute about 190 per cent of GDP (Haley, Low and Toh, 1996) making Singapore's trade bigger than India's and nearly two-thirds of China's. Consequently, Singapore's governmental leaders initially claimed that Singapore did not represent any model – except one in public housing and town planning (Goh, 1977). Goh Keng Swee, one of Singapore Incorporated's architects, repeatedly insisted that Singapore's contribution did not involve policies but the inflexible determination needed to implement them. However, in the last decade, Singapore has offered a regional model of social organization and economic growth.

Offering model of social organization

As Haley, Low and Toh (1996) identified, Singapore's self-image as a corporation carries strong implications and assumptions of social organization. Socially, first Prime Minister Lee Kuan Yew argued for a Confucian, rigidly hierarchical, stabilizing society in Singapore of mandarin bureaucrats on top, hardworking, disciplined, blue collars on the bottom, and leading businessmen and a closely-watched professional class in between (Krause, 1988; Redding, 1990). The unabashedly authoritarian government (exclusively from the ruling People's Action Party (PAP) that has governed Singapore since independence in 1965) serves as the major stakeholder in Singapore Incorporated, constituting agenda setter and often agenda achiever. This internalizing of markets through hierarchies, as an MNC would, carries both costs and benefits: its benefits, as noted by Singapore's government, translate to increased efficiency and strategic speed; its costs, as also noted by Singapore's government and foreign MNCs, contribute to a relative lack of initiative, entrepreneurship and creativity (Tripathi, 1996b), and an inflexible bureaucracy (Haley, Low and Toh, 1996).

Because of its characteristics, a viable combination of high growth, social development and authoritarian policy, Singapore offers an officially accepted model for China's social organization. In 1992, China's Deng Xiao Ping stated (quoted in Margolin, 1993: 96), 'Guangdong Province may reach in 20 years the level of Asia's four tigers, in terms not only of economic prosperity, but also of social order and behavior. We can overtake them … We can take inspiration from the Singapore social order, and do better.' Through the China-Singapore Suzhou Industrial Park, Singapore is training Suzhou officials in operational methodologies. Singapore's Lee Kuan Yew has argued that with adequate universal housing, crime drops, contributing to social and political stability. Consequently, using Singapore's exacting standards as a reference, Chinese cadres are writing blueprints for environmental and building regulation and land-use planning. They are also studying Singapore's CPF and Housing Development Board (HDB) as ways to finance a solution to China's housing shortage. As Chan Soo Sen, the park developer's CEO, confirmed, '[the Chinese] are impressed by Singapore's ability to steer through economic revolution with the social fabric basically intact' (Kohut, 1996: 28).

The Singaporean government closely supervises the Virtual Singapore's values and development in Suzhou. David Lim, head of the China–Singapore Suzhou Industrial Park Development Company (CSSD) constructing the park, formerly headed other flagship projects for Singapore Incorporated: the Jurong Town Corporation (that develops and manages Jurong township, Singapore's premier industrial zone), and the Port of Singapore Authority (that develops and manages Singapore's prized port). The 120 Singaporean executives and technicians in Suzhou have started feeling the pressures. 'We're working under a microscope, being closely monitored by our government and our people', said CSSD's general manager Goh Toh Sim, who relocated his family to Suzhou (Law, 1996). He typically worked thirteen-hour days.

The Singaporean transfers of software to China encounter continuing technical and cultural hurdles. The CSSD faces technical problems such as ensuring that the industrial park's two 50-megawatt thermal power plants produce to full capacity; and devising an economical way of piping and treating water from nearby Lake Tai. The CSSD also faces cultural obstacles when transplanting the Singaporean way to the Virtual Singapore it is building. For example, the CSSD and SIPAC, the industrial park's local government, share the same lakeside building. The Singaporean portion appears modern and businesslike; the Chinese side has smelly toilets, beds for people to nap and a red propaganda banner strung across the conference room. However, SIPAC differs from the typical Chinese state organization: about 100 employees staff its ten bureaux; in contrast, about 1000 employees staff the much smaller totally Chinese managed Pudong Development Zone in Shanghai.

The Singaporean transfer of software to China also entails diplomacy. Humiliated by Western powers in the nineteenth century and by Japan in the twentieth, China bristles at any foreign presence that recalls its painful past. For nearly a century till the Second World War, the colonial powers, including the USA, ran sectors of Shanghai by their own rules and for their own pleasure and profit. In the China-Singapore Suzhou Industrial Park, Singapore Incorporated deals tactfully with that delicate issue by emphasizing repeatedly that China writes the rules. Chinese officials regularly go to Singapore for a few months to work in various governmental departments and to learn the Singaporean way. The Chinese return home to reflect on the lessons and then go back to Singapore once again to draft the regulations for Suzhou.

Offering model of economic growth

Since the 1970s, policy-makers and academics have touted Singapore as an economic model for its economic growth; economic zones; public housing and town planning; technological upgrading; public transportation; traffic and environmental management; successful demographic transition; cleanliness; absence of corruption; efficiency, bureaucratic transparency and freedom of red tape; magnificent airport and national airlines; and strategic direction (Emmersen, 1982; Margolin, 1993). In the 1970s, the new United National Party government of Sri Lanka attempted to model Colombo's Free Trade Zones on Singapore's Jurong township, and its national airline on Singapore International Airlines. After he retired from government, China invited Goh Keng Swee, designer of Singapore's economy, 'to set up economic zones and a tourist industry' (Rajaratnam in Ang, 1991). As indicated in the earlier section, the Singapore–Johore–Riau Islands growth triangle provides an alternative strategy from the Virtual Singapores for Singapore Incorporated's regionalization. Yet, Singapore's strategy and performance in the growth triangle's economic zone have contributed greatly to global perceptions of it as an economic model. Moreover, bilateral treaties, with Singapore as growth node, rather than a tripartite arrangement between Malaysia, Indonesia and Singapore, have created the growth triangle: consequently, the growth triangle serves as an economic model for the Virtual Singapores' dealings with the developing countries' host governments and with the MNCs operating in the region.

Singapore Incorporated's goals for the growth triangle involve maximizing its comparative advantages by exploiting factor endowments in the region. The three partners appear to have complementary factor endowments: Singapore has high-quality human capital and a well-developed infrastructure; Johore has land and semi-skilled labour; Batam and Bintan in the Riau Islands have land and low-cost labour. The differences in factor endowments affect operating costs: for example, in Johore, unskilled labour costs approximately twice that in the Riau Islands, and one-fifth that in Singapore (recent steep devaluations in the regional currencies *vis-à-vis* Singapore's have increased the discrepancies). MNCs operating in the region can therefore maintain their capital and knowledge-intensive operations in Singapore, and their labour-intensive and spatially driven operations in Johore or Batam. Proximity of MNCs' operations to Singapore allows for better monitoring and controlling of operations and easier transhipping of intermediate and final goods. Alternatively, to obtain the greatest competitive advantage, MNCs can locate production facilities according to their production-factor intensities in the various locations: for example, they can locate their specialized and highly-technical operations in Singapore, their less-technical operations in Johore and their labour-intensive, assembly operations in Batam. The creation of a wider manufacturing base, with different factor endowments in each node, provides an incentive for MNCs to consider the region as a whole for investment – a prime consideration for Singapore with the region's smallest domestic market and the highest operating costs. With adequate logistical support, Singapore Incorporated hopes to encourage this interlinked, wider manufacturing-base model among the MNCs in the Virtual Singapores.

In the growth triangle, and in the Virtual Singapores, Singapore Incorporated also hopes to capture manufacturing and scale economies in services. Singapore's financial and business services sector has links to global markets and can provide ancillary services for industrialization. Industries in developing countries, tightly bound to Singapore through managerial, operational and logistical systems, encourage numerous spillovers to the Singaporean economy's other sectors and more transactional efficiencies through larger networks. Conversely, the developing countries obtain a cheaper developmental strategy through Singapore's service network and greater scale economies accrue to all. In the growth triangle, Johore's and the Riau Islands' natural beauty can also combine with Singapore's tourist traffic to market the region as a complete product: as the Singapore Tourist Promotion Board advises, visitors to

Singapore can have short holidays in the adjoining countries' resorts in addition to their normal Singaporean stopovers.

For Malaysia and Indonesia, the growth triangle entails accepting Singapore's important role in their national development, and consequently incorporating some Singaporean models and methods – especially those regarding town and land planning and the use of advanced technologies. Singapore Incorporated hopes to have the same significance in the other developing countries that host the Virtual Singapores. Singapore values this pivotal role as regional economic model because of its stark economic vulnerabilities. One economic vulnerability involves its greatest strength – its world-class port. The port's cranes daily unload nearly 300 container vessels at an average of twelve hours per vessel; annually about 12 million containers change hands. Despite improvements, and US$3 billion in modernization efforts by 1998, 70 per cent of the port's cargo neither originates from Singapore nor is destined for it – posing the greatest threat to the port's future as rival ports originate in Malaysia and Thailand (Tripathi, 1997).

Transfers of hardware

Hardware transfers from Singapore of manufacturing facilities and personnel aim at maintaining local firms' participation and preventing the MNCs' exodus from Singapore. Despite the recent economic downturn, the costs of doing business in Singapore have risen sharply with rapid economic growth for two and a half decades. The constraints of limited labour and land have greatly increased their costs which, together with a generally appreciating Singapore dollar (till 1997), have squeezed profit margins. Singaporean employees enjoy the second highest wages in Asia after the Japanese: the average Singaporean blue-collar worker earns nine times as much as a comparable Thai worker (recent steep devaluations in the Thai currency have increased the discrepancy). In Singapore, changes in labour productivity have not matched real wage increases, implying an increase in real labour costs. Since 1987, foreign labour has also become increasingly expensive because of the foreign workers levy and the imposition of a 40 per cent ceiling on the number of foreign workers that companies can hire. Similarly, office rents rose 15 per cent in 1995 to an annual average of S$863 per square metre, making Singapore one of the ten most expensive cities in the world for office space (Tripathi, 1996a). Industrial land in Singapore costs about 186 per cent more than in Malaysia, 173 per cent more than in Thailand and 757 per cent more than in China (Tripathi, 1995). Consequently, local firms and MNCs have to decide whether to upgrade their operations in Singapore, redistribute their labour-intensive operations elsewhere or do both.

Maintaining local firms' participation
As domestic costs escalated in the early 1990s, the EDB and the Committee to Promote Enterprises Overseas began to implement incentives for local private firms to invest in the region. Through many assistance schemes, the EDB gives local firms a total business development package that caters to them from cradle to maturity. The Virtual Singapores in the developing countries of China, Vietnam, Indonesia and India allow Singapore Incorporated to build its external economy and to complement its internal economy by involving local private firms.

Singapore has less capital and people to spread in the region than other Asian newly industrialized economies. Therefore, Singapore Incorporated has drawn together its old strategic alliance of statutory boards, GLCs and MNCs to blaze the trail. When MNCs and GLCs move abroad, the government extends the local industry upgrading programme (LIUP) to enable these stakeholders to upgrade local contractors' technologies. Local construction and management firms help to build and to operate the industrial parks. Moreover, the government has set aside nearly US$1 billion to invest directly in foreign manufacturing projects and to share in their returns, as with Daimler-Benz's operations in Vietnam; the government uses these foreign equity partnerships to make strategic investments with local, private firms as well as to accelerate their development along strategic thrusts. Thus, Singapore can keep its economy expanding and its local firms competitive in slower economic times.

Preventing MNCs' exodus

The possibility of highly volatile movements in short-term and long-term capital flows, including foreign direct investment, accentuates Singapore's extreme economic vulnerability. As a Singaporean Member of Parliament stated, 'At present a significant proportion of our GDP is non-indigenous, meaning that our technological base is weak' (*Straits Times*, 1995). Rising domestic costs affect MNCs just as they do local, private firms; and labour shortages, especially of skilled and tertiary-educated workers, have resulted in MNCs arguing for larger quotas of foreign workers. Peebles and Wilson (1996) identified this crucial weakness of Singapore: Singapore experiences peculiar economic vulnerabilities that first-world countries do not; foreign, and especially US-owned, MNCs dominate its manufacturing base. These MNCs have no vested interests in Singapore; if economic or political circumstances force the MNCs to leave, Singapore can not fill the void (Peebles and Wilson, 1996: 241).

Many MNCs, though lauding Singapore's business environment, fear that operating there may cleave them from their Asian markets. For example, in 1994, Siemens held its corporate board meeting in Singapore, its first outside Europe in 147 years. Yet, Singaporean smiles melted when Siemens announced its next wave of investments – US$1 billion for China and India, US$1.5 billion for the rest of Asia, and only US$215 million for Singapore. Prime Minister Goh Chok Tong requested Siemens to at least establish a regional headquarters in Singapore; yet, CEO Heinreich von Pierer declined explaining that Beijing and not Singapore provided promising markets. As Goh recalled his conversation with von Pierer, 'his comments sent a chill down my spine' (Tripathi, 1995). Clearly, Singapore had to join forces with Asia's developing nations – or lose to them in the race for investments.

By cloning itself overseas through the Virtual Singapores, Singapore intends to forestall any large-scale exodus among the 5000 MNCs operating there. Singapore hopes that as overall Asian business grows, MNCs will maintain and perhaps expand their regional headquarters in Singapore – and operate existing factories, if only to train managers and workers for their new plants abroad. Singapore Incorporated's abilities to control the MNCs' foreign operations and to channel resources obviously increase in the Virtual Singapores that it manages.

The next section explores the implications of the Virtual Singapores for structural and organizational changes in Asia.

■ Implications for restructuring Asia's competitive environments

The 1997 world competitiveness ranking by the Swiss-based International Institute for Management Development (IMD) once again ranked Singapore as the world's second most competitive economy after the USA. Singapore retained top honours in internationalization and government and improved to top place in management. However, people and finance slipped. The World Competitiveness Project's director, Stephane Garelli said, 'The US and Singapore seemed to have reached cruising speed in world competitiveness with good rankings in almost all factors ... The challenge for Singapore is what will come next. To develop even more, it must develop new horizons' (Aggarwal, 1997). Without the USA's diversity or resources, Singapore is using the Virtual Singapores to develop new horizons – with attendant ramifications for structural and organizational changes in the region. This section explores some implications for structural and organizational changes in Asia resulting from the Virtual Singapores' services and strategies.

First-class travel

Chan Soo Sen, the Singaporean CEO of the Suzhou industrial park's developer in China, likened a company entering China to a passenger on a jetliner that cannot avoid bumpy weather. 'In the first-class section, you still will feel more comfortable', said Chan (Kraar, 1996). In other words, by operating in the developing countries' Virtual Singapores, MNCs cannot reduce the political risks of bumpy weather; however, they can obtain top accommodations and experienced flight attendants. Of course, when the jetliner crashes, all passengers crash, including those in first class.

Services for regional governments

In its Virtual Singapores, Singapore offers the regional governments of China, Vietnam, India and Indonesia credibility with MNCs, and therefore jobs for their workforces and prosperity the Singaporean way. For example, the nationalistic Indonesians had attempted fruitlessly for years to lure foreign MNCs. In 1990, spotting an opportunity, Singapore's government leaders offered to help, provided that they could remove bureaucratic barriers as well as tons of earth. They convinced the Indonesian government to exempt the Batamindo Industrial Park from an Indonesian ban on 100 per cent foreign ownership; and relieved international investors from the usual, long paper chases for countless permits, a system reeking of corruption. Eager to show results before the Indonesians changed their minds, the GLC, Singapore Technologies, worked around the clock to build the Batam park and to get some corporate tenants in eleven months. Singapore Incorporated also ensured that the Virtual Singapore had its own utilities and international phone links, services that MNCs often find erratic in other parts of Indonesia. Since 1990, Singapore has filled the Batamindo Industrial Park with over eighty-seven manufacturers – including AT&T, Seagate Technology, France's Thomson, and Japan's Sumitomo Electric.

Services for MNCs

In its Virtual Singapores, as indicated earlier with Daimler-Benz in Vietnam, Singapore also serves as middleman for the MNCs. The Batamindo Industrial Park has become a model for Singapore Incorporated's technique of insulating MNCs from local

bureaucrats. Foreign investors in each Virtual Singapore deal with a single organization – run by Singaporeans as well as local officials – that promises to break through
bottlenecks. Siemens, for instance, simply wrote two letters, and the Batamindo
Industrial Park's administration promptly attended to all aspects in setting up the
MNC's computer-chip plant.

Singapore's government officials attempt to plug into the host countries' power structures and to keep political leaders involved in assuring that a pro-business environment exists in the Virtual Singapores. For example, in Suzhou, Chinese officials
demanded money from the MNCs under regulations posted nowhere. Consequently,
the Singaporean government polled the MNCs to discover what fees the Chinese were
charging, compiled a list of hundreds of fees, and submitted the list to Suzhou's
authorities. After long discussions about the need for a pro-business environment,
Suzhou's government officials pared the voluminous list to twenty-eight required
fees. For instance, MNCs in the China–Singapore Suzhou Industrial Park no longer
have to pay a termite fee for unrequired protection against an infestation not found in
the park's steel buildings.

New economic space

Even before the Asian economic crisis, Singapore's GDP growth had slowed to 7 per
cent in 1996 after 8.8 in 1995 and 10.5 in 1994; and growth in productivity in 1996
slipped to its lowest point in a decade, 0.7 per cent, from 3.6 in 1995. Yet, real wage
rates grew by 3.6 per cent in 1996 from 3.8 in 1995; and unit labour costs in manufacturing grew 3 per cent in 1996, reversing three straight years of decline (Wong, 1997).
To maintain Singapore's high growth rates and extremely high labour costs, Singapore
has undertaken efforts to carve new economic space; these efforts entail managing the
Singaporean way with ensuing changes in MNCs and competitive environments.

Control over information
Singapore Incorporated functions efficiently and swiftly through extremely tight governmental control of information. The Singaporean government has transplanted
these practices, for the most part, to the Virtual Singapores. In April 1997, the Freedom
House ranked Singapore's news media as among the most completely controlled in
the world (only Indonesia and China had more controlled news media) (*The Economist*,
1997). Since 1979, this New York based organization has conducted an annual survey
of print and broadcast media in most countries of the world. The survey measures
press freedom by assessing the impact of laws, administrative decisions, and economic
or political influences on the news media's content. The Singaporean government's
control over its domestic media adds to securities analysts' pressures to avoid negative reports. 'As long as there are restrictions on the free flow of information, they can't
expect to be a major funds-management and stock-brokering center', said William H.
Overholt, Bankers Trust's managing director in Hong Kong (*Business Week*, 1995: 28)

The Singaporean government also aims to guarantee access to privileged technical
information (which may endanger relations with local hosts or hurt Singaporean companies) through interlocking directorates with MNCs. For example, disk-drive manufacturer Seagate Technology protested the presence of Singaporean government
officials on its board that also sat on the competing board of the GLC, Singapore
Technologies.

Control over sourcing

Through incentives and equity partnerships, Singapore Incorporated aims to control sourcing of the MNCs that operate in the Virtual Singapores. The incentives aim to encourage MNCs with regional headquarters in Singapore to source from Singapore when manufacturing in the Virtual Singapores. For example, the EDB in 1996 announced the manufacturing headquarters (MHQ) incentive for MNCs with substantial manufacturing in Singapore. The MHQ incentive complements the operational headquarters (OHQ) incentive and the business headquarters (BHQ) incentive. The MHQ incentive encourages the MNCs to provide manufacturing support services to their plants in the Virtual Singapores from Singapore. The related logistics programme encourages MNCs to set up their products' regional distribution centers in Singapore. The communications and media cluster aims to develop Singapore as the Asia-Pacific hub for the MNCs to deliver region-wide services, to develop and to market new and innovative capabilities and to create content. Equity partnerships between the EDB and MNCs, such as Hitachi Semiconductor in the China-Singapore Suzhou Industrial Park, also enable strategic investments in Singaporean supporting industries. Of course, the MNCs in the Virtual Singapores do not have to source from Singapore – but, increasing efficiencies and economies of scale, with a corresponding relinquishing of the MNCs' strategic independence, follow central sourcing.

Bumpy weather

Despite the careful charting of their courses, the Virtual Singapores appear to be travelling in bumpy weather, concomitantly reducing their potential for structural and organizational changes in Asia.

Insufficient diversification

Investments in developing countries incur high returns and equally high attendant risks. Singapore Incorporated, with mostly Asian linkages, has not appeared to diversify investments sufficiently. In 1998, because of the regional economic crisis, Singapore suffered a recession. About 30 per cent of its exports go to other Association of South East Asia Nations (ASEAN) countries; 80 per cent constitute intermediate and capital goods designed for the region's exporters. Since the Asian crisis, despite depreciating approximately 15–20 per cent against the US dollar, the Singaporean dollar has strengthened between 30–195 per cent against regional currencies, greatly weakening its exports (Osman, 1998). Additionally, ASEAN's exports have dropped by 5 per cent just between February and May 1998; the exports will likely drop much further. Investment analyst Nicholas Brooks of Santander (Singapore) argued that if ASEAN's economies fail to improve soon, Singapore Incorporated's export machine will grind to a halt, with permanent detrimental effects on its growth (Sprague and Shameen, 1998).

Additionally, Asia has absorbed over 60 per cent of Singapore's foreign direct investments. China, a major investment destination for Singapore, remains one of the fastest growing economies in the world with about 7 per cent annual GDP growth (Sprague and Shameen, 1998); yet, over 30 per cent of Singapore Incorporated's investments have gone into the financially-troubled ASEAN countries (Department of Statistics, Singapore, 1996). Consequently, the Singapore Government is now encouraging investments in unrelated developing economies such as Latin America and Eastern Europe (Ibrahim, 1998).

Local politics

Finally, despite the Virtual Singapores' zest and drive, Asian competitive environments show inertia and resistance that even Singapore Incorporated has trouble overcoming. For example, traditional political squabbling between China's central and municipal governments has delayed the Virtual Singapore's development in Suzhou. In December 1997, in his strongest expression of unhappiness over the China–Singapore Suzhou Industrial Park's progress, Singapore's Senior Minister Lee Kuan Yew wished that Wuxi and its officials had been placed in Suzhou. He said that in a recent survey of Chinese industrial zones, the China–Singapore Suzhou Industrial Park had achieved the top rank in foreign investments, industrial sales and foreign exchange earned per industrial land's square mile. Despite Chinese President Jiang Zemin's instructions to make the industrial park a model township, Suzhou's municipal officials had deliberately obstructed the park's projects (Chua, 1997). Suzhou's officials had been diverting investments meant for the Virtual Singapore to the New District, a nearby rival industrial park set up in 1990 and wholly managed by Suzhou's government. Alternatively, the China-Singapore Suzhou Industrial Park was set up in 1994 with Beijing's governmental approval. The Suzhou New District, like the local Virtual Singapore, hosts high-tech industries and residential areas.

■ References

Aggarwal, N. (1997). S'pore is world's second most competitive economy again. *Straits Times Weekly Edition*, 29 March, p. 20.
Ang, H. S. (1991). Dialogues with S. Rajaratnam. *Shin Min Daily News*.
Business Week (1995). Asia's supercities. 24 April, 26–9.
Chua, L. H. (1997). SM Lee unhappy over Suzhou Park progress. *Straits Times Weekly Edition*, 6 December, p. 1.
Department of Statistics, Singapore (1996). *Singapore's Direct Investment Abroad, 1994*. Occasional Paper on Financial Statistics, DOS.
Economic Development Board of Singapore (1995). *EDB Yearbook 1995*, EDB.
Economic Development Board of Singapore (1996a). *EDB Yearbook 1995/96*, EDB.
Economic Development Board of Singapore (1996b). *Regionalisation 2000*, EDB.
Economic Development Board of Singapore (1997a). Singapore to develop resources and enterprises for the next phase of regionalization. Press release, 21 January.
Economic Development Board of Singapore (1997b). *EDB Yearbook 1996/97*, EDB.
Economic Development Board of Singapore (1998). Singapore's industrial parks in the region. Press release, May.
The Economist (1997). Freedom of the press. Emerging-market indicators. 10–16 May, p. 112.
Emmerson, D. K. (1982). *Pacific Optimism*. (1 and 2), UFSI Reports, Hanover, USA.
Fernandez, W. (1998). S'pore is still No. 2 country to invest in. *Straits Times Weekly Edition*, 9 May, p. 24.
Goh, K. S. (1977). *The Practice of Economic Growth*. Federal Publications.
Haley, U. C. V. (1996). Joining forces in international competition: the case of Singapore Incorporated. Paper presented at the 'Changes in firm boundaries in response to government policy changes' session, 16th Annual International Strategic Management Society Conference, Phoenix, Arizona, November.
Haley, U. C. V, and Haley, G. T. (1997). When the tourists flew in: strategic implications of foreign direct investment in Vietnam's tourism industry. *Management Decision*,

special issue on Strategic management in the Asia Pacific: perspectives from the region, **35** (8), 595–604.

Haley, U. C. V., Low, L. and Toh, M. H. (1996). Singapore Incorporated: reinterpreting Singapore's business environments through a corporate metaphor. *Management Decision*, special issue on Strategic management in the Asia Pacific, **34** (9), 17–28.

Ibrahim, Z. (1998). Look beyond present crisis: PM. *Straits Times Weekly Edition*, 16 May, p. 24.

Kohut, J. (1996). A bridge to Singapore. *Asia Inc.*, March, p. 28.

Kraar, L. (1996). Need a friend in Asia? Try the Singapore connection. *Fortune*, 4 March, (4), 86–95.

Krause, L. B. (1988). Hong Kong and Singapore: twins or kissing cousins? *Economic Development and Cultural Change*, s45–s66.

Lau, D. C. (1963). *Lao Tzu. Tao te ching*. Penguin Books.

Law, S. L. (1996). Lion and dragon. *Asiaweek*, 21 June.

Lee, T. Y. (1991). *Growth Triangle: The Johor-Singapore-Riau Experience*. Institute of Southeast Asian Studies.

Margolin, J. L. (1993). Foreign models in Singapore's development and the idea of a Singaporean model. In *Singapore Changes Guard. Social, Political and Economic Directions in the 1990s* (G. Rodan, ed.) 84–98, St Martin's Press.

Osman, A. (1998). S'pore stronger from regional crisis. *Straits Times Weekly Edition*, 9 May, p. 4.

Peebles, G. and Wilson, P. (1996). *The Singapore Economy*. Edward Elgar.

Redding, S. G. (1990). *The Spirit of Chinese Capitalism*. Walter de Gruyter.

Sprague, J. and Shameen, A. (1998). Economic immunity is not an option. *Asiaweek*, 8 May, 48–9.

Straits Times (1995). 4 March, p. 34.

Straits Times Weekly Edition (1997). Beri rates S'pore workers tops – again. 12 April, p. 4.

Tripathi, S. (1995). Singapore's cost crunch. *Asia Inc.*, June.

Tripathi, S. (1996a). Singapore swing. *Asia Inc.*, February, 38–44.

Tripathi, S. (1996b). No can do, lah. *Asia Inc.*, October, p. 20.

Tripathi, S. (1997). The peninsula paws back. *Asia Inc.*, January, 51–5.

Wong, D. (1997). Economy will continue to recover, says MTI. *Straits Times Weekly Edition*, 22 February, p. 24.

Chapter 13.1

The Vietnam–Singapore Industrial Park

Usha C. V. Haley

Despite Vietnam's recent economic woes (see Chapters 14.1 and 19.1), the Vietnam–Singapore Industrial Park (VSIP), the Virtual Singapore situated 17 km north of Ho Chi Minh City (and discussed in Chapter 13) appears healthy, confirming Singapore's central investment role in that economy (see Chapter 14). The VSIP has drawn twenty-eight companies from ten countries till August 1998, after only twenty-six months of operations; about 40 per cent of these companies originate from Singapore. With a total investment of US$370 million, the companies represent industries such as engineering, food, office equipment, electrical and electronics, pharmaceuticals and supporting activities like packaging. Five of the companies have invested in the VSIP since the beginning of 1998: Two of the newcomers come from Japan, and one each from Singapore and Taiwan (Economic Development Board, 1998).

Following the other Virtual Singapore's developmental patterns in Asia (as elaborated in Chapter 13), the Singaporean government has worked hard to simplify policies and procedures for setting up operations in the VSIP, as well as to draw investment incentives from the Vietnamese government. Citing examples of measures implemented first for the VSIP and eventually all over Vietnam, Vietnam's Vice-Minister for Planning and Investment, Nguyen Nhac, said enterprises exporting and processing agricultural and manufacturing products using high technology will enjoy profit tax rates of 10 to 15 per cent, profit tax exemptions of up to four years and reductions of profit tax by 50 per cent for four succeeding years. Some projects can enjoy tax holidays of up to eight years from the time they make profits (Economic Development Board, 1998). The government has widened the scope of import-duty exemptions, at present applicable to only the establishment, expansion, replacement and renewal of technology, to include construction materials that manufacturers cannot make locally and which the VSIP will use. The Vietnamese government has also increased the types of enterprises allowed to buy foreign currency in the lists of infrastructure projects, essential import substitutes and important projects contributing more than US$8 million to the State Budget per year. Nhac said in joint ventures, Vietnam would show more flexibility regarding equity participation: in the first few years, the Vietnamese partners do not have to contribute 30 per cent of the capital. In the first six months of

1998, the number of wholly owned foreign enterprises has increased. Nhac underscored that joint ventures with problems can obtain assistance. For example, certain projects can convert to 100 per cent foreign ownership, and some enterprises with foreign capital can borrow from Vietnamese banks.

Nhac also announced his Ministry's approval of the VSIP's Phase II development of 191 hectares, bringing the total development to date to 315 hectares. The VSIP's land rentals have fallen. As in Suzhou (Chapter 13), the host and Singaporean governments are working on a plan to implement one level of prices and charges for both domestic and foreign enterprises, including prices for water, telecommunications and electricity.

The VSIP's development appears unusual as Vietnam's investment climate has generally turned hostile towards foreign investment after the Asian crisis (see Chapter 19.1). Nhac said, 'I see [the VSIP] as a model for other industrial parks in Vietnam' (Economic Development Board, 1998). The Virtual Singapores aim to serve as models to perpetuate Singapore's regional influence (Chapter 13); therefore for Singapore, this goal at least appears on track so far.

▓ Reference

Economic Development Board (1998) VSIP: A model industrial park in Vietnam, Press Release, July.

Chapter 14

When the tourists flew in: strategic implications of foreign direct investment in Vietnam's tourism industry[1]

■ Usha C.V. Haley and George T. Haley ■

When the tourists flew in
The Finance Minister said
'It will boost the Economy
The dollars will flow in.'

The Minister of Interior said
'It will provide full
and varied employment
for all the indigenes.'

The Minister of Culture said
'It will enrich our life ...
contact with other cultures
must surely
Improve the texture of living.'

The man from the Hilton said
'We will make you a second Paradise;
for you it is the dawn
of a glorious new beginning!'

When the tourists flew in
our island people
metamorphosized into
a grotesque carnival
– a two-week sideshow

[1] A version of this chapter was presented at the 1st International Conference on Sustainable Tourism in Vietnam, held in Hué, Vietnam, 22–23 May 1997. The first author thanks the participants from the Vietnamese Government in the training programme at the Australian National University's (ANU's) Managing Business in Asia (MBA) Programme for their insightful feedback on a seminar she delivered on the topic; she also thanks the ANU's MBA programme for support and facilities to conduct this research. Both authors gratefully acknowledge suggestions from Mark Dodgson and Geoffrey Wall, and continual support from Comet. This chapter has been published previously by MCB University Press Limited: Haley, U. C. V. and Haley, G. T. (1997). When the tourists flew in: strategic implications of foreign direct investment in Vietnam's tourism industry. *Management Decision*, **35** (8), 595–604.

When the tourists flew in
our men put aside
their fishing nets
to become waiters
our women became whores

When the tourists flew in
what culture we had went out the window
we traded our customs
for sunglasses and pop
we turned sacred ceremonies
into ten-cent peep shows

When the tourists flew in
local food became scarce
prices went up
but our wages stayed low

When the tourists flew in
we could no longer
go down to our beaches
the hotel manager said
'Natives defile the sea-shore'

When the tourists flew in
the hunger and the squalor
were preserved
as a passing pageant
for clicking cameras
– a chic eye sore!

When the tourists flew in
we were asked
to be 'side-walk ambassadors'
to stay smiling and polite
to always guide
the 'lost' visitor …
Hell, if we could only tell them
where we really want them to go!'

(Cecil Rajendra, quoted in Richter, 1989: 190–1)

■ Introduction

Governments no longer ask should we encourage tourism – but, rather, how fast can the tourism industry grow? Yet, traditional policies of growth have proved unable to curtail the concurrent growth of socially undesirable industries and environmental degradation in most high-tourist destinations. The Vietnamese Government has targeted the tourism sector in its economy for strategic foreign direct investment (FDI). We provide some suggestions on how a centrally directed economy can maintain sustainable tourism – and, what kinds of FDI it should try to attract to do so. Experiences in similar and related markets and industries in Asia provide indications of the policies necessary to develop a sustainable, socially and ecologically desirable tourism industry through appropriate balancing of key stakeholders' goals. First, we define sustainable development in the context of tourism and indicate its relevance for Vietnam. Next, we analyse some economic and social costs and benefits associated with tourism; we also interpret recent governmental policy's influence. Finally, we provide policy recommendations for the future of sustainable and economically viable tourism development in Vietnam.

■ Sustainable development of Vietnam and tourism

Tourism forms the largest industry in the world contributing approximately 11 per cent to global gross domestic product (GDP), employing about 11 per cent of the world's population, having a current, average turnover of US$2500 billion, and growing at about 12 per cent per annum (Stoessel, 1997; World Travel and Tourism Council). In 1995, East Asia and the Pacific, including Vietnam, contributed 35 per cent to the total, worldwide increase of tourists' arrivals (World Tourism Organization).

In this section, we define sustainable economic and social development in Vietnam in the context of tourism. As Butler (1993: 29) indicated, sustainable tourism is tourism in a form which can maintain its viability in an area for an indefinite period of time; however, sustainable development in the context of tourism is tourism

> which is developed and maintained in an area (community, environment) in such a manner and at such a scale that it remains viable over an indefinite period and does not degrade or alter the environment (human and physical) in which it exists to such a degree that it prohibits the successful development and wellbeing of other activities and processes. (Butler, 1993: 29)

The latter definition explicitly acknowledges tourism as an integral component of national development.

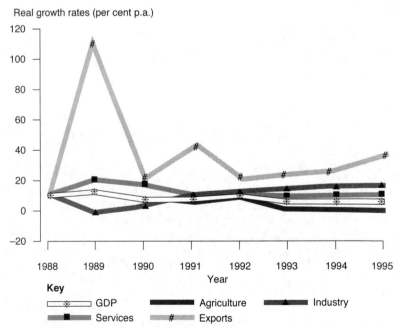

Figure 14.1 Vietnam's changing economic structure, 1988–95
Source: *Asia Pacific Profiles*, 1996

Although researchers and policy-makers comprehend particular aspects of tourism, they often misperceive how the variables interact within economic and political systems (Hall and Jenkins, 1995: 96). These variables, and their effects on strategic decision-making, become even more murky in rapidly developing and changing environments such as Vietnam (Haley, 1996; Haley and Haley, 1997a; Haley and Tan, 1996). Figure 14.1 indicates real-growth rates hovering around 10 per cent per annum in the Vietnamese economy.

We argue that tourism has multiple facets that involve providing a range of inter-related goods and services by public and private sectors. Tourism also constitutes a dynamic, changing industry that requires medium and long-range planning (Rajotte, 1978); it involves many levels of inter-relationships and co-ordination – at local, state, national, regional and international levels (Shaw and Williams, 1994). Unfortunately, researchers and policy-makers have concentrated generally on what markets to tap and what resources to develop for tourism – and have ignored frequently who is developing tourism resources and how they are doing so (Richter, 1989). As Figure 14.2 indicates, the tourism industry includes several stakeholders – investors (private and governmental), tourists (business and social), indigenous populations and host governments – all with diverse, sometimes-conflicting goals. A full understanding of development and policy instruments, including those in the context of tourism (Aislabie, 1988; Pearce, 1995; Rajotte, 1978) must include some understanding of these diverse stakeholders' goals (Haley, 1991; Haley and Haley, 1997b; Haley, Low and Toh 1996). Allied industries with high stakes run the gamut from airlines to infrastructural development, and from accommodation to shopping and entertainment. For example, the growing tourism industry in

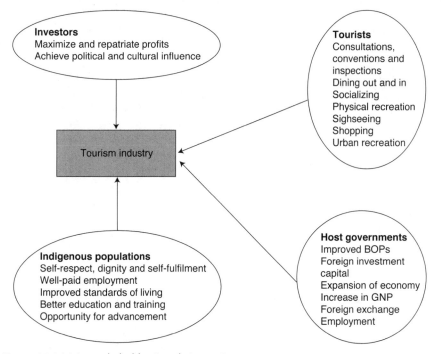

Figure 14.2 Major stakeholders' goals in tourism

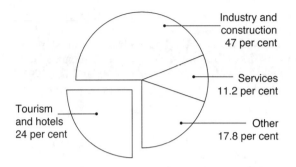

Figure 14.3
Sectoral FDI in Vietnam,
1991–95
Source: Asia Pacific Profiles,
1996

Vietnam supports many allied industries in neighbouring countries such as Thailand and Singapore; consequently, these countries have interests in sustaining tourism in Vietnam.

In 1986, the Communist government of Vietnam launched Doi Moi, or Renovation, as a policy to reform the economy; from the early 1990s, tourism expanded dramatically in Vietnam with the government gradually opening its command economy to market forces and inviting FDI. In 1990, about 25 000 foreign tourists visited Vietnam; in 1995 about 1.35 million foreign tourists visited Vietnam – a rise of about 33 per cent from the previous year – and brought in around US$818 million (Ihlwan, 1996). The Vietnamese government aims to attract 3.5 million foreign and about 11 million domestic tourists by the end of the twentieth century. As Figure 14.3 indicates, from 1991 to 1995, about 24 per cent of the FDI into Vietnam flowed into tourism. In 1996, the government planned to attract US$6 billion of FDI, of which US$1.6 billion was targeted for the tourism sector (Xinhua News Agency, 1996). The Vietnam National Administration of Tourism estimates that revenues from tourism will reach US$2.6 billion in the year 2000 and about US$11.8 billion in 2010. In 1994, tourism represented 3.5 per cent of Vietnam's GDP, the government estimates that this proportion will grow to 9.6 per cent by the year 2000 and 12 per cent by 2010 (Vu, 1997).

In 1995, Hong Kong, Taiwan, Singapore and Japan ranked generally as the biggest investors in Vietnam and in tourism specifically (*Asia Pacific Profiles*, 1996): Figure 14.4 shows the major investors in Vietnam in 1995. By April 1997, preliminary statistics revealed that Singapore formed the biggest investor in Vietnam with US$4.7 billion of cumulative FDI; Taiwan with US$4.6 billion and Japan with US$2.6 billion of FDI also ranked among the biggest investors in Vietnam (*Business Times*, 1997). As Figure 14.5

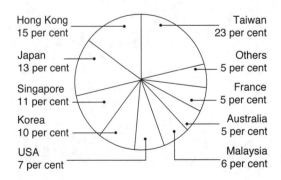

Figure 14.4
Major investors in Vietnam, 1995
Source: Asia Pacific Profiles, 1996

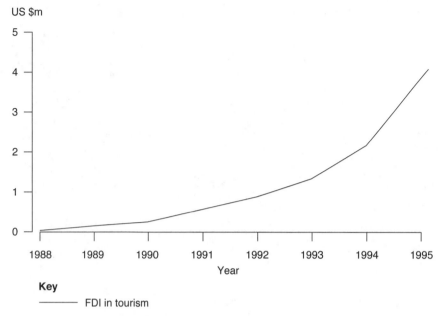

Figure 14.5 Cumulative FDI in tourism in Vietnam, 1988–95
Source: Adapted from Erramilli et al., 1997

shows, from 1988 to 1995, cumulative FDI in the tourism sector exceeded US$4 billion.

The Vietnamese government has recognized the importance of planning for and understanding tourism; indicators include the government's six-point strategy for tourism (Vu, 1997) and the first, international, policy conference on sustainable tourism in Vietnam held in Hué in May 1997. In the next section, we will examine some of the drivers behind the Vietnamese tourism industry and their positive and negative effects on development.

■ Benefits and costs from tourism

As the previous section indicated, the Vietnamese government plans to develop the tourism industry as part of a balanced economy, as a renewable resource, and in a manner that strengthens Vietnamese society (Publishing House TRE, 1991; Thanh, 1992). Consequently, the tourism industry must generate more employment than it destroys, complement local and domestic industries, and maintain the physical and cultural environments' integrity. This section elaborates on some economic and social considerations that may influence sustainable development in Vietnam in the context of tourism.

Key economic considerations

As Figure 14.6 shows, Vietnam's exports, and by implication its relative competitive strengths, emphasize primarily agriculturally intensive products – although this proportion has reduced since 1986. Figure 14.7 shows Vietnam's increasingly deteriorat-

Per cent of merchandise exports

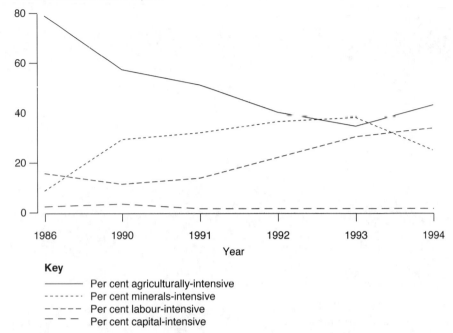

Key
—————— Per cent agriculturally-intensive
··········· Per cent minerals-intensive
− − − − Per cent labour-intensive
— — — Per cent capital-intensive

Figure 14.6 Vietnam's merchandise exports by inputs, 1986–94
Source: *Asia Pacific Profiles*, 1996

US $m

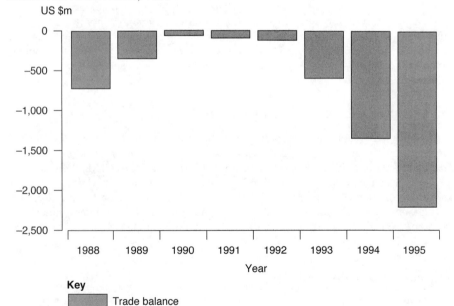

Key
[█] Trade balance

Figure 14.7 Vietnam's trade balance, 1988–95
Source: *Asia Pacific Profiles*, 1996

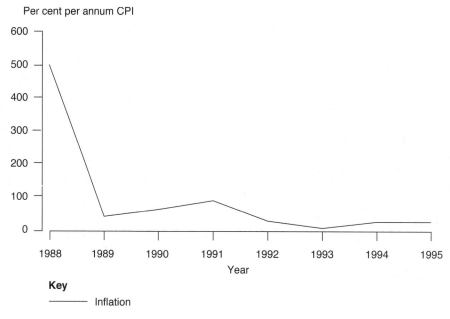

Per cent per annum CPI

Figure 14.8 Inflation in Vietnam, 1988–95
Source: Asia Pacific Profiles, 1996

ing trade balance as the country strives to develop. Some economic benefits of tourism include (Aislabie, Stanton and Tisdell, 1988; Harris and Nelson, 1993) obtaining more foreign exchange for Vietnam; extending existing infrastructure within Vietnam; developing other, inter-related, local products and resources; spreading development geographically and across industrial sectors; complementing other economic activities' products; and increasing full-time, part-time and seasonal employment, thereby helping Vietnam to achieve its goal of 5 per cent unemployment in cities and not more than 20 per cent underemployment in rural areas (*Asia Pacific Profiles*, 1996).

Conversely, through dynamic, ripple effects, tourism may also increase inflation (which, as Figure 14.8 shows, the government has increasingly controlled since 1988); increase unemployment; increase susceptibility to political changes, rumours, spread of diseases and economic fluctuations as it assumes more importance in the economy; increase unbalanced, economic development; and, increase visual pollution and destruction of resources. Astute, policy measures need to acknowledge and to shape tourism's relationships, especially with employment, renewability of resources and foreign exchange.

Employment
According to the General Statistical Office of Vietnam (GSO), in 1995, Vietnam's total, active, labour force constituted 33 million people; approximately 1.1 million Vietnamese annually enter the labour force. In 1995, the GSO classified about 20 per cent of the labour force as unemployed and about 40 per cent as underemployed;

approximately 72 per cent of the labour force worked in agriculture, and approximately 1 per cent in tourism (General Statistical Office of Vietnam).

For Vietnam, the tourism industry can create jobs in two ways (Aislabie, Stanton and Tisdell, 1988; Forsyth and Dwyer, 1994). First, tourism can create jobs immediately through employing local citizens in hotels, restaurants, and entertainment and tourist services that cater directly to tourists. Second, tourism can create jobs through multiplier effects. For example, by creating demand for local products supplied to establishments that would not have existed without tourists, tourism can create employment in related, service industries; tourism also can create jobs to serve the additional demand from otherwise unemployed, local citizens working in the industry. The tourism industry, however, also can destroy jobs, or reduce job creation, and to the extent it does, policy makers have to adjust the multiplier effects (Cohen, 1995).

First, tourism can destroy jobs when tourists visit sites primarily for their pristine beauty. These tourists usually prefer seeing old forests to logged forests, meadows to cultivated fields, and coral reefs to fishing fleets. If tourism displaces farmers, loggers, fishermen or other productively employed individuals, it destroys these individuals' jobs and those of individuals in related service and support industries.

Second, underemployment often dampens tourism's multiplier effects in developing economies such as Vietnam (Ecologically Sustainable Development Working Groups, 1991). To the extent that underemployed people in Vietnam can extend their efforts and increase their productivity within their jobs, the tourism industry's growth will fail to employ additional people in related, service industries, or in those industries and businesses indirectly affected by tourism.

Third, tourism can destroy jobs through currency-exchange value effects. If tourism increases demand for the local currency, and drives up the local currency's value in foreign exchange markets, it will drive up the price of the country's exports. The more expensive exports will encounter decreased demand in foreign markets, thereby affecting jobs in the country's export industries.

Recently, the Vietnamese Central Bank has loosened restrictions on the trading of the Vietnamese dong, indicating a possible, planned move to a managed-float system. A floating dong may help Vietnam's trade balances, and by expanding money supply, stimulate local demand and increase employment; however, it may also adversely affect employment. According to the new measures, the dong will trade for as much as 5 per cent above or below the government's guideline rate (*Asian Business Review*, 1997). Under a floating exchange rate (which Vietnam does not yet have) and with a successful tourism industry, tourists purchasing the dong can drive up its demand, thereby increasing its price. This appreciation may make Vietnamese exports more expensive in foreign markets, and imports cheaper in Vietnam. Fewer exports could reduce employment in traditional, export industries which may offset employment gains created by tourism. The fixed-currency system restricts the dong's appreciation; consequently, Vietnamese exports did not become more expensive in foreign markets and its imports did not become cheaper at home. In the short term, with a fixed exchange rate, jobs otherwise lost in export industries due to the dong's appreciation will remain and not offset jobs created by tourism. However, given Vietnam's large trade deficits, a successful tourism industry will probably not result in the dong's significant appreciation, even if the government allows the currency to float.

Resources' renewability

Managing environmentally oriented tourism facilities as renewable, rather than finite, resources poses unique challenges (Hunter and Green, 1995). In Vietnam, with some of the most verdant natural spots in the region, the tourism boom is fuelling fears of ecological damage. As Vietnam's Ministry of Agriculture and Rural Development revealed, forest areas have already reduced from 14 325 000 hectares, or 43.7 per cent of the country, in 1943 to 8 631 000 hectares, or 26.1 per cent of the country, in 1994; resort developments must surely reduce this proportion further (Pham, 1997). Consequently, environmentalists have protested against resort developments and the attendant proliferation of water and chemical-intensive golf courses in the subregion (Gill, 1996).

Other challenges revolve around co-ordinating the industry's profits with the industry's seasonality and cycles. Seasonality makes imperative a situation where tourists' facilities must earn crucial portions of revenues and profits during limited periods in the year. During peak seasons, seasonal facilities may frequently operate at or near full capacities even though they raise prices. However, during the balance of the year, seasonal facilities must continue to cover fixed costs, such as maintenance and repairs, while revenues significantly fall through reduced volume, reduced prices, or both. Consequently, managers must build seasonal facilities that can generate sufficient revenues during peak seasons to carry the facilities' debt burdens through slack seasons. Additionally, as tourist areas achieve success, property values rise. More expensive land has to attain greater returns per square metre to achieve profitability; hence, usually, the facilities' carrying capacities become denser. The resulting difficulties appear readily visible in popular, beach resorts such as Pattaya in Thailand and Bali in Indonesia. In these tourist areas emerge large, glossy hotels and heavily degraded environments; relative slums also arise as inflated land prices force local residents from old neighbourhoods, within reasonable distances of tourist areas where they work, into densely packed residential ghettos.

Table 14.1 shows the environmental degradation that can typically arise at beach resorts; the kinds of pollution vary through each zone of tourists' activities. Table 14.2 shows tourists' waste-water production in Pattaya, a beach resort near Bangkok, Thailand; it also reflects the peak seasons' relative effects on commercial and residential waste-water production. Waste-water production during Pattaya's peak seasons ranged from 1.65 to 2.29 times the average over the entire year (Manopimoke, 1992). Comparisons for the averages of the non-peak with the peak seasons would appear more dramatic. Despite developing countries' scarce resources, policy makers have to incorporate seasonal, cost considerations in tourists' facilities. Typical decisions include trade-offs between inevitable environmental degradation and absorbing waste-water or solid-waste treatment facilities' excess capacities and maintenance costs during off-peak seasons.

In 1995, approximately 72 per cent of FDI in tourism in Vietnam flowed into the construction of hotels (Erramilli et al., 1997). In 1996, Vietnam had 51 000 hotel rooms with more than half of them up to international standards; the number of hotel rooms should rise to 76 000 by the year 2000 (Xinhua News Agency, 1996). To prevent a glut, Vietnam has begun to limit FDI in hotels. The government encourages FDI in the construction of entertainment sites, large tourist villages and ecological resorts, but not large hotels. For example, the Vietnam National Administration of Tourism announced that the country needs ten or fifteen large tourist areas, each with an investment of US$200–300 million. However, the government still invites construction of hotels in targeted areas such as Hanoi, Ho Chi Minh City, Hai Phong and some others (Xinhua News Agency, 1996). Policy lessons from Bali in Indonesia indicate that by limiting hotels' and tourist resorts' sizes (though not their quality), Vietnam should expend fewer scarce resources, increase beneficial multiplier effects and retain greater control of development: small guest houses need less capital, create greater backward linkages, increase multiplier effects, and increase informal employment more than large, five-star hotels do (Wall, 1993).

Table 14.1 Environmental degradation of a beach resort

Tourists' activities	Coastal environments	Environmental problems
Accommodation and service-sector zone	Hinterland	Visual pollution, water pollution, solid waste
Transit zone	Dunes	Sand loss, shore erosion
Recreational activity zone	Beach	Solid waste, beach loss
Recreational activity zone	Sea	Marine pollution, coral reef damage

Source: Adapted from Manopimoke (1992).

Table 14.2 Waste-water production in Pattaya

| Year | 1000m^3 per day | | |
	Average occupancy	Peak occupancy	Peak/average
1986	7 557	14 282	1.90
1987	8 895	14 970	1.68
1988	11 394	18 770	1.65
1989	13 204	23 396	1.77
1990	18 661	42 800	2.29

Source: Adapted from Manopimoke (1992).

As tourism develops, the government also needs to maintain well-used infrastructure, such as roads and telephone lines. Recently, Prime Minister Vo Van Kiet of Vietnam called for mass mobilization of the country's workforce to modernize crumbling infrastructure. In an interview with the official Vietnam News Agency, the Prime Minister gave few details but analysts believe that all citizens of working age will toil for a fixed number of days each year (*Asian Business Review*, 1997). Failing, inadequate infrastructure can prove a major impediment to the tourism industry's expansion in Vietnam. However, one wonders if a non-specialized mobilized workforce can expand and renovate to acceptable, international standards, rail lines, ports, airport terminals, runways and other infrastructure important to tourism.

Foreign exchange

Tourism can either bring foreign exchange into Vietnam or leak it out of the Vietnamese economy. Ultimately, policy should encourage foreigners to spend more in Vietnam than Vietnamese spend in the foreign countries (either as tourists or to purchase essential resources and skills or to augment infrastructure). One driver behind the tourist explosion in ASEAN countries seems to revolve around the vast amounts of surplus capital generated every year from illegal activities such as prostitution and drug trafficking. For many illegal activities, laundering cash in real estate, hotels, casinos and golf courses seems to offer lucrative and safe solutions; although these illegal activities create an underground economy, they do not generate foreign exchange for Vietnam and the government must adequately regulate them.

Key social considerations

At its most sublime, tourism has the potential to broaden education; increase international peace and understanding; dissolve language, social, class, religious and racial barriers; and increase appreciation of one's own and extraneous sociocultural elements (Cohen, 1995; Harris and Nelson, 1993). However, tourism may equally increase misunderstanding, stereotyping, xenophobia, demonstration effects and social pollution; fuel the commercialization of culture and religion; and, contribute to prostitution, conflicts and crime (Pearce, 1995). Although most foreign investors in Vietnam maintain majority control (Erramilli et al., 1997), the government has begun to limit foreign ownership of hotels: all three-star, joint-venture hotels must have at least 30 per cent of Vietnamese investment (Xinhua News Agency, 1996). In addition, alarmed by the growth of the sex industry along with growing tourism, the government has launched a campaign to eradicate 'social evils' (Gill, 1996). Effective, policy measures need to acknowledge and to shape tourism's relationships, especially with sociocultural values.

Sociocultural values

Excessive and uncontrolled development of tourism tends to create cultural degradation (Hall and Jenkins, 1995; Pearce, 1995). Local populations may exhibit severe resentment towards tourists as rising property values force locals into ghettos. The local communities' cultural values may also weaken: a portion may identify with the tourists' cultural values and wish to possess the same luxuries; concentrations of tourists and wealth may tempt some locals into undesirable professions; or too many tourists may erode well-respected cultural and historical shrines. As island developments indicate, the cumulative effects of tourists' contributions to cultural degradation may assume significant proportions.

A trip by us, in May 1997, to Tu Duc's tomb, constructed between 1864 and 1867 in Hué, revealed desecration and mutilation of statues, of the stele, the largest in Vietnam, enumerating the longest-reigning Nguyen king's exploits, and pollution. Some statues, including one of an exquisite, life-size, stone horse in the Honor Courtyard, seemed to have been broken within a week of a previous visit. The tomb overflows with stories on its construction, its symbolic resonance and historical significance: for example, extinct animals' tracks, made on then setting concrete in the now overgrown paths, speak eloquently of the whirlwind construction that almost led to a labour revolt. Yet, no signs or guidebooks tell these stories. Most of Vietnam's major tombs, including another Nguyen king's, Minh Mang's, majestic and architecturally superb tomb in Hué, appear overgrown and in dire disarray; many seem to have experienced recent plundering, and all manifest grave need of renovation. Such degradation of physical, cultural and social environments will hasten tourism development's fall and disrepute. The industry will also suffer if the degradation continues to destroy the areas' physical and cultural attractions; it will spiral into disrepute if the local authorities, desperate to maintain the industry's jobs and tax revenues, allow the markets to turn towards the more undesirable niches. The long-term social and economic effects could have enormously detrimental consequences for host nations (Rajotte, 1978).

Some sociocultural issues involve policies emphasizing different types of tourist developments. As we indicated earlier, the Vietnamese Government is encouraging the development of large, resort areas (Xinhua News Agency, 1996) that often include large, hotel complexes. Large resorts offer many quality and price levels to accommodate several budgets and frequently include their own commercial complexes. Their hotels' high-business volumes, and tendencies to collect in close proximity, also ensure that the large resorts will generate a significant amount of solid and liquid wastes, as well as social and cultural pollution. Alternatively, the Vietnamese government could emphasize building smaller resorts, aimed at niche markets: at the lower end, these smaller resorts will generally have local ownership and management; and, at the higher end, will tend to emphasize smaller hotels at the super-premium level (such as the Banyan Tree). In Bali, small guest houses decreased migration stimuli, increased host–guest interactions, increased local control, and had fewer land, water, energy and waste disposal needs than five-star hotels, thereby providing a more harmonious sociocultural alternative (Wall, 1993).

In Vietnam, as Table 14.3 indicates, individual, tourism projects' sizes and complexities have increased dramatically since 1988. In 1992, the average FDI project in tourism in Vietnam approximated US$9 million; this ballooned to US$67 million in 1995 (Erramilli et al., 1997). The growth in projects' sizes correlates with growth in estimated-completion times: in 1988, the average tourism project took about eight years to complete; in 1995 projects' estimated completion times averaged twenty-seven years, indicating their complexity and scales (Erramilli et al. 1997). These large, complex projects will prove very difficult for the Vietnamese government to control and to monitor. The next section discusses possible actions that the Vietnamese government can take to promote sustainable development in the context of tourism.

■ Policy recommendations

Vietnam has some innate assets that encourage the development of its tourism industry. The country has a fascinating history, miles of beautiful beaches and scenic, interior areas, as well as a complex allure for many owing to its recent wars for independence. While largely agricultural, Vietnam enjoys over 90 per cent literacy and a significant proportion of its population has technical skills, education and training. With the Viet people forming the majority, Vietnam also includes many minority peoples and cultures, including fifty-four ethnic tribes that offer diverse, cultural events to attract tourists. Economically, however, Vietnam lacks the infrastructure and industrial development to generate the greatest possible returns on its assets. As the

Table 14.3 FDI projects in tourism in Vietnam

Year	Number of FDI projects in tourism	Tourism projects as per cent of total FDI projects
1988	5	13.5
1989	12	17.1
1990	19	17.1
1991	31	20.0
1992	35	17.9
1993	33	12.5
1994	43	12.6
1995	30	8.0

Source: Adapted from Erramilli et al. (1997)

previous sections indicated, the tourism industry's growth will bring many economic and social changes to Vietnam: the government has to monitor routinely and to evaluate these changes to prevent and to cure (Harris and Nelson, 1993; Marsh, 1993; Nelson, 1993).

FDI in tourism in Vietnam is resulting in large, tourist developments with large-scale economies and long time horizons: these patterns reflect investors' goals to maximize and to repatriate profits, as well as to achieve political and cultural influence (Haley, Low and Toh,1996). Yet, other stakeholders, such as Vietnam's indigenous people and government, may not obtain commensurate benefits and may shoulder unforeseen costs. For effective, balanced growth, the Vietnamese government has to question who is developing the tourism industry and how they are doing so. Some economic questions that need routine answers include: which stakeholders (governmental and private) receive income from tourists? Which stakeholders pay costs from tourism? How have indigenous populations benefited from the industry? What patterns of business initiation, bankruptcies and profits permeate the Vietnamese tourism industry? Some social questions also need routine answers: what kinds of jobs (quantity and quality) is tourism creating? Who is migrating in and out of the communities? What complaints do major stakeholders voice about tourism? Who are the tourists (numbers, proportion of repeat visitors, lengths of stay)?

From our analysis, we recommend that to promote sustainable development in the context of tourism, the Vietnamese government should:

- develop and implement new economic and social indicators that define national well-being as sustainable development

- design and implement public consultation techniques and processes to involve all major stakeholders in making decisions on the tourism industry

- create tourism advisory boards that involve all stakeholders

- identify support industries for tourism in which Vietnam can have a conceivable advantage – and encourage their development to ensure increased employment

- include tourism in land-use planning, especially *vis-à-vis* agricultural uses

- develop standards and regulations for economic and social impact assessments, and monitoring and auditing of existing and proposed tourist developments

- ensure that the carrying capacities of tourists' facilities reflect sustainable levels of development and are monitored and adjusted appropriately

- limit individual, tourism projects' sizes to enhance strategic control over development

- interpret sites' significance and weave them into story-telling efforts

- continue to design and to implement educational and awareness programmes that sensitize people to the issues of sustainable development in the context of tourism

- develop adequate tools and techniques to analyse tourism's effects on heritage sites and ancient monuments as an integral part of cultural and environmental impact assessment

- enforce regulation for illegal trade in historic objects and crafts, unofficial archeological research and the desecration of sacred sites.

■ References

Aislabie, C. J. (1988). Tourism issues in developing countries. In *Economics of Tourism. Case Study and Analysis* (C. A. Tisdell, C. J. Aislabie and P. J. Stanton, eds) pp. 345–78, The Institute of Industrial Economics.

Aislabie, C. J., Stanton, P. J. and Tisdell, C. A. (1988). Themes in tourism research: an overview. In *Economics of Tourism. Case Study and Analysis* (C. A. Tisdell, C. J. Aislabie and P. J. Stanton, eds) pp. 1–37, The Institute of Industrial Economics.

Asia Pacific Profiles (1996), The Australian National University, Canberra.

Asian Business Review (1997). Vietnam. The region. April, p. 13.

Business Times (1997). Go ahead for 6 in Viet industrial park. *Business Times Online*, 1 April.

Butler, R. W. (1993). Tourism – an evolutionary perspective. In *Tourism and Sustainable Development: Monitoring, Planning and Managing* (J. G. Nelson, R. Butler and G. Wall, eds) pp. 27–43, Department of Geography Series, Waterloo, Canada.

Cohen, E. (1995). Contemporary tourism – trends and challenges. In *Change in Tourism. People, Places, Processes* (R. Butler and D. Pearce, eds) pp. 12–29, Routledge.

Ecologically Sustainable Development Working Groups (1991). *Final Report – 'Tourism'*. Australian Government Publishing Service.

Erramilli, K., Luu, T., Gilbert, L. and Hooi, D. H. (1997). Foreign direct investment patterns in the Vietnamese tourism sector. Presentation at 1st International Conference on Sustainable Tourism in Vietnam, Hué, Vietnam, 22–23 May.

Forsyth, P. and Dwyer, L. (1994). Modeling tourism jobs. Occasional Paper No. 2, Commonwealth Department of Tourism, Australian Government Publishing Service.

Gill, T. (1996). Indochina tourism: Asian tigers invest with gleams in their eyes. Inter Press Service English News Wire, 04-01-1996.

Haley, G. T. and Haley, U. C. V. (1997b). Making strategic business decisions in South and SouthEast Asia. Proceedings of the 1997 International Conference on Operations and Quantitative Management, Jaipur, India.

Haley, G. T. and Tan, C. T. (1996). The black hole of South-East Asia: strategic decision making in an informational void. *Management Decision*, **34** (9), 37–48, special issue on Strategic management in the Asia Pacific.

Haley, U. C. V. (1991). Corporate contributions as managerial masques: reframing corporate contributions as strategies to influence society. *Journal of Management Studies*, **28** (5), 485–509.

Haley, U. C. V. (1996). The MBTI personality inventory and decision-making styles: identifying and managing cognitive trails in strategic decision making. In *Developing Leaders. Research and Applications in Psychological Type and Leadership Development* (C. Fitzgerald and L. K. Kirby, eds) pp. 187–223, Consulting Psychologists Press.

Haley, U. C. V. and Haley, G. T. (1997a). Investing in sustainable tourism in Vietnam: some policy implications. Presentation at 1st International Conference on Sustainable Tourism in Vietnam, Hué, Vietnam, 22–23 May.

Haley, U. C. V., Low, L. and Toh, M. H. (1996). Singapore Incorporated: reinterpreting Singapore's business environments through a corporate metaphor. *Management Decision*, **34** (9), 17–28, special issue on Strategic management in the Asia Pacific.

Hall, C. M. and Jenkins, J. M. (1995). *Tourism and Public Policy*. Routledge.

Harris, J. E. and Nelson, J. G. (1993). Monitoring tourism from a whole economy perspective: a case from Indonesia. In *Tourism and Sustainable Development: Monitoring, Planning and Managing* (J. G. Nelson, R. Butler and G. Wall, eds) pp. 179–200, Department of Geography Series, Waterloo, Canada.

Hunter, C. and Green, H. (1995). *Tourism and the Environment. A Sustainable Relationship?* Routledge.

Ihlwan, M. (1996). Tourist numbers to Vietnam jump 33 pct. *Reuters*, 01-24-1996.

Manopimoke, S. (1992). The environment in a tourist economy: a case study of Pattaya. Background report, 1992 Year end conference on Thailand's economic structure: towards balanced development?, 12–13 December, Chon Buri, Thailand.

Marsh, J. (1993). An index of tourism sustainability. In *Tourism and Sustainable Development: Monitoring, Planning and Managing* (J. G. Nelson, R. Butler and G. Wall, eds) pp. 257–8, Department of Geography Series, Waterloo, Canada.

Nelson, J. G. (1993). An introduction to tourism and sustainable development with special reference to monitoring. In *Tourism and Sustainable Development: Monitoring, Planning and Managing* (J. G. Nelson, R. Butler and G. Wall, eds) pp. 3–23, Department of Geography Series, Waterloo, Canada.

Pearce, D. (1995). Planning for tourism in the 1990s. An integrated, dynamic, multiscale approach.', In *Change in Tourism. People, Places, Processes* (R. Butler and D. Pearce, eds) pp. 229–44, Routledge.

Pham, T. L. (1997). The ecotourism in Vietnam: perspective and challenges. Presentation at 1st International Conference on Sustainable Tourism in Vietnam, Hué, Vietnam, 22–23 May.

Publishing House TRE (1991). *Vietnam – Investment and Tourism in Prospect*. Publishing House TRE.

Rajotte, F. (1978). A method for the evaluation of tourism impact in the Pacific. Monograph, Center for South Pacific Studies, University of California, Santa Cruz.

Richter, L. K. (1989). *The Politics of Tourism in Asia*, University of Hawaii Press.

Shaw, G. and Williams, A. M. (1994). *Critical Issues in Tourism. A Geographical Perspective*. Blackwell.

Stoessel, H. (1997). Impact on socioeconomic, cultural and environmental development. Presentation at 1st International Conference on Sustainable Tourism in Vietnam, Hué, Vietnam, 22–23 May.

Thanh, N. B. (1992). *Vietnam. Foreign Investment and Tourism*. Law Commission of the National Assembly, Hanoi.

Vu, T. C. (1997). Vietnam tourism master plan with environment and resource management strategy. Presentation at 1st International Conference on Sustainable Tourism in Vietnam, Hué, Vietnam, May 22–23.

Wall, G. (1993). Toward a tourism typology. In *Tourism and Sustainable Development: Monitoring, Planning and Managing* (J. G. Nelson, R. Butler and G. Wall, eds) pp. 45–58, Department of Geography Series, Waterloo, Canada.

Xinhua News Agency (1996). Vietnam to limit foreign investment in hotel sector. Xinhua News Agency, 08-24-1996.

Chapter 14.1

How the Asian crisis has affected Vietnam

■ Usha C. V. Haley ■

Vietnam has suffered from the impact of Asia's economic crisis, with a drop in foreign direct investment (FDI) and trade blunting the country's formerly healthy economic growth. In 1997, because of the Asian economic crisis, committed FDI into Vietnam fell to US$5 billion (Haley and Haley, 1998; see also Chapter 13.1). In 1996, the Vietnamese government attracted US$8.8 billion of FDI of which US$0.9 billion was to be targeted for the tourism sector (Haley and Haley, 1998)

In late 1998, data seem scanty and sometimes contradictory, but overall, they suggest far higher unemployment than the official 6 per cent rate. In the capital Hanoi, the state media reported a record unemployment rate of 8.6 per cent, the highest since economic reforms began a decade ago (Associated Press, 1998). In 1997, according to the Vietnamese labour ministry, 170 000 people nationwide, about 10 per cent of the country's workforce, lost their jobs (Marshall, 1998).

Faced by severe problems at home, companies with investments from Southeast Asia, South Korea and Taiwan have up to September 1998 fired about 30 000 workers. The Vietnamese government reported that 10 per cent of construction workers and about 30 per cent of workers in the leather, shoe, textile and garment industries have lost their jobs in 1998. To ease the unemployment pressures, the government in July approved a national unemployment program to create 5 million new jobs by 2000. The government promised to spend about US$343 million from the state budget, foreign aid and other sources to create the new jobs (Associated Press, 1998).

The Vietnamese dong's non-convertibility has protected the nation's economy a little from the region's financial crisis. Yet, the economic crisis is seeping in. The government has devalued the dong in small, steady steps, but it still has not fallen as much as neighbouring currencies. Consequently, exports have become less competitive, and labour less cheap. These economic developments, combined with the painstakingly slow reforms of Vietnam's investment climate, have prompted many foreign multinational corporations to leave (see Chapter 19.1).

■ References

Associated Press (1998). Vietnam's jobless rate rises to 7 per cent amid Asia turmoil, 26 September.

Haley, U. C. V. and Haley, G. T. (1998). Investing in sustainable tourism in Vietnam: Implications for governmental policy. *Journal of Vietnam Studies* **1** (1), 18–31.

Marshall, S. (1998). With layoffs soaring, Vietnam braces for unemployment crisis. *Wall Street Journal,* 22 September.

Part Four

World Wide Web resources on regional change

Chapter 15

The best World Wide Web resources on regional change in the Asia Pacific

■ Usha C. V. Haley ■

These carefully chosen and repeatedly checked World Wide Web (WWW) sites provide free access to additional information in English on the Asia Pacific region and countries generally, and on topics covered by individual chapters in Section B (as noted). I have not included fee-based or non-English sites.

■ General Asia Pacific regional information (Section B)

APEC:
http://www.apecsec.org.sg/
ASEANWEB:
http://www.aseansec.org/
Asia Pacific links:
http://www.stanford.edu/group/APARC/links/
Asian Continent Informational Resources:
http://www.vuw.ac.nz/~caplab/asiavl/WWWVL-AsianCont.html
Asian Studies WWW Virtual Library:
http://coombs.anu.edu.au/WWWVL-AsianStudies.html
Business Resources on the Web: International Business:
http://www.idbsu.edu/carol/BUSINTL.HTM
International Business Resources:
http://ciber.bus.msu.edu/busres.htm
International Trade Administration Information:
http://www.ita.doc.gov/
Library Congress Federal Research Division Country Studies Area Handbook Series:
http://lcweb2.loc.gov/frd/cs/cshome.html
Virtual International Business and Economic Sources:
http://libweb.uncc.edu/ref-bus/vibehome.htm
Web of Culture:
http://www.webofculture.com

▥ Political, economic and financial risks of Asia Pacific (Chapters 2 and 2.1)

Business Environment Risk Intelligence:
http://www.beri.com
Campbell Harvey Country Risk Analysis:
http://www.duke.edu/~charvey/Country_risk/couindex.htm
Political Economic Risk Consultancy:
http://www.asiarisk.com/

▥ Statistical information on Asia Pacific (Chapters 3 and 3.1)

Asian Development Bank Web:
http://www.adb.org
Bank of International Settlements:
http://www.bis.org/
IFC Emerging Markets Data Base (EMDB):
http://www.ifc.org/EMDB/EMDBHOME.HTM
IMF Dissemination Standards Bulletin Board:
http://dsbb.imf.org/index.htm
International Trade Centre:
http://www.intracen.org/
International Trade Web Resources:
http://www.fita.org/webindex.html
Resources For Economists on the Internet:
http://econwpa.wustl.edu/EconFAQ/EconFAQ.html
Statistical Data Locators:
http://www.ntu.edu.sg/library/statdata.htm
World Bank Group:
http://www.worldbank.org/

▥ Asia Pacific banks/financial information/financial crisis (Chapters 4 and 4.1)

Asian Financial Crisis:
http://www.hiid.harvard.edu/pub/other/asiacrisis.html
CNNfn the Financial Network:
http://www.cnnfn.com/news/worldbiz/asia/
Excite Asian Market Crisis:
http://nt.excite.com/topics/business/asian_markets_crisis
Financial Data and Resource Locators (including banks):
http://www.ntu.edu.sg/library/financial.htm
Infocast Limited:
http://www.infocast-mdf.com/
Morgan Stanley Capital International:
http://www.msci.com
Responding to the Crisis – The World Bank and Asia:
http://www.worldbank.org/html/extdr/asian_crisis/default.htm
What Caused Asia's Economic and Currency Crisis and its Global Contagion:
http://www.stern.nyu.edu/~nroubini/asia/AsiaHomepage.html
Yahoo! News – Business Headlines – Asian Economy:
http://headlines.yahoo.com/Full_Coverage/Business/Asian_Economy

■ European Union's investments in Asia/Innovation in Asia Pacific (Chapters 5 and 5.1)

Asia BizTech:
http://www.nikkeibp.asiabiztech.com/
Business Researcher's Interests:
http://www.brint.com/country.htm#IntAsia
EU/ASEAN Relations
http://www.ntu.edu.sg/library/eu/

■ Australian investments in Asia (Chapters 6 and 6.1)

Australian Bureau of Statistics:
http://www.statistics.gov.au
Australian Department of Foreign Affairs and Trade:
http://www.dfat.gov.au/
Australian Trade Commission Online:
http://www.austrade.gov.au/

■ Chinese culture/morality (Chapters 7 and 7.1)

Chinapoint: Profiles of China and Hong Kong:
http://www.chinapoint.com/news/business/asia/news.htm
Chinese Philosophy:
http://www-personal.monash.edu.au/~sab/index.html
East Asian Language and Thought:
http://www.human.toyogakuen-u.ac.jp/~acmuller/index.html
Internet Guide for China Studies – Philosophy and Religion:
http://sun.sino.uni-heidelberg.de/igcs/igphil.htm#confucianism

■ Asia Pacific business news/developments (Chapters 8 and 8.1)

Asia Inc.:
http://www.asia-inc.com
Asiaweek:
http://cnn.com/ASIANOW/asiaweek
The Australian:
http://www.theaustralian.com.au
Excite Asia News Report:
http://nt.excite.com/topics/world/asia_news_report
Far Eastern Economic Review Interactive Edition:
http://www.feer.com
News and Newspapers on the Internet: Singapore and Asia:
http://www.ntu.edu.sg/library/asia-n.htm#en-asia
Singapore Business Times Online:
http://business-times.asia1.com.sg/
Vietnam Business Journal:
http://www.viam.com/

■ Singaporean business environments/industrial parks (Chapters 9, 9.1, 12, 12.1, 13 and 13.1)

China–Singapore Suzhou Industrial Park:
http://www.cs-sip.com/
EDB Homepage:
http://www.sedb.com.sg
Information Technology Park – Bangalore:
http://www.asianconnect.com/itpark/
Singapore Inc Homepage:
http://www.singapore-inc.com
Singapore InfoMap:
http://www.sg
Singapore Trade Development Board's Globalink:
http://www.tdb.gov.sg/index.html
Statistics Singapore DataShop:
http://www.ecomz.com/singstat/

■ Japanese business environments (Chapters 10 and 10.1)

Global Window – Japan:
http://www.anderson.ucla.edu/research/japan/mainfrm.htm
The J-Guide:
http://fuji.stanford.edu/JGUIDE/
Japan Economic Foundation:
http://www.jef.or.jp/index.html
Japanese External Trade Organization (JETRO):
http://www.jetro.go.jp/top/index.html

■ New Zealand's business environments (Chapters 11 and 11.1)

Introduction to Investment in New Zealand:
http://www.rmmb.co.nz/investnz/Welcome.html
New Zealand: Commerce & Economy:
http://www.lincoln.ac.nz/libr/nz/nzcomm.htm
BIZinfo – National Business Information Service:
http://www.bizinfo.co.nz/

■ Vietnamese business environments (Chapters 14 and 14.1)

ANU Vietnam Virtual Library:
http://coombs.anu.edu.au/WWWVLPages/VietPages/WWWVL-Vietnam.html
Asia Gateway.com:
http://www.asiagateway.com/vietnam/index/.html
Vietnam Business – Economy News:
http://www.cgtd.com/global/vietnam.html
Vietnam Economy:
http://vneconomy.com.vn

Section C
Organizational change

Part Five

Foreign multinational corporations' strategies

Chapter 16

Skills for successful international assignments to, from and within Asia and the Pacific: implications for preparation, support and training[1]

Gary Fontaine

International assignments from anywhere, to anywhere – whether in business, diplomacy, employment, technology transfer, education, or whatever – typically involve journeys to 'strange lands'. They are encounters with new ecologies: new and diverse sociocultural, physical, and biological environments. That certainly is the case with assignments to, from, or in a region as ecologically diverse in these respects as Asia and the Pacific: from Perth to Tokyo, Chiang Mai to Auckland, Suva to Calcutta, Honolulu to Jakarta, Beijing to Los Angeles, Seoul to Kuala Lumpur, Singapore to Cebu. Those new ecologies present several significant challenges to assignment success. To the degree that assignees are able to deal effectively with these challenges, their assignments will be successful. To the degree that they are unable to meet one or more of them, their success will be less than optimal – often they fail altogether.

Thus effective preparation, support, and training for international assignments need to be based on sound research-supported models of the skills required to meet the challenges of those assignments for the assignees themselves, their families accompanying them, those managing them, and the hosts with whom they are working. Though there has been less theoretical development than desirable in the intercultural/international assignment field, there are models of varying degrees of comprehensiveness from which to choose (e.g. Barna, 1983; Black, Mendenhall and Oddou, 1991; Furnham and Bochner, 1986; Gudykunst, 1991). One such model (Fontaine, 1989; 1993a) is described here along with its implications for the skill-related objectives of assignee preparation, support and training.

---

[1] This chapter has been published previously by MCB University Press Limited: Fontaine, G (1997). Skills for successful international assignments to, from and within Asia and the Pacific: implications for preparation, support and training. *Management Decision*, **35** (8), 631–43.

■ The ecology of international assignments

As noted earlier, the ecology of an international assignment consists of the sociocultural, physical, and biological environment in which tasks on that assignment are completed. The ecology might involve, for instance, the skills, expectations and relationships of the task participants, the characteristics of the physical resources available, and the health, safety and security conditions of the assignment site, respectively. There are several characteristics common to the ecologies of most international assignments (Desatnick and Bennett, 1977; Fontaine, 1989) (see Figure 16.1). For example such assignments are usually characterized by travel to a place different from home; they typically involve special problems associated with time differences and communication; there are important cultural differences in the people and how they live and do business – particularly in how they resolve conflict, since some conflict is almost unavoidable interculturally; there is often less organizational, social and technological support than at home; and assignees usually are more responsible for providing the structure of their daily, weekly and monthly activities. These characteristics essentially define what 'international assignments' are and set them apart from their domestic counterparts.

Other ecological characteristics differentiate one international assignment from another (Fontaine, 1989). For instance, the specific character of each of the above will do so (e.g. assignment to Thai versus Australian culture with a tropical or temperate climate). In addition, assignments may differ in organizational context (e.g. business, diplomacy or foreign study); degrees of power assignees have relative to their hosts;

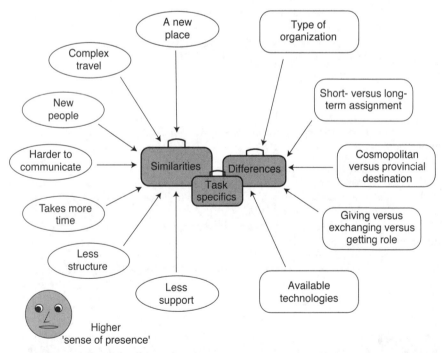

Figure 16.1 The ecology of international assignments

the standard of living they find; and the type and novelty of the communication, transportation, manufacturing, educational, or other technologies needed to get tasks done. Of particular importance can be differences between assignments in duration (e.g. three days, three months or three years), whether the destination is a cosmopolitan urban area with ample resources for support, entertainment, recreation, and so forth or a provincial one with very few; the availability of a supportive expatriate community; and a culture/language that eases or hinders entry into host country support groups.

▨ The three challenges faced on international assignments

As indicated, international assignments to anywhere, from anywhere typically involve journeys to new ecologies. Those new ecologies present assignees with at least three key challenges. To the degree these challenges are dealt with successfully, those assignments will be successful; to the degree they are not, success is much less likely.

The first challenge: coping with 'ecoshock'

Those on international assignments commonly experience a package of physiological, psychological and social symptoms including: poor perceptual-motor co-ordination and short-term illness; anxiety or nervousness, often with no specific identifiable source; depression manifested in boredom, fatigue, wishing to sleep all the time, withdrawal from others or the inability to get interested in anything; irritability and other mood changes, often over matters that otherwise might appear minor; fears of being taken advantage of, cheated or discriminated against; feelings of vulnerability to disease, accidents, crimes and failure; lowered effectiveness of thought processes particularly in judgement and decision making; and breakdowns in old social relationships and difficulty in establishing and maintaining new ones. These symptoms can directly affect the quality of their experience, their performance, and their motivation to stay. The symptoms are produced by assignees' physiological and psychological reactions to a new, diverse, or changed ecology – a reaction that I refer to as 'ecoshock'.

Ecoshock is caused by more than simply encountering a new culture and thus this first challenge requires more than coping with 'culture shock' (Adler, 1975; Furnham and Bochner, 1986; Oberg, 1958) alone. Though cultural differences are often very important on international assignments, they represent just part of the new ecology encountered. As indicated in Figure 16.1, the ecology of an international assignment presents us with new arrays of activity and experience in a number of different categories. Encountering these arrays produces at least three reactions in assignees that together contribute to the package of symptoms described above.

Initially, at least, these new arrays can produce a change in our physiological state away from normal. Assignees to, from or in Asia and the Pacific area are likely to encounter major ecological changes ranging from travel distance to climate and topography to foods and smells – particularly if they are travelling between tropical and temperate latitudes – in addition to the myriad cultural differences associated with the region. Travel dysrhythmia or 'jet lag' is one such example of a primarily physiological reaction that occurs when we are confronted with light or darkness at a biologically irregular time resulting in desynchronization of several important circadian rhythms such as those regulating eating, sleeping, body temperature, and kidney and liver functioning. We are learning more about other physiological changes produced on assignments by new characteristics of the physical environment in particular, e.g. temperature, humidity, altitude, ultraviolet rays, food, alcohol, and so forth.

The new stimulus arrays presented on international assignments also produce changes in stress levels away from those optimal for performance and satisfaction. Most commonly these are increases in stress produced by the unpredictability of ecology due to cultural and other ecological differences – we are often faced with a threat to our competence in even the most mundane tasks. Further, we are stressed if our structure of activities is removed and – we are not plants – our removal from the social networks, on which we depend for needs ranging from identity to companionship, can be the largest source of stress on an assignment.

In addition, the new ecology of an assignment often changes our attentional focus away from the specially favoured activities and experiences with which our optimal moods are associated. That is, we are deprived from what we like to think, see and do. And we are often confronted with what we don't like. For example, a long-term assignment to Adelaide can deprive us of mountain hikes that might be key to maintaining our positive moods or we may simply detest the heat, pollution and noise in the summer in Tokyo. We may be deprived of our specially favoured activities and experiences because:

- they simply are not available in the destination
- they are available but culturally inappropriate for us to participate in them
- we may be distracted from them by other experiences or activities or
- we may find that the extra burdens of surviving and getting the job done abroad place them in a lower priority.

Back home most of us do not live 'James Bond' lives. We may not normally participate in our specially favoured activities and experiences daily, weekly, or even monthly – but frequently enough for our lives to be satisfying and to 'keep going'. Consequently, on an assignment we may not notice their absence for many months – perhaps not for a year or more. Thus, long after our bodies have adjusted to physiological reactions to the new ecology and long after ambient stress levels have diminished as the destination becomes familiar and predictable, we still just 'don't like the place or the people'. There is ample evidence that serious symptoms of ecoshock are more likely after one or two years than one month (Fong and Peskin, 1969; Lefley, 1989). Mismatches between our specially favoured activities and experiences and those encountered in the destination abroad may be responsible for much of that delayed effect.

Coping with physiological reactions produced by the new ecology principally involves time and patience for the body to adjust itself. Coping with the stress produced principally involves time and patience to allow the ecology to become more predictable (though stress management skills may help). On the other hand, coping with mismatches identified above requires more than time or patience alone. Without active intervention these mismatches can produce an increasing deterioration of adjustment over time. Intervention should involve improving assignees' skills of attentional regulation and attentional flexibility.

Attentional regulation is the skill to re-establish participation in specially favoured activities and experiences by manipulating the ecology to reduce the distractions, finding situations in which their cultural inappropriateness is less a problem, or organizing time or social networks to allow participation in them sufficiently. Assignees can, for instance, learn not to be disturbed by traffic noise in the open architecture of the tropics as they listen to their favourite music or they may find a double-wall, air-conditioned apartment to reduce the noise. Joining a golf club can commit them to play golf when there may be other 'more important' things to do. Or the potential for useful 'networking' such clubs may provide can help them rationalize that it is an important thing to do.

But attentional regulation may still not be enough to maintain optimal moods abroad. One frequently hears the complaint from those abroad that 'there is nothing to do here' (and they may be talking about Hong Kong, Singapore, Los Angeles or Sydney!) or 'I'm bored and going crazy'. What they often really mean is that there is nothing familiar to do! None of their familiar specially favoured activities exist. The new ecology abroad may simply not provide the kinds of activities and experiences that assignees or their families enjoy, however well they can regulate their attention. In such cases they need to be more flexible. They need to have or to develop the skill to derive optimal moods from a broader variety of activities and experiences. This attentional flexibility allows them to adapt their preferences to those supported by the overseas ecologies they encounter. There may not be any golf courses there, but assignees may find that strolls in a wooded park or table tennis or an afternoon playing mahjong can functionally replace golf. The key here is to learn what it is about golf that provides the optimal mood – walking on freshly cut, tailored grass with its distinctive sweet smell, watching the flight of a perfectly struck ball, or companionship or the challenge of competition – and then to find it in other activities.

The second challenge: developing strategies to complete effectively tasks in a new ecology

The shared perceptions of the world and strategies for completing the tasks of living and working in it are developed at home within a familiar, relatively stable ecology. To the degree to which these shared perceptions are appropriate to – or tailored to – that ecology, the tasks are completed successfully and we are productive, successful people. If the ecology remains familiar and stable, these perceptions continue to be effective and our strategies become habits or 'our way' of doing business and we become very good at it. Most commonly this is the case at home. Because our way continues to work and because most of those around us do it that way, too, our way becomes 'the way' to do business. But we usually forget that it works – not because it is 'the' way – but only because it remains appropriate to the ecology in which it was developed. On international assignments the ecology changes and the appropriateness of 'our way' becomes problematic. International assignees are faced with the second challenge: Given that we expect and are skilled in doing tasks one way and those in the new culture expect and are skilled in doing them another, how are we going to do them well together? Do we continue to do things our way, or try to adopt 'their way', or compromise, or what?

Rather than selecting specific strategies based on doing things our way, their way, or compromising (i.e. some combination of our way and their way), dealing with this second challenge requires a more generic strategy in which these – or frequently other

– specific strategies are selected based on what is most appropriate to the new, overseas task ecology (Fontaine, 1989, 1991). This is necessary because the international character – at least – of the ecology makes it somewhat of a 'strange land' to all participants (hosts included!) and thus habitual strategies developed at home are unlikely to be optimally effective. I have labelled shared perceptions by task participants about specific strategies for completing particular tasks as microcultures. If they are tailored to the characteristics of the international assignment ecology, I have called them 'international microcultures' (IMCs). They also represent one meaning of the term 'third cultures' (Casmir, 1993). Use of them is the optimal strategy for job effectiveness on international assignments in contexts ranging from business to diplomacy. That also has been a conclusion of Hofner-Saphiere (1996) in her recent systematic study of productive, real life, global business teams in Asia and elsewhere.

To meet the second challenge of successfully getting their job done assignees to, from, or in Asia and the Pacific need to develop IMCs accommodated to the full range of relevant ecological characteristics of each assignment task. Many of the most significant characteristics are cultural. 'Western' cultures such as Australia, New Zealand, the UK, Canada and the USA place primary value on the individual; while Asian cultures place relatively more value on the relationship or some form of collective (Triandis, 1995). Cultures such as Australia, New Zealand, Canada and the USA expect people to express their opinions honestly, i.e. to convey them accurately to others, while more collectivist cultures place a greater emphasis on maintaining harmony and face. In many cultures (particularly individualistic ones like the USA) the decision to do business is based primarily on the quality of the deal; while in others (particularly more collectivist ones like China, Japan or the Philippines) the decision is based more on the long-term quality of the relationship envisaged. In high-power-distance cultures (the Philippines, India, Hong Kong, or Singapore) managers make decisions and subordinates do not expect, are not trained, not paid, and usually do not appreciate being asked to participate; in low-power-distance cultures (Australia, New Zealand, North America) responsibility for decisions is more distributed (Hofstede, 1984). Some cultures (notably Japan, with the UK and USA somewhat less so) are high in work centrality (or a related dimension Hofstede, 1984, calls 'masculinity') in which an employee's work is the centre of his or her life; cultures lower in work centrality distribute their allegiance more to include family, friends, community activities and so forth outside the job. In cultures such as the USA and Japan people generally prefer to structure activities mono-chronically or 'one at a time;' others are more polychronic (the Philippines, Indonesia, Malaysia, India), preferring to engage in several topics or activities interwoven over time (Dodd, 1991; Hall, 1981).

Because confrontation with these and other important cultural differences on assignments to, from and in Asia and the Pacific area is unavoidable, conflicts in relationships essential to business success are almost inevitable. IMCs must have effective means of resolving the conflict that occurs in them and thus 'salvaging' the relationships before they 'sink' the task and the assignment. But unfortunately – almost unfairly – there are major cultural differences in the strategies and skills to do that (Fontaine, 1990). In more individualistic, direct and low-context cultures (Australia, New Zealand, USA) if a person has a complaint against another, the burden of explicating that complaint is on the offended person. He or she may not do it, but the burden is on them. Typically the complaint is made verbally and the participants 'talk about it' – the earlier the better (before the conflict festers or worsens!). If they have trouble talking about it, there are workshops or books to help them 'communicate'. 'Talking about it' usually means analysing it and developing solutions. The offender, if motivated, then alters his or her behaviour and often the conflict is resolved. It does not by any means always work, but it is the expected strategy. In more collectivist, high-context cultures such as those in Asia, the burden of 'explicating' the complaint is on the offender. The offended person will indicate that there is a complaint – he or she will be late for work, pout, fail to turn in a report, etc. – but the expectation is that the offender will then figure out what the complaint is. And in more role-conscious, collectivist cultures, people are generally pretty good at figuring out what they have done – in terms of violating role expectations. The offender, if motivated, often will then alter his or her behaviour and the conflict is resolved. It does not always work in these cultures either. The key here is that the complaint itself never needs to be talked about, or even referred to, in any way! In fact, to do so is seen as only further disrupting relationship harmony. If the complaint is verbalized it's more likely to be as part of the ending stage of the relationship – when all else has failed.

Problems occur when those with different expectations for how to resolve conflict come together in a task group. And it is most importantly a problem of skills. Assignees trained in Western cultures simply do not normally have the skills to recognize how they have violated the role expectations of those from a more collectivist culture. Should they recognize that there is a complaint, they quickly attempt to talk about it openly – asking 'what's wrong?' This is read by the offended host, at best, as a further disruption of the relationship or, at worst, as indicative of its end! And assignees from Asian cultures simply are not raised to be comfortable with the kind of intensive, direct, one-on-one, 'honest' verbal exchanges so common in the early stage of conflict resolution in Western cultures. As a consequence, it is not unusual for problems produced by differences in conflict resolution strategies, to be a bigger threat to the business relationship than whatever initially produced the conflict! Thus, again, building IMCs that can 'salvage' business relationships, without exacerbating the conflict in them, is a critical skill on international assignments in Asia and the Pacific area, as well as elsewhere.

An IMC is not usually just some mixture of our way or their way to do a particular task. They would only comprise an IMC if they were ecologically appropriate. But such can be the case, as shown in the following illustration.

> Royal Nepal Airlines Corporation (RNAC) developed a cooperative agreement with an airline from a European country in which the latter would provide technical, marketing, operations, and publicity assistance. A Project Chief was assigned to RNAC who coordinated three other compatriots as advisors to three RNAC departments. The general strategy of the European airline was to help RNAC do it 'our way'. In spite of initial optimism by both parties, however, the agreement was eventually terminated. With one exception there had been no significant improvement in the performance of any unit. That exception was the Training Section of the Maintenance Department. Their advisor was responsible for implementing a structure based on that of his own airline and specified in a detailed manual. In that lone unit, however, the 'our way' strategy worked. In terms of the above discussion it is revealing to see why. Most units in RNAC were largely staffed by long-time company personnel who were resistant to outside input. Their resistance was further hardened by what they saw as an arrogant 'tone' to the way the input was provided – the advisors apparently treated the Nepalese personnel rather like inexperienced 'students' than 'professionals' seeking assistance. The Training Section, uniquely, was staffed by newly-hired engineers who had recently completed

their university education. They had yet to develop a unit 'culture', were anxious for a structure that would provide them with some explicit programme direction, and wanted to see themselves in a meaningful role in the company that would facilitate career growth. The very detailed manual for their unit, provided by their advisor, defining an ambitious role for training was just what they were looking for. They adopted it energetically, overlooking that 'tone' with which it was provided.

In this case 'our way' worked, but not because it was the effective strategy for delivering assistance in the cooperative agreement (in all but the Training Section it failed!). It worked because in this one unit it was responsive – apparently fortuitously – to the ecology (Bhawuk, 1988).

More commonly IMCs require inclusion of perceptions for doing tasks that extend beyond simply 'ours' or 'theirs' to include a broader range of 'others' as might be appropriate to the task ecologies. This is seen in the following illustrations:

An American-based food products company in the Philippines was having serious problems associated with the sabotage of production equipment by workers. The largely expat[riate] American management staff correctly assumed that the sabotage reflected worker complaints. Their strategy for discovering the specifics of the complaints was to hold several management-worker meetings promoted for that purpose and to install several 'complaint boxes' at various locations around the plant – common American practices.

Unfortunately the meetings were poorly attended and for over six-months they didn't receive a single complaint in the boxes (and a couple of the boxes were sabotaged as well!). The managers 'our way' strategy was not working. But they didn't have the knowledge of the workers' culture, generally, or job expectations, in particular, to figure-out the basis of the complaint and an appropriate response, as Filipino managers probably would have been able to do. Thus the American managers didn't have the skill to do it their way.

The solution occurred sometime later on the advice of a consultant hired for other purposes. He suggested what basically amounted to hiring informants that would work in production, yet be tasked in part with reporting worker complaints to the management. It worked. The workers – who were, of course, perfectly aware of what was going on with the 'spies' – were happy with the arrangement and its effectiveness in getting their complaints across. The managers were happy because they now understood the complaints, could respond to some of them, and the sabotage disappeared.

The complaint resolution strategy constituted an IMC accommodated to that particular task in that particular company at that particular time. It is not necessarily recommended for anyone else:

Earlier in my own career I was faced with providing in-house communication seminars to middle management personnel in a traditional, Chinese family-owned company in Hong Kong. My typical strategy in presenting such seminars – my 'our way' – was to use a very interactive, participatory style in which much of the communication behavior examined is elicited from seminar participants during the session. From my previous experience, however, I knew that the participants would be more familiar with a formal, lecture format and probably be uncomfortable with an interactive one (particularly in English rather than Cantonese). I was tempted, then, to try do it their way.

But there were other ecological characteristics to be considered. First, I was not particularly effective at doing it their way: I was (then!) too young to receive the ascribed status needed to give a lecture legitimacy in Chinese culture. I needed to achieve that legitimacy by demonstrating my competence to them. Second, I knew that often Chinese management personnel – aware of, but unexposed to, a growing emphasis on participation – are sometimes anxious to try it out, away from the office, in the less threatening ecology presented by a Western trainer in a hotel meeting room. Finally, the latter motivation notwithstanding, I expected that they would be reticent to try it out using English in front of the other participants. So the strategy I selected was one more tailored to the actual ecology confronted in that particular seminar. I integrated lectures on key issues in English with participatory small group sessions in which the language used was Cantonese. I was able to place a few participants found to have American educational backgrounds in different work groups as facilitators. I demonstrated my competence by illustrating issues that participants had actually experienced in these groups. They had the opportunity to try out a more participatory style in their own language and in non-threatening small groups. The strategy was to develop an IMC. The outcome was, I believe, a successful seminar.

An IMC – like any microculture – is associated with a particular occurrence of a task and will differ from that associated with other occurrences of that type of task as the task ecology differs. An IMC, in other words, is not a generalized strategy applied to many occurrences of a task. For example, the IMC used to negotiate a particular 'petroleum rights' treaty will nearly always differ from that used with other 'petroleum rights' treaties negotiated at other times and with other participants.

Because an IMC is tailored to a particular task ecology, participant perceptions and behaviours in it are not necessarily consistent with those across this and other types of tasks at the level of national or even organizational culture. This explains the common observation that our foreign hosts do not behave as expected, given their organizational or national culture, and is why appreciation of the task ecology of international assignments is so critical. That ecology may differ significantly from the national or organizational ecologies and associated cultures to which our expectations of their behaviour are tied. In diplomacy for instance, Kimmel (1989) notes that relying on the stereotypic 'national negotiating styles' commonly taught to foreign service personnel 'may be of interest to those studying national images, but ... are likely to blind negotiators to important nuances and changes in the other actor's negotiating behaviour and make them prisoners of their own images'. He explicitly stresses the need to develop IMCs as a basis for effective negotiation.

To some degree, assignees can prepare in advance of an assignment for the culture they will encounter through some form of cross-cultural training. However, the development and use of IMCs typically requires knowledge of the task ecology abroad at a level of detail far in excess of what is available in advance. Assignees may need to know, for instance, the task objectives and their importance from all participants' perspectives, details of the facility in which the task takes place and the resources available, the participants' personalities, motives, skills, relationships with each other, and so forth. To a significant degree, assignees must assess what is necessary in terms of these or other characteristics, identify a broad range of possible options for dealing with them, and select the most desirable options to constitute an IMC 'on the spot'.

The key skill in doing it 'on the spot' involves effective use of assignees' sense of presence – the experience we all commonly have on an international assignment in which we have a heightened awareness of everything around us (see again Figure 16.1). It is the international business equivalent of 'street smarts'. If you ask people in, or returning from, an international assignment what the experiences are like – especially what differentiates them from those at home – they report a sense of 'immediacy', a sense of 'involvement', 'participation', of being active 'out in the world'; a 'total awareness' of everything around them; everything seems very 'real and vivid' and they feel 'very much alive'; and they report that they tend to think and act in 'new and innovative ways' (Fontaine, 1993b). One skill assignees need to meet the second challenge is to use that sense of presence to establish the necessary, possible and desirable – as described above – required for the development of IMCs essential for the tasks required to do their job.

Use of a sense of presence is certainly not the only skill associated with IMC development. Because IMCs, like any culture, involve shared perceptions in task relationships, assignees need social skills to build relationships and maintain them long enough for IMCs to develop. Because IMCs are most commonly negotiated among diverse members, communication skills – particularly those critical to intercultural communication – are needed. The latter include ritual exchange, perspective sharing, context matching, agenda matching and language skills. Together with use of a sense of presence, they represent the central skills in a 'package' necessary for the second challenge. A key to developing IMCs is recognizing ecological parallels across different types of tasks (e.g., negotiation versus interview) and responding to those parallels in selecting a strategy, rather than selecting it based solely on the type of task and the strategy typically used with that type of task in the past. That is, assignees must base IMCs on the ecological characteristics of the task, not the type of task alone. While the type of task certainly is an important characteristic of the task ecology, it is by no means the only important one. Those who are good at putting together IMCs are those who are good at recognizing the parallels between a current task ecology and those ecologies in the past with which they have been involved, or about which they otherwise have adequate information.

We need much more research, however, on the process by which IMCs are developed. Current research by Westney (1996) is promising in this regard. She suggests that a key role in this 'knowledge creation' process – i.e. what works and does not work in new ecologies – is increasingly being played by short-term international assignees. These are personnel assigned abroad for periods generally less than six months and selected for their professional knowledge (e.g. engineering, accounting, product development, etc.) rather than international management expertise. They may not be assigned to a specific 'job' *per se*, but rather are tasked with visiting foreign subsidiaries, joint ventures, or partners to learn how they operate. They carry the knowledge acquired back home or to other sites abroad. The knowledge is often location-specific information about a working IMC and the ecological characteristics to which it is accommodated. Often there can be ecological similarities or analogies elsewhere to which this specific knowledge can be usefully applied. Knowledge can also be learned about the necessity of accommodating strategies to ecologies and it can be applied back home or in any other international site. That is, these assignees bring back new tools and the knowledge of when to apply them!

■ The third challenge: maintaining the motivation to continue

The third challenge involves the motivation to continue dealing with the first two challenges in the face of almost inevitable ecoshock and performance difficulties, fatigue and frustration. This may continue to be challenging long after much of the stress produced by the unfamiliar ecology is gone, but the depression, mood changes, irritability, poor performance and so forth produced by changes in attentional focus remain and grow. Maintaining motivation is particularly critical on international assignments because the development and use of IMCs to meet the second challenge may take much more time and effort than relying on the habitual 'our ways' of home. IMCs may be new and require training or practice; their occurrence may be more fortuitous, than planned; and they may require a lot of trial and error. Assignees need to be motivated to 'stick with it' long enough for luck or trial and error to have a chance!

There is a vast range of motives that sends people abroad, keeps them there, and lures them back abroad again. Some of these motives are more extrinsic in nature, i.e. the assignment provides some benefit apart from the international character of the ecology itself (Black, Mendenhall and Oddou, 1991). These might include the 'official' reason for the assignment ('it's part of the job'), or the money, promotion opportunities, or acquisition of new knowledge or skills. Other motives might be more intrinsic, i.e. the benefit is inherent in the international character of the assignment. These might include the business activity itself, sightseeing, trying new foods, exploring or adventuring, the special treatment and status often received abroad, or the heightened experience of the sense of presence mentioned earlier.

Recent work by myself and colleagues has identified six factors – or clusters – of reasons given by assignees for why they go abroad in contexts such as business and foreign study. In a sense each factor constitutes a type of traveller, although, of course, any given assignee will usually be characterized by more than one of these types. Each type is described below in terms of the reasons that have been found to be included in that factor:

- *A job-motivated traveller.* Job-motivated travellers go abroad for career benefits such as higher salaries, promotions, training, education, or business or professional contacts; to teach or to help others as part of their job; for the opportunities to apply their knowledge or skills; or simply because it is required by their employer. In all cases the reason has something to do with the performance of their job.

- *A rest and recreational traveller.* Recreational travellers go abroad for the entertainment, sports, hobbies or recreational activities; for rest, relaxation, or emotional release; or because they like flying in the planes, staying in the hotels, or eating in the restaurants. Keep in mind that these are assignees with some job or other career-related activity abroad. They are not just taking a vacation! That reminder applies to the following types as well.

- *An explorer.* Explorers go abroad to see and experience different peoples – their appearance, values, life-styles and cultures; to visit different places – climates, scenaries, cities or countrysides; for the new experiences it provides – the novelty and adventure; to learn more about the world and, interestingly, more about themselves.

- *A presence seeker.* Presence seekers go abroad because when abroad their experiences are real and vivid; they seem aware of everything happening around them every minute; and they seem to think or act in new ways. That is, presence seekers go abroad for the more frequent or heightened sense of presence they experience there; they go abroad because that's where they feel most alive! As noted earlier, the novel ecology that assignees typically encounter abroad produces a sense of presence and thus often supports this motivation.

- *A collector.* Collectors concentrate on bringing things back home. These 'things' include material goods such as clothes, paintings or artefacts, but they also includes slides and stories of adventures, friendships, romances and sexual experiences to bring home to 'show and tell' to others or simply add to their life's 'treasure chest'. They acquire the 'stuff ' of being abroad – material goods, relationships and activities.

- *A family traveller.* Family travellers go abroad to be with a family member or members who are also abroad or to accompany friends or co-workers. They – unlike all the others – might really want to stay at home. They go abroad, however, to fulfil a relationship obligation or because they do not want to be left at home.

As noted above, in reality any given assignee is not usually just one type of traveller, but rather is some combination of types. That combination constitutes his or her motivational profile. Some assignees may be primarily rest and recreational, explorer, presence-seeking travellers. Others may be more collectors or job motivated. And, of course, any given assignee's motivational profile may well change over time: The package of motivations that brought them abroad may not be the same as the one that keeps them there, nor the one that brings them back abroad again.

There is, however, evidence that motivational profiles are remarkably similar for assignees quite diverse in job context (e.g. business or foreign study), age, and nationality (Fontaine, 1993c). Recent data indicate that the motivational profile of the average international assignee is strongest in explorer, rest and recreation, and presence-seeking. While job-oriented issues are certainly important to these assignees, they do not appear to be the ones most significant in assignees' self-reports of why they go abroad on assignments.

The activities and experiences actually encountered abroad may deviate substantially from those that assignees expect to encounter, value, and on which their motivation to go on the assignment is based. When there is a mismatch between an assignee's motivational profile and the activities and experiences actually encountered, ecoshock with its associated physiological, psychological, and social consequences can occur. And there frequently are such mismatches as indicated, for example, by Everett and Stening's (1989) research on Japanese assignees. As we saw earlier with respect to analogous mismatches between specially favoured activities and experiences and those encountered abroad, without active intervention the mismatches between the motivation to go abroad and the activities and experiences encountered is likely to continue to erode the motivation to stay.

Thus, maintaining motivation is a critical challenge that must be dealt with for a successful international assignment. That notwithstanding, we know less about this challenge than the other two. Much more research is needed into not so much the motivational profiles of the average assignee in Asia and the Pacific, but the most successful assignees. Likewise, much more research is needed on the skills associated with maintaining motivation. It would seem apparent, however, that these skills would include at least the following:

• The skill to pick the 'right' assignment based on the match between the assignee's motivational profile and the assignment ecology. Mismatches between the two can affect not only the degree of ecoshock experienced, but the motivation to continue the assignment. Careful use of both organizational screening and assignee self-selection is thus implied. There are, of course, many contexts in which such assignment choice is unavailable. In those cases the following skills also become important.

• The skill to adapt an assignee's motivational profile to the assignment ecology, i.e. we do not adapt the ecology, we adapt the assignee. From a behavioural science point of view that certainly is a challenge in itself! At least in the short term. However, there is at least anecdotal evidence that many 'old hands' at international assignments are able to do just that: They are able to find new reasons to go to or be where they must go or are! They may do this either by finding new motives more compatible with the assignment ecology or, perhaps, rekindling older motives more 'dormant' in their profiles. The following skills may help as well in this regard.

• Skills of attentional regulation and flexibility can help assignees either find innovative ways to satisfy the package of motives they brought with them, or to expand that package to include motives better supported by the ecology they encounter – they will need to either find times and places to make friends in the host culture (if that proves to be a frustrated motive for going there) or take up shell collecting (if that is more easily available)! For many assignees specially favoured activities and experiences centre on family, friends and other social relationships. In such cases, attentional regulation and flexibility can be social skills for maintaining existing social relationships and developing new ones. Several such skills are described in the following section. These can be necessary so that an assignee is not driven to return home early because of dissatisfactions with the impact of the assignment on their ongoing relationships. New relationships can also provide new reasons or motives for staying!

This list of skills is simply suggestive; it most likely is not exhaustive. But these or other skills to maintain the motivation to continue to try on an international assignment may be the most pivotal skills of all to assignment success – and the longer the assignment the more pivotal they become!

■ Skills for developing and maintaining social support on an assignment

The initial motive that brought an assignee abroad (e.g. getting a promotion or escaping from home) may be insufficient to keep him or her there long enough to deal successfully with the first two challenges. Useful organizational intervention can include supporting existing social support groups (e.g. the family, co-workers) so that an assignee is not motivated to return home early because of relationship problems or the participants' dissatisfactions, and enmeshing the assignee in new social groups (Briody and Chrisman, 1991) from which new motives to remain can evolve, stemming from rewarding group activities, relationships with its members or other benefits of participation. Assignees can also be screened for, or trained in, the social skills necessary to develop and maintain support groups abroad (Adelman, 1988; Fontaine, 1996). Some of the more important of these skills are described below.

Identifying the social support provided at home

This skill involves identifying the range of social support needs being provided for at home. The need to identify personal support requirements by examining the functions of support groups at home may seem obvious but, in my experience, few assignees have ever thought much about it. As is true of much else in our lives, we often don't give much thought to, or recognize the importance of, social support until it is disrupted or gone! Many people don't fully appreciate the importance of social support in their lives until they find themselves on an international assignment.

Identifying social support needs on the assignment

This skill involves predicting social support needs on the assignment based on the previous examination of needs at home. Rarely are all of assignees' support groups relocated with them – they may be accompanied by their family, perhaps by some of their workmates, probably not by their friends or other support groups (e.g. recreational, hobby or self-help groups to which they may belong). Based on an assessment of which groups are accompanying them, they can identify what needs will go unfilled on their assignment, and consequently what their support requirements will be. Assignees need to learn that on longer-term assignments the chances of home-country support groups (those not accompanying the assignee abroad) continuing to play important support needs are considerably diminished. Assignees must recognize that the effectiveness of mediated support over time and distance is usually overestimated. Most needs occur immediately and locally – and support is most effective if immediate and local as well.

Identifying social support opportunities available on the assignment

This is essentially an exploring or scouting skill (Steele, 1980) involving an identification of the support groups accompanying assignees (e.g. family members or workmates), what the organization provides in terms of home culture (those from the home culture resident abroad) and host culture (those from the destination culture) personnel and dependants, and what is available in the wider community in terms of both home and host culture groups (e.g. an expatriate community or support groups and activities sponsored by the host community). It is often necessary to identify a broad range of support options abroad because: assignees may require more support than at home; find their success rate in getting into groups is lower; or find that the groups encountered abroad may function quite differently in terms of support than similar groups back home (see below).

Matching unfilled needs with available support

This is probably the key social support skill on international assignments. It requires assignees to know their support needs and to know what opportunities are available. But, most importantly, it requires making the match. On the one hand, making the match should be based on an understanding of the resource requirements of the needs (e.g. physiological, psychological, social) and the resources provided by available support groups. Then needs and groups are matched on resources which the group provides, rather than on the type of group. It is important for assignees to understand that the same type of group abroad may not provide the same resources provided at home. At home, a university may provide just the kinds of recreational opportunities required for optimal moods; abroad, the university may provide for no recreation at all. At home, a church may provide baby-sitting services; abroad, it may provide only religion. At home, bars might be a good place to meet the opposite sex; abroad, that may only be the case if you are willing to pay for meeting them. Making the match may well involve matching different groups to the same need (assignees may meet the opposite sex in church – or a tennis club – instead). One reason why successful assignees often appear to live very different life-styles overseas is that they find they require very different support groups to fill their needs.

Maintaining existing relationships

Often, of course, 'making the match' produces the recognition that at least some social support needs require the maintenance of ongoing social relationships. Typically these are with home-country and home-culture groups. As described earlier, maintenance of the former is made more problematic over time by distance and communication barriers and maintenance of the latter is made difficult since they too are usually experiencing ecoshock. Further, for a variety of reasons, assignees involved in international lives often find themselves in intercultural relationships – marriages or work groups. These relationships often have special challenges of their own to successful maintenance (Fontaine, 1990; Romano, 1988). A key to maintaining any relationship during times of change – or intercultural relationships any time – is recognizing differences in perception (attitudes, values, etc.) that may cause relationship problems and developing consensual solutions to those problems. Again, the quality and stability of a relationship is not based solely on the number of its problems, but significantly on the partners' ability to solve them (e.g. Ting-Toomey, 1994).

Developing, maintaining and dissolving new relationships

'Making the match' can often involve developing, maintaining, and – when necessary – dissolving relationships with new support groups. Usually these are home-culture groups at work or in an expatriate community and/or host-culture groups at work or in the wider host culture. The selection of home-culture versus host-culture groups is heavily dependent on ecological characteristics of the assignment (e.g. is there an available expatriate community or are there mechanisms for easing entry into host-culture groups?) There can also be important concerns about the impact of each on adjustment. While emphasis on building relationships with home-culture groups might be most advisable for short term assignments, in the longer term, over-reliance on such groups may hinder the adjustment to the new culture required for a successful, long-term assignment (Kim, 1987).

An important skill in establishing relationships abroad is being able to put oneself 'in the right place at the right time'. Assignees need to know where the behaviour settings are that provide opportunities to meet relevant others and develop relationships (e.g. meetings of professional societies, cocktail parties, sports' clubs, dinners, etc.). These settings vary considerably from culture to culture and the skill to find them is usually based more on clever planning than spontaneity. Further, assignees need to know how to access the settings (e.g. get invitations or tickets). A prerequisite to initiating inter-actions, once in the appropriate behaviour settings, is having sufficiently high self-confidence (Coopersmith, 1967) – at a time when it is often eroded by ecoshock. Some assignees seem to be skilled at quickly personalizing a place and having a sense of belonging that bolsters their confidence. This is particularly important for those who must relocate frequently to very different ecologies.

Once contacts have been made and interaction initiated, other skills are needed to maintain the relationships. Internationally, home-culture support groups may tolerate a lot of deviance because they need all the people they can get. It takes lots of expatri-ates to put on a golf tournament. They'll forgive assignees for anything – probably even cheating – as long as they participate! Host-culture groups can be less forgiving. They may not need assignees at all and with an assignee's first mistake may dissolve back into the city!

Finally, assignees need to remember that their assignment will end (hopefully suc-cessfully). They will have to say 'goodbye'. Thus, they need to have relationship dis-solution (or transition) skills as well. How they say 'goodbye' can be important. It will affect how those in the expatriate community and in the host culture remember the assignee. International communities are small and mobile – assignees may run into the people elsewhere and need them again. And how assignees say 'goodbye' can also impact on how those left behind – particularly host-culture groups – treat the next person that comes along on assignment to that destination.

▓ Preparation, support and training for international assignments

As noted earlier, preparation, support and training for personnel on assignments to, from and in Asia and the Pacific – rather than being a rather inconsistent and haphaz-ard collection of objectives, programmes and techniques – need to be focused on a sound model of the challenges and skills required for success on those assignments. And they need to do so in terms of the specific assignment ecology in which assignees find themselves. One such model has been presented here. The skills identified by this model are summarized in Figure 16.2. There are a variety of programmes through which human resource managers can help assure that their assignees to, from or in Asia and the Pacific area have those skills:

- Screening and self-selection programmes for prospective assignees based on pos-session of the skills identified by this or other models of the challenges of interna-tional assignments to the region – or at least the knowledge of and willingness to learn those skills.

- Orientation programmes to provide information about all aspects of the assignment ecology, particularly about the cultural and other ecological characteristics relevant to the development of IMCs. Such programmes can also provide information about the challenges they will face and the necessity to meet them.

- Organizational and social support programmes for assignees and their families with a particular concern on buffering ecoshock and facilitating IMC development.

Skills for coping with ecoshock

Attentional regulation

Skills for maintaining motivation

Patience

Attentional flexibility

Identifying motivation profile-destination ecology match

Broadening stress-coping tool kit

Preparation, support and training for successful international assignment

Identifying the social support provided at home

Use of a sense of presence to build IMCs

Identifying social support needs abroad

Communication skills in ritual exchange, perspective sharing and language, context and agenda matching

Identifying social support opportunities abroad

Matching unfilled needs with available support

Skills for dealing with diversity

Social skills–particularly in conflict resolution

Skills for developing and maintaining social support

Figure 16.2 Skills for success abroad that need to be addressed in preparation, support and training

- Training programmes for assignees, their families, their managers, and their hosts designed to help assignees acquire the skills identified throughout this chapter – and elsewhere – to cope with ecoshock, develop IMCs, and maintain motivation.

Assistance to managers in developing such programmes tailored specifically to needs in Asia and the Pacific area is available from a growing range of experienced professionals and much of their knowledge is presented in a recent state-of-the-art handbook on the subject (Landis and Bhagat, 1996). In my experience, brief two- or three-hour orientations that simply alert assignees to the challenges and relevant skills can be useful – then they are more likely to recognize and deal with them. But we can usually do much more. For instance, two-day training seminars for personnel (at the executive, manager or staff levels) with a one-day programme for spouses is in appropriate time and expense parameters for most companies. These seminars allow for greater elaboration of the challenges, more detailed tailoring to assignment and task ecologies, and inclusion of techniques for guiding participants in developing or improving relevant skills. A typical outline for such a programme would include:

- an overview of the basics in terms of the requirements for doing business successfully in Asia and the Pacific area

- the ecology of the specific destination

- the challenges to success on their assignment

  – skills for coping with ecoshock

  – skills for effectively completing tasks in a new ecology

  – skills for maintaining motivation

- dealing effectively with intercultural conflict in the workplace

- developing and maintaining social support; techniques for bringing it all 'back home' to the job and a plan to continue improving necessary skills over the course of an assignment

- access to a package of resources to which they can continue to refer over the course of their assignment and career. This is increasingly easy with the expansion of access to the Internet and WWW.

The seminar objectives of such a programme come to fruition, of course, not with the seminar's conclusion, but only to the degree the participants take the identified challenges and skills back to their job. Back in their job they must devote the same time and effort to the development of these skills as they would to any other skills more traditionally deemed essential to their careers.

■ References

Adelman, M. B. (1988). Cross-cultural adjustment: a theoretical perspective on social support. *International Journal of Intercultural Relations*, **12** (3), 183–204.

Adler, P. S. (1975). The transitional experience: an alternative view of culture shock. *Journal of Humanistic Psychology*, **15** (4), 13–23.

Barna, L. M. (1983). The stress factor in intercultural relations. In *Handbook of Intercultural Training* (D. Landis and R. W. Brislin, eds), vol. 2, Pergamon.

Bhawuk, D. P. S. (1988). 'Incharge', Technical facility, RNAC. Presentation at the East-West Center, Honolulu.

Black, J. S., Mendenhall, M. and Oddou, G. (1991). Towards a comprehensive model of international adjustment: an integration of multiple theoretical perspectives. *Academy of Management Review*, **16**, 291–317.

Briody, E. K. and Chrisman, J. B. (1991). Cultural adaptation to overseas assignments. *Human Organization*, **50** (3), 264–82.

Casmir, F. L. (1993). Third culture building: a paradigm shift for international and intercultural communication. In *Communication Yearbook 16* (S. A. Deetz, ed.) pp. 407–28, Sage.

Coopersmith, S. (1967). *Antecedents of Self-esteem*. Freeman.

Desatnick, R. L. and Bennett, M. L. (1977). *Human Resource Management in the Multinational Company*. Nichols.

Dodd, C. H. (1991). *Dynamics of Intercultural Communication*. Wm. C. Brown.

Everett, J. E. and Stening, B. W. (1989). The overseas assignment preferences of Japanese managers. *Environment and Behavior*, **21** (2), 151–74.

Fong, S. L. M. and Peskin, H. (1969). Sex-role strain and personality adjustment of China-born students in America. *Journal of Abnormal Psychology*, **74**, 563–7.

Fontaine, G. (1989). *Managing International Assignments: The Strategy for Success*.

Prentice-Hall.

Fontaine, G. (1990). Cultural diversity in intimate relationships. In *Intimates in Conflict* (D. Cahn, ed.) pp. 209–24, Earlbaum.

Fontaine, G. (1991). Managing intercultural effectiveness. *Australian Journal of Communication*, **18** (1), 52–65.

Fontaine, G. (1993a). Training for the three key challenges encountered on all international assignments. *Leadership and Organization Journal*, **14** (3), 8–14.

Fontaine, G. (1993b). The experience of a sense of presence in intercultural and international encounters. *Presence: Teleoperators and Virtual Environments*, **1** (4), 1–9.

Fontaine, G. (1993c). Motivational factors of international travellers. *Psychological Reports*, **72**, 1106.

Fontaine, G. (1996). Social support and the challenges of international assignments: implications for training. In *Handbook of Intercultural Training* (D. Landis and R. Bhagat, eds) 2nd edn, Sage.

Furnham, A. and Bochner, S. (1986). *Culture Shock: Psychological Reactions to Unfamiliar Environments.* Methuen.

Gudykunst, W. B. (1991). *Bridging Differences.* Sage.

Hall, E. T. (1981). *Beyond Culture.* Anchor Press.

Hofner-Saphiere, D. M. (1996). Productive behaviours of global business teams. *International Journal of Intercultural Relations*, **20** (2), 227–59.

Hofstede, G. (1984). *Culture's Consequences: International Differences in Work-related Values.* Sage.

Kim, Y. Y. (1987). Facilitating immigrant adaptation: the role of communication. In *Communicating Social Support* (T. L. Albrecht and M. B. Adelman, eds) pp. 192–211, Sage.

Kimmel, P. R. (1989). *International Negotiation and Intercultural Exploration: Toward Cultural Understanding.* US Institute of Peace.

Landis, D. and Bhagat, R. (eds) (1996). *Handbook of Intercultural Training*, 2nd edn. Sage.

Lefley, H. P. (1989). Counselling refugees: the North American experience. In *Counselling across Cultures* (P. B. Pedersen, J. G. Draguns, W. J. Lonner and J. E. Trimble, eds), University of Hawaii Press.

Oberg, K. (1958). *Culture Shock and the Problem of Adjustment to New Cultural Environments.* US Department of State, Foreign Service Institute.

Romano, D. (1988), *Intercultural Marriage: Promises and Pitfalls.* Intercultural Press.

Steele, F. (1980). Defining and developing environmental competence. In *Advances in Experimental Social Processes* (C. P. Alderfer and C. L. Cooper, eds) pp. 225–44, Wiley.

Ting-Toomey, S. (1994). Managing conflict in intimate relationships. In *Conflict in Personal Relationships* (D. D. Cahn, ed.), Erlbaum.

Triandis, H. C. (1995). *Individualism and Collectivism.* Westview Press.

Westney, E. (1996). *Cross-border Management of R&D.* Panel discussion of knowledge creation, JAIMS and the Sasakawa Peace Foundation, Honolulu.

Chapter 16.1

Family support for expatriate employees

■ Usha C. V. Haley ■

Overseas assignments' failure rates are forcing multinational corporations (MNCs) with expatriate employees in the Asia Pacific to pay more attention to family support, despite the added costs. To make their expatriate-management programmes more cost-effective, and to identify and to retain expatriate employees, MNCs appear more willing than before to consider foreign assignments' financial and human costs: the costs of replacing expatriate employees far outweigh the costs of providing orientation visits and reimbursement for job-hunting and career-counselling services.

For MNCs, expatriate assignments typically cost three times more than employing a domestic employee. Consequently, two-thirds of the MNCs in a Price Waterhouse (PW) survey of eighty-one Australian and New Zealand MNCs were exploring ways of supporting expatriate employees and their families (Marshall, 1998). In their reasons to reject overseas assignments, nearly 80 per cent of the MNCs' employees nominated family concerns as the primary reason, followed by dual-career concerns, location, career risks and too-lengthy assignment times.

Family difficulties often abruptly shorten expatriate assignments. Because of the substantial costs involved in finding replacements, MNCs also want to minimize the risks of choosing the wrong candidates. The PW survey showed that the Australian and New Zealand MNCs seemed more willing in 1998 than in 1996 to pay for pre-assignment orientation visits and spousal-support programmes – strategies to reduce the overseas assignments' failure rates. More MNCs also partially or fully reimbursed primary and secondary education costs (82 per cent compared with 68 per cent in 1996) and increased financial support for pre-schoolers (50 per cent from 21 per cent). A greater number of the MNCs (18 per cent compared with 15 per cent in 1996) compensated for losses of spousal income, even though the compensations seemed small – between A$5000 and A$10 000 a year. Multinational corporations with no spousal assistance comprised 12 per cent of the sample in 1998 as compared with 18 per cent in 1996.

Price Waterhouse is developing methodologies for clients interested in considered, strategic approaches to planning and managing international assignments. A survey of European expatriates conducted by PW in 1997 showed just under half of the MNCs measured their international assignments' costs and only 4 per cent evaluated returns on investment. In the same survey, the reason that expatriate employees highlighted most commonly for assignments' failures included mismatched expectations (nearly 60 per cent); for their spouses, social, intercultural and emotional reasons appeared as the most common. Therefore, about 20 per cent of repatriated employees wanted to leave their jobs and their employers on their return.

■ Reference

Marshall, K. (1998). Keeping workers happy so they carry on abroad. *Australian Financial Review*, 26 June, p. 63

Chapter 17

Boxing with shadows: competing effectively with the Overseas Chinese and Overseas Indian business networks in the Asian arena[1]

■ George T. Haley and Usha C.V. Haley ■

■ Introduction

He who in action sees inaction and in inaction sees action, he is wise among men. (Lord Krishna explaining the meaning of work to Arjuna in the Bhagavad Gita)

Foreign multinational corporations (MNCs) investing in or expanding business operations in China, South and Southeast Asia often find themselves sparring with local business groups. These business groups constitute unknown and unpredictable competitive opponents for many foreign MNCs: the local business groups' operations differ from familiar competitive behaviours; and their managers subscribe to novel assumptions about environments and strategies (Haley, 1997a; Haley and Haley, 1997; Shigematsu, 1994). Consequently, many foreign MNCs do not anticipate their local competitors' reactions, miss with their punches and are knocked out of the competitive arena (Haley, 1997a): most foreign direct investment projects in Asia and with Asian partners fail to achieve projected expectations. This chapter serves as a preparatory primer for organizational restructuring in the turbulent Asian arena by indicating how MNCs' managers may compete successfully with local business groups.

Through established procedures, Asian and Overseas Asian business people create specific kinds of social networks composed of family members, friends and trusted colleagues that influence business operations and environments (Haley, 1997a, 1997b; Haley and Haley, 1997). These social networks appear as clusters of interconnected firms that we refer to as business networks. In South and Southeast Asia, two major overseas Asian business networks, the Overseas Chinese and the Overseas Indians, hereafter collectively referred to as 'the Networks', dominate and influence competi-

[1] This chapter has been published previously by MCB University Press Limited: Haley, G. T. and Haley, U. C. V. (1998). Boxing with shadows: competing effectively with the Overseas Chinese and Overseas Indian business networks in the Asian arena. *Journal of Organizational Change Management*, **11** (4), 301–20.

tive environments. The Networks have also become major investors in China and India (*The Economist*, 1996) and with very few reported bankruptcies (unlike the Korean *chaebols*), appear to be successfully weathering the recent Asian economic crisis (Vatikiotis and Daorueng, 1998). To compete successfully in the Asian arena, MNCs' managers must understand these Networks' moves and be able to predict their punches.

First, we measure the sparring rings in Asia by exploring the historical conditions that contributed to the Networks' fighting stances and to Asian business environments. Next, we spotlight specific Asian competitors by elaborating on cultural differences between the Networks. In the ensuing section, we predict the Networks' movements in the ring by analysing their unique management and strategic decision-making styles. Finally, we prepare for the bell, by discussing the implications of the Networks' business practices for MNCs' strategies and organizational restructuring in the Asian arena.

■ Measuring the ring: historical and environmental influences on competitive environments in Asia

Haley (1997a) and Haley and Haley (1997) indicated some important characteristics that distinguish successful Overseas Chinese and Overseas Indian business networks' firms operating in South and Southeast Asia:

1 Little differentiation exists between the controlling families and the firms.

2 The firms have very strong familial and informal networks.

3 The firms exhibit good relationships with the often enormous public sectors in these countries.

4 The firms appear highly diversified often undertaking unrelated diversification, thereby contravening mainstream, Western theoretical notions.

In this section, we elaborate on the historical circumstances that generated the competitive rings in which foreign MNCs must spar – specifically comprising the environments that perpetuate the Networks' firms unique characteristics and strategic stances.

Strategic decision-making in Asia differs from that in the West (Haley, Tan and Haley, 1998; Hofstede, 1994); these differences mould the Networks' management and decision-making styles and practices. Researchers have posited various explanations for the differences that emerge between Asian and Western strategic decision-making. For example, Haley and Tan (1996) and Haley and Haley (1997) suggested competitive advantage as a possible explanation. Hofstede (1994) argued that ethnic and cultural factors separated decision-making styles; alternatively, Haley and Stumpf (1989) traced differences in decision-making to personality-type differences. Later, Haley (1997c) detected significant personality-type differences between managerial cadres from different countries thereby supporting Hofstede's arguments.

A potent understanding of the Networks' styles probably incorporates facets from the diverse explanations. However, Haley and Tan's (1996) categorization of Asia as an informational void relative to the amount of information available in industrialized economies lies unquestioned. This informational void has led to a unique, strategic-management style for many Asian firms. Consequently, the major differences in Asian decision-making stem from the information that Asian decision-makers have available and desire: this information often differs significantly from that used by Western managers and strategic theorists (Haley, 1997a; Haley and Tan, 1996). This section explores some of the historical and environmental influences that have bolstered the informational void in the Asian arena.

Traditionally, three major business clusters have dominated the Asian economic arena: government-linked corporations (GLCs), either wholly or partly controlled by regional governments, family firms and manufacturing-based MNCs. In South and Southeast Asia, the family firms have generally been controlled by Indians, Overseas Indians and Overseas Chinese. Historically, none of the three clusters in Asia have desired local-market information, and have generally adapted their strategies to their information-poor environments.

GLCs usually began as suppliers of products and services in protected, domestic markets. For GLCs, strategic planning synchronized with governmental plans for economic growth and development. Market information rarely comprised a critical success factor; hence, information gathering did not assume top priority. Although MNCs first entered Asia over two centuries ago, those in manufacturing had the greatest impact and entered primarily after the Second World War; this latter group invested mainly to rationalize manufacturing costs for products intended for Japan and the West. Not seeking to serve local markets, the manufacturing-based MNCs neither needed nor sought more local-market information (Haley, 1997a; Haley, Tan and Haley, 1998).

The Overseas Chinese business networks (hereafter referred to as the Overseas Chinese) probably constitute the single, most dominant, private business grouping in Asia outside of China, Japan and South Asia. The Overseas Chinese form 3.5 per cent of Indonesia's population, 29 per cent of Malaysia's, 2 per cent of the Philippines', 10 per cent of Thailand's, and 77 per cent of Singapore's – yet control respectively 73 per cent, 69 per cent, 50–60 per cent, 81 per cent and 81 per cent of listed firms by market capitalization in these countries (Vatikiotis, 1998). Increasingly, the Overseas Chinese are facing fierce competition from the manufacturing-based MNCs, now interested in the rapidly growing and increasingly prosperous local markets, and from the Overseas Indian business networks (hereafter referred to as the Overseas Indians).

Many Overseas Chinese started as merchants and traders that moved into property-related businesses, and then into any business deemed profitable. Their firms generally exhibit an entrepreneurial, intuitive and fast decision-making style, and paternalistic management. The founders of the Overseas Chinese firms generally had little formal education and even less formal, Western-style business education: their business education originated from their experiences (Chan and Chiang, 1994). Table 17.1 presents a small sample of Overseas Chinese families and the businesses in which they operate.

Today, the Overseas Indians form an extremely viable business force in Asia. For example, Indian businessmen account for one-tenth of Hong Kong's exports, even though they comprise less than 1 per cent of its population (Cragg, 1996). Yet, efforts to chart the Overseas Indians' influence often fail. Few from this business network assume prominent or high-profile public positions, often preferring to operate behind the scenes. Also, where the business climates allow, Overseas Indians tend not to

Table 17.1 Some families and businesses in the Overseas Chinese business networks

Family/leader	Primary businesses
Hong Kong	
Li Kai Shang	Ports and infrastructure, retailing, manufacturing, telecommunications, property development, energy, finance and investment
Peter Woo/Pao family	Real estate, cable television, infrastructural development, transportation
Indonesia	
Liem Sioe Liong	Cement, processed foods, flour milling, steel, banking, real estate, investments
Eka Tjipta Widjaja	Diversified
Oei Hong Leong	Beer, tyres, consumer products
Mochtar Riaddy	Property, banking, insurance
Suhargo Gondokusumo	Agri-industries, property
Prajogo Pangestu	Timber, car assembly
Malaysia	
Robert Kuok	Plantations, sugar and wood processing, media, hotels
Quek Leng Chan	Finance, diversified
Lim Goh Tong	Casinos, real estate
Vincent Tan	Leisure, manufacturing, investment
Philippines	
Lucio Tan	Beer, tobacco, banking, investments
Henry Sy	Retailing, cement, investments
Alfonso Yuchengco	Banking, insurance
Antonio Cojuangco	Telecommunications, real estate
John Gokongwei	Real estate, diversified investments
Singapore	
Kwek Leng Beng	Real estate, hotels, financial services
Lee family	Banking, plantations
Thailand	
Chearavanont family	Agri-business, real estate, telecommunications
Kanjanapas family	Real estate, transport, finance
Ratanarak family	Cement, banking, telecommunications
Sophonpanich family	Banking, real estate, investments
Lamsam family	Banking, real estate

report specifically their firms' structures. Some families, like the Hindujas, have a reputation for extreme secrecy about business operations, discussing them only in encrypted fax and e-mail messages, taking long walks in parks to avoid being overheard and sometimes (as in the case of Srichand Hinduja) refusing to divulge return addresses on business correspondence. These tendencies often obfuscate researchers' and competitors' efforts to ascertain the firms' ownership, structure and strategies.

Almost all Indian émigrés arrived in their new homelands with few material assets.

Often beginning as traders or retailers, they formed close communities for support and to create natural markets for goods and services (Haley and Haley, 1997). Like the Overseas Chinese, the Overseas Indians also generally adopt an entrepreneurial and fast decision-making style (Gidoomal and Porter, 1997). Frequently, the Overseas Indians decide to invest, to expand, and to compete mainly on business sense, experience, and individual propensities for risks (Piramal, 1996; Shigematsu, 1994). Protected competitive environments and the informational void in which these firms operate have bolstered the Overseas Indians' decision-making propensities (Haley and Haley, 1997). Table 17.2 presents a small sample of Overseas Indian families and the businesses in which they operate.

Table 17.2 Some families and businesses in the Overseas Indian business networks

Family/leader	*Primary businesses*
Hong Kong	
Harilela family	Property development and management, financial trading, hotels, restaurants
Amitabha Chowdury	Media
Mahabir Mohindar	Media
Indonesia	
Lakshmi Mittal	Steel
Malaysia	
Ananda Krishnan	Telecommunications, multimedia, property development, gaming
Singapore	
Chanrai family	Steel, textiles, hotels, fashion
Jhunjhnuwala family	Hotels, property development
Thakral family	Textiles, electronics, trading, hotels, property development
Philippines	
Hiro Asanadas	Textiles, garments
Nari Genomal	Textiles, garments
John Daswani	Textiles, garments
Chanrai family	Textiles
Ferdinand Nanki Hiranand	Restaurants
Robin Wasvani	Lens manufacturing
Thailand	
Bharat and Vijay Shah	Diamonds, real estate, construction, movies

With difficult business decisions, when additional information seems necessary, the Overseas Chinese and Overseas Indians usually depend upon their webs of friends and government officials for information (Haley, 1997a). Trust and loyalty form central concerns for the Networks. Desired information often reflects subjective views or beliefs that raise the managers' confidence in their decisions (Haley and Haley, 1997). Availability of suitable managers seems to prompt the direction of the Overseas

Indians' diversification much more than detailed understandings of the industries (Gidoomal and Porter, 1997): Overseas Indians often expand into industries in which they feel that trusted people have the skills to manage the new ventures successfully. As Table 17.2 shows, many Overseas Indians have undertaken unrelated conglomerate diversification, though not as consistently as the Overseas Chinese.

The Networks' somewhat-holistic, intuitive, decision-making styles conform well to information-scarce environments including those providing poor quality market-survey data; these styles concurrently serve to exclude new entrants without the established communities' experiences and webs of contacts. For instance, many Asian banks have historically served particular communities or networks, not geographic areas; these community bases persist today. Consequently, in Indonesia, for example, individuals applying for business loans from banks often find that the information in their applications has been transferred to the banks' related firms, controlled by the Overseas Chinese, in the same business as the applicants'; and that the related firms often have even implemented the submitted business plans for entering the applicants' projected markets (East Asia Analytical Unit, 1995)!

The Overseas Indians often prefer to use internal labyrinths of business contacts over outside sources of funding to finance their ventures (Gidoomal and Porter, 1997). When borrowing from these internal contacts, interest rates competitive with prevailing banks' rates accrue. The business contacts issue *hoondies* or bills of exchange that constitute private financial circles' instruments to control and to honour debts. Each *hoondie* has payment dates and maturity dates. Despite bypassing traditional banking systems, the *hoondie* system based on honour and reputation appears functional and continues in South Asia and wherever Overseas Indians operate.

Many researchers and managers attribute the rapid growth of the Networks' businesses in South and Southeast Asia to their unique processing and channeling of information (Gidoomal and Porter, 1997; Haley and Tan, 1996). Chu and MacMurray (1993) argued that in Southeast Asia, decision-making speed and control of information constitute primary competitive advantages for the Overseas Chinese, aiding them in seizing major business opportunities; similar advantages accrue to the Overseas Indians (Piramal, 1996). Thus, the informational void in Asia exists because of historical business practices and participants' goals. As the key decision-makers have not desired more objective information, the region resembles an informational black hole for those who do (Haley and Tan, 1996). Consequently, the Networks' firms roam the ring with a sound knowledge of their sparring partners' capabilities and their ring's size and floor characteristics; yet, new entrants have little reliable information about their local competitors' boxing styles and slugging power, or about the ring's slippery spots. The next section elaborates on the cultural influences that have shaped the Networks' fighting stances.

▓ Differentiating the competitors: cultural influences on the Networks

Foreign MNCs operating in Asia often assume that the Networks' firms should demonstrate strategic and operational characteristics similar to the now well-studied and relatively well-understood Japanese firms. These assumptions about their competitors' behaviours cause many missed punches in the Asian economic arena. This section elaborates on the region-specific characteristics that differentiate the Overseas Chinese and Overseas Indians' cultures from their Japanese competitors' and each other.

Like the Japanese, most of the managed Asian economies have depended primarily on export-led growth. Japanese firms have always formed Japan's principal sources of exports; until recently, Japanese exports focused mainly on North America and Europe. Alternatively, with the exception of South Korea, manufacturing-based MNCs have formed the non-Japanese Asian nations' principal sources of exports to Western nations; local firms have concentrated on the local markets that Western MNCs now perceive as so important (Haley and Tan, 1996). Firms from most Asian nations, outside of Japan, have built their size and managerial expertise within the informational void described in the previous section – rather than in competition with Western MNCs as Japanese firms did. Table 17.3 summarizes some significant cultural differences between the Chinese, Indians and Japanese; these cultural differences have influenced the Networks' firms, their concepts of loyalty as well as the bases for commercial trust in business dealings with them.

Table 17.3 Cultural similarities and differences between the Chinese, Indians and Japanese

Attributes	Chinese	Indian	Japanese
Firm			
Merchants	Reviled	Specialized	Exalted
Primogeniture	None	Very strong	Strong
Firm's life-span	Short	Medium	Long
Loyalty			
Family definition	Blood	Blood	Role
Focus	Individual	Group	Institution
Intensity	Low	High	High
Filial piety vs patriotism	Opposed	No relationship	Equivalent
Commercial Trust			
Ethical foundation	Five relationships and social harmony	Dharma	Mutual self-interest
Ethical focus	The 'way'	Family	Service to father figure
Expectations of benefits	Immediate and up front	Immediate and up front	Long-term and delayed

▪ Firm-related attributes

Merchants

The Japanese, Chinese and Indian cultures exhibit divergent attitudes towards merchants. The Japanese culture incorporates an economic philosophy of growth that exalts merchants. A major influence on the Overseas Chinese, the Confucian culture, also includes an economic element; however, Confucian economics incorporates a subsistence philosophy that exalts peasants and reviles and persecutes merchants. For example, ancient Chinese customs prohibited merchants from wearing silks and riding horses or in wagons; these customs required merchants to dress in coarse fabrics and travel on foot. Confucian philosophers frowned upon merchants whom they perceived as excessively concerned with profits rather than the 'way' (Lau, 1995; Waley, 1996); the philosophers also saw merchants as mobile, and thus unreliable supporters of rulers. Not surprisingly, innumerable waves of Overseas Chinese flooded South and Southeast Asia over the centuries: every wave corresponded to a period of persecution against the merchants.

Alternatively, since ancient times, Indian cultures have encouraged and provided specialized places for thriving merchant classes. Many Overseas Indians come from the Vaisya or Jain merchant castes of India that encouraged business within the broad Hindu system. Others emanate from small, highly prosperous, niche, non-Hindu communities, such as the Parsis, that local rulers protected and encouraged. Several Overseas Indians, such as the Shah brothers from Palanpur, in the Western state of Gujarat, have parlayed their traditional occupations, in their case that of diamond merchants, into major multinational operations: today, the Shah brothers rank among the world's largest diamond dealers with operations in Belgium, Thailand and India (Piramal, 1996).

Primogeniture and firms' lifespans

Another difference between Chinese, Japanese and Indian customs revolves around primogeniture or the emphasis on single heirs, usually the eldest sons. These customs have influenced firms' lifespans. Confucian customs emphasize large families and ban primogeniture; consequently, an ancient Chinese saying prophesies that 'no fortune survives the third generation'. Most of today's major Overseas Chinese firms have survived only as far as the second generation of managers (Chu and MacMurray, 1993). Alternatively, Japanese customs emphasize primogeniture; however, according to customs, the eldest sons need not necessarily inherit regardless of competence, and consequently, the Japanese firms have built concentrated and continued wealth. Japanese firms, especially large ones such as Mitsubishi, have survived for a considerable time in some form. Some of Japan's major firms began hundreds of years ago as family firms that evolved through growth into the Japanese *keiretsu* conglomerates. The Indians emphasize primogeniture even more than the Japanese do. Many Overseas Indian firms have evolved from traditional, small, family businesses into third or fourth-generation family-controlled conglomerates (*Business Today*, 1998). The eldest sons often succeed their fathers as heads of the family firms, regardless of their competence or aptitudes, thereby debilitating top-management cadres and increasing the need for professionalization. Consequently, Gidoomal and Porter (1997) noted that succession forms a major concern among the Overseas Indian firms.

■ Loyalty-related attributes

Family, focus and intensity

In Japanese cultures, loyalties, though very strong, have functional bases: family members owe filial loyalties to the breadwinners, not to the actual fathers. Conversely, in both Chinese and Indian cultures, family members owe filial loyalties to the fathers, regardless of who actually constitute the breadwinners; members of the Networks' cultures share highly personalized, as opposed to functional, bases for loyalties. The

Indian cultures glorify loyalties that members may transfer to groups within the extended families and their businesses. In the Chinese cultures, however, loyalties accrue to individuals; members often do not transfer loyalties to friends or employers and hence employees' loyalties do not survive individual managers.

Patriotism

The relationships that the Japanese, Chinese and Indians perceive between individuals and societies also differ; these associations affect the ways in which the Overseas Chinese and Overseas Indians contribute to their adopted and native countries. A Japanese adage posits that 'to be a good patriot is to be a good son'. Alternatively, the equivalent adage in China argues that 'one cannot be both a good patriot and a good son'. In Indian cultures, no relationship exists between patriotism and filial piety.

■ Trust-related attributes

Ethical foundations

Concepts of ethics differ significantly between the three cultures (Haley, 1997b; Haley and Haley, 1997), affecting the bases of commercial trust. Although the Japanese view contractual duties as binding and familial and friendship ties as helpful, ties of personal and corporate self-interest prove paramount; trust in commercial relationships derives from perceived, mutual self-interest. Hence, the numerous social gatherings in which potential business associates seek out similarities in outlooks, perspectives and values.

In Confucianism, the major ethical influence on the Overseas Chinese, five relationships define ethical duty:

1 Sovereign and minister.

2 Father and son.

3 Husband and wife.

4 Elder brother and younger brother.

5 Friends.

If relationships fall outside the above categories, then Confucian necessities to maintain social harmony, rather than normative ethical desires, regulate relationships. As Cheung Kim Hung, editor-in-chief of Hong Kong's leading Chinese-language news weekly summarized, 'In Chinese business circles, the emphasis is on harmony. People agree to compete or not to compete' (Cheng and Vriens, 1996: 48). However, without familial or established friendship ties, trust rarely exists in commercial relationships with the Overseas Chinese: to work well with them, foreign business associates must build noncommercial ties of friendship or family. Hence, the Indonesian bankers from the previous section (that forward strangers' loan applications as strategically important information to their business networks) are acting in accordance with Confucian ethics, despite violating Western ethics: strangers do not fall within the Confucian five relationships' purvey and often cannot disrupt social harmony in their disappointment and anger.

Dharma, which loosely translates from the Sanskrit to the natural law and incorporates duty, assumes centrality for many South Asian communities including the Overseas Indians. *Dharma* covers duties to families, to business partners, and to societies. Many Overseas Indians view succeeding financially as a familial duty (Gidoomal and Porter, 1997), especially for the eldest son. This association with familial duty transforms success into religious obligation. As Gidoomal and Porter (1997: 17) note, 'as virtue brings its rewards, success as a religious obligation often becomes a religious blessing'; thus, among South Asians, financial rewards from business success provide overtones of personal virtue for successful people. At the turn of the century, American businessmen, drawing on arguments from social Darwinism, also associated financial success with virtue (Heilbroner and Singer, 1984); alternatively, South Asians strive for financial success primarily as fulfillment of familial duty. *Dharma* provides a special intensity to the Overseas Indians' drive and work ethics.

Ethical focus

The three cultures' ethics demonstrate different normative focal points. To the Overseas Chinese influenced by Confucian philosophies, individuals should behave in manners appropriate to their stations in life within the five relationships' frameworks; the Confucian philosophers refer to these collectively appropriate behaviours as the 'way'. To the Japanese, individuals should serve their superiors (their father figures), and through their superiors, patriotically, their emperors. But, to South Asians, including the Overseas Indians, families should provide the central concerns: codes of *Dharma* regulate the duties of individuals to their families.

Expectations of benefits

The Overseas Indians and Overseas Chinese differ from the Japanese in their expectations of benefits from contractual relationships. Among the Overseas Indians, legal principles and the rule of law appear to mold trust in commercial relationships. However, neither the Overseas Indians nor the Overseas Chinese will enter or maintain contractual relationships without minimal benefits and the expectations of making profits: when the benefits and expectations fade, so do contractual duties for the most part. Unlike the Japanese, although the Overseas Chinese and the Overseas Indians will invest time, money and effort, they expect to see tangible benefits up front (Redding, 1996; Shigematsu, 1994). Piramal (1996) and Gidoomal and Porter (1997) attributed local populations' animosities toward the Overseas Indians in Africa and the UK to the group's hard-edged negotiating style and its undisguised interest in making profits commensurate with its efforts. The Overseas Chinese, whose history includes many episodes of persecution in Southeast Asia, also exhibit similar negotiating styles and expectations (Redding, 1996). Because of their experiences with foreign populations, both groups emphasize earning fairly immediate, tangible returns and maintaining substantial holdings of liquid assets (Haley, 1997a).

Although familial and friendship ties oil commercial relationships in Indian cultures, most Overseas Indians view contractual duties in commercial relationships as ethically binding as Westerners do (Gidoomal and Porter, 1997). Thus, commercial partners with signed contracts can have some confidence that the Overseas Indians will follow the contracts' terms. However, with the Overseas Chinese, signed contracts may often begin, rather than end, negotiations (Haley and Tan, 1996); consequently, commercial partners should expect some quibbling over the contracts' terms.

The next section elaborates on some of the unique ring movements of the Overseas Chinese and Overseas Indians.

■ Their fighting arsenal: the Overseas Chinese and Overseas Indian business networks' strategic management styles

Drawing on their observations and study of Asian top managers, Haley and Tan (1996) and Haley and Haley (1997) posited that the following characteristics seem common to Overseas Chinese and Overseas Indians' strategic-management practices and styles:

• hands-on experience

• lateral transfers of knowledge

• reliance on qualitative information

• holistic information processing

• action-driven decision-making

• emergent planning.

This section elaborates on the fighting arsenal that the Networks' firms bring to the ring.

Hands-on experience

To make decisions quickly, without detailed analyses of hard data, managers must approximate hands-on line managers who know at first hand the firms' work routines and processes as well as the products, markets, business environments and industries. Without this intimate knowledge of the businesses, managers will not have the necessary perspectives and insights to make timely decisions. Consequently, many senior managers from the Networks remain active in all aspects of their firms; their successors often depend on their elders' experiences more than on professional managers' expertise. This level of experience and involvement contributes to making the right decisions without the supporting information most Western managers would desire. Kazuo Wada (1992) provided an example of a top manager from Hong Kong who responded within fifteen minutes to an offer by Li Kai Shang, chairman of Hutchinson/Cheung Kong, to enter into a major joint venture; the manager's confidence in Li's judgement and word, and his in-depth knowledge of the business and markets under consideration, allowed him to make such a rapid decision.

Lateral transfers of knowledge

Managers often have difficulties making decisions within new environmental contexts. However, the Networks' firms frequently diversify into totally different, non-core businesses (see Tables 17.1 and 17.2), contravening given business wisdom of staying within firms' core businesses. To succeed in industries in which they have no prior experiences, managers must generalize from past experiences in other industries, and apply those generalizations in the new contexts. The abilities to tackle new problems in different situations involve conceptualization skills different from analytical skills. Successful Networks' managers often see the big pictures, and intuitively separate winners from losers (Haley, 1997a). Chu and MacMurray (1993) argued that conglomerate diversification in Asia must change; yet, many managers in the region feel that it forms a major reason for their firms' enviable growth rates and risk-absorbing capacities.

Qualitative information

Many of the Networks' managers appear to take unnecessary risks by not doing sufficient research or analyses before acting; these appearances prove misleading. The managers often process myriad bits of information and consider several alternatives in depth before they act. They differ from Western managers in that they may conduct their analyses, almost entirely, internally: though they articulate their decision-making, the Networks' managers may not present the results in written, analytical forms.

The Networks' managers almost always use external sources of information in making strategic decisions. Haley and Tan (1996) indicated that managers actively seek out critical information that will affect their decisions: however, the Networks' managers rarely seek published information, generally preferring qualitative, even subjective information supplied by friends, business associates, government officials, and others in whose judgment and character they trust. They prefer to visit localities personally to check on information rather than to rely on secondary information. Their local contacts can often supply up-to-date, accurate, unpublished information superior to available, published or traditional, primary, research alternatives. For example, on learning through his family's contacts that a foreign country would soon ban imports, Ram Gidoomal of the Inlaks Group committed his family's firm to sell a frozen-chicken consignment to the country's buyers (Gidoomal and Porter, 1997). Market research would not have revealed the information in time for his firm to react; his trust in his contacts allowed him to take advantage of the opportunity and to make a huge profit.

Holistic information processing

Conventional, analytical problem-solving stresses sequential, systematic and step-by-step approaches to decision-making. These approaches work best when managers can obtain needed information. In informational-void situations, the analytical models often prove unworkable. With experience-based intuitive models, managers take general approaches to problems, define parameters intuitively and explore solutions holistically: such approaches resemble Asian thinking and learning and the Networks' managers appear to subscribe to them. The intuitive models provide alternative modes of decision-making that frequently work well, especially in those markets where they evolved: the models reduce risk, not through formal data-collection and analyses, but through collection of subjective information and incremental approaches to investments (Haley, Tan and Haley, 1998).

The initial investments in foreign markets by the Networks' firms almost never endanger the firms' survival if they fail. Consequently, the Shah brothers could walk away from their failed US$3 million investment in a diamond-cutting factory in Nepal; however, they continued to take investment risks, learning from their failed negotiations with the Nepalese government. Without what Western managers would consider adequate information, the Shahs empowered brother Vijay to invest US$5 million to start BV Diamond Polishing Works in Thailand, reportedly the world's largest diamond-cutting and polishing factory. Vijay Shah drew on his experiences in the diamond business and with regional governments, on assurances from the Thai government, and on his feel for the market's potential to make his investment decision. Peter Meeus, director of Beurs voor Diamanthandel, one of Antwerp's four diamond bourses, when speaking of the Shahs' decision-making style, said,

> Vijay can take risks. I remember when they were thinking of setting up a factory in Bangkok – many were going to Thailand at the time – but everybody went in for small [stone] sizes, Jewish and Indians, but not Vijay. He thought they should be polishing medium stones. Everybody thought he would fail, but that factory is doing very well. (Quoted in Piramal, 1996: 323)

Action-driven decision-making

Speed constitutes a key characteristic of decision-making in Asian business. Top managers often make key decisions without consulting anyone, preferring action to discussion. Many stories exist of well-known Networks' managers who decide on important matters in minutes and implement the results almost immediately. This speed reflects the managers' empowerment and accountability. As the managers often have great latitude in deciding matters, long debates and committee meetings rarely occur. In the above mentioned example, Ram Gidoomal, under time constraints, committed significant financial resources from the Inlaks Group, including the most expensive ship-charter contract in its history, without contacting other directors (Gidoomal and Porter, 1997); he could do so because his family's faith in him provided him with the authority and power to act.

The decision-making models used by the Networks' managers reflect authoritative management. However, when responsibility coincides with authority, projects often progress faster in emerging and rapidly developing markets. These conclusions prompted Kazuo Wada to move Yaohan's headquarters from Japan to Hong Kong, and the international headquarters for all operations outside of Hong Kong and China, to Singapore; he maintained only the headquarters for domestic Japanese operations in Japan. Wada has now similarly moved Yaohan's headquarters to Shanghai to reflect China's importance in the firm's future plans. Similarly, after wringing lucrative incentives, tax benefits and financial benefits from the Thais, Vijay Shah completed his Thai diamond factory in ten months – under schedule and in record time.

Emergent planning

The Networks appear to engage in what Mintzberg (1987, 1994) and Mintzberg and Waters (1985) termed emergent planning (Haley, Tan and Haley, 1998). Strategies bubble-up through individual firms and also collectively through the Networks (Piramal, 1996). Typically, news, rumors or insider information will reach the Networks' managers and create interest. The managers will then seek confirming evidence, gauge available resources, make and implement decisions. As further information becomes available, the managers will modify strategies. The firms' strategies emerge from the managers' and the firms' learned business behaviours. If managers feel they need strategic partners, the firms will seek them out, preferably within their respective Networks; the potential partners' decisions to join hinge largely on their confidence in the proposing managers' judgment and abilities. After studying strategic-planning practices in Singapore and Malaysia, Ghosh and Chan (1994) also concluded that the planning activities of the Networks' firms appear *ad hoc* and reactive. 'CEO's personal knowledge of market' seemed the only market-related factor of any importance contributing to success in planning.

As in other emergent planning (Mintzberg, 1994), the Networks' managers detect discontinuities, know their businesses intimately, manage patterns and reconcile changes with continuities. First, through their webs of associates, the managers determine potential changes in governmental policy or environments that can cause discontinuities and force strategic changes (Haley, 1997a). Second, the managers emphasize knowing their businesses through hands-on experience, and active, intimate participation in all important aspects of their firm's activities, products and markets (Haley and Tan, 1996). Because of this reliance on intimate, intuitive understandings of businesses and environments, strategic planning in the Networks emphasizes line management (Haley, Tan and Haley, 1998). Third, the managers rely on perceptions of holistic information, viewed as patterns; the patterns help the managers to infer the firms' present and future relationships with environments and to optimize benefits. By discerning general patterns of behaviours and requirements for success, the managers often extrapolate experiences across unrelated products and markets (Haley and Tan, 1996). Finally, through their webs of associates, the managers seek to enhance patterns of change and continuity – where possible pursuing preferential treatment, and lobbying for or against laws and regulations that affect their privileged positions within desired markets and industries. For example, the Philippines' Cojuangco Group has had great success in influencing or leveraging industry structures and regulations in its home markets; by skillful lobbying, the Cojuangco Group has amassed enormous wealth through key governmental franchises, such as the long-distance telephone franchise in the Philippines.

Like top boxers, the Networks' firms seek to enter the ring with established advantages over their opponents. The Networks' firms endeavor to control the ring through forming alliances, to manipulate opponents through controlling information, and to paralyse competitors through hiding their strengths and weaknesses. The next section discusses some implications for organizational change in the Asian arena and for MNCs' restructuring.

■ Waiting for the bell: implications for multinational corporations sparring in the Asian arena

The Networks' firms with their unique fighting arsenal and movements have profound influences on sparring in the Asian arena. This section identifies some implications for successful organizational change and restructuring by MNCs to improve their odds for success.

Reconstructing the ring

We have argued that the Networks form institutionalized mediums for political, social and economic activities; they serve as social constructions that reflect normative prescriptions for cohesive groups' formations. By placing the Networks in a comparative perspective, and showing differences and similarities between the Overseas Chinese and Overseas Indians, we have indicated that fuller understandings of the Networks must question Western economic and sociological theories and consequently, managers' formal understandings of the Asian competitive arena.

To enhance understandings of the Asian arena, researchers should enquire more specifically into how the Networks shape industrial structures. Many Asian developing countries' economic hierarchies arise from the Networks that control so much of these economies (Haley and Haley, 1997). Specific strategies to fashion the Networks appear to precede and to condition the capitalist markets' establishments (Redding, 1996). Consequently, in order to understand and to predict the markets' evolution and development, researchers must more-fully comprehend the Networks' institutional and developmental roles in these markets.

The Network firms' strategies do not seem suited to all industries; their managerial practices have instituted wide-ranging structural changes that sometimes offer foreign MNCs advantages. For example, across East Asia, the financial crisis has adversely affected banks and forced the Overseas Chinese families that control them to reanalyse and to sell. Thailand had not granted a new full-service banking licence in forty years, creating a family-directed plutocracy of fifteen families such as the Wanglees, that rivalled the Finance Ministry in their power. But today, many blame that insular system for the country's financial troubles. As noted earlier, family banks often make loans based on relationships – giving more weight to a patriarch's reputation and the collateral of his name than to business plans and the firm's cash flow. Critics say such outdated practices allowed the Thai firms to rack up too much debt and to pump air into real estate and stockmarket bubbles. The Thai government is determined to change the system, clearing a path for Western banks in this long-cloistered market. The International Monetary Fund has made an overhaul a central condition of its US$17.2 billion bailout package. The changes are already striking. The central bank nationalized four banks in 1998, wiping out founding-family shares. One other bank has been sold to the Dutch banking giant ABN-AMRO and another to the Development Bank of Singapore. The era of family banking is over says Amaret Sila-On, head of a government body overseeing disposal of non-performing bank assets. 'Whether the families like it or not, Thailand now needs professionals at the helm' (quoted in Kahn, 1998).

Reanalysing the competitors

To more fully comprehend their Asian competitors, researchers need to develop theories that reflect the Networks' unique business practices and styles as well as their strengths and weaknesses: superimposed understandings from US business networks fail to explain the Networks adequately. For instance, the Asian Networks show much more resilience than the individual firms that make up the Networks (Redding, 1996); through interlocking directorates, marriages and joint ventures they often coalesce their interests to present one institutional interest to governments and competitors. By contrast, US business networks appear relatively weak and generally represent individual firms' short-term institutional interests (Mizruchi and Schwartz, 1987). Through an institutional perspective, the Asian economies appear network-based whereas the US economy appears firm-based. The Networks' configurations also differ systematically across the Overseas Indians and the Overseas Chinese; researchers can trace the differences to the distinctive and institutionally rooted ways in which the Chinese and the Indians form social groups. Unlike the Western network theories propagated by researchers such as Nohria and Eccles (1992), the Overseas Chinese and Overseas Indians do not seem to draw on practices or theories of voluntarism and individualism: the Networks seem normative, relational, hierarchical and substantive. Future researchers should enquire and elaborate on these characteristics to develop useful theories of the Networks and their movements in the Asian arena.

Rechoreographing movements

The Networks' firms and their unique decision-making styles influence MNCs' competitive environments and should influence their Asian strategies. Unlike Japanese firms, the Networks' firms move quickly and expect rapid decisions from their potential partners; MNCs that follow standard operating procedures will lose good opportunities in the Networks' markets. However, to move rapidly, MNCs cannot delay researching markets until they perceive potential opportunities: MNCs must have the information substantially on hand and 'leverage to beat the odds' (Slywotsky and Shapiro, 1993) – that is, MNCs must generate multiple returns on investments from the same information. The Networks' unique strategic management and information-processing styles give them advantages in the Asian economic arena. To spar effectively against the Networks, MNCs must restructure and change key operations and processes.

First, MNCs' managers must determine which markets they aim to serve. While appropriate information appears scarce, it exists. For MNCs, research constitutes an investment that will produce substantial returns both in earning future profits and in avoiding future losses. The information should reveal potential products, markets and major competitive players. For example, several accounting firms in Hong Kong conduct 'due diligence' research on Chinese firms to reveal their often disguised or undisclosed operations. The MNCs using these data can then determine which of those players would prove legitimate, beneficial business partners and which would not. MNCs should use information to move into products and markets alone, or rapidly with joint ventures should they identify appropriate partners.

Second, as rapid decisions assume critical importance, MNCs' managers must have close links in each Asian country and ready access to top corporate management to speed internal decision-making. Using more local employees with strong local connections, and building trust-based relationships, constitute some of the ways through which MNCs may establish stronger links to relevant information. When MNCs cannot find appropriate Asian local managers, managers from other emerging economies may prove suitable. For example, Phillips selected a highly trusted and historically successful Mexican executive, Reinaldo Wences, from its Latin American operations as general manager of its Singaporean regional headquarters: Phillips assumed that the Latin American business environment's high uncertainty, poor information base, and highly personal, autocratic style of management would better prepare top managers for Asia than the European business environment would; in this instance, judging from sales and profits, Phillips appears to have made the appropriate appointment.

Third, the competitive environments created by the Networks favor experience-based training and line managers over staff-based managers for MNCs' top management positions. Line-management experiences provide managers with the essential, in-depth familiarity with markets and operations to react rapidly in highly fluid, uncertain situations. Line managers also often better understand their senior counterparts, with similar operational experiences, at most Asian firms (Haley and Tan, 1996). Consequently, line management experiences should help MNCs' managers to build quickly local links with senior Asian managers. Also, MNCs' managers without line-management experiences will have based strategic decisions on formal data analyses that Asian competitors and partners generally do not undertake; consequently, these managers often will experience great difficulties in judging some strategies and propositions as valid or reliable.

Fourth, understanding the Networks should help MNCs to manage more effectively intellectual-property rights in Asia. Widespread lack of respect for intellectual-property rights severely affects product management in Asia. Among the Overseas Chinese and their government supporters, no historical or cultural precedence supports intellectual-property rights: Confucian economic philosophy ignores intellectual property. Consequently, local legal authorities often ignore intellectual-property-rights grievances even when central governments supposedly support the rights. These differences in perceptions of rights, and attendant costs to MNCs, must influence MNCs' needs to move production as close as possible to major markets. Currently, in Asia, India, Singapore, Thailand, and Malaysia appear most successful in protecting intellectual property rights.

Finally, MNCs' managers should recognise that Asian relationships evolve seemingly unpredictably. Unlike other business networks, the Overseas Chinese acceptance of individuals can vary with events over which the individuals have no influence; acceptance includes the individuals – and others that affect situations in which the individuals interact with the Overseas Chinese. MNCs' managers have limited freedom to undertake some behaviours that may help to cement their positions with Overseas Chinese and Overseas Indians. For example, often the MNCs' managers cannot involve their families in business relationships as completely as the Networks do. Consequently, MNCs' managers must learn to recognize the cues emanating from the Networks' managers as indicators of relationships' conditions at any instance. Trust in relationships with the Networks may provide an environment for assessing cues; yet, trust arises slowly and focuses on individuals or management groups rather than institutions. Foreign MNCs' (especially US MNCs') practices of rotating managers every two or three years may pull them out of the ring just as they are forming trust-based relationships with competitors and collaborators, thereby hindering the MNCs from becoming fighting fit for the Asian arena.

■ References

Business Today (1998). India's business families: can they survive? Sixth anniversary issue, January–February.

Chan, K. B. and Chiang, C. (1994). *Stepping Out. The Making of Chinese Entrepreneurs.* Prentice-Hall.

Cheng, A. and Vriens, H. (1996). Superman vs China. *Asia Inc.*, **5** (12), 42–9.

Chu, T. C. and MacMurray, T. (1993). The road ahead for Asia's leading conglomerates. *McKinsey Quarterly* (3), 117–26.

Cragg, C. (1996). *The New Maharajas. The Commercial Princes of India, Pakistan and Bangladesh.* Random House.

East Asia Analytical Unit (1995). *Overseas Chinese Business Networks.* AGPS Press, Department of Foreign Affairs and Trade.

The Economist (1996). A survey of business in Asia. 9 March.

Ghosh, B. C. and Chan, C. O. (1994). A study of strategic planning behaviour among emergent businesses in Singapore and Malaysia. *International Journal of Management*, **11** (2), 697–706.

Gidoomal, R. and Porter, D. (1997). *The UK Maharajahs: Inside the South Asian Success Story.* Nicholas Brealey.

Haley, G. T. (1997a). A strategic perspective on Overseas Chinese networks' decision making. *Management Decision*, **35** (8), 587–94.

Haley, G. T. (1997b). The values Asia needs. *Business Times*, Editorial and Opinion Section, 24 December, p. 6.

Haley, G. T. and Haley, U. C. V. (1997). Making strategic business decisions in South and Southeast Asia. *Conference Proceedings of the First International Conference on Operations and Quantitative Management*, Jaipur, India, vol. 2, pp. 597–604.

Haley, G. T. and Tan, C. T. (1996). The black hole of Southeast Asia: strategic decision making in an informational void. *Management Decision*, **34** (9), 37–48.

Haley, G. T., Tan, C. T. and Haley, U. C. V. (1998). *The New Asian Emperors: The Overseas Chinese, Their Strategies and Competitive Advantages.* Butterworth-Heinemann.

Haley, U. C. V. (1997c). The Myers-Briggs type indicator and decision-making styles: identifying and managing cognitive trails in strategic decision making. In *Developing Leaders: Research and Applications in Psychological Type and Leadership Development* (C. Fitzgerald and L. Kirby, eds) pp. 187–223, Consulting Psychologists Press.

Haley, U. C. V. and Stumpf, S. A. (1989). Cognitive trails in strategic decision making: linking theories of personalities and cognitions. *Journal of Management Studies*, **26** (5), 477–97.

Heilbroner, R. L. and Singer, A. (1984). *The Economic Transformation of America: 1600 to the Present*, 2nd edn. Harcourt Brace Jovanovich.

Hofstede, G. (1994). Cultural constraints in management theories. In *International Review of Strategic Management* (D. E. Hussey, ed.) vol. 5, pp. 27–47, John Wiley.

Kahn, J. (1998). Asian crisis humbles Thai dynasty. *International Herald Tribune*, 17 April, p. 2.

Lau, D. C. (1995). *Mencius Says.* Federal Publications, Pte Ltd.

Mintzberg, H. (1987). Crafting strategy. *Harvard Business Review*, July–August, 66–75.

Mintzberg, H. (1994). The fall and rise of strategic planning. *Harvard Business Review*, January–February, 107–14.

Mintzberg, H. and Waters, J. (1985). Of strategies, deliberate and emergent. *Harvard Business Review* (6), 257–72.

Mizruchi, M. S. and Schwartz, M. (1987). *Intercorporate Relations: The Structural Analysis of Business.* Cambridge University Press.

Nohria, N. and Eccles, R. G. (1992). *Networks and Organizations: Structure, Form and Action.* Harvard Business School Press.

Piramal, G. (1996). *Business Maharajas*. Viking Penguin.

Redding, S. G. (1996). Weak organization and strong linkages: managerial ideology and Chinese family business networks. In *Asian Business Networks* (G. G. Hamilton, ed.) pp. 27–42, Walter de Gruyter.

Shigematsu, S. (1994). The study of overseas South Asians: retrospect and prospect. Working paper, Graduate School of International Development, Nagoya University, Japan.

Slywotsky, A. J. and Shapiro, B. P. (1993). Leveraging to beat the odds: the new marketing mind-set. *Harvard Business Review*, September–October, 97–107.

Vatikiotis, M. (1998). The Chinese way. *Far Eastern Economic Review*, 26 February, p. 45.

Vatikiotis, M. and Daorueng, P. (1998). Survival tactics. *Far Eastern Economic Review*, 26 February, 42–5.

Wada, K. (1992). *Yaohan's Global Strategy: The 21st Century is the Era of Asia*. Capital Communications Corporation Ltd.

Waley, A. (1996). *Confucius: The Analects*. Wordsworth Editions Ltd.

Chapter 17.1

Boxing with shadows – round two

■ George T. Haley ■

Despite the amazing changes occurring in Asia, our observations on business networks in Asia from Chapter 17 continue to hold. However, the regional changes covered in the first section provide windows of opportunity for multinational corporations (MNCs) to score some significant points in their continuous bout with the local Overseas Chinese and Indian networks operating in Asia.

In our book *New Asian Emperors*, we (Haley, Tan and Haley, 1998) argued that one of the Asian networks' great competitive advantages stemmed from their virtual monopoly on knowledge of local markets and conditions. Presently, everyone is starting from scratch. The markets are dithering from the knockout punches that landed right on several Asian economies' seemingly glass jaws over the past eighteen months. However, although we all know the Asian markets will recover, no one – even in the business networks – knows when the markets will recover or how they will evolve when they do so. Furthermore, when projecting markets' post-crisis evolutions, MNCs possess considerable advantages in market-research technology over most of the networks' companies. The MNCs must start investing now in knowledge acquisition and in leveraging that knowledge to beat the odds.

The Asian business networks have also enjoyed a traditional advantage in their close relationships with government authorities. The changes taking place now are loosening the business networks' hold on local government authorities in several countries, such as Thailand. In other countries, such as Malaysia and Indonesia, reformers are finally gaining significant support, possibly enough to challenge the old guards and their anointed successors. The business networks are working to build relationships with all future potentially prime political players within the various governments; but the MNCs can establish relationships also. If MNCs start to build relationships with rising political players now before those players commit to particular business networks, the MNCs will build from a more equal, favourable basis than they could have before. Though MNCs can probably never establish the strong relationships with governing authorities that the business networks can, they can build significant relationships to offset any future inroads that competitors from the business networks may drill.

Finally, the tremendous secrecy prevalent in the Asian business networks prevents outsiders, such as MNCs' executives, from knowing potential partners' true financial probities, trustworthiness and uprightness; even due diligence investigations can fail in some cases. The present crisis, in its disruptive momentum, provides an excellent opportunity to observe the business networks' companies. Though secretive, the companies with serious financial difficulties due to poor management will become apparent, especially those large enough to constitute legitimate partners for MNCs. Monitoring the region's business press should provide sufficient data (see the WWW resources in Chapter 15). The strains of conducting business during a crisis should also display trustworthy and upright partners. (Trustworthiness and uprightness constitute uniquely Asian cultural concepts dealing with appropriate behaviours and are discussed in detail in Haley, Tan and Haley, 1998.) By observing the business networks and seeing who continues to belong to a network, and who continues to work on their business projects, MNCs can see which of the businessmen and women the business networks consider as truly trustworthy and upright.

Though the present economic crisis generally presents a significant blow to business operations in Asia, to Western companies seeking to enhance their staying power in the boxing arena, it offers many blessings to add to their arsenal of punches and moves. So far, the Asian business networks have straddled Asia as the unquestioned regional economic powers. Mohammed Ali entered the ring against George Foreman's overwhelming power only after studying Foreman's fighting style and developing his rope-a-dope strategy. Now more than ever, the Western MNCs have to study their Asian markets and competitors so that they can develop their own innovative strategies for the Asian arena.

■ Reference

Haley, G. T., Tan, C. T. and Haley, U. C. V. (1998). *New Asian Emperors: The Overseas Chinese, their Strategies and Competitive Advantages.* Butterworth-Heinemann.

Chapter 18

Foreign companies and Chinese workers: employee motivation in the People's Republic of China[1]

■ Terence Jackson and Mette Bak ■

■ Introduction: the challenge of motivating Chinese employees

At the end of 1978, during its 'third plenum', the Chinese Communist Party Central Committee gave economic reform top-level priority. Following the Second Session of the Fifth National People's Congress on 1 July 1979, foreigners were permitted by law 'to establish equity joint ventures together with Chinese companies, enterprises or other economic organizations ... within the territory of the People's Republic of China, on the principle of equity and mutual benefit' (PRC, 1987).

Since the beginning of these economic reforms in 1979 the Chinese economy has exploded, with an average annual growth rate in gross national product (GNP) of 10 per cent over the last decade, with the attainment of 20 per cent in the coastal areas designated 'special economic zones' (EIU, 1994). Foreign direct investment more than doubled between 1987 and 1990 (Kelley and Shenkar, 1993), despite a slow-down after the Tiananmen Square incident, with an estimate of more than 150 000 joint ventures in China. Much of this investment comes from Hong Kong (68.2 per cent in 1992) and other countries of Eastern Asia, with European countries, and even the USA (with 4.6 per cent in 1992) badly represented.

Despite this economic growth, there are indications that productivity has been a problem. This may have implications for the attractiveness of China to foreign investors, despite low labour costs. A study undertaken in the mid-1980s indicated that productivity levels were 60–70 per cent of those in Hong Kong (Locket, 1987). A recent study (Turcq, 1995) indicates a steady rise in productivity relative to wage increases over the ten years from 1980 to 1990. But many of the problems and failures

[1] This chapter has been published previously by MCB University Press Limited: Jackson, T. and Bak, M. (1998). Foreign companies and Chinese workers: employee motivation in the People's Republic of China. *Journal of Organizational Change Management*, 11 (4), 282–300.

of international joint ventures in China have been associated with problems in the area of human resources management, and particularly in performance motivation and staff retention (Child, 1994; Child et al., 1990; Henley and Nyaw, 1990; Kelley and Shenkar, 1993; Wang, 1992; Wang and Satow, 1994).

Bjoerkman and Lu (1997) report that at a recent round-table discussion with the government of the People's Republic of China (PRC), 59 per cent of participants from foreign invested enterprises (FIE) concluded that recruiting and retaining managers (a significant input into human resource management) was the most significant problem facing FIEs in China. This represented twice the number who considered Chinese bureaucracy to be the major issue. Findings drawn from a study of sixty-seven Sino-foreign international joint ventures by Lu, Child and Yan (1997) show the highest cause of perceived difficulties occurring because of differences in management styles (according to twenty-six of the fifty-one foreign managers surveyed), and the second highest perceived cause of difficulties being human resource management in areas such as pay, welfare and arrangements of accommodation (eighteen out of fifty-one foreign managers). In this study, Chinese managers saw the highest cause of difficulties being expatriate managers without knowledge of the Chinese environment (twenty-nine out of the fifty-six Chinese managers surveyed), and the second highest cause being different management styles (eighteen out of fifty-six Chinese managers). In both sets of accounts within the sixty-seven international joint ventures, human resource management and related issues such as management styles were seen as the main causes of difficulties within the general management of such enterprises. These issues have major implications for the way Chinese workers are motivated within the enterprise, and the motivation of workers has an important impact on the success of the enterprise within China.

It may be that Western concepts of motivation are not relevant in a socialist China where people have been motivated perhaps only to do what was best for the country, with little overlap in practice to industrial productivity. Over the last two decades Chinese state enterprises have gone through a number of market-related reforms, in order to develop institutions pursuing profit and productivity rather than ideological, political or specifically social goals (Boisot and Child, 1988; Chen, 1995a; Jackson, 1992; Walder, 1986). With the changing face of China's social and economic infrastructure, motivational patterns may be changing. Perhaps they must change in order to facilitate additional increases in productivity, which will encourage further investment from the West. But it may be naïve none the less to think that Western managers can enter China with an armoury of motivational techniques which have proved useful back home.

This chapter sets out to look at Western approaches to motivating employees and to show why these approaches may not work in a Chinese context. Chinese work values and motivation are compared to these approaches and propositions advanced to indicate how Chinese employees may be motivated by Western MNCs, and then to compare these with current practices and attitudes within foreign firms and joint ventures in China. For the latter, a study carried out in Beijing by one of the authors (Bak, 1995) among thirteen foreign enterprises is drawn on. Evidence seems to indicate, from these results, that some Western practices may be inadequate. We then offer some practical suggestions for structural changes which may help in addressing these issues on motivating Chinese employees in the hope that this will provide useful input into foreign managers' conceptual and strategic resources.

■ Western motivational theories: are they applicable to Chinese employees?

The static-content theories of motivation are standard reading in Western textbooks, and form the basis of management training programmes. They underline our assumptions about motivating employees in the Western hemisphere. The best known theories are those of Maslow (1958/1970), Herzberg (1968), McClelland (1987) and McGregor (1960), and largely address the question 'What outcomes are attractive to an individual and why?' The development of incentive schemes within Western companies tends to focus on the satisfaction of such needs identified by Maslow and Herzberg through job design, participation in decision making, promotion opportunities, working conditions and pay.

Yet Maslow's (1958/1970) hierarchy of needs has been criticized as reflecting a particular individualist view of the world (Hofstede, 1980) with 'self-actualization' being at the top of the pyramid. Nevis (1983) suggests a revision of the hierarchy in the Chinese situation to reflect group loyalty and national unity which may need to be addressed even before physiological needs – where self actualization is in the service of the community; where individual esteem (achievement, independence, reputation and prestige) may not be a relevant concept in a highly collectivist society; and, where 'face' is more related to belongingness rather than to individual esteem.

These comments must also have implications for Herzberg's (1968) theory of hygiene factors where extrinsic factors, such as working conditions and money, when absent may cause demotivation. Motivators or intrinsic factors include content of the task, achievement, responsibility and growth. Belongingness may well be a 'hygiene' factor in this sense, where if this is absent little else is particularly meaningful.

McClelland's (1987) motivation theory suggests that people are differently motivated towards achievement, power, affiliation and avoidance, where the achievement motive is key to McClelland's view of economic development. Such achievement involves the creation of more efficient ways of doing things and solving problems, the preference for tasks which reveal successful performance, and the taking of personal responsibility for performance. These are concepts which may not apply to Chinese achievers. While there is some evidence to suggest that achievement is relatively important in China (Specter and Solomon, 1990; Stewart and Chong, 1990) this could be related, for example, to the need to achieve output quotas rather than reflecting any intrinsic satisfaction. When we consider, however, that in other Chinese societies outside the PRC, the proportion of entrepreneurs is high, and is an explanation of their economic success, we could conclude that Chinese culture does have a tradition which allows the development of high achievers (the Overseas Chinese are well documented in Chen, 1995b). Alternatively, it could be argued that those who left China, where traders were traditionally seen as being of low status, could only be successful outside of mainland China.

The power motive (McClelland, 1987) may also not be very strong in mainland China. The distance between the middle ranks and the high ranks is huge, with the latter being mainly unattainable, whereas advancing to the middle levels does not bring increased power of any significance. There are, however, little or no specific research findings in this area. Affiliation, on the other hand, has played a key role in China through work units (in urban areas) and production brigades (in rural areas). These took care of housing, children's education, marriages and often the timing of employees' child bearing. The social aspects of motivation within the job situation in China may therefore be significant.

The avoidance motive (McClelland, 1987) may be high in China, and may be a real problem for productivity: the fear of being punished for mistakes seems to be deep rooted in the mainland Chinese. Schermerhorn and Nyaw (1990) call this 'learned helplessness'. A person learns from an experience of past inadequacies to feel incapable of future success. A senior manager who is already a victim of learned helplessness does not expect initiative from middle managers. This may lead to passivity in the workplace and even a need for a high level of supervision. This is connected to a lack of achievement where taking risks is avoided, a high level of uncertainty avoidance, and in McGregor's (1960) terms, a preponderance of management styles and techniques which favour Theory X, rather than Theory Y. The former assumes that most workers dislike work and therefore try to avoid it. They must be controlled and coerced into achieving organizational goals. The latter assumes that employees seek responsibility, can make decisions and will exercise self-control when properly motivated. Evans, Hau and Sculli (1989) suggest that Theory X is more applicable in this context, whereas Theory Y may be more applicable in the West.

To understand more fully why Western assumptions of employee motivation may not work in China, it is important to first understand Chinese work values within the context of broader theories of cultural differences. We can then move on to propose approaches to the ways in which companies may formulate motivational policies and practices by reviewing motivational processes in the Chinese context.

■ Chinese work values

The normally cited 'classic' work on cultural values (Hofstede, 1980) is silent when it comes to the PRC. The more recent Chinese Cultural Connection (1987) brings Hofstede's work up to date, but only by adding a fifth dimension (Hofstede, 1991), which provides limited additional information to our current knowledge of China's work-related values. Even the more modern work of Trompenaars (1993) is surprisingly silent on such key areas as collectivism-individualism when it comes to China. Of course, Hofstede (1980) draws on data from Hong Kong and Taiwan to describe Chinese characteristics. But we should be wary of generalizing from these societies which have been exposed to Western ideas and practices for some time. However, it is likely that such value dimensions as collectivism–individualism, power distance, uncertainty avoidance, masculinity–femininity, as well as long term–short term ('Confucian dynamism'), have some relevance in the mainland China context and can help us to understand those aspects of motivation which are related to work values.

Power distance, for example, is high in China, with the unapproachability of the top stratum, but with distances between middle management, supervisors and workers being somewhat smaller (Locket, 1987; Warner, 1993). A person who advances through the system beginning as a worker, then up to foreman and finally middle management will gain comparatively little power and influence, and this may therefore not be a motivator. Also power structures are not well installed because of a lack of managers, and may take shape as a result of necessity. The respect for hierarchy and authority may well be rooted in Confucianism, together with a regard for age as a source of authority which is largely unknown in business in the West.

A view of uncertainty avoidance in China is not so clear cut. Hofstede's (1980) work indicates a lack of need to avoid ambiguity in Chinese cultures, and this may reflect the fact that China itself (as could be argued of Hong Kong) is relatively free of a highly regulated legal code, and has traditionally been ruled by men (power distance) rather than by laws (uncertainty avoidance), but more recent work (Chimezie, Osigweh and Huo, 1993) indicates a strong avoidance of uncertainty among Chinese, with a strong desire to maintain social order with a degree of predictability. But Hofstede (1991) in his later work argues that uncertainty avoidance may be an irrelevant concept which is linked to the question of 'truth'. Truth is not a relevant issue in Eastern thinking. The Chinese manager may well be motivated to save 'face' and to tell the other person what they want to hear, rather than what may be regarded as the absolute truth in Western eyes.

Masculinity–femininity is also a value dimension for which there is little direct information on China. Chinese cultures in Hofstede's IBM studies had medium scores for this dimension. The concept of masculinity represents an emphasis on competition and the centrality of work in one's life. Japanese managers, for example, score high on masculinity (Hofstede, 1991). The meaning of work study (MOW International Research Team, 1986) also indicates a high centrality of work for Japanese individuals. It is the degree of importance of working which influences employee motivation, and this is an area of information which is lacking in the context of China.

As one would expect, collectivism is high in Chinese cultures, with the main group of reference being the family (collectivism is target specific [Hui, 1990]). This is rooted in both Confucianism and the ancient land system which ensured the farmer and his family were immovable for economic reasons. Mao attempted to weaken this influence, but perhaps it will be the increasing economic prosperity of China which may further weaken collectivism. A different approach is worth noting here in that Chen, Meindl and Hunt (1997) suggest that increased economic success may be paralleled to a weakening of horizontal collectivism or interpersonal cohesion, and the strengthening of vertical collectivism or corporate loyalty and identification: an aspect which may be important in the development of corporate identity as we discuss below. Hofstede (1991) indicates a positive correlation between individualism and per capita GNP. Individualism may well be on the increase in China (Nevis, 1983) as no doubt it has already been in Hong Kong. The implications for this in motivational terms may be a higher emphasis on individual achievement rather than the mutual reliance of the group or collective.

However, rather than the short-term achievement orientation of many Western societies, China is characterized by long-term values (Hofstede, 1991) such as thrift and perseverance. This is believed to sustain steady economic growth (Hofstede and Bond, 1988) which has been borne out until recently by the 'economic miracles' of some of the Asia Pacific countries. Certain 'quick fix' management approaches, suggested by many Western management specialists, may therefore not provide motivators in a Chinese context. Different perspectives on time between China and the West also have implications for the perception of objectives, where the achievement of short-term objectives as an indicator of individual achievement may not be appropriate. This has implications for the introduction of individually based reward systems founded on goal achievement. A connected factor is that of locus of control (from Rotter, 1966), where Eastern cultures have a fatalistic view of destiny, where cause and effect is more likely to be attributed to external factors than internal factors which can be controlled by the individual. With a view that the individual has little control over short-term objectives, goal-based individual reward systems may not be appropriate.

As we indicated above, many researchers believe that the value system in China is changing. For example, Cyr and Frost (1991) argue that Chinese workers are shifting towards a value system which is more goal-achievement oriented rather than egalitarian. However, an empirical study of work values in eight different countries including China (Elizur et al., 1991) indicates a low importance in China of 'instrumental' values, such as pay, benefits, convenient working hours and working conditions. Taiwan scores high on the same instrumental values, which may indicate that the low importance of these factors in China is resulting from several decades of socialist influence rather than any fundamental Chinese cultural characteristic (assuming it is possible to separate these). Moreover, Vertinski et al. (1990) point out the greater weight traditionally placed upon ascribed rather than achieved status in Chinese society, as being a reflection of Confucian values. The limited empirical evidence of motivational indicators in the PRC does not therefore provide unequivocal evidence that China is moving towards an achievement society. It is therefore necessary for MNCs to consider specifically Chinese approaches to motivating employees, if they are to develop adequate personnel policies and practices within China.

■ How might Chinese workers be motivated?

There is evidence from studies undertaken in China, and among Chinese cultures, that particular motivational considerations apply in the Chinese context, and that certain motivational techniques have been successfully developed and employed. Child (1994) believes (following Tung, 1991) that the way Chinese enterprises motivate employees can be understood within Katz and Kahn's (1978) model of 'rule enforcement', 'external rewards' and 'internalized motivation'. By expanding this model slightly, we can produce at least a partial explanatory model of motivation which may be employed in the Chinese context, and from this to make certain propositions about how MNCs may better motivate their Chinese employees, as follows.

Rule enforcement (acceptance of the legitimacy of role prescription and organizational directives)

Rather than the use of rules and role prescriptions being seen as addressing uncertainty avoidance, it may be regarded as a form of role protection in the Chinese context. Child (1994) provides the example of job descriptions carrying little motivational content in terms of tasks or objectives to be achieved, but as an insurance against being asked to take on additional and unknown duties and against being overworked. This may also be indicative of the avoidance motive, in not wanting to take risks because of a deep-seated fear of punishment. However, the reverse side of the coin is the incentive to find ways around tightly enforced regulations in state enterprises in order to facilitate their running. Therefore, in order first to provide employees with a psychologically safe foundation from which to work effectively:

Proposition 1: There is a need to structure work tightly around well defined parameters which are documented, communicated and accepted by employees and supervisors, with an emphasis on role protection as well as task performance.

External rewards (attaching of incentives to produce desired performance outcomes)

Material incentives have been used by China's economic reformers in order to stimulate performance (Child, 1994). In terms of reward systems there is evidence that money is important in China as a motivator for employees. Also individual bonuses have existed in China since 1978 (Locket, 1987) and performance-related bonus incentives schemes since 1983 (Cyr and Frost, 1991). Cyr and Frost (1991) report on a survey undertaken in Eastern China in 1989 which indicates that workers would rather function in a system where pay is based on individual performance. However, there has been a tendency towards low differentiation of pay in an egalitarian reward system, reflecting a need to minimize competition and foster harmony in the workplace: a reflection of a strongly collectivist culture. Where pay differentials exist they are often based on length of service, perhaps reflecting respect for old age. It is also the case that state enterprise employees' wage structures are extremely complex and based on a whole number of different subsidies, bonuses and allowances (Henley and Nyaw, 1987; Laaksonen, 1988). Employees may be reluctant to leave this type of system in favour of a less socially supportive one. Although there is contradictory information about the desirability of performance-related pay, we know that there is a strong tradition of status accorded by ascription rather than achievement, and often based on age and length of service. Even in European countries which are more ascriptive than the UK or USA, managing by objectives (MBO) type systems have been largely unsuccessful, particularly when related to pay (for the example of France, see Barsoux and Lawrence [1990]) as young, high-performing newcomers to the organization may be rewarded more highly than those of a higher status in the organization. Individual performance incentives also often ignore the longer-term, group-focused performance which may be more important in a collectivist society, and instead focus on the short-term performance of individuals in isolation. Also within Chinese society, there is an expectation that the enterprise will take care of employees through housing and other social benefits, which must have a strong loyalty effect. On an understanding that performance is short term, while loyalty and belongingness are long term:

Proposition 2: Systems of pay should retain a strong element of reward through loyalty and seniority, as well as 'belongingness' elements such as housing allowances.

Internalized motivation (the internalization of organizational and political cultural factors)

A major source of internalized motivation in China has been through political indoctrination and campaigning (Tung, 1991). For example, there have been a number of 'emulation campaigns' in communist China following the Soviet pattern where workers are encouraged to strive to become 'labour heroes'. Chimezie, Osigweh and Huo (1993) describe this as an attempt to appeal to high performers who might otherwise feel inhibited to perform in an exemplary manner in an egalitarian culture. Such practices largely have been discredited since the events in Tiananmen Square in 1989.

However, a modern day equivalent can be seen in Japanese companies in China which send their best workers to Japan in order to learn from example and from being exposed to a foreign culture (Ireland, 1991). Through this exposure and emulation there is more willingness to change.

In addition, by building on a sense of belongingness and loyalty of Chinese workers, there is a good opportunity to develop internalized motivation from developing corporate identity through a strong organizational culture (see Child, 1994). Indeed, foreign companies may have a particular kudos for Chinese workers, and this could be built on to encourage long-term loyalty. Effective supervision would involve doing by example. New patterns of behaviour (including creativity and innovation) could be encouraged by emulation, both in the workplace and on training courses in China and, where appropriate (particularly for managerial and supervisory staff who can act as role models) abroad. Hence:

> Proposition 3: A focus should be placed on building corporate identity through effective induction and subsequent training programmes in order to promote 'the way we do things around here', as well as developing supervisors who can act as role models in developing and changing work-related behaviour towards that supported by the corporate culture.

Intrinsic motivation (the intrinsic attractiveness of the job)

In a study of six Chinese enterprises in 1985 and again in 1990, Child (1994) found that employees were satisfied with the intrinsic job content and challenge, and opportunities to enjoy social relationships in the workplace. However, there was dissatisfaction with the prospects for advancement and promotion. This led him to conclude that enterprises could unleash a considerable motivational potential by creating opportunities for employees to advance. This bears out the known historical problems of hierarchy and advancement which we have discussed above. If we take the total employment experience of Chinese employees and examine how we might develop the attractiveness of this, it could well be in the formulation of a career path for those who have successfully taken on board those work behaviours which are seen as appropriate to the organizational culture, and who themselves can act as role models in supervisory and management positions. Hence:

> Proposition 4: In order to develop loyalty, identity with the organization, requisite work related behaviour and intrinsic motivation for the total employment experience, a clear career path should be visible for employees who can develop effectively as future role models.

We now turn to the practices operated by foreign MNCs in China, to see how they try to motivate Chinese employees, and then to evaluate these practices against their apparent successes or failures.

▓ How do foreign enterprises motivate Chinese workers?

Following the above discussion on the appropriateness of motivational practices with Chinese workers, what do foreign companies in China actually do? An in-depth survey of motivational policies and methods used in thirteen international enterprises in China (see Table 18.1) was carried out by M. Bak in Beijing, by interviewing key managers who were most directly involved in the formulation of motivation policies and their implementation (principally human resource managers, chief executives and production managers as appropriate to the enterprise), both foreign and PRC Chinese. These key managers, who had been subjected to Western practices, had some familiarity with data collection methods and interview techniques and were familiar with the management of indigenous Chinese employees. They were seen as the best source of information.

Table 18.1 Companies surveyed in Beijing

Company	Type of organization	Nationality of parent company	Sector
ABB	Joint venture	Swiss/Swedish	Electrical engineering and manufacturing
AEG	Representative office	German	Electro-electronics
Beijing Toronto Hotel	Joint venture	Chinese	Hotel
Coopers & Lybrand	Joint venture	American	Auditing
EAC	Representative office	Danish	(LOTS) graphics divisions
ICI	Foreign company	British	Chemicals
Jardine Matheson-E-Jian Technical Services Co. Ltd	Joint venture	Hong Kong	Building services
Jianguo Hotel	Joint venture	American	Hotel
Jing Guang Centre	Joint venture	American	Hotel
Maersk (China) Shipping Co. Ltd (A.P. Moller Group)	Foreign company	Danish	Shipping
Northern Telecom	Foreign company	Canadian	Telecommunications
Novo Nordisk	Foreign company	Danish	Pharmaceuticals/biotechnology
Price Waterhouse	Joint venture	American	Auditing/taxation/consulting

First order data collection from Chinese workers and management was felt not to be suitable. Shenkar and Von Glinow's (1994) review of the literature provides almost insurmountable methodological problems, which the current authors felt were beyond the scope of this study to address. These include for questionnaires: unfamiliarity; a tendency to complete mid-range values; failure to distinguish among variables and the production of halo effects far more likely than for Western respondents; problems with answering hypothetical questions; using the group rather than self as the frame of references; and reporting a desired rather than an actual state. For interviews problems include: reserving the most important points to the end; and 'face' introducing distortions (see also Adler, Campbell and Laurent, 1989; Bond and Hwang, 1986; Metzger, 1977; Young, 1982).

Managers were asked to describe the type of motivational techniques and methods they actually employed, and the rationale for doing so. In order to avoid a direct examination of methods company by company, we have generalized the results from the thirteen companies as far as possible, and have pointed out exceptions where appropriate. We have subsequently classified their responses in terms of the modified Katz and Kahn (1978) model outlined above, as follows.

Rule enforcement

We first look at role allocation and performance by looking at the way responsibility is given and the way performance is directed through goal setting and appraisal, and then enforcement through sanctions for non-performance, and reinforcement through praise.

Responsibility

Generally there is a guarded attitude towards giving too much responsibility on the available evidence that workers like guidance and there is some fear of making mistakes resulting in inaction. Particularly older workers prefer clear instructions, although it was noted that many younger workers also prefer such an approach. Motivation is also seen as rising when more responsibility is given to employees in their own area. However, this is seen to come with experience, where, depending on the individual, more responsibility may be given. There is little evidence of precise job descriptions being used, and instructions seem to relate to the job at hand. General rules of conduct exist in some companies, and in one company these are made clear in a two-day induction session: no spitting, no smoking, how to dress and cut your hair (an in-house hairdresser is employed).

Goal-setting and appraisal

Several companies use goal-setting extensively, and see it as useful. This involves the setting of individual targets, face-to-face performance discussions, and weekly to annual appraisals, depending on the company.

Pressure and punishment

Direct punishment was only found in the hotel sector where some of the companies punish their staff for bad behaviour and not working. Deductions from salary or bonuses are seen to give positive results. For some offences up to three warnings can be given before dismissal. Penalty schemes for non-attendance at training sessions are also in operation. The use of pressure and punishment of this kind was not identified in companies outside the hotel industry.

Praise

Companies seem not to praise their employees very often. Individual praise in front of the group is not often used deliberately except in the hotel industry. A view elsewhere is that this may be negative or embarrassing.

External rewards

Incentives within the companies surveyed involve packages which include to a greater or lesser extent, money, bonus systems, and welfare benefits.

Money

Generally money is seen as important for recruiting and retaining employees, but not as a real motivator. It is seen as a hygiene factor in that it keeps staff in the company.

Bonus systems

By law, a large part of an employee's salary comprises bonuses and subsidies. This overlaps to a certain extent with the welfare package. Despite this, one company pays a fixed salary only. Some companies offer performance-related bonuses. One company has established smaller units or profit centres where performance measurement is undertaken monthly, and on which basis a bonus is paid to employees within the profit centre, with an element of the bonus reflecting also the performance of the company as a whole. Generally, it is seen that bonuses relating to individual performance would improve motivation, but this is not widespread.

Welfare package

This is seen as necessary but is not believed to motivate. The provision of housing in state companies causes problems when foreign companies do not provide housing. By moving to a foreign company, employees lose their house. There is therefore pressure on foreign companies to provide housing or an associated benefit. Company provision of local housing also may cut down on commuting time, which may benefit productivity. Some companies provide housing loans. For example, one company provided a ten-year tax free loan to key staff who had been in the company for at least five years. This type of provision is not seen as so important for younger employees living with parents. As Chinese workers give up benefits when they move to a foreign company, this has implications for recruitment.

Internalized motivation

There is evidence that some efforts are being made by foreign companies to engender corporate loyalty and belongingness through internalizing factors of motivation, which combine elements of example setting, training and social-building initiatives. However, the evidence that companies are deliberately attempting to foster identification with the company is not overwhelming.

Identification with company

Managers from at least two companies thought that working for a foreign joint venture or Fortune 500 company engendered pride in its employees. One company has a desire to promote a company culture without being specific about how they should do this, although the training aspects described below can be seen to contribute to corporate identity. One company also involves employees more by use of a suggestion box, a communication letter which did not last very long due to turnover and lack of resources, service campaigns, honesty campaigns, a smiling campaign, and badges and certificates for best workers.

Training

Most companies report some form of training as part of their motivational programme. Examples include lunchtime learning where the company buys lunch while courses in computing, languages or technology may be conducted. On-the-job training for one company takes place in China, while their top engineers are sent to Europe for one month a year to attend special courses. One company has set up a (transient) business school in China based at local hotels for a few days at a time, with a view to setting up a permanent classroom in the near future.

This type of activity is seen as enhancing the 'Western spirit', providing better qualifications and chances of promotion, and in some cases a chance of going abroad to train. There is also a danger of losing employees when they go abroad, and one company has adopted the practice of sending only married men abroad, to try to ensure that they return home. Other companies use the incentive of promotion on their return home. However, one hotel reported having to compel staff to attend training courses. When forced to participate, employees argue that they prefer to learn the handouts by heart, although the purpose might be to teach them to work in unforeseen circumstances. Punishment is given for non-attendance at training courses in this instance.

Setting a good example

It is generally seen as important that the supervisor or manager should set a good example to employees, although this is not viewed particularly as a general policy. It is seen more importantly as motivating employees to do the job, as often when the boss is away employees are reluctant to work.

Staff outings and activities

Several companies regard staff outings as motivators. Some companies encourage employees to organize these themselves, others have an impressive list of company-organized activities, including sports, dancing, birthday parties, annual staff parties, events with relatives, and seminars.

Intrinsic motivation

We use the term intrinsic motivation widely here to refer to the total employment experience. Under this heading the job itself, including working conditions, job design and social aspects of work, as well as career, can be identified as providing some degree of intrinsic motivation from the sample of companies examined.

Working conditions

There are some differences of opinion regarding the importance of working conditions. Generally Chinese workers are used to a lower standard from state-owned companies and tend to have low expectations. Therefore air conditioning, for example, is believed by one company not to be overly important. In another company, employees in the hot summer prefer to stay in the cool office rather than to go home. So environmental factors are likely to serve as an added bonus if available. There is also a view that Chinese employees expect a European working environment if working for a European company, and therefore expectations are generally high. In this vein, the availability of computers is used in one company to feed the perception by Chinese workers of computers as a status symbol. This may also be seen as a mechanism to enhance identification with a foreign company.

Job rotation and enrichment

Lip-service seems to be paid to job rotation and enrichment schemes, as there is little evidence of these being used, or when used being particularly effective. When managers were probed, one mentioned the possibility of sending a secretary from Beijing to work in Shanghai. In another company the human resource department recommends job rotation for its Chinese workforce. However, supervisors and managers around the company have resisted implementing such a scheme.

Social life at work

This aspect was not spontaneously mentioned by interviewed managers. One said that he spends longer talking to workers (including small talk) than in the West. He also spends more time with his local staff on social events outside normal working hours (such social events and activities have been discussed above under internalized motivation, and overlap with this aspect). There does not seem to be any mechanism used to encourage and foster the social dimension of work at the workplace, and this aspect seems to be left to extramural activities.

Promotion and career in company

Rapid promotion through an extensive staff ranking system is seen in one company as a very important motivational mechanism. As the company is successful in China, it can offer more opportunities with the growth of the company. All other companies were silent on the positive use of career planning and promotion as a motivational tool.

How successful are Western motivational techniques in China?

We now address the question of whether or not the motivational techniques used by foreign MNCs and joint ventures in China have the desired effects of motivating Chinese employees. We know that there are problems generally of productivity and retention of staff, as we noted above. Especially, some of the companies sampled report high turnover rates, and a lack of flexibility in their financial resources to be able to introduce some of the measures they would like. One of the high performers in China has a well-developed career planning and promotion policy as we saw, and this seems to have positive repercussions for its ongoing success. We are largely unable to compare directly financial success with the use of specific motivational techniques. This is simply because financial information is not readily available, and because of the methodological difficulties in establishing a connection between these variables in the presence of so many other contributing factors. We therefore evaluate motivational policies both in terms of the companies' own admissions of success or failure in the area of human resource management, and against the four propositions regarding good practice which we outlined above.

Rule enforcement

We first proposed (*Proposition 1*) that companies should structure work parameters tightly within a well-communicated statement which seeks to protect the employee within the role defined. Information coming from the sample companies suggests that this is not happening. Rule enforcement relates more to instructions for individual tasks, some goal-setting, and the use of punishment and praise in at least one sector. Companies report a reluctance of employees to take on responsibility or to show initiative, and to be involved in participative decision-making. They also report a need to supervise staff closely in order for them to work effectively (which may also be indicative of other problems). It would seem that the issues associated with rule enforcement and role protection are not therefore being directly addressed.

External rewards

Proposition 2 suggests that a system of pay should retain a reward for loyalty and seniority as well as a 'belongingness' element such as housing allowances. Yet companies are reporting problems associated with a lack of an effective reward systems, such as staff turnover (often directly identified with pay) a lack of productivity (sometimes associated with housing problems) and a general lack of loyalty to the company through job-hopping to get more pay. We saw above that motivational practices in companies centre on pay as a hygiene or holding factor and concentrate on a fixed salary plus some element of performance bonus, and reluctantly welfare provision such as benefits for housing. This does not seem to be seen as a motivational pushing influence or incentive.

Internalized motivation

In *Proposition 3* we suggest that corporate identity should be inculcated by effective induction and training programmes, and the development of supervisors as role models. We noted above that companies in our sample were keen to promote a company culture, but this was only generally addressed through training, and to a certain extent through organizing out-of-work social activities. We have already indicated that companies identify a problem of a lack of loyalty and subsequent turnover, and it may be that companies are not doing enough in this area. One company even reports that employees have to be made to go to training sessions. This may be that the training is viewed as irrelevant, or that it does not have an effect of inculcating corporate identity. The other side of the coin is that training may be effective in developing transferable skills (companies report a lack of experience and relevant skills among recruits, particularly when they come from the public sector). This can only add to employees' subsequent attraction to other foreign companies after a couple of years' experience and training in one foreign company, and may result in job-hopping.

Intrinsic motivation

Our final *Proposition 4*, suggests that a clear career path should be identifiable for employees in order to encourage them to develop as future role models and to instil intrinsic motivation for the total employment experience. Yet only one company really took career development seriously, and this was one of the most successful companies in our sample. Other companies identified a lack of resources in order to accomplish this. Other indicators of a lack of intrinsic motivation reported by companies were absenteeism, particularly at busy times and false expectations of a European working environment and attractiveness of the job, causing employees to become bored and disillusioned.

To summarize, the problems of motivation and performance identified by companies include high levels of turnover, absenteeism, lack of productivity and a reluctance to take on responsibility and make decisions without guidance. These seem to be ongoing issues which must reflect on the efficacy of current organizational policies on motivating Chinese employees.

■ Recommendations

It is hoped that the current study will provide a useful starting-point both for Western managers who are confronted with the issues of managing a Chinese workforce, and for researchers who wish to further examine and verify the findings within this study. It is important that the weaknesses within this study are identified. China comprises 9.6 million sq km with huge differences between north and south, between coastal and inland regions, between urban and country areas, between special economic zones and areas not so designated, and between Beijing and the other major cities of Shanghai, Tianjin, Shenyang, Wuhan and Guangzhou. What pertains in one area may not be the case in another. We have also obtained information from managers who are most involved in decisions regarding motivational policies and practices. A further study among Chinese employees in order to get their views on motivational practices would be desirable in order to further validate our findings, although such a study would have to surmount the methodological problems involved in collecting data which we listed above.

We have provided a partial model for understanding motivational issues within the Chinese context by modifying that of Katz and Kahn (1978), and through this have provided suggestions for how companies may tackle the problems of motivation. There are two problems with providing firm advice to managers within this context. First, China is a complex country and difficult sometimes for outsiders to comprehend; and second, China is in transition and therefore constantly changing. Bearing this in mind and taking into account the recommendations and discussion above, we close with specific structural and policy recommendations which follow from our four propositions. We indicate how these might be reflected in specific human resource practices aimed at motivating Chinese employees in foreign joint venture companies:

1 Organizational rules and procedures should be well documented and communicated in order to reduce risk and ambiguity. This should provide a strong element of 'security' for employees by informing them of rules of conduct, the parameters and scope of their jobs, and expectations in terms of performance and quality. This reflects a need to protect employees within defined roles and rules, and should be operationalized in human resource practices by:

   (a) providing clear job descriptions as well as clear instructions for specific tasks. As confidence levels grow alongside experience in a foreign company, participation in the decision-making process could produce high levels of motivation, for carefully selected employees;

   (b) experimenting with praise and goal setting in order to raise confidence levels.

2 Structural reward systems should include a 'loyalty' element which inculcates 'belongingness', and reflects seniority, rather than directly addressing an achievement motive, which may not be as relevant as in a Western setting. This should include provisions such as housing allowances. Additional human resource practices should include:

(a) ensuring money is commensurate with an employee's standing in the organiza- tion, as this may well be seen as a measure of success for individuals and for their family.

3 A strong corporate identity should be fostered, and human resource policy should reflect a desire to inculcate both common work values, and a belongingness to the company through:

(a) developing effective induction programmes which draw the new employee closer to the company;

(b) developing subsequent training programmes which reflect the way things are done in the organization, while taking care not to concentrate too heavily on training for skills which are easily transferable to other enterprises;

(c) focusing on developing role models: supervisors who are trained in the way of the company, and can gain standing in the organization by representing the values and practices of the organization;

(d) as a foreign manager, working hard, not coming in late, not drinking tea all day, and expecting Chinese employees to copy your positive behaviour;

(e) not getting too hung up on job enrichment programmes: these seem to have only limited success when they focus on individualistic values. Focusing on team- working may be more productive.

4 Attention should be paid to developing clear career paths as part of human resource planning as well as through a need to develop loyalty, identification with the orga- nization, required work-related behaviour and intrinsic motivation for the total work experience. Human resource managers should therefore:

(a) present clear options for career development: this seems to be a major motivator, although significantly lacking in current motivational design. Career paths should be particularly visible for those who can develop as effective role models.

The current study therefore indicates that the human resource strategy of foreign enterprises should clearly reflect a consideration of well defined rule enforcement; external rewards which are appropriate to the Chinese situation and reflect belong- ingness; internalized motivation through identification with the corporation; and intrinsic motivation which focuses on the total employment situation. In addition, this and other studies discussed above have identified a lack of sensitivity by Western managers on human resources issues, and a lack of understanding of motivators in the Chinese situation. For example, the study by Lu, Child and Yan (1997) identifies dif- ferences in management style as a primary cause of problems. It would seem that those responsible for human resource management are not sufficiently aware of what may work and what may not work in a Chinese situation. Steps should therefore be taken to develop appropriate training programmes prior to expatriate assignments, and provide opportunities for Western managers to reflect on their experiences subse- quently in the job with colleagues, both Western and Chinese. It is probably through these measures which companies operating in China can most effectively and directly make the necessary changes to ensure optimal motivation and performance from Chinese employees.

■ References

Adler, N. J., Cambell, N. and Laurent, A. (1989). In search of appropriate methodology: from outside the People's Republic of China looking in. *Journal of International Business Studies*, **70** (1), 61–74.

Bak, M. (1995). Optimisation of human resource management in international environments: guidelines for success in motivating Chinese employees. European Research Project (unpublished Master's dissertation), EAP European School of Management, Oxford.

Barsoux, J.-L. and Lawrence, P. (1990). *Management in France*. Cassell.

Bjoerkman, I. and Lu, Y. (1997). Human resource management practices in foreign invested enterprises in China: what has been learned? In *Advances in Chinese Industrial Studies* (S. Stewart and A. Carver, eds) vol. 5, pp. 155–72, JAI Press.

Boisot, M. and Child, J. (1988). The iron law of fiefs: bureaucratic failure and the problem of governance in the Chinese economic reforms. *Administrative Science Quarterly*, **33**, 507–27.

Bond, M. H. and Hwang, K. K (1986). The social psychology of Chinese people. In *The Psychology of the Chinese People* (M. H. Bond, ed.) Oxford University Press.

Chen, C. C. (1995a). New trends in reward allocation preferences: a Sino–US comparison. *Academy of Management Journal*, **38**, 408–28.

Chen, C. C., Meindl, J. R. and Hunt, R. G. (1997). Testing the effects of vertical and horizontal collectivism: a study of reward allocation preferences in China. *Journal of Cross-Cultural Psychology*, **28** (1), 44–70.

Chen, M. (1995b). *Asian Management Systems*. Routledge.

Child, J. (1994). *Management in China during the Age of Reform*. Cambridge University Press.

Child, J., Boisot, M., Ireland, J., Li, Z. and Watts, J. (1990). *The Management of Equity Joint Ventures in China*. China–EC Management Institute.

Chimezie, A., Osigweh, Y. and Huo, Y. (1993). Conceptions of employee responsibility and rights in the US and People's Republic of China. *International Journal of Human Resources Management*, **4** (1).

Chinese Cultural Connection (1987). Chinese values and the search for culture-free dimensions of culture. *Journal of Cross-Cultural Psychology*, **18** (2), 143–64.

Cyr, D. and Frost, P. (1991). Human resources management practice in China: a future perspective. *Human Resource Management*, **30** (2), 199–215.

EIU (1994). *Economist Intelligence Unit Quarterly Reports China and Mongolia*, 4th Quarter.

Elizur, D., Borg, I., Hunt, R. and Beck, I. M. (1991). The structure of work values: a cross-cultural comparison. *Journal of Organisational Behaviour*, **12**, 21–38.

Evans, W. A., Hau, K. C. and Sculli, D. (1989). A cross-cultural comparison of managerial styles. *Journal of Management Development*, **8** (3), 5–13.

Henley, J. S. and Nyaw, M. K. (1987). The development of work incentives in Chinese industrial enterprises – material versus non-material incentives. In *Management Reforms in China* (M. Warner, ed.) Frances Pinter.

Henley, J. S. and Nyaw, M. K. (1990). The system of management and performance of joint ventures in China: some evidence from Shenzhen special economic zone. *Advances in Chinese Industrial Studies*, **1** (B), 277–95.

Herzberg, F. (1968). *Work and the Nature of Man*. Staples Press.

Hofstede, G. (1980). *Culture's Consequences: International Differences in Work-Related Values.* Sage.

Hofstede, G. (1991). *Cultures and Organisations: Software of the Mind.* McGraw-Hill.

Hofstede, G. and Bond, M. (1988). The Confucian connection: from cultural roots to economic growth. *Organisational Dynamics,* **16** (4), 4–21.

Hui, C. H. (1990). Work attitudes, leadership styles and managerial behaviour in different cultures. In *Applied Cross-cultural Management* (W. E. Brislin, ed.) Sage.

Ireland, J. (1991). Finding the right management approach. *China Business Review,* January–February, 14–17.

Jackson, S. (1992). *Chinese Enterprise Management,* De Gruyter.

Katz, F. and Kahn, R. (1978). *The Social Psychology of Organisations.* Wiley.

Kelley, L. and Shenkar, O. (eds) (1993), *International Business in China.* Routledge.

Laaksonen, O. (1988). *Management in China: During and after Mao.* Walter de Gruyter.

Locket, M. (1987). China's special economic zones: the cultural and managerial challenges. *Journal of General Management,* **2** (3), 21–31.

Lu, Y., Child, J. and Yan, Y. (1997). Adventuring in new terrain: managing international joint ventures in China. In *Advances in Chinese Industrial Studies* (S. Stewart and A. Carver, eds) vol. 5, pp. 103–23, JAI Press.

McClelland, D. C. (1987). *Human Motivation.* Cambridge University Press.

McGregor, D. (1960). *The Human Side of Enterprise.* McGraw-Hill.

Maslow, A. (1958/1970). *Motivation and Personality,* 2nd edn. Harper and Row.

Metzger, T. A. (1977). *Escape from Predicament.* Columbia University Press.

MOW International Research Team (1986). *The Meaning of Working: An International Perspective.* Academic Press.

Nevis, E. (1983). Cultural assumptions and productivity: the United States and China. *Sloan Management Review,* **24,** 17–29.

PRC (1987). Law of the PRC on Chinese-foreign equity joint ventures. *The Laws of the PRC.*

Rotter, J. B. (1966). General expectancies for internal versus external control of reinforcement. *Psychological Monographs,* **80** (1), Whole No. 609.

Schermerhorn, J. R. and Nyaw, M.-K. (1990). Managerial leadership in Chinese industrial enterprises. *International Studies of Management and Organisation,* **20** (1–2), 9–21.

Shenkar, O. and Von Glinow, M. A. (1994). Paradoxes of organisational theory and research: using the case of China to illustrate national contingency. *Management Science,* **40,** 56–71.

Specter, C. N. and Solomon, J. S. (1990). The human resource factors in Chinese management reform. *International Studies of Management and Organisation,* **20** (1–2), 69–83.

Stewart, S. and Chong, C. H. (1990). Chinese winners: views of senior PRC managers on the reasons for their success. *International Studies of Management and Organisation,* **20** (1–2), 57–68.

Trompenaars, F. (1993). *Riding the Waves of Culture: Understanding Cultural Diversity in Business.* Nicholas Brealey.

Tung, R. L. (1991). Motivation in Chinese industrial enterprises. In *Innovation and Work Behavior* (R. M. Steers and L. W. Porter, eds) 5th edn, McGraw-Hill.

Turcq, D. (1995). The global impact of non-Japan Asia. *Long Range Planning,* **28** (1), 31–40.

Vertinski, I., Tse, D. K., Wehrung, D. A, and Lee, K.-H. (1990). Organisational design and management norms: a comparative study of managers' perceptions in the

People's Republic of China, Hong Kong and Canada. *Journal of Management*, **16** (4), 853–67.

Walder, A. G. (1986). *Communist Neo-traditionalism*. University of California Press.

Wang, Z. M. (1992). Managerial psychological strategies for Chinese-foreign joint ventures. *Journal of Managerial Psychology*, **7** (3), 10–16.

Wang, Z. M. and Satow, T. (1994). Leadership styles and organisational effectiveness in Chinese-Japanese joint ventures. *Journal of Managerial Psychology*, **9** (4), 31–6.

Warner, M. (1993). Human resources management with Chinese characteristics. *International Journal of Human Resources Management*, **4** (1), 45–65.

Young, L. W. L. (1982). Inscrutability revisited. In *Language and Social Identity* (J. J. Gumperz, ed.) Cambridge University Press.

Chapter 18.1

China in the wake of the Asian crisis

■ Terence Jackson and Mette Bak ■

Among the widespread economic slowdown projected for the region as a result of the financial crisis and currency devaluation in Southeast Asia and Korea, China's trading results for the first quarter of 1998 were unexpected. Official figures indicated that exports increased 13.2 per cent to US$40 billion between January and March. The trade surplus during this period was US$10.6 billion. Foreign investment increased by 10.1 per cent for contracted investment and 9.7 per cent for actually used foreign investment. Although Asian countries were buying less from China, exports with other continents increased by 17 per cent in the first quarter of 1998.

State Statistics Bureau figures also suggest that the economy grew by 7.2 per cent in the first quarter, although this is below the target of 8 per cent growth for 1998 set by Chen Jinhua, the minister in charge of the State Planning Commission. Other macro-economic goals set down include investment in fixed assets to increase by 10 per cent, retail prices controlled within 3 per cent, imports and exports to reach US$345 billion, the natural population growth to be confined to 1.06 per cent, and the registered unemployment rate should be about 3.5 per cent in the urban areas (the real rate is a much higher 7 to 8 per cent). This within a general policy of promoting development while maintaining stability.

Job creation has become a priority with 11–13 million unemployed in 1997, 13–15 million in 1998 and a likely 15–18 million in 1999. Although GDP has grown by 12 per cent per year between 1991 and 1996, unemployment has increased annually by around 1 per cent. This is the highest since the founding of the People's Republic. State enterprises are due to lay off 8–10 million workers in the next three years, with large influxes of migrant rural workers, 22 million surplus workers in the state sector and 4 million government staff to be laid off as a result of streamlining.

China is the second largest recipient of foreign direct investment (FDI) in the world next to the USA. One hundred and forty thousand foreign invested enterprises operate in China, with 21 001 being approved for operation in 1997. FDI totalled US$49.5 billion in 1997, up 15 per cent from 1996. This has directly created jobs for 17.5 million people (10 per cent of the non-agrarian population). It is against this backdrop that this chapter can be viewed.

Foreign companies are continuing to play a significant role in China's economy, and continuing to provide employment. With the general decline of employment in the state sector, foreign managers will play a role in developing and managing people not used to the demands of competitiveness and results orientation. The attraction of China to foreign companies may diminish not only through a continuing demise of the Asian economy, but also through lack of productivity of Chinese workers. There is, therefore, an even bigger need for foreign managers to understand employee motivation in order to develop the capabilities of people and the effectiveness and profitability of foreign invested enterprises in China.

■ WWW sources

http://www.chinapoint.com/news/business/asia/china/economy.htm
16 September 1998
http://www.ccpit.org/engVersion/cp_info/cp_infor.html 16 September 1998

Chapter 19

Effective leadership in joint ventures in Vietnam: a cross-cultural perspective[1]

■ Truong Quang, Fredric William Swierczek and Dang Thi Kim Chi ■

■ Introduction

To try to stimulate economic growth, Vietnam implemented in 1987 what was one of the most investment-friendly laws in Southeast Asia. Because of this law, many international companies have started operations in Vietnam. According to recently published statistics, Vietnam has attracted 1784 projects with a total investment capital amounting to US$31.7 billion as of February 1998 (*Vietnam Economic Times*, 1998a). Table 19.1 lists the major investors.

This pattern has not changed very much over the past years (Haley and Haley, 1997: 597). The most controversial investors in Vietnam are those from Taiwan, Korea and Hong Kong with which there have been many labour disputes. The USA and France have also been associated with a number of problem joint ventures.

However, Vietnam is facing a crisis of foreign investment. Even before the regional economic crisis there were signs of a slowdown, particularly of foreign direct investment (FDI). New commitments last year ran to US$4 billion dollars – less than half of the previous year's US$8.7 billion (Stier, 1998: 9).

The problem of declining FDI in investment while dramatic is less important than the slow implementation of projects. As of February 1998, with over ten years of *doi moi*, US$30.4 billion dollars of projects have been licensed, of this only US$12.4 billion has been implemented (*Vietnam Economic Times*, 1998b). This is a 40 per cent implementation rate. Even in the two priority cities for investment, Hanoi has received US$13 billion and implemented 5 billion (41 per cent) and Ho Chi Minh City gained US$9 billion, but only 4 billion has been allocated (44 per cent). For the year 1997, Hanoi's performance was worse. US$913 million worth of licences were given but only 34 per

[1] This chapter has been published previously by MCB University Press Limited: Quang, T., Swierczek, F. W. and Chi, D. T. K. (1998). Effective leadership in joint ventures in Vietnam: a cross-cultural perspective. *Journal of Organizational Change Management*, 11 (4), 357–72.

cent were implemented while Ho Chi Minh City received US$1.8 billion with 47 per cent implemented (Chung, 1997; 21).

Table 19.1 Top ten foreign investors in Vietnam

Rank	Country	Projects	Total capital $ (billions)
1	Singapore	175	6.20
2	Taiwan	304	4.10
3	Hong Kong	191	3.74
4	Japan	218	3.57
5	South Korea	191	3.13
6	France	91	1.48
7	Malaysia	60	1.35
8	USA	69	1.23
9	Thailand	78	1.10
10	British Virgin Islands	54	1.04

Source: *Vietnam Economic Times* (1998a: 11).

There have been a number of high-profile withdrawals, for example Chrysler which abandoned a US$190 million car plant, or Total which withdrew from Vietnam's multi-billion refinery project.

In terms of foreign investment failures from 1988 until November 1997, 694 projects were dissolved and 44 expired, out of 4514 projects. This is an official failure rate of 16 per cent (Thu, 1998: 24). The failure rate of joint ventures is conservatively estimated at twice this rate.

In early February 1998 nearly 800 foreign businessmen identified the current foreign investment problems which have not changed in five years:

1 Inadequate implementation of the legal framework.

2 Red tape and bureaucracy.

3 Unfair treatment in costing projects.

4 Import/export tariffs.

5 Corruption.

Vi Le, Commercial Counsellor of Australia, described the present investment climate in Vietnam:

> There have been too many high profile failures or withdrawal cases, too many disputes between joint venture partners, too many problems associated with the lack of transparency in the law which allows for too many different (and changing) interpretations by bureaucrats which in turn create unforeseen delays and costs for investors. (*Saigon Times*, 1998: 18)

In such a culturally complex business environment, expatriate managers are not only judged with respect to their technical and international business knowledge and experience, but also on their personal characteristics and leadership skills. Insufficient knowledge and limited understanding of each partner's culture often create open and long-lasting conflicts between international managers and local counterparts and employees. In the worst cases, this leads to the failure of the business partnership (Quang, 1997).

This chapter explores the role of effective leadership in the context of a dynamic business environment. Vietnam is an interesting case because:

1 Vietnam is the first Communist country to join the Association of South East Asian Nations (ASEAN); a free market economic grouping in the Asia-Pacific region.

2 Vietnam insists on its own formula of 'a market economy with a socialist character'.

3 Economic growth, considerably high in the last three years (8.2 per cent on average), has not been supported by a consistent and institutionalized foreign investment framework.

4 The managerial competency of local managers is generally limited, which requires a high influx of expatriates to fill the gap.

5 The nature of effective leadership has not been clearly identified in Vietnam.

Understanding effective leadership may help international and local managers in Vietnam to achieve better results in the very complex business and cultural environment characteristic of joint ventures.

■ Culture and joint venture success

Co-operative ventures are increasing in international business because of the well-known imperatives to be simultaneously global and local. The role of culture in the success and failure of joint ventures is still not well researched, despite the seminal efforts of Lane and Beamish who recognized that: 'many Western corporations seek co-operative ventures as a quick fix to global competitiveness without understanding the relationships being established and the behavioural and cultural issues involved' (Lane and Beamish, 1990: 88).

Not developing this understanding is the root of poor performance and the eventual failure of the joint venture:

> Failure stems from the influence of culture on behavior and management systems which create unresolved conflicts. Compatibility between partners is the most important factor in the endurance of a global alliance. Differences between national cultures, if not understood, can lead to poor communication, mutual distrust and the end of the venture. (Lane and Beamish, 1990: 88)

Any partnership will involve the interaction of at least two different cultures. How the cultures blend will determine the future development of the venture:

> The full potency of culture can be seen during the implementation of an international joint venture when two disparate cultures are forced to become one. As a matter of fact, the establishment of an international joint venture always results in the crossing or the interaction of parental cultures ... When cultures cross, a cultural shock can occur, often

accompanied by negative effects on organizational involvement and work climate. (Meschi and Roger, 1994: 199)

This clash of cultures is captured in the cultural distance involved between the partners. The less distance, the more compatible the partners will be, and the more successful will be the international joint venture (Bowditch and Buono, 1989). Cultural distance can be measured according to the categories developed by Hofstede (1980), power distance, individualism, uncertainty avoidance, masculinity and long-term orientation. For example:

1 Power distant cultures have less trust and greater organizational controls.

2 Long-term cultures value trust because it supports business results (Shane, 1992: 299).

Since trust is a major dimension of effective partnership, those cultures which emphasize trust would minimize the impacts of cultural distance. In high trust ventures, organizational controls are often based on shared values such as duty or obligation to others (Shane, 1992: 300).

Cultural distance is most clearly shown in terms of communication. This causes problems, particularly when the partners do not share a common working language. The local values, beliefs and norms for getting the jobs done are generally constrained by the international partner's approach to managing the joint venture (Walters, Peters and Dess, 1994: 8).

Partnership criteria

From the perspective of joint ventures, the selection of partner, generally the local partner, is of paramount importance. One of the major studies on partnership describes this issue: 'Studies typically cite the need for selecting the "right" or "proper" partner, one which is "complementary". Indeed, it has been argued that a lack or erosion of complementarity is the most important factor undermining the effectiveness of the international joint venture process' (Geringer, 1991: 42).

Partnership selection distinguishes between criteria for partners associated with operational skills and resources which a venture requires for its competitive success (i.e. task related) and criteria associated with efficiency and effectiveness of partners' co-operation (i.e. partner related) (Geringer, 1991: 45).

According to Geringer (1991: 46), these partner-related criteria include:

• partner's national or corporate culture

• favourable past association

• compatibility

• trust.

However, Geringer (1991) only concentrates on task-related criteria, which is understandable, but leaves the relationship aspects very much neglected. This is a significant gap because the relationship aspects of the partnership seem to be the most relevant for success:

> Partnership will be based on mutual interests, trust and the management of ongoing relationships. Alliances and joint ventures will focus executive behaviour on working collaboratively, communicating and gaining consensus (Lane and Beamish, 1990: 88).

For long-term results, commitment, willingness to work with the local partner as well as management skills and problem-solving are required. However, multinational managers have not learned these relationship skills (Lane and Beamish, 1990: 99). A review of successful alliances has identified the following important criteria:

1 An alliance is effective when the driving forces are complementary.

2 It should also have complementary strengths – strategic synergy.

3 Both partners should share a co-operative spirit – the importance of 'chemistry'.

4 Partners are willing to address new risks, and are committed to flexibility and creativity.

5 Partners should have compatible styles of management and corporate cultures.

6 Partners and managers should be able to interact well with their counterparts (Lynch, 1994: 40).

This review suggests various propositions which will be considered in this research. These are listed in Table 19.2.

Table 19.2 Propositions on leadership style and successful joint ventures

---

1 Joint ventures will be more successful where there is a higher degree of compatibility in the leadership styles of the partners.

2 Joint ventures will be more successful where there is a greater emphasis on closing the cultural distance and on developing a multi-cultural foundation for management.

3 Joint ventures with a leadership style which emphasizes trust, communication and mutual objectives will be more successful.

4 Joint ventures in which the partners emphasize a relationship style based on teamwork and collaboration will be more successful.

5 The greater the complementarity of leadership styles of the partners in the joint venture the greater the likelihood of success of the joint venture.

6 The greater the emphasis of multicultural leadership characteristics and skills in the joint venture, such as flexibility, empathy, understanding problem-solving, communication and relationship building, the greater the likelihood of success of the joint venture.

■ Joint venture management characteristics

What are the key characteristics a manager should have to be effective in joint ventures? There has been considerable emphasis in the literature on such characteristics:

Global competent managers need a new and broader range of skills than has the traditional expatriate. Global managers cannot focus on a single country and culture, and they cannot be limited to managing relationships between headquarters and a single subsidiary. They will have to learn about many foreign cultures' perspectives, tastes, trends, technologies and approaches to conducting business. They will have to be skillful at working with people of many cultures and perspectives. (Adler and Bartholomew, 1993: 44)

Global managers use cross-cultural skills on a daily basis. It will not just be a new set of values or a more prepared orientation to new cultural situations. Cross-cultural management represents a more effective form of international management. Such managers will be able to combine many beliefs and backgrounds into a creative organizational culture rather than simply integrating into the dominant culture of the headquarters' nationality (Adler and Bartholomew, 1993: 44).

A study assessing the effective cross-cultural management style of Masters in Business Administration (MBA) graduates in International Business from 1977 to 1992 suggests several characteristics are important: flexibility, empathy, tolerance for ambiguity, problem solving, self-reliance and responsiveness to challenges (Feldman and Thomas, 1992: 291).

Intercultural problems between joint venture partners leads to failure (Stening and Hammer, 1992: 78). To be effective the appropriate joint venture should emphasize relationships – satisfy interpersonal needs, understand feelings, empathize with employees, work with local partners effectively and develop cross-cultural teams (Haley, 1997; Stening and Hammer, 1992: 82).

For example, a study of 291 American managers in Japan and Thailand, and Japanese managers in the USA and Thailand showed that Japanese managers had a less favourable attitude towards their intercultural experience and their social skills than American managers (Stening and Hammer, 1992: 86). Because of this limitation, Japanese managers were less effective in intercultural interaction or in managing joint ventures.

The more important factors of effective leadership tend to be what actions managers take to facilitate cross-cultural understanding and relationship building. In general, most international managers are not well prepared to manage in joint ventures despite their recognition of the appropriate characteristics and skills required. These examples of research on management styles and skills suggest support for the leadership propositions outlined in Table 19.2.

■ Research methodology

This study was designed based on the ASEAN Perspectives on Excellence in Leadership (APEL) research project, which was undertaken by the University of Brunei Darussalam in 1991. Over 350 managers in ASEAN, excluding Vietnam, participated in this survey. The purpose of APEL was 'to study the perceptions of excellence in leadership within both private and public sector organizations in ASEAN countries' (Selvarajah et al., 1995: 29).

The research used the same ninety-four item questionnaire designed for the APEL project. To consider leadership styles in joint ventures, this study included both Vietnamese and international managers. The survey covered four dimensions, i.e.

leadership characteristics, leadership behaviours, organizational demands and environmental awareness.

A total of 200 questionnaires were sent to local and international managers in Hanoi and Ho Chi Minh City, the two major centres for joint ventures in Vietnam. In total, 127 managers working for 35 joint ventures returned surveys. Over half were Vietnamese. The international managers represented respondents of ten different countries, namely Asia, North America and Europe.

About half of the respondents were 36 years old or younger. Most were male, only one quarter were women. They were mostly employed in companies with over 500 employees and had more than ten years' experience in managerial positions.

Two statistical methods were used to analyse the data collected:

1 Factor analysis: to determine the underlying, common themes or relationships in leadership. Varimax rotation was used to determine the interpretation of the factors. To reduce the emphasis on quantitative analysis only the factors are identified, the relevant variables which make up the factors are not included.[2]

2 The t-test: to test the significant differences between Vietnamese and international managers on the factors which were established from the factor analysis.

The analysis will be based on the conceptual framework as outlined in Figure 19.1. As Figure 19.1 illustrates, joint ventures in Vietnam will face a variety of organizational demands for change to achieve better results. One influence on change will come from factors in the environment such as policy changes to improve the foreign investment climate. Another influence on organizational change will be the leadership characteristics of the joint venture management, which would support changes in performance such as sufficient responsibility and an open, practical orientation to change.

The key dimension of effective leadership in joint ventures will be the requirements

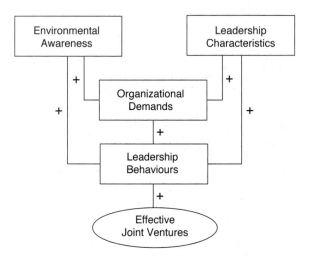

Figure 19.1. Leadership dimensions and effective joint ventures

[2] The factor analysis is not included in this chapter. However, it is available from the authors via e-mail: qtruong@ait.ac.th

that organizational demands such as performance, productivity and strategic vision will have on leadership behaviours. To change to a performance-oriented organization will require a leadership style which emphasizes teamwork, delegation and a strong people orientation.

Successful joint ventures will likely have this profile. Unsuccessful joint ventures will be characterized by a negative profile of leadership behaviour based on control. This research will compare the two groups of managers in joint ventures on the same leadership dimensions to assess their similarities and differences.

■ Overview of leadership

The statistical analysis of the responses reveals the most critical characteristics, knowledge and actions that are important for managers in joint ventures. The respondents ranked the top ten important statements that they perceived as most contributing to effective leadership. A five-point scale was used in ranking the importance of statements.

Table 19.3 shows the top ten leadership characteristics for managers in Vietnam. They represent characteristics related to personal qualities (dependable, honest, responsible). Most, however, are related to managerial behaviours (strategic vision, logical problem-solving, consistent decision-making). The small difference between 4.45 and 4.24 demonstrated in Table 19.3 can be interpreted that all respondents perceived these qualities as important.

Table 19.3 Most important characteristics of leadership in Vietnam compared to ASEAN

Top ten characteristics	Vietnam ranking	
1 Be dependable and trustworthy	4.45	
2 Be honest	4.43	(1)[a]
3 Have a strategic vision for the organization	4.34	(2)
4 Have confidence in dealing with people	4.30	(4)
5 Be logical in solving problems	4.29	
6 Be consistent in making decisions	4.26	
7 Adapt to changing working conditions	4.25	
8 Organize work time efficiently	4.25	(7)
9 Adjust organization structure and rules to the realities of practice	4.24	
10 Accept responsibility for mistakes	4.24	

Note: [a] Parentheses indicate the ranking of the value from ASEAN respondents (the full data for the ASEAN Leadership study is in Selvarajah et al., 1995)

Only a few similar characteristics were clearly reflected in the ranking of importance of Vietnamese managers compared to the findings of the ASEAN managers. For example, 'be honest' was shared as a very important characteristic for excellent leaders (ranked first in ASEAN, second in Vietnam). Both groups of managers also showed a similar concern for strategic vision and organizing work efficiently. However, Vietnamese managers tended to give more weight to managerial behaviours than their ASEAN counterparts. They shared a concern for relationships, for example confidence in dealing with people.

The most striking difference between the Vietnamese managers and their ASEAN counterparts is that managers in Vietnam ranked 'be dependable and trustworthy' at the top of the list. This was not mentioned in the top-ten list of ASEAN leaders. This highlights that Vietnamese managers regard 'trust' as a key success factor, especially in joint ventures with foreign partners (Quang, 1997).

Table 19.4 presents the least important leadership characteristics. The low ranking of 'sharing power' was an interesting finding for Vietnam, which indicates an authoritarian orientation. Other power-related characteristics were also not important. Emphasis on the heart or feelings is ranked lower than expected, given the Vietnamese cultural emphasis on feelings.

Table 19.4 Least important characteristics of leadership in Vietnam compared to ASEAN

Least important characteristics	*Vietnam ranking*	
1 Behave in accordance with his or her religious beliefs	2.58	(4)[a]
2 Ignore personal morality in the interest of the organization	3.03	
3 Work for long hours, even at home	3.20	(1)
4 Give priority to short-term goals	3.31	
5 Share power	3.36	
6 Be strict in judging the competence of employees	3.38	
7 Manipulate people in order to achieve goals	3.40	
8 Be formal when dealing with employees at work	3.46	(6)
9 Use rank and power to get things done	3.50	
10 Follow the heart – not the head – in compassionate matters	3.52	(2)

Note: [a] Parentheses indicate the ranking of the value from ASEAN respondents (the full data for the ASEAN Leadership study is in Selvarajah et al., 1995)

For the ASEAN counterparts, there were only four similar rankings. They shared 'working long hours', 'following the heart', 'formality and religious beliefs'. The comparison of Vietnamese managers showed that they are much more different than their ASEAN peers, although there are a few common values.

These findings have important implications for leadership in joint ventures between Vietnam and ASEAN. Vietnam's style of leadership does not match very well with that in the region. This will make the compatibility of management in joint ventures more difficult to attain in ASEAN joint ventures. Some indications of this issue are problems in joint ventures with Thai or Malaysian partners.

■ Leadership characteristics in Vietnam

Leadership characteristics refer to the personal values, skills, beliefs, attitudes and behaviours of the manager, irrespective of profession or organization (Selvarajah et al., 1995: 39).

The findings demonstrate that joint venture leadership in Vietnam should be open and fair in its managerial style. At the same time, they should pay equal attention to the competitive performance of the joint venture.

▉ Comparing leadership in joint ventures

To compare the perspectives on leadership of Vietnamese managers with their international counterparts a test of significance is used. While different cultural backgrounds are represented in the sample of international managers, past analysis using cluster analysis indicates that Asians, North Americans and Europeans tend to have more similarities than differences in management style, but are very different from the Vietnamese respondents (Nga, 1997). International managers indicate a professional orientation based on education and experience, which is similar across cultures. There is evidence of a convergence of managerial styles. In Vietnam, local managers are in the early stages of developing professionalism. They tend to reflect the past influence of the command economy and other influences, such as Confucian values (Doanh and Nguyen, 1995: 29).

Another reason for the comparison is that in Vietnam, there is a 'we-they' mentality that exists between foreign partners and Vietnamese partners:

> In interviews with expatriate managers with verifiable successful experience in Vietnam, they say it takes three years to acquire the necessary knowledge of local conditions, to build up trust and to develop the right kind of relationships.

> Those relationship are important. Foreigners tend to put a lot of emphasis on spending their precious time dealing with and negotiating the more formal legal aspects of their Vietnam business ventures instead of spending more time on the really productive aspects such as making friends, building relationships and getting to know how things actually happen. (Sears, 1997: 29)

The foreign managers in Vietnam, no matter what their national backgrounds, see themselves as different, and Vietnamese counterparts, no matter their experience, see themselves as uniquely one culture. The emphasis here is to illustrate the Vietnamese expectations of leadership in contrast to the professional expectations of the international managers.

Table 19.5 shows that there were several significant differences between the two groups of managers. Vietnamese managers identified 'open communication' and 'being positive' as more important. Their international counterparts considered 'being practical' and 'ethical' as more important. Both Vietnamese and international managers agreed that the most important quality for leadership in cross-cultural situations is that they should accept responsibility. Characteristics such as making the joint venture competitive were also shared. The Vietnamese managers, in particular, stressed more open communication than their international counterparts. They believe that such a skill was vital to the organization to guarantee employees' productivity and the quality of performance. Surprisingly, ethical behaviour was rated the lowest for both groups of managers. Vietnamese managers considered this even lower than international managers.

The implications of these findings for organizational change relate to process versus structure. International managers will emphasize formal procedures to guide practice. Their Vietnamese counterparts will emphasize communication and positive relationships. Ethical issues are minimized.

Table 19.5 Comparing leadership characteristics

Leadership characteristics	Vietnamese	International
1 Responsibility	4.28	4.26
2 Open communication	4.14	3.93*
3 Competitive	3.98	3.96
4 Positive	3.88	3.57*
5 Practical	3.84	4.00*
6 Emotional	3.54	3.67
7 Ethical	3.14	3.44*

Note: * significant at 0.05.

■ Leadership behaviour

In this section, factors related to leadership behaviour were assessed. Leadership behaviour refers to the values, attitudes, actions and styles of managers that are specific to the performance of the management task (Selvarajah et al., 1995: 40).

Table 19.6 indicates that there were several significant differences between Vietnamese managers and their international counterparts. Vietnamese managers stressed more time management and approaches to manipulate subordinates. International managers significantly emphasized decision making and delegation.

Table 19.6 Comparing leadership behaviours

Leadership behaviours	Vietnamese	International
1 Teamwork	4.21	4.18
2 Logical	4.19	4.01
3 People oriented	4.05	4.01
4 Time management	3.95	3.55*
5 Objectives	3.88	3.71*
6 Decision-making	3.80	4.05*
7 Delegation	3.59	3.74*
8 Specific details	3.74	3.75
9 Manipulation	3.41	3.23*
10 Sharing power	3.06	3.36*

Note: * significant at 0.05.

Both groups of managers favoured the 'people oriented' and 'teamwork' approach in management. They also used specific decision-making skills, including logical approaches, objectives and specific details.

There is one major difference between the two groups of managers. Vietnamese managers do not emphasize sharing power. This reflects a managerial style characteristic of a 'high-power-distance' culture. This contradicts the emphasis on teamwork and delegation. Vietnamese managers do not perceive these actions as sharing power.

In joint ventures, international managers will expect to include their counterparts in decision-making and delegation, which involves the sharing of power. There is an interesting difference of perspective for Vietnamese managers involving the use of authority. These managers have a positive view of the authoritarian style because it involves taking action that will accomplish objectives. Paradoxically, in the past system of the command economy, managers had no authority, they were only instruments of state policy. Manipulation of subordinates is not perceived as a negative behaviour but as a way of accomplishing objectives.

▪ Organizational demands

Organizational demands relate to the way a manager reacts or responds to organizational goals, roles, rules, structures, demands, pressures, rewards and the requirements for performance (Selvarajah et al., 1995: 41). Seven factors were identified as critical for evaluating the leader's adaptation to organizational demands: performance, strategic vision, adaptability, deadlines, productivity, long-term orientation and politics (see Table 19.7).

Table 19.7 Comparing responses to organizational demands

Organizational demands	Vietnamese	International
1 Deadlines	4.11	3.74*
2 Strategic vision	4.04	4.11
3 Adaptability	4.04	4.03
4 Long-term orientation	3.79	3.61
5 Performance	3.59	4.02*
6 Productivity	3.58	3.39*
7 Organizational politics	3.35	3.34

Note: * significant at 0.05.

The Vietnamese and international managers did not differ significantly on such factors as having a strategic vision and adaptability to the environmental conditions. However, the Vietnamese emphasized responses related to organizational efficiency such as deadlines (significantly different), productivity and long-term goals. Both groups of managers gave less importance to organizational politics. There was a significant difference concerning performance. It is indicative that the Vietnamese managers showed less concern for performance than international managers, but this gap in leadership style was also related to the heritage of a command economy.

These results indicate that there was less similarity between international managers and their Vietnamese peers when it comes to performance. The significant differences relate to time and productivity, which were not considered important by Vietnamese managers in the past system.

The implications of these findings for organizational change are that there would be compatible perspectives on implementing a long-term strategic vision, but not on performance and adapting the organization for improved productivity. Resistance might be expected because Vietnamese managers do not have the same commitment to performance.

Environmental awareness

Environmental influences are factors outside the organization that have influences on the operation and success of the organization (Selvarajah et al., 1995: 41). Three factors were identified as important: environmental awareness, multicultural orientation and political and social impact on work (see Table 19.8).

Table 19.8 Comparing environmental awareness

Environmental awareness	Vietnamese	International
1 Political and social impact	4.10	3.78*
2 Environmental awareness	3.91	3.78
3 Multicultural orientation	3.57	3.76*

Note: * significant at 0.05.

Vietnamese managers considered being responsive to political realities as important for managers who want to be successful leaders in a changing economy like Vietnam. Environmental awareness included items such as 'economic indicators for planning purposes' and 'response to the expectations of the customers'.

Overall, there was a significant difference between the two groups of managers. Successful leadership for the international manager depends largely on developing a multicultural approach to the joint venture, which emphasizes mutual understanding of each manager's culture and management style. The effective leader must recognize, evaluate and anticipate social trends which have an impact on the organization.

Both groups of managers indicated an awareness of the organizational environment but emphasized different dimensions. Vietnamese managers emphasized the external political impact on the organization. This means that organizational change might be very cautiously implemented as Vietnamese managers wait for the right political indicators or clues. International managers focused on the need to develop a shared perspective of values and the need to create a common organizational culture which would be a blend of the Vietnamese culture and the international management perspectives.

Conclusions and implications

In conclusion, the results of the survey are compared to the propositions listed in Table 19.2.

For *Proposition 1*, there are mixed results for compatibility. International managers and their Vietnamese counterparts share an emphasis on responsibility and competitiveness. There are significant differences between the managers on open communication, practicality and a positive orientation, which would reflect an incompatibility of style and could lead to failure of the joint venture.

Proposition 2 focuses on reducing the cultural differences in the joint venture and developing a multicultural perspective. This is supported by shared leadership behaviours, such as teamwork and being people oriented. This leadership style would create shared values and minimize differences in the joint venture.

Trust, communication and mutual objectives are stressed in *Proposition 3*. Here, there are major differences between international managers and Vietnamese managers concerning objectives, decision-making, delegation and sharing power. These differences will be the biggest source of failure in joint ventures.

Proposition 4 also has mixed results. There is compatibility between the managers for teamwork and relationships but not for collaboration-related behaviours, such as sharing power and delegation. Vietnamese managers do not value this approach because it is perceived as weak. This is a source of conflict which would limit the success of the joint venture.

Proposition 5 emphasizes the balance between different leadership styles. There is a complementarity of international and Vietnamese managers concerning strategic vision, adaptability and long-term orientation. However, there is a major gap in the orientation to performance. This will have a major limitation on the future success of the joint venture because the Vietnamese managers will tend to fall back on control, not results. International managers will focus on results.

Multicultural leadership is the focus of *Proposition 6* and international managers emphasize this significantly more than their local counterparts. The mixed results for compatibility, complementarity, collaboration and performance will limit the potential success of joint ventures in Vietnam. However, there are also shared orientations on responsibility, teamwork, people orientation, productivity and competitiveness which could support success if the joint venture would change in the direction of relationships.

In terms of organizational change, the emphasis should be on process. Teamwork and relationships are seen by Vietnamese subordinates as important features of organizational design to carry out decisions, but not as a means of sharing power. International managers will have to demonstrate strongly the need to delegate and manage through participation. Communication on a mutual basis will also have to be encouraged. This is a major weakness for both international managers and their Vietnamese counterparts.

There will be the temptation for some international joint ventures to emphasize structural change, such as control, regulation and deadlines, as an approach to enforce performance. This reflects a lack of trust and a task orientation which does not fit the Vietnamese situation very well. This type of change is not likely to be successful.

In our experience working with joint ventures, the most problematic and least successful joint ventures are those that emphasize their own culture such as Korean, Taiwanese, French or American and those that emphasize control or only a task orientation. The examples of successful joint ventures, such as ABB and Unilever, emphasize building relationships, creating a mutual understanding and shared values. In organizational change, they are more adaptive, focused more on teamwork and they provide a stronger role for local managers. From the perspective of organizational learning, successful joint ventures promote the management development of Vietnamese managers and reduce the involvement of expatriates. These joint ventures enhance their strategic capability by having a long-term commitment and a vision for the joint venture which will be implemented by Vietnamese managers with effective leadership skills.

■ References

Adler, N. and Bartholomew, S. (1993). Is the expatriate executive extinct? *Crossborders*, Summer, 44.

Bowditch, J. and Buono, F. (1989). *The Human Side of Mergers and Acquisitions*. Jossey-Bass.

Chung, V. (1997). On location. *Vietnam Economic Times*, 18–21 April, p. 36.

Doanh, L. D. and Nguyen, M. (1995). How will Vietnam develop its own business culture. *Vietnam Economic Times* (15), p. 29.

Feldman, D. and Thomas, D. (1992). Career issues facing expatriate managers. *Journal of International Business Studies*, **23**, 271–94.

Geringer, J. (1991). Strategic determinants of partner selection in international joint ventures. *Journal of International Business Studies*, **22**, 41–62.

Haley, U. C. V. (1997). The MBTI and decision-making styles: identifying and managing cognitive trails in strategic decision making. In *Developing Leaders: Research and Applications in Psychological Type and Leadership Development* (C. Fitzgerald and L. Kirby, eds) 187–223, Consulting Psychologists Press.

Haley, U. C. V. and Haley, G. T. (1997). When the tourists flew in: strategic implications of foreign direct investment in Vietnam's tourism industry. *Management Decision*, **35** (8), 595–604.

Hofstede, G. (1980). *Culture's Consequences: International Differences in Work-Related Values*. Sage.

Lane, H. and Beamish, P. (1990). Cross-cultural co-operative behavior in joint ventures in LDCs. *Management International Review*, **30** (special issue), 87–102.

Lynch, R. (1994). Designing business alliances that fit. *World Executive's Digest*, **15** (10), October, 34–40.

Meschi, P. and Roger, A. (1994). Cultural context and social effectiveness in international joint ventures. *Management International Review*, **34** (3), 197–215.

Nga, N. T. (1997). Human resource issues in joint ventures in Vietnam. In *Understanding International Joint Ventures in Vietnam* (F. W. Swierczeck, U. Bumbacher and T. Quang, eds) 166–205, Management of Technology Information Centre.

Quang, T. (1997). Successful international equity joint ventures in Vietnam: a conflict management approach. In *Understanding International Joint Ventures in Vietnam* (F. W. Swierczeck, U. Bumbacher and T. Quang, eds), Management of Technology Information Centre.

Saigon Times (1998). An integral part. 14 February, 8–18.

Sears, K. (1997). Lessons to learn. *Vietnam Economic Times*, **46**, December, p. 29.

Selvarajah, C. T., Duigan, P., Suppiah, C., Lane, T. and Nuttman, C. (1995). In search of the ASEAN leader: an exploratory study of the dimensions that relate to excellence in leadership. *Management International Review*, **35** (1), 29–44.

Shane, S. (1992). The effect of cultural differences in perceptions of transaction costs on national differences in the preference for licensing. *Management International Review*, **32** (4), 295–311.

Stening, B. and Hammer, M. (1992). Cultural baggage and the adaptation of expatriates. *Management International Review*, **32** (1), 77–90.

Stier, K. (1998). Vietnam: keeping faith. *Asian Business*, **34** (4), April, 9–11.

Thu, T. (1998). New wave to improve investment climate. *Saigon Times*, 4 February, 22–5.

Vietnam Economic Times (1998a). Foreign investment by country and territory. **49**, March, p. 11.

Vietnam Economic Times (1998b). Foreign invested projects by province. **49**, March, p. 10.

Walters, B., Peters, S. and Dess, G. (1994). Strategic alliances and joint ventures: making them work. *Business Horizons*, **37** (4), 5–10.

Chapter 19.1

Implications of the Asian crisis for official ideology and investments in Vietnam

■ Truong Quang and Fredric William Swierczek ■

Contrary to what the Vietnamese Communist Party would have you believe, the bureaucracy is not the driving force of change in Vietnam and is more often than not an impediment. Indeed, change slows when the Party has the budgetary outlays to maintain the status quo and accelerates when the funds begin to run out. Given this equation, the IMF's and World Bank's millions may actually discourage reform.

... In the early 1990s, private companies gained strength as SOEs weakened due to lack of state resources. Then, in the mid-1990s, the pork came pouring in: tax revenues, bank credits, import tariffs, foreign investment and overseas aids all offered largesse, which, not surprisingly, went mainly to SOEs. Also not surprisingly – given the Party's proven inability to avoid over-indulging when times are good – the boom years ended in tears. (Fforde, 1998)

The East Asian economic crisis is turning its fury toward Vietnam despite the perceived insulation Vietnam's authorities expected to enjoy. The official growth rate was reduced from 9 per cent to 6–7 per cent for 1998. The more realistic projection may be closer to 4–5 per cent. Export growth has dropped from 25–28 per cent in 1997 to 10 per cent in 1998 (Keenan, 1998). Exports are affected by rising costs and declining competitiveness. The currency has been devalued by 7 per cent but this is just the first step. Inflation and unemployment is growing (see also Chapter 14.1).

Foreign investment projects are declining for the second year in a row. To date 1998 project approvals amounted to $1.1 billion (see also Chapter 13.1). This is a decline of 20 per cent less than 1997 for the same period. Unfortunately the decline will be worse because the 1998 total includes a $700 million project in Dalat which will not be implemented (Keenan, 1998). However, this is not the first time that foreign investment in Vietnam was inflated by large projects that were implemented slowly or not at all. In 1996, out of an expected $8.8 billion investment, two projects valued at $3.1 billion were not realized (Hornstein, 1998). The current rate of utilizing foreign investment capital is less than 10 per cent.

Given the dramatic changes in East Asia why is Vietnam so slow to reform? Even before liberation in 1975, policy directions in Vietnam were characterized by a tension between maintaining ideological purity and opening up to the economic realities in the Asia Pacific region. The tension has continued in the period of *doi moi* or Renovation (since 1986). This tension colours much of what takes place in leadership changes in the party and the administration as well as policy alternatives for example in foreign investment, privatization (*Co phan hoa*, or equitization in the Vietnamese version) and administrative reform. At some times the purists are ascendant, at other times the reformers take precedence. Overall, however, ideological supremacy is still the major influence guiding Vietnamese policy.

Related to this is a strong cultural influence relating to regulation. This has its foundation in Confucian thought of a well-ordered universe articulated in the procedures of a mandarinate. This was extended by the French colonial bureaucracy administering the Napoleanic Code with more of an emphasis on prohibiting activities than encouraging independent actions. Both of these trends are compatible with the command and control orientation of present-day Vietnam.

During the period 1989–90, when the Soviet Union and other socialist Eastern European states changed, Vietnam took solace that it maintained its Marxist purity. Now with the East Asian economic crisis, it believes that its ideological perspective has been vindicated.

Vietnam always finds a justification to move slowly and inhibit reform. This issue is clearest in foreign investment and more recently in equitization. Equitization is Vietnam's approach to reduce government ownership of industrial sectors. It is a very good illustration of the tensions of reform. It is expected that equitization would increase private share ownership, increase profitability and create jobs. However, it only focuses on small- and medium-sized enterprises (SMEs) and not the major state enterprises.

Vietnam's Central Commission on Equitization has plans to equitize 1000 firms by the end of 1999. So far only 200 have agreed, twenty-nine have actually been equitized and only seventeen have been studied in depth. The average time to equitize has been two to three years with the longest taking six years and seven months.

The slow process is intentional. According to D. K. Dan of the State Enterprise Reform Committee:

> Our policies are not really as attractive as we need them to be because they are full of complex procedures involving organisations which are badly co-ordinated. All our procedures have been shown to be rather cumbersome, particularly in the matter of assessing the value of enterprises which sometimes takes as much as three years. (*Vietnam Economic Times*, 1998: 14)

The Party's General Secretary Le Kha Phieu has guaranteed that equitization will be a slow, steady, thorough and careful process.

Equitization is related to leadership because of the nature and style of managers involved. Large state-owned enterprises (SOEs) do not have sufficient management ability and are characterized by the old command and control mentality. Managers in the SMEs are more entrepreneurial, committed to their companies and learn faster.

The performance of the seventeen equitized enterprises as evaluated by the Mekong Project Development Facility (MPDF) of the World Bank-IFC was very positive: 'They were favorably impressed with the perspective, dynamism, and leadership of the managers they interviewed' (*Vietnam Economic Times*, 1998: 17).

There is some positive signs for the opening up of the state enterprise sector but the Vietnamese authorities still do not support the policy initiatives necessary to allow the private sector to grow (Tan, 1998). Until this situation is resolved, the leadership of enterprises will not become competitive and Vietnam will suffer the effects of the East Asian crisis with more severity.

In the long run, Vietnam is still attractive to foreign investments and overseas assistance, which together with its almost untapped internal strength (*noi luc*) would undoubtedly re-emerge from this period of crisis as one of the most promising emerging economies. But, as long as corruption continues to be epidemic, the bureaucracy cumbersome, the banking system inefficient, the majority of the SOEs loss-making and the SMEs very infantile, the slogan currently exhorted by the government to 'turn to our internal strength' remains lip-service. Hence, the prospect of developing the country, relying largely on the country's own resources, as a substitute for foreign investments and overseas assistance, seems too unrealistic to be achieved.

References

Fforde, A. (1998). Handouts won't help Vietnam. *Asian Wall Street Journal*, 16 September.
Hornstein, A. (1998). Vietnam is feeling pressure. *Knight Ridder/Tribune Business News*, 21 August.
Keenan, F. (1998). Vietnam: reality check. *Far Eastern Economic Review*, 3 September, p. 57.
Tan, L. D. (1998). An enterprising outlook. *Vietnam Economic Times*, August, p. 19.
Vietnam Economic Times (1998). In the driving seat: smaller companies are at the vanguard of the equitization process, August, 14–17.

Part Six
Local companies' strategies

Chapter 20

A strategic perspective on Overseas Chinese networks' decision-making[1]

■ George T. Haley ■

■ Introduction

Academic journals (Nakamura, 1992; Hofstede, 1994; Redding, 1995; Haley and Tan, 1996) and the popular press (Kohut and Cheng, 1996; Seagrave, 1996; Weidenbaum and Hughes, 1996) have recently published a great deal about Overseas Chinese networks' (hereafter referred to as the Networks) management and decision-making styles. The authors have either tried to describe the decision-making processes, explain the styles' various consequences, or explain their origins and significance; the authors have generally made little effort to place the Networks' strategic decision-making style in any of strategic-planning's theoretical constructs. Many argue that the Overseas Chinese do not conduct strategic planning. This chapter will place the Networks' strategic-management style in established, strategic-planning constructs. By doing so, the chapter aims to enhance strategic understanding of the Networks' capabilities, strengths and weaknesses.

First, this chapter briefly reviews some of the literature on the Networks' management style and strategic decision-making processes. Second, it succinctly analyses some of the major, theoretical, strategic-planning constructs and incorporates the Networks' decision processes in these constructs. Finally, it proposes a best-fit scenario and discusses some implications of the Networks' strategic-planning style for those companies that compete against, or co-operate with, the Networks' firms.

[1]The author wishes to thank the guest editor, Dr Usha C.V. Haley, the anonymous reviewers and Comet for their many points of advice which helped to improve the quality of the chapter tremendously. Any errors are solely the responsibility of the author. This chapter has been published previously by MCB University Press Limited: Haley, G.T. (1997). A strategic perspective on overseas Chinese networks' decision making. *Management Decision*, **35** (8), 587–94.

■ The Overseas Chinese networks' strategic management style

Nakamura (1992) argued that strategic decision-making in East Asia, including that of the Overseas Chinese of Taiwan, Hong Kong (at the time), Singapore, and many of the ASEAN countries, was developing along the same lines as strategic decision-making did in Japan. Though some similarities appear, Haley and Tan (1996) highlighted the many dissimilarities between the Overseas Chinese and the Japanese; Haley and Tan (1996) effectively argued that Western managers would seriously err if they depended on their understandings and experiences with Japanese firms to deal with the Networks. This section highlights some major research findings on the Networks' business operations.

The Overseas Chinese form one of four major business clusters in South-East Asia; the others include government-linked corporations (GLCs) and foreign multinational corporations (MNCs) (Haley and Tan, 1996), and a fourth, gaining increasing influence, the Overseas Indians (Haley and Haley, 1997). The Networks constitute the single, most dominant, private business grouping in Asia outside the Asian giants of Japan, China and India. Figure 20.1 depicts the Overseas Chinese populations of the established, non-communist economies of South-East Asia; the relative economic influence of the Overseas Chinese in these economies, depicted in Figure 20.2, far outstrips their shares of population.

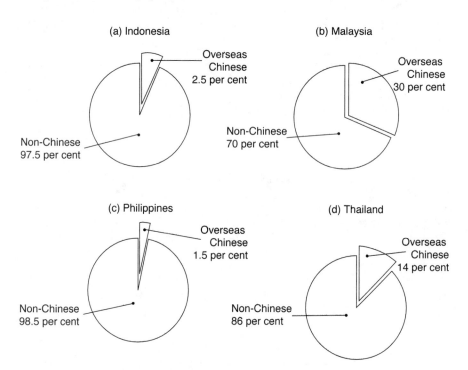

Figure 20.1 Overseas Chinese share of population
Source: Redding, G. (1995); Kohut, J. and Cheng, A. T. (1996).

The Overseas Chinese have tended to follow conglomerate diversification. Generally, they began as merchants, expanded into real estate and then moved into any business where they perceived substantial profits. The important characteristics that distinguish successful, local companies operating in South and South-East Asia are:

- The companies appear highly diversified; often, they undertake unrelated diversification, contravening mainstream theoretical notions.

- The companies have good relationships with the often enormous, public sectors in these countries.

- The companies have very strong familial and informal Networks.

- Managers tend to use subjective information as inputs to decision-making.

The Salim Group of Indonesia, the largest of the Overseas Chinese firms, demonstrates the above characteristics (East Asia Analytical Unit, 1995; Kohut and Cheng, 1996).

- Salim has interests in cement, processed foods, flour milling, steel, banking, real estate, investments, pharmaceuticals, information technology, chemicals, shipping, general manufacturing and vehicle assembly.

- Salim's close ties to the government in its home base of Indonesia are shown by its government contracts for flour milling (at an estimated fee of 300 per cent of world prices), its sharing exclusive rights to import cloves into Indonesia with one other

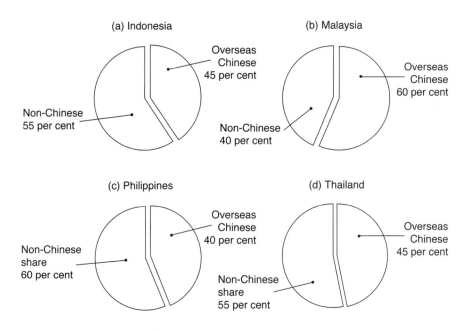

Figure 20.2 Overseas Chinese share of economy
Source: Redding, G. (1995); Kohut, J. and Cheng, A. T. (1996).

company, and the many Salim companies that have the government as a minority shareholder.

• Salim has close ties, as manifested by joint ventures, management contracts and strategic alliances, with Indonesia's Lippo Group, Ciputra Group, Sinar Mas Group, Barito Group, and Ongko Group, Malaysia's Robert Kuok, Taiwan's Koo family, and Thailand's Sophanpanich family, among others.

Researchers have offered many explanations for the differences between Asian and Western strategic decision-making. Hofstede (1994) argued for culture as a dominant variable in decision-making styles. Haley and Stumpf (1989) found differences in decision-making traceable to personality types; later Haley (1997) found evidence that significant personality-type differences may exist across managerial cadres from different nations, thereby implying that personality types rather than culture may capture many national differences in decision styles. Many authors have traced the Networks' decision-making style to Chinese culture's Confucian belief structures (Hsu, 1984; Pan, 1984; Redding, 1995), and this aspect needs further study. Haley and Tan (1996) suggested competitive advantage as a possible explanation, as it tends to exclude new entrants without the established communities' experience and connections.

The true situation probably includes all the different explanations. However, few question Haley and Tan's (1996) observation that the amount of data available to decision-makers about Asian markets resembles an informational void relative to the amount available on industrialized economies. Whatever the reason, many major Asian firms exhibit a unique strategic-management style. The Asian firms' somewhat holistic, intuitive, decision-making style appears well suited to information-scarce environments or environments where market-survey data seem highly suspect. As decision-makers have not generally desired more information, the region is an informational void for those who do.

Many attribute the rapid growth of the Networks' businesses in Southeast Asia to their speed of decision-making (Chu and MacMurray, 1993). This speed, and the Networks' dominant control of information, facilitate the Networks' efforts to seize business opportunities and constitute major, competitive advantages (Haley and Tan, 1996; Redding, 1995). The Networks' management also tends to exhibit personal, rather than professional corporate characteristics. For example, Ghosh and Chan (1994), in their study of strategic-planning behaviours among firms in Singapore and Malaysia, classified planning activities as *ad hoc* and reactive. The only important, market-related factor that they found centred on the 'CEO's personal knowledge of market', which was the fourth-most-important contributing factor to success in planning. Their findings reflect the Networks' idiosyncratic styles (Haley and Tan, 1996; Redding, 1986), specifically the 'CEO's personal knowledge' of the market assumes importance, not the firm's or the marketing manager's.

Very few empirical studies exist of Asia's holistic/intuitive decision-making styles. Drawing on their observations and study of Asian executives, Haley and Tan (1996) found the managers rely most on the following:

• *Hands-on experience*. To make decisions quickly, without detailed analyses of hard data, managers must be experienced line managers who know the firm's work routines and processes, and know the product, market, business environment and industry at first hand. Senior Asian businessmen get involved in all aspects of their firms' activities and remain active in them until they retire.

- *Transfers of knowledge across businesses*. Asian companies often engage in unrelated diversification, running contrary to business wisdom regarding staying in one's core business. Executives who succeed in unfamiliar industries possess intimate knowledge of the business environments in which they operate. This knowledge allows them to generalize from past experience, recognize patterns of similarities and dissimilarities in the different businesses they enter, and apply those generalizations in the new context.

- *Qualitative information*. Many Asian executives process myriad bits of information and consider several alternatives in-depth before they act; they differ from Western executives in that their analyses appear almost entirely internal. Though their decision-making may be highly articulated, Asian executives rarely present the results in written, analytical form. Asian executives may also not seek published data on which to base their decisions: they use qualitative, often subjective, information supplied by friends, business associates, government officials and others in whose judgement and character they trust. Their subjective-data preferences, though not most Western managers' choices, generally offer more accurate reflections of reality than quantitative data from the region would.

- *Holistic information processing*. In an informational void, conventional, analytical problem-solving that stresses sequential, systematic, and step-by-step approaches to decision-making often prove unworkable. In the Networks' experience-based intuitive model, managers take a general approach to problems, define parameters intuitively and explore solutions holistically.

- *Action-driven decision-making*. Speed constitutes a key characteristic of decision-making in Asian business. The Asian decision-making model reflects authoritative management and speed as well as the executives' empowerment and accountability. When one person has both responsibility and authority, a little authoritativeness can get work done faster. A loss caused by action often proves more acceptable than a loss caused by inaction.

The next section considers dominant, Western, strategic-planning systems' requirements.

■ Strategic planning and the Networks

Unlike the Asian strategic-management style elaborated in the previous section, a determining factor in Western management revolves around the wealth of information available for anyone with the desire and wit to find and to use it. Table 20.1 summarizes some of the dominant characteristics of strategic systems propounded by prominent theorists.

Hofer and Schendel (1978) are among the earliest conceptualizers of a classic, strategic-planning system. Michael Porter's system also uses many of the same building blocks for strategy. First, both systems depend on abilities to acquire large amounts of relatively high-quality internal and external information. Both systems demand analytical rationalism, depending on largely-sequential collection, analysis and interpretation of data to generate the above-mentioned information. Managers collect, analyse and interpret the data in fixed, perceptual constructs of the relationships between the firms and their environments. By emphasizing threats and opportunities in the firm's external environments, the systems assume that managers can measure and understand the relationships between firms and environments through collecting and analysing data in the positivist framework.

Table 20.1 Planning characteristics of strategic constructs

Strategic theorists	Staff/line dependent	Data/experience dependent
Hofer and Schendel	Staff	Data
Porter	Staff	Data
Prahalad and Hamel	Staff/line	Data/experience
Mintzberg	Staff/line	Data/experience

Second, both systems depend largely on extensive staff to collect, to collate and to analyse large amounts of data to understand business situations and to generate recommendations for strategic action. Frequently, staff have no line management or operational experience; their understandings of business situations revolve around their familiarity with the data and the analytical techniques – not with the operations' nuances and relationships with stakeholders. The systems separate minds and hands (Mintzberg, 1987, 1994).

The Networks' firms employ and use fewer staff than Western firms: for example, Hong Kong firms' average sizes shrank by 59 per cent from 1954 to 1984, although their operations expanded during this period (Redding, 1986). Consequently, strategic management concepts proposed by Hofer and Schendel, and Porter, seem inappropriate to explain their strategic-planning practices. The dearth of quality, quantitative data in most Asian environments reinforces this situation.

Prahalad and Hamel (1990) argue for a more internal focus where firms' successful strategies exploit core competencies, or key skills refined and honed in their drives for success. Unlike Hofer and Schendel, and Porter, Prahalad and Hamel make no pronouncements about how to plan. Strategic planning drawing on core competencies may or may not depend on large amounts of high-quality information and huge staff. However, Prahalad and Hamel (1990) state that a firm's core competency must:

1 provide potential access to various markets

2 make an important contribution to the perceived benefits a firm provides its customers

3 be difficult to imitate.

While the Networks' firms have pursued conglomerate diversification, they have instinctively developed, used and protected their core competency – their decision-making style. The Networks' decision-making style provides them with access to a variety of markets as their conglomerate diversification demonstrates. Examples of this diversification abound, as Table 20.1 shows. Thailand's Chearavanont Family (CP Group) went from poultry farming into real estate and telecommunications;

A strategic perspective on Overseas Chinese networks

Indonesia's Oei Hong Leong (Widjaja's son and controller of China Strategic Investment Group) operates in beer, tyres and consumer products; the Philippines' Lucio Tan is involved in beer, tobacco, banking and diversified investments; and Malaysia's Robert Kuok operates in plantations, sugar and wood processing, media and hotels – and has recently begun moving into the utilities industry. The Networks, through their management style, prosper and produce goods in an informational void that they create and perpetuate, thereby providing perceived benefits to customers. Finally, competitors cannot imitate this decision-making style as the Networks maintain secrecy on their sources of information. Because they lack the Networks' web of contacts, and have inadequate access to soft, insider information, most potential independent competitors fail in the region. In this instance, the 'complex harmonization of individual technologies and production skills' (Prahalad and Hamel, 1990), refers to the Networks' specialized knowledge and information, combined with managerial decision-making skills, to produce the firms' strategic and operational actions.

Table 20.2 Families and businesses in the Overseas Chinese networks

Family/leader	Primary businesses
Indonesia	
Liem Sioe Liong	Cement, processed foods, flour milling, steel, banking, real estate, investments
Eka Tjipta Widjaja	Diversified
Oei Hong Leong	Beer, tyres, consumer products
Mochtar Riaddy	Property, banking, insurance
Suhargo Gondokusumo	Agri-industries, property
Prajojo Pangestu	Timber, car assembly
Malaysia	
Robert Kuok	Plantations, sugar and wood processing, media hotels
Quek Leng Chan	Finance, diversified
Lim Goh Tong	Casinos, real estate
Vincent Tan	Leisure, manufacturing, investment
Philippines	
Lucio Tan	Beer, tobbacco, banking, investments
Henry Sy	Retailing, cement, investments
Alfonso Yuchengco	Banking insurance
Antonio Cojuangco	Telecommunications, real estate
John Gokongwei	Real estate, diversified investments
Thailand	
Chearavanont Family	Agri-businesses, real estate, telecommunications
Kanjanapas Family	Real estate, transport, finance
Ratanarak Family	Cement, banking, telecommunications
Sophonanich Family	Banking, real estate, investments
Lamsam Family	Banking, real estate

Source: East Asia Analytical Unit (1995); Haley and Tan (1996); Kohut and Cheng (1996).

Mintzberg's theoretical construct seems to capture many facets of the Networks' strategic planning processes and modes. Mintzberg states that strategic plans are both directed and emergent – and that strategic plans often evolve from the collective, behavioural patterns of firms' employees (Mintzberg, 1987, 1994; Mintzberg and Waters, 1994) as they react to environmental stimuli. He argues that the best planning requires both directed and emergent strategic planning.

With the Networks, emergent strategic planning appears to come to the forefront. This occurs because of Networks' and the Overseas Chinese characteristics. Haley and Tan (1996) described how the founders of most Network firms, though highly intelligent, had little formal education and even less management education. Hence their decision-making evolved in a different perspective of what constitutes acceptable data than most Western managers have; the Networks' managers used data drawn from their experiences, advice from trusted friends, and their perceptions of the situations.

With soft data, strategy emerges from the Network executives' interactions with their environments. For a typical Networks' firm, news, rumours or insider information will reach an executive and create interest. The executive will then seek out confirming evidence and gauge available resources. The executive will analyse the situation, make and implement decisions. As the implementation proceeds, further information will become available and the executive's strategy will emerge and be fleshed out; he or she will either stand firm, continue along the same path, or make the strategic alterations deemed necessary. The strategies which the firm follows will emerge from the executive's and the firm's learned business behaviours. If the executive feels the need for a strategic partner, the firm will seek one out. Though major Overseas Chinese firms are family based, and each major firm is a significant conglomerate, potential partners in the Networks will base their decisions largely on the confidence and trust they have in the proposing executives' judgement and managerial abilities. This bubbling-up process is a key and unique element of the Networks' strategic planning: while this bubbling-up process occurs on an intrafirm basis in most firms, in the Networks it also occurs on a suprafirm basis.

Wada (1992) cited an example of the bubbling-up process when he described how a Chinese businessman in Hong Kong decided on a multi-million dollar investment – fifteen minutes after he received a phone call offering him the opportunity. The time frame indicates that the businessman analysed data comprising largely personal experiences, rumours, soft information, and trust in the individual who made the offer. In this situation, the investment strategy bubbled up into the Network through the proposing individual.

Mintzberg (1987) argued that strategic planning without the mind's activities seems as incomplete and imbalanced as when strategic planners ignore the hand's activities. He postulated that strategic planning consists of four activities:

1 detecting discontinuities

2 knowing the business

3 managing patterns

4 reconciling change and continuity.

The Networks' strategic-planning methods emphasize line management through depending on soft data and on intimate, intuitive understandings of the business and its environments. As Haley and Tan (1996) described, its managers disdain the separation of planning and doing. Other similarities appear between Mintzberg's construct of strategic planning and that of the Networks.

First, Mintzberg specified detecting discontinuities as the essence of strategic planning; Haley and Tan (1996) discerned this process when analysing how the Networks' managers use contacts in local governments and communities as primary sources of data. Through their web of associates, the Networks' managers determine potential changes in government policy or environments which can cause discontinuities and force divestment or changes of business strategies. These activities also reflect the managers' intimate knowledge of the markets and business environments that Mintzberg argued is the crux of crafting strategy.

Second, knowing the business is another of Mintzberg's characteristics and translates directly into the hands-on experience identified by Haley and Tan (1996). The Networks' managers emphasize active, intimate participation in all important aspects of their firms' activities and product/markets. They also stress getting one's hands dirty in the firms' operations – and the need to deal with more than descriptive statistics.

Third, Mintzberg argued that business strategists' primary duties included perceiving and managing the emerging patterns of firms' operations and markets. Haley and Tan (1996) similarly identified managing patterns in the Networks' holistic information processing. In both instances, the strategists rely on perceptions, not on hard data or on collective manifestations of it that could display significant distortions. These perceptions of holistic data, viewed as patterns, lead the strategists to infer the firms' present and future relationships with their internal and external environments; the perceptions also present avenues to manage effectively the firms' resources and to optimize present and future benefits.

Haley and Tan (1996) also detected how the Networks manage patterns in the transfer of knowledge. They identified how the Networks' managers extrapolate what they have learned and experienced in one product/market to different, unrelated product/ markets. By considering similarities and dissimilarities of the different product/ markets, the managers are also considering similarities and dissimilarities in the patterns of behaviour and requirements for success in the venues.

Finally, Mintzberg argued that in order to optimize a firm's performance, the strategist must encourage the emergence of some patterns, and delay, or even prevent the emergence of other patterns – thereby reconciling change and continuity. Through their web of associates, most especially local-government associates, the Networks' managers seek information – and, where possible, also pursue preferential treatment and lobby for or against the promulgation of laws, regulations and privileged positions in desired markets and industries. In this fashion, the Networks' managers strive to enhance patterns of change and continuity that enhance their strengths and minimize their weaknesses. For example, the Philippines' Cojuangco Group has been enormously successful in influencing or leveraging industry structure and regulation in its home markets; it has amassed enormous wealth by obtaining key governmental franchises, such as the long-distance telephone franchise in the Philippines (Chu and MacMurray, 1993).

■ Competitive implications

The previous sections have highlighted the Networks' strategic-planning styles and elaborated on its theoretical connotations and constructs. These arguments have strong implications for the Networks' and competitors' strategies and behaviours. Some of the major implications include the following.

Strategic competitiveness

The Networks' strong defensive positions

The Networks follow defensive competitive strategies, however aggressive they may seem because of decision-making speed. Their strategies seek to generate profits through maintaining an environment that shields their core competency and competitive advantage – the informational void. Without the informational void, the Networks' firms could face severe challenges from non-Network, local firms, and from foreign MNCs with competitive advantages in product and process technology, R&D, advertising and promotional skills, distribution and finances. The informational void gives the Networks' firms the ability to compete with foreign MNCs by trading their contacts for the MNCs' advantages. The informational void also reduces the Networks' domestic competition by hindering the growth of non-Network businesses: these local, non-Network businesses would compete directly against the Networks in the various product/markets, and would provide foreign MNCs with alternative local, Asian strategic partners.

The Networks' poor offensive positions

Unlike Japanese firms, few of the Networks' firms appear likely to develop strong competitive positions in the foreign MNCs' home markets, barring significant investments in managerial personnel. The Networks' core competency becomes both their strength and weakness. Until the Networks' firms develop a core competency less dependent on their home environments, as the large Japanese and Korean firms did, they will fail as strong competitors outside the seemingly maze-like management environments serving as their bastion. The Networks' core competency implies that foreign MNCs investing in research, data acquisition and contacts, can attack competitors from the Networks in their home bases: conversely, the majority of the Networks' firms will have difficulties retaliating against the MNCs in the MNCs' home markets.

Strategic planning

Line rather than staff planners for MNCs

Foreign MNCs in Asia would benefit by emphasizing planning through line management in their Asian operations. Line managers will encounter many of the same difficulties in becoming acquainted with the Asian environments as staff planners; however, line managers should have better knowledge of the MNCs' internal operational workings, and could better locate initial, common bases for relationships with the Networks' managers – both should have intimate familiarity with business operations and their problems. The Networks' managers would also probably find the line managers' business experiences of more interest and value than the staff managers' experiences.

Human resource practices

Rotation of staff for MNCs

The core competency of the Networks' firms also implies that many foreign MNCs' practices of rotating executives in foreign postings every two or three years will prove counterproductive in fighting the competition. First, the rotations diminish the MNCs' abilities to employ emergent strategies in Asia. This effect occurs because the MNCs' executives often fall short of gaining the intimate knowledge of the market in the product/market equation: they cannot recognize the emerging patterns in the environments or in the firms' local operations and, consequently, cannot generate effective Asia-based emergent strategies. Second, firms do not build contacts, humans do. When MNCs rotate employees out of Asian countries, they lose the employees' contacts. The damage may prove minimal because in the short period of two or three years, the employees could not have had opportunities to build substantial numbers of influential contacts. However, if after three years, MNCs' executives had socialized with the local business communities effectively and built contacts, the MNCs were probably only starting to get substantial returns from those executives. These two reasons appear especially valid when the MNCs choose to operate in Asia without local partners.

Staff's characteristics for MNCs.

Multinational corporations should select managers for their Asian operations from among those who show exceptional ability to operate effectively under high levels of uncertainty. Without the kind of plentiful, high quality, hard data that they generally utilize, foreign managers of Asian operations must face business problems head on without the kinds of analytical and informational support they normally rely on in their planning and decision-making.

Staff's morale in the Network

Bright, non-family managers working for the Networks' firms usually wish they worked for someone else, providing opportunities for MNCs. Recent surveys have shown that executives of the Networks' firms in Hong Kong feel out of place and dissatisfied with their employment; most would prefer to work for companies where they could contribute to corporate strategy and aspire to top managerial positions (*The Economist*, 1996). However, the Networks' firms usually buy their managers' loyalties through substantial annual performance bonuses and generous retirement schemes.

▓ References

Chu, T. C. and MacMurray, T. (1993). The road ahead for Asia's leading conglomerates. *McKinsey Quarterly*, **3**, 117–26.

East Asia Analytical Unit (1995). *Overseas Chinese Business Networks.* AGPS Press, Department of Foreign Affairs and Trade, Australia.

The Economist (1996). The limits of family values, in a special Survey of Business in Asia, March 9–15, 12–22.

Ghosh, B. C. and Chan, C. O. (1994). A study of strategic-planning behavior among emergent businesses in Singapore and Malaysia. *International Journal of Management,* **11** (2), 697–706.

Haley, G. T. and Haley, U. C. V. (1997). Making strategic business decisions in South and Southeast Asia. *Conference Proceedings of the First International Conference on Operations and Quantitative Management, Vol. 2,* Jaipur, India, 597–604.

Haley, G. T. and Tan, C. T. (1996). The black hole of Southeast Asia: Strategic decision-making in an informational void. *Management Decision,* **34** (9), 37–48.

Haley, U. C. V. (1997). The Myers-Briggs Type Indicator and decision-making styles: Identifying and managing cognitive trails in strategic decision making. In *Developing Leaders: Research and applications in Psychological Type and Leadership Development,* C. Fitzgerald and L. Kirby (eds), Consulting Psychologists Press, 187–223.

Haley, U. C. V. and Stumpf, S. A. (1989). Cognitive trails in strategic decision-making: Linking theories of personalities and cognitions. *Journal of Management Studies,* **26** (5), 477–97.

Hofer, C. W. and Schendel, D. (1978). *Strategy Formulation: Analytical Concepts.* West Publishing Co.

Hofstede, G. (1994). Cultural constraints in management theories. *International Review of Strategic Management,* Vol. 5, D. E. Hussey, (ed.), John Wiley & Sons, 27–47.

Hsu, P. S. C. (1984). The comparison of family structure and values on business organizations in oriental cultures, a comparison of China and Japan. *Proceedings of the 1984 AMA Conference, Singapore,* 754–68.

Kohut, J. and Cheng, A. T. (1996). Return of the merchant mandarins. *Asia Inc.,* March, 22–31.

Mintzberg, H. (1987). Crafting strategy. *Harvard Business Review,* July/August, 66–75.

Mintzberg, H. (1994). The fall and rise of strategic planning. *Harvard Business Review,* January/February, 107–14.

Mintzberg, H. and Waters, J. (1985). Of strategies, deliberate and emergent. *Strategic Management Journal,* **6,** 257–72.

Nakamura, G.-I. (1992). Development of strategic management in the Asia Pacific Region. *International Review of Strategic Management,* Vol. 3, D. E. Hussey, (ed.), John Wiley & Sons, 3–18.

Pan, C. C. H. (1984). Confucian Philosophy: Implication to management. *Proceedings of the 1984 AMA Conference, Singapore,* 777–81.

Prahalad, C. K. and Hamel, G. (1990). The core competence of the corporation. *Harvard Business Review,* May/June, 79–91.

Redding, G. (1986). Entrepreneurship in Asia. *Euro-Asia Business Review,* **5** (4), 23–7.

Redding, G. (1995). Overseas Chinese networks: Understanding the enigma. *Long Range Planning,* **28** (1) 61–9.

Seagrave, S. (1996). *Lords of the Rim,* Bantam.

Wada, K. (1992). *Yaohan's Global Strategy, the 21st Century is the Era of Asia.* Capital Communications Corporation.

Weidenbaum, M. and Hughes, S. (1996). *Bamboo Network.* Martin Kessler.

Chapter 20.1
Strategic adaptation for a mid-life crisis

■ George T. Haley ■

Asia's economic collapse seems to have brought on a mid-life crisis for the Overseas Chinese companies. As declining Asian economies devastate Asian-generated profits for all companies operating in the region, one can easily forget the prowess of the Overseas Chinese companies that dominate and depend so heavily upon the region. Rarely does a day go by without some notice of an Overseas Chinese company suffering tragedy (a notable example is the Salim group in post-Suharto Indonesia). Yet, dismissing the Overseas Chinese companies would appear akin to the American automobile industry's dismissing those first, small Hondas and Toyotas as toys.

In our book, *New Asian Emperors*, my co-authors and I highlighted the history of the Overseas Chinese and their strategic-planning processes' evolution (Haley, Tan and Haley, 1998). The business-focused history, though extremely short, communicates the tremendous resiliency and adaptability of the Overseas Chinese. Yet, the weaknesses of most Overseas Chinese companies include their strategic planning processes' dependence on their home region's business and economic environments. The present regional economic decline should provide the stimulus for the Overseas Chinese to throw off this limitation and build globally competitive and competent companies. The Overseas Chinese already have several models which they can follow, including Acer Computers, the largest computer company headquartered outside the US or Japan and the world's third largest personal computer (PC) manufacturer (for a more complete discussion of Acer see Haley, Tan and Haley, 1998; see also Chapter 23).

Acer's founder and CEO, Stan Shih, told us how he and his people built the company into an international powerhouse in the computer industry. A crucial aspect of Acer's strategy involved assimilating what its management observed in the West – the large, US fast-food companies' production processes! As we related (Haley, Tan and Haley, 1998: 91):

> Shih borrowed a concept from the fast-food industry: the company ships pre-processed ingredients to outlets to minimize preparation time; and the company makes the product just-in-time to maintain freshness and consistency. Acer manufactures components, such as caseworks, power supplies, keyboards and monitors at its plants in Taiwan and Malaysia and ships them to regional assembly facilities. Acer air freights

more technology and price-sensitive items such as motherboards, while locally procuring other components such as disk drives and memory chips.

Simultaneously, some of Acer's business practices appear vintage Overseas Chinese. Acer has expanded through building a network of largely, locally owned and managed companies around the world held together by mutual self-interest, personal ties and, to an extent, cross-ownership of shares in each others' companies. Acer also places a premium on speedy decision-making and rapid deployment of resources. Stan Shih indicated to us his use of market research (Haley, Tan and Haley, 1998: 95): 'We use it in a small way. We believe in doing things quickly. We do discuss things amongst ourselves a lot, it is like a team kind of gut feel. We implement and change things quickly. It is all implementation in the market place.' Few more apt descriptions exist of the Overseas Chinese method of strategic planning and management.

Acer also counteracts the criticism that the Overseas Chinese can prosper only so long as they obtain technology and products from others; this criticism stems from the short-term focus that so many, though not all, of these companies have. Acer has its own successful technological and product-research department that has effectively developed proprietary technology and licensed it to high-tech companies around the world. Many changes in managerial practice at Acer occurred in response to various crises the company faced over the years. Consequently, the present crisis faced by Southeast Asia's Overseas Chinese companies will stimulate the better companies to change some practices, thereby minimizing subsequent crises' effects on their companies. As I indicated in Chapter 20, a supra-company bubbling-up process occurs in the Overseas Chinese business networks; this bubbling-up process provides a distinctive overtone to strategic planning among the Overseas Chinese companies. The strategies of companies that are successfully weathering the Asian financial crisis, such as Acer, are presently bubbling up among the business networks.

▩ Reference

Haley, G. T., Tan C. T. and Haley, U. C. V. (1998). *New Asian Emperors: The Overseas Chinese, their Strategies and Competitive Advantages*. Butterworth-Heinemann.

Chapter 21

International strategies of corporate culture change: emulation, consumption and hybridity[1]

■ R. I. Westwood and P. S. Kirkbride ■

■ Introduction

The intensification of globalization and the internationalization of business have meant a more profound encounter between, and interpenetration of, different organization and management systems (OMS). A strategic issue confronting all internationally active organizations – both those entering into foreign markets and for local organizations engaging with foreign organizations and their systems – is how to manage effectively the intersection of different OMS. Some companies, such as McDonalds, have adopted the view that their management systems are culture-free and can be transplanted anywhere in the world (see Puffer, 1992). Such culture-free approaches have been criticized as being ethnocentric and of neglecting international differences in management and organizational behaviour. Certainly, corporations have been increasingly warned not to assume the universality and cross-cultural transferability of their OMS (e.g. Adler, 1991; Guillén, 1994; Hoecklin, 1995; Hofstede, 1980; Ouchi, 1981; Trompenaars, 1993). As Fligstein and Freeland (1995: 33) have noted 'despite all of the discussion of globalisation of the world economy and the so-called multinationalisation of corporations, different societies continue to have distinctive organisational arrangements'.

The focus of this chapter, however, is not on Western multinational companies' strategic responses to cross-cultural engagements, but rather on the less attended to issue of local companies' strategic responses to their encounters, in their practice and in international educational and media representations, with foreign modes of management. Whilst encounters between different OMS are an interaction, it should be recognized that they often take the form of the abutment of dominant systems from the Western,

[1] This chapter has been published previously by MCB University Press Limited: Westwood, R. I. and Kirkbride, P. S. (1998). International strategies of corporate culture change: emulation, consumption and hybridity. *Journal of Organizational Change Management*, **11** (6), 554–77.

developed world (particularly the US) with those of newly developed, developing or less developed countries. There is a tendency for the systems of economically, politically or culturally dominant countries to be more invasive through their power as exemplars, their active or passive promotion, or through mimesis. A trend has developed whereby local business communities emulate aspects of foreign systems. Certain organization and management practices, such as total quality management, process-re-engineering and – the focus of this chapter – organizational culture change, have taken on the quality of cultural products to be deployed and consumed around the world.

Are such strategies of emulation and the underlying logic of dominance and assimilation, which support the convergence thesis, the only option? An alternative is to propose a divergence thesis whereby local systems maintain their distinctiveness and promote an indigenized approach, resisting the march of the dominant systems. The Asian Values and Neo-Confucian arguments would be a recent version of this perspective. Absent from both these positions is the recognition that increasingly OMS are in interaction with each other and are mutually penetrative. This opens up the less extreme and more plausible options for various types of adaptation, modification, synthesis and hybridity. Local OMS are situated in a complex dynamic wherein they are increasingly exposed to international business and the management practices of others – to which they need to respond – whilst at the same time being emergent out of and constituted by their own sociocultural and institutional context – to which they must also respond. The strategies they adopt and the mode of management and business they develop need to reflect this confluence and the multi-stakeholders involved.

The specific aspect of the intersection of different OMS dealt with in this chapter is the symbolic representational practices of corporate culture change. At one level, then, this paper addresses, by way of an illustrative case, the strategic corporate culture change initiatives of a large Chinese owned and managed company in Hong Kong (HK). The change was presented by the company as a necessary strategic response to the evolving situation, especially from the viewpoint of its increasing engagement with international companies and its international competitiveness. However, there are indications that received conceptions of what a modern organization should be like and a fashion-conscious modelling of desired representations of such an entity also impelled the change.

The presenting problem is how to bring about a change in organizational culture and the role of symbolic manipulation in that process. This is complicated by the company's use of symbolic forms derived from US cultural sources to represent and drive the change – a strategy of emulation. The chapter questions the efficacy of these symbolic representations in bringing about changes in the values and behaviour of the workforce. We argue that such a trajectory threatens to take the company away from persisting traditional Chinese values in the community thus rendering it as out of tune with that culture. This makes problematic the change process and the meaningfulness and effectiveness of the espoused corporate culture. If the symbolic forms fail to resonate with the organizations' membership and the change effort is of limited efficacy, the value of pursuing a cultural change project by using such symbolic forms is in doubt.

The above critique only holds if it is assumed that the intended targets for the symbolization of the corporate culture are the employees. In one sense this was the case, but the company may have had another agenda too. If one considers that organizations have multiple stakeholders, then the problem of culture change is not only one of influencing the values and behaviours of employees, but also of symbolically representing the company in a favourable light to other stakeholders so as to secure prestige, legitimacy, and/or support. Much of the corporate culture change literature has focused on the impact on employees, where the orthodoxy suggests that a corporate culture can be constructed, symbolized and engineered so as to transform employee values and behaviour thereby enhancing individual, and ultimately, organizational performance. There is, however, emerging recognition of companies' efforts to use symbolic forms to influence other stakeholders. For example, Haley (1991) has discussed the attempts to influence investors through symbolic activity and more recently addressed the symbolic representation of Singapore Inc. to its various stakeholders (Haley, Low and Toh, 1996). Whilst the main thrust of this chapter is on the disjuncture between espoused culture and the employees, this alternative agenda relating to a wider stakeholder group is also pursued.

The case with which this chapter deals is deployed as a heuristic for exploring the above issues conceptually and is not intended as an empirical investigation of them. The material for the case was developed as part of a larger, ongoing study of organizational symbolism in Chinese contexts. The authors were able to secure access to the company on that basis. Interviews with senior managers and some lower level staff were conducted during 1993–94 to determine what symbolic forms were present in the company, their derivation, and their intended use and force. In addition, we also had direct observation of the symbolic forms and access to documents and other artefacts in which they were manifest. Some of these were subjected to content analysis in a search for themes and deep structures. Our continuing investigations reveal that these symbolic forms all remain in use at the company and there has been no need to update our analysis of their content. Details about the company and its cultural symbolic forms will be provided shortly.

■ Encounters between US and Chinese OMS: dominance, mimesis, hybridity

Hong Kong, being the site of an intense confluence of Eastern and Western influences, is an exemplar of the type of intersections and engagements outlined above. It is a confluence not confined to the British and Chinese, although that is highly significant historically, but a truly cosmopolitan one. As a consequence, there is a dynamic and complex nexus of various OMS in HK that abut or interpenetrate one with the other. The extent of influence and penetration is highly contingent and not historically stable. The British system was dominant for a while, but no longer. More recently the USA has enjoyed more influence, although at times challenged by Japan – as the rest of Asia looked to its successes – and latterly by mainland China for reasons of political and economic expediency. The recent Asian economic crisis, particularly Japan's collapse into recession and the faltering in China's economic growth, has the USA, and the economic supranational organizations over which it exerts such influence, back on centre stage. The influence of the US OMS in HK, and indeed globally, is partly because the size and success of its system elevates it to the status of exemplar and standard – readily available for comparison and emulation. Readily available not only through active presence and practice, but also since the USA is the pre-eminent constructor of management research, theory and pedagogy, which it successfully promulgates internationally.

Hong Kong's organizational landscape has evolved in this context and is composed of a number of varying elements. There is a small, but economically significant, number of *hongs*: large diversified companies of British heritage that have continued the traditions of their founding *taipans*. Hong Kong is also home to a large, diverse set of foreign-based companies, which often sustain their domestic organization and management approaches. The USA and Japan have been most prominent in recent years. Mainland Chinese companies are the newest, but in many respects the most significant, feature of the landscape. Then there are the local HK Chinese companies of varying types and sizes.

Despite this confluence of influences, HK remains first and foremost a Chinese society with 95 per cent of the population being ethnic Chinese. It remains imbued with aspects of traditional Chinese culture in which the Confucian ethos continues to shape values (Bond, 1986; Kirkbride and Westwood, 1993; Lau and Kuan, 1987). In terms of OMS, it has increasingly been recognized that a distinctive form exists among the Nanyang (Southeast Asian) Chinese communities (Chao, 1990; Chen, 1991; Chen, 1995; Hamilton, 1997; Kirkbride and Westwood, 1993; Oh, 1991; Redding, 1984, 1990; Redding and Hsiao, 1990; Redding and Wong, 1986; Safarian and Dobson, 1996; Westwood, 1992a, b, 1997; Westwood and Chan, 1995; Whitley, 1992; Wong, 1985). Without going into detail (for which see the above citations) this form is characterized by paternalism, personalism, nepotism, relationship-centredness, avoidance of formalization, high centralization, structural simplicity, conflict avoidance and the pursuit of harmonious relationships, and distinctive and extensive forms of networking. The roots reside in traditional Chinese values, particularly Confucian – leading some to propose the Neo-Confucian Hypothesis as an explanation of this form of economic organization (Chen, 1995; Hofstede and Bond, 1988; Kahn, 1979; Redding, 1990). It is a form most apparent in the small, owner-managed enterprises that still make up more than 90 per cent of HK's establishment population, but even larger publicly listed companies have a distinctive form derived from these traditions (Whitley, 1992).

However, this rather traditional form is under pressure to change as internationalization and other developments in HK's macro-environment continue to evolve, and particularly in the light of the fresh challenges posed by the recent economic crisis. There are, for example, a growing number of large Chinese owned and operated companies, some of multinational status. This type of company, more than any other, is at the nexus of international influences apparent in HK and other parts of Asia: constructed at a meeting point of traditionalism and modernism. Their mode of operation and international involvement exposes them in a more significant way to Western business/management practices. There is strategic pressure to move from traditional, personalistic forms to more modern, professional ones – or at least, and this is important, to construct a self-presentation in the international arena that symbolises that (see Haley, Tan and Haley, 1998).

Pressure for change comes from the intersection with the international business community, but also from other quarters. For example, HK's management education and training system, like others worldwide, is heavily imbued with American influences:

either directly through the deployment of their pedagogic paraphernalia, or indirectly since many of HK's management educators receive their own education at US universities. Furthermore, many of the leaders of HK's larger companies are very aware of US management models and the values accompanying them. Often they have received a business education in the USA or have in other ways been exposed to the US system. The promulgated imagery of US business and management exerts a strong influence and is an object of desire for some local Chinese operators. New business/management ideas and practices developed in the USA become quickly available in Asia. There is a fashionableness about being seen to be familiar with and adopting the latest management ideas emanating from the USA. The corporate culture idea is one such 'export' that has taken hold in HK and other parts of Asia. It began to surface in HK in the mid to late 1980s, first among foreign multinationals and then among large utility and transport companies that, then, were still managed by expatriates. Some larger, locally owned companies have followed suit, including the one discussed in this chapter. We contend that such cross-cultural mimetic and consumptive processes with respect to aspects of business and management practice are becoming more widespread in the Asian region. There are dangers in such trajectories. The trends and fads of US management theory and practice are constructed out of the particular set of issues and relevancies within that society and may have no resonance in other cultural settings. Changes in the OMS in HK and Asia are inevitable, but need to be constructed in the light of indigenous systems and values.

Although the penetration of US management has been extensive in HK and parts of Asia, the nature of the engagement is complex; more so than the simplifying dichotomies of culture-bound versus culture-free, or convergence versus divergence imply. We reject the view that US-derived OMS are universal or culture-free and that their promotion internationally will bring about global homogenization. A radical divergence thesis, that sees indigenous cultures and their social formations persisting in pristine form, untrammelled by globalization processes and the interpenetrations they embody, also has limitations. An engagement between elements of two or more cultural systems is, just that, an engagement. As the post-colonial literature demonstrates, even under conditions of colossal colonial invasiveness there is rarely a monolithic imposition of one system upon another. The options are not merely assimilation or eradication: there are demonstrated strategies of appropriation, adaptation, mimesis and hybridity (see for example Bhahba, 1994; Thomas, 1994). Thus, whilst in HK there are elements of imitation and fashion-following after the Western image, there is also a counter-movement of differentiation and a search for distinctiveness through indigenous formulation and practice. This is sometimes induced by a willed distancing from a colonial past and a regenerated sense of cultural identification and pride, especially since the reunification. Furthermore, traditional cultural values are not easily shed, even in turbulent times, and their influence on managers and business operators' perceptions, orientations and action, persist.

These interactive, interlocking and mimetic aspects of management systems have been relatively neglected in the comparative management literature – this, despite early signalling that alternative forms may emerge out of the intersection of business systems (Ouchi, 1981). The exception has been with respect to Japanese–Western engagements (e.g. Oliver and Wilkinson, 1992) where the depiction of Japan as a borrower and adapter of Western technologies and management has undergone a reversal in the last couple of decades. At another level, whilst there are arguments that a new world order is emerging centred on economic rationalism and the logic of late capitalism, it has been pointed out that capitalism has its variants and homogenization is not a necessary consequence (Berger, 1986; Clegg and Redding, 1990; Hamilton, 1997).

■ Cultural symbolization: cultural items and their consumption

The notion of organizational culture has had an explosive impact since the early 1980s (for recent critical overviews see Jeffcutt, 1997; Martin and Frost, 1996). Given the concerns of this chapter, it should be noted that a focus on the success and distinctiveness of Japanese business triggered the interest, and that from the outset warnings were made about the embeddedness of organizational cultures in the wider culture and the limits this placed on transfer and emulation (Ouchi, 1981; Pascale and Athos, 1981). However, since then the issue of the cross-cultural relevance and applicability of notions of organization culture has not received the attention it deserves (Adler and Jelinek, 1986: 81): partial exceptions include Lau (1995).

Whilst the literature on corporate culture is characterized by diversity and debate, the current orthodoxy has been labelled integrationist and rests on unitarist notions and the view that culture change is a matter of engineering values (Martin and Frost, 1996). Part of the 'engineering' process involves the construction, presentation and manipulation of symbols that express the aspired to value orientations. It is this perspective that has received the widest exposure and been most heavily promulgated in foreign situations, including Asia and HK.

The case company seems to have accepted this view of culture and attempted to engineer a culture change in which the development and presentation of symbolic forms played a crucial part. The role of symbols and symbolization in the formation and maintenance of corporate cultures has been recognized from the outset (Deal and Kennedy, 1982; Pondy et al., 1983; Trice and Beyer, 1993). However, the mechanisms by which symbols are supposed to effect change in people's values and behaviour have not been adequately conceptualized. There are vague pronouncements that the symbols embody desired cultural values thus reinforcing the intended message and facilitating internalization. This presupposes that the symbols are so invested with the correct meanings, and that such meanings are transferred to the employees, have resonance with the individuals and can be internalized into their own value set. Since a change is involved, it must also be assumed that the new values being symbolized replace, complement or modify existing ones in some manner. This is difficult enough even where there is some commonality between symbol producers and symbol consumers, and shared understanding of the symbols and their meanings. However, in the case examined, the mode of symbolization draws heavily on US significations and values in a highly mimetic manner, and in ways not in tune with the culturally constituted world in HK. We question whether the consumption of that representation by the local workforce engenders the intended meanings and accompanying attitudinal and behavioural changes.

This chapter, then, provides a critical appraisal of the symbolization of corporate culture by one of the larger locally owned organizations in HK with modernizing aspirations. We chose the company because such a change effort reflects the tensions generated by the intersections and dichotomies of values and orientations outlined above.

We will pursue some of the images and practices of corporate culture that have emerged in these particular circumstances, focusing specifically on their symbolic manifestation and presentation. We raise questions about the nature of the symbolism employed: its cultural specificity, the values and practices it invokes, and its mimetic and consumptive qualities.

▣ Kut Cheung and its espoused culture

Family traditions

The Kut Cheung Company (KC) was founded by Henry Chen in 1971 in a manner which already marks some of the tensions suggested above (names of the company and of persons have been changed for reasons of confidentiality). Henry is the third son of an immigrant entrepreneur from Guangdong province who moved to HK after the Second World War. The father established the Golden Tiger Property Company in 1955 and it is now a major company in the territory. His first son, following Chinese family business traditions, took over the company from the patriarch, while the second also pursued business interests under Golden Tiger's corporate umbrella. Returning from studying overseas, Chen originally took over a family-controlled spinning mill. However, differences of opinion led to Chen branching out on his own, a somewhat atypical move in the Chinese family business context. None the less, family cohesiveness enabled him to borrow family funds to establish his own construction company and for all business in the first two years to come via existing family concerns. Beginning with only five employees, the company has continued to grow independently until today where it stands as a major construction and property group. It is a typical Chinese networked business (Whitley, 1992) with a complex web of subsidiary companies anchored around the core business – manifest in the Kut Chung Construction and Materials Ltd Group. This latter achieved a turnover of HK$4732 million in 1998 with profits attributable to shareholders of HK$313 million (Annual Report). It has a workforce in excess of 3000 almost all of whom are ethnic Chinese.

Chen has sought to cultivate an approach to corporate culture that is both distinctive for a Chinese-run business in HK and mimetic with respect to contemporary Western symbolizations of corporate practice. We deal here with the presentational and symbolic aspects of his approach to corporate culture change. What follows is a descriptive account of fragments of that symbolic representation.

Fragments of Kut Cheung's corporate culture

The change effort began when Chen initiated a strategic business consolidation and corporate reorientation programme in the form of a three-day top-management retreat. One tangible outcome was a corporate mission statement (CMS), the generation of which was already unusual for a Chinese firm in HK at that time (Kirkbride and Tang, 1989). This CMS contains the following five key corporate value statements, each amplified with additional commentary:

- *Profit* – to achieve sufficient profit to provide an attractive return to our shareholders and to finance our growth.

- *Customers* – to provide our clients with quality service and products.

- *Our people* – to provide an environment whereby our people can excel, develop and grow with the company.

- *Management philosophy* – to provide an environment that encourages and rewards merit and team effort.

- *Corporate culture* – to cultivate a set of shared beliefs on which all our policies and actions are based.

This CMS may look familiar, a sense of *déjà vu* that is not surprising once one learns that Chen instructed retreat participants to bring, in addition to their normal business reports and data, copies of *In Search of Excellence* (*SOE*) (Peters and Waterman, 1982) as a basic reference!

The company reproduces the CMS in a variety of published formats. A lot of effort and resources are expended in promoting the espoused corporate culture through this and other mechanisms. Irrespective of its specific meanings and symbolic content, the KC CMS – qua mission statement – already symbolizes modern Western management, and beyond that a whole complex array of values, orientations, practices, rationalities and logics. It invokes a distinctive discourse circulating in the academic/practitioner language community of the contemporary US business world. But there is immediately a problem here. Its localized symbolic force rests largely on the distinctiveness it marks in the context of the Chinese business community. The fact that CMS's are rare in that community gives it a difference that highlights this symbolic quality. However, a fuller interpretation is only really possible because the CMS indexes a particular text, through Peters and Waterman, and on to a vast corporate culture discourse prevalent in the US business/academic community. Such esoteric textual and symbolic properties are not available to everybody the CMS is directed at, most notably the workers at KC.

To a degree, the whole of Chen's espoused corporate culture change project works in this way. The constructed imagery of the CMS and other aspects of corporate culture identity at KC further mark the distinctiveness already embodied by his break from the family business. The company is differentiated from most Chinese-run businesses in HK. But more than that, the symbolic representations collectively conspire to declare that KC, and importantly Chen himself, is participating in modern management and all that connotes. Paradoxically, this distinctiveness is established through a fairly explicit mimicry of a particular representation of US business practice. A difference is symbolically established only by the immediate creation of a relation of similarity, becoming both distinctive and commonplace in one move.

The language of the CMS is pregnant with further meanings and symbols many of which, given their mimetic qualities and indexing of a particular US discourse surrounding corporate cultures, are quite accessible to Western academic audiences. Such symbolic connections have received adequate articulation in the literature and do not need reiteration here. We will, however, comment further on aspects of the CMS later. Let us return to other key symbolic fragments of KC's corporate culture.

One of the most interesting elements of the presented culture is its logo. From early in its history the company had taken Jonathan Livingston Seagull (*JLS*), from Bach's (1972) book of the same name, as the inspiration for its corporate logo. The logo is a simple, stylized depiction of a white bird (a seagull) in flight with wings outstretched.

It is set on an orange disk, with both wing tips touching the radius of the disk on opposite sides. Below the bird two white lines segment the disk: one very thin, lying about a quarter of the way up, the second thicker and lying just below the first. The intended meaning of this symbol is best indicated by its description in a corporate video:

> Here at KC we also have a logo of our own. KC, a name which is becoming better and better known in HK as synonymous with an efficiently organized, fast growing company. These qualities work in perfect harmony with the spirit of the Jonathan Livingston Seagull that has become very much a part of KC philosophy. The Jonathan Livingston Seagull – in flight, soaring ever upward towards the infinity of the blue sky, symbolizes a constant quest for self-betterment and perfection. This symbol has become to all of us at KC an inspiration, something with which to identify, and a focal point for our thoughts. At KC, we too believe that perfection is the goal for every effort, and that the constant quest for improvement is a source of stimulus and challenge. This spirit of Jonathan Livingston Seagull prevails everywhere at KC, where already the concrete rewards of our corporate struggle for improvement can be seen all around us.

Part of that final sentence is literally true. The logo is used extensively at KC: displayed in all manners of printed materials, on the sides of vehicles, construction site placards, in lobbies and corridors. KC has also adopted as a slogan a specific quotation from the book: 'The most important thing in life is to reach out and touch perfection.' As Chen's wife, Rita (also a director of the company) said in an interview:

> My husband and I read JLS in the early years of our construction company, and found that it also reflected our aspirations about the kind of company we wanted to create. The Seagull is now our company logo and the book is part of the reading material used for the orientation program for our new staff.

Notably, the name of Chen's first son is ... Jonathan!

That a Western 1970s cult book should turn up as the inspiration for the symbolic depiction of a large Chinese company in HK, is rather odd. The power of the symbols is severely reduced if the intended meaning can only be unearthed by staff being given copies of the book to read! However, the company bombards its members with the logo and key quotation and this association may be sufficient to imbue the logo with the right meanings and enable members to accomplish the correct reading.

The corporate culture symbolized in the CMS and logo is reinforced in several other ways. As noted, quite sophisticated corporate videos are used to promote the culture. KC also produces two in-house publications that heavily feature the culture statement and the logo as well as interviews and stories which reinforce the culture. There is also a KC Club, which organizes picnics, outings and community service volunteer work. Many of the prescribed accoutrements, used then, are of corporate culture manufacture.

One of the videos, used in employee orientation sessions and company promotions, reiterates themes in the logo and CMS. It begins with shots of a seagull gliding in a peerless blue sky, the sun glinting off its wings. The voice-over intones: 'Soaring through an endless sky Jonathan Livingston Seagull was in a constant search for perfection. That same search, that same ambition, is exemplified today in HK's Kut Cheung Group.' The video goes on to present symbolically the key corporate values as articulated in the CMS. It does so with a tightly edited mixture of text, voice and imagery that conspire to provide a symbolic gestalt around the core values. For example, the value of profit is presented with a textual presentation of the CMS element with a voice-over declaring the salience of the profit motive for a business enterprise. This is supported by on-screen images of piles of various currencies and a lingering close-up of bank notes. A little later a weighing scale is graphically depicted which has the words 'economy, effectiveness and efficiency' resting on one side and a large dollar sign on the other. The segment closes with a close-up of the dollar sign filling the screen. It would be instructive to provide a frame by frame account of the symbolism of the company's videos, but space does not permit.

Another fragment concerns the symbolism of architecture. KC is headquartered in a custom-built tower in a core business district. Designed and built by KC in a high-tech style, it is a multi-storey, hung-glass-walled construction that stands gleaming alongside a forest of other gold-glassed, reflective-glassed and concrete buildings housing international companies of the likes of the Bank of America, Kumagai-Gumi, Caterpillar and so on. It again symbolizes a modern international company, given further credence by this shoulder-rubbing with some essential bastions of that world. It features all the appropriate accoutrements: atrium, marble tiling, gleaming stainless steel, modernist design furniture, open plan offices, and the state-of-the-art gadgetry of the electric office.

The company's structural design is also of symbolic significance as a representation of Chen's espoused corporate culture. First, unlike many other Chinese companies, the owner's family members (other than Chen's wife) do not populate KC at the top. Second, the company is organized on divisional lines. At the top is KC Group Limited which co-ordinates the group's activities and provides a variety of corporate services to group companies. Various divisions and subsidiaries are under the corporate umbrella. The divisional structure provides a degree of autonomy and decentralization for operating units not common in more typical Chinese businesses (Redding, 1984; 1990; Whitley, 1992). The corporate staff units also add a degree of differentiation and structural complexity rare in traditional Chinese companies. Many of the services offered by these units would simply not be found in other companies, or if they were, would not be formalized as at KC. Again, with its structure, the company marks out its distinctiveness, differentiates itself from the more typical Chinese business, and more closely follows a form and design of the modern American corporation.

The leadership style at KC is espoused as being participative and informal in nature, as stated in the CMS: 'We are committed to consultative and participative management rather than management by directive.' The CMS also reveals that KC intends to encourage extensive delegation and a climate of informal, open communication. This espousal is very different from the centralization and autocratic management styles found in typical Chinese enterprises. It is also not as overtly paternalistic as its counterparts and it is more dependent on formalistic arrangements.

Lastly, KC uses a full battery of standard, modern, Western managerial practices: human resource planning, job analysis, standard recruitment and selection processes, an appraisal system, training and development on an extensive scale, a Hay job evaluation scheme, etc. Such management practices further symbolize and support the aspired to distinctiveness and modernity of KC contra traditional Chinese companies. The existence of these managerial practices, and certainly the level of formalization that accompanies them, is, again, rare amongst Chinese businesses in HK.

■ On the extensionality of Kut Cheung's corporate symbolization

The mimesis of culture: ready-mades and intertext

Much of the symbolism at KC must be viewed as highly individualized; as creating and signifying a pattern of meaning of relevance and significance only to Chen and his immediate cohorts. Although the symbolic construction has this private quality, the intention, of course, is to extend it into the public domain. However, there are aspects of the symbols, their mode of construction and presentation that suggest that such extensionality into a domain shared by the members of his organization and some other stakeholders is, at best, problematic. If symbols are 'signs which express much more than their intrinsic content; they are significations which embody and represent some wider pattern of meaning' (Pondy et al., 1983). What wider patterns of meaning are accessed by the symbolism circulating at KC?

The mimetic qualities of Chen's approach to, and symbolization of, culture change have already been noted. The core symbols are not culled from his own conscious or unconscious, nor emergent from the cultural significance of his own organization or the Chinese community at large. Rather they have the quality of ready-mades taken up and imported (from alien milieux) into his company. They are taken, at an immediate level, from two distinctive sources: Bach's *JLS*, and Peters and Waterman's *SOE*. At this level the mimesis is direct and obvious.

The logo and key statements of corporate philosophy are, at this first level, a symbol of the book *JLS*. The esoteric nature of these symbols is such that they require the support of the whole book (as required reading for new members) to provide a position of intelligibility likely to foster the intended meanings. This is an obscure text even in the West and likely to be even more alien to any kind of HK audience except students of contemporary Western literature; and certainly not the Chinese workers of KC. The reading provided by the Chens is itself a particular one. The notion of the pursuit of perfection is certainly central to Bach's text but is by no means the only reading locatable there.

The use of *SOE* is a little more indirect but more pervasive. The inclusion of the book at the initiating retreat, led to a conception of corporate culture and its symbolization that is a clear reflection of the content and ideas contained within it. There are significant parallels between the CMS of KC and that of Hewlett-Packard (H-P), which receives comprehensive treatment in the book. There is a second order mimicry here then: KC on H-P. *SOE* is certainly less esoteric than *JLS* but is not as widely read in HK as in, say, the USA, and certainly is not a recurring element in the business discourse of HK, particularly in the Chinese sector.

The mimetic process extends beyond this immediate level. The symbols of KC operate via a kind of intertext which works through the two ready-mades on to a broader discourse. The CMS and other symbolic elements directly and indirectly mark *SOE* as an access to one such complex discourse that popularly articulates distinctive perspectives on organizations and management in the USA. *SOE* is an exemplar of that discourse which is extended in all manner of academic and practitioner media. It is a discourse that runs around the central metaphor of organizations as cultures (Morgan, 1986). It not only promotes certain concrete approaches to management and organization, but also reflects and symbolizes distinctive values deemed appropriate for modern organizations and instrumental for organization effectiveness. It urges that organizations need 'strong cultures' characterized by particular qualities and values (these vary but are epitomized by Peters and Waterman's eight key attributes of 'excellence'). There is a prescriptiveness here in which good cultures are strong cultures and must exhibit these kinds of characteristics.

But what can these patterns of meaning indexed and symbolized at KC mean for the organizational members, most of whom are not aware of, and have not (prior to Chen's intervention) been exposed to, this discourse and its symbolic forms. The only likely position of intelligibility by which they can accomplish an intended reading is the intraorganizational one provided by the company's supporting paraphernalia. The meaning and power of the symbols is likely to be diminished by this inaccessibility.

The consumptive experience of corporate culture

To obtain a theoretical angle on this disjuncture of symbolic construction and reception we turned to some work on the symbolism and semiotics of advertising and consumerism (see for example Hirschman and Holbrook, 1981, 1992; Levy, 1982; McCracken, 1986; Mick, 1986). McCracken's (1986) discussion of the cultural significance and meaning of consumer goods, in particular, provides insight into the processes of corporate culture creation and transmission. His concern is with the transfer of cultural meaning with respect to consumptive items. The typical trajectory is from the 'culturally constituted world'[2] to the consumptive item and from thence to the individual consumer. Advertising is one mechanism by which a transference along this trajectory is accomplished.

An advertisement provides a symbolic frame in which there is an intended contiguity between some valued/desirable aspect of the culturally constituted world and the particular consumptive item such that the consumer is able to read the relationship and so transfer the value from the culturally constituted world to the consumptive item. This only works, of course, through the known and shared values and qualities of the culturally constituted world being successfully attached, in the consumers' reading, to the unknown values and qualities of the consumptive item.[3] We can see this as analogous to the attempted construction of a corporate culture. The construction, presentation and reception of a corporate culture can be viewed as a consumptive process. Chen is trying to renew his organization and invest it with certain values and qualities. These are, ostensibly, presented with the intention of bringing about a change in the attitudes and behaviour of the organizational consumer. The symbolic

[2] The 'culturally constituted world' is defined as: 'the world of everyday experience in which the phenomenal world presents itself to the individual's senses fully shaped and constituted by the beliefs and assumptions of his/her culture. This constitution is accomplished in two ways. Firstly by the culture acting as a 'lens' through which phenomenal experience is mediated and made useful. Secondly ... culture is the 'blueprint' of human activity, determining the co-ordinates of social action and productive activity, and specifying the behaviours and objects that issue from both' (McCracken, 1986: 6). It should be noted that McCracken does not view this as a naturally occurring and passive process; he is fully cognizant, for example, of the role of the reader in the active interpretation and construction of meaning.

[3] This part of the process only deals with the transfer of meaning from 'culturally constituted world' to the consumer good. The symbolic coding accomplished here will then have a significant bearing upon the transfer from the item to the individual consumer. But certainly if the symbolic coding in the construction phase is not effective, then a reading that results in the intended reception/production of meaning is not likely to occur.

representations are intended to give meaning to the values and beliefs so promoted; to make them resonant, palatable and acceptable to the membership. Following McCracken (1986), they are better able to do so if they align with particular values and beliefs of the culturally constituted world.

In one sense this is indeed what happens. The ready-mades are already part of some people's culturally constituted world. The symbolism at KC indexes a broad terrain, invoking on the one hand the whole corporate culture discourse circling in US academic and business arenas and, on the other, through Bach, another culturally constituted world with an additional set of distinctive values and assumptions. However, the culturally constituted world(s) so invoked are essentially alien to the intended audience. The intended consumptive items (the values, attitudes and behaviours) the organization is intending to transfer to its members are represented by symbolic forms that invoke culturally constituted worlds not known and shared by the members. Transference is unlikely to be readily accomplished.

This lesion in the espoused project becomes more apparent when one considers some of the traditional, and still influential, features of Chinese culture and the mismatch between those and the values being put forward in KC's corporate culture symbolization.

A cultural schism

Hong Kong's Chinese cultural heritage

Any attempt to delineate Chinese culture here would be audacious, instead we only make reference to literature that deals with Chinese culture with respect to work and organizations and makes some attempt to link these to their historico-cultural roots.

A handle on the work-related values of the Chinese might initially be found via Hofstede's (1980) cultural dimensions. This shows HK as being a relatively large power distance, very weak uncertainty avoiding, moderately masculine, collectivist culture. The most significant differences between HK and the USA are in individualism and power distance where the USA is an extreme individualistic culture and has a smaller power distance. This values orientation for the Chinese is supported by other studies (Bond and Hwang, 1986; Hofstede and Bond, 1984; Westwood and Everett, 1987).

The collectivist nature of Chinese culture has been widely attested to: the significant point of reference for people is the collectivity rather than the individual self; the interests of the collective supersede those of the individual; and a sense of identity is achieved via membership of, and reference to, the group rather than by self-reference. This receives support from the work of Redding (1984, 1990), and Redding and Wong (1986) in the more specific context of Chinese businesses where collectivism is reported as an orientation that mediates organizational relationships and influences behaviour patterns.

The traditional Confucian ethos continues to infuse Chinese value systems. The Doctrine of the Mean (Chung Yung) urges the individual to adapt to the collectivity and to control their own emotions, avoid confusion, competition and conflict (Hsu, 1949). This is associated with the primary philosophical/moral precept of harmony, of which collectivism is viewed as a necessary corollary. The maintenance of harmonious relationships within the social collectivity is the prime mover and people must subjugate their individual desires and interests to that end. The psychological literature further supports this. In review, Yang (1986) reports dominant psychological attributes of social harmoniousness and relationship centredness in studies with Chinese subjects. Such collectivism is contrasted with the individualism and egocentrism of Western culture.

Large power distance implies the existence and acceptance of power differences and inequalities in society. There is philosophical and moral support for this from a Confucian ethic that has at its core a legitimized and expected set of unequal but reciprocal relationships – emperor/minister; husband/wife; father/son; older brother/younger brother; friend/friend – with the moral imperatives of filial piety and fidelity. These relationships are linked to the key Confucian values of *Li* and *Jen*. *Li* refers to the ethic of propriety and prescribes these social relationship structures and impels the individual not to challenge or disturb the role system. The concept of *Jen* confirms that individuals should not be considered as separate entities but as inextricably bound up with the social context, the clan and the family. Individuals are expected to conform to these structures and relationships and the accompanying behavioural prescriptions. Again, psychological research suggests a disposition of conformity amongst the Chinese (Wong, 1982; Yang, 1986). Studies on authoritarianism (Ho and Lee, 1974; Yang, 1970) and compliance (Hiniker, 1969) also offer empirical evidence supporting the traditional values of respect for authority and conformity to prescribed social structures and behaviour patterns. These psychological dispositions and moral and philosophical injunctions have continued to receive reflexive reinforcement in the socialization practices and structural patterns of Chinese society over the last two thousand years.

Chinese organizations are configured by a legitimized hierarchy based upon status overlaid with a system of reciprocal personal relations and ritual. It is the tacit (Confucian) social ethic and the prescribed set of relations that orders and controls the system, not an abstract and impersonal rule system – as in the Western bureaucratic model. Acceptance of, and compliance to, this form of structure and governance has been deeply rooted in Chinese organization and persists down to the present day. A distinctive style of management and organization for Chinese organizations develops out of and is in tune with the central cultural traditions, as indicated above. The typical Chinese family business is characterized by: a paternalistic management philosophy; high levels of centralized decision-making centred on the owner-manager and his immediate family; low levels of formalization; personalism; loyalty and obedience to the owner-manager based on the natural rights of the patriarch; and an implicit, tacit mode of order and control. The collectivist orientation, which in HK is focused on the family, is seen as underwriting much of this. Indeed, one author (Lau, 1984) captures the animus of HK society with the concept of utilitarianistic familism. As Redding argues 'most successful organizations in the Chinese case have managed to develop a particularly powerful family atmosphere which releases higher levels of motivation and trust' (Redding, 1984: 15). These value orientations also begin to articulate a framework for a distinctive Chinese organizational culture.

This sketch of Chinese values and psychological dispositions, and the suggested cultural heritage that continues to inform Chinese values and orientations with respect to organization and administration, raises some seductive questions that have a bearing upon KC's corporate culture project.

Cultural impediments to a correct reading

It is argued that the culturally constituted world of the HK Chinese, even in the arena of business, is informed by these persisting Confucian values and traditional social structures and relationships. Such a culturally constituted world is symbolized in innumerable ways within society and entrenched in socialization practices. The corporate symbolism at KC, however, signifies distinctively US discourses and values that attach to, what for the HK Chinese is, an alien culturally constituted world; one symbolized via a set of references that are obscure and esoteric and unlikely to produce the meanings the company seeks to promote. Organizational consumers would have great difficulty in transferring meanings from this alien culturally constituted world to the consumptive items of desired organizational values and behaviours. Certainly a correct reading would prove difficult and always be in danger of invasion by alternative meanings locatable in the culturally constituted world of Chinese values and forms.

More explicitly, we can see that at certain points in the symbolisation of KC's corporate culture there is a signification of values and perspectives at odds with the core values and orientations of Chinese culture. This is most apparent in those parts of the CMS advocating consultative, participative and decentralized systems – e.g.: 'We are committed to consultative and participative management rather than management by directive' and 'We encourage proper delegation of authority and decision-making at the lowest possible levels'.

The video reinforces this with images of meetings with many different types of employees taking part, and is further symbolically reinforced by the open-plan design of offices, structural design and expressed management style. This symbolic depiction clashes with aspects of the Chinese culturally constituted world such as: large power distance; respect for authority; traditional relationships and hierarchical structures; the Confucian prescription to accept and accede to laid down and established unequal relationship patterns; and with the reported authoritarianism.

There are similar discontinuities with respect to collectivism, although the situation is somewhat more complex. The symbolism around *JLS* suggests an individualistic value system. The lone bird seeking self-growth and perfection, itself symbolises the narcissistic preoccupations of the West in the 1970s. The seagull has no specific symbolic meaning in Chinese culture – the crane, the peacock and the phoenix do, but none of them resembles the logo. In the CMS, and elsewhere, there are further marks of individualism. For example, 'We want our people to get the recognition each of them deserves and to be proud of their accomplishments' and 'We support the concept of superior compensation for superior performance'. We contend, therefore, that the logo and the symbolism around *JLS* are culturally alien to a Chinese audience and are largely indexing an individualistic values set at odds with Chinese collectivism.

It is apparent, just from these examples, that the symbolism of KC's corporate culture is severely at odds with some of the characteristics of traditional Chinese organizations as discussed in the literature. Most notably, the traditional preference for highly centralized decision-making does not square with KC's pronouncements about decentralization. The autocratic management styles, with clear and largely unquestioned management prerogative, is also disjunctive with the prescriptions in the CMS for participation and consultation. Paternalism is apparent in the KC project but to a lesser degree than in more traditional companies. KC aspires to much higher levels of formalization than is common, and to an extent replaces the personalistic forms of relationships pervading traditional companies, with more legalistic and impersonal systems. In some respects the treatment of staff is more in line with the concepts of rights apparent in the West and less guided by a moral order rooted in Confucian precepts.

A work ethic is apparent in both orientations but its antecedents and interpretation are different. The Nanyang Chinese work ethic has its roots in the particular historic material conditions of those people. The work ethic symbolized in KC's corporate culture, however, stresses the enjoyment of work, recognition, achievement and self-satisfaction: that is, intrinsic motivation. This may not resonate with the motivational pattern of the highly pragmatic, instrumental and materialist ethos of the HK Chinese in which extrinsic factors are far more significant. The intrinsic orientation links with another whole US management discourse about work meaning and motivation.

There are, in summary, major disjunctures between the symbolic presentation of the espoused corporate culture at KC and the wider cultural context in HK where traditional Chinese values continue to exert a significant influence.

■ Conclusion

This chapter offers an analysis that reflects the complexities of the international intersection of OMS. It is not only multinationals from the leading economies that need to strategize their responses to such engagements and intersections, but also local organizations in contexts such as HK and Asia. There are complex dynamics at work with forces impelling a measure of convergence and divergence operating simultaneously. On the one hand there is the continued diffusion, if not imposition, of modes of business and management from the dominant economies, particularly the USA. This is facilitated both by factors emanating from those economies, such as their management education industries, and by the receptivity of local élites. On the other hand, local organizations cannot be other than elements within their local social and institutional systems and must function in ways that resonate with that. There are, furthermore, forces for divergence as resistances to Western business and economic dominance impel a move towards asserting distinctiveness and indigenization of OMS. Within this complex nexus multiple strategies, multiple motives and multiple stakeholders are in play. At times there are elements of the imposition of one system upon another. Then there are strategies of emulation and mimesis. At other times there are more or less deliberate trajectories of differentiation and rejection of external systems. Perhaps more often than is commonly acknowledged, the intersection of OMS results in neither of these, but rather in processes of appropriation, modification and hybridity. The case and the discussion surrounding it reflect the complexity of these strategic options. It should not be assumed that only one strategic response is in play within the same company at the same time. Indeed, we would suggest that the case company is engaging in different strategies with respect to its different stakeholders.

Companies like KC stand very much at the confluence of Western and traditional Chinese values. Their size, mode of operation, international exposure, and adoption of modern Western structures and practices, generate pressures that impel them away from the parameters of their local culture. It is an organizational form that is becoming more prevalent across Asia as the forces of internationalization and globalization gather momentum. Although KC was one of the first Chinese operated companies to construct a corporate culture, there has been a discernible trend through the 1990s of large local firms seeking to project a more modern and professional image. This is still a relatively small and élite group, but influential. They remain distinctive in an enterprise population still characterized by traditional Chinese values and practices within which such notions of corporate culture have limited appeal. The trend has been more noticeable in such areas as banking and finance, retail and the hospitality industry, but is emergent in manufacturing, construction and other heavy industries. For example the retail group, Giordano, has developed and projected a corporate culture and style of business that symbolizes a modern, Western approach. One of the largest local banks, Hang Seng, initiated a major corporate culture change in the mid-1990s to transform its traditional Chinese image to one more in tune with its international competitors. Locally owned hotel groups, such as New World International, have increasingly presented an image that makes them indistinguishable from their international counterparts. These have followed such companies as Cathay Pacific, the Mass Transit Railway Corporation and Stan Shih's Acer Group in Taiwan, which developed formal corporate cultures in the 1980s. There are convergent forces at play in such contexts. This trend reflects two things. First, there is an emulation of Western management practices since they are perceived as attractive and viable models and bring kudos among peers within this elite group of HK senior managers and owners. Second, there is a strategic imperative derived from the fact that these companies increasingly have to interact in the international business arena and to project an image appropriate to that.

At one level then, this chapter deals with a Chinese organizational leader apparently attempting to construct an organizational corporate culture and to autonomize it through the employment of a range of esoteric symbols and which index some particularly Western organization and management discourses. We have argued that these symbols access a culturally constituted world that is at odds with that of at least one major stakeholder group to which they are projected – the employees. We question whether the aspired to meanings will successfully transfer to them. There is evidence of this from the interviews with lower level staff whom, whilst knowledgeable about the existence of the various symbols, were not knowledgeable about their derivation and meanings. Remember that the vast bulk of the workforce is ethnic Chinese. In a further partial test of the cultural disjuncture we asked sets of ethnic Chinese university students to describe the meaning of a symbol approximating the corporate logo (a monochrome version of the seagull in flight). Many meanings were generated but none reflected the company's intended one. The efficacy of the change effort with respect to this stakeholder group is questionable. This raises doubts about the value of emulating or transplanting Western notions and practices of corporate culture into different cultural contexts, especially when those contexts have forms of management and cultures that do resonate with wider cultural values.

The US corporate culture project can be taken at face value as a mechanism to secure the unitarism and compliance required for effective collective performance and as a reflection of the perceived failure of other forms of achieving that, such as bureaucratic and command models. Traditional Chinese businesses have little trouble supporting a governance system that serves the interests of owners and managers and in which dominance and compliance are readily accomplished. This is achieved by drawing upon the presumed virtues and veracities of the shared traditional cultural value system that legitimates power inequalities, paternalistic rule and the rest. This alternate rationality of dominance has its own symbolic forms, one of which is the depiction of the business as a family with all the attendant obligations, duties and structural and behavioural implications that brings. There is, however, none of the deliberate engineering of or self-conscious absorption with, overt symbolic forms in the orders and structures apparent in traditional Chinese business that has accompanied the corporate culture project in the West. The question that then poses itself is why a Chinese owned company finds it necessary to eschew that form of organization and emulate the Western model – especially when the strategy has involved a symbolization process that is radically at odds with the likely resonance of its own workforce. The preceding analysis suggests that such a mimetic strategy will run into difficulties – if the motivation is genuinely to instigate a corporate culture within the organization along those lines.

This holds if the typical Western rhetoric about the purpose of corporate culture, as being one of inducing change in the values and behaviour of organization members, is accepted. However, if one takes a multi-stakeholder view then different audiences and intentions with respect to the construction and presentation of the corporate culture arise. As has already been implied, Chen was keen to project a certain image of himself and his company as being modern, international and up to date with regard to contemporary management practice. In this sense the culture change was intended to cultivate an image for external audiences. This has strategic implications since the organization had positioned itself as an international company. This meant that it either had to form relationships with other international companies or consortia, or compete with them for tenders and contracts. The corporate culture is an effort to signal that KC is a modern, international company suitable for transactions with these other players. The company is also a major contractor for government work; it was also important to project a modern and credible image to this highly significant stakeholder group. In the light of the economic crisis in Asia, the perceived need to be seen as a company of this type and not one mired in traditional and old-fashioned Asian practices has perhaps increased. In this regard, other stakeholder groups are also of relevance. Since much of the Asian crisis is linked to poor financial and banking practices, projecting a modern, international image is of greater significance in securing good relationships with banks and other funding bodies in order to secure financing and credit. The projected image is also aimed at the Chinese business élite in HK. There is kudos in being seen to be up to date with international practice and the corporate culture exercise helps to present that image. Finally, many talented, young graduates in HK aspire to work for modern international companies and avoid the personalism and restricted opportunities often to be found in more traditional local companies. The corporate symbolization serves a function with respect to this stakeholder group in enhancing the chances of recruiting the best talent.

This may have been the real agenda behind the corporate culture project at KC and for other companies in the region that have pursued a similar path. This would suggest that the construction of the culture for the organization's internal audience was not the prime motive. In this sense, the culture is a veneer, a superficial masque that reflects out to the external stakeholders and not inwards to the organization members (see also Haley, 1991; Haley, Tan and Haley, 1998). Our interviews with staff partly supports such a conclusion since they were of the view that the espoused culture had little meaningful impact on the day-to-day operation and management of the company. It is also reflected in the fact that the company expended a considerable amount of effort and resources in promoting its image externally through media presentations, corporate videos and other mechanisms.

There are important implications that derive from this analysis. First, the mimetic aspect of KC's experience and the problem of a disjuncture of the symbolization of corporate culture with indigenous cultural values raise doubts about the ability of such strategies to internally transform organizations. Local organizations, if they are seduced by the notion of corporate culture and genuinely want to change their internal cultures, ought to at least attend to the values and other features of their indigenously culturally constituted world and evolve a corporate culture that is in tune with it. However, as we have seen, this is not the only rationale for corporate cultures in these contexts. Thus, second, from a multi-stakeholder view, the function of corporate cultures takes on a different hue. This provides a different rationale and legitimization for the change effort. It is this that is likely to drive other organizations to follow a similar path. The current economic crisis may be a factor that strengthens rather than weakens this strategic imperative. Third, there is not usually a mere imposition of US systems or a direct copying. There are processes of hybridity at work. As in many things in HK, the surface image has a Western veneer, but the deep structures and processes remain Chinese. Companies like KC have significant stakes in China now; indeed, Chen has political interests there as well as business ones. In many respects it is the stakeholder groups there that in the longer term are of most significance and one can expect this situation to add to the complexity but also to increasingly drive strategic responses and the form of OMS that evolve. These complex and subtle interactive effects will continue to play out in the international business scene. The types of interactions and engagements intensified by global processes, and the responses, adaptations, modifications and hybridities they give rise to, require much more empirical and theoretical attention in organization studies than has hitherto been the case.

References

Adler, N. J. (1991). *International Dimensions of Organizational Behaviour*, 2nd edn. PWS-Kent.

Adler, N. J. and Jelinek, M. (1986). Is 'Organizational Culture' Culture Bound? *Human Resource Management*, **25** (1), 73–90.

Bach, R. (1972). *Jonathan Livingston Seagull*. Pan.

Berger, P. L. (1986). *The Capitalist Revolution*. Basic Books.

Bhabha, H. (1994). *The Location of Culture*. Routledge.

Bond, M. H. (ed.) (1986). *The Psychology of the Chinese People*. Oxford University Press.

Bond, M. H. and Hwang, K. K (1986). The Social Psychology of the Chinese People. In *The Psychology of the Chinese People* (M. H. Bond, ed.) Oxford University Press.

Chao, Y. T. (1990). Culture and work organization: the Chinese case. *International Journal of Psychology*, **25**, 583–92.

Chen, C. H. (1991). Confucian style management in Taiwan. In *Management: Asian Context* (J. M. Putti, ed.), McGraw-Hill.

Chen, M. (1995). *Asian Management Systems*. Routledge.

Clegg, S. R. and Redding, S. G. (eds) (1990). *Capitalism in Contrasting Cultures*. De Gruyter.

Deal, T. and Kennedy, A. (1982). *Corporate Cultures: The Rites and Rituals of Corporate Life*. Addison-Wesley.

Fligstein, N. and Freeland, R. (1995). Theoretical and comparative perspectives on corporate organization. *Annual Review of Sociology*, 21–43. Annual Reviews.

Guillén, M. (1994). *Models of Management: Work, Authority, and Organization in Comparative Perspective*. University of Chicago Press.

Haley, G. T., Tan, C. T. and Haley, U. C. V. (1998). *The New Asian Emperors: The Overseas Chinese, their Strategies and Competitive Advantages*. Butterworth-Heinemann.

Haley, U. C. V. (1991). Corporate contributions as managerial masques: reframing corporate contributions as strategies to influence society. *Journal of Management Studies*, **28** (5), 485–509.

Haley, U. C. V., Low, L. and Toh, M. H. (1996). Singapore Incorporated: reinterpreting Singapore's business environments through a corporate metaphor. *Management Decision*, **34** (9), 17–28.

Hamilton, G. G. (1997). *Chinese Capitalism? The Economic Organization of Chinese Societies*. Routledge.

Hiniker, P. J. (1969). Chinese reactions to forced compliance: dissonance, reduction or national character? *Journal of Social Psychology*, **77**, 157–76.

Hirschman, E. C. and Holbrook, M. B. (eds) (1981). *Symbolic Consumer Behaviour*. Association for Consumer Research.

Hirschman, E. C. and Holbrook, M. B. (1992). *Postmodern Consumer Research: The Study of Consumption as Text*. Sage.

Ho, D. Y. F. and Lee, L. Y. (1974). Authoritarianism and attitudes towards filial piety in Chinese teachers. *Journal of Social Psychology*, **92**, 305–6.

Hoecklin, L. (1994). *Managing Cultural Differences: Strategies for Comparative Advantage*. Addison Wesley.

Hofstede, G. (1980). *Culture's Consequences: International Differences in Work-related Values*. Sage.

Hofstede, G. and Bond, M. H. (1984). Hofstede's cultural dimensions: an independent validation using Rokeach's value survey. *Journal of Cross-Cultural Psychology*, **14** (4), 417–33.

Hofstede, G. and Bond, M. H. (1988). The Confucius connection: from cultural roots to economic growth. *Organizational Dynamics*, **17**, 4–21.

Hsu, F. L. K. (1949). Suppression versus repression: a limited psychological interpretation of four cultures, *Psychiatry*, **12**, 223–42.

Jeffcutt, P. (1997). *Culture and Symbolism in Organizational Analysis*. Sage.

Kahn, H. (1979). *World Economic Development: 1979 and Beyond*. Croom Helm.

Kirkbride, P. S. and Tang, S. F. Y. (1989). Personnel management in Hong Kong: a review of current issues. *Asia Pacific Human Resources Management*, **27** (2), 43–57.

Kirkbride, P. S. and Westwood, R. I. (1993). Hong Kong. In *Managers and National Culture* (R. D. Peterson, ed.) Quorum.

Lau, C. M. (1995). Organizational development practices in Hong Kong: current state and future challenges. *Asia Pacific Journal of Management*, **12** (1), 101–14.

Lau, S. K. (1984). *Society and Politics in Hong Kong*. The Chinese University Press.

Lau, S. K. and Kuan, H. S. (1987). *The Ethos of the Hong Kong Chinese*. The Chinese University Press.

Levy, S. J. (1982). Symbols, selves, and others. In *Advances in Consumer Research* (A. Mitchell, ed), vol. 9, 542–53, Association for Consumer Research.

Martin, J. and Frost, P. (1996). Organizational culture war games: the struggle for intellectual dominance. In *Handbook of Organizational Studies* (S. Clegg and C. Hardy, eds) Sage.

McCracken, G. (1986). Culture and consumption: a theoretical account of the structure and movement of cultural meaning of consumer goods. *Journal of Consumer Research*, **13**, June, 71–84.

Mick, D. G. (1986). Consumer research and semiotics: exploring the morphology of signs, symbols, and significance. *Journal of Consumer Research*, **13**, September, 196–213.

Morgan, G. (1986). *Images of Organization*. Sage.

Oh, T. K. (1991).Understanding managerial values and behaviour among the Gang of Four: Korea, Taiwan, Singapore and Hong Kong. *Journal of Management Development*, **10** (20), 45–56.

Oliver, N. and Wilkinson, B. (1992). *The Japanisation of British Industry: New Developments in the 1990s*. Blackwell.

Ouchi, W. (1981). *Theory Z: How American Business can Meet the Japanese Challenge*. Addison-Wesley.

Pascale, R. T. and Athos, A. G. (1981). *The Art of Japanese Management*. Simon and Schuster.

Peters, T. and Waterman, R. H. (1982). *In Search of Excellence*. Harper and Row.

Pondy, L., Frost, P. J., Morgan, G. and Dandridge, T. C. (1983). *Organizational Symbolism*. JAI Press.

Puffer, S. (ed.) (1992). *The Russian Management Revolution: Preparing Managers for the Market Economy*. M. E. Sharpe.

Redding, S. G. (1984). Varieties of the iron ricebowl. *The Hong Kong Manager*, May, 11–15.

Redding, S. G. (1990). *The Spirit of Chinese Capitalism*. De Gruyter.

Redding, S. G. and Hsiao, M. (1990). An empirical study of Overseas Chinese managerial ideology. *International Journal of Psychology*, **25**, 629–41.

Redding, S. G. and Wong, G. Y. Y. (1986). The psychology of Chinese organizational behaviour. In *The Psychology of the Chinese People* (M. H. Bond, ed.) Oxford University Press.

Safarian, E. and Dobson, W. (eds), (1996). *East Asian Capitalism: Diversity and Dynamism*. Hong Kong Bank of Canada Papers on Asia, vol. 2, University of Toronto Press.

Thomas, N. (1994). *Colonialism's Culture*. Blackwell.

Trice, H. and Beyer, J. (1993). *The Cultures of Work Organizations*. Prentice-Hall.

Trompenaars, F. (1993). *Riding the Waves of Culture: Understanding Cultural Diversity in Business*. Nicholas Brealey.

Westwood, R. I. (1992a). *Organizational Behaviour: Southeast Asian Perspectives*. Longman.

Westwood, R. I. (1992b). Rationale and structure. In *Organizational Behaviour: Southeast Asian Perspectives* (R. I. Westwood, ed.). Longman.

Westwood, R. I. (1997). The impact of culture on business and management in Asia. In *The People Link: Human Resource Linkages Across the Pacific* (A. E. Safarian and W. Dobson, eds) Hong Kong Bank of Canada Papers on Asia, vol. 3, 13–72, University of Toronto Press.

Westwood, R. I. and Chan, A. (1995). The transferability of leadership training in the East Asian context. *Asia Pacific Business Review*, **2** (1), 68–92.

Westwood, R. I. and Everett, J. (1987). Culture's consequences: a model for Southeast Asian management? *Asia-Pacific Journal of Management*, **4** (3), 187–202.

Whitley, R. (1992). *Business Systems in East Asia: Firms, Markets and Societies.* Sage.

Wong, S. L. (1985). The Chinese family firm: a model. *The British Journal of Sociology*, **36** (1), 58–72.

Wong, T. (1982). Aggression, personality and political culture. *Bulletin of the Hong Kong Psychological Society*, **9**, 5–17.

Yang, K. S. (1970). Authoritarianism and the evaluation of the appropriateness of role behaviour. *Journal of Social Psychology*, **80**, 171–81.

Yang, K. S. (1986). Chinese personality and its change. In *The Psychology of the Chinese People* (M. H. Bond, ed.) Oxford University Press.

Chapter 21.1

Asian corporate symbols in rapidly changing times

■ R. I. Westwood and P. S. Kirkbride ■

Organizations have always made use of symbols to signify aspects of their history or primary values and orientations (see also Chapters 9 and 9.1). From the insignia of military units, to the intense symbolic paraphernalia of religious organizations, to the logos, vision statements and other elements of the symbology of the contemporary corporations, symbols have been a key part of organizations' representations to themselves and their stakeholders. Symbolism requires the nexus of three elements: the symbol itself, what it refers to and a person who perceives and interprets. The person perceiving the symbol needs to be able to recognize the symbol, grasp what it refers to and understand the meaning that is embedded in the relationship between the two. Without this association the symbol remains devoid of meaning. Symbols can be enormously powerful when they trigger collective memories, values and orientations towards significant aspects of people's life-worlds. One need only consider national flags or core religious symbols, such as the cross or the crescent, to appreciate this power. For organizational symbols to function they need to resonate with the audience such that associations between symbols and what they intend to signify can be made and appropriate meanings distilled. There must be a connection between the memories, experiences and life-world of the perceiver and the symbols deployed. Chapter 21 deals with a Chinese company that deployed symbolic forms, as part of their strategic corporate culture change, that were imported from an alien, Western symbolic system. The resonance with the audience was diminished and the intended meanings lost.

Many Asian organizations have made use of corporate symbols, but they have frequently used symbols that connect to the common experiences and meaning frames of people within their cultural context. For example, Hong Kong's Hang Seng Bank has used an ancient Chinese coin as its corporate logo, and the Japanese Sakura Bank makes use of a symbolized form of the peach blossom. An interesting case from Hong Kong, which parallels the example explored in the chapter, is that of the Great Eagle Construction Company. The name more literally in Chinese means Eagle master and is derived from the names of the founder and his wife. The founder was Mr Lo Ying Shek, and *ying* means eagle. The wife's name was Lo Lai Kwan, with *kwan* meaning master. The logo is a piece of classic Chinese calligraphy containing the two characters for *ying* and *kwan*. However, the characters are arranged hierarchically with that reflecting the male origin above that reflecting the female. This corresponds to the patriarchal hierarchy of traditional Chinese culture. The third son of the family now runs the company. The other sons have all gone into separate businesses. Some have deployed logos and other symbols that subtly reference the Great Eagle; others have gone for more modern, international symbols, which have no particular historical, or local significance. This is somewhat unusual in the Chinese context. The independence of the sons and their businesses is reflected in the use of non-traditional symbols.

In a sense this last example is illustrative of the trend in Asia. As the pace of internationalization increases, local companies are increasingly adopting Western or broadly international management and business trends. One consequence is the deployment of symbols that are no longer anchored to the local culture. This is either being done in sheer emulation or as a strategic ploy to present a modern, international image to international or internationally oriented stakeholders. The danger is that we are left with a global corporate landscape populated by culturally detached symbols devoid of meaning.

Chapter 22

An examination of strategic foreign direct investment decision processes: the case of Taiwanese manufacturing small- and medium-sized enterprises[1]

■ Ho-Ching Wei and Chris Christodoulou ■

■ Introduction

In the 1980s there were both economic and non-economic factors impacting on Taiwan's economy and creating a worsening business environment (Chiang, 1994: 23). The main economic factor was Taiwan's huge trade surplus which had caused the appreciation of the New Taiwan (NT) dollar, the introduction of hot money into the economy and an increase in the money supply. As a consequence, Taiwan's industries had their competitiveness eroded due to the increases in operating costs, for example, real estate and labour costs. The main non-economic factor was the removal of martial law which then led to a growing labour movement, an environment protection movement, political confrontation between the ruling party and the opposition parties, and a deterioration of public security. The resulting instability also contributed to the deterioration of the investment climate.

Due to the worsening business environment in Taiwan in the 1980s, many manufacturing enterprises, the majority being labour-intensive, small- and medium-sized enterprises (SMEs), were moving out to other developing countries (Kao *et al*, 1992, p. 12). The major purpose for their overseas investments was to seek competitive advantages that had been lost in Taiwan.

Private foreign direct investment (FDI) made by Taiwanese firms in Association of South East Asian Nations (ASEAN) countries was popular. From 1963 to 1993, the total FDI amount (excluding the FDIs in China which the Taiwanese government defines as indirect investments), approved by the Taiwanese government was US$4.02 billion, of

[1] This chapter has been published previously by MCB University Press Limited: Wei, H.-C. and Christodoulou, C. (1997). An examination of strategic foreign direct investment decision processes: the case of Taiwanese manufacturing SMEs. *Management Decision*, **35** (8), 619–30.

which 51 per cent (US$2.05 billion) was in the ASEAN countries (Huang *et al*, 1994, p. 36). The FDI in these countries reached its peak in 1991, when it reached US$703 million, then it declined from 1992 onwards. In 1992 the FDIs in ASEAN countries declined to US$289 million, and most of the recent overseas investments have been to China. From 1991 to 1993 the total FDI amount approved by the Taiwanese government was US$3.36 billion. Huge capital outflow into China has now forced the government to re-examine its policy with regard to China.

To understand the stream of FDI from Taiwanese manufacturing SMEs, this chapter examines the FDI determinants and significant variables involved in the FDI decision processes of Taiwanese manufacturing SMEs and explores the implications for the Taiwanese owner managers, the Taiwanese government and the interested host countries and companies.

Operational definitions

Small and medium-sized enterprises (SMEs)

The definition of an SME differs from time to time and from country to country. In this research a Taiwanese manufacturing SME is defined as:

1 registered capital: not more than 40 million NT dollars;

2 employees: not more than 200;

3 a current factory licence.

Foreign direct investments (FDI)

An FDI is a term which is sometimes used interchangeably with terms such as foreign investment and overseas investment. In this context it is defined as either equity or capital investment by a Taiwanese company in a new or existing overseas enterprise. A portfolio, for example a stock investment, would not be considered as an FDI.

■ Conceptual framework

Figure 22.1 is the conceptual framework utilized for this research. There are three dimensions of factors which will affect an SME in making an FDI decision. They are external environments surrounding an SME, the networks around owner managers and the owner-managers' background. From a long-term view, these factors will influence each other.

An SME is surrounded by international, national and task environments. Changes from these environments may cause the SME to adopt new strategies to adapt to new circumstances (Bourgeois and Eisenhardt, 1988; Hitt and Tyler, 1991; Porter, 1980). For instance, entry barriers set by one country may force an SME to set up manufacturing facilities in that country in order to enter the market or to maintain its market share; a country's worsening political and economic environments, or an industry in decline, may cause firms to consider establishing in other countries to improve their competitive advantages. When such pressures occur, the owner managers will consider the company's objectives and may start thinking strategically. Meanwhile, the owner-managers' attitudes (Gupta, 1984; Hambrick and Mason, 1984; Hitt and

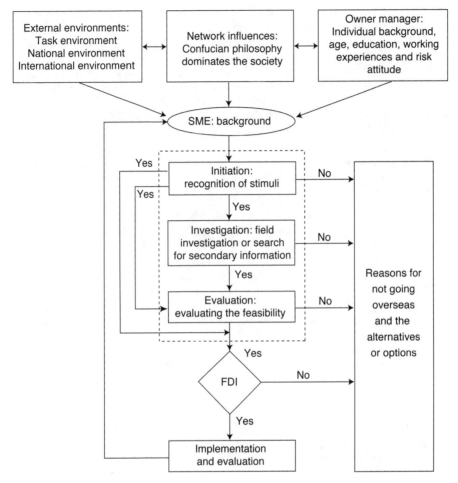

Figure 22.1 FDI conceptual model

Tyler, 1991) and the social (Meyer, 1994) and industrial network (Bodur and Madsen, 1993) influences will affect their thinking and performance.

In this research there are three kinds of networks under survey. They are the social network, the industrial network and the network of relations between business and government. Social networks and industrial networks are dominated by Confucian philosophy (Chen, 1994; Wen and Hsiao, 1988) that focuses on human relations. Government has played an important role in Taiwan's economic development. The business–government relationship is also explored to examine the government's role in FDI.

The FDI decision-making process is examined using a framework which incorporates the concepts developed by Mintzberg and Aharoni. Mintzberg, Raisinghani and Theoret (1976) examined twenty-five cases of decision-making and identified a basic structure which underlies an 'unstructured' decision-making process. Aharoni (1966) in his doctoral research entitled *The Foreign Direct Investment Decision Process* classified the FDI decision-making process into three phases, namely: the decision to look abroad, the investigation process and the decision to invest. These phases are similar to those of the Mintzberg model of identification, development and selection phases. In this research, the FDI decision-making process is examined according to the following phases: initiation and preliminary thinking, investigation, and evaluation and final decision-making. The model is similar to those of Aharoni and Mintzberg; however, the titles of the three phases were amended into a frame-work readily understandable by the Taiwanese respondents.

■ Research method

Research samples

Almost half (408 projects) of the officially approved Taiwanese FDI projects (858 projects), between the period of 1963 to 1993, were from the Electronic and Electric Appliances industry (Huang *et al.*, 1994, p. 13). The investment amount was about one-third (US$1.1 billion) of the total Taiwanese FDI amount (US$4.02 billion). Meanwhile the average FDI investment scale of the Electronic and Electric Appliances industry is small when compared to industries such as the Chemical Materials industry (6.05 per cent of total FDI projects and 26.31 per cent of total FDI amount) and the Basic Metal industry (1.59 per cent of total projects and 11.1 per cent of total FDI amount). The Electronic and Electric Appliances industry is therefore a suitable industry for studying the FDI decisions of Taiwanese manufacturing SMEs. In this research the population list was obtained from the *Manufacturing Directory* (Chinese National Federation of Industries, 1994) of the Chinese National Federation of Industries.

Two major factors were considered in order to select the sample universe: high refusal rate in Taiwan and the data requirements. In total 100 companies from the Electronic and Electric Appliances industry were selected at random from the Manufacturing Directory (Chinese National Federation of Industries, 1994) by geographic location based on an anticipated response rate of 30 per cent.

The questionnaires

Two semi-structured questionnaires were designed to gather data about respondents' decision-making processes, their perspectives about external and internal environments and finally their backgrounds. Questionnaire 1 was designed for those owner managers who had made FDIs and questionnaire 2 for those who had no FDIs or who were in the process of undergoing a FDIs feasibility study. Questionnaires were originally written in English and later translated into Chinese both for the pre-test and for the full fieldwork.

Since all the sample firms were in Taiwan, it was difficult to pre-test the questionnaires in Taiwan from Australia. For this reason, a small group of Taiwanese business migrants in the Melbourne area of Australia were used as pre-test respondents. These Taiwanese migrants with backgrounds in business were chosen because they had similar backgrounds to the owner managers of the sample firms. Six pre-test respondents were chosen and the pre-tests were held in Melbourne from December 1994 to January 1995.

The field interviews

The field research undertaken in Taiwan began in mid-February 1995 and continued over a period of three months till mid-May. The length of the interview depended on the number of questions the respondents were asked and on their willingness to talk. The average interview time for all respondents was about eighty-five minutes, with some as long as two and a half hours and others only about thirty minutes.

Table 22.1 Distribution of sample firms

Categorization	Number of firms
Firms accepting interviews	35
• Firms who had overseas investments (the *go* group):	18
1 Still had the investments	17
2 Divested of the investments	1
• Firms who had made no overseas investments (the *no-go* group):	17
1 Never considered an FDI	6
2 Rejected an FDI after investigation	5
3 Was considering an FDI	6
Firms refusing interviews	27
Invalid sample	38
1 Companies moved to other areas	2
2 Subsidiaries of large multinational companies	4
3 Companies had been closed	6
4 Unknown situation: firms might have moved overseas or be temporarily dormant	26
Total	100

An analysis of sample firms

Table 22.1 shows the distribution of the sample firms. A total of thirty-five companies participated in this survey. There were eighteen companies who had made a *go* decision on their most recent FDI investigations and the other seventeen companies were categorized as a *no-go* group which included: six companies who had never considered an FDI; five companies who had made a *no-go* decision after considering or investigating the feasibility of an FDI; and six who were still investigating the feasibility of an FDI. One of the eighteen *go* companies has subsequently withdrawn from its FDI.

In total, twenty-seven companies refused to participate. These companies included those which: did not refuse to participate directly but the researcher was unable to contact the owner managers; and those of which the owner managers were not in Taiwan and no one else in the company was familiar with the decision process. Table 22.2 shows the reasons for the companies not accepting an interview.

Table 22.1 indicates that thirty-eight of 100 sample firms fell into the category of invalid sample. Some twenty-six companies were classified as invalid because their situation was unknown. These companies were still listed in the *Manufacturing*

Table 22.2 Reasons for not granting an interview

Reasons	Cases	%[a]
1 Owner managers gave no reasons	4	14.8
2 Owner managers were not in Taiwan	3	11.1
3 Investigator could not reach owner managers	5	18.5
4 Owner managers were not interested in the survey	5	18.5
5 Owner managers were busy and had no time to be interviewed	6	22.2
6 The company was going to close or cut back on Taiwan operations so would not tell the story	2	7.4
7 It was company policy not to take part in interviews or surveys	2	7.4
Total	27	100

Note: [a]figure is rounded

Directory (Chinese National Federation of Industries, 1994) and still held a manufacturing factory licence in Taiwan. A checking of the telephone directory and the member list of the Taiwan Electric Appliance Manufacturer's Association (TEAMA) was unable to identify these companies. During the interview processes, many interviewees mentioned that there were many companies which had completely moved to China and had closed down their Taiwanese activities. Kao *et al.* (1994: 169–71) surveyed 2503 Taiwanese companies operating in China and found that 20.7 per cent (a figure very close to the findings of this research) had closed their Taiwanese companies by January 1993. It has been assumed that most of the companies that were considered as an unknown situation have totally moved to China or ceased their business activities in Taiwan.

Response rate

In total thirty-five companies participated while twenty-seven refused to participate. On the basis that thirty-eight companies of the original population sample were considered invalid, the effective response rate was fifty-six per cent. The comparison of the distribution of respondents with the original geographic distribution (see Table 22.3) illustrates that the sample was representative of the geographic distribution of SMEs

Table 22.3 A comparison of population and true sample distributions by location

Location	Population No. of firms	%	Samples in this research No. of firms	%
Taipei City	994	15	7	20
Taipei Hsien	3715	58	23	66
Taoyuan Hsien	1265	20	4	11
Hsinchu City	447	7	1	3
Total	6421	100	35	100

■ Results

Characteristics of responding firms

The average history of the responding companies was 14.5 years while the company with FDI was 13.8 years and the company with no FDI was 15.3 years. Table 22.4 shows the characteristics of the responding firms. Eight firms had foreign operation

Table 22.4 Summary of characteristics of responding firms

| | FDI decision | | | |
| | Go | | No-go | |
Variable	N	%[a]	N	%[a]
Internationalization				
Per cent of sales as direct exports*	–	60	–	37
Foreign operation experiences***				
• Yes	8	44	0	0
• No	10	56	17	100
Import of raw materials				
• Yes	11	61	10	59
• No	7	39	7	41
Company size				
Full-time employees				
• Under 10	2	11	1	6
• 10-49	14	78	16	94
• 50 and above	2	11	0	0
Capital				
• Under NT$5 million	2	11	3	18
• 5 million to 9.9 million	9	50	7	41
• 10 million and above	7	39	7	41
Annual sales amount**				
• Under NT$50 million	7	39	12	70
• 50-99.99 million	5	28	2	12
• 100 million and above	6	33	3	18
Characteristics of organization				
Own R&D				
• Yes	15	83	11	65
• No	3	17	6	35
Own financial capital				
1) Short term				
• Yes	11	61	12	71
• No	7	39	5	29
2) Long term				
• Yes	8	44	10	59
• No	10	56	7	41
Domestic investments:				
1) R&D				
• Yes	14	78	11	65
• No	4	22	6	35
2) Manufacturing facilities				
• Yes	15	83	11	65
• No	3	17	6	35

Notes: Significance: * < 0.1; ** < 0.05; *** < 0.01; [a]Rounded

experiences in addition to their most recent FDI, of which four had one, three had two
and one had four FDIs. The major raw materials or components were imported from
Japan followed by the USA and China. Two internationalization variables, direct
export percentage and foreign operation experiences, had a significant influence on
the FDI decision. A company with previous foreign operation experience has a higher
possibility of making a positive FDI decision in its most recent FDI investigation. Also
a company with a higher sales proportion generated from direct export has a higher
possibility of making a positive FDI decision. The company's capital was not
significant in making a positive FDI decision. However, the higher a company's sales,
the greater the likelihood that the company will make a positive FDI decision.

The most recent FDI

In this research the respondents were asked to describe their most recent FDI
investigation. Table 22.5 shows a summary of the most recent FDI investigations made
by the respondents. Of the most recent FDI investigations, 39 per cent of the *go* group
were made before 1993, whereas only 9 per cent of the *no-go* group were made before
1993. A total of 98 per cent of FDI investigations were in the Asia Pacific area. The most

Table 22.5 Summary of the most recent FDI evaluations

	FDI decision			
	Go		No-go	
Variable	N	%[a]	N	%[a]
*FDI year***				
• Before 1993	7	39	1	9
• 1993 to 1995	11	61	10	91
Destination				
• China	14	78	8	80
• Others	4	22	2	20
Legal form				
• Sole proprietor	6	33	5	45
• Joint venture	12	67	6	55
Proposed FDI activities				
Sales and marketing				
• Yes	9	50	7	64
• No	9	50	4	36
Assembly				
• Yes	9	50	6	55
• No	9	50	5	45
Production				
• Yes	12	67	8	73
• No	6	33	3	27
Research and development				
• Yes	4	22	2	22
• No	14	78	9	78

Notes: Significance: ** < 0.05; [a]Rounded

important reason for the companies considering China as an FDI location was the same language and the similar culture.

Characteristics of respondents

Table 22.6 summarizes the characteristics of the respondents – except risk attitude. Two significant variables in the set of personal characteristics should be noted. First, an owner manager with a finance background had a higher possibility of making a positive FDI decision than owner managers with other backgrounds. Second, the risk attitude of owner managers of the *go* group as perceived by themselves was ranked as substantial risk-taking (mean 4.33 on a six-point scale), whereas only one owner manager of the *no-go* group answered this question and he ranked himself as very risk-avoiding (mean 1.0). It should be noted that a comparison of the two groups in risk attitude should be avoided due to an insufficient sample of the *no-go* group.

Table 22.6 Summary of characteristics of respondents

| | | | FDI decision | |
| | *Go* | | *No-go* | |
Variable	N	%[a]	N	%[a]
Gender				
• Male	16	89	16	94
• Female	2	11	1	6
Owner manager				
• Yes	17	94	14	82
• No	1	6	3	18
Age				
• Under 36	2	11	3	18
• 36-45	6	33	9	53
• 46-55	8	45	3	18
• Above 55	2	11	2	11
Education				
• Compulsory	2	11	3	18
• High school or vocational high	6	33	9	53
• Junior college	7	39	4	23
• College or university	3	17	1	6
Functional background				
• Finance**	6	33	1	6
• Production and R&D	5	28	10	59
• Sales and marketing and other	7	39	6	35
Working experiences				
• 15 years and under	3	17	5	29
• 16-20 years	5	28	7	41
• 21-25 years	7	39	2	11
• Above 25 years	3	17	3	18

Notes: Significance: ** < 0.05; [a]Rounded

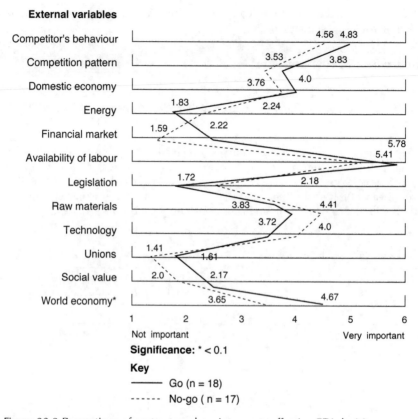

Figure 22.2 Perceptions of past external environments affecting FDI decision

External environments

Past changes

Figure 22.2 shows the perceptions of the past external environment between the *go* and *no-go* groups. The respondents pointed out that the most important potential change in Taiwan, during the period of 1990 and 1995, was the availability of labour. Both groups of *go* and *no-go* ranked it as very important to their companies. The other important areas which were ranked above mid-point of the scale are: competitor's behaviour, world economy, raw material, domestic economy, technology and consumption pattern. The changes in immediate task environment were recognized as more important to companies than those in national and international environments.

The world economy was the only variable with a significant difference between the two decision groups. The *go* group ranked the world economy as being of substantial importance compared to mild importance for the *no-go* group. The most likely reason for this difference is that the *go* group relies more heavily on exports and hence they are much more sensitive to the world economy.

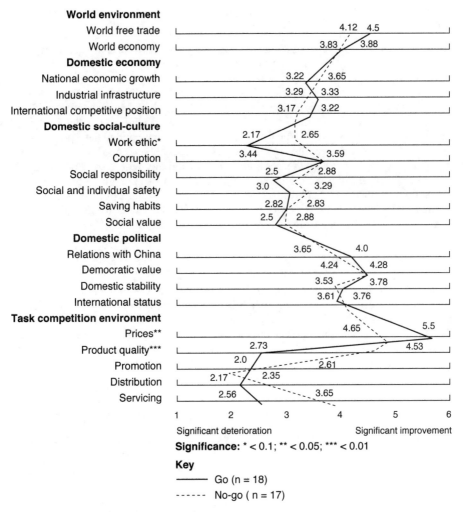

Figure 22.3 Perceiving future external environments

Future perception

Figure 22.3 summarizes the respondents' perceptions of their external environments in the next five years. Both groups perceived that the world environment would improve in terms of both world free trade and world economy. With respect to the economic, social-cultural and political variables concerned with Taiwan's future, the domestic economy was generally ranked to be unchanged or to undergo a mild deterioration. The domestic social-cultural environment was thought to be substantially deteriorating except for corruption and social and individual safety, which were perceived as remaining unchanged. The respondents have, however, given a higher mark to domestic politics as they believe that Taiwan would have a stable or slightly improved political environment over the next five years. The perception of the work ethic was significantly different between the two groups. The *go* group expected that the work ethic in Taiwan would deteriorate significantly more than the *no-go* group anticipated.

There are only two variables of the task environment which were ranked important to the respondents. They are price and quality competition. Both groups identified that price competition in their main market was substantially strong and the *go* group felt that price competition was significantly stronger than that of the *no-go* group. The *go* group felt that quality competition was not so strong but the *no-go* group ranked it significantly higher. From the results, it appears that the higher the level of price competition, the higher will be the possibility that a company will make a positive FDI decision. On the contrary, the higher the level of quality competition a company perceives, the higher will be the possibility that a company will make a negative FDI decision. These findings support the viewpoint that most FDIs made by Taiwanese SMEs are to reduce costs and to meet keen price competition from their competitors, whereas Taiwanese SMEs which compete on quality are trying to keep their high-quality product manufacturing in Taiwan.

FDI decision process

Table 22.7 identifies what stage in the decision process the respondents had reached. Five firms had undertaken preliminary thinking, of which two were still considering an FDI. Three firms were undertaking a field survey to obtain further information. Two firms were evaluating the feasibility of FDI, of which one had not yet reached a decision. Only one company had completed the whole decision-making process and made a negative decision.

Table 22.7 Responding firms in each step of decision processes

| | | No-go group | |
| | | Firms made negative decision | Firms are continuing investigation |
Steps	Go group N	N	N
Initiating and preliminary thinking	N/A	3	2
Investigation and collecting information	N/A	Nil	3
Evaluation of feasibility	N/A	1	1
Made an FDI decision	18	1	N/A

Note: There are six firms which had never considered an FDI.

The reasons why the six responding companies had never considered an FDI were: the owner managers were preparing to hand on the businesses to the next generation and the future planning of the companies depended on the heirs; and the companies were relying 100 per cent on the Taiwan market and it was not necessary to have an FDI. The reasons why the five companies had rejected an FDI were: they felt difficulty in controlling overseas activities; the companies lacked management talent; there was no niche to import back the products made overseas; they were preparing to shrink the business; they were preparing to upgrade the technology or to shift to another industry; and there were other reasons such as diversifying the sources of purchasing to reduce costs.

Initiation and preliminary thinking

All the *no-go* group respondents indicated that external stimulus from environmental changes was the major initiation force which made them think about the possibility of an FDI, while 88 per cent of the *go* group identified environmental changes as the major initiation force. The other forces were internal stimulus from the company's growth (60 per cent of *no-go* group and 83 per cent of *go* group) and external stimulus from friends and/or customers (40 per cent of *no-go* group and 61 per cent of *go* group).

Table 22.8 Major reasons for considering an FDI

| | FDI decision | | | |
| | Go | | No-go | |
Variable	N	%ᵃ	N	%ᵃ
Labour shortage in Taiwan*				
• Yes	14	78	11	100
• No	4	22	0	0
High labour and other costs*				
• Yes	13	72	11	100
• No	5	28	0	0
Worsening business environment in Taiwan				
• Yes	9	50	4	36
• No	9	50	7	64
Prominent host market potential				
• Yes	7	39	4	36
• No	11	61	7	64
Followed customers to go overseas				
• Yes	7	39	2	18
• No	11	61	9	82

Notes: Significance: *< 0.1; ᵃRounded.

Table 22.8 shows the major reasons given by the companies on why they considered the possibility of an FDI. The most important reasons were labour shortage and high labour costs and other costs in Taiwan. The *no-go* group had stronger feelings about these two reasons than the *go* group. The major reasons for considering an FDI highlight the benefits sought from an FDI, that is, low production costs and abundant labour supply in the host country.

Investigation

Only one company (of the *go* group) expressed that they had engaged in formal long-term planning and the planners were responsible for investigating the feasibility of the

FDI. Only two companies (of the *go* group) had prepared a formal feasibility report and the planning horizon was five and ten years respectively. The total time in investigating the feasibility and preparing the final report averaged 13 months, while it took 11.67 months for the *go* group and 19.5 months for the *no-go* group. This variable was significant between the two groups. Table 22.9 shows the major findings about investigators, investigation methods and important information gathered about the host country. The only significant variable was information relating to regulations and laws gathered by the respondents. The *no-go* group focused much more on this variable than the *go* group.

Table 22.9 Major findings of investigation process

| | FDI decision | | | |
| | Go | | No-go | |
Variable	N	%[a]	N	%[a]
Person carried out investigation				
• Myself	9	50	3	50
• Myself and business partner	3	17	1	17
• Business partner	4	22	1	17
• Formal corporate planners	1	6	Nil	Nil
• Myself and management	1	6	1	17
Investigation methods				
• Field visit to host country				
• Yes	18	100	6	100
• No	0	0	0	0
• Get information from friends/customers				
• Yes	15	83	6	100
• No	3	17	0	0
• Information offered by host governemnt				
• Yes	4	22	0	0
• No	14	78	6	100
Information gathered about the host country				
• Market situation				
• Yes	10	56	3	50
• No	8	44	3	50
• Social-cultural background				
• Yes	9	50	4	67
• No	9	50	2	33
• Political situation				
• Yes	4	22	2	33
• No	14	78	4	67
• Economic factors				
• Yes	12	67	6	100
• No	6	33	0	0
• Regulation and laws*				
• Yes	8	44	6	100
• No	10	56	0	0

Notes: Significance: *<0.05; [a]Rounded.

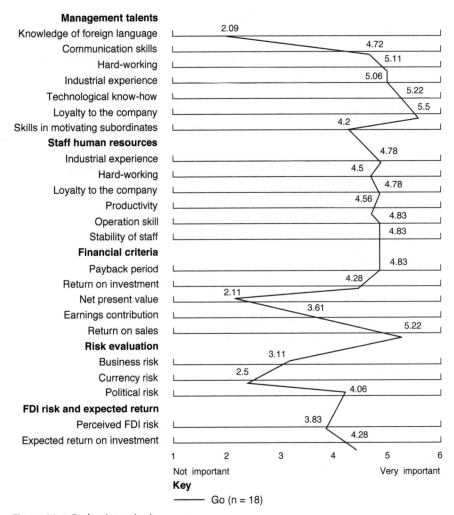

Figure 22.4 Evaluation criteria

Evaluation

Figure 22.4 represents the evaluation criteria ranked by the *go* group. The criteria included management talents, staff human resources, financial criteria and risk analysis. The group was proud of its management loyalty (5.5). The highest-ranked criteria for staff human resources were operation skill (4.83) and stability of staff (4.83). The most important financial evaluation method was return on sales. Political risk analysis was ranked as substantially important in risk analysis. The average expected return on investment was 38.22 per cent. The most important measure for assessing potential income of an FDI was earnings after foreign taxes followed by earnings after foreign taxes available for repatriation. Of the respondents, 72 per cent mentioned that their companies used a *go/no-go* method to evaluate an FDI rather than using a multiple alternative choice method.

There were only three firms of the *no-go* group which responded to the evaluation criteria questions; hence any comparison between the two groups needs to be treated with caution. The ranking of the evaluation criteria by the three companies was similar to the *go* group except for the hardworking characteristics of staff (3.33), the stability of staff (3.67) and the currency risk (1.0). All of them did not analyse currency risk.

Table 22.10 Major findings of final decision-making process

Variables	Go group N	%
Taiwan government's policies		
• Not important at all	15	83
• Mildly important	2	11
• Very important	1	6
Relations between Taiwan and host country		
• Not good	8	44
• Good	10	56
Decision method		
• Formal meeting called for all partners	9	50
• Decision made only by owner manager	7	39
• Decision made only by few critical partners	2	11
Critical people in decision-making		
• Only myself	8	44
• All partners in Taiwan	3	17
• Major partners in Taiwan and host country	3	17
• Major partners in Taiwan	4	22

Final decision-making

Table 22.10 shows that the Taiwanese Government's policies had little influence on the most recent FDI decision. Nearly half the respondents considered themselves as the critical person in making the final FDI decision. In 50 per cent of the cases, a formal meeting involving all partners was held to make the decision, whereas in nearly 40 per cent of the cases, the owner manager made the decision. The average time, identified by the companies, from their first thinking about an FDI to the final decision-making was 15.7 months, of which 13 months were spent on investigation and preparing reports. The average time to make the final decision after the investigation was 2.7 months. The respondents were pretty evenly split about whether the relations between Taiwan and the host country for an FDI were either on a good or poor basis.

Figure 22.5 shows the objectives for undertaking an FDI. The most important objective was cost reduction followed by seeking stability of the business, internal growth, profitability, survival and customer satisfaction. Three objectives were under the scale mid-point (3.5), namely social responsibility, business image and cash flow.

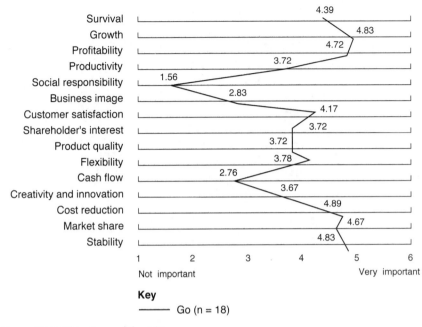

Figure 22.5 Objectives of the FDI

The importance of networks

Table 22.11 shows the importance of the owner-managers' social and industrial networks. Although the majority of the respondents indicated that they personally had influenced the FDI decision very much, there were some influences which came from their networks.

Eight respondents mentioned that their FDI decisions were highly influenced by the networks, especially by their business partners. A total of twelve respondents replied that they were substantially influenced by their networks, especially by their friends. Only five respondents said that they were not influenced by anyone at all in making the FDI decision. It was very interesting that two of the five companies had collected information from their networks during the decision processes. Another interesting thing was the changing nature of business and government relations. Only one of thirty-five respondents indicated that the company had received assistance from the government during the past five years. That was a low-interest loan for the purchase of a plant. The other thirty-four firms mentioned that they had never received or considered any government assistance. Of the respondents, 81 per cent stated that the Taiwanese government's policies would not affect them at all. Only 4.8 per cent indicated that these policies were very important to the company during the FDI decision process. There were 10 per cent who indicated that they had considered the government's policies and that the FDI decisions were substantially influenced by these policies.

Table 22.11 The influences from owner-managers' networks

No.	FDI decision group	Influences from networks on FDI decision				Information from networks
		Very low	*Mild*	*Substantial*	*Very high*	
1	G	2,3,4,5		1		Y
2	NG	1,2,4,5			3	Y
3	G	2,3,5	1		4	Y
4	G	1,3,4,5		2		Y
5	G	2,3,4,5		1		Y
6	G	2,4,5			1,3	Y
7	NG	1,3,4	2,5			Y
8	NG	1,2,3,4	5			Y
9	G	2,4,5		1	3	Y
10	G	1,2,4,5		3		Y
11	NG	1,2,3,4,5				N/A
12	NG	3,4,5	2	1		N/A
13	NG	2,4	5		1,3	N/A
14	G	2,3		1,5	4	Y
15	NG	1,2,3,4,5				N/A
16	G	1,2,3,4,5				Y
17	G	3,4,5		1,2		Y
18	G	2,4	1,3,5			Y
19	NG	2,3,4,5		1		Y
20	G	1,2,4	3,5			N
21	G	1,2,4,5	3			N
22	NG	1,2,3,5		4		Y
23	G	2,4,5		1,3		Y
24	NG	4	1,2,5	3		Y
25	G	1,2,4,5			3	N
26	G	1,2,4	5		3	Y
27	G	2,4,5	1,3			Y
28	G	1,2,3,4,5				Y
29	NG	1,2,3,4,5				N/A

Note: G: go; NG: no-go; 1: friends; 2: family; 3: partner; 4: customers; 5: staff; Y: yes; N: no; N/A: not applicable due to not answering question

Further FDI plans

Eighteen (51 per cent) of the respondents replied that their companies would have a further FDI plan in the next five years. Eight (44 per cent) of them were from the *no-go* group and ten (56 per cent) were from the *go* group.

The most important reasons for the companies considering a further FDI, in order of importance, were: Taiwan's worsening business environment, the need to consider the future of family and children, and the tendency to follow customers who go overseas.

All eight companies from the no-go group, which were planning a further FDI in the next five years, perceived that Taiwan's business environment was worsening and that this was the main reason for going overseas. In the meantime, only half of the companies from the *go* group took it as the reason for them to plan another FDI. Five owner managers (two from the *go* group and three from the *no-go* group) mentioned that they were considering giving their families a much more comfortable living environment, such as quality of life and personal security. The other minor reasons mentioned were the need to secure the company's market share, and the desire to stabilize supply of raw materials.

◼ Summary

This research into Taiwanese SMEs in the Electronic and Electric Appliances industry was able to show that the more a company is internationalized in terms of previous foreign operation experiences and percentage of direct export to total sales, the greater is the likelihood that the company will make a positive FDI decision. It was also shown that the companies with higher sales have a greater likelihood of making a positive FDI decision. The companies with greater exports were also found to be much more sensitive to the world economy.

Owner managers who have a finance background are more likely to make a positive FDI decision, whereas those with a production background are more likely to make a negative FDI decision. In about half the cases, the FDI decision was made solely by the owner managers, but friends and partners do appear to exert influence, through the social networks, on the FDI decision-maker.

Those who have made a positive FDI decision perceive that the work ethic in Taiwan is deteriorating. It also appears that the companies investing in China are those which seek to compete on price, while the companies which keep all their operations in Taiwan appear to be those which mainly compete on product quality. The major benefits being sought in an FDI appear to be low production costs and abundant labour supply in the host country. The most important reasons for the companies selecting China as the FDI host country are that they have the same language and cultural similarities. Of the most recent FDIs by Taiwanese SMEs, 78 per cent in the electronic and electric appliances industry are in China. In recent years the Taiwanese government's policies appear to be having little influence on Taiwanese SMEs' FDI decisions.

The most important functions being evaluated when investigating a prospective FDI are, in order of importance, production, sales and marketing, assembly and research and development. In evaluating the decision to make an FDI, the most important financial criterion is return on sales with return on investment and political risks being important considerations.

Of the companies who never considered an FDI, the reasons given were: the owner managers were preparing to hand on the businesses to the next generation and the future planning of the companies depended on the heirs; and the companies were relying 100 per cent on the Taiwan market and it was not felt necessary to have an FDI. The reasons given by the companies which rejected an FDI were: they felt difficulties in controlling overseas activities; the companies lacked management talent; there was no niche to import back the products made overseas; they were preparing to shrink the business; they were preparing to upgrade the technology or to shift to another industry; and there were other reasons such as diversifying the sources of purchasing to reduce costs.

Implications

This research has some important implications for the Taiwanese manufacturing SMEs, the Taiwanese government and other interested parties.

The Taiwanese SMEs

1 *Management of human resources is a critical factor for an FDI of the Taiwanese SMEs.* When facing FDI opportunities, an SME must consider who will be in charge of the overseas operations. A company should foster the development of management staff to handle the necessary operations as part of its approach to developing an FDI project.

2 *Taking care of the networks around the owner managers is important.* Networks are important to the Taiwanese SMEs' FDI decision outcomes. The owner managers should take care of the networks around them especially those which stimulate them to come to consider an FDI.

3 *Collecting information directly from the host government is important to the FDI decision.* Many SMEs do not like to use the information offered by the government of the host country. But direct dialogue with the host country government and/or the collection of information directly from the host government has been shown to be one of the major information collection methods for the *go* group.

4 *An FDI is an international learning process for a company and the owner manager.* This research shows that the companies with previous FDI operations experience have a shorter FDI decision-making time than the companies with no previous FDI experiences. This result attributes the learning process to the previous FDI decision-making processes. SMEs should try to learn from their previous FDI decision-making processes.

The Taiwanese government

1 *Taiwanese FDIs did not cause the Taiwanese industries to decline.* Many Taiwanese scholars and government officials are seriously concerned about the probability of decline (or in Taiwanese terminology, hollowing out) of Taiwanese industries due to the rise of FDIs. This research found that most companies with FDIs continued to invest domestically. The number of the companies which continued to invest domestically in the *go* group was even higher than that in the *no-go* group. This might imply that the companies with an FDI were continuing to upgrade the competitive abilities of their Taiwanese companies. From this research, the issue of causing Taiwanese industries to decline as a result of FDIs did not occur.

2 *Interference is not the best policy for Taiwanese FDIs in China: improving Taiwan's business and social-cultural environments is the best way to encourage Taiwanese SMEs' 'leaving roots in Taiwan.'* Of the thirty-five responding companies twenty-six (74 per cent)

will have a further FDI in the next five years. This figure includes the existing eighteen companies which already had FDIs but excludes the companies which were investigating an FDI during the time of interviews and might make the decision after the interviews. The major reason for this growing trend of FDI was the deteriorating business and social-cultural environments in Taiwan. The best policy for the Taiwanese government is to encourage SMEs to stay in Taiwan by seeking to improve the Taiwanese environment for business.

3 It is important to reconstruct the manufacturing SMEs' confidence in the government. The loss of trust and confidence in the Taiwanese government is another reason for SMEs going overseas, in addition to the deteriorating business environment in Taiwan. The best method for the government to reconstruct the SMEs' confidence is to coordinate the roles of the large-scale businesses and the SMEs and to set up communication channels for SMEs with the Taiwanese government.

The interested parties

An interested host country or company should pay attention to the above-stated suggestions for both the Taiwanese SMEs and the Taiwanese government. An interested company may attract joint ventures from a Taiwanese SME by offering its strengths. A potential competitor should pay attention to the synergy of Taiwanese SMEs' networks and the flexibility of their decision-making processes. The following are also important.

1 *The host country government's policies and attitudes affect the Taiwanese FDIs.* Most respondents mentioned that they had faced some barriers in dealing with countries other than China, especially those arising from cultural and language factors. In comparison with other countries, China was felt to have fewer barriers for the respondents. In China's case, because of the same language and similar culture, the respondents felt that they did not have communication problems and most of them were able to collect information from the Chinese government. Meanwhile, China's active attitude in attracting Taiwanese FDIs might be another factor which has encouraged the investigators to contact the government directly. All the respondents who collected information directly from the host government were in the *go* group. This might also mean that a company is more likely to make a positive FDI decision if the host government can communicate directly with the SME.

2 *Different country-specific advantages will attract different Taiwanese FDIs.* The FDI investigations in China and Southeast Asian countries are tending to focus on the use of abundant supplies of labour and land, and cheap labour costs. On the contrary, investigations in the countries other than China and Southeast Asia tend to focus on the market potential and political stability of the host country. The countries which are interested in Taiwanese FDIs may use a booklet explaining the do's (expectations for the FDI) and the don'ts (the regulations and the FDIs which are not welcome, such as industries that may pollute the environment) for the potential Taiwanese SME investors' references. This will assist the SMEs in collecting the right information about the host country especially those concerning cultural factors. This also offers an indirect communication channel for the host country and the Taiwanese SME investors.

3 *The Taiwanese companies are likely to adopt joint ventures with local partners in the FDIs.* This research has shown that FDIs in countries other than China were likely to be joint ventures with local companies. An increased level of FDI in developed countries and countries other than China is to be expected. The reason is that the Taiwan–China relationship is likely to have tensions. The main functions for these future FDIs is likely to be sales and marketing, R&D and production. The companies which are interested in joint ventures with a Taiwanese business need to develop mutual trust and the appropriate Taiwanese networks before the project can proceed.

Directions for future research

Although this chapter has presented many findings about the FDI decision process of Taiwanese manufacturing SMEs, there are some limitations. First, a further survey of industries other than the electronic and electric appliances industry would be worthwhile for future research. Results from industries such as the chemical industry, which have increased their FDIs both in projects and value would be valuable to compare with the results from this research. Second, in this chapter most determinants and significant variables have been explained item by item. In practice it is desirable to measure some concepts by using multiple indicators rather than only one single variable. Further statistical analyses such as factor analysis and regression analysis should be used to examine the effects of groups of variables on the FDI decision. Third, the influences from an owner-manager's networks need to be further examined. Fourth, the comparisons between the Taiwanese FDI decisions in China and other developing countries and developed countries would be worthwhile, to understand how universal are the models of Taiwanese SMEs' decision-making processes.

■ References

Aharoni, Y. (1966). *The Foreign Investment Decision Process.* Harvard University.

Bodur, M. and Madsen, T. K. (1993). Danish foreign direct investment in Turkey. *European Business Review*, **5**, 28–43.

Bourgeois, L. J. III and Eisenhart, K. M. (1988). Strategic decision processes in high velocity environments: four cases in the microcomputer industry. *Management Science*, **34** (7), 816–35.

Chen, C. H. (1994). *Cooperating Network and Life Structure: Social-Economic Analysis of Taiwanese Small and Medium-Sized Enterprises.* United Publishing. (In Chinese.)

Chiang, P. K. (1994). *The Economic Development of the Republic of China on Taiwan: Issues and Strategies.* Ministry of Economic Affairs.

Chinese National Federation of Industries (1994). *Manufacturing Directory.* CNFI. (In Chinese).

Gupta, A. K. (1984). Contingency linkages between strategy and general manager characteristics. *Academy of Management Review*, **9**, 399–412.

Hambrick, D. C. and Mason, P. A. (1984). Upper echelons: the organization as a reflection of its top managers. *Academy of Management Review*, **9**, 93–106.

Hitt, M. A. and Tyler, B. B. (1991). Strategic decision models: integrating different perspectives. *Strategic Management Journal*, **12**, 327–51.

Huang, R. C. et al. (1994). *Taiwanese Manufacturing Industry's Strategies in Facing of Asia*

Pacific Regional Economy, Council for Economic Planning and Development, (In Chinese.)

Kao, C. *et al.* (1992). *An Empirical Study of Taiwan Investment on Mainland China*. Commonwealth Publishing. (In Chinese.)

Kao, C. *et al.* (1994). *The Taiwan Investment Experience in Mainland China – A First-Hand Report*. Commonwealth Publishing. (In Chinese.)

Meyer, G. W. (1994). Social information processing and social networks: a test of social influence mechanisms. *Human Relations*, **47** (9), 1013–47.

Mintzberg, H., Raisinghani, D. and Theoret, A. (1976). The structure of 'unstructured' decision processes. *Administrative Science Quarterly*, **21**, 246–75.

Porter, M. (1980). *Competitive Strategy*. The Free Press.

Wen, C. Y. and Hsiao, S. H. (1988). *Chinese: Concepts and Behaviours*. Chi-Liou. (In Chinese.)

Chapter 22.1

Taiwanese small- and medium-sized enterprises in post-crisis Asia

■ Ho-Ching Wei and Chris Christodoulou ■

Taiwanese small- and medium-sized enterprises (SMEs) play an important role in Taiwan's economic development process (also see Chapter 13). According to the Taiwanese government's early policies, SMEs were designed and formed to export, whereas the large-scale enterprises served as upstream suppliers to the SMEs (Medium and Small Business Administration, 1992: 11). Small- and medium-sized enterprises are mainly international and large businesses are mainly domestic. In 1995, SMEs comprised 97.97 per cent of all the firms in Taiwan, contributed to 79.75 per cent of the nation's total employment, and the ratio of SMEs' exports to the nation's total exports was 50.65 per cent, valued at US$56.5 billion.

■ Taiwanese small- and medium-sized enterprises and the government

As indicated in our research (Chapter 22), many factors contributed to Taiwanese SMEs' outward foreign direct investment (FDI) decisions. More recently, an important factor contributing to the Taiwanese SMEs' moves to other countries is the deteriorating relationship between the Taiwanese government and the SMEs. The major reasons for the deteriorating relationship are: a) the worsening business environment in Taiwan, b) SMEs having difficulties in accessing financial resources, c) impractical laws and regulations applied to businesses and d) lack of communication channels between the government and the SMEs (Wei and Christodoulou, 1998: 245–52). The continuing deterioration of the Taiwanese business environment is illustrated by the following aspects: In 1996, a kidnapping for ransom occurred every 2.5 days in Taiwan, a 50 per cent increase over 1995. In August 1997, the Parliamentary Cabinet was forced to resign in response to the worsening social, safety and business environments in Taiwan.

■ International environments

Three months after the research described in Chapter 22 was completed, Taiwan's relation with China deteriorated. From 1995 to 1996, China fired missiles four times into the

Taiwan Strait as a warning to the Taiwanese independence movement. The Taiwanese government then adopted the 'Go South' policy and encouraged Taiwanese firms to transfer their investments to Southeast Asian countries. President Lee Teng-Hui also urged business people to adopt an attitude of *jie ji yong ren* (that is, to avoid undue haste and to exercise forbearance) towards China. Under this policy, the Taiwanese government became more conservative in its approach towards China and more restrictive regulations on investments in China were announced (Wei and Christodoulou, 1998).

However, the SMEs did not appreciate the *jie ji yong ren* policy. A recent survey of Taiwanese businesses with FDI shows that 50.32 per cent of the respondents were seeking that the Taiwanese government relax its policies on investing in China (*The China Press*, 1998: 18). Of the respondents, 71.12 per cent indicated that they already had FDI in China, a figure similar to our research findings. This suggests that the Taiwanese SMEs' investments in China are continuing to increase.

In early 1997, many of the Southeast Asian countries faced a severe financial crisis that seriously impacted on their economies. As a consequence, many of the Taiwanese firms who invested in the Southeast Asian countries have been affected and many of them have complained about the Taiwanese government's recent policy of encouraging investment to 'Go South'. From January to August 1998, Taiwanese exports to the Asian area dropped to US$33.31 billion, a 17.4 per cent decline compared to US$40.34 billion in the same period of 1997 (Ministry of Economic Affairs, 1998).

■ A review of the respondents

In 1997, when the authors tried to contact the owner-managers who had participated in the research covered in Chapter 22, it was apparent that they were continuing to move their businesses out of Taiwan or to set up new subsidiaries in Western countries. Some had completely closed down their operations in Taiwan and hence we do not know if these businesses moved out of Taiwan or simply failed.

The process of Taiwanese firms using FDI to gain competitive advantages is clearly continuing. As described in detail in Chapter 22, the first stage is usually to seek labour-cost advantages in the host countries, and at this stage Taiwanese SMEs usually import goods manufactured in China and/or in Southeast Asian countries. This stage is usually followed by Taiwanese firms seeking technological and market-size niches in host countries. Both Western countries and China have attracted FDI at this stage. The final stage for some is that they move out all their operations from Taiwan; this may occur faster if the relationship with China continues to deteriorate.

■ References

Medium and Small Business Administration (1992). *A Flying Dragon: The Guidance and Growth of Small and Medium-sized Business*. Ministry of Economic Affairs.

Ministry of Economic Affairs (1998). Export by area.
http://www.tptaiwan.org.tw/st/areae.htm

The China Press (1998). Businesses ask for refrozen policy on jie ji yong ren. 8 September, p. 18.

Wei, H. C. and Christodoulou, C. (1998) The Changing Relationship Between the Taiwanese Government and Small and Medium-sized Enterprises, *Asian Studies Review*, **22** (2), 239–60.

Chapter 23

The evolution of multinational firms from Asia: a longitudinal study of Taiwan's Acer Group[1]

■ Peter Ping Li ■

Multinational enterprises (MNEs) have been the primary force behind the trend toward globalization. Besides the multinational enterprises from the developed countries, there has been an accelerating proliferation of the MNEs from the developing countries, some of whom are becoming notable global players (Heenan and Keegan, 1979; Tolentino, 1993). This is especially salient among the newly industrialized countries in Asia (Yeung, 1994a). Despite their growing importance, we know very little about the MNEs from the developing countries, especially the process of their evolution from obscurity to prominence (Lecraw, 1993; Yeung, 1994b). To close the gap, this study focuses on one primary question: what is the evolutionary pattern of the MNEs from the developing countries? The specific purpose of this study is to shed light on the intriguing links between organizational change and competitive advantage among the MNEs from the developing countries. We want to explore where they obtain their initial competitive advantages despite the liability of being based in the developing countries and how they develop new advantages. This study is part of a growing trend to emphasize the dynamic organizational process (see Barnett and Burgelman (1996) for a review).

■ The working model

To study the evolutionary pattern of the MNEs from the developing countries, we need to develop a model that is capable of describing, explaining and prescribing not only the 'spatial' pattern of MNE evolution (i.e. the antecedent, activity and consequence of MNE evolution) but also the temporal pattern of MNE evolution (i.e. the simultaneity, directionality and rhythm of MNE evolution). One way to do that is to synthesize the extant MNE theories with strategy analysis (Andrews, 1971) and the

[1] This chapter has been published previously by MCB University Press Limited: Li, P. P. (1998). The evolution of multinational firms from Asia: a longitudinal study of Taiwan's Acer Group. *Journal of Organizational Change Management*, 11 (4), 321–37.

evolutionary perspective (Barnett and Burgelman, 1996).

The 'spatial' pattern of MNE evolution

Synthesizing the theory of strategic analysis (Andrews, 1971) and that of international production (Dunning, 1988, 1995), we can identify five essential 'spatial' variables concerning MNE evolution:

1 external context;

2 internal profile;

3 ultimate intent;

4 strategic choice; and

5 market effect (Li, 1994, 1995).

External context refers to the set of location-specific and industry-specific environmental factors. Internal profile refers to the set of firm-specific factors. Ultimate intent refers to a firm's mission, which is the core of corporate culture. Strategic choice refers to a firm's key decisions and actions to achieve its ultimate intent by matching its external context and its internal profile. Market effect refers to a firm's performance in the marketplace as the direct result of its strategic choice. For MNEs, the above 'spatial' factors extend beyond the confines of a single country (Dunning, 1988, 1995).

To further operationalize strategic choice, a four-dimension typology can be used (see Li, 1994):

1 Strategic target as the operationalization of ultimate intent (e.g. to maximize revenue volume or profit margin).

2 Strategic thrust as the operationalization of both ultimate intent and strategic target (e.g. to cut cost or enhance value).

3 Strategic posture as the operationalization of ultimate intent, strategic target and strategic thrust (e.g. how to configure marketing mix and location mix).

4 Strategic mode as the operationalization of ultimate intent, strategic target, strategic thrust and strategic posture (e.g. how to co-ordinate activities across various functions, businesses and locations).

The strategic choice of MNEs is based on three factors:

1 A firm's unique ownership advantage over its foreign competitors.

2 The location advantage of the host countries.

3 The organizational advantage of internal control (Dunning, 1988).

In sum, the above variables define the 'spatial' pattern of MNE evolution, i.e. the issues of 'what', where', and 'how' with regard to the growth of MNEs.

The temporal pattern of MNE evolution

Synthesizing the evolutionary perspective (Barnett and Burgelman, 1996; Riegel, 1979) with the model of internationalization process (Johanson and Vahlne, 1977, 1990) and that of the investment development cycle (Dunning, 1988), we can identify three basic temporal variables:

1 Simultaneity – the measure of absolute time when events occur concurrently;

2 Directionality – the measure of absolute time when events occur sequentially; and

3 Rhythm – the measure of relative time when events recur at different intervals.

We use these three variables to define the concurrent, sequential and recurrent relationships between the 'spatial' variables as the temporal pattern of MNE evolution.

To further operationalize directionality, we synthesize the models of internationalization process and investment development cycle (Dunning, 1988; Johanson and Vahlne, 1990). There are two macro-level stages of MNE evolution: pre-MNE stage – before a firm's initial direct investment overseas; and MNE stage – after a firm's initial direct investment overseas. The pre-MNE stage can be further divided into three micro-level sub-stages:

1 Pre-export sub-stage – before a firm's initial exports, but imports and joint ventures with foreign partners at home are possible.

2 Immature exports – after a firm's initial exports, but the exports are largely irregular and unstable.

3 Mature exports – when a firm's exports become regular and stable.

The MNE stage can be further divided into two micro-level substages:

1 Immature MNE – when a firm's foreign direct investment is driven more by the location-specific factors than by the firm-specific factors.

2 Mature MNE – when a firm's international operation is driven more by the firm-specific factors than by the location-specific factors.

In sum, these variables define the temporal pattern of MNE evolution, i.e. the issues of 'when' and 'at what pace' with regard to the growth of MNEs.

■ Methodology

Many MNE scholars have called for more and better-guided longitudinal case studies of MNEs (e.g. Andersen, 1993; Parkhe, 1993). Different from the method of cross-sectional study, the method of longitudinal case study offers the best prospect for advancing our knowledge about organizational process (Eisenhardt, 1989; Yin, 1989). For the purpose of this study, we chose to adopt the case study method.

Case selection

The case for our study is Taiwan's Acer. We considered several criteria in selecting this case. First, we limited our selection to the MNEs from the Asian developing countries in global high-tech industries because they offer the best prospect for studying the evolutionary pattern of the MNEs from the developing countries, especially the process of developing technology-based competitive advantages. Second, we limited our selection to the MNEs that have already become successful global players so as to study the complete process of becoming major global players. We selected Acer because it met the above criteria (Engardio and Burrows, 1996; Hanrahan, 1994; Kraar, 1995).

Data collection

We collected data for this study from archival documents including corporate brochures, corporate annual reports, books, newspaper or magazine reports and case studies. Approximately 1500 pages of archival data were collected. Data from various sources were coded using typical content analysis procedures (Yin, 1989). First, we identified specific events as the basic unit of analysis. Second, we coded the events into five groups according to the five 'spatial' variables in the working model; finally, we re-coded the events into three groups according to the three temporal variables in the working model. Only those data that were corroborated from multiple sources were used in our study.

■ The case evidence

Acer was founded in Taiwan in 1976; by 1997, Acer had become the fifth biggest computer-maker in the world. Acer experienced three major 'takeoff' phases. The phase of 1976–86 witnessed Acer's first takeoff when it became the largest computer firm in Taiwan; the phase of 1986–95 witnessed its second takeoff when it became one of the top computer firms in the world; and its third takeoff phase started in 1995 when it decided to become one of the leading electronics firms in the world. However, Acer's take-off phases (i.e. the overall pattern of its organizational evolution) did not overlap perfectly with its stages of internationalization (i.e. the special pattern of its multinational evolution), so we modified the working model in two areas by evoking the metaphor of human life cycle (Van de Ven and Poole, 1995). First, we further divided the stage of 'immature MNE' into two parts: 'infant MNE' stage – when a newly-born MNE experiences its initial success; and 'teenage MNE' stage – when the initially successful MNE gets into serious trouble. Second, we renamed the stage of 'mature MNE' as 'adult MNE'. For a summary of the case evidence, please see Table 23.1.

Acer at its pre-MNE stage

Pre-export stage (1976–77).

Acer (then Multitech) was set up in Taiwan in 1976 when Apple was born in the USA. As a start-up firm, Acer had a good management team and strong Research and Development (R&D) team (Stan Shih, CEO and co-founder of Acer, had a good R&D and managerial background, so did other founders to various degrees), but Acer had

Table 23.1 The pattern of Acer's internationalization

'Spatial' pattern	Temporal pattern		
	Pre-exports (1976-77)	Immature exports (1977-81)	Mature exports (1981-84)
Ultimate intent From local to global and from follower to leader	To survive as start-up	To accumulate capital and experience	To be one of the best in its home country
External context From local to global and from task-specific to general	Underdeveloped capital market at home Birth of PC industry in world (little competition)	(more competition)	IBM launched PC-XT
Internal profile From individual to organization and from capability to commitment manufacturing	Good management team Good R&D team Little capital No manufacturing		Capital infusion Starting
	No unique product Premature venture Strong corporate culture (simplicity, frugality, trust, egalitarianism, team, shared vision and shared interest)	First Chinese terminal	PC-based kit series IBM clone
Strategic choice From micro to macro and from means to end	To grow fast To balance cost and value To focus on low-end niche market at home		
	Acting as importer and local distributor Controlling via strong culture Setting up joint ventures	Exporting from the USA as an exclusive agent First Chinese terminal for its home market	Exporting to the USA (under OEM deal) Starting to diversify (e.g. publishing)
Market effect From short term to long term and from failure to success	Survived Annual growth of 100% No exports yet	Limited exports	Regular exports of its own products

'Spatial' pattern	Temporal pattern		
	Infant MNE (1984–87)	Teenage MNE (1987–92)	Adult MNE (1992–now)
Ultimate intent From local to global and from follower to leader	To be the leader both at home and abroad	To be one of the best in the world	To be one of the best in the world
External context From local to global and from task-specific to general	Improved capital market at home Intense competition in the PC industry	Booming stock market at home Game rules changed in the PC industry	
Internal profile From individual to organization and from capability to commitment	Good management team Strong R&D capability (e.g. 2nd 32-bit clone in the world) More capital Good manufacturing Innovative products Good corporate culture (simplicity, frugality, trust, egalitarianism, team, shared vision and shared interest) Lacking global experience Lacking global brand	Complacent management Initial public offering of its stocks (IPO) Eroding corporate culture (largely due to a flood of new people and its past success) Name change	Wakened management Restoring its corporate culture Having a global brand
Strategic choice From micro to macro and from means to end	To expand abroad To emphasize value To focus on higher-end niche market (lab in the USA) Entering Southeast Asia and West Europe Further diversification (e.g. retail, ASIC, etc) Hiring international experts	To expand aggressively Entering Latin America Aggressive acquisition Starting formal control	Three strategic initiatives (a) Fast-food process re-engineering to gain operating efficiency; (b) Client-server form restructuring to build network organization; (c) Global-local balance to reprogramme mentality
Market effect From short-term to long-term and from failure to success	Annual growth of 75% Dominating home market Balanced overseas markets OEM as a half of its sales	Profits starting to drop First annual loss in 1991 Failed in its first attempt to globalize	Profits starting to increase The 5th biggest computer company in the world Annual growth of 60%

neither capital nor products of its own. Acer was set up prematurely owing to the financial troubles in another company, where some of the founders worked. The capital market was not well developed in Taiwan at that time, and the government would not financially support firms without new high-tech products in hand. As a result, Acer decided to be a local distribution agent for foreign vendors and a designer for local clients. If Acer had not been set up prematurely, it might have been an exporter at birth. In this pre-export phase, Acer already had its first international experience by being an importer of foreign products. This was also a part of its pre-manufacturing phase as it did not set up its own manufacturing facility until 1981. Acer achieved its primary target at this stage (to survive).

Immature export stage (1977–81).

With more experience in local distribution, Acer was ready to expand. In 1977, Acer set up its first international office (a joint venture) as an exporter of microprocessors from the USA. In 1978, Acer became the exclusive agent for Texas Instruments (TI) in Taiwan and made a huge profit by distributing TI chips to electronic toy makers until the Taiwanese government banned the business in 1982; it also began export trade by selling the US-made chips to Europe and started setting up sales offices (joint ventures) in major cities in Taiwan. It offered training and publications in Taiwan about microprocessors. In 1980, Acer introduced Taiwan's first Chinese-based cathode-ray tube (CRT) terminal that won a national award. Acer achieved its primary target at this stage (to accumulate capital and expertise for the computer business). Acer had its first net profit in 1978; from 1977 to 1981, it grew about 100 per cent annually, largely due to the sales of its Chinese-based CRT terminals and TI chips in Taiwan. This was Acer's immature export phase because most of its sales were at home; it had no product of its own to export regularly, and it had no manufacturing facilities either.

Mature export stage (1981–84).

With the capital and expertise accumulated in prior stages, Acer was able to come up with its own products for both domestic and overseas markets. When IBM launched its PC-XT in 1981, Acer introduced its Microprofessor-I (microprocessor-based learning kit that was a hit at home and abroad), so Acer started its regular exports. Acer set up its first manufacturing facility in the Hsinchu Science-based Industry Park that was sponsored by the government to attract MNEs and overseas Chinese entrepreneurs for high-tech firms (it is interesting to know that this subsidiary became Acer's parent company in 1987). Acer launched Microprofessor-II in 1982 (when Compaq launched the world's first IBM-compatible clone), and Microprofessor-III in 1983; both generated many orders from overseas. In 1983, Acer hosted its first international distributor meeting attended by over forty dealers from twenty nations. In the same year, Acer began to export Microprofessor-II to the USA, but the products were seized at the US customs owing to Apple's charge of intellectual property right violation. One year after the first IBM-compatible clone was introduced by Compaq, Acer introduced its own clone at the end of 1983, and began exporting to the USA via original equipment manufacturer (OEM) orders in early 1984 (the shipment was seized again at the US customs on the request of IBM). To fill the export order, Acer had to license an operating system software from DRI in the USA. Owing to the two instances, Acer set up a law office and started to pay a close attention to intellectual property rights protection. Despite all this, Acer became the biggest computer firm in Taiwan by 1983. Acer's annual growth was about 100 per cent in 1981–84 largely due to the sales of the Microprofessor series.

Acer experienced a take-off in this period. Acer started to expand into related businesses such as technical publishing and venture capital investment. After a government-sponsored visit to the Silicon Valley, Acer was inspired to set up a venture capital investment firm. Based on personal ties, Multiventure Investment Inc. was founded as a joint venture between Acer and Continental Engineering with a stock swap. With this capital infusion, Acer began the process of modernizing its financial control system; it extended its stock purchase policy to every employee (Acer used to require its top managers to buy Acer's stocks when they came in). Acer also set up Third Wave Publishing as a technical publishing firm in 1983, and Acer Peripherals (for OEM orders) in 1984. This was Acer's mature export phase because it had its own regular products to export (via both OEM order and its own brand). Acer achieved its primary target at this stage (to become one of the biggest and best computer firms in Taiwan). From the experiences of foreign trade, Acer acquired its initial capabilities to become a multinational company.

Acer at its MNE stage

Infant MNE stage (1984–87).

Soon after its founding in 1984, Multiventure Investment Inc. invested in a start-up in the Silicon Valley, a research lab which led to the world's second 80386-based computer in 1986 after Compaq's first. This was Acer's first, yet indirect, attempt to invest overseas, suggesting its status as a newly born MNE. It also started actively hunting for top executives with extensive international experience (so-called 'parachuting squad'). Early in 1985, Acer's top management took a promotional tour around Southeast Asia, resulting in the establishment of sales offices in Indonesia, Malaysia, Singapore and Thailand; it also built its first European warehouse in Amsterdam and its first European sales office in Germany. In 1986, Acer set up its Japanese subsidiary and promoted the sales office in Germany to a subsidiary. By then, Acer had exported to over thirty countries in the world; at the same time, Acer set up Acer Land, the first franchised computer retail chain in Taiwan. In 1987, Acer entered the application-specific integrated circuit (ASIC) business by setting up Acer Laboratories.

IBM introduced its 16-bit PC-AT model in 1984; early in 1986, Acer introduced its clone of PC-AT and started to export in large volumes. It took Acer about two years to introduce a clone of IBM's PC-XT or PC-AT, but it leapfrogged IBM in introducing a 32-bit computer to the market in 1986, which gave Acer worldwide instant fame. By 1987, Acer had received five big awards for its innovations in Taiwan and one international award in Germany, indicating the recognition of Acer's R&D capabilities not only at home but also abroad. As a result of the publicity of its 32-bit computer, Acer received many big OEM orders from Unisys of the USA and ICL of Britain (later Unisys licensed Acer's technology, the first time for a Taiwanese firm to transfer technology to US firms). However, IBM began to put more pressure on the computer firms in Taiwan to license its technologies, among whom Acer suffered the most (e.g. Acer paid at least $9 million in a settlement with IBM in 1989 concerning its PC-AT technology).

In this period, Acer's annual growth rate was lower than before (about 75 per-cent from 1984 to 1987 in contrast to about 100 per cent from 1977 to 1984). This slowdown was largely due to its bigger revenue base. Acer achieved its key target at this stage (to gain large market share both at home and abroad). Acer dominated its home market with a 50 per cent share of branded microcomputer sales. Its international sales accounted for over 85 per cent of its total revenue in 1987, a third of which went to North America and another third to Europe. But Acer still lacked brand recognition overseas. By 1987, about 47 per cent of Acer's worldwide sales were OEM orders. Besides, some problems were developing at this stage (e.g. the impact of the 'parachuting squad' and Acer's aggressive expansion of its corporate culture and organizational structure).

Teenage MNE stage (1987–92)

This was Acer's most hectic and troubled phase in its history so far (the most interesting for our research). After Acer's first ten-year plan (1986–96) was announced, Acer was on a fast track of expansion, especially in the international area. This plan called for more international managers, internationally recognized brands, international channels, capital from foreign sources, and higher value-added products. Acer found it too slow to develop in-house, so it began to acquire from outside, resulting in a series of miscalculated moves.

For higher value-added products and better known brands, Acer acquired Counterpoint (a minicomputer firm in the Silicon Valley) in 1987. However, the computer technology moved so fast that Counterpoint's minicomputer soon became obsolete. This occurred again in 1990 when Acer acquired Altos (a firm specializing in the high-end multiuser UNIX computer network) for $94 million (plus the initial loss of $20 million). Acer also acquired a marketing firm in Los Angeles for half a million in 1989 as a service center in the USA, but it cost Acer over $20 million due to the initial loss. Another failure was Acer's buy-out of the German joint venture in 1991. All the failed acquisitions were 100 per cent ownership acquisitions (as a result, Acer later shifted back to joint ventures as the primary mode of market entry).

Acer also had other acquisitions and many large investment projects during this period of time that increased its financial burden and reduced its profitability. In 1989, it bought Kangaroo Computer BV in The Netherlands as the centre of its European operations; it set up a joint venture with TI for memory chips (Acer's initial investment was $85 million); it joined other firms to set up an international distributor of high-tech products; it built its first overseas manufacturing plant in Malaysia (all in the same year); Acer also expanded into the ASIC business. In addition, Acer changed its name and brand (from 'Multitech' to 'Acer') in 1987 for $1 million, and it launched an advertisement campaign in 1991 with a budget of $20 million.

To pay for all the acquisitions and investment projects, Acer had its initial public offering in 1988. Many international investors poured their money into Acer (only 10 per cent of Acer's stocks were initially offered, so Acer employees still owned over 70 per cent). This offering and a subsequent issue of new stocks coincided with a spectacular bull market, so all Acer employees became rich overnight. With this euphoria, little attention was paid to the signs of emerging trouble (Acer's profits dropped in 1988, the year of its first offering, and culminated in Acer's losses in 1991 and 1992). Given this momentum, Acer's traditional structure of decentralized and informal control fuelled further expansion by each division and subsidiary. By then, the relationship between the 'parachuting squad' and other managers began to deteriorate, further eroding Acer's co-operative culture. Overexpansion and cultural erosion (due to complacency) became serious problems.

At this critical moment, Stan Shih picked Dr Liu, a twenty year IBM veteran, as Acer's new president in 1989 to spearhead its internationalization. Liu's IBM background led to some major errors (e.g. his insistence on 100 per cent control of Altos and the German distributor and his bias in favour of formal control and larger computers). Liu came at a wrong time when the negative effect of the aggressive expansions since 1986 eroded Acer's culture and structure while the new rules of competition in the computer industry emerged (because of the increasing power of microprocessors and the growing popularity of low-cost distribution such as mail order and discount stores, both of which led to a revolution towards disintegration). Both Shih and Liu ignored this trend, so Acer's internal problems exploded under the external pressure. Liu's initial task was to restructure Acer for an international takeoff, but he had to struggle for survival when Acer's problems exploded. He tried his best to squeeze more efficiency out of Acer's old structure, but that was not enough. Under the internal pressure due to the huge loss, Liu left in 1992. However, Liu left with at least three major contributions to Acer that made it possible to restructure successfully later. The first contribution was the introduction of profit centres as part of Acer's new structure, in which each strategic business unit (SBU) was responsible for its own R&D and manufacturing while regional business units (RBUs) were responsible for their marketing. Such a structure greatly improved the efficiency of Acer's operation at that time. Liu's second contribution was the adoption of a merit-based policy, by which the star performers were promoted on fast tracks, but the poor performers were demoted or dismissed. Liu's third contribution was being a role model for responsible and efficient management. In short, Liu introduced Acer to world-class standards.

There were also positive results in Acer at this period. Acer increased its R&D budget to about 5 per cent of its sales (very high in Taiwan) and its marketing budget to 6-7 per cent of the sales; it invented the Chip-up technology and licensed it to many US firms including Intel; it launched its notebook computers; it successfully penetrated the Latin American markets; it increased the sales under its own brand to 60–70 per cent; and it had diversified markets (28 per cent of the sales in Europe, thirty per cent in the USA, 30 per cent at home and the rest in other regions). However, Acer failed to achieve its basic target at this stage (to become a mature global player). Acer resembled a troubled teenager who was experiencing the pain of adolescent growth.

Adult MNE stage (1992–95)

Both Shih and Liu offered to resign, but Shih was asked to stay. This shocked everybody in Acer as a wake-up call. The 331 management team finally united around Shih to undertake a fundamental reconstruction by adopting three key strategic initiatives:

1 fast-food process.

2 client-server structure.

3 global-brand with local-touch mentality.

The first initiative was intended to reengineer the operating process so as to improve efficiency; the second initiative was intended to restructure the organizational structure so as to support the fast-food process and enhance effectiveness; and the third initiative was intended to reprogramme the managerial mentality so as to support the fast-food process and the client-server structure.

Shih was inspired by the efficient operation of fast-food chains so he applied that concept to the microcomputer business. The process would start with planning (after careful market research) to produce major 'ingredients' at a few large manufacturing sites; then, shipping the ingredients to the assembly sites close to customers (shipping standard ingredients by sea and time-sensitive ingredients by air over the world or sourcing ingredients locally whenever possible); and finally, delivering 'fresh' computers by customized orders. This is a fast, efficient and low-risk process. In three years, thirty-four so-called 'uniload' assembly sites in each of its major markets around the world were set up, so Acer could offer 'fresh' (just-in-time by order) products at low cost.

Inspired by the concept of client-server computer architecture (which was consistent with Acer's corporate culture), Shih restructured Acer into a network organization. As a closely knit network of entrepreneurs as managers, Acer designed a new structure with the headquarters and operating units as both clients and servers for diverse functions contingent on the need of clients and the expertise of servers; there were no more fixed and hierarchical relationships (a server may be more capable in certain areas than a client, but the server had no control over the client; the server played the role of assistant or consultant for the client). To adopt this structure, each operating unit was given total authority and full responsibility for its own performance; all units were advised to take full advantage of the common resources (such as the corporate brand and credit, collective procurement and collective marketing whenever necessary); and all the units were asked to share their resources with one another whenever possible. The headquarters' role shifted from that of boss or parent to that of referee and broker; as a result, the staff at Acer's headquarters was reduced from 300 to ninety (only for legal functions and institutional sales). Acer would hold annual summit meetings with all the unit heads to co-ordinate operations and build consensus with the help of the CEO. This structure leveraged the strength of a whole system while allowing each unit to take initiatives (a web-like network that interconnects all the distinctive centres of excellence).

As if the client-server structure was not radical enough, Acer pushed forward by adopting a revolutionary approach to globalization (the 'fourth way' that was different from the traditional approaches adopted by American, European or Japanese MNEs). This was a modified version of Acer's unique success formula (i.e. shared interest, shared ownership and shared management between strategic partners as the underlying core of Acer's overall strategy). With this mentality, Acer developed the '21-in-21' plan (to spin off twenty-one subsidiaries as publicly-listed companies wherever they are located at the turn of the century). The first spin-off came in 1995, when Acer Computer International became a public company in Singapore, and others would follow in the coming years. It was Acer's goal to reduce its shares in these localized firms to a minority level (less than 50 per cent); Shih said, 'Some people talk about control with 51 per cent ownership. But I control through an intangible approach, common interest.' In the same spirit, Acer would form a joint venture with local partners whenever possible. This approach proved extremely successful in making Acer the top brand in each country, and instrumental to Acer's strategy to encircle the markets of the developed world by first occupying those of the developing countries. As a result, Acer was No. 1 or No. 2 in many developing countries (e.g. being No. 1 in Africa, East Asia except Japan and Korea, the Middle East, and Russia; being No. 2 in

Latin America, and No. 3 in India). As a borderless network of companies, Acer united these spin-offs and joint ventures by developing their shared interest in Acer's global brand, its global R&D capability, its global marketing capability, and the interlocking ownership among the spin-offs and joint ventures.

Acer more than achieved its primary target at this stage (to turn around). Acer became a world-class player as the result of the three radical initiatives (e.g. Acer's Aspire home system, as the direct result of the initiatives, was responsible for turning Acer America from trash into a treasure). By 1995, Acer was operating eighty offices in thirty-eight countries with over 15 000 employees supporting numerous dealers in over 100 countries; it grew 57 per cent annually from 1992 to 1995 to a total revenue of US$5.8 billion. Acer reached its matured adulthood by that time.

■ Discussion

The explanations of the case evidence

Explaining the pre-MNE stage

Acer was successful in its pre-MNE stage. Its success was due to an interactive effect of three 'spatial' variables (i.e. external context, internal profile and strategic choice). Acer entered a newly born industry at the early phase of its life cycle, so Acer competed in a relatively level field where there were no immense gaps between the MNEs from the developed and developing countries in regard to technological level, brand recognition, country-of-origin image, market channel access, production cost, supporting industries and trade policies. Acer also benefited from some support from its government that intended to support its national high-tech industries (e.g. through industrial parks and trade missions). Despite its humble start, Acer seized all these opportunities and gained its initial competitive advantages.

Acer had a sound strategy. It chose a *posture* of seeking emerging niche market segments (e.g. the microcomputer business); emphasizing cost-effective R&D (e.g. adapting the available foreign technologies) and 'poor-man' marketing (e.g. utilizing media coverage as free advertising); and early international involvement (e.g. as an importer and distributor for foreign venders and as an exporter in export trade; equally important, importing advanced technologies from overseas). It also chose a *mode* of integrating competition and co-operation through shared interests and trust (e.g. shared vision; employee-as-owner policy; leaders as role models; and 20 per cent minority veto power); formalizing financial control but keeping other areas informal; and using joint ventures as the mode for market entry and R&D operation. Underlying this strategy was Acer's corporate culture, which included the values of the common man (i.e. modesty and frugality; e.g. 'poor-man' marketing) and beliefs in the good man (i.e. egalitarianism, self-control, teamwork, and trust due to shared interest and shared vision; e.g. minority shareholders' veto power).

Explaining the MNE stage.

Acer rode a boom-bust-boom rollercoaster at its MNE stage. This is due to the joint effect of the 'spatial' variables (external context, internal profile, ultimate intent, strategic choice and market effect). Acer was initially cautious in international expansion, so it performed well in its infant-MNE stage; at its teenage-MNE stage, Acer became complacent (e.g. the over-expansion and insensitivity to market changes). At its adult-MNE stage, Acer overcame its complacency by going back to its cultural roots (i.e. the values of the common man and the beliefs in the good man). The central element defining Acer's performance at its MNE stage was the link between its strategic choice and its corporate culture. Acer suffered when it went away from its cultural roots, and it prospered when it came back to its cultural roots. The crucial link between its strategy and culture was severed when Acer became complacent (due to its early success); this complacency eroded Acer's corporate culture, and led it to overexpansion. Acer's internal problem was exacerbated by the external changes at that time (i.e. the sudden change in the rules of competition in the computer industry). The external changes served as the catalyst for Acer to reconnect its strategy to its cultural roots.

Corresponding to the boom-bust-boom performance cycle, Acer's strategy went through a similar cycle:

1 Its *target* shifted first from market share to profit margin, and then from profit-margin back to market share.

2 Its *thrust* shifted first from cost to value, and then from value back to cost.

3 Its *posture* shifted from home orientation to host orientation, and then from host orientation back to balanced orientation.

4 Its *mode* shifted from informal control to formal control, and then from formal control back to informal control.

The pattern of strategic change coincided with the boom-bust-boom performance cycle (i.e. a fit between strategy and culture led to a boom, while a misfit between the two led to a bust).

The implications of the case evidence

The sources of the initial competitive advantages

The case evidence suggests that the competitive gaps between the MNEs from the developed and developing countries do exist, but the MNEs from the developing countries can take full advantage of the international differences by obtaining the advanced technology and the abundant capital from the developed countries (as Acer did in its early stage of evolution – as a local agent for foreign vendors and taking advantage of the Chinese Americans for technology and capital). By combining the imported technologies and capital with the cheap labour at home, the MNEs from the developing countries acquire their initial competitive advantages (as Acer did with its initial exports). Unlike the MNEs from the developed countries who derive their competitive advantages largely from their home countries, the MNEs from the developing countries have to develop their initial advantages by combining the location-specific advantages of their home countries with the location-specific advantages of the developed countries (Dunning, 1988). Besides, the international gaps may be also used to create competitive gaps between the local firms (those who are international would enjoy certain competitive advantages over those who remain local).

The strategies to develop new competitive advantages

The case evidence suggests that fatalistic view that the MNEs from the developing countries would suffer from permanent disadvantages fails to appreciate the real character of MNEs as global players that can transform the location-specific advantages into firm-specific advantages (i.e. the MNEs can internalize the location-specific advantages). In this aspect, there is no between-group difference in strategy among the MNEs from the developed and developing countries. They all have to develop global brands, global marketing channels, global R&D capabilities, global sourcing capabilities as well as global management teams. As indicated by the case evidence, however, the strategy to utilize the global ethnic network or the mode of joint venture seems to be more significant to the MNEs from the developing countries than to those from the developed countries. Further, the evidence shows that a creative design of organizational structure is an integral part of strategic choice. It also suggests that a fit between strategic choice and corporate culture is the key to a firm's long-term success. Consequently, the MNEs from the developing countries must pay a close attention to their organizational structures and corporate cultures. Finally, the case evidence suggests that the fit between strategy and culture is not always easy to maintain, thus organizational evolution may take the form of a spiral composed of both incremental and punctuated changes. The MNEs from the developing countries should effectively manage the spiral process.

The fit between strategy and culture as the key to success

The case evidence suggests that it is important to appreciate the role of corporate culture. Among the five 'spatial' variables, the relationship between strategic choice and corporate culture (as the central element of internal profile) is the most fundamental as the deep structure (i.e. the basic link between the inter-related parts of a system (Gersick, 1991)). The anchor of the deep structure is corporate culture since it is more stable than strategy, and it affects strategy more than strategy affects it. The case evidence shows that a fit between strategy and culture will lead to a good performance (i.e. a boom during the period of incremental change), while a misfit between strategy and culture will lead to a poor performance (i.e. a bust during the period of punctuated change). Thus, a firm's strategy should be compatible with the firm's corporate culture, and such a link appears to be the key to its long-term success, especially when the core elements of that culture are in line with the new rules of the competitive game (e.g. the fit between Acer's three strategic initiatives – fast-food process, client-server structure and spin-off policy; Acer's good-man beliefs, and the trend towards the network form and business disintegration, led to Acer's recent turn-around).

The evolutionary pattern of MNEs

The case evidence suggests that a firm's pattern of internationalization is an integral part of its overall organizational evolution, but the former does not always match the latter. The case evidence shows that the evolution of MNEs tends to follow a pattern of spiral progression (i.e. effective at first, ineffective afterwards, and effective again). This spiral pattern of organizational evolution results from the spiral process of organizational learning. The case evidence shows that accumulation of knowledge via learning is possible, but this accumulation does not always follow the linear pattern of incremental evolution; it also goes through periods of punctuated revolution. During the period of incremental evolution (when the interplay of the 'spatial' factors is well-synchronized, e.g. Acer's infant-MNE and adult-MNE stages), organizational learning is continuous; thus organizational evolution is smooth. However, during the period of punctuated revolution (when the interplay of the 'spatial' factors is poorly synchro-nized, e.g. Acer's teenage-MNE stage), organizational learning is disjointed, thus orga-nizational evolution is turbulent. In sum, the overall pattern of organizational evolution is a combination of, or an alternation between, incremental and punctuated changes. The challenge to all MNEs is how to manage effectively the shifts between these two kinds of change.

Conclusion

This study seeks to explore the evolutionary pattern of the MNEs from the developing countries via a case study of Taiwan's Acer Group. The case evidence suggests that the MNEs from the developing countries can gain their initial competitive advantages by combining the location-specific advantages of their home countries and the developed countries. These MNEs should further develop their new competitive advantages by tapping their global ethnic networks and using joint ventures as the primary mode of market entry. The case evidence also shows that the MNEs from the developing coun-tries will evolve in a spiral pattern characterized by a mix of incremental and punctu-ated changes. It seems almost inevitable and often necessary for MNEs to fail from time to time as long as they can learn from the mistakes and overcome the difficulties by drawing strength from their cultural roots. Further study is needed to corroborate the findings of this case study.

For the current crisis in Asia, this study also offers at least two significant implications. First, similar to Acer's phase of troubled teenage-MNE, Asia is suffering from its past success, which has led to Asia's complacency and over-expansion, causing the current crisis in Asia; in fact, Asia's 'deep structure' (i.e. the fundamental links between its eco-nomic, political, social and cultural systems) is undergoing a punctuated revolution. Second, the challenge to Asia is to find a good way, just as Acer did, to shift from an old deep structure to a new one. The key to this transition is to reconnect the other ele-ments of the deep structure to the cultural roots – the anchor of deep structure. These are the two lessons other Asian MNEs can learn from the case of Acer. It is interesting to note that many ethnic-Chinese businessmen blame the stray from the traditional Chinese way of doing business for the current crisis in Asia, and they believe that the key to survival is to return to the traditional Chinese values (see Vatikiotis and Daorueng, 1998). Though it may be too early to draw any final conclusions at this time, the case of Acer seems to lend some support for the above argument.

References

Andersen, A. O. (1993). On the internationalization process of firms: a critical analysis. *Journal of International Business Studies*, 2, 209–31.
Andrews, K. R. (1971). *The Concept of Corporate Strategy*. Irwin.
Barnett, W. P. and Burgelman, R. A. (1996). Evolutionary perspectives on strategy. *Strategic Management Journal*, 17 (special issue), 5–19.
Dunning, J. H. (1988). The eclectic paradigm of international production: a restatement and some possible extensions. *Journal of International Business Studies*, 19, 1–49.
Dunning, J. H. (1995). Reappraising the eclectic paradigm in an age of alliance capital-ism. *Journal of International Business Studies*, 26, 461–91.

Eisenhardt, K. M. (1989). Building theories from case study research. *Academy of Management Review*, **14**, 532–50.

Engardio, P. and Burrows, P. (1996). Acer: a global powerhouse. *Business Week*, 1 July, 22–4.

Gersick, C. J. G. (1991). Revolutionary change theories: a multilevel exploration of the punctuated equilibrium paradigm. *Academy of Management Review*, **16**, 10–36.

Hanrahan, C. (1994). The fourth way. *World Executive Digest*, 17–18 March

Heenan, D. A. and Keegan, W. J. (1979). The rise of third world multinationals. *Harvard Business Review*, **1–2**, 101–9.

Johanson, J. and Vahlne, J. E. (1977). The internationalization process of the firm – a model of knowledge development and increasing foreign market commitments. *Journal of International Business Studies*, 23–32.

Johanson, J. and Vahlne, J. E. (1990). The mechanism of internationalization. *International Marketing Review*, **7** (4), 11–24.

Kraar, L. (1995). Acer's edge: PCs to go. *Fortune*, 30 October, 187–204.

Lecraw, D. J. (1993). Outward direct investment by Indonesian firms: motivation and effects. *Journal of International Business Studies*, **3**, 589–600.

Li, P. P. (1994). Strategic profile of indigenous MNEs from NIEs: the cases of South Korea and Taiwan. *The International Executive* **36**, 147–70.

Li, P. P. (1995). Inevitability, desirability and resolvability of paradox: a dialectical approach to global strategy. Presentation at the Academy of Management Annual Meeting, Vancouver.

Parkhe, A. (1993). 'Messy' research, methodological redispositions, and theory development in international joint ventures. *Academy of Management Journal*, **18**, 227–68.

Riegel, K. F. (1979). *Foundations of Dialectic Psychology*. Academic Press.

Tolentino, P. E. (1993). *Technological Innovation and Third World Multinationals*. Routledge.

Van de Ven, A. H. and Poole, M. S. (1995). Explaining development and change in organizations. *Academy of Management Review*, **20**, 510–40.

Vatikiotis, M. and Daorueng, P. (1998). Survival tactics. *Far Eastern Economic Review*, 26 February, 42–5.

Yeung, H. W. (1994a). Transnational corporations from Asian developing countries: their characteristics and competitive edge. *Journal of Asian Business*, **10** (4), 17–58.

Yeung, H. W. (1994b). Third World multinationals revisited: a research critique and future agenda. *Third World Quarterly*, **15**, 297–317.

Yin, R. K. (1989). *Case Study Research: Design and Methods*. Sage.

Chapter 23.1

Acer's strategy from post-crisis Asia

▓ Peter Ping Li ▓

It is interesting to note that Taiwanese firms have generally fared better than other Asian firms so far in the current Asian crisis, so has Taiwan's overall economy. Unlike all other economies in East Asia, Taiwan is still growing at a reasonable pace (see also Chapter 22.1). As for Acer, its total turnover in 1997 was US$6.5 billion, a healthy 10.2 per cent growth despite the Asian crisis; but this growth paled in comparison with its immediate past (from 1992 to 1995), in which it enjoyed an annual growth of about 70 per cent. Acer has lowered its goal to an annual growth rate of 20 per cent. Acer's challenges are not confined to the Asian region; its operations in the USA face intensified competition that has led to Acer's heaviest losses in years.

The sharp decline of Acer's sales started during the second half of 1996, particularly in its core business (i.e., its computer system business); its profit fell dramatically beginning in the second quarter of 1997, largely due to the loss of Acer's US operations and its semiconductor business (which used to be a joint venture between Texas Instruments and Acer, but now is 100 per cent owned by Acer).

Despite all the above difficulties, Acer has become the third largest PC manufacturer in the world, and the seventh best-known PC brand in the world. Acer has adopted a new strategy to achieve its goal of becoming one of the top five computer firms in the world (see also Chapter 20.1).

First, Acer plans to expand its software business so much that it will account for about 15 per cent of Acer's total turnover and about one-third of its total profit. To accomplish that, Acer has begun the development of Aspire Park, a Utopian community that harmonizes futuristic technology, a humanistic spirit and a bucolic setting. Nestled in the midst of spectacular countryside scenery 30 miles from Taipei, Aspire Park will combine residential, recreational and educational facilities along with those for business and research. This represents Acer's new thinking about brain power; to Acer, brain power is not limited to technology, but also art, so Aspire Park is a model for a new lifestyle that blends technology, art and natural environment together so as to harmonize nature, people and technology.

Second, Acer plans to expand the scope of its operation from computer products to 3C products (i.e., computer, consumer electronics and communication systems).

Third, Acer plans to launch a new computer platform, X computer. X computer is a task-specific computer, rather than a general-purpose computer as conventional computers are now. Since X computer is application-specific, its cost will be lower while its performance will be higher.

Fourth, Acer has been restructured into five subgroups: Acer International Service Group; Acer Sertek Service Group; Acer Semiconductor Group; Acer Information Products Group and Acer Peripherals Group, so as to best implement its overall strategy.

Recognized as one of the best companies in Asia (e.g., Acer's CEO, Stan Shih, led the 1997 *Asiaweek* Business Hall of Fame, and Acer was ranked second among Asia's top fifty most competitive companies by a survey of 4500 companies across fourteen countries in 1997), Acer represents a new breed of Asian firms that differs from the traditional Asian firms in many aspects, as identified below and indicated in Chapter 23:

1   Acer is not family-owned.

2   Acer is not centrally controlled.

3   Acer is not a widely diversified conglomerate.

4   Acer is not dependent on government connections or corruption.

5   Acer is a high-tech firm.

6   Acer has its own brand.

7   Acer is not opportunistic or speculative.

8   Acer is not extravagant and arrogant.

The above are the lessons that many Asians can learn from Acer.

Chapter 24

Defending against multinational corporation offensives: strategy of the large domestic firm in a newly liberalizing economy[1]

■ Ranjan Das ■

■ Introduction

During the last two decades or so, economic activities have become increasingly global. Multinational corporations (MNCs) have played a major role in this process of globalization. Despite their long experience in international business, MNCs now face new challenges not only in technological, political and economic terms, but also from the strategic initiatives being taken by MNCs and domestic firms of newly industrializing countries which now have the motive and growing financial power to confront large corporations from developed countries. Domestic firms of countries such as China, India and Central and Eastern Europe are well aware of the advantages and disadvantages of their respective nations and are in a position to act on their own or in co-operation with well-known MNCs from advanced countries to enhance competitiveness of their own firms. Today MNCs from developed countries face a number of new challenges which differ significantly from what they were used to, even a decade and a half ago.

Dunning (1993), while examining business prospects of MNCs during the next ten to fifteeen years, observed three key patterns for example: continuing eminence of MNCs from USA, Japan and Western Europe in world trade and commerce; further shrinkage of corporate and national boundaries as a result of ongoing technological and organizational innovations; and continuing conflicts between national governments and political parties over the balance between economic integration and political sovereignty. While these issues are bound to influence MNC strategies in the future, another factor rising in the consciousness of domestic firms is the need to enlist MNC support in order to pursue their own ambitions of becoming globally dominant. MNCs will have to accept this new reality. The determination of host country firms to develop and implement a strategy that aims to defend their entrenched position in the

---

[1] This chapter has been published previously by MCB University Press Limited: Das, R. (1997). Defending against MNC offensives: strategy of the large domestic firm in a newly liberalizing economy. *Management Decision*, **35** (8), 605–18.

domestic market is an issue that MNCs will have to examine while reviewing their own options for foreign market servicing.

This chapter will take a look at the growing economic power of emerging nations and the implications so far as worldwide strategies of MNCs are concerned. It will then identify a range of strategic choices that MNCs can initiate to exploit opportunities that are opening up in newly liberalizing economies, as well as factors that influence such choices. The paper will then provide a framework that will describe a set of 'defensive' strategies which domestic firms can pursue to respond adequately to the offensive strategies of MNCs. Finally, the chapter will detail the managerial implications of the findings and also provide directions for future research.

■ Emerging nations

There are already signs of a shift in economic power from the industrial economies that dominated the past one and a half centuries to emerging nations in Asia and the Far East. Major technological changes, the phenomenon of globalization and the drive taken by these nations have brought about this new equation. With the opening up of more and more economies, particularly in the Third World and former Soviet Bloc countries, there is now more promise of rapid growth so far as developing countries are concerned. A recent World Bank Report (*The Economist*, 1994) shows that while rich industrial countries are poised to grow only at the rate of 2.7 per cent per annum during 1994 to 2003, developing countries are expected to grow during the same period at the rate of 4.8 per cent per annum (growth during 1974 to 2003 will be 3 per cent per annum). Likewise, share of world output of rich industrial countries is projected to come down from 47 per cent in 1995 to 37–38 per cent in the year 2020. Of all the developing countries, those in Asia are poised to grow very rapidly and an estimate shows that by 2020 China will be the world's largest economy. The list of the top fifteen economies by 2020 is likely to include as many as seven Asian countries including India, Thailand, Indonesia and Taiwan (the others are China, Japan and South Korea). Porter's study (Porter, 1990) took a look at Japan and South Korea and identified inherent competitive advantages of these two countries, as well as specific actions taken by them to become formidable rivals in increasingly advanced industries and segments. Dunning provided a different perspective on Porter's concept of national competitive advantage and argued that foreign inward and outward investments, driven mainly by MNCs, affect the way a nation undertakes resource allocation and usage.

■ Multinational corporations and domestic firms

There is thus a reversal of roles already, so far as world trade is concerned. MNCs from rich countries are now facing a large number of competitors from emerging nations. However, the good news is that developing countries are likely to account for two-thirds of the rise in world imports during the period 1995–2020 and this means an increase in the number of customers for advanced nations. In other words, developing countries are going to be the key source of growth for advanced countries as well as the MNCs that originate from them. Rich countries need not worry that China, India and other select emerging economies may move ahead of some of today's Group of Seven (G-7) countries but there is definitely a need to understand the strategies of these emerging nations, as well as the companies that originate from them, in order to develop an alternative approach to fight new competition. The urgency to understand the strategy of companies of the developing world is felt more now than ever before because underneath their so called 'defensive' strategies to face competition from MNCs of advanced countries, the pace of which has certainly increased after the liberalization of individual economies, there also lies a clear intent to occupy pre-emptive positions in specific market segments in the medium- to long-term future. Japan has already shown the power of such strategic intents to capture market leadership in various products and services (Hamel and Prahalad, 1989) and this trend is likely to persist. The pace at which companies of the developing world will move may be something not experienced before. The collective efforts of these companies belonging to developing nations such as India, China or Indonesia have the potential to make their respective countries catch up at a faster rate than what happened in the case of the USA *vis-à-vis* the UK, or Japan *vis-à-vis* the USA. And herein lies the importance of understanding the strategies of the domestic firms of developing nations in responding to the initiatives of MNCs from currently advanced countries. Such an understanding can give useful insights to these MNCs in shaping and driving their future worldwide strategy with regard to:

• configuration of international value chains including decisions on which components, subassemblies or finished products are to be produced in which country;

• driving down strategic costs, not just by shifting production off-shore but also benchmarking high productivity and best operating practices being followed by companies belonging to emerging nations;

• clarity in relation to markets to be targeted for future growth as well as in deciding with whom to collaborate and with whom to compete in order to increase global share of markets and to achieve greater economies of scale; and

• diversification of financial investments taking into account the fact that returns from investments in emerging countries are likely to be higher than the same from mature, slower growing, advanced countries.

As MNCs take a fresh look at their worldwide strategy and operations in order to remain viable under the new world economic order, they will need to appreciate the growing importance and power of developing nations, particularly those from Asia. During 1988 to 1994, ten developing countries, including seven from Asia, received a total foreign direct investment (FDI) of over $120 billion. In 1993 alone, developing countries had received FDI close to $80 billion *vis-à-vis* $100 billion received by rich industrial countries. This trend points to the growing role of MNCs in enhancing the competitiveness of companies from emerging nations by way of providing much needed technology, management capabilities and funds. Given this pattern, it is important for MNCs to understand the strategies and intents of domestic firms of developing countries as a prelude to formulating their own strategies under the new dispensation.

■ Multinational corporation offensives in a liberalizing economy

During the last ten to fifteen years, economies across the world have been liberalizing at a rapid pace and MNCs are constantly reevaluating their strategies to exploit new opportunities. While the initiatives undertaken by MNCs in response to such liberalization can be country or region specific, there are certain underlying common patterns behind such moves. This section will identify these patterns in the context of liberalization and reforms undertaken by India during 1991–95.

The new economic policy adopted by the government of India in mid-1991 was based on the twin principles of deregulation of the government's economic interventionist functions and encouraging competition. The main thrust of this policy was to ensure free flow of investment, product, technology and managerial personnel across national borders leading to greater integration of the Indian economy with the rest of the world. Various Indian regulations in the areas of industrial licensing, monopoly and restrictive trade practices, foreign exchange regulation, import and export, capital markets, external commercial borrowing, Companies Act, convertibility of rupee in current accounts, etc., have already been changed extensively to facilitate liberalization and deregulation and more are in the offing.

The reforms that took place in India during the first five years had a beneficial effect on a number of fronts. One key progress was in the field of FDI which has increased steadily over the past five years. Total FDI during 1991–96 was around Rs.500 billion (i.e. US$14 billion), 48 per cent of which was from the USA, 30 per cent from Europe, 14 per cent from East Asia and 8 per cent from Japan (*Business Today*, 1997a). FDI inflow during April to October 1996 at Rs.42 billion (i.e. US$1.1 billion) was a 13 per cent improvement over the corresponding period in the previous year (*Business Today*, 1997b), though significantly lower than FDI of Rs.170 billion (i.e. US$4.9 billion) approved during the said period. The FDI figure given here excludes portfolio investments made by foreign institutional investors (FII) which hovered around US$2 billion during 1995–96. It needs to be mentioned here that during the fiscal year 1995–96, FDI inflow to India at US$2 billion was quite insignificant in comparison to US$90 billion received by all developing countries together, of which China alone received US$38 billion. These figures, however, need not be disappointing, since China started its reforms process in 1979 and it took ten years to achieve a FDI of US$3 billion (Pike, 1996).

Reforms have also given a boost to the number of joint ventures (JVs) entered into by Indian companies. For example, between April 1991 and May 1996, as many as 4190 JVs were signed (*Business Today*, 1996a). Some of the countries with whom such JVs were entered into were the USA (908), Germany (478), the UK (440), The Netherlands (248), Japan (192), Singapore (181), Italy (178), Switzerland (178), France (143) and South Korea (141). A majority of these JVs were in electrical equipment (767), chemicals (369), food processing (372), financial services (293), industrial machinery (254), textiles (233), telecom (183), transportation (164), consultancy (153), engineering (146), metals (127), fuels (117), and hotel/tourism (101).

India's commitment to the reforms process has continued to remain at a fairly satisfactory level, five years after commencement of the same, even though investors and multilateral agencies belonging to developed countries still feel that not enough has yet been done. In the latest spate of reforms initiated during 1996–97, notable steps were – further widening of the list of industries where automatic approval for up to 51 per cent of equity would be allowed, approval for foreign equity up to 74 per cent in the infrastructural sector, consideration of proposals for investment up to 100 per cent of foreign equity subject to meeting certain specific conditions, allowing FIIs to invest up to 30 per cent in equity of domestic public limited companies as well as in unlisted companies and debt funds (including government securities), private sector participation in infra-structure, setting up of the Telecom Regulatory Authority of India and granting the telecom sector the status of infrastructure (thereby enabling it to get a number of fiscal benefits), etc. The government of India has also simplified foreign investment approval procedures and set up a Foreign Investment Promotion Council to attract FDI. A disinvestment commission was constituted to advise the government regarding disinvestment of government holdings in public sector units. A takeover code has been introduced to facilitate mergers and acquisitions. The Companies Act 1961 is proposed to be amended soon, to enable buyback of shares and raise the overall ceiling for intercorporate loans and investments. The health insurance sector is also proposed to be opened up to private sector competition.

In addition to economic reforms and liberalization, there are other factors which make India, along with other Asian countries, a potential target for increased MNC activities. Naisbitt (1995) identified certain key trends which are applicable to Asia in particular. For example, Asian countries are becoming consumer focused and market driven, getting increasingly urbanized, using technology to replace labour, deriving an Asian approach to management as distinct from the same followed by the West and are beginning to establish networks with other nations to face the rest of the world. Many of these trends are also applicable to India and it is no wonder that leading MNCs are making it a point to ensure that they have a strong presence in India.

MNCs have already taken a number of actions to exploit the new opportunities.

Some of these initiatives are:

- Increasing the equity holding, from 40 per cent to 51 per cent and above, in existing subsidiaries and associate companies to ensure greater control of operations and strategy. Some notable cases, which took place during 1992–96, are The BOC Group, Glaxo, ABB, Philips, Pepsico, Colgate Palmolive, Honda, Whirlpool and many others, all of whom increased their equity to 51 per cent and above (*The Economic Times*, 1993a).

- Setting up new ventures with 100 per cent ownership – a new phenomenon after liberalization was introduced. For example, Sony has set up a wholly-owned subsidiary for manufacturing one million television sets per year by 2000; similarly, GE Capital Services, USA has already set up a 100 per cent subsidiary to oversee GE's six joint ventures in India (*Business Today*, 1997c).

- Buying up major Indian brands and distribution networks as a prelude to launching own brands. Examples include Coca-Cola buying India's largest soft drinks brands (1992), Heinz buying Glaxo India's food business (1994) and Unilever buying soaps and detergent business of the Tata Group as well as major Indian ice-cream brands (1994) (*The Economic Times*, 1994a).

- Using India's competitive advantages in certain fields to strengthen its world-wide position. For examples, General Motors is sourcing auto components from India (*Business India*, 1994) while ABB has similar plans for circuit breakers and power-line communication equipment. On the same basis, other MNCs are tapping India's low-cost advantages in software, colour television and computers. Some MNCs are going a step forward and tapping India's research and development (R&D) pool in select areas. A few interesting examples are General Electric (polymers), Du Pont (agricultural chemicals), Philips Semiconductors (VLSI design), United Technologies (aircraft engine), Unilever (basic research), etc. (*Business World*, 1997).

- Restructuring existing outfits to improve competitiveness and focus and make them market driven. Some examples are: ABB acquiring and merging Flakt India Ltd (in 1994), the largest producer of pollution control equipment in India (*The Economic Times*, 1994b), Ciba Geigy selling its Indian oral product division to Colgate India Ltd (in 1994), Glaxo India selling its food business to Heinz USA (*Business Standard*, 1994), the BOC Group divesting its Indian welding business (in 1991) to concentrate on core activities and reducing manpower by more than 70 per cent during 1991–95 through a voluntary retirement scheme (Das, 1993), and Siemens undertaking business process re-engineering to improve cost competitiveness and customer service at its Western India plant (during 1995) (*Business Today*, 1995a).

- Using strategic alliances and joint ventures to access the growing Indian market. For example, in 1992, Hewlett Packard formed a joint venture with HCL Limited, one of the leading Indian computer and office equipment manufacturers, and set up a new company called HCL-HP Limited (*The Economic Times*, 1994a). Likewise, Samsung Group of South Korea put up a 51:49 joint venture with an Indian company (*Business World*, 1995a); Unilever Group entered into a strategic alliance with Lakme India (in 1995), the largest manufacturer of cosmetics in India (*Business World*, 1995b), while Mercedes-Benz, Peugeot and General Motors entered the Indian auto market through collaborations with auto manufacturers in India (*Business Today*, 1996a). Other instances are: GE of USA setting up six joint ventures in various fields such as consumer appliances, financial services, lighting equipment, medical systems, etc., and Matsushita putting up a joint venture with an Indian company for manufacturing colour televisions (*Business Today*, 1996b).

The above set of actions taken by various MNCs during the first four years of reforms shows the following patterns so far as their strategic choices are concerned.

- The choice of a right entry route is critical to the future success of an MNC as observed by Root (1987), Davidson (1985) and Killing (1992). A unified framework linking country risk, country familiarity, the stage of the country's development, technology and transaction cost was provided by Hill, Hwang and Kim (1990). who postulated that a particular entry decision cannot be viewed in isolation and that such decisions are considered in relation to the overall strategic posture of the firm. Another factor, observed from strategies adopted by MNCs in India, is their desire to occupy a pre-emptive position in chosen market segments before other MNCs or domestic groups can do so. MNCs, which already had subsidiaries or affiliates prior to initiation of the reforms process in the host country, work towards this objective by repositioning their firms in terms of cost, quality and customer service. The approaches followed by Coca-Cola, Hewlett Packard (both new entrants) and Philips (in operation in India for many years) highlight this particular thinking.

- In businesses which are primarily brand and distribution intensive and where domestic firms have already established strong market positions, MNCs prefer to access a growing domestic market through acquisition of existing entities/brands or setting up joint ventures with majority holding. Entry through acquisition of strong domestic brands helps in giving the incoming MNC a decent market share right from the beginning. This route also enables MNCs to fill product gaps which they may have in their range. Unilever buying Indian detergent and ice-cream brands, Coca-Cola buying India's largest Indian soft drinks brands or Heinz buying Glaxo India's food business are examples of this. The joint venture route is chosen by MNCs in cases where there is a need to have local participation for tactical reasons (such as for bidding in telecom projects) or where outright purchase of brands and distribution rights is not feasible in the short run or where the local partner has certain core competencies which are valuable to the concerned MNC. The cases of Hewlett Packard setting up a joint venture with one of India's largest computer manufacturers, HCL Limited, or GE of USA setting up a series of joint ventures with various Indian partners are examples of this.

- Increase of equity holding in existing affiliates by MNCs indicates not only their long-term expectation of the prospects of the host country but also their desire to integrate operations of the affiliates more closely with the rest of the organization world-wide. Integration of the activities of the subsidiary helps the latter achieve improvement in a number of areas such as productivity, efficiency, quality and customer services, which in turn enhance its profitability and competitiveness. Sharp improvements in results achieved by BOC India and Philips India during the last four years in all these areas corroborate this observation.

- While improving the competitiveness of its subsidiary *vis-à-vis* pre-liberalization days by making available best operating practices, MNC headquarters also ensure that the strategy and organization adopted by the local subsidiary follow, by and large, the same pattern as pursued by the parent. Unilever Group's plan to organize its world-wide business along food and non-food lines was also adopted in India, leading to a number of mergers and divestments among its group companies in India. BOC India divested its welding business, in which it was involved for more than fifty years, in line with its parent company's policies. Likewise, Glaxo India divested its food and agro-chemical business. To facilitate the implementation of various new initiatives, MNC subsidiaries also effect changes in their organizational structures as well as administrative systems of rewards and punishment, planning and control, etc., whose designs reflect, by and large, the principles adopted by the headquarters. The planning, information and control systems as well as organizational structure at BOC India underwent a number of changes to bring it in line with that of the parent company (Das, 1993). A similar approach was also followed by Glaxo Wellcome's Indian subsidiary.

- Faced with declining cost competitiveness of their operations in various countries, MNCs evaluate their outsourcing decisions on an ongoing basis and look for new production sources for driving down costs and improving quality. Countries which possess selective advantages in specific fields but which were not conducive to foreign investment earlier, may become attractive due to changes in the host government's policies. When such a change takes place, MNCs re-evaluate their outsourcing decisions leading to possible shifts in their sources of supply. Decisions taken by General Motors and a number of software companies to outsource from India, point to the strategy of these MNCs to further augment their global competitiveness by exploiting India's cost advantages.

- In situations where the size and growth of the domestic market, as well as the pace of reform, are yet to reach the desired level, MNCs are normally willing to wait longer to get the target return if they assess the potential to be bright. The upfront promotional investments being made in India by Pepsico, Coca-Cola and Procter and Gamble to build strong brand position, even though current volumes are not satisfactory, are instances of MNCs putting more emphasis on long-term market creation than short-term financial gains. Other examples include Daewoo of South Korea, which is planning to invest up to $4 to $5 billion dollars (*Business World*, 1995c, d) and ABB which is planning to invest $300 million dollars over the next five years to consolidate their positions in India. A similar intention has been expressed by Sony which has not only set up a 100 per cent subsidiary in India but has also commissioned an entertainment venture.

According to Ring, Lenway and Govekar (1990), firms doing business in international markets conform to two basic imperatives – namely economic and political. They observed that actions taken to deal with political imperatives are a function of the impact of such imperatives on the firm as well as the latter's strategic pre-disposition. Ghoshal (1987) also identified four kinds of risks confronted by MNCs namely, macro-economic, policy, competitive and resources. MNCs entering India for the first time, as well as those already operating for some time, have examined the level of each of these risks and assessed whether the future looks stable or adverse *vis-à-vis* the present. The projections made by World Bank, General Agreement on Trade and Tariffs (GATT) and United Nations Center for Trade and Development (UNCTAD) along various dimensions such as projected size of economy, country's share of world exports of manufactured goods, share of world output, GDP growth, inflow of FDI as well as history of political stability of the concerned host country are taken into account while developing strategies.

Based on these observations and also on the patterns seen in India so far as MNC offensives are concerned, a framework indicating the key variables that are taken into account by MNCs to formulate their strategies for dominating the host country market is given in Figure 24.1 The framework identifies four broad parameters: MNC pre-disposition; risk profile of host country; future scenario; and choice of strategic platform that significantly influences extent of MNC offensive in a host country. The factors that come under each of these parameters are described in the framework. It needs to be stressed that of the four parameters, choice of strategic platform (a firm-specific decision) determines to a great extent the intensity of MNC offensive. For example, it is expected that all other factors remaining the same, the MNC offensive will be of a very high order in cases where strategic platforms are defined around high intensity of intent, large size of investment, longer time frame so far as returns are concerned and close integration within the world-wide MNC system.

Domestic firms, particularly those which had been operating only in the home market prior to the commencement of reforms, will need to respond to the emerging opportunities opened up as a result of deregulation and also defend fresh offensives of MNCs triggered by the same deregulations in order to remain viable. The next section deals with this important subject.

▨ Strategic responses of the domestic firm

Most domestic firms are accustomed to operate primarily in their country of origin. Only a handful of these companies have some exposure to international business

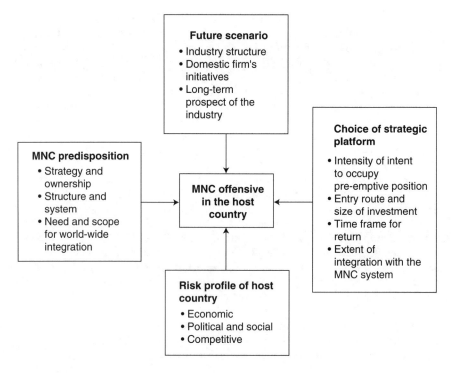

Figure 24.1 Factors influencing MNC offensives

through limited export activities or operating a joint venture formed with the help of overseas principals. A protected domestic market helps in reaping profits but lack of competitive pressure results in inefficiency, absence of customer focus and inadequate innovation in all aspects of business. When the reforms process gets under way and liberalization of economic policies becomes a way of life, domestic firms face three strategic choices:

1 *Reposition and rejuvenate* existing portfolio and operations to combat new competition and grow in the deregulated environment.

2 *Withdraw* from businesses where current competencies are inadequate to deal with future competitive battle and *redirect* resources so released to new opportunities that are compatible with competencies available.

3 *Globalize* with a view to exploiting opportunities available in the international market as well as for defending domestic position.

These three key choices are evaluated by domestic firms against three critical imperatives that need to be addressed in order to respond to the newly liberalized regime. These three critical imperatives are:

1 *Exploit* new opportunities in domestic and global markets.

2 *Combat* increased competition from other domestic firms as well as MNCs (existing and new entrants).

3 *Overcome* firm-specific constraints that had not been addressed in the past.

Figure 24.2 links the three strategic choices referred to above with the three critical imperatives. These strategic choices can be pursued by domestic firms, singly or in combination, to respond to the three imperatives. The strategies adopted by domestic firms in India explain this linkage as outlined in Figure 24.2.

■ Reposition and rejuvenate

Many Indian firms, faced with rising MNC offensives in the post-deregulation phase, have already initiated actions to reposition and rejuvenate their organizations with a view to achieving greater competitiveness in such areas as cost, quality and customer service. The list of actions includes strategic alliances and joint ventures (to acquire new competencies or for getting access to international brand names), streamlining and right-sizing existing operations, changing business portfolios and altering the configuration of the value chain through mergers and acquisitions and divestitures, effecting financial reengineering and undertaking organizational development. The following examples explain this particular strategy adopted by domestic firms in India, in response to MNC offensives:

- Indian Oil Corporation Ltd (IOCL), a government of India company, having a turnover of Rs.430 billion (i.e. US$12 billion) is a *Fortune* 500 company and is facing problems of increased competition resulting from deregulation (already certain segments of the petroleum industry have been deregulated and the rest are expected to be deregulated progressively). The problem is accentuated by the fact that while the changed scenario now needs IOCL to be extremely proactive, the company still has to operate under the restrictive guidelines applicable to public sector units where no reform worth its name has yet taken place. This is reducing IOCL's ability to introduce rapidly far-reaching changes in operations to enhance competitiveness. The IOCL also understands that its current position as market leader (55 per cent market share in petroleum products) will be threatened greatly unless it invests in infrastructure such

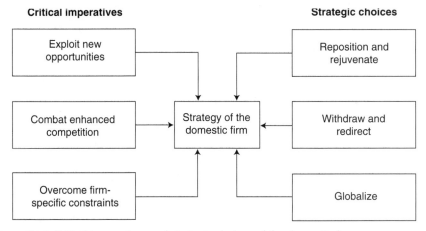

Figure 24.2 Critical imperatives and strategic choices of the domestic firm

as pipelines and port facilities and puts up additional refining capacity. There is also the need to downsize the organization – in terms of the number of employees – as well as simplify its systems and procedures in order to debureaucratize and make the company responsive to market needs. For overcoming the government's bureaucratic control on new investment areas, IOCL has entered into 50:50 joint ventures with leading international companies in post 1991–92 in areas such as port development, refining and aviation lubes. In automobile and industrial lubricants, it has entered into a joint venture with Mobil. The company is also planning to diversify into new fields such as power and petrochemicals where it has certain synergies. Side by side, an action plan is currently being drawn to make the organization lean and trim and the structure, systems and processes more market focused. (The observations on IOCL are based on the author's consulting assignment with the company).

- The Tata Iron and Steel Company Limited (TISCO), having a turnover of above Rs.50 billion per year (i.e. US$1.5 billion), is the largest private sector steel company in India. It has undertaken a number of actions that will lead to greater competitiveness in meeting global challenges. The company has not only completed substantial modernization in the five-year period 1991–96 but it has also moved to a new organizational form wherein each Strategic Business Unit (SBU) will have different market specific missions and accountability. A series of programmes on organizational development has been initiated to make the company proactive and market sensitive. In addition, the company is also working towards downsizing the number of employees. It is also setting up a modern steel plant with international capacity and efficiency norms in order to have a major presence in India and the global steel market (*Business India*, 1996).

- In the automobile industry the two oldest companies, Hindustan Motors and Premier Auto, have floated separate companies in joint ventures with a subsidiary of General Motors (USA) and Peugeot (France) respectively, the objective being to introduce new generation cars in the Indian auto market. Another example of repositioning and restructuring in the Indian automobile industry is the case of DCM Toyota Ltd which used to manufacture light commercial vehicles. The company, faced with a declining performance and seeing opportunities in the passenger car segment, entered into a joint venture with Daewoo Motors of South Korea during 1993–94 which resulted in changing the product mix of the company as well as altering the capital structure (the promoters' share came down from 51 per cent to 11 per cent and a nominee of Daewoo Motors became the Chairman of the company) (*The Economic Times*, 1994c, d).

- Leading Indian computer manufacturers such as Wipro Group and HCL Group, both of which have strong brand and distribution networks in India, recognized quite early the impending opportunities in information technology and also their relative inability to face single handedly the global competition that was to sweep India after deregulation. Both the companies are highly entrepreneurial and cost competitive. They decided quite early to enter into joint ventures with leading MNCs to strengthen their Indian market positions and also learned the skills and competencies needed to become a global player. HCL tied up with Hewlett Packard in 1992 to form a joint venture company and transferred its computer and related product business to the new company. Wipro also entered into a series of joint ventures with a number of well-known companies.

▣ Withdraw and redirect

One option available to domestic companies is to withdraw from those businesses where competition from MNCs would be difficult to withstand in the long run. Companies that may need to consider this option include those that operate mainly in products which are culture independent, which are brand and distribution intensive requiring continuous and heavy investment, and which face competition from international giants. The strategy of divestment requires as much careful thinking as acquiring a new business and may turn out to be extremely lucrative since MNCs planning to enter the domestic market through acquisition are willing to pay a significant premium for buying strong domestic brands. The following examples illustrate this point:

• Parle Products (turnover Rs.4 billion or US$114 million) sold its Indian soft drinks brands (having 55 per cent market share) and distribution rights to Coca-Cola USA because it felt that it would be difficult to operate in an industry which was going to be dominated by two international giants namely Coke and Pepsi. Good sense told the owner to sell the business while the going was still good (*The Economic Times*, 1993b).

• Manufacturers of 'Kwality' brand of ice-creams sold their brand and distribution rights to Brooke Bond Lipton India Ltd (a Unilever Group company now merged with Hindustan Lever Ltd, the flagship company of the group in India) to ensure a steady revenue for their businesses. These ice-cream manufacturers noted that the Indian ice-cream market was going to be extremely competitive and the critical factor for success would be marketing and distribution capabilities. Under the arrangement entered with Brooke Bond Lipton, the manufacture of ice-creams will continue to be with the original owners but brand and distribution rights would be with Unilever (*The Economic Times*, 1994a).

▣ Globalize

Another strategy a domestic firm may pursue, in the face of competition from MNCs, is to globalize its activities. The importance of globalization cannot be overemphasized and it is increasingly felt that companies which formulate a strategy without a global perspective in mind run the risk of competitive decline. This is because most industries are becoming global and there is a continuous need to acquire new competencies to face global competition. Pursuing a global strategy enables a firm to keep in touch with shifting customer preferences at the international level, monitor activities of international competitors, identify patterns of technology development in advance, source components and subassemblies from cost-competitive countries and build global brand and distribution dominance. Being global-minded in strategy formulation and benchmarking the best international rivals are essential elements of a defensive strategy. Large domestic firms in India have understood the importance of pursuing a global strategy with a view to protecting their market position, as can be seen from the following examples:

• Ranbaxy, the largest drug manufacturer in India having a turnover of about Rs.7 billion (i.e. US$200 million), is defending its current market position by pursuing a global strategy that involves setting up joint venture projects in strategic locations.

It has an extensive marketing network in three continents and fully owned subsidiaries in four continents. Its strategic alliances, particularly with leading US firms, is allowing Ranbaxy to access US and other markets. Ranbaxy will also supply its low-cost products to its international partners (*Business India*, 1994).

- A V Birla Group (turnover Rs.50 billion, i.e. US$1.5 billion), which started globalizing its activities since the early 1970s, is now the largest player in the world in the field of viscose fibre and the sixth largest in carbon black. It is continuing to pursue this globalization strategy along with strengthening its Indian activities, which together are making the entire group strong in financial terms (*Business India*, 1994).

- Other Indian companies and groups are also increasingly pursuing global strategy as part of their plans to strengthen their domestic position in the post-deregulation phase. Notable examples are: Arvind Mills (denim manufacturing), Ispat Group (iron and steel), Essar Group (steel), Thapars (paper mill), Lupin and Dr Reddy's Laboratory (both pharmaceuticals) and Ceat (truck tyres) (*Business India*, 1994). In some of these cases, the preference has been for acquisition of existing capacity or entering into joint venture agreements to overcome two major challenges of globalization, as mentioned by Rosenzweig (1994), namely challenges of scale and challenges given by existing competitors operating in the country where entry is being made. A V Birla Group, for example, has set up most of its new ventures as green-field projects (except for a Polish buyout).

- The increasing desire of large Indian firms to achieve a critical scale of operation in the global context and participate in all the trading zones is quite clear from the fact that at the end of 1994, 524 joint ventures and 300 wholly-owned subsidiaries were either in operation or were at different stages of implementation. Indian companies are also locating their overseas activities in strategic locations that give them access to markets in Europe or in the North American Free Trade Agreement (NAFTA) region. For example, Arvind Mills has put up a denim plant in Mauritius from which it can easily access the European market. Similarly, a number of Indian companies are planning bases in Mexico that will open up doors to the NAFTA region (*Business India*, 1994; *Business World*, 1992).

Data on Indian companies show that when a domestic firm refocuses its strategy to defend against MNCs through pursuit of one or more of the above three strategic choices, certain patterns emerge.

Making pre-emptive investment

One of the approaches followed by a large domestic firm is making pre-emptive investments in new opportunity areas hitherto not opened to the private sector and where even MNCs have not invested due to policy restriction. For a developing country, one area that normally has long-term growth potential is the infrastructure sector where the scale of investment is generally very high. Large domestic firms having a good track record of performance and capacity to mobilize technology and funds can create entry barriers not only for other domestic firms but also for MNCs which are keen to enter this sector. The speed of action taken by domestic firms in this regard can outpace the MNCs. In India, infrastructure has been opened to the private sector only recently and large domestic firms and industrial houses such as Reliance Industries (turnover Rs.60 billion, i.e. US$1.7 billion) and Essar (turnover Rs.15 billion, i.e. US$430 million) have indicated their plans of making a number of infrastructural investments very quickly. Help of MNCs is being selectively sought for technical support as well as equipment supply, but the lever of control in the proposed new ventures shall remain with these firms. On the same basis, many other domestic firms in India are embarking on large-scale investments in a number of new fields and a study (*Business Today*, 1994) shows that during the first three years of reforms, as many as eighty projects were announced by Indian companies, each requiring a minimum investment of Rs.5 billion (i.e. US$143 million). The total investment in all such proposed projects, as estimated in the study, was close to Rs.1,850 billion (i.e. US$53 billion). While many of these projects are yet to take shape mainly due to funding constraints and procedural difficulties originating from the government of India, domestic Indian firms are fairly clear about the need for rapid implementation of these projects in order to gain pre-emptive market control.

Attaining critical size

While formulating the strategy to defend domestic position, a key concern of the local firm is to attain a critical size that is needed not only to face domestic or global competitors but also enhance bargaining power *vis-à-vis* suppliers of foreign technology and know-how. Size of the firm can act as an entry barrier to new aspirants and it enhances capability to mobilize resources at a rapid rate. Keeping in view the importance of size to combat competition and exploit new opportunities, domestic companies and industrial houses in India are working consciously to increase their size in terms of assets, turnover and profit through fresh investments and also going in for mergers and acquisitions. A study (*Business World*, 1995e) shows that as of 1995, twenty of the largest industrial houses in India had each an asset base between Rs.14 billion (i.e. US$400 million) and Rs.190 billion (i.e. US$5.5 billion). The list of these twenty major industrial houses and companies include only two MNC affiliates namely ITC Limited (in which BAT Industries, UK holds 32 per cent equity) and Hindustan Lever Limited (a subsidiary of Unilever). One interesting feature is that out of the top twenty industrial houses and companies that dominated the Indian industrial scenario in 1976, ten have lost their position to newly emerging Indian groups such as Reliance Industries (petro-chemical and textile), Essar (steel, oil and shipping), RPG Enterprises (power, tyre, entertainment, etc.), Bajaj (automobile) and Mallyas (liquor and engineering), all of which are extremely ambitious and are in a hurry to move up the ladder as far as size of assets, turnover and profitability are concerned. MNCs need carefully to watch these new groups. Reliance Industries, owned by Ambani Group, which occupied sixty-seventh position two decades ago, is now the third largest industrial house having an asset base of over Rs.66 billion (i.e. US$1.9 billion) and turnover of Rs.60 billion (i.e. US$1.7 billion). The route to attain critical size rapidly is not restricted only to making investments in domestic projects or acquiring domestic firms. Ambitious Indian companies are also growing through overseas investments and international acquisitions, as has been seen in the cases of A V Birla Group, Essar, Arvind Mills and Ranbaxy.

Creating 'national,' brands

The importance of investing in brand and distribution networks for creating and sustaining competitive advantages is well known. Hamel and Prahalad (1994) cited many instances of how Japanese companies were able to dominate world trade and commerce by building layers of advantages, the most important of which was brand and distribution networks. According to them, Japanese companies understood quite early the importance of these two factors (in addition to cost and quality competitiveness) which their Western counterparts were slow to learn. Domestic firms of a developing country are fortunate to have these experiences of Japanese and Western companies properly documented and thus are in a position to use this learning while formulating their strategy to defend against MNCs. In India, for example, there is far more awareness today about the need to create brand equity than there was before the reforms were introduced in 1991. As MNCs such as Unilever, P&G, Revlon, Kellogg's, Whirlpool, ABB, etc. are stepping up their advertising and promotion budget to push new brands and strengthen existing ones, Indian companies are also rising to the occasion and committing resources to create their own brands and distribution networks. Even though the list of top advertisers in India is still dominated by affiliates or subsidiaries of MNCs, the picture is fast-changing as Indian firms are realizing the importance of brands in protecting domestic position and building international presence. BPL Group (turnover Rs.18 billion, i.e. US$500 million), which has a strong presence in the consumer appliance business (colour televisions, washing machines, refrigerators, etc.), has chalked out a plan to spend Rs.2 billion (i.e. US$60 million), 11.4 per cent of turnover, in media buying alone to build and support its brands in the face of rising competition from MNCs such as Whirlpool, Electrolux, Sony and Matsushita, all of which are planning major offensives in India. The same approach is increasingly being followed by other Indian companies and a recent study (*The Economic Times,* 1996) shows that the advertising business in India grew by a phenomenal 49.5 per cent in 1994–95 *vis-à-vis* a very high rate of growth of 37 per cent achieved during the previous two years. With increasing urbanization and consumerism and opening up a number of private and public sector television channels (at present there are more than forty channels compared to only one national network owned by the government of India before the reforms started), a clear trend is already visible among domestic firms in India to make investments for creating and strengthening brands. The aim is not just to protect the domestic position but also to create an 'Indian' brand. There are already some success stories among Indian brands which have occupied important international positions in such areas as moulded luggage (VIP Industries), whisky (UB Group), small capacity boilers (Thermax), two-wheelers (Bajaj Auto), rayon fibre (A V Birla Group) and denim (Arvind Mill). While a lot still needs to be done by Indian domestic firms to improve quality, cost and customer services in addition to making investments in creating brand equity and strengthening distribution networks, it is clear that domestic firms need not go through a long learning process to understand the importance of brands in defending against MNCs.

Exploiting national competitive advantage

Every country has certain competitive advantages and disadvantages defined in terms of factor condition, demand condition, existence of related and supporting industries and strategy, structure and rivalry among the domestic firms (Porter, 1990). While a certain level of national competitive advantage is a must for achieving a strong international position in a particular field, it depends ultimately on the domestic firms to take the initiative in spotting and seizing new opportunities in areas where the nation has an advantage. Such firms can defend against MNCs by exploiting the competitive advantages of the nation and also overcoming its disadvantages by tapping the resources available overseas. Indian companies, in their desire to become internationally competitive, are now following this twin route. For example, many domestic firms are resorting to importing capital goods as well as raw materials and components, whenever needed, to achieve the desired level of competitiveness. Imports by India are now rising in dollar terms at the rate of around 30 per cent per annum, implying a pressure on the country's balance of payment position, but the good news is that the bulk of the imports are taking place in the areas of capital goods and raw materials which indicates the domestic firms' intention of improving the competitiveness of their operations by overcoming India's selective disadvantages. While tapping the advantages of other countries, these firms are also using Indian advantages in such areas as low-cost labour, availability of technical and scientific manpower, fairly developed supporting industries and the existence of a large domestic market. There is a greater awareness today to set up overseas ventures (wholly owned as well as subsidiary) to tap the advantages of advanced countries and to use them as listening posts to understand and disseminate the competitive activities of global players. To facilitate this learning process and also to ensure the smooth flow of products and information across domestic and international outfits, companies such as Ranbaxy have designed appropriate organization and administrative systems and hired managers of different nationalities who are helping in realizing the advantages of both home and host countries in an effective manner.

Adopting internationally accepted best practices and augmenting core skills

Prior to liberalization, most domestic firms had neither the intention nor the compulsion to become internationally competitive. As a result, when liberalization put into motion the reforms process and MNCs invaded the domestic market with their superior products, technology, operating practices and marketing capabilities, domestic firms, not geared up to meet the challenges, were likely to be adversely affected. However, a high-performing firm having a clear intention to reposition itself in the deregulated regime, can adopt a different route and work out a blueprint to improve competitiveness and strategic posture. Such a blueprint invariably takes a global perspective and avoids an incremental approach. The emphasis is on leapfrogging to the best international practices, be it in operations, marketing or distribution and no time is lost in 'reinventing the wheel'. For example, leading firms in India are now taking professional help from international consultants such as McKinsey, Andersen Consulting, Coopers and Lybrand, KPMG Peat Marwick and Price Waterhouse to restructure their companies on international lines and adopt best practices wherever needed. Using the services of well-known international consultants is helping Indian firms access best international practices and benchmarks and also model their organizations and management systems in line with the latest global trends. A study (*Business Today*, 1995a) on the recent assignments handled by leading international consultants in India shows that McKinsey helped RPG Enterprises, the fifth largest industrial group in India with an asset base of over Rs.65 billion (i.e. US$1.8 billion), to restructure its business portfolio. The Industrial Finance

Corporation of India Ltd and Industrial Development Bank of India, which are large financial institutions, hired the services of Andersen Consulting and KPMG Peat Marwick respectively to reposition their organizations and acquire new competencies. The Tata Iron and Steel Company Ltd, the largest private sector steel company in India, took the services of Arthur D. Little to reposition the company in the highly competitive global steel industry (*Business India*, 1996). Arthur D. Little also helped Colour Television Manufacturers' Association in developing an action plan to defend against global brands such as Sony and Akai. IOCL took the help of Solomon Assocates Inc., USA, to evaluate its competitiveness in various operational areas *vis-à-vis* well-known international oil companies. Many Indian firms are divesting non-core activities to focus on a few select areas, where they have capabilities, in line with international trends and the concept of core competence developed by Prahalad and Hamel (1993). Some Indian companies are also putting up world-scale plants with international efficiency norms and in this effort, international consultants are providing the necessary information to facilitate leapfrogging to best operating practices. Easing restrictions on the import of capital equipment, technology, as well as raw materials and components, is also helping Indian firms to upgrade their competencies in general. Firms that are failing to see this need for leapfrogging to best operating practices will be slow to achieve international competitiveness and this will negate their efforts to defend against MNCs.

Effecting change in core values and improving quality of management

Another key effort on the part of domestic companies trying to defend against MNCs is to question the basic assumptions which dominated the mindset of the organization for a long period. The aim here is to effect a change to make the organization ready to face new realities. Central to this transformation process are efforts made to change the core values relating to quality and productivity, customer focus, people orientation, information sharing and learning. This, in other words, implies development of a new theory of business (Drucker, 1994). While current practices may have been successful in the past under a protected environment where international competition was not allowed to come in, customers were taken for granted and people were treated more as pawns rather than as a vital resource. Under the newly deregulated scenario, domestic firms need to question the relevance of long-held values. Without developing a set of fresh core values and effecting a transformation of the organization to the new mode, efforts to defend against MNCs, pursuing market-driven strategy and sharply focused relevant values will not be successful. Indian firms have already started realizing this and some of them are now redefining their core values as part of their overall strategy and organizational renewal process (*Business World*, 1995f).

Ranbaxy has sharply focused its corporate mission to become a research-driven international company, while A V Birla Group is trying to integrate its domestic and global operations by adopting a similar management structure, systems and practices, the aim being to build the same set of values across the organization while accepting the inherent assymetry that exists at different locations. On the whole, Indian firms are realizing that they not only need to improve the fundamentals of business and step up investments in technology, brand and distribution networks, but also alter the mindset and core values of the organization if the benefits of various initiatives undertaken are to be fully exploited. The number of in-company training and reorientation programmes is on the rise in leading Indian firms to effect this change in core values. One other key factor is the quality of the management team and its leadership that drive the efforts of the domestic firm to defend against MNCs. Needless to say, the quality of management is going to distinguish domestic firms that will be able successfully to defend their market position against MNCs from those who will not. With the passage of time, the scope and scale of the resource base of a company will become less important for success compared to how such resources are managed. A domestic firm needs to keep this particular issue in mind as it embarks on mobilizing new resources – be it funds, technology, brand or distribution networks. Reliance Industries, the largest private sector company in India, in its effort to drive to the future, has built up a high-quality team of young, multiskilled, globally oriented managers to lead the group (*Business Today*, 1995b). They have redesigned their organization and systems in a manner that encourages horizontal communication and empowerment of the front line. To upgrade the quality of management, the company is hiring managers of different nationalities with global-scale salary. Many managers are being trained in a six-month residential training programme at one of the business schools in India. In order to achieve its global ambition, the company is attracting the best talent from the domestic industry and is paying 15–20 per cent higher salaries than the industry average. Like Reliance, other leading industrial houses such as Tata, Bajaj, RPG Enterprises and Godrej have initiated moves to alter respective core values and upgrade the quality of management as part of their repositioning strategy.

▮ Role of the government

Whether a domestic firm will be successful in defending its market position by pursuing one or more of the strategies mentioned above ultimately will depend on the firm's own capability, but the government can play a key role in strengthening the efforts at the firm level. While it is accepted that the government should progressively move away from actual conduct of business, it must ensure that existing policies in various areas do not hinder large domestic firms becoming bigger and efficient. Increasing the scale and scope of operations at a rapid rate is a must to achieve world-scale economy and exploit technical, managerial and administrative competencies. The efforts of the US government during the 1960s and 1970s to restrict the size and growth of AT&T, GM, IBM, Xerox and Du Pont led to a decline of these companies in such areas as technology and product development (Ghoshal, 1995a). Governments of countries whose domestic firms are defending against MNCs must be aware of possible adverse implications of various policies they are formulating on efforts of domestic firms to achieve international competitiveness. The argument that allowing one or two domestic firms to become very big will mean lowering competition should not be used to tie the hands of domestic firms to expand and grow. Competitive pressures on such firms can still be maintained through the removal of entry barriers of all kinds, including allowing imports without giving any protection to domestic firms. Another role of the government in the same area is to withstand the pressure of international agencies to curb the influence of local large firms. From the point of view of MNCs, the presence of local large firms is not only an entry barrier but is also a potential threat since such firms will have a growing ability to retaliate internationally against offensive strategies initiated by MNCs in the domestic market. In addition to large industrial houses in the private sector, large Indian public sector companies such as IOCL, Steel

Authority of India Ltd, Oil and Natural Gas Commission and Bharat Heavy Electricals Ltd, have the technology, as well as managerial competence, to become global players. With the right governmental support and non-interference from the bureaucracy, these firms have the potential to become successful MNCs like any other large MNCs from advanced countries. Developing countries such as India are fortunate enough to have quite a few large companies in the private and public sector who are already pursuing strategic initiatives (referred to previously) to defend their domestic position. Favourable support from the governments of such countries, on the lines followed in Japan or South Korea (Porter, 1990) but without giving any protection, will go a long way to developing large and strong domestic firms. When this takes place, developing countries stand to gain in terms of higher bargaining power, so far as attracting FDI or importing foreign technology and know-how is concerned. It is high time that policy makers of developing countries reorient their thinking processes and attitudes towards large domestic firms and recognize that socioeconomic growth of a country comes, as observed by Nobel laureate Herbert Simon and echoed by Ghoshal (1995b), from its organizations. In today's context, the wealth of a nation is synonymous with the wealth of its organizations and to ensure that large domestic firms play their due role in the country's development, the government of a developing country must provide the required support. The government of India seems now to have understood this important requirement and recently proposed that it would delegate required managerial autonomy to nine leading public sector units of the country.

■ Managerial implications

This chapter gave an overview of MNC offensives and responses of large domestic firms to the same in the context of a liberalizing economy. It was argued that as MNCs step up their offensives to get a dominant position in the newly liberalized economy during the initial years of reforms, large domestic firms tend to adopt a defensive posture that is based on careful strategic thinking and driven by an ambition to dominate the domestic and global markets. The resourcefulness and commitment of large domestic firms to pursue this approach in response to MNC offensives are quite visible in the case of India.

Managers of both MNCs and large domestic firms should find the conclusions useful in formulating their respective strategies, particularly those operating in a newly liberalizing economy. Outlining the offensive strategies of MNCs, as well as defensive strategies of domestic firms, should help managers of such firms to assess moves and intentions of the opponents. MNCs, already facing growing competitive threats from domestic firms of Third World and newly-industrializing countries, will need to reassess their future strategic initiatives in the context of defensive moves by domestic firms. The focus of this article, in trying to specifically conceptualize the strategy of domestic firms in a newly-liberalizing economy such as India can be of special interest to those MNCs which are looking for such markets for rapid growth. Understanding the proactive and well thought out strategies of leading domestic firms of the host country will be a critical success factor for continued dominance of MNCs in the future. This chapter should help them in this effort.

Managers of domestic firms will also have a difficult time unless they are able to gauge correctly the various 'offensives' that are likely to be initiated by incoming MNCs, including the rationale thereof, and develop a set of strategic moves that not only neutralizes the new competitive threats but also dominates them in their aim to achieve a pre-emptive position in ongoing global market share battles. The identification of possible strategic options available to domestic firms during the early phase of reforms, as outlined in this chapter, should be handy to their managers in dealing with emerging competitive rivalry.

Although the chapter draws its evidence from the Indian context, applicability of the conclusions is expected to be wide since patterns and processes of liberalization in many developing countries tend to follow, by and large, similar routes. Specifically, MNCs planning to enter India will find significant information and references regarding the nature and scope of reforms that have already taken place in India and how foreign investors and companies, as well as large domestic firms in India, have responded during the past five years of reform.

■ Future research directions

In this chapter, two different but interrelated issues have been addressed – first the range of strategic options that are available to an MNC to exploit the opportunities available to it during the first few years of reforms initiated by the host country and factors that influence its choice process; the second issue is the nature of alternative strategic moves that can be made by the large domestic firms belonging to the host country and the patterns that underlie these options. Two related questions that can be taken up by future researchers in this field, are:

1 What kind of MNCs are likely to make offensive moves when an economy opens up for the first time and what relative influence will each of the factors, mentioned in Figure 24.1, have on their decisions in this regard?

2 What kind of domestic firms are likely to be successful against an MNC offensive during the first phase of reform and how can MNCs, entering for the first time into a newly liberalizing economy, identify such companies well in advance in order to chalk out a successful offensive strategy?

Both the incoming MNCs and existing domestic companies will benefit if the above two questions are researched against the back-drop of the findings of this chapter.

■ References

Business India (1994). Window to the World, 9–22 May, p. 68.
Business India (1996). The big comeback, 3–16 June 1996, 54–60.
Business Standard (1994). 5 July.
Business Today (1994). Managing mega projects, 22 August–6 September, 64–73.
Business Today (1995a). The firms, 7–21 July, 64–75.
Business Today (1995b). Inside Reliance, 7–21 September, 66–75.
Business Today (1996a). New management principles of partnering, 7–21 October, 91–101.
Business Today (1996b). 22 September–6 October
Business Today (1997a). Interview with Chairman of Foreign Investment Promotion Council, 7–21 February, p. 117.
Business Today (1997b). Economic indices, 7–21 March 1997, p. 70.
Business Today (1997c). Will M&A be GE Cap's real assets? 7–21 February, 42–3

Business World (1992). Global gambit, 29 December 1992–11 January 1993, 36–41

Business World (1995a). Samsung sets its sights on India, 18–31 October 1995, 60–2.

Business World (1995b). Lakme adds on international tint, 29 November–12 December, 56–7.

Business World (1995c). The scent of Daewoo's dollars, 31 May–13 June, 58–60.

Business World (1995d). The Koreans are coming, and how, 6–19 September, p. 123.

Business World (1995e). Clans in crisis, 24 August–6 September, 22–34.

Business World (1995f). Stepping out, 3–16 May, 44–51.

Business World (1997). A new beaker for multinational R&D, 1–15 March.

Das, R. (1993). Case Series on BOC India Ltd.

Davidson, W. H. (1985). The location of foreign investment activities: country characteristics and experience effects. *Journal of International Business Studies*, **16**, Summer, 5–21.

Drucker, P. F. (1994). The theory of business. *Harvard Business Review,* September–October, 95–104.

Dunning, J. A. (1993), *The Globalization of Business – The Challenge of 1990s.* Routledge, 295–6.

The Economic Times (1993a). 23 March, p. 9.

The Economic Times (1993b). Should industry fear MNCs? 22 October.

The Economic Times (1994a) Corporates jump on the multinational bandwagon to prevent getting waylaid, 21 July.

The Economic Times (1994b). 12 August.

The Economic Times (1994c). 20 September.

The Economic Times (1994d). Stepping aside, 29 September.

The Economic Times (1996). Sixth A&M agency report, 4 January, p. 13.

The Economist (1994). The global economy, 1 October.

Ghoshal, S. (1987). Global strategy: an organizing framework. *Strategic Management Journal*, **8**, 425–40.

Ghoshal, S. (1995a). Role of the large firms in liberalized economy. *The Economic Times,* 23 September.

Ghoshal, S. (1995b). Knowledge is the critical resource. *The Strategist Quarterly,* October–December.

Hamel, G. and Prahalad, C. K. (1989). Strategic intent. *Harvard Business Review,* May–June, 63–76.

Hamel, G. and Prahalad, C. K. (1994). *Competing for the Future.* Harvard Business School Press.

Hill, C. W. L., Hwang, P. and Kim, C. (1990). An eclectic theory of choice of international entry mode. *Strategic Management Journal*, **11**, 117–28.

Killing, P. J. (1992). How to make a global joint venture work? *Harvard Business Review*, **60**, May–June, 120–7.

Naisbitt, J. (1995*). Megatrends: The Eight Asian Megatrends That Are Changing the World.* Nicholas Brearly.

Pike, F. (1996). The new Government: a foreigner's view. *Business India,* 17–30 June, 96–7.

Porter, M. (1990). *The Competitive Advantage of Nations.* Macmillan, 69–78.

Prahalad, C. K. and Hamel, G. (1993). The core competence of the corporation. *Harvard Business Review*, **68** (3), 79–91.

Ring, P. S., Lenway, S. A. and Govekar, M. (1990). Management of political imperatives in international business. *Strategic Management Journal,* **11**,141–51.

Root, R. R. (1987). *Entry Strategies for International Markets.* DC Heath.

Rosenzweig, P. (1994). The new 'American challenge': foreign multinationals in the United States. *California Management Review,* Spring, 107–23.

Chapter 24.1

India's post-crisis business environment and the strategies of domestic firms

■ Ranjan Das ■

The Asian financial crisis, experienced during the last full year, has turned into a region-wide recession. While Indonesia, Thailand, Korea and Malaysia were most affected and recorded negative growth during the first half of 1998, the growth of Japan, China and Hong Kong has either stagnated or slowed down. Russia and Brazil are the latest countries to fall prey to the after-effects of the Asian financial crisis (also see Chapter 3.1).

India, unlike other Asian countries, has not been affected as adversely as initially feared. While Paul Krugman of MIT termed it 'lucky' during the course of the speech he delivered at the National Management Convention held in Calcutta on 18 September 1998, the reality is that Indian policy-makers consciously adopted a number of conservative approaches over the last few years that turned out to be beneficial when the crisis erupted. Examples of such policies were: putting limits on total external borrowings and specifying the end uses of such foreign loans; ensuring that banks are not overly exposed to real-estate investments and stock markets; maintaining current account deficits within 1.5 per cent to 1.8 per cent of gross domestic product (GDP); and not opting for full convertibility in spite of international pressures and the partial floating of the Indian currency with periodic intervention by the Reserve Bank of India as needed. India's low level of exports, expressed as a percentage of its GDP, also helped in the sense that while the Southeast Asian crisis was triggered by the poor export performance of concerned countries, India was not affected as she was less export dependent.

The performance of the Indian economy during the last three years is, however, a matter of concern with GDP growth declining to 5.1 per cent during 1997–98. While GDP growth during 1998–99 is expected to improve to around 6.5 per cent, it is still below the minimum level of 8 per cent to 9 per cent required to make the Indian economy vibrant. Exports as a percentage of GDP have been hovering between 9.1 per cent and 9.7 per cent from 1995–96 to 1997–98. Exports to the Association of South East Asian Nations (ASEAN) and South Asian Association for Regional Co-operation (SAARC) countries declined during 1997–98, but exports to other trading blocs such as the Commonwealth of Independent States (CIS), North American Free Trade Agreement (NAFTA), European Union (EU), Organization for Economic Co-operation and Development (OECD) and the Organization of Petroleum-Exporting Countries (OPEC) have improved. As against this, imports from all the trading blocs, except OPEC, improved during 1997–98 *vis-à-vis* 1996–97. In general, imports were 13.1 per cent to 13.6 per cent of GDP from 1995–96 to 1997–98.

The current account deficit was contained at the level of 1.5 per cent to 1.8 per cent of GDP, but the gross fiscal deficit rose to as high as 8 per cent during 1997–98, clearly indicating the Government of India's continuing inability to reduce its expenditure. On the monetary front, the Government of India has been able to control liquidity levels, soften interest rates and generally contain inflation (except during the second half of 1997–98). Foreign currency reserves also improved in recent months and stood at over US$25 billion at the end of September 1998. The inflow of foreign direct investment (FDI) at US$3.2 billion during 1997–98, though an improvement over the 1996–97 level, was still insignificant compared to the US$38 billion received by China and the total FDI flow to developing countries of US$120 billion.

How does the future look so far as India is concerned? India needs to do a lot in terms of opening up her economy, unlocking all under-performing assets belonging to the public sector units through disinvestments and extensive reforms, drastically cutting down government expenditures, and improving the physical and social infrastructures by a substantial degree. While India's large domestic market, English-speaking population, decent and impartial legal system, and institutionalization of democracy as the country's political system are positive features, the pace of economic and administrative reforms and the quality of infrastructure are out of line with the requirements of international business. The lack of political consensus on the direction and pace of reforms and the inability to access foreign funds at the level that China could do remain India's biggest problems. However, given the fact that India is not severely affected either by the recent Asian financial crisis or sanctions imposed in the wake of nuclear tests, there are some signs that the long-term attractiveness of the Indian economy may not be depressed. A recent foreign-currency bond issued by the State Bank of India successfully fetched over US$4 billion. HSBC Securities has of late upgraded India's asset allocation from 11 per cent to 17 per cent and downgraded Hong Kong from 48 per cent to 42 per cent. Morgan Stanley Dean Witter's Research team has identified India as the 'relative outperformer' of the Asia Pacific region and observed that India is 'operating under normal circumstances unlike most other Asian economies'. Foreign investors are taking renewed interests in India and there are indications that they are turning bullish on India again. On the whole, it appears that a general impression is gaining ground that while India may not be moving fast enough in undertaking reforms and improving its infrastructure, she may still be able to grow at the rate of 6 per cent and above (in sharp contrasts to the negative growth of several countries) by virtue of her adopting the slow-and-steady principle.

Chapter 24 takes a look at multinational corporation (MNC) offensives and also the defensive strategies adopted by domestic firms, and proposes two frameworks that explain strategic initiatives undertaken by such firms. The chapter also makes a series of observations indicating patterns or rationales underlying the defensive strategies adopted by the domestic companies. The conclusions and framework provided in the chapter do not, however, relate to specific macroeconomic, political and industry contexts in which such firms operate or are likely to operate. This being so, the conclusions of the chapter, published initially in late 1997, continue to remain applicable even after the recent Asian financial crisis. However, certain additional observations can be made regarding the likely impact of the recent developments on some of the factors referred to in the chapter. These are:

1 So far as MNC offensives are concerned, two of the key factors that influence such offensives, 'Risk profile of the host country' and 'Future scenarios' have undergone significant changes during the period under reference. There is more uncertainty on both these fronts and, as a result, the intensity of fresh MNC offensives in the Asian region, over the next twelve months or so, is likely to be lower. Many MNCs may like to wait and to watch for some time before undertaking fresh offensives. However, the situation in the case of India may be different in the sense that India has not been affected as adversely as other Asian countries (for the reasons stated before) and, as a result, MNCs may continue to find India as attractive as before and maintain their offensive stances. This will mean that domestic Indian companies will have to be alert and also protect themselves against attempted takeovers by foreign companies: it is well known that Indian companies are traditionally undervalued.

2 Large domestic firms are likely to perceive the Asian financial crisis as an opportunity to strengthen their 'defensive' strategies. Specifically, for companies belonging to India (that has experienced to a lesser degree the impact of the Asian financial crisis), there is an opportunity to acquire modern technology and plant and machinery from countries like South Korea, at a comparatively lower cost, and use the same to reposition and to rejuvenate their respective companies. There is also an opportunity for such firms to go 'global' through acquiring companies in countries like Malaysia and South Korea whose currencies have depreciated sufficiently enough to make such acquisitions attractive. There are, of course, two negative fall-outs (a) exports from these large domestic Indian companies to Asian countries undergoing the current financial crisis are likely to become non-competitive, and (b) there is every likelihood that these Indian companies will face 'dumping' from the countries whose currencies have depreciated significantly and whose need to earn foreign exchange is extreme.

3 As a result of the Asian financial crisis, there will be a surge in merger and acquisition (M&A) activities in Asian countries over the next three to four years. According to a recent McKinsey report, a huge US$60 billion is expected to be involved in M&A and corporate restructuring activities in the Asian region, of which India will account for US$8 billion. Seventy per cent of these US$60 billion will be spent through local companies in Asia, implying that domestic Indian companies will be undertaking M&A and corporate restructuring as well as globalizing in a major way over the next three to four years.

4 In Chapter 24, a brief reference has been made to the role of the governments of the developing countries in making their large national firms more competitive. Under the changed scenarios, the governments of developing countries will need to act much faster, not in terms of giving more protection to domestic companies, but rather in helping such companies to capitalize on the opportunities referred to in 2 above, so that by the time things clear up, large domestic firms are ready not only to defend but also to take position in overseas market segments where the MNCs

have significant market share. National governments can and should do a lot to help their domestic companies in their efforts to become powerful global players.

As mentioned, the findings of Chapter 24 remain applicable even after the Asian financial crisis but the above observations provide additional perspectives incorporating the impact of the crisis. The update also gives an overview of how India has responded.

Part Seven

Local governments' strategies

Chapter 25

Electricity industry reform: a case analysis in Australia[1]

■ Lindsay Nelson and Peter J. Dowling ■

■ Introduction

Electricity supply industry (ESI) deregulation is taking place throughout the world, where typically public monopolistic ownership is being replaced by a privatized system in which previously vertically integrated functions have been disaggregated and competition introduced. Although deregulation appears to be a product of the late 1980s, the idea of substituting competition for the regulation of utilities with a natural monopoly was argued some years ago by Demsetz (1968). Under deregulation it is assumed that marketplace competition provides sufficient controls to replace regulation.

Electricity is already privatized, or privatization is being considered in twenty-nine countries (Victorian Government, 1995: 4). In the USA, electricity has for many years been dominated by large regionally based, vertically integrated utilities, mostly privately owned. New rules contained in the Energy Policy Act 1992 encourage competition by obliging existing companies to give newcomers access to existing transmission grids. In some quarters it is thought that these changes could take years to clear the appeal courts, (*The Economist*, 1993) leading to speculation whether the prospect of free competition is entirely welcomed by the players. Debate is currently about whether competition in the wholesale market is being limited by the fact that the industry is still vertically integrated and the utility is the sole purchaser of electricity and major supplier of generation within its allotted area (Lewis and Besser, 1995).

The USA started reform from a position of private ownership, but in the UK where the electricity industry was nationalized, things could not have been more different. Following the announcement of plans to privatize electricity in 1988, the industry was completely reorganized within three years. Yet, as Yarrow (1991) observes, with many

---

[1] This chapter has been published previously by MCB University Press Limited: Nelson, L. and Dowling, P. J. (1998). Electricity industry reform: a case analysis in Australia. *Journal of Organizational Change Management*, **11** (6), 481–95.

issues to be resolved by government, its original privatization objectives of depoliti-cizing decision-making in the industry seem unlikely to be achieved. In the restruc-tured industry, vertical integration was abandoned in favour of four separate functions: generation, transmission, distribution and supply.

Critics say that privatization in the UK was inspired not by public disquiet but a polit-ical agenda (Parker, 1997) and carried out with indecent haste, leading to undervalued assets and predatory foreign investors (Cory and Lewis, 1997). They also raise the issue of whether privatization has really delivered expected efficiencies and consumer benefits. Typical problems associated with privatization in the UK experience are excessive shareholder profits, the need for effective competition and the problem of takeovers (Parker, 1997). The latter point appears to negate the philosophy of compe-tition. On the positive side, costs appear to have been reduced throughout the UK according to Burton (1997).

In Australia, the development of electricity infrastructure and retail supply has tradi-tionally been the responsibility of state governments. Following overseas trends, however, the states moved to restructure the electricity industry in the early 1990s, with a view to lowering costs and enhancing efficiency. Included in the changes mooted was a plan to form a national electricity grid in 1991 (Office of State Owned Enterprises, 1994: 4). These moves were given greater impetus in 1993 with the release of a report on competition and subsequent agreement in 1995 by all Australia's states to implement a national competition policy (Government Prices Oversight Commission, 1996: 4). Experience overseas, outlined above, indicates that there is no single, preferred model for the electricity industry or how it should operate, which helps to explain the fact that there is variation between states in Australia.

However, reforms in Australia differ only in detail. The traditional role of government appears to have changed course from one of providing infrastructure for broadly based social as well as economic development, to that of pursuing narrowly defined financial returns for the enterprise and its private or public shareholders. The mecha-nism for achieving this goal is making provision for competition, in the belief that this will also benefit consumers by keeping prices down. These changes have in most cases involved restructuring away from vertical and horizontal integration and a preference for private over public ownership. This follows trends in other countries such as the USA and UK. Similar to experience from overseas there is growing evidence of con-sumer concerns which, it is claimed, are being neglected (Johnston, 1995: 35). Benvenuti and Walker (1995), Walker (1995) and the Federal Bureau of Consumer Affairs (1995) document other examples of consumer issues. Power blackouts in New Zealand and Queensland in 1998 have added to disquiet over the prospect of further privatization.

Such concerns have led to the creation of control mechanisms to regulate the industry and to establish an ombudsman in some states (Victorian Government, 1995: 12–17). These wider contextual factors converge in the following discussion which deals with the subject of the case study, referred to as TasElec.

TasElec was created in 1914 when the state government of Tasmania took over a pri-vately owned company which had been attempting to build a hydroelectric scheme in the central highlands, and appointed an engineer, as its chief executive (Read, 1986: 35). Over the ensuing seventy years a number of dams were constructed to produce hydroelectricity by exploiting a combination of abundant rainfall and rugged terrain. In doing so it became a large, powerful organization in an age when Tasmania, along with other states in Australia, clung to the belief that industrialization would follow from having ample supplies of electricity. Davis (1995) calls this the myth of hydro-industrialization. Relying on heavy borrowings to finance the construction of dams and power stations, it incurred large debts which account for about 40 per cent of its expenses (Government Prices Oversight Commission, 1996: 25–6).

During the 1970s, however, TasElec was challenged over (natural) environmental issues connected with flooding a lake and, later, the proposed damming of a river. Increasing confrontation over the environment and debt burdens combined to start reforms aimed at bringing accountability and a commercial focus to the organization. Nevertheless, TasElec's public image was not good; some idea of the fall from grace and eroded credibility of the utility may be gained from sentiments such as the following: 'the past abuse of monopoly power by the [organization] is legendary. For decades it controlled much of the economic agenda of the State and, when it felt it was necessary for its own good, deliberately undermined Ministers and Governments' (Kohl, 1994: 1).

In the aftermath of these problems, which climaxed in the mid-1980s, the existing chief executive – an engineer – was not reappointed but was replaced with someone from outside, a pattern which has continued.

By this time events related to ESI deregulation and competition were overtaking TasElec, obscuring its immediate history of confrontation. Reforms completed in 1995 removed much of its power. From mid-1998 it was disaggregated into three separate companies in preparation for privatization. The most significant changes, however, took place in the preceding six years when TasElec reduced its staff from over 5000 to about 1600 and undertook change to bring about the commercial orientation demanded as a preliminary to privatization. The management of these changes known as 'commercialization' is the focus of this chapter.

▦ Methodology

Case studies are a form of field research but should not be thought of as a subset of other research strategies such as experiment; according to Yin (1989: 28) case studies should not be confused with the flawed one-shot post-test-only design as a quasi-experimental design. The case study, Yin (1989) goes on to say, is now recognized as a separate research strategy having its own research designs.

Case studies comprise a single unit analysis based upon depth that is both holistic and exhaustive (Ball, 1996: 75–6), which retains the meaningful characteristics of realistic events. Thus a case study as defined by Yin (1994: 13) is an empirical inquiry that:

- investigates a contemporary phenomenon within its real-life context; especially when
- the boundaries between phenomenon and context are not clearly evident.

In the present study, the purpose is not to examine the particular effects of deregulation and competition on TasElec compared with organizations in other parts of

Australia or further afield. Instead, the aim is to treat deregulation and competition as simply the catalyst of change in which the focus is on management issues erupting from a combination of Yin's (1989) criteria for single cases. TasElec was required to meet the challenge of moving from a public utility to a corporate entity, thence through disaggregation with a view to being privatized. On the first of Yin's (1989) criteria, this can be seen as a critical case for testing theory. Second, on several grounds this represents an extreme or unique case. The uniqueness stems not so much from economic theory underpinning competition as the historical and other contextual ingredients of the situation. The main component of uniqueness arises from the central part TasElec formerly played in Tasmania's vision of economic development and the philosophy of hydro-industrialization followed by successive governments. Third, this is a revelatory case in so far as given the juxtaposition of historical factors and the relatively closed environment of TasElec, it has not previously been accessible to investigation. Finally, an embedded research design was selected, enabling units of analysis within the organization to be examined.

Interviews were conducted with twenty-five existing managers and key people associated with implementing the commercialization. Two former chief executives and three retired senior engineers were also included. In addition, five former employees who played significant roles in the commercialization were located and agreed to be interviewed. Finally, four outside consultants who were engaged to assist with change processes were also interviewed. These interviews were of between 45 minutes and one hour in duration. In some cases they were supplemented with follow-up interviews to clarify certain points as questions arose. Interviews were audiotaped and written transcripts produced for computer analysis.

Documentary evidence was gathered from several sources. Internally, TasElec made available records such as statistical data, annual reports, in-house newsletters and certain other information as required. Access to the organization's library was freely available. From external sources, former employees allowed personal documents to be copied. Historical evidence was gathered from newspaper records, parliamentary records and newspaper clippings of parliamentary proceedings.

◼ Change theory

Leifer (1989) sees change as normal and simply a natural response to environmental and internal conditions, arguing that change is consistent with open systems in which learning occurs and describes the stable state as a myth. On this basis, all organization theory, through the classical, human relations and contingency periods, is connected with change. Dunphy (1996), who regards these periods as early attempts to understand change, supports this view.

The scale of change varies from small to great, variously termed incremental or fine-tuning to transformational, radical, revolutionary or frame-breaking (Dunphy and Stace, 1990; Nadler and Tushman, 1989; Tushman, Newman and Romanelli, 1986; Tushman and Romanelli, 1985). The question of the magnitude of change is taken up by Greenwood and Hinings (1996: 1024) in the context of institutional theory, who draw a distinction between convergent and radical change on the one hand and revolutionary and evolutionary change on the other. Where the former varies from fine-tuning (convergent) to frame-bending (radical), the latter is defined by temporal factors stretching from swift change affecting all parts of the organization simultaneously (revolutionary) to slow, gradual change (evolutionary). This permits the possibility of having massive change but over an extended time frame, whereas it might have been assumed that massive change was necessarily over only a short time period. On this basis, change at TasElec can be placed at the radical end of the scale. Although not entirely clear from Greenwood and Hinings (1996), change at TasElec may be regarded as evolutionary since the time scale extends from about 1988 for some years, even though the principal commercialization processes took place from 1992 onwards. One of the most significant points to be increasingly recognized is that static models of organizations are being displaced by dynamic models, but which also reflect the discontinuous nature of organizational change (Fombrun, 1992; Greenwood and Hinings, 1988; Pettigrew, 1985). Periods of incremental change sandwiched between more violent periods contributed to the illusion of stability once taken for granted. Romanelli and Tushman (1994) develop this idea further in their punctuated equilibrium model of organizational transformation. These developments in theory suggest limitations to contingency approaches which carry the assumptions of static models of change. Dawson (1994), for example, mentions several difficulties with contingency theory and points out empirical evidence which appears to be at odds with the Dunphy and Stace (1990) model of change. He sums up the main problems with contingency theory being the tendency to impose unidirectional rational models on what is a complex and dynamic process (Dawson, 1994: 22).

The what and how of change, although implied in early change theories going back to Lewin (1951) appear to have developed side by side. Rajagopalan and Spreitzer (1997) note the lack of empirical or theoretical synergy between content and process schools, and propose an overarching framework to bring them together. Having made their point regarding a lack of synergy, it may be a little unfair not to point out that contextualists do in fact also recognize the content or substance of change (Dawson, 1994; Pettigrew, 1985). Contextualists would argue that the critical factor is what happens to content as change processes unfold. Returning to Rajagopalan and Spreitzer (1997), however, they suggest an integrative model, fusing rational, learning and cognitive approaches into what they term a multi-lens framework. Pertinent to the present study is that their framework hinges upon not just a fusion of approaches, but also the need to adjust managerial behaviour during the change process.

According to Dunphy the strategic approach to change is the dominant model at present, using the: 'metaphor of a marketplace where organizations are acting as purposive competitors, with flexibility, adaptation and innovation being increasingly critical to their success (Dunphy, 1996: 825). In assessing the strategic model he points out that although the rationalistic version was criticized, strategic change can also be emergent and adaptive, suggesting that both versions may be true. Dunphy (1996) goes on to admit, however, that there is no single unified theory and in evaluating several approaches to organizational change outlines three main types. First, there are those who advocate the one best way such as Peters and Waterman (1982), and Beer, Eisenstat and Spector (1990); second, there are contingency models which hold that several avenues of change are available (Dunphy and Stace, 1990; Nutt 1989; Stace and Dunphy, 1994; Strebel, 1992) and third, there are the contextualists who argue that because each organization is unique interventions must be handcrafted (Pettigrew, 1985, 1990, 1992).

In viewing organizations as purposive (Dunphy, 1996) it follows that management exercises a level of control and direction over change. An intriguing question is whether change is controlled externally or from within. Explanatory theories and their underlying metaphors, it seems, can be attached to both. Although there seem to be no universally accepted classification of change theories, there are areas of general similarity. Van de Ven and Poole (1995) in their examination of processes of change, distinguish between life cycle, evolution, dialectic and teleological theories, proposing that the interplay between them produces a wide variety of more complex theories of change and development. Narayanan and Nath (1993) on the other hand, describe six: life cycle, population ecology, innovation, planned change, resource dependence and institutional theory of imitation.

From these exemplars can be detected representative positions which are commonly found: life cycle and evolution, for example, emphasize the powerful impact of the external environment on organizations. On the other hand, approaches such as innovation and teleological focus on internal aspects. This bifurcation concerns not just whether the source of change is external or internal, but the extent to which the organization itself is able to exercise control. If, for example, the metaphor of evolution is accepted this means that the environment selects organizations which are themselves powerless to change (Morgan, 1986).

Taking what Pettigrew (1990) calls a holistic approach, strategic change processes need to be understood in terms of content, context and processes but not as the rational linear model often assumed due to a myriad of other social and political variables which impact on change strategies but which are overlooked by this latter model (Whipp, Rosenfeld and Pettigrew, 1988). Further, as argued by Morgan (1986), we should think of causal loops not straight-line causation. Taking this a stage further could be the need not just to use the contextualist's methodology in analysing change, but also to apply it as a map in implementing change.

The contextualist framework employed by Pettigrew (1985) and developed by Dawson (1994, 1996) permits change to be visualized as dynamic rather than static, having a temporal setting and which has multiple causes acting as loops rather than simple lines. This enables change to be understood as a discontinuous phenomenon having the benefits, without the limitations, of rational contingency models. The essential features of this approach are contained in Figure 25.1, adapted from Dawson (1996) who conceptualizes the determinants of change as context, politics and substance:

1   *The substance of change.* This can be thought of as the content or the 'what' of change. In the present chapter this is represented by the actions of both state and commonwealth governments to reform the electricity industry.

2   *The politics of change.* This refers to the exercise of power over and within the organization. It includes activities such as consultation, negotiation, conflict and resistance. The sources may be external or internal.

3   *The context of change.* This involves linkages between temporal variables in the external and internal environment. The internal environment include the six areas listed in Figure 25.1. These contextual variables, however, should not be seen in isolation from other processes. As pointed out by Pettigrew (1985: 36), crucial to the contextualist approach is the interplay between variables in the vertical analysis

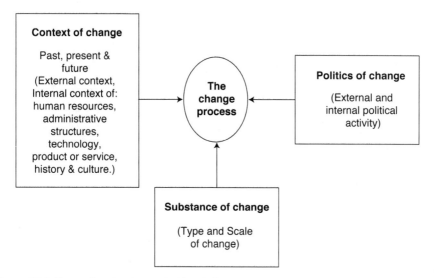

Figure 25.1 Determinants of organizational change
Source: Adapted from Dawson (1996): 65.

(inner and outer environments) and processes under observation in the horizontal (temporal) analysis.

Case study: TasElec

Analysing this case ahistorically, deregulation could be seen as the starting point, but this would divorce events from their temporal and contextual realities. The preceding years, when a vision of hydro-industrialization was pursued, should not be ignored because of the controversy and changes they precipitated. Whilst the focal point here is the change known as commercialization, the case study illustrates how strategies need to be handcrafted and adjusted as change processes unfold. The following analysis is grouped under the areas listed in Figure 25.1, but it should be remembered that substance, context and politics interact holistically.

The substance of change

For political reasons relating to (natural) environmental controversy, the direction of TasElec was transformed in the mid-1980s. The dam-building era ended but only after intervention by the Commonwealth Government and the High Court of Australia (see Davis, 1982; Gee, 1994; Montgomery, 1993). The immediate effects were a dramatic loss of staff as existing projects reached completion and the need for a redirected vision to replace that of hydro-industrialization (see Davis, 1995).

TasElec entered a period of uncertainty as governments grappled with swiftly moving global trends stemming from a minimalist state approach to competition and market forces. In this climate, the government, as owner of TasElec, wanted an increased return on investment, particularly in view of the large debts trailing over from previous borrowings for power schemes. Simultaneously, the responsible minister seemed

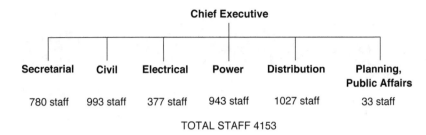

Figure 25.2 Organizational structure, 1988 (traditional)

determined to decrease the sweeping powers enjoyed by TasElec to set the agenda on power policies and their implementation.

The first wave of reforms brewed from this time and culminated in 1995 with Acts of Parliament corporatizing TasElec, controlling its governance, and removing its powers in respect of the ESI policy, planning, regulation and pricing. This brought a measure of accountability to TasElec which had been missing since its inception in 1914. In spite of disquiet in Parliament going back some forty years, over TasElec's excessive use of its powers, it took a major crisis to bring about these changes – changes which, incidentally, were strongly resisted by TasElec, which first ignored complaints raised by outsiders, and then conducted open campaigns to fight proposed changes while simultaneously not co-operating with official inquiries such as the 1974 Lake Pedder Committee of Enquiry (1974).

Up to 1987, TasElec had a structure virtually unchanged (see Figure 25.2); then new structures were imposed as construction work was phased out and staff numbers depleted. The commercialization structure is shown in Figure 25.3, but still further iterations were effected up to 1998 (see Figure 25.4) immediately before the present disaggregation.

As worldwide ESI trends clarified, strategies for introducing competition in Australia took shape and commercialization was introduced in 1992. The vehicle for this was to establish a new TasElec in parallel with the old and appoint staff on the basis of merit and needs of the metamorphosed organization. A change management team was estab-

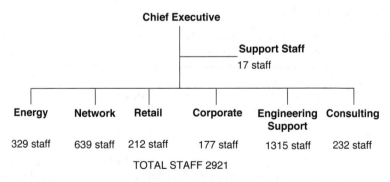

Figure 25.3 Organizational structure, 1992 (commercialization)

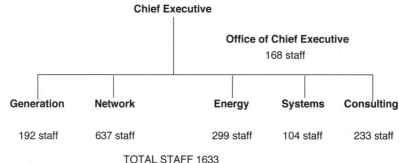

Figure 25.4 Organizational structure, 1998

lished along with a series of transition teams to assist in the transformation. At the same time, change processes which included restructuring, efficiency reviews and total quality management (TQM) programmes were commenced to spearhead change. Redundancies, which began in 1989 as the construction of the last power schemes reached completion, continued under commercialization. Displaced employees were offered early retirement, depending on age, or declared redundant. The thrust and focus of change was to set up and work towards commercial goals, as expressed in this mission statement: 'We're in the electricity business. We are to give our customers high quality, competitive services, sensitive to our environments and profitable for Tasmania.'

The substance of change thus represented a major challenge to co-ordinate and to control a number of strategies at the same time. Importantly, to think of commercialization as a single cause in isolation from the multiple causation of past events and traumas is to underestimate the complexity of the task facing management. To succeed in the commercialization changes, therefore, TasElec needed to take into account both present and historical factors converging as causal loops. The fact that only 23 per cent of existing staff were around at the time of commercialization suggests that management achieved a reorientation to business values more by changing people than changing culture. As a result, TasElec lost skills and corporate memory it could ill afford to lose. Consequently, a number of former employees were brought back as consultants to write procedural manuals for guiding recently appointed, inexperienced staff.

The politics of change

External politics in this case were marked by a turnaround from wilful indifference by political leaders to concerns raised by the public before 1980, to barely concealed hostility towards TasElec top management during the 1980s. Tensions and undercurrents continued after the removal of the last civil-engineer CEO in 1987 and his replacement by an outsider. At the time when TasElec was given commercial goals, it seems paradoxical that the relationship between the CEO and government should sour over interference, to the point where the CEO resigned. After years of political non-intervention, the government now gave TasElec a great deal of attention. History had overtaken commercialization: political tensions and interference had their genesis not so much in this critical period of change as in the remembered intransigence of TasElec during environmental confrontation of the 1980s.

In the mean time, within TasElec, staff were faced with two issues. The public one was to embrace change even if this meant turning their backs on an engineering heritage that had nurtured employees for decades. At the personal level, they were faced with trying to survive during a period of upheaval and sustained downsizing. Many blue-collar workers had no choice, but others could not adjust to the change in direction and chose early retirement or redundancy. It is this group that presents management problems during change transitions. It is easy to believe that TasElec was better off for having shed these staff, however, a widespread view of management today is that many of these people had skills and qualifications that should have been retained. Building on this point is the fact that a number of people used this period of flux to bolster their own situation by manoeuvring for the best positions in the new TasElec. For some, commercialization provided a lifeboat for survival whilst the real issues of change were ignored as much as possible.

Retrenchments were handled smoothly with the assistance of outside specialist consultants. A generous package and sensitive conduct of this phase helped to avert what could have been a major union-management confrontation. During the period of environmental controversy groups formed, comprising existing employees, former politicians and a former CEO, for the purpose of exerting pressure on government to proceed with unchecked further hydro development. However, once this battle was lost employees accepted the end of the dam-building era. Thus they had a period of several years to accept the idea of eventual job loss, only forestalled as existing construction work ran out. This was an important interim period which allowed staff to psychologically prepare for eventual retrenchment. Events therefore tended to assist management during what could have been an industrially difficult programme. However, downsizing seemed to dominate the attention of management, deflecting them from concentrating on other issues relevant to commercialization processes. Internal power and politics, for example, were allowed to occur unmoderated, as the best positions in the new TasElec were sought.

The context of change

These issues form part of the contextual milieu. Commercialization, as already pointed out, consisted of several programmes: downsizing, TQM, efficiency reviews, working in teams and a number of restructurings. All this was being conducted in a climate of political sensitivity, moving later to tension and hostility in the upper echelons of government and management. With the passage of time, commercialization lost momentum and collapsed. An internal blueprint guided the initial phases but there was no follow-up action to revitalize the programme or make adjustments in light of unfolding events. Just as contextual analysis insists that vertical levels (the inner and outer factors) and horizontal levels (temporal connections between past, present and future) be recognized (Pettigrew, 1985), then it is argued that similar factors need to be taken into account by management as change programmes progress. Had this been done, then momentum might not have been lost.

Momentum collapsed in two crucial areas. First, after the vision of hydro-industrialization disbanded, it was replaced with a vacuum. A business orientation, expressed in financial terms, did not represent a new vision. This is a matter of continuing unease among surviving managers, who seek a holistic expression of what TasElec is trying to achieve. This vacuum affected the sustainability of commercialization. Second, change was done in the name of competition but this was more rhetoric than reality because there are no signs of competitors entering the market. This is something over which management has no control and the problem becomes one of how best to maintain a level of enthusiasm and preparedness for battle in the face of a continuing *status quo*.

The penetration of change was patchy. In the first place it lacked drive to go down to the workplace level. The manager in charge of these changes reports that line managers lacked the people skills to achieve change effectively at the lower levels of the hierarchy in TasElec. In spite of undertaking a strong campaign of communication led by the CEO, management failed to ensure that rank and file workers understood what was happening and how they could translate higher level goals into their ordinary day-to-day work lives. Commercialization also failed to affect significantly some areas within TasElec. A separate repository was incorporated into the new structure to accommodate a group of civil engineers, who remained relatively untouched by change. They represented to many other managers within TasElec the last outpost of a past empire, but who managed to avoid being contaminated by commercial reality. Some other pockets, such as information technology, were also seen as élitist and leading protected lives. These perceptions were widespread and, whether entirely accurate or not, presented an issue senior management needed to recognize and face, even if it was uncomfortable.

Degrees of uncertainty during change processes are to be expected, but management fuelled cynicism and mistrust by focusing on the level of managers rather than ordinary workers as already mentioned. Telephone hot lines handled staff queries but this strategy needed reinforcing with a stronger effort to make direct contact with their employees. Moreover, instances occurred where, as in the case of a workshop, having been told that jobs would continue, workers found later that the entire work area would close.

■ Conclusions

This could be described as a classic instance of a static model being applied to change, resulting in the process getting bogged down and matters being allowed to drift along because they were not part of the original plan. It is clear from the case analysis that managers needed to adjust the master plan of change as issues and problems emerged. Instead, plans remained operational even when it became evident that modification was required. The handcrafting of change, therefore, needs regular reassessment and revitalization. This, it is argued, is a natural extension of Pettigrew's (1985) work and is one of the points made by Rajagopalan and Spreitzer (1997).

One of the major difficulties facing any organization contemplating change is the question of control over external variables. This is brought into sharp focus here, due to the fact of government ownership where issues related to control vacillated and, at the very time the organization needed some operational freedom, it was denied. In these circumstances the organization needs to exert every effort to take charge of its own destiny rather than allow the external environment to control the change. This is not just a reiteration of the strategic (Dunphy, 1996) or innovation (Daft, 1982, 1989, 1995) models of change, but more closely resembles the ideas expressed by Morgan (1986) in relation to autopoiesis. It seems evident that environmental forces can always be expected to impact on organizational plans for change, but the difficulty for management is to control the unfolding events as much as possible, as change progresses. A clear lesson from this analysis is the value of building sufficient forethought into any radical change. This shows retrospectively with TasElec in so far as its period of violent confrontation in the 1970s and 1980s could have been prevented had the framing legislation had adequate checks and balances to ensure it was held accountable. The same applies now in moving towards competition and privatization. If measures are not included beforehand to hold an organization accountable for its activities, then it could well prove extremely difficult to achieve this later.

▩ References

Ball, S. J. (1996). Case study. In *The Social Science Encyclopedia* (A. Kuper and J. Kuper, eds) 2nd edn, Routledge.

Beer, M., Eisenstat, R. and Spector, B. (1990). *The Critical Path to Corporate Renewal.* Harvard Business School Press.

Benvenuti, J. and Walker, D. (1995). *Switched Off: Case Studies of Consumers' Experiences with Energy and Water Utilities.* Consumer Advocacy and Counseling Association of Victoria.

Burton, N. (1997). A City View of the UK electricity supply industry. *Power Engineering Journal*, April, 51–7.

Cory, B. and Lewis, P. (1997). The reorganization of the electricity supply industry: a critical view. *Power Engineering Journal*, April, 42–6.

Daft, R. L. (1982). Bureaucratic versus nonbureaucratic structure in the process of innovation and change. In *Perspectives in Organizational Sociology: Theory and Research* (S. B. Bacharach, ed.) JAI Press.

Daft, R. L. (1989). *Organization Theory and Design*, 3rd edn. West.

Daft, R. L. (1995). *Organization Theory and Design*, 5th edn. West.

Davis, B. W. (1982). The Tasmanian parliament, accountability and the Hydro-Electric Commission: the Franklin River controversy. In *Parliament and Bureaucracy* (J. R. Nethercote, ed.) Hale and Irenmonger.

Davis, B. W. (1995). Adaptation and deregulation in government business enterprise: the Hydro-Electric Commission of Tasmania. *Australian Journal of Public Administration*, **54** (2), 252–61.

Dawson, P. (1994). *Organizational Change: A Processual Approach.* Paul Chapman.

Dawson, P. (1996). Beyond conventional change models: a processual perspective. *Asia Pacific Journal of Human Resources*, **34** (2), 57–70.

Demsetz, H. (1968). Why regulate utilities? *Journal of Law and Economics*, **11**, 55–65.

Dunphy, D. (1996). Corporate strategic change. In *International Encyclopedia of Business and Management* (M. Warner, Ed.) vol. 1., 822–28, Routledge

Dunphy, D. and Stace, D. (1990). *Under New Management: Australian Organizations in Transition.* McGraw-Hill.

The Economist (1993). America's electricity industry: when sparks fly. **326** (7799), 20 February, 68–9.

Federal Bureau of Consumer Affairs (1995). Utility reform – the consumer and the community. Conference proceedings, Royal Exhibition Building, Melbourne, 20 October.

Fombrun, C. J. (1992). *Turning Points.* McGraw Hill.

Gee, H. (1994). Lake Pedder. *Habitat Australia*, May, 8–10.

Government Prices Oversight Commission (1996). *Hydro-Electric Commission*

Retail Prices Investigation: Background Paper. Government Prices Oversight Commission.

Greenwood, R. and Hinings, C. R. (1988). Organizational design types, tracks and the dynamics of strategic change. *Organization Studies*, **9** (3), 293–316.

Greenwood, R. and Hinings, C. R. (1996). Understanding radical organizational change: bringing together the old and the new institutionalism. *Academy of Management Review*, **21** (4), 1022–54.

Johnston, C. (ed.) (1995). *Consumer Rights and Utilities*, Law Foundation of NSW.

Kohl, B. (1994). Local government as electricity retailers. Paper presented to *Electricity in Tasmania: New Directions. The Second Public Symposium for 1994*, Launceston, 12 November.

Lake Pedder Committee of Enquiry (1974). *Final Report of Lake Pedder Committee of Enquiry April 1974: The Flooding of Lake Pedder*. Australian Government Publishing Service.

Leifer, R. (1989). Understanding organizational transformation using a dissipative structural model. *Human Relations*, **42** (10), 899–916.

Lewin, K. (1951). *Field Theory in Social Science*. Harper and Row.

Lewis, S. M. and Besser, J. G. (1995). The competitive generation market has been assumed, not proven. *Electricity Journal*, **8** (3), April, 70–3.

Montgomery, B. (1993). Looking back in anger. *The Australian Magazine*, 26–27 June, 16–28.

Morgan, G. (1986). *Images of Organization*. Sage.

Nadler, D. A. and Tushman, M. L. (1989). Organizational frame bending: principles for managing reorientation. *Academy of Management Executive*, **3**, 194–204.

Narayanan, V. K. and Nath, R. (1993). *Organization Theory: A Strategic Approach*. Irwin.

Nutt, P. (1989). Selecting tactics to implement plans. *Strategic Management Journal*, **10** (2), 145–61.

Office of State Owned Enterprises (1994). *Reforming Victoria's Electricity Industry*. Office of State Owned Enterprises.

Parker, M. (1997). The privatisation of the UK electricity industry: a case of unfinished business. *Power Engineering Journal*, April, 47–50.

Peters, T. and Waterman, R. (1982). *In Search of Excellence: Lessons from America's Best Run Companies*. Harper and Row.

Pettigrew, A. (1985). *The Awakening Giant: Continuity and Change in Imperial Chemical Industries*. Blackwell.

Pettigrew, A. (1987). Context and action in the transformation of the firm. *Journal of Management Studies*, **24** (6), 649–70.

Pettigrew, A. (1990). Longitudinal field research on change: theory and practice. *Organization Science*, **1** (3), 267–92.

Pettigrew, A. (1992). The character and significance of strategy process research. *Strategic Management Journal*, **13**, 5–6.

Rajagopalan, N. and Spreitzer, G. M. (1997). Toward a theory of strategic change: a multi-lens perspective and integrative framework. *Academy of Management Review*, **22** (1), 48–79.

Read, P. (1986). *The Organization of Electricity Supply in Tasmania*. University of Tasmania.

Romanelli, E. and Tushman, M. L. (1994). Organization as a punctuated equilibrium: an empirical test. *Academy of Management Journal*, **37** (5), 1141–66.

Stace, D. and Dunphy, D. (1994). *Beyond the Boundaries: Leading and Re-creating the Successful Enterprise*. McGraw-Hill.

Strebel, P. (1992). *Breakpoints: How Managers Exploit Radical Business Change*. Harvard Business School Press.

Tushman, M. L., Newman, W. H. and Romanelli, E. (1986). Convergence and upheaval: managing the unsteady pace of organizational evolution. *California Management Review*, **1** Fall, 29–44.

Tushman, M. L. and Romanelli, E. (1985). Organizational evolution: a metamorphosis model of convergence and reorientation. In *Research in Organizational Behavior* (L. L. Cummings and B. M. Staw, eds) vol. 7, 171–222, JAI Press.

Van de Ven, A. H. and Poole, M. S. (1995). Explaining development and change in organizations. *Academy of Management Review*, **20** (3), 510–40.

Victorian Government (1995). *Reforming the Electricity Supply Industry: A Brighter Future for all Victorians*. Victorian Government, Department of Treasury and Finance, Privatisation and Industry Reform Division.

Walker, D. (1995). *Regulation of Victoria's Energy and Water Utilities: An Analysis of the Protection of Consumers and the Public Interest*. Consumer Law Centre.

Whipp, R., Rosenfeld, R. and Pettigrew, A. M. (1988). Understanding strategic change processes: some preliminary findings. In *The Management of Strategic Change* (A. M. Pettigrew, ed.) Blackwell.

Yarrow, G. (1991). Should the market rule? *Institutional Investor*, **25** (12), October, S55–S56

Yin, R. K. (1989). *Case Study Research: Design and Methods*, revd edn. Sage.

Yin, R. K. (1994). *Case Study Research: Design and Methods*, 2nd edn. Sage.

Chapter 25.1

Concerns about Australian privatization programmes

Lindsay Nelson and Peter J. Dowling

Australia is pursuing a programme of privatization in which competition is regarded as giving consumers the protections previously provided under a regulated regime of public ownership. Examples include the privatization of the Commonwealth Bank and the partial sale of Telstra, Australia's telecommunications carrier.

Privatization is also being progressively introduced in the electricity industry where desegregation into generation, distribution and retail has been added in an effort to open up markets to competition. Victoria's privatization commenced in 1993 and, what was formerly seen as rapid expansion to other states, appears to have stalled in light of recent political events. Concerns over issues related to the reliability of electricity supply to consumers, and company profits leaving Australia in the case of foreign ownership, are not assuaged by the appointment of regulators to oversee the industry. Moreover, recent problems in other utilities have done little to maintain public confidence in privatization and/or corporatization. Examples include problems over the quality of drinking water in Sydney and lengthy disruptions to Melbourne's gas supply following damages caused by an explosion. Press reports indicate possible legal class actions being mounted in both cases.

State governments see the sale of electricity utilities as an attractive way of reducing their debt levels. However, non-conservative (Labour) governments in New South Wales, Queensland and Tasmania seem unlikely to proceed with the sale of these power assets. In Tasmania, the state election was fought over the issue of privatizing the electricity utility in which the successful party opposed its sale. In South Australia, opposition parties have combined in resisting moves to pass enabling legislation.

Issues now being raised publicly include whether a) in order to meet requirements for a competitive marketplace, utilities should necessarily be privatized, and b) short-term consumer gains in retail price wars are offset by longer-term costs of system maintenance and problems associated with implementing a national electricity grid.

This resistance to change appears to demonstrate that although the push for privatization follows global trends and may seem rational, important elements not to be overlooked are consumers who, as stakeholders, have views which need to be recognized. These are contextualist factors that should be taken into account as critical to the successful implementation of any change. In Chapter 25, we have argued that at the micro level of organizations, contextual factors are similarly important when introducing change.

Chapter 26

Transforming the tax collector: re-engineering the Inland Revenue Authority of Singapore[1]

■ Siew Kien Sia and Boon Siong Neo ■

> Change has a face of its own. It can conjure up such strong feelings in us. But if change has a face, it also has a heart. For at the heart of change are its people ... (Excerpt from IRAS News, no.8)

■ Introduction

Whether it is pursued out of sheer anxiety about the current business crisis, or in anticipation of competitive pressures, there is no lack of evidence of the exponential interest in both commercial and government organizations about applying business process re-engineering (BPR) to achieve quantum leaps in organizational performance. However, the scale of transformation accompanying BPR has brought about much challenge to traditional change management practices. Successful implementation of BPR is elusive. As suggested by several studies (Hall, Rosenthal, and Wade, 1993; Hammer and Champy, 1993), as much as 70 per cent of BPR projects failed. The cause has been primarily traced to change management issues that arise from the paradigmatic shift in work processes, performance measurement, and skill requirements.

Given the limited understanding about change management issues in large-scale transformation, the call by both academics and practitioners (e.g., Terez, 1993) is to move away from anecdotal research into more field-based case study research. Much of the literature on BPR is descriptive, elaborating on new organizational blueprints and why they are important in today's competitive world, but fails to provide guidance on how to manage the migration to the new organizational form. This chapter provides a comprehensive account of the re-engineering experience of the Inland Revenue Authority of Singapore (IRAS). As echoed by the findings of several case

---

[1] This chapter has been published previously by MCB University Press Limited: Sia, S.K. and Neo, B. S. (1998). Transforming the tax collector: re-engineering the inland revenue authority of Singapore. *Journal of Organizational Change Management*, **11** (6), 496–514.

studies (e.g., Barlett and Goshal, 1995; Cooper and Marcus, 1995), the IRAS case reveals that the hard issues in BPR projects are often the soft human issues. Our aim is to help clarify these softer change management issues, both positive and negative, that can be drawn from IRAS's experience. IRAS's experience can help other firms anticipate and prepare for what they will experience as they ascend the learning curve of re-engineering.

◼ Inland Revenue Authority of Singapore

The history of tax administration[2] in Singapore goes back to 1947 when the Income Tax Ordinance was enacted. Since then, IRAS (then known as Inland Revenue Department or IRD) has evolved as the main vehicle through which government collects revenue and implements economic policies. With Singapore's economic growth, limited resources increasingly strained IRD. Our interviews with key officials of the IRAS took place between 1995 and 1997. 'If every year you have x number of tax cases to do, we were only doing half of x,' the Commissioner noted to us. At the end of 1990, the tax authority had yet to settle accounts with 35 000 or 50 per cent of corporate tax cases; 52 000 or 45 per cent of small business; and 380 000 or 40 per cent of individual taxpayers. All these amounted to a staggering $1.14 billion revenue in arrears. Backlog creates more backlog. The vicious cycle set IRD back a few months each year in terms of their assessment efforts. Many taxpayers were unhappy. One telephone survey rated IRD among the lowest in terms of public satisfaction (*Straits Times*, 19 October 1991), which was clearly unacceptable in a government that is obsessed with efficiency and competitiveness (Haley, Low and Toh, 1996). Coupled with other change drivers (see context chart in Figure 26.1), the IRAS embarked on an enterprise-wide organizational transformation to relook at everything they did and question it.

Historically, the tax authority had been operating over a few geographical locations, each focusing on a specific tax type. The physical separation had perpetuated a highly compartmentalized, divide-and-rule management structure. The systems and the mind-set of people were very much by tax types. For example, there had been cases where income tax returns were repeatedly sent to deceased taxpayers by the income-tax branch even though estate duty had been settled with the estate duty branch. Other examples include separate processing of a tax refund and the chasing of another tax assessed by different tax divisions, causing much unhappiness among the taxpayers. As noted by the Commissioner to us, 'There was no one then who saw the whole organization. Everyone was strongly anchored in the depth of knowledge and no one was concerned with the wider interests of the organization. These places were not working as one.'

The re-engineering efforts in IRAS revamped the traditional tax-type organization into process structures, eliminating 'hand offs' across tax types. Embedded in the heart of the re-engineering is a $69 million Inland Revenue Integrated Systems (IRIS) – an elaborate computer program that allows the handling of all tax types to be dealt with in an integrated one-stop service manner. All transactions are now fed through IRIS. Only exceptions to the embedded 600 to 800 rules are thrown out for manual reviews. On

---

[2] Unlike the 'pay as you earn' tax system in many countries, income tax in Singapore is assessed and paid after the end of each calendar year from which the income is derived. The motivation for voluntary compliance in tax filing under such a system is much lower, requiring substantial efforts by the tax authority to enforce tax compliance.

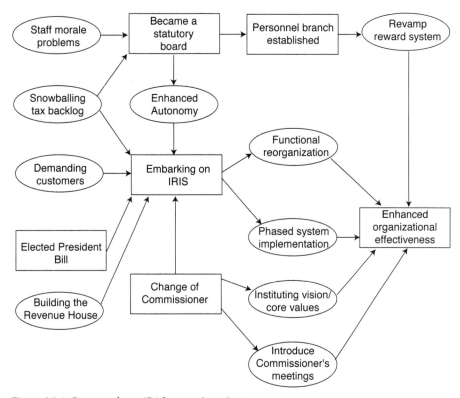

Figure 26.1 Context chart: IRAS re-engineering

average, about 80 per cent of the tax transactions pass through the processing pipeline without any human intervention. The other 20 per cent that require special attention are routed out to specific tax officers according to the required skill levels. The new efficiency offered by the document imaging system also contrasts sharply with the previous system where the 'avalanche of papers'[3] required 'an army of office attendants' simply to move files (as the Senior Deputy Commissioner told us). The application of various technologies – workflow management, intelligent character recognition, three-tier client-server, FCP gateways, super LAN – makes IRAS one of the world's most technologically advanced tax administrators.[4] A few examples of the operational improvements IRIS brought are shown in Table 26.1.

Within the business processes, simultaneous changes in the requirements for information, competence, authority and reward were also made (see Table 26.2). Underlying the re-engineered system were significant changes to the strategic focus of IRAS along the following themes:

---

[3] 'There are papers, papers everywhere ... ,' one external consultant told us. The tax base of 1.3 million taxpayers amounts to approximately 3 million records. It was estimated that 20 million documents were processed annually, posing significant problems in storing, retrieving and physically moving these documents.

[4] IRAS was awarded the 'Plexus Application Excellence Award' by Recognition International during the AIIM (Association of Information and Image Management) Conference 1995, San Francisco.

Table 26.1 Improvement in work flow after re-engineering

Process	Then ...	Now ...
Accessing files	Officers often had to find out which officer was holding onto the folder and then wait for 2–3 *days* to have the folder routed to them.	Multiple officers can access the same folder at the same time. These imaged documents take *less than 10 seconds* to retrieve.
Composition of letters	Either type the letter with a word processor or write the letters and send them to be typed by clerks. Took up to *1–2 days*.	Correspondence management tool enables officers to draft letters easily by providing a selection of templates. The entire process takes *15–30 minutes or overnight* (batch printing).
Return status inquiry	With IMS, officers could tell if a return had been received or supplied out. To ensure the physical copy of the return, they would have to manually note down the batch and entity IDs and then notify the processing centre to locate that particular return. The process could take as long as *1–2 days*.	With the return Status dialogue, an officer can know within minutes the precise status of the return. If the officer needs to look at the return, he/she can simply retrieve the imaged document through Adhoc Browse dialogue in *less than 10 seconds*.
Routing of work	Whenever one officer needed to route a piece of work to another officer, he/she would leave the files in his/her Out tray. The files would be manually routed. It could take 1–2 *days* before the second officer received the files.	The first officer simply creates a sub-work item through the Work Item Creation dialogue and routes it to the second officer to receive the item *within minutes or half a day* (depending on the internal work supply schedule.)

'Triage' – segmentation of transaction streams

The Commissioner noted to us: 'The old process had a tremendous bureaucratic load. An entire process is often needed to take care of exception cases – 0.1 per cent of the normal transactions.' By applying different procedures to different versions of the same transactions, IRAS attempts to match the profiles of the transaction streams to

Table 26.2 Changes in information, competence, authority and rewards

	Before	*After*
Information	No common source of information Fragmented and limited by tax type specialization Redundant preparation of data by tax officers Highly specialized by tax types	Common source of information Integrated across tax types Responsive, on-line and simultaneous access to data by tax officers
Competence	Highly specialized by tax types Little matching of job complexity and skills of tax officers All-encompassing review Relationship with taxpayers: weak to none, desk-bound Vague mythical, complex interpretation of the Act	Generalists / strong cross-tax types co-ordination Automated matching of job complexity and skills of tax officers Review by exceptions Relationship with taxpayers: frequent field visits, streamlined Decisive practice guide to give business certainty
Authority	Vague individual accountability Narrow supervisory span of control (5–7) Long apprenticeship (about 6 months) Limited involvement of tax officers in work improvement teams	Strong individual accountability with clear targets Expanded supervisory span of control (15–20) Shorter apprenticeship (from 3 weeks to 3 months) possible with the streamlining of job complexity All officers are required to be in work improvement teams
Rewards	Tagged to broadbase indications Fixed bonus for everyone Fixed scale pay increment and promotion No addition performance bonus	Performance discriminated at the individual level, within and across divisions Variable bonus for different tax officers ranging from 0–6 months Pay increment and promotion are on a salary range which allows differential increments One-off performance bonus

the costs of employing specific procedures more carefully. Only specific transactions are subjected to the old process now. The rest are managed in a somewhat simplified manner. One example is the modification of tax forms. Previously, one standard Form B (eight pages) attempted to cater to all taxpayers. Now, Form B is used for taxpayers with trade income. A new Form B has been created for other taxpayers. Form B1 is further split into a few subsections. Most taxpayers only need to complete the first section (two pages). Taxpayers, who have additional sources of income or updates in personal details, etc., may attach the additional sections as necessary.

Another example is the mass-property appraisal system that splits property valuation into two main streams. For benchmarked properties, the practice of valuation via physical inspections continues. For homogeneous properties, valuations are now estimated from the respective benchmarked properties. Physical inspections of homogeneous properties are only performed upon specific events, e.g., renovations. The Chief Valuer reflected on the change to us: 'We had to shift from spending too much time on noting fine property differences which will not materially enhance the accuracy of valuations and instead follow how people think in the marketplace – making fast decisions and getting more done through confident broad-based approximations.' Similarly, the provision of 'one-stop' service for Taxpayer Services (TPS) is also made possible with a triage arrangement. Routine and general enquiries across tax types are now routed to TPS Section 1, while special or more complicated cases are referred to TPS Section 2 (for individual income tax and business income tax) and TPS Section 3 (for corporate income tax and goods and services tax).

Encouraging voluntary compliance

The Commissioner told the managers in a speech for the planning workshop: 'We will make it easy and help taxpayers to comply. We must believe that taxpayers will comply voluntarily if they are convinced that they are paying only their fair share. Nothing more, nothing less.' Much has been done to brush up the image of IRAS as an excellent tax administrator, respected for its professionalism, integrity, and fairness, e.g., having a new logo, and designing new uniforms for counter staff. Indeed, the rules embedded within IRIS automatically seek out entitled tax reliefs for taxpayers who have omitted them accidentally. Many policies have been implemented to encourage voluntary compliance from taxpayers. For example, the simplification of tax forms to make things as simple as possible for taxpayers to conform. Sole proprietor and partnership businesses only need to submit a four-line statement in their tax returns showing their turnover, gross profit/loss, allowable deductions and adjusted balance. Businesses whose annual turnover is less than $500 000 need no longer attach their statements of accounts to their tax returns. The twelve months instalment payment scheme also helps taxpayers to plan their spending to minimize potential tax delinquency. Moreover, while the previous position was to remain mythical and vague in interpreting the Income Tax Act to allow leeway for decision-making, the compilation of *COMPASS* practice notes (a monthly IRAS publication circulated to interested external parties on a subscription basis) is intended to 'give business certainty as much as possible'. 'We have been a lot more open ... We no longer have to hide behind the law' the Senior Deputy Commissioner told us. Dialogues with trade associations/professionals and field audits are also conducted to clarify tax laws with taxpayers. It is to help taxpayers comply with the laws, not so much as to rap knuckles.

Re-balancing front-end and back-end procedures

The re-engineering efforts in IRAS also saw an interesting shift towards relaxing front-end procedures with an increased emphasis on deferred or ex-post review. The Commissioner justified his filer assessment policy in an interview with us: 'Our basic assumptions about taxpayers will have to change. Then we regard[ed] 80 per cent of the taxpayers as potential evaders and 20 per cent as OK. Perhaps we have to regard 90 per cent of them as OK and 10 per cent as potential evaders.' Hence, instead of raising tax queries and challenging income declared by taxpayers in their tax returns, tax officers now try to accept the honesty of taxpayers as far as possible (without reference to prior year documentation, for example) and taxpayers are simply assessed based on what they file. Moreover, non-graduates like polytechnic diploma holders, are increasingly being empowered to do tax review and assessment. 'We expect every Singaporean to be able to fill in the tax forms, and yet we employed graduates to review them,' the Commissioner commented on the wasteful use of graduates. This relaxation of front-end control is, however, compensated with a much closer co-ordination with the other departments for feedback on the adequacy of the front-end system. One TPS manager told us her awareness of such issues: 'Are we allowing too much to flow through?' Tax officers at TPS for example, also monitor the trend of enquiries. If they find an unusual trend regarding specific issues, immediate notification will be made to the Tax Processing division for actions/rectification.

The relaxation of front-end checking is also complemented with a significant enhancement of back-end taxpayer audit and investigation functions. As noted by the Commissioner in an interview with us,

> We are now using the tax processing concept and exceptions are flagged out for review. More and more, we are also allowing taxpayers to input data themselves into our computer systems, as in telefile/ Internet filing. But this must be done without compromising the long-term compliance level of taxpayers. The (new) organization structure will better institutionalize check[s] and balance[s]. For this reason, a great deal more of senior management attention would [be] put into these areas.

The emphasis on back-end audit is evidenced by the size of the Taxpayer Audit Division, which has grown from twenty people in 1993 to 100 in 1996, and is now stabilizing at 200 people in 1998. The audit strategy has also changed from an all-encompassing catch-all audit that identified even isolated cases of exceptions to selective audits that target specific patterns. This switch of strategy has seen the recent investigation into specific groups of doctors, property speculators, freight forwarders and company directors. Significant efforts are also under way to build a strong audit presence through field audits, proactive dialogues with professionals/trade associations, and media publicity of prosecuted cases.

Cross-tax types fertilization is also affected through circulation of probable markers of income omissions to various audit teams, monthly experience-sharing sessions, cross-training, joint audit teams and annual Tax Audit Conferences where the different technical branches come together to set out audit strategies. As noted by the Divisional Director for Taxpayer Audit to us, the audit teams now function in a manner that 'the left hand knows what the right hand is doing!' The IRIS audit module also pre-fetches specific information about the taxpayers, e.g., asset ownership, and pre-computes basic statistics about taxpayers. With the support from data warehousing and data mining software, the existing half-blind audit approach has been enhanced to identify taxpayers who should be audited. As an indication of its emphasis on expert competency, IRAS has also put in place a parallel career-advancement route for tax specialists and non-specialists (e.g., managers). The aim is to ensure that people with strong technical inclination will have equal opportunity of advancement. Such a system requires that some senior tax specialists' jobs be bigger than some of the Branch Heads' jobs. In fact, the IRAS Board has approved a policy to peg the earning of IRAS's top specialists to those of private-sector tax partners or principals.

▓ Organizational effectiveness

The above changes in strategic focus have contributed to the organizational effectiveness of IRAS. The results of re-engineering were remarkable, as indicated by the performance indicators in Table 26.3.

Table 26.3 Performance indicators before and after re-engineering

	Before	*After*
Tax collection	$9.3 bn (FY 92/93)	$13.4 bn (FY 94/95) $13.9 bn (FY 95/96)
Income tax arrears	$967 m (FY 92/93)	$761 m (FY 94/95)
Property tax arrears	$106 m (FY 92/93)	$53 m (FY 94/95)
Tax and penalty collected by field audit	$0.04 m	$18 m
Additional collection from tax investigation	$8 m	$13 m
Cost of collecting each dollar of tax revenue	$0.81 (FY 92/93) $0.88 (FY93/94)	$0.82 (FY 94/95)
Tax return processing	7 months	5 months
Staff strength	About 1715	About 1514 (March 1995)[5]
Staff turnover	11 per cent (1991)	10 per cent (1995)
Staff mix (ratio of graduates to non-graduates)	32	12
Taxpayer satisfaction	Survey (1991) Rated among the lowest in the civil service	Survey (1994) 9 out of 10 taxpayers rated service as courteous and efficient Average walk in waiting time <10 mins Turnaround time for correspondence < a month, with 6 out of 10 letters within 2 weeks >90 per cent successful phone enquires

Note: FY = financial year.

On the negative side, the implementation of IRIS has created a much more stressful and competitive work environment – to the extent that some upstream processes carelessly pushed the workload downstream, creating another form of hand-offs. The IRAS had to fine-tune the performance criteria a few times to align the overall objectives. The IRAS is beginning to realize the potential benefits of evolving to a further

---

[5] The reduction translated to saving of $3.5 million per year in payroll costs. Note, however, that personnel cost (inclusive of performance bonus, etc.) has increased by 17 per cent on average per annum for the last three years even though personnel numbers have fallen by 12 per cent.

segmentation by taxpayers' profiles (i.e., both cross-tax type and cross-functional design for different segments of taxpayers) to enable more value focused tax administration. Given the much greater dependence on IRIS, social interaction among co-workers has reduced significantly, generating some unhappiness among staff. The stability of the computer systems was also erratic. In fact, poor network reliability has forced the tax operation to be down on a few occasions.

Overall, however, these negative consequences were tolerable. The Commissioner was presented with the Meritorious Service Medal - one of the highest honours in the 1995 Singapore National Day Awards – for his role in leading the re-engineering efforts in IRAS. The IRAS also won the 1996 National IT Award for public sector organizations. The award was given by the National Computer Board in honour of organizations in Singapore which are committed to achieving business excellence through the use of information technology.

■ The re-engineering journey

The IRAS managed the re-engineering with the involvement from two other major parties, i.e., National Computer Board (NCB – quality assurers) and Andersen Consulting (AC – major vendor and consultant). At its peak, the project team comprised more than 200 full-time staff: about 150 from AC, thirty from NCB, and sixty to eighty dedicated user representatives from IRAS. A rough timeline of the transformation roadmap from late 1991 to 1996 is shown in Figure 26.2.

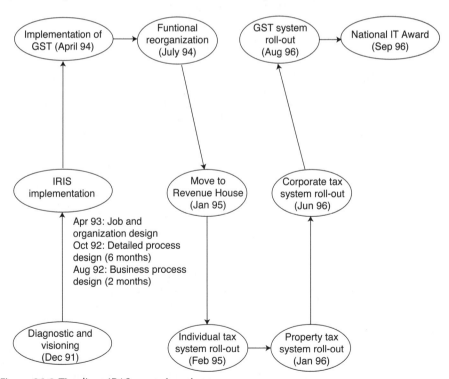

Figure 26.2 Timeline: IRAS re-engineering

With the facilitation of external consultants, focus groups by functional activities (e.g., collection and assessment) were formed to get an in-depth understanding of the business issues. The average size of each group was about ten to twelve, including two consultants and at least one representative from the different tax types. A few sessions were conducted, and each session lasted about half a day. Subsequently, a two-day off-site visioning workshop was conducted. All senior management, divisional heads, and a handful of younger staff participated. One young officer told us that the workshop had a number of 'warm, soul-searching sessions that examined why we are where we are today and gathered what we have heard or seen and crystallize[d] these thoughts into concrete ideas'. Guided by an understanding of the issues on hand and the vision statements, four new focus groups were formed to analyse the changes required in each of the key organizational components, i.e., strategy, people, technology and business process.

Sub-work groups were formed for each of the twelve business processes identified (e.g, taxpayer identification, return generation, return review, payment processing) within the new tax administration model. For example, current processes were studied to identify commonalties (e.g., registration and assessment) and differences (e.g., property tax valuation) across tax types to facilitate new process designs. The IRAS users were involved either as functional experts in specifying user requirements and systems testing or as system officers in assisting the streamlining of processes, i.e., questioning the assumptions behind user requirements and mediating between users and developers, e.g., determining what is within the project scope. Typically, the team leaders would provide the strawman design while IRAS staff provided feedback and refinement over many iterations. Pocket benchmarking to identify industry best practices was also initiated where appropriate, e.g., through the evaluation of mail-handling process in express courier companies.

As the project progressed, little internalization of the new design occurred, however, as the real impact had yet to be felt. Doubts and uncertainties to the impending change was noted in comments such as 'It won't work for us!' 'We won't know if this high level design will work until we go down to details!' Eventually, IRAS had to extend the user requirement phase by an additional three months in parallel with actual system-development work, simply to give the people a higher comfort level about the feasibility of the new design and to gather the people's support. Even though the documentation of these detailed studies were not used at all in the actual system-development project, the Project Director noted these additional efforts and time were absolutely necessary. As part of the strategy to generate enthusiasm for IRIS's feasibility, a few quick-hit initiatives were also implemented, e.g., twenty-four hour deposit of cheques, twelve-month instalment payment scheme, and sending of assessment by ordinary mail instead of registered mail.

Earlier in the process, there were few who challenged the *status quo* and pushed for new changes. The Project Director and his team of officers took up the role of constantly challenging users' views. One controversy, for example, was the relaxing of decision rules regarding refund approvals. Previously, tax refunds were first routed back to tax assessors for a second look to be doubly sure before refund officers processed the payment. The re-engineered system eliminated these reworks and let the refund officers process the refunds directly. Amidst the heightened sentiment of risk aversions, challenges to the *status quo* were articulated in remarks like – 'Why the unnecessary backward flow?' 'Shouldn't assessors be confident of their assessments in the first place?' And, 'Why not route back possible cases of over-assessment also to be fair to taxpayers?' A clearing-house staff committee chaired by the Senior Deputy Commissioner and comprised mainly of divisional heads was established to address disputes over proposed changes.

Towards the end of process design, the morale of the project team members who were working fourteen-hour days was also becoming an issue. Many staff resigned or left the project. Visits to the project site by CEOs and senior officers were arranged to boost the morale of the project team. The *IRIS Connection*, an informal newsletter was initiated as a means of free expression for members of the project team. Articles contributed included project-related news, group activities, announcements (weddings, birthdays, babies, etc.), holiday news, jokes, cartoons and quotations. The newsletter also featured profiles of fellow team members, with photographs at play or with families and friends. Many social events, e.g., junk cruise, barbecues, baby photo competition, red and white day, sushi-making sessions and healthy breakfast treats, were also organized. The aim was to promote casual, friendly relationships among project team members and to balance the otherwise tense and hectic working atmosphere. Special contribution-based bonuses were also given to IRAS project team members. 'Otherwise, you can't find enough energy for the project,' the Project Director noted, reflecting on the multiple 'valleys of despair' they had gone through.

By the end of 1996, IRIS was fully operational. A few additional modules around IRIS were introduced in 1997–98. These included the data warehousing/mining applications for taxpayer audit, financial accounting and personnel systems, integration with external agencies and, more recently, the Internet/ telephone tax filing system.

Managing people issues in re-engineering change

Various process design and project management issues (as noted above) surfaced during the transition. However, they were far less complicated and painful than the daunting people issues IRAS had to deal with. While technical and rational actions (e.g., objective design validation, incentive bonus) could often be taken for process design/project management matters, handling-people issues required greater sensitivity as radical re-engineering brought both psychological and political disruptions to people's turf and jobs. In charting the new organizational structure to support the re-engineered processes, for example, drawing the new boxes and lines generated much controversy. Not all activities fell neatly into the process-organization structure. For example, should taxpayer identification be placed under tax processing or compliance? Should the collection of property tax be subsumed under the Property Valuation and Assessment branch or the Payment Collection branch? Problems arose when debt enforcement was reluctant initially to take over non-filer management. Sometimes, classifications into functional structures were more for historical reasons than by strict functional definition, e.g., a branch with officers that had the expertise or resources in performing a specific task would take over the job even though it was strictly not within the branch's functional duties. At other times, the status differentials also rendered certain classifications infeasible, e.g., the proposal to group the International Tax Treaty (supposedly the cream of tax specialists) under the Legal branch was rejected outright.

In addition, the migration to the new functional structure raised much uncertainty about who fits where. There were problems in matching the new organizational structure with the available resources. In some cases, they had to make do with two different persons filling a role. The allocation of people resources was particularly sensitive, given that everyone wanted to retain good people for him/herself. One frustration in setting up a new TPS function was noted by an AC employee that we interviewed: 'Everyone agrees that it is a good idea to set up TPS, but no one wants to give up his/her staff!' As noted by the Commissioner, 'the allocation of money is probably less important than the allocation of people'. There were also disputes about job sizing. For example, investigation officers claimed their jobs were larger than the audit officers. How different is the specialized assessment work performed by TPS officers (for cases with less than $500 000 turnover) and Specialized Assessment officers (cases above $500 000 turnover)? Many anonymous letters were circulated around claiming unfair treatments by the management and that loyalty was no longer valued by IRAS.

Build an information system for change

The IRAS dealt with these issues by establishing a variety of communication channels, e.g., system owners meetings, staff committees, and briefing sessions with divisional/branch heads. Simultaneously, help desks, suggestion box, questions and answers (*IRAS News*), and 'Dialogue with IRIS' (*Eye on IRIS*) were established to gather employee feedback and to address employees' concerns in a transparent manner. Three separate organization climate surveys have been conducted thus far, measuring from the employees' perspective, dimensions such as morale, training, core values, communication and leadership. One officer noted that she no longer has the lost in the crowd feeling: 'The barriers to communication are not so obvious, the walls are not so thick now.' One manager noted the importance of communication in managing change: 'sometimes, we spent more time talking than doing', he told us.

The fast capturing of this ground level information/feedback was further complemented with the more intensified co-ordination among the management to act. The previous divide and rule management structure has given way to the integrative Commissioner's meetings (CMs) – weekly sessions where all divisional heads were brought together to identify problems, challenge ideas, and thrash out issues. The role of CMs was to co-ordinate across divisions, to manage the overlapping areas, and to ensure all divisions pull in the same direction, and not one group pulls forward and another backward. To encourage interaction among the management and the tax specialists, the concept of a lunch club has also been initiated. Every Tuesday, Thursday and Friday, a small room near the cafeteria has been reserved for managers and tax specialists to socialize during their lunch hours. The informal atmosphere has seen an encouraging number of managers and specialists mixing around during these hours. Thus, the information system for change enabled quick identification and resolution of issues before they grew out of control. Sometimes, a series of clearing-house arbitration committees were established to mediate the negotiations among conflicting parties. These committees were often chaired by senior and respected figures in the organizations who had the authority to push things through. In other situations (e.g., drawing the functional boundaries and grouping grey areas logically, sizing jobs), the involvement of external consultants has made the process more acceptable to tax officers.

Smooth the change transition

As part of the migration strategy to cope with these uncertainties and iron out potential problems, an interim organizational structure was implemented half a year before the implementation of the IRIS system. The interim structure was essentially the same as the old structure in term of physical location and system/work supports except that it now followed the reporting lines of the new organization structure. For example, tax officers handling taxpayer inquiries remained at the same place and continued to perform their normal duties. But the reporting line was to a new head for TPS. The strategy was to give people time to adjust to the organizational changes first before the introduction of system changes as in IRIS. An organization migration work group was formed to manage staff expectations and morale. IRIS the mascot, a lively and cheerful character, was created to sell IRIS as a smart, efficient, tireless personal helper, whizzing around to complete tasks. A video production on IRIS was also made. To prepare tax officers to handle inquiries across tax types, a series of skill-bridging courses on income tax, property tax, and goods and service tax (GST) was organized. Monthly project updates and concerted efforts to sell IRIS were made through *Eye on IRIS* or *IRAS News*, the two in-house publications. The Commissioners had also assured all employees that there would be no retrenchment of any sort as a result of the re-engineering.

Tackle the old entrenched culture

Many of the people issues could be traced to the deeply entrenched bureaucratic culture in IRAS. The results of an anonymous change readiness survey showed that most employees had been with the IRAS for a long time, had little change experience, were loyal only to their functional heads, were narrow in their organizational view, and were hesitant to be open/collaborative. Recognizing these problems, the new Commissioner set out to change the organization culture. Excellent Tax Administration for the Twenty-first Century (ET21) was introduced to create an IRAS culture where service excellence and continuous performance improvement are a way of life. Four subcommittees have been set up to meet the four functional elements in ET21, i.e., a staff well-being committee, a quality action circle committee, a quality service committee and an organizational review committee. The IRAS also attempts to enhance employee voices through various communication channels. The Staff Suggestion Scheme, for example, requires that each staff member contributes at least two suggestions for improvement a year. Each division has a discretionary budget to reward staff. Higher-level awards have also been established. A quarterly tea session is held to present the best suggestion awards. Reflecting a change to a proactive culture among tax officers, the number of staff suggestions jumped from 214 in 1994 to 3019 in 1995. Comments like, 'Oh! That is workable, let us send the suggestion in!' are fairly common in the day-to-day work of the tax officers. Moreover, each staff member is also required to participate in the quality action circles, working on any projects with other colleagues of their own choice. Every tax officer was also exposed to personal effectiveness courses and total quality training.

Clarify organizational vision

The vision that drove the entire re-engineering efforts in IRAS was to be an excellent tax administration, respected for its integrity, fairness and professionalism. The IRAS had consistently brought down these high concepts to the operational level in an attempt to clarify the organizational vision. Almost every organizational strategy was articulated along this vision. The intensification of the field-audit strategy, for example, was articulated as a professional means of handling disputes instead of incessant phone queries of taxpayers in the old desk-audit approach. The mass-property appraisal system was 'sold' as being fair to taxpayers as the valuation of every property is now appraised annually. There had also been cases where refunds were made to taxpayers who omitted specific claims or relief, again illustrating their attempts to be fair to taxpayers. Even the controversial performance-based reward system was framed as being fair to IRAS employees. Integrity was often referred to support the need to maintain taxpayer confidentiality and their readiness to take tough actions against tax evaders. Posters with catchy phrases (e.g., 'Fairness, that's what the taxpayers deserve ... ') and an inspirational video were produced. The core values were constantly communicated through regular in-house newsletters which featured how IRAS staff had applied the core values in their daily work. Such interpretations guided the tax officers in coping with the uncertainties that come with job changes. One manager noted during our interview , 'as long as you are in line with the core values, you can do anything you want'. Positive reinforcement of such behaviours is also provided through the core-value awards, presented to employees who have demonstrated themselves as strong role models. These tax officers are nominated and voted by all IRAS staff.

Inculcate a system of accountability and discipline

The management processes saw a flattening of hierarchical structure with an expanded span of control. While a supervisor was in charge of five to seven officers previously, now he or she supervises between fifteen and twenty officers. The shift is towards inculcating individual accountability with clear performance targets. The consistent message from the management is that everyone has a role to play in organizational performance. Extensive mechanisms that build individual accountability exist, from the Commissioner right down to the support officers. One interesting accountability mechanism is the annual planning workshops, i.e., a two to three days events where directors of the respective branches present their plans and established targets for the coming year to the entire IRAS staff. The planning workshops are more than a means of giving the employees a sense of the overall direction of the organization. It also seeks public commitment from the tax officers to achieve the aggressive targets established.

Thirty-two organizational performance indicators have been established, e.g., tax processing efficiency, debt management efficiency and effectiveness, and quality of taxpayer services. These performance measures are then cascaded downward and the specific expectation communicated to the individual officers through the annual performance review at the beginning of the year. A new sheet has been added to the performance review form documenting the lists of individual targets for the coming year in order of importance, follow-up discussion in mid-year review, and subsequent changes in targets, if any. Previously, the performance-review process was closed and little did tax officers know about their performance, their strengths and weaknesses, and the performance expected of them. Such accountability mechanisms eventually cascaded down to the work level. In Return Review Branch, for example, specific quantitative goals are established for the tax officers, e.g., assigned cases per week per officer of 150 and expected turnaround time is that 90 per cent of cases should be completed within the first week while the remaining 10 per cent within the second week. The embedded workflow management system in IRIS enables the immediate gathering of information such as number of cases allotted, open, closed and ageing information which were not possible before that. One manager noted, 'The computer system now chases after you!' IRIS also automatically captures and compiles performance statistics by individual and in aggregate. Indeed, one management issue managers faced was the setting of a reasonable and yet sufficiently challenging performance benchmark for individual tax officers.

To provide inducement for individual accountability, IRAS has revamped the reward system such that good performers can be compensated adequately. Performance evaluations are taken seriously, with individual employees being ranked within divisions and across divisions. Constructive suggestions, idea contributions, and research projects are all taken into consideration. The variable bonus now ranges from zero to six months. In addition, pay increment and promotion are no longer on fixed scales but on a salary range which allows differential increments. The IRAS is also the only organization in the public sector to make a once-off special payment to officers who have made special contributions. 'We should be very clear about the relative worth of each person we have and the compensation scales be adjusted to reward these people. We are more discriminating now,' the Corporate Services Director told us. In 1994, IRAS paid out $10 million in additional bonuses, $9 million in year end bonuses and $1 million in once-off performance bonuses.

▨ What have we learned from the Internal Revenue Authority of Singapore?

The case of IRAS gives us a unique glance into the complexity of managing large-scale change. In particular, it shows how IRAS coped with the essential yet delicate people issues by building an information system for change, smoothing the change process, tackling the old entrenched culture, clarifying organizational vision and inculcating a system of accountability and discipline. There are a few lessons to be drawn from their transformation experience:

1 The major success factor in the IRAS change effort is its recognition that the people resource issue is at the heart of change. The Commissioner noted during the planning workshop in 1995, 'what we can do, and what we must succeed in doing, is to retain and over time increase our share of better quality people ...To retain people, we must create the space for good people to grow and be challenged ... ' One manager reiterated, 'we have no problem if people leave during the transition, but we will be concerned when good people leave'. One indication of its conscious effort to guard against the loss of its people resource is in identifying three generations of management succession. Over 100 high-potential staff at different levels were identified throughout IRAS. Many of these young 'future leaders' were involved in the visioning workshops and subsequently appointed as system officers in re-engineering teams. Some of them even had direct access to divisional directors in co-ordinating the implementation of IRIS. Occasionally, they were also asked by the

Commissioner to attend the CMs and to take minutes of the discussions. These tax officers were allocated by the staff committees into challenging positions for wide exposure as part of a competency model for leadership. Indirectly, 'champions of change' were planted throughout the entire organization in 'walking the talk.' This pool of people formed the core 'infrastructure' with which IRAS copes with the various change management issues. The Commissioner told us in an interview,

> I don't expect all will welcome the change, given a project this size. There will be those who are faint-hearted or cynical. We will try to win them over. But what you need is a handful of good people to support you, a handful to support those who support you ... That should be sufficient.

2 Many basic principles of managing change (e.g., Kotter and Schlesinger, 1979; Schein, 1980) were reiterated in IRAS. However, the applications of these change management principles by IRAS were fragmented and rather haphazard (see Table 26.4). Clearly, managing the large-scale transition proved more difficult than IRAS has anticipated. Managers proceeded in a hit or miss fashion, implementing the most visible bits while missing other bits of the change management models. For example, the tensions which emerged between the managers and tax specialists could have been highlighted through a stakeholder analysis. Hence, some of the people issues that arose could have been due to the lack of a comprehensive perspective from all major change models. This is particularly true in managing large-scale change as the multiple perspectives will provide a more complete view of the complex change phenomena (e.g., critical inputs to change, phases of change over time, organizational elements to be tackled, stakeholder analysis, interactions among change actions, and the vision-driven change process). Future research should pursue the development of an integrated model of change management.

3 While the experience of IRAS suggests a need for a more integrated change management model, it also highlights the other parts of change management that are simply not predictable. This is particularly so for large-scale projects like IRAS which must take into account multiple variables over a long implementation time frame. Additional complexity can be due to external factors, e.g., the government's decision to introduce a GST in the midst of re-engineering stretched the resource constraints unexpectedly. Complexity can also be the emergent responses to planned change actions. For example, the early actions by the Commissioner to develop managers with broader organizational views (e.g., his comments that the old divide and rule structure 'can't produce managers, only good tax specialists') backfired with an exodus of tax specialists (e.g., resignations) and widespread rumours that quality was no longer important. The chaotic situation persisted until a parallel career path for tax specialists was instituted. The IRAS case thus suggests the applicability of an improvisational model of change (Orlikowski and Hofman, 1997) in managing large-scale change, in contrast to the static and linear change assumptions in traditional models. The inability to anticipate all responses and to coordinate multiple things simultaneously alludes to the need for an ongoing process of learning and experimentation in change management. Large-scale organizational change, in particular, should therefore recognize the need to strengthen the internal capability for change. In the case of IRAS, these capabilities to tackle emergent changes were in the form of building the information system for change (e.g., the CMs, the establishment of arbitration committees), nurturing people

Table 26.4 Fragments of change management principles noted in IRAS

Input perspective	Process perspective	Output perspective
Pre-conditions for successful change management, for example: + Senior management commitment (Bashein, Markus and Riley, 1994; Hall, Rosenthal and Wade, 1993) • Empowered staff (Bashein, Markus and Riley, 1994) + Sufficient budget (Bashein, Markus and Riley, 1994) + Adequate motivation for change (Kotter, 1995) + Powerful coalition (Kotter, 1995)	Phases of change over time: + Change process must have three sequential phases: unfreezing, moving, refreezing (Lewin, 1951) Elements in change process: • Integrated business models: change process must balance strategy, technology, individual roles and culture, management processes and structure, systems, style, staff, skills, shared values Stakeholders in change process: • Stakeholder analysis: to analyse the perceived benefits accrued to identified stakeholders and their expected commitments to change. (Freeman, 1984) Interactions among change actions: – Matrix of change: highlight the interaction among different change initiatives, thus providing guidelines for the pace, sequence, feasibility and location of change (Brynjolfsson, Renshaw and Alstyne, 1997)	+ Vision-driven change process through a series of future states (Beckhard and Harris, 1987)

Notes: + Strong evidence of application in IRAS.
• Some evidence of application in IRAS.
– No evidence of application in IRAS.

resources, and providing slack resources like full-time dedicated re-engineering teams and the use of contract workers.

Thus, reflections on the transformation of IRAS indicate that the reality of large-scale organizational change is highly complex. Specific strategies may come together only towards the end of a change process rather than at the beginning. While part of the complexity can be reduced through an integrated model of change management, the others can only be dealt with by building the internal capabilities for change. At the heart of change, it is the pool of people resource that matters. Organizations planning large-scale change should therefore not treat people issues lightly.

■ References

Barlett, C. A. and Goshal, S. (1995). Rebuilding behavioral context: turn process reengineering into people rejuvenation. *Sloan Management Review*, Fall, 11–23.

Bashein, B. J., Markus, M. L., and Riley, P. (1994). Preconditions for BPR success and how to prevent failures. *Information Systems Management*, Spring, 7–13.

Beckhard, R. and Harris, R. (1987). *Organizational Transitions*, 2nd edn. Addison-Wesley.

Benjamin, R. I. and Levinson, E. (1993). A framework for managing IT-enabled change. *Sloan Management Review*, Summer, 23–33.

Brynjolfsson, E., Renshaw, A. A., and Alstyne, M. V. (1997). The matrix of change. *Sloan Management Review*, Winter, 37–54.

Caron, J. R., Jarvenpaa, S. L. and Stoddard, D. B. (1994). Business reengineering at CIGNA Corporation: experiences and lessons learned from the first five years. *MIS Quarterly*, **1** (3), 233–50.

Chalykoff, J. and Nohria, N. (1990). The Internal Revenue Service: automated collection system. Harvard Business School, Case No. 9-490-042.

Cooper, R. and Marcus, M. L. (1995). Human reengineering. *Sloan Management Review*, Summer, 39–50.

Davenport, T. H. (1993). *Process Innovation*. Harvard Business School Press.

Davenport, T. H. and Nohria, N. (1994). Case management and the integration of labor. *Sloan Management Review*, **35** (2), 11–23.

Davenport, T. H. and Short, J. (1990). The new industrial engineering: information technology and business process redesign. *Sloan Management Review*, **31** (4), 11–27.

Freeman, R. E. (1984). *Strategic Management: A Stakeholder Approach*. Pitman/Ballinger.

Haley, U. C. V., Low, L. and Toh, M. H. (1996). Singapore Incorporated: reinterpreting Singapore's business environments through a corporate metaphor. *Management Decision*, special issue on Strategic management in the Asia Pacific, **34** (9), 17–28.

Hall, G., Rosenthal, J. and Wade, J. (1993). How to make reengineering really work. *Harvard Business Review*, November–December, 119–31.

Hammer, M. (1990). Re-engineering work: don't automate, obliterate. *Harvard Business Review*, **68** (4), 104–12.

Hammer, M. and Champy, J. (1993). *Reengineering the Corporation*. Harper Collins.

Jarvenpaa, S. L. and Stoddard, D. B. (1994). CIGNA Corporation, Inc.: managing and institutionalizing business reengineering. Harvard Business School, Case No. 9-195-097.

Kotter, J. P. (1995). Leading change: why transformation efforts fail. *Harvard Business Review*, March–April, 59–67.

Kotter, J. P. and Schlesinger, L. A. (1979). Choosing strategies for change. *Harvard Business Review*, **57** (2), 106–14.

Lewin, K. (1951). *Field Theory In Social Science*. Harper and Row.

Miles, M. B. and Huberman, A. M. (1984). *Qualitative Data Analysis: A Sourcebook Of New Methods*. Sage.

Orlikowski, W. J. and Hofman, J. D. (1997). An improvisational model for change management: the case of groupware technologies. *Sloan Management Review*, Winter, 11–21.

Schein, E. (1980). *Organizational Psychology*. Prentice-Hall.

Scott Morton, M. S. (ed.) (1991). *The Corporation of the 1990s: Information Technology and Organizational Transformation*. Oxford University Press.

Terez, T. (1993). A manager's guidelines for implementing successful operational changes. In *Business Process Reengineering: Current Issues and Applications*, compiled by Institute of Industrial Engineers, Industrial Engineering and Management Press, 215–18.

Yin, R. K. (1989). *Case Study Research: Design And Methods*. Applied Social Research Series. Sage.

Chapter 26.1
Singapore's drive for efficiency

■ Siew Kien Sia and Boon Siong Neo ■

> We have an appreciation of how fragile we are. There is nothing special about this island. It is just one of the 18,000 islands in the region ... The only thing that makes it special is that the place is revved up to 99 per cent of what it is capable of. Unless you can run at that efficiency, there is no reason to be here ... (Brigadier-General Lee, Deputy Prime Minister, in Knoop et al., 1995: 11)

It is in this cultural context of the constant fear of losing out that the little island of Singapore has grown to be known for its no-nonsense commitment to competitiveness and efficiency (see also Chapter 9). In many ways, the Singapore government itself takes the lead in driving total productivity improvement focusing not only on labour costs, but also infrastructure, invention of leading edge technologies, and the quality of business/operational processes. The overall labour productivity for the third quarter in 1997, for example, improved by 3.5 per cent compared to a mere 0.7 per cent increase in 1996. The unit-business-cost index also reduced correspondingly from 125.6 in 1996 (base year = 1988) to 121 (Ministry of Trade and Industry, 1997). Other efforts can be seen in the reorganization of the Productivity and Standards Board and the establishment of the Singapore Quality Awards to promote business excellence and continuous productivity improvement.

The government's drive for efficiency is also evident in the setting up of various autonomous agencies, statutory boards and even privatization to operate vital utilities and public services. These organizations have broader flexibility in resource utilization and human resource management, but at the same time they are more accountable to established performance targets. The objective is to motivate public servants to adopt a management style that is more like that of a private company, emphasizing both operational efficiency and a high level of customer service. A PS21 (Public Service in the Twenty-first Century) programme has also been launched in all ministries and statutory boards to look into four key areas: quality service, organizational review, work improvement teams/suggestions, and staff welfare. Simultaneously, information technology is positioned as one major strategic thrust. Various programmes have been introduced. These include the IT2000 plan to develop a national information infrastructure, Civil Service Computerization Program, Singapore One – a nationwide broadband network that enables interactive/multimedia applications – and, more recently, the attempts to make Singapore an electronic commerce hub (as indicated in Chapter 12).

The transformation of the Inland Revenue Authority of Singapore (IRAS) is simply an example how one government agency attempted to renew itself to be in line and relevant with the various national initiatives. For example, the re-engineered system in IRAS enabled it to lead the integration of information across various government agencies for further efficiency, e.g., the single billing of property tax and television licence fees and the auto-inclusion of salary data for government employees. The IRAS has also gone into electronic commerce recently by enabling electronic tax filing through its web site. Indeed, the successful transformations at IRAS and other efficient agencies have directly or indirectly served as the transformation models for others. The Commissioner who led the re-engineering at IRAS has been promoted and since moved on to manage the Ministry of Health and the Monetary Authority of Singapore. His influence in initiating radical reforms there should be seen. A number of other government agencies are also undergoing massive re-engineerings currently, e.g., the Immigration Department, the Prison Department, the Port Authority of Singapore, Changi Airport and the Singapore General Hospital. Similarly, more publicly listed and private organizations are jumping on the re-engineering bandwagon. A recent 1997 survey of thirty-three re-engineering projects in Singapore (Lim, Ng and Yap, 1998), reveals the following statistics on the types of companies embarking on re-engineering projects (see Figure 26.1.1) and the targeted process for re-engineering (see Figure 26.1.2).

In many ways, these re-engineering efforts share many characteristics of the transformation experience at IRAS: top-down driven, heavy leverage on information technology, strong customer-service orientation, etc. But at the same time, these organizations face significant challenges in managing the scale of change. As noted in the ranking of

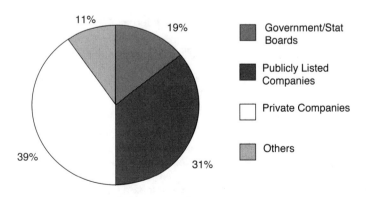

Figure 26.1.1 Types of companies embarking on BPR projects

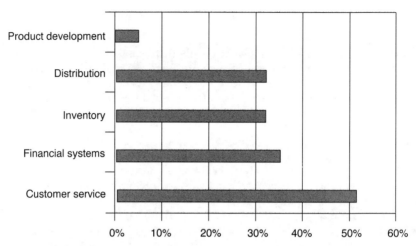

Figure 26.1.2 Targeted process in BPR projects

Table 26.1.1 Ranking of problem severity

Problem category	Severity ranking	Major issues
Change management	1	• Manager's failure to support the new rule • Failure to anticipate and plan for resistance to change • Absence of human resource policies to cultivate required values
Culture	2	• Organizational culture was conservative thus resisting change • High value placed on conformity thereby inhibiting creativity • A culture of intolerance towards failure discouraging risk-taking
Project management	3	• Difficulty in measuring re-engineering project's performance • Failure to commit the required resources • BPR took too much time • Lack of external consultant support for BPR
Process analysis and modelling	4	• Difficulty in modelling and simulating the proposed changes to the process • Too much emphasis on analysing the existing process
Process identification and selection	5	• Proposed changes to the process were too incremental, not radical enough • Identification of candidate processes not based on strategic planning
Management support	6	• Lack of senior management support • Lack of a BPR project champion
Technological	7	• Limited database infrastructure • Lack of IT expertise in the organization

problem severity (see Table 26.1.1), the major problems encountered in re-engineering are people management issues rather than technical process analysis or technological competence issues. For example, the inflexible compensation schemes, conservative hiring/retrenchment human resource policies, and the generally conformative culture in local organizations, pose significant difficulties in aligning people to new process designs. The findings reaffirm the elusiveness of effective change management. While some organizations have achieved dramatic improvements, the re-engineering effectiveness of others remains ambiguous. Reflecting on the successful transformation experience of IRAS may thus be a good insight to effective change management practices in this region.

On a more macro perspective, the transformation of IRAS provides a glimpse of how Singapore as a nation harnesses the organizational changes in its own civil-service engine to propel innovation, process streamlining, and IT adoption in the generally less forthcoming private sector. The fact that Singapore has been able to achieve consistently high growth and maintain competitiveness is probably reflective of some success of these policies. The World Economic Forum has again ranked Singapore as the world's most competitive country in 1997. However, there are potential dangers of using business process re-engineering (BPR) as a social-rule system, i.e., the process of legitimization requires everyone to 'talk the talk.' For example, there may be an unspoken taboo in the social norm on questioning the appropriateness and implementability of the BPR process. Thus, generalizing the successful transformation experience of IRAS across cultures, states or even to the future, will require careful assessment.

■ References

Knoop, C., Applegate, L. M., Neo, B. S. and King, J. (1995). Singapore Unlimited: building the national information infrastructure. Harvard Business School, Case No. 9-196-012.
Lim, Y. H., Ng, C. S. and Yap, K. L. (1998). Business process reengineering in Singapore. Applied Research Project (97/98), Nanyang Technological University.
Ministry of Trade and Industry (1997). *Economic Survey of Singapore: Third Quarter 1997*. Ministry of Trade and Industry.

Part Eight

World Wide Web resources on organizational change

Chapter 27

The best World Wide Web resources on organizational change in the Asia Pacific

■ Usha C. V. Haley ■

These carefully chosen and repeatedly checked World Wide Web (WWW) sites provide free access to additional information in English on Asia Pacific corporations and organizations generally, and on topics covered by individual chapters in Section C (as noted). I have not included fee-based or non-English sites.

■ General Asia Pacific corporate/organizational information (Section C)

ABW Company Directory:
http://www.asianbusinesswatch.com/comp.html
AsiaOne Business Center:
http://www.asia1.com.sg/bizcentre/
Asia Pacific Management Forum:
http://www.apmforum.com
Asia-Pacific.com:
http://www.asia-pacific.com
Asian Business and Trade Directories:
http://www.ntu.edu.sg/library/doing.htm#dir-sg
Asiaweek 1000:
http://www.pathfinder.com/asiaweek/98/1120/aw1k1-50.html
Fortune Global 500:
http://www.pathfinder.com/@@T5C5BwYAJzFz03Oj/fortune/global500/
    index.html
International Business Guide Worldclass Supersite:
http://web.idirect.com/~tiger/supersit.htm
IPAnet:
http://www.ipanet.net/
Kompass:
http://www.kompass-usa.com/inet.html

Publicly listed companies in Asia:
http://www.irasia.com/listco/index.htm
Trade Zone Directory Reference International:
http://www.tradezone.com/trdzone.htm
Wright Research Centre:
http://profiles.wisi.com

▓ Human resource management in Asia Pacific (Chapters 16 and 16.1)

Baker and McKenzie – Publications, Asia Pacific, Employment and Compensation:
http://www.bakerinfo.com/BakerMcKenzie.html
Expat Singapore:
www.expatsingapore.com
International HR Links:
http://www.shrm.org/hrlinks/intl.htm
Salary Calculator:
http://www2.homefair.com/calc/salcalc.html

▓ Asian business networks (Chapters 17, 17.1, 20 and 20.1)

South Asian Diaspora:
http://library.berkeley.edu/SSEAL/SouthAsia/diaspora.html
World Chinese Business Network:
http://www.wcbn.com.sg

▓ Business operations in China (Chapters 18 and 18.1)

Business opportunities in China:
http://www.ntu.edu.sg/library/china/
Chinapages.com:
http://www.chinapages.com
China Window:
http://china-window.com/window.html
Inside China Today:
http://www.insidechina.com
World Trade Data Base:
http://www.wtdb.com/

▓ Business operations in Vietnam (Chapters 19 and 19.1)

Vietnam: a suitCASE study:
http://www.ntu.edu.sg/library/vietcong/
Vietnam Online:
http://www.vietnamonline.net/

■ Business operations in Hong Kong (Chapter 21 and 21.1)

Hong Kong Trade Development Council:
http://www.tdc.org.hk/
Hong Kong WWWVL:
http://www.asiawind.com/hkwwwvl/

■ Business operations in and with Taiwan/Acer Group (Chapter 22, 22.1, 23 and 23.1)

The Acer Group:
http://www.acer.com
Foreign Trade Statistics of Taiwan:
http://www.cetra.org.tw/english/statistics/indexset.htm
Trade Port – Market Research Reports – Taiwan:
http://www.tradeport.org/ts/countries/taiwan/mrr/index.html

■ Business operations in India (Chapters 24 and 24.1)

Corporate Information on India:
http://www.corporateinformation.com/incorp.html
India Business Net:
http://www.indiabusinessnet.com/
India WWW Virtual Library:
http://webhead.com/WWWVL/India/
Trade India:
http://www.trade-india.com/

■ Governmental operations in Australia/privatization (Chapters 25 and 25.1)

Australian Commonwealth Government:
http://www.fed.gov.au/
Australian Government Directory:
http://www.agd.com.au/
Electricity Industry Reform:
http://www.isr.gov.au/resources/electricity-reform/index.html

■ Governmental operations in Singapore/IRAS (Chapters 26 and 26.1)

Singapore Infomap – Government:
http://www.sg/govern.html
Internal Revenue Authority of Singapore:
http://www.iras.gov.sg/

Appendix: abbreviations

ABDU Annual Business Directory Update
AC Andersen Consulting
AIG American International Group
AIIM Association of Information and Image Management
ANU Australian National University
ANZCERTA Australia-New Zealand Closer Economic Relations Trade Agreement
APEC Asia-Pacific Economic Cooperation
APEL ASEAN Perspectives on Excellence in Leadership
ASEAN Association of South East Asian Nations
ASIC application-specific integrated circuit
BERI Business Environment Risk Intelligence Inc.
BHQ business headquarters
BIBF Bangkok International Banking Facility
BIE Bureau of Industry Economics
BPR business process re-engineering
BRIE Berkeley Roundtable on the International Economy
CEO chief executive officer
CER Closer Economic Relations
CHH Carter Holt Harvey
CIS Commonwealth of Independent States
CM Commissioner's meeting
CMS corporate mission statement
CPF Central Provident Fund
CPIB Corrupt Practices Investigation Bureau
CRT cathode-ray tube
CSSD China–Singapore Suzhou Industrial Park Development Company
DBS Development Bank of Singapore
DRAM dynamic random access memory
DTI Department of Trade and Industry
EAP European School of Management in Paris
EC Economic Community
EC European Community
ECA Employment Contracts Act
EDB Economic Development Board
EEO equal employment opportunity
EIU Economist Intelligence Unit

EPA Economic Planning Agency
ESCP Paris Graduate School of Management
ESI electricity supply industry
ESRC Economic and Social Research Council
ET21 Excellent Tax Administration for the Twenty-first Century
ETM elaborately transformed manufacturing
EU European Union
F&P Fisher and Paykel Industries Ltd
FDI foreign direct investment
FIE foreign invested enterprise
GATT General Agreement on Tariffs and Trade
GDP gross domestic product
GLC government-linked corporation
GNP gross national product
GSO General Statistical Office
GST goods and services tax
HDB Housing Development Board
HK Hong Kong
HOS Home Ownership Scheme
HRM human resource management
ICFTU International Confederation of Free Trade Unions
ICOR incremental capital output ratio
ICRG International Country Risk Guide
IDS Innovation Development Scheme
IFC International Finance Corporation
IMC international microculture
IMD International Institute for Management Development
IMF International Monetary Fund
INSEAD European Institute of Business Administration
INTAN Malaysian National Institute of Public Administration
IOCL Indian Oil Corporation Limited
IOD Institute of Directors in New Zealand
IPMNZ Institute of Personnel Management New Zealand
IPS Institute of Policy Studies
IRAS Internal Revenue Authority of Singapore
IRD Inland Revenue Department
IRIS Inland Revenue Integrated Systems
ISICS Institute of Socio-Information and Communication Studies
IT information technology
ITRI Industrial Technology Research Institute
JAIMS Japan America Institute of Management Science
JETRO Japan External Trade Organization
JIT just in time
JLS Jonathan Livingston Seagull
JOCM Journal of Organizational Change Management
JTC Jurong Town Corporation
JV joint venture
KC Kut Cheung Company
LIUP local industry upgrading programme

M&A mergers and acquisitions
MBA Managing Business in Asia
MBO managing by objectives
MD Management Decision
MDF medium density fibreboard
MHQ manufacturing headquarters
MIGA Multilateral Investment Guarantee Agency
MIT Massachusetts Institute of Technology
MITI Ministry of International Trade and Industry
MNC multinational corporation
MNE multinational enterprise
MPDF Mekong Project Development Facility
MSC multimedia super corridor
NAFTA New Zealand Australia Free Trade Agreement
NAFTA North American Free Trade Agreement
NCB National Computer Board
NGO non-governmental organization
NIDA National Institute of Development Administration
NIE newly industrializing economy
NIFA National Innovation Framework for Action
NMP nominated Member of Parliament
NSTP National Science and Technology Plan
NT New Taiwan
NUS National University of Singapore
NWC National Wages Council
NYU New York University
NZIM New Zealand Institute of Management
NZOQ New Zealand Organization for Quality
OECD Organization for Economic Co-operation and Development
OEM original equipment manufacture
OHQ operational headquarters
OHQ overseas headquarters
OIC Overseas Investment Commission
OMS organization and management systems
OPEC Organization of Petroleum-Exporting Countries
OPIC Overseas Private Investment Corporation
PAP People's Action Party
PC personal computer
PERC Political and Economic Risk Consultancy
PLE Promising Local Enterprise
PR public relations
PRC People's Republic of China
PRI Political Risk Index
PRS political risk services
PS21 Public Service in the Twenty-first Century
PW Price Waterhouse
R&D research and development
RBU regional business unit
RDAS Research and Development Assistance Scheme

RHQ regional headquarters
RISC Research Incentive Scheme for Companies
RNAC Royal Nepal Airlines Corporation
SAARC South Asian Association for Regional Co-operation
SAR Special Administrative Region
SBU strategic business unit
SDF Skills Development Fund
SEZ special economic zone
SHE Shin-Etsu Handotai
SIPAC Suzhou Industrial Park Administrative Committee
SME small or medium-sized enterprise
SMEA Small and Medium-sized Enterprise Agency
SOE In Search of Excellence
SOE state-owned enterprises
SPC statistical process control
SPRU Science Policy Research Unit
SSPO Singapore Software Project Office
TEAMA Taiwan Electric Appliance Manufacturer's Association
TI Texas Instruments
TISCO Tata Iron and Steel Company Limited
TNC transnational corporation
TPS taxpayer services
TQM total quality management
TQMI Total Quality Management Institute
TRI Technology Resources Industries
UNCTAD United Nations Conference on Trade and Development
UNDP United Nations Development Programme
UNESCAP United Nations Economic and Social Commission for Asia Pacific
UNIDO United Nations Industrial Development Organization
VOC volatile organic compound
VSIP Vietnam–Singapore Industrial Park
WWW World Wide Web

Index